WILSON, CLEMENCEAU, LLOYD GEORGE
and the
ROADS TO PARIS

ROBERT F. KLUEGER

B&K

Bridge & Knight Publishers

Copyright © 2021 Robert F. Klueger

www.rfklueger.com

Publisher's Cataloging-In-Publication Data
(Prepared by The Donohue Group, Inc.)

Names: Klueger, Robert F., author.
Title: Wilson, Clemenceau, Lloyd George and the roads to Paris / Robert F. Klueger.
Description: Hoboken, New Jersey : Bridge and Knight Publishers, [2021] | Includes bibliographical references and index.
Identifiers: ISBN 9781736387306 (hardback) | ISBN 9781736387313 (paperback) | ISBN 9781736387320 (ebook)
Subjects: LCSH: Wilson, Woodrow, 1856-1924. | Clemenceau, Georges, 1841-1929. | Lloyd George, David, 1863-1945. | Treaty of Versailles (1919 June 28) | Heads of state--20th century--Biography. | World War, 1914-1918--Peace. | LCGFT: Biographies.
Classification: LCC D412.6 .K58 2021 (print) | LCC D412.6 (ebook) | DDC 909.820922--dc23

Library of Congress Control Number: 2021906877

ISBN: 978-1-7363873-0-6 (Hardback)
ISBN: 978-1-7363873-1-3 (Paperback)
ISBN: 978-1-7363873-2-0 (eBook)

*This Volume is dedicated
to the loving memory of
Patricia Ann Klueger*

CONTENTS

PART TWO: THE WAR

PART THREE: PARIS

INTRODUCTION

The great Hall of Mirrors of the Palace of Versailles was packed with the delegates from twenty-nine countries, secretaries, newspapermen, soldiers and guests on this Saturday, June 28, 1919. In this same room, in January, 1871, Chancellor Otto von Bismarck had proclaimed the German Empire following the defeat of France. It was five years to the day that a Serb nationalist had assassinated the Austrian Archduke Franz Ferdinand and his wife, the terrorist act that had lit the fuse that resulted in the Great War. More than six months had elapsed since the Germans had agreed to the Armistice. They were gathered here to sign the treaty that would put the war to an end.

The treaty itself, bound in a brown leather case, sat on a table in the center of the hall. At exactly 3:07 P.M. the German delegates, Dr. Hermann Müller, the new foreign minister, and Johannes Bell, the colonial secretary, entered the hall and were shown to their seats. The long table opposite the one on which the treaty sat was reserved for the delegates of the victorious Allies. Seated directly in front of the table was the prime minister of France, Georges Clemenceau. To his left sat David Lloyd George, the prime minister of Great Britain. To his right sat Thomas Woodrow Wilson, the twenty-eighth president of the United States.

Precisely at 3:10 P.M. Georges Clemenceau rose. "The session is open," he began. "The allied and associated powers on one side and the German Reich on the other side have come to an agreement on the conditions of peace. The text has been completed, drafted and the president of the conference has stated in writing that the text that is about to be signed now is identical with the 200 copies that have been delivered to the German delegation. The signatures will be given now and they amount to a solemn undertaking faithfully and loyally to execute the conditions embodied by the treaty of peace. I now invite the delegates of the German Reich to sign the treaty."

There was total silence as the two Germans came forward. They were shown where to sign. Dr. Müller signed at 3:12 P.M. Johannes Bell signed one minute later. They revealed no expression, but their hands trembled as they signed. And with that (except for the required ratifications by the respective legislatures) the Great War—"the war to end wars"—which had cost upwards of ten million lives, was at an end.

The three men who sat in silence as they watched the Germans sign led three very different nations. For France and Great Britain, the war had begun on August 4, 1914. The United States had not entered the war until April, 1917 and its *doughboys* did not see action until the end of that year. The British had lost a half million men in France and Flanders and in the North Atlantic, but its homeland had not been invaded. France had been brutally occupied for more than four years, with villages flattened and farms and fields in ruins. It had lost 1,500,000 men. The British and the French shared one fate: the war had impoverished them. The war had made the United States richer and stronger.

The three men who watched the Germans sign the treaty had traveled very different roads to get to this place. Clemenceau had traveled the longest road; he was seventy-seven. He had trained to be a medical doctor, as had his father, and like his father had devoted himself more to politics than to medicine. He had been elected to the National Assembly and had become the mayor of Montmartre when he was twenty-nine, just as Prussia and its German allies were crushing the French armies. When the National Assembly voted to approve the treaty of peace with the new German Empire, the treaty that severed Alsace and Lorraine from France, Clemenceau was one of 117 *protestataires* who refused to sign. More than once his political career had seemed to have floundered, only to rebound. He was the last of the 117 *protestataires* to survive.

David Lloyd George had grown up in poverty in rural Wales. When he was five—in 1868—he saw landlords summarily dispossess tenant farmers who had the temerity to vote against the Tories. It made him a Liberal by instinct and a lifelong hater of landlords. He never went to university, or even to high school. Apprenticed to a firm of solicitors at fourteen, he was first elected to the House of Commons at twenty-seven, where he would spend the rest of his life. He was the only Welshman, and the only solicitor, ever to become prime minister.

They were very different men. Woodrow Wilson spent the first fifty-six years of his life cloistered in academia, as a student, professor and administrator. He went from president of Princeton University to president of the United States in the span of two years. Lloyd George and Clemenceau would travel the world, Clemenceau having known Karl Marx, John Stuart Mill, Claude Monet, Ulysses S. Grant and Émile Zola, among others, *before he was thirty.* Clemenceau was a life-long atheist, Lloyd George gave up any belief in the hereafter when he was eleven, while Wilson's religious belief was the centerpiece of his life. Wilson was a devoted husband and father, Clemenceau a divorced *boulevardier* while Lloyd George had frequent affairs and kept a mistress for half of his adult life. Clemenceau was devoted to the arts; Lloyd George and Wilson evidenced no interest whatever. Clemenceau was fluent in English; neither Lloyd George nor Wilson could speak a foreign language. Clemenceau and Lloyd George had learned to master their respective national legislatures; Wilson had never entered one. Lloyd George's Liberalism, and Clemenceau's belief in the ideals of the French Revolution, were inbred. Wilson had begun as an instinctive conservative and ended up as the leader of the Progressives.

But in more significant ways, they were very much alike. All three were thoughtful, insightful and brilliant men. All three possessed the gift of articulate expression that gave them the ability to move men to their ways of thinking, and this ability propelled their political careers. Each would lead his nation to triumph in the First World War, and then represent his nation in Paris for the most consequential summit conference of the twentieth century.

This is their story.

PART ONE

ROADS

1

YOUNG REVOLUTIONARY

You're going to have your hands full with this boy yet.

—Dr. Benjamin Clemenceau

On July 3, 1866, the armies of Prussia and other north German states crushed the armies of Habsburg Austria. The war had lasted all of six weeks. Just as important is what Prussia's leader—Chancellor Otto von Bismarck—then did *not* do: He did not march on Vienna. Instead, he forged an alliance with his defeated foe.

The significance of Prussia's defeat of the Austrians is that suddenly the locus of power that the Habsburgs had enjoyed for almost four hundred years over the various kingdoms, principalities, dukedoms and free cities of the German Confederation shifted away from Vienna to Berlin. Bismarck was quick to consolidate Prussian control over the new North German Confederation, integrating the Prussian military into the armies of the various states.

Nowhere was the shock of Prussia's ascendancy felt more acutely than in Paris, and by its emperor, Louis-Napoleon—Napoleon III—the nephew of the great emperor. Throughout France, Austria's defeat was viewed as much as a defeat for France as for Austria, and as a French humiliation. Prussia, a country that most Frenchmen had viewed as a sleepy land of poets (Flaubert had once termed the Prussians "a people of dreamers") was suddenly awake and menacing. Louis-Napoleon's Spanish-born empress, Eugenie de Montijo, best summed up France's fears when she told Prussia's ambassador: "[W]e are in danger of seeing you in Paris one day unannounced. I will go to sleep French and wake up Prussian."[1] The usually level-headed Adolphe Thiers, the leader of the Republicans who would later become France's indispensable man, insisted that the only way to save France was to declare war on Prussia immediately.

With Austria's defeat, Bismarck had succeeded in consolidating the North German Confederation under his control, but there would be no unified German nation until the south German states—Bavaria, Württemberg and Hesse-Darmstadt—fell under his control. In order to achieve that Bismarck needed a war with France. But in order to ensure that neither Great Britain or any of the Italian states would come to France's aid, Bismarck had to coax Louis-Napoleon into declaring war on Prussia. Bismarck bided his time, waiting for an opportunity. Four years later, in 1870, he found it.

A dispute arose between France and Prussia over the vacant Spanish throne. Bismarck's candidate, the Prussian Prince Leopold Hohenzollern-Sigmaringen, would have united Spain with Prussia and its king, the Hohenzollern Wilhelm I. After Austria's defeat, it would have further isolated and humiliated France. Leopold was thus unacceptable to Louis-Napoleon. On July 2, 1870, Paris awoke with the news that Leopold had accepted the Spanish throne. It was as if a dam had burst. Louis-Napoleon dispatched his ambassador to Bad Ems, Wilhelm I's summer resort on the Rhine, to demand that Wilhelm order Leopold to withdraw his candidacy. The two met in the park as Wilhelm took his morning stroll. The meeting was courteous and correct, but Wilhelm said he considered the matter closed, doffed his hat, and walked off. He then had an aide issue a report of the meeting to Bismarck. When Bismarck read the report he turned to his great military chief, Field Marshal Helmuth von Moltke, the man who had engineered the Austrian defeat, and asked if Prussia was ready for war. Moltke assured him that it was. Bismarck then repaired to a side table, took a pencil from his pocket, and began editing the report. When he was done, the edited report appeared to read as if Wilhelm had disrespected Louis-Napoleon. Bismarck then let the press have the edited report.

On July 14, Paris learned of what became known as the "Ems telegram." Hostile crowds began to form in Paris, screaming *"Au Berlin."* The next day, France declared war. It was a war for which France was completely unprepared. Troops arriving at railway stations often had to wait days for a train to take them to their appointed destinations. Once supplies were finally loaded onto trains, there was often no provision for offloading the supplies at their destination. The army was short of everything, from tents to cooking pots. If weapons were delivered, they were often unaccompanied by cartridges. Officers had no maps, and were reduced to requisitioning maps from local schools.

After some minor skirmishing, the war erupted in earnest on August 6, 1870. By September 1, it was effectively over. On August 29, Marshal Patrice MacMahon, 62, found himself surrounded by 250,000 Prussians, Bavarians, Württembergers and Hessians at Sedan, seven miles from the Belgian border. At the same time, the army of General Francois Achille Bazaine, 59, was surrounded and under siege near Metz. MacMahon had been injured in the fighting, and the role of negotiating the surrender fell on Gen. Emmanuel Wimpffen, who on September 1 rode out to meet Bismarck himself. Perhaps remembering the lenient treatment Austria had received, Wimpffen argued that Draconian terms would result in nothing but endless war between Prussia and France. Bismarck's response is revealing. He said that Prussia could not rely on the good will of an unstable country like France. "One can rely on nothing in your country," he said. It would be different if France had a stable monarchy, like Austria, where they could rely on the word of the monarch. But with France, "we must have land, fortresses and frontiers which will shelter us for good from enemy attack."[2] Bismarck had opposed marching on Vienna; he favored a march on Paris as a way of punishing the French people. The siege at Metz would continue until October 29, when Bazaine surrendered his half-starved army of 133,000 men. One of the men captured at Sedan was Louis-Napoleon himself.

With the fall of Louis-Napoleon, many in France assumed that the war was over. After all, it had been Louis-Napoleon's Second Empire that had declared war on Prussia; with his overthrow, continued warfare would be pointless. That was not, however, how Bismarck or the man in the street in Berlin saw it. To them, this was a war against the people of France. Bismarck told a friend that there would be no peace unless France ceded Metz (the capital of Lorraine) and Strasbourg (the capital of Alsace), "to guard against a new French offensive war we must possess the two fortresses."[3]

On September 4, before a cheering crowd at the Hôtel de Ville, the new government of France, the "Government of National Defense," was proclaimed by Jules Favre, 61, a republican lawyer who had spent his career opposing Louis-Napoleon and had opposed going to war over the Ems telegram, and Léon Gambetta, 32, a radical journalist and lawyer. It was the beginning of the Third French Republic, and it would last for seventy years. But no sooner did the Government of National Defense come into existence that it fractured into moderate and radical factions, the moderates wishing to make peace and the radicals—led by Gambetta—refusing any accommodation with the invaders. Three days later, the Germans began their advance on Paris. By September 20, they had completely encircled of the city; Paris was cut off from the world. The inhabitants awaited the invasion that never came. Bismarck intended to starve them into submission.

On September 18, in the "Galerie des Glaces"—the Hall of Mirrors—in the palace of Versailles, then the temporary headquarters of the Prussian government, Wilhelm I, the King of Prussia, was proclaimed the emperor—*kaiser*—of a united Germany. A visitor to Versailles today sees no evidence that the German nation was created on French soil.

The following day, Favre and Bismarck met in the Rothschild chateau at Ferrieres, an eastern suburb of Paris. Before the meeting, Favre told an Austrian diplomat: "Bismarck will not take a province, for that will make a durable peace impossible."[4] He was perhaps remembering the lenient terms Bismarck had given the Austrians. Favre had a reputation for tearing up easily, and when Bismarck informed him that there would be no peace unless France ceded Strasbourg and Metz, Favre burst into tears, proclaiming, "You are trying to destroy France." But Bismarck was adamant that the turnover of Alsace and Lorraine was essential for Germany's security: "I am sure that very soon we will have a new war with you, and we want to do so with all the advantages."[5] Favre refused to cede any territory, and the meeting ended.

Prior to the investment of Paris being completed, Favre dispatched a few elderly politicians to Tours, 146 miles southwest of Paris. It was feared they could not withstand the rigors of the siege. There matters stood until October 7, when Gambetta climbed into a hot air balloon and defied the siege, landing safely in Tours. His daring escape became the emblem of the resistance. He took charge as soon as he arrived, forming the "Army of the Loire," comprised of raw recruits, escapees from the siege at Metz and soldiers who had never made it to the front during the chaotic mobilization. But when Metz finally fell and the Germans could concentrate their forces on the Loire, Gambetta's little army lost all chance of relieving the siege.

But Bismarck, ensconced in Versailles, soon began to feel the stresses of the siege. He accused von Moltke of meddling in political matters. Moltke believed Bismarck—decked out as he was in a military uniform—was intruding in military matters. The aging emperor was caught between them and grew increasingly irritable as the siege continued and the capitulation he expected did not come. Prussia had been seen as the victim when France declared war. Now Bismarck feared that Germany would lose whatever good will it had earned. Winter was coming and provisioning his 800,000 soldiers was beginning to affect his economy. Bismarck wanted to negotiate peace.

By the end of January, 1871, Paris was down to a two-day supply of bread. Favre wrote Bismarck requesting that they renew negotiations. His request was granted, and Favre immediately headed to Versailles. They agreed to a three-week armistice, to permit the calling of national elections which would elect a government empowered to negotiate a permanent peace. The armistice would cover all of France, including the

Army of the Loire. The siege would be lifted in the interim, and the provisioning of Paris would begin. They agreed that if peace could not be negotiated, the 300,000-strong National Guard in Paris would be disarmed and marched off into captivity. The military party in Versailles, including von Moltke, thought the terms too lenient.

National elections were held on February 8. There was little time for an election campaign, and candidates did not present a platform. Most of the candidates were local notables who, if nothing else, were recognized as men of substance and probity. In some cases the choice was clear, with the word "Peace" or "War" appearing beside the candidate's name. Most of France outside Paris wanted peace, and the result of the election was an overwhelming victory for the peace-at-any-price conservatives. One wag referred to it as "an assembly of country bumpkins," including monarchists who remained faithful to one or the other of the two branches of the Bourbon dynasty that had ruled France until 1848. The big losers were the Bonapartists and the followers of Gambetta. The biggest winner was Adolphe Thiers. Candidates were permitted to stand in multiple prefects; Thiers was elected in twenty-six. He was seventy-three, small, white-haired, and resembled an owl. He was conservative: "[B]y tastes and habits and associations I am an aristocrat."[6] The election revealed the rift between Paris and the rest of France that had been papered over by Louis-Napoleon's Second Empire. Republican Paris was faithful to the spirit of the original revolution of 1789. It was bourgeois, secular and anti-clerical. With the exception of Lyon and Marseilles, the rest of France was rural (70% of France was still peasants), deeply conservative, illiterate (primary education was not made compulsory until 1882) and in the grip of the Catholic Church. Thiers was made the head of the new government, but was denied the title of president. He became "head of the executive power." Thiers retained Favre as foreign minister.

Thiers and Favre arrived in Versailles on February 21 to negotiate the preliminary treaty. Bismarck demanded all of Alsace, including Strasbourg, and most of Lorraine, including Metz. He demanded an indemnity of five billion francs, payable one billion francs in 1871 and the balance within three years following the approval of the preliminary treaty. The Germans would occupy France, partially withdrawing only as payments were made. The French would bear the cost of supporting their German occupiers. Most, but not all, of the French forces would retire below the Loire, and most, but not all, of the Germans would evacuate Paris. They agreed they would meet in Brussels to negotiate a definitive treaty. On February 26, Bismarck, Thiers and Favre signed the preliminary treaty, as did representatives of the South German States, "having taken part in the present war as allies of Prussia, and now being part of the German Empire." The consolidation of the German states into one nation was now complete.

Thiers presented the preliminary treaty to the new National Assembly, meeting in Bordeaux, on February 28. Victor Hugo rose and made an impassioned speech in opposition, saying that Paris had given its mandate to vote against the dismemberment of the Fatherland. He predicted that one day France, bent on revenge, would rise up and not only retake Alsace and Lorraine but would go on to conquer the left bank of the Rhine. Gambetta warned: "If we conclude such a humiliating peace, revolution will break out in Paris."[7] As most of the newly-elected delegates were committed to peace, there was no chance that the treaty would not be approved, and on the following day the delegates approved the treaty, 546-107. The twenty-three delegates from Alsace and Lorraine abstained, and then resigned their seats.

The 107 delegates who refused to approve the peace treaty would be forever known as the *protestataires*. One of them was the twenty-nine-year-old mayor of Montmartre, Georges Clemenceau.

His father was a country doctor, as were his grandfather and great grandfather, and more out of family tradition than anything else, he became one too. The region in which he was born, the Vendee, hard by the Bay of Biscay, was one of the most rural and desolate in France, notable for the *bocage*, the rugged, wooden land of sunken roads, mud walls and secluded villages. In later years, Georges Eugene Benjamin Clemenceau would say that he could ride for two or three miles without seeing the sun. "Its charm won me, its charm has held me."[8] Throughout his life, he would return again and again to the Vendee.

He was born on September 28, 1841 in the Vendeean village of Mouilleron-en-Pareds, fifty miles southwest of Nantes, at the home of his mother's parents, the second of six children and the eldest son. His parents, Benjamin Clemenceau and the former Emma Gautreau, differed from most of the French in one important respect: Neither were members of the Roman Catholic Church. Emma's parents were Protestants, as were many other Vendeeans. Benjamin was a lifelong atheist, who would pass his atheism on to his son. Another difference: the region was staunchly royalist; Benjamin was an ardent revolutionary. Portraits of Robespierre and Saint Just, the "Angel of Death" of the Reign of Terror, adorned the walls of the Clemenceau household in l'Aubraie. "My father made a cult of the Revolution," Clemenceau would remember.[9]

In 1843, Benjamin moved the family to Nantes, where he practiced medicine as little as he could, reserving most of his time for politics. Clemenceau attended a small private school. When he was twelve he enrolled in the local *lycee* in Nantes. Much of his education consisted of long walks and dinner conversation with his father. He received no religious instruction; his father forbad it. He studied English in school and at home, and was soon fairly fluent. He wept at a performance of *Uncle Tom's Cabin* in Nantes. Lincoln was one of his earliest heroes.

Benjamin's revolutionary politics made him an opponent of Louis-Napoleon's Second Empire. Like many others, Benjamin would not forgive Louis-Napoleon for snuffing out the 1848 revolution with his 1852 *coup d'etat*. In 1858, the year in which Clemenceau enrolled in the Preparatory School of Medicine and Pharmacy in Nantes, Louis-Napoleon decided to purge France of his opponents, real or imagined. Every district was given a quota of revolutionaries to arrest and deport, and Benjamin's name appeared on the local list. Deportation to a penal colony in Algeria could have amounted to a death sentence. The seventeen-year old Clemenceau visited his father in jail in Nantes, vowing "I will avenge you." Benjamin replied: "If you want to avenge me, work." Benjamin was transported to Marseilles, the last stop before shipment to Algeria. That is as far as he got. A hue and cry erupted at the deportation of a popular member of the community, and Louis-Napoleon, sensitive to public opinion, rescinded the sentence. Upon his release, Benjamin said to the prefect of police, referring to his son: "You're going to have your hands full with this boy yet."[10]

In 1861, Clemenceau enrolled at the Faculty of Medicine at the University of Paris. He found a flat on the rue de l'Estrapade in the Latin Quarter. Benjamin accompanied him to Paris for the express purpose of introducing his son around in republican circles. One of Benjamin's friends, Etienne Arago, would briefly serve as mayor of Paris and would be instrumental in launching Clemenceau's political career.

Clemenceau made friends easily, and quickly befriended many young republicans who would later become some of the leading lights of radical politics. He became friends with Charles Longuet, later to become a participant in the Commune and who would go on to become Karl Marx's son-in-law. He met Charles Delécluse, a leader of the Commune who would literally die on the barricades. He befriended two contemporaries, Victor Jaclard, a union organizer who later served as deputy mayor of Montmartre under Clemenceau, and Émile Zola. Around Etienne Arago's table he first met Claude Monet. But the man whom he would be closest to throughout his life was August Scheurer-Kestner, a wealthy Alsatian industrialist. Clemenceau courted Scheurer-Kestner's sister-in-law, Hortense Kestner, ardently and unsuccessfully. It is possible that the failure of this courtship was instrumental in Clemenceau boarding a ship bound for New York.

Within one month of arriving in Paris, Clemenceau and a group of friends founded a student newspaper, *Le Travail, journal littérature et scientifique*. The reference to "*littérature et scientifique*" was an attempt to conceal from Louis-Napoleon's censors that the newspaper was purely political. In the February 16, 1862 issue, Clemenceau wrote: "We are strong because we fight for an idea...we can be forced to conceal our thought, but not to compromise it."[11] One of the members of *Le Travail's* staff was Émile Zola. Clemenceau thought little of his journalism, and advised him to seek a career elsewhere. ("You will never be a writer.")[12] The attempt to hide *Le Travail's* purpose from the police failed; they closed it after nine issues.

While attending medical school, Clemenceau fell under the influence of Auguste Blanqui (1805-1881), an ardent and lifelong revolutionary, who was then enduring one of his many prison sentences at the hands of the Second Empire. Clemenceau visited him in prison frequently during 1862 and 1863. Blanqui thought enough of Clemenceau to entrust him with the mission of picking up a printing press in Brussels and returning it to Paris for use in Blanqui's subversive activities. Blanqui's relations with Clemenceau cooled briefly after Blanqui learned that Clemenceau was a friend of Delécluse, an enemy of Blanqui. They were later reconciled.

During this period Clemenceau became a devotee of the positivist philosophy of Auguste Comte, a philosophy that dove-tailed perfectly with his father's revolutionary thought. Comte taught that anything knowable had to be amenable to the scientific method. This left no room for such "superstitions" as theology and metaphysics.

On February 24, 1862, Clemenceau and a group of his friends from *Le Travail* staged an anti-government rally at the Place de la Bastille. They had posted notices in workers' neighborhoods inviting them to attend. Few workers showed up, but the police did. They managed to sing a few revolutionary songs before the police, brandishing nightsticks, broke up the rally and arrested the organizers. Clemenceau fled, but was found in hiding two days later. He was tossed into a paddy wagon and hauled off to the rat-infested Mazas prison. Benjamin came up from Nantes in an unsuccessful attempt to have him released. Most fathers would have been at least annoyed that his son was spending his time at revolution rather than on his studies. Not Benjamin, who prided himself in his son's work. Clemenceau was formally charged with violating an 1848 law banning "riotous assemblies." He received a thirty-day sentence, but got no credit for the time he had already spent in Mazas awaiting trial. His total jail time amounted to seventy-three days.

Clemenceau's political activities and his courtship of Hortense Kestner did interfere with his studies, but in 1865 he was finally awarded a medical degree. His thesis, *De la generation des éléments anatomiques* was less about medicine than about philosophy. In keeping with his positivist philosophy, he rejected the idea of a soul, because life processes were so mathematical that "there is not a moment for the introduction of the soul into the embryo."[13] He successfully defended the thesis, claiming many years later that the only reason he was able to do so was that only one of his examiners had read it.

Sometime in early 1865 Clemenceau formed the thought of visiting America, ostensibly to "see democracy in action." We cannot know how much of the decision was based on the failed courtship of Hortense Kestner or just youthful wanderlust, but in July Clemenceau, accompanied by Benjamin, sailed for London. There they met John Stuart Mill. Clemenceau agreed to translate Mill's *Auguste Comte and Positivism* into French. In exchange, Mill's publisher agreed to issue a second printing of Clemenceau's doctoral thesis.

In early September, 1865, Clemenceau, 24, boarded the steamer *Etna* in Liverpool, bound for New York, intending only a short stay. He remained for four years, his sojourn interrupted by a number of trips back to France. He found an apartment at 215 W. 12th street in Greenwich Village. He felt right at home in the neighborhood, as it was "more characteristic of Paris than New York...it reminded one strongly of the Latin Quarter."[14] He frequented Pfaff's Restaurant at 653 Broadway, a haunt for bohemians, where writers, actors, journalists, illustrators and artists whose "habits of dress, speech and thought were deemed unconventional."[15] Pfaff sought out a French-speaking clientele, providing its patrons with foreign newspapers. Pfaff reserved a large oval table for his bohemians, and it was at this table that Walt Whitman would bring drafts of his poems. In Paris Clemenceau had befriended Edward H. House, the drama critic of the New York *Tribune*, then edited by Horace Greeley, and House introduced him to Greeley. Pfaff's was slightly past its prime as the gathering place for New York bohemia by the time Clemenceau got there, thinned out by competition and the Civil War. It is doubtful that he met Whitman, but he did meet Charles Halpine, an Irish-born poet, editor of the *New York Times* and local politician, who showed him around. He met Charles Anderson Dana at the *New York Sun*, and through Dana obtained interviews with Secretary of State William Seward and with General Grant at Army headquarters, where Clemenceau unwisely positioned himself beside the cuspidor; Grant spat tobacco juice in his direction throughout the interview. He also obtained an interview with the man who would become his hero, Sen. Charles Sumner of Massachusetts. He roamed all over the east, traveling as far south as South Carolina. He spent a month in Chicago. He witnessed a lynching.

In order to supplement his father's meager allowance, Clemenceau secured a job as a foreign correspondent for *Le Temps*, a liberal Paris daily. Because Clemenceau had a police record, *Le Temps* deemed it prudent to publish "Letter from the United States" under a pseudonym. There were ninety-five letters in all, the first dated September 28, 1865, and the last August 1, 1870.[16] They are extraordinary on a number of levels. For one, they exhibit the remarkable depth of knowledge Clemenceau, a twenty-four-year-old foreigner, possessed with respect to the most arcane aspects of American political procedure. More importantly, they are a mirror into the unflinching prejudice for social justice Clemenceau would carry with him through life. As such, the letters are a guide to his political career. All of the letters concern themselves with the principal political issues of the day, such as the radical Republican attempt to push Reconstruction and President Johnson's attempt to slow it, which resulted in Johnson's impeachment, and the election campaign of 1868. One yearns for more of Clemenceau's views of life in New York and what he saw and heard around the table at Pfaff's, but there is very little of that. He was all business.

He probably wrote the letters seated in the Astor Library on Lafayette Street or in the Cooper Union on Astor Place. Not all of the letters were written in New York, as he made numerous trips back to France, and none of the letters after June, 1869 were written in New York; he had permanently returned to France by then.

In his first letter, dated September 28, 1865, he reported favorably on a speech delivered by Sen. Sumner, calling him a "distinguished, upright and popular statesman." In the speech, Sumner had recommended keeping the military power in the southern states "until the spirit of revolt has entirely died out."[17] The letter continues: "There is a feeling that the South is now at the mercy of the North, and that for the first time the opportunity is at hand to quell definitely, once and for all, the temper of oligarchical pride which worked such division to the Republic."[18] In that first letter, Clemenceau advised his Parisian readers that: "the people of the United States have a peculiar faculty for adjusting themselves to circumstances and learning by experience, suddenly changing their course and thus nearly always disappointing prophets of disaster. The Americans will quickly find out how to remedy them. They will lose their way temporarily among the problems which beset them, trying out and abandoning unsatisfactory solutions, but in the end, when truth and justice have taken some kind of shape and revealing themselves to the eyes of the world, the people will seize them."[19]

In his letter dated December 23, 1865, he let his optimism (and his prejudices) show clearly: "No one has any doubt that the blacks will have the right to vote, nor that slavery is abolished. It should be so, and it will be so."[20] In keeping with his positivist philosophy that there is a certain inevitability to the march of history, he advised his readers: "It is certain from now on that the political equality of the two races is only a question of time. There has been a continual growth of opinion toward this end."[21]

Clemenceau parted company with the radical Republicans on the issues of protectionism (calling the North's protectionism "misguided self-interest") and Sunday closing laws, reporting that the New York State Court of Appeals had upheld a law requiring the closing of cabarets on Sunday.[22] He attended a Republican meeting where Horace Greeley was present. "It was decided there, between prayers, that morality, the

Bible, Providence, as well as order and propriety, demand that every Sunday New York take on the aspect of a cemetery."[23] He warned that the Republican view on liquor was also politically harmful; German voters might desert the Republicans: "the Germans… most of whom would not mind giving the blacks the vote, are not willing to vote for men who will take away their glass of beer in the name of religion." But in the same letter he predicted: "The Republican candidate will certainly be elected to succeed [President Johnson] and will have the glory of finishing the work so valiantly begun by Abraham Lincoln."[24]

Clemenceau was briefly back in Paris in February, 1866. While there, he joined a society called, "Act According to your Beliefs," and took a pledge never "to receive any sacraments for birth, marriage or death."[25]

In October, 1867, Clemenceau reported on by-elections in Ohio and Pennsylvania, both carried by the Democrats. The conventional wisdom was that the Democrats would prevail in the general election in 1868, but he predicted (correctly) that "when the national elections come along, it will be seen that the retrogression was only momentary."[26] He also reported that the by-elections had hurt the presidential ambitions of Chief Justice Salmon P. Chase: "Probably Mr. Chase will never be president of the United States, and I doubt if the country loses much. When a man occupies a position of such importance as that of Mr. Chase, and is not satisfied with it, it is a bad sign."[27]

From January, 1868 until May, 1868, Clemenceau reported to his readers on the impeachment of President Johnson. Initially, Clemenceau supported Johnson's go-slow approach to Reconstruction, but soon Clemenceau turned against him. "The Democrats are leaving him on all sides…A little while longer and he will be politically dead, like Pierce, Buchanan and Fillmore."[28] He gave his Parisian readers, all living under a dictatorship, a glimpse into the drama of American democracy at work, reporting on the House of Representatives' impeachment managers entering the Senate chamber: "'Hear! Hear! Hear!' shouted the sergeant-at-arms, 'Let no one speak under pain of imprisonment, while the House of Representatives presents to the Senate of the United States the articles of impeachment drawn up against Andrew Johnson, President of the United States.'" The presiding officer in any impeachment is, of course, the Chief Justice: "Yesterday…at one o'clock in the afternoon, the Chief Justice appeared before the Senate. 'Senators,' he said, 'I come at your request to assist you in organizing as a court of impeachment, and to proceed to the trial of Andrew Johnson, President of the United States.'"[29] In this same letter, he reported on the failing health of one his heroes, Rep. Thaddeus Stevens, who had to be carried to his desk in the House chamber: "If it were not for the smoldering in the depths of his piercing eyes, one might imagine life had already fled from that inert body, but it still nurses all of the wrath of a Robespierre."[30]

In early April, Clemenceau was still confident of Johnson's conviction. But by mid-May, he was less sure, advising his readers that a vote of two-thirds of the Senate was required to convict. There were fifty-five senators, forty-four of whom were Republicans. Thus, he feared, if only eight deserted, Johnson would escape conviction. In his letter dated May 22, he reported that Johnson had indeed been acquitted, by a vote of 35 to 19 to convict, one vote short of the two-thirds needed. "One more vote, and he would have been deposed…The amusing part of the whole affair is that the Democrats are almost as disappointed as the radicals. They did not foresee the acquittal of Mr. Johnson and abandoned him at the first sign of danger, attempting to disentangle his cause from theirs as soon as he was accused."[31]

Benjamin now asked his son to return to France. He refused, and Benjamin cut off his allowance. Through a friend, he got a job teaching French at Miss Aiken's Seminary for Young Ladies, a girls' finishing school in Stamford, Connecticut. When Catherine Aiken learned he could ride, she extended his duties to include teaching horsemanship to the young ladies. He took the train to Stamford on Monday morning, taught classes on Monday and Tuesday, and returned to New York Tuesday evening. One can imagine the effect that the dashing mustachioed young man with the French accent had upon his charges. His students loved him enough to present him with a copy of Washington Irving's *Sketches* at the 1868 commencement exercises. One teacher recalled: "He flirted with practically every girl in the school with the exception of little demure Mary Plummer."[32] By the spring of 1868, eighteen-year-old Mary Plummer and he were engaged. Mary, an orphan, was supported by her uncle, Horace Taylor, a New York banker. Taylor insisted on a church wedding. Honoring the vow he had taken to the "Act According to your Beliefs" society, Clemenceau refused. On June 27, 1868, Clemenceau sailed for France without her, and did not return until November. All of the letters he wrote to *Le Temps* during this period were actually written from France.

With the impeachment over, Clemenceau's letters began to concentrate on the election campaign. He made no attempt to hide his bias for the Republican Grant over his Democrat opponent, Horatio Seymour of New York: "[I]f Mr. Seymour is cherishing the vain hope of winning against General Grant, he is reckoning without the patriotism of the American people…If the Reconstruction laws were annulled, according to the wishes of the Democrats, all the questions once settled would recur, and the South would again possess the power which it lost by defeat…They were not heeded in defeat, and it is incredible that they would be heeded after victory."[33] Clemenceau's optimism was of course misplaced. The Reconstruction laws would be nullified years after Clemenceau returned to France. But his prescience cannot be faulted. "All the questions" that he assumed had been settled would indeed be re-litigated in the decades to come.

In his letter dated June 12, 1868, he reported that General Grant held the view that he intended to do no more as president than execute the laws enacted by Congress. "The fact that these views should be honestly and sincerely entertained by a victorious general of immense popularity is a peculiarly American trait."[34]

On August 5, 1868, he informed his readers that the Russian ambassador was in Washington, "having received yesterday from Mr. Seward a check for fifteen million francs, the purchase price for Russian America. It is said that important coal mines have recently been discovered in this region." He also noted that Indian wars had flared up in Kansas and Colorado.[35] One week later, Clemenceau eulogized his hero, Thaddeus Stevens: "He was often accused of narrowmindedness. The truth of the matter is that he put on blinders in order to see more clearly, and he continued to wear them all his life."[36] He could not have known that he was describing his own future political career.

In covering the election campaign, Clemenceau first advised his readers of the now-discarded American tradition that the candidates themselves did not campaign. But he could not conceal his joy and amusement at what he saw: "Untrammeled freedom of speech and of the press is here, freedom to jeer, to insult and deride and bear false witness, to arouse hatred and scorn of anything and anybody…If by some good luck some violent enemy is on the spot and feels that he his strongly enough supported by a few comrades, the occasion is perfect. Orator can vociferate against orator…Grotesque and extravagant as it is, it must be less dangerous than it appears, since people who indulge in it have yet to call on any outside aid to rescue themselves."[37] In early October he witnessed a huge Republican parade in Philadelphia, predicting that "As Pennsylvania goes, so goes the Union."[38] The next day, he was on hand for a Democratic parade in New York City. "[The] goddess of liberty" was represented by "a powerfully built Irish girl, wearing her red cap with an audacious air, one hand resting on a pike staff, while she held some broken chains with the other."[39]

His letter of November 4, 1868, began: "General Grant is elected."[40] But he over-optimistically predicted that the election "guarantees the failure of reaction, and it is an assurance that the negroes will not be left at the mercy of their former masters. America intends to make, and will make, out of its slaves, men, free men, citizens."[41]

In January, 1869, Clemenceau returned to France. While there, he learned that Horace Taylor had relented and had agreed to allow Mary Plummer to be wed in a civil ceremony. Clemenceau returned to New York in May, and they were married on June 23, 1869 in Horace Taylor's home on Fifth Avenue. Mayor Oakey Hall performed the ceremony. A few days later, the couple sailed for France. He would not return for fifty-three years.

In one of his last letters to *Le Temps*, (April 12, 1870) written when he had already returned to France, he wrote: "With the admission of Texas, the last of the rebel states to re-enter the fold, and with the ratification of the Fifteenth Amendment, the American Revolution is over…The rash violation of justice which unleashed it has been both punished and expiated…as long as justice is disregarded, the avenging spirit lives on, and there can be only one way of ending all questions: that is to solve them with justice."[42]

The Franco-Prussian War erupted six weeks later.

Clemenceau and his new bride took up residence in his father's home in L'Aubraie. Clemenceau set up a little medical practice, but the transition was difficult for Mary. Her French was poor, and the stark, rural Vendee was nothing like New York, even in the 19th century. Benjamin was cool towards her, but she did receive the support of Clemenceau's sisters and mother. Their first child—Madelaine—arrived in June, 1870.

When Clemenceau learned that Louis-Napoleon had declared war on Prussia, he decided to go to Paris to see what was happening. He arrived on September 1, the very day that Marshal MacMahon surrendered at Sedan. He stayed with a friend from his student days at 19, rue Capron, in the 18th *arrondissement,* the Montmartre section of northeast Paris. News of MacMahon's defeat—and the capture of Louis-Napoleon—reached Paris on September 3. The next day, a crowd gathered outside the legislature, the *corps legislatif,* demanding the creation of a republic. Clemenceau was in the crowd. Wearing a red *kepi* of the Parisian National Guard, he followed Léon Gambetta to the Hotel de Ville (in effect, Paris' city hall) where Gambetta proclaimed the creation of a republic.

The temporary Government of National Defense appointed Benjamin's friend, Étienne Arago, whom Clemenceau had befriended during his student days, as the mayor of Paris. Arago was tasked with appointing the mayors of the 20 Paris *arrondissements,* and as major of the 18th Arago chose the twenty-nine-year-old Clemenceau, whose administrative experience totaled zero. The 18th was the second most populated of the twenty *arrondissements,* totaling 130,456 in the last census.[43] It was working-class, with many of its poor having been displaced from the city center by Baron Haussmann's urban renewal. It was a hotbed of left-wing extremism.

Clemenceau got busy. With the Prussians closing in on Paris, he formed a committee to enforce the conscription laws. He placarded the walls warning that shirkers from military service would be prosecuted to full extent of the law. He supervised the distribution of rifles and bullets. On September 20, the encirclement of Paris was complete and the siege began. He created committees on health and hygiene, organized relief, the distribution of milk, food and medicine. This was also his first opportunity to put his life-long anti-clericalism into action. When he learned that schoolteachers were sending their students to mass during school hours, he issued a circular: "You are to receive the children for teaching and watching over them, not for sending them to church during school hours."[44] The only teacher who obeyed the circular was the revolutionary Louise Michel, "The Red Virgin of Montmartre," known to some as "the French *grande dame* of anarchy."

On September 23, Clemenceau posted an appeal to the citizens of the now-besieged Montmartre: "Shall France be swallowed up and disappear, or shall she resume her former rank in the vanguard of the peoples? That is the question facing us today and it is up to us to answer it.

"The enemy is at the gates of the city. The day is not far off, perhaps, when our breasts will be the last rampart of *la patrie*. Each of us knows his duty. We are the children of the revolution. Let us be inspired by the example of our fathers in 1792, and like them, we shall conquer. *Vive la France! Vive la Republique!*"[45]

During a midnight inspection of the fortifications along the rue Andre, he found the guard asleep and the artillery unattended. He reprimanded him, and returned every three hours to inspect. He reported the guilty to the General Trochu, the commanding general of Paris.[46]

When the news broke that Thiers had been seeking foreign assistance for an armistice, which would include the cessation of Alsace-Lorraine and the payment of an indemnity, he posted the following: "The municipality of the 18th *arrondissement* protest with indignation against an armistice which the Government could not accept without committing treason."[47]

As the appointments for mayors of the *arrondissements* were of questionable validity, it was determined that the mayors should stand for election. On November 5, Clemenceau was elected as mayor of Montmartre, defeating a *government supported* candidate.

On December 20, Clemenceau wrote Mary, in English: "We have armed and equipped the *Garde Nationale*, organized a new army. We have fortified Paris in such a manner that the Prussians did not dare attack our walls, now the time has come when we may go and attack them…I guess the Prussians will soon find that they have a hard nut to crack, as a Yankee would say."[48]

Of course, von Moltke never attacked the city, waiting for the inhabitants to starve. A meeting of the government and all of the mayors of the *arrondissements* was called.

Clemenceau demanded that the war be continued at all costs. On January 26, the government accepted the armistice terms. Clemenceau told his subordinates: "You have been cruelly abandoned. All resistance has been made impossible."[49]

One of the terms of armistice was that France would hold immediate elections for a new legislature which would appoint a government to conduct formal peace negotiations. Clemenceau stood from Montmartre and was elected. All of the elected representatives from Paris were republicans and most of them—like Clemenceau—opposed the armistice. On February 16, 1871, he took his seat in the new National Assembly meeting in Bordeaux. He was now both an administrator and a legislator. The National Assembly met in secret. Only three days into his career as a legislator, he tried—without success—to have the meetings opened to the public, claiming that restrictions on public access were "a heritage of imperial traditions."[50] When the deputies from Alsace and Lorraine resigned their seats, having lost their constituents, Clemenceau, along with Victor Hugo, Louis Blanc and others, signed a letter to them: "We declare that the National Assembly and the people of France are incompetent to make a single one of your constituents a Prussian subject; like you, we hold in advance as null and void any act or treaty, any vote or plebiscite, by which any part of Alsace or Lorraine should be ceded. Whatever happens, the citizens of those two areas will remain our compatriots and our brothers."[51]

On March 1, the Prussians had their victory march through Paris. Clemenceau urged the people of Montmartre not to resist it, ordering this poster be put up:

> "Citizens:
>
> "One last trial has been reserved for us, a fearful and humiliating trial—that of seeing the enemy enter Paris.
>
> "We have been handed over without conditions.
>
> "All resistance has been rendered hopeless. Any act of aggression would be fatal to us.
>
> "If any of you still believe it to be their duty to die and to bury their wives and children under the ruins of the city, let them think of the futile results of so hopeless a struggle, let them think above all of the Republic.
>
> "Only the Republic can revenge and repair our disasters..."[52]

On that same day, he was one of 107 *protestataires* who voted against the law that authorized the terms of the peace treaty. March 1 was momentous in another respect: On that day, the National Guard hauled two hundred guns up to the heights of Montmartre, fearing that they might otherwise fall into the hands of the Prussians.

Bismarck had warned Jules Favre that he would rue not having disarmed the National Guard, and it was now the most powerful military force in France, save for the Prussians themselves. The Paris garrison of the National Guard, the *Comite Central de la Garde National*, was the most radical, the bourgeois elements having fled the city at the beginning of the siege.

On March 8, Adolphe Thiers, the "Chief of the Executive Power," ordered the Montmartre guns be turned over. The National Guard refused. Clemenceau attempted to mediate the dispute between Thiers and the National Guard, and may have met Thiers personally in an effort to hammer out a compromise. No compromise was possible; retrieving the guns was part of Thiers' overall effort to bring all of Paris under government control. By March 17, Thiers realized he would have to use force to recover the guns. He proclaimed "You will approve our recourse to force, for it is necessary, at all cost…the very basis of our well-being, should be reborn."[53] Thiers gave the order to recover the guns to two brigades, commanded by two generals, Paturel and LeComte. By 4 A.M. on the morning of Saturday, the eighteenth, they had marched up the hill to the Montmartre heights and had taken possession of the guns. It was then that they realized that they had forgotten to bring with them sufficient horses to bring the guns down the hill. A lone National Guard trooper, Turpin, was wounded. As luck would have it, Louise Michel happened by, and she attended to Turpin's wounds. She then managed to run through the two brigades' lines down the hill unmolested, yelling "treason!" all the way. Soon, all of Paris was aware of what was happening up in the Montmartre.

With daybreak, a mob formed in Montmartre, surrounding the inexperienced troops and shouting cheers to the republic. LeComte ordered his troops to fire on the mob, then rescinded the order as being futile. In fact, some of the beleaguered troops began to switch sides, raising their rifle butts in the air, a sign that they were joining the mob. At this point, Clemenceau appeared, demanding that Turpin be removed to hospital. LeComte refused to let Turpin be moved. Clemenceau warned LeComte that he had better remove the guns as quickly as possible. The mob grew larger, and uglier. LeComte was isolated, then dragged from his horse. Ominously, he was taken to a National Guard post commanded by a Captain Simon Mayer. Captain Meyer went to Clemenceau's office to report that he held LeComte prisoner. Clemenceau instructed Captain Meyer that he was responsible for LeComte's safety, but the "Vigilance Committee of the 18th *Arrondissement*" an outfit with no legal standing whatever, fearing that Clemenceau would order LeComte released, ordered Captain Mayer to transfer LeComte to another National Guard post in the rue de Rosiers.

By 4 P.M., the mob had a second captive. Gen. Clement Thomas, a retired National Guard commander, appeared on the scene. Tall and white-bearded, he was known to have assisted in the suppression of the 1848 revolution. The mob demanded the execution of both generals. Both were taken out into the garden at 6 rue de Rosiers and executed. Clemenceau arrived on the scene, wearing his sash of office, pleading *"Pas de sang, mes amis, pas de sang!"* ["No blood, my friends, no blood"]. He was advised that he was too late. In a later account of the events he wrote: "All were raving like savage beasts without realizing what they were doing. I observed then the pathological phenomenon that one might call blood lust…It was one of those nervous outbursts, so frequent in the Middle Ages, which still occur among masses of human beings under the stress of some powerful sensation."[54] He did not go into the house where the now-mutilated bodies lay, fearing that if he did he would not come out alive.

Clemenceau later met with the Vigilance Committee, who agreed to release their remaining prisoners after dark. One of Clemenceau's deputies, Col. A.J. Langlois, testified before before a National Assembly inquiry that Clemenceau had exposed his life: "If you had seen how he treated the assassins…you would find it hard to understand how he was not shot."[55] Years later, Clemenceau reflected that "it was a good initiation into the stupidity of public life…I found myself between two groups that both wished me dead."[56] The National Assembly inquiry cleared Clemenceau of wrongdoing, but not before one witness, an army officer, suggested that Clemenceau shared culpability for the officers' deaths. Clemenceau promptly challenged the officer to a duel—with pistols. These affairs were usually concluded with both parties firing symbolic shots in the air. Not this one. Clemenceau said to his accuser: "I could kill you, but you are a French soldier, and I shall content myself with giving you a warning."[57] With that, he shot the soldier in the thigh.

In the days that followed, Clemenceau and the other mayors tried to conciliate the *Comite Central*. Clemenceau warned them: "Paris has no right to revolt against France and must recognize absolutely the authority of the Assembly. The *Comite* has only one means of getting out of this impasse: give way to the deputies and the mayors who are resolved to obtain from the Assembly the concessions demanded by Paris."[58] The *Comite's* demands were modest; mostly, they wanted to hold elections in Paris and wanted to appoint their own officers. But Clemenceau and the other mayors would soon learn that conciliation was not possible; Thiers wanted to crush the insurgency, and to the extent that he entered into negotiations it was only to buy time to build up his forces. Clemenceau introduced a bill authorizing municipal elections for Paris. But this Assembly, elected on February 8 during the siege and controlled by monarchists, was in no mood to conciliate with Paris. The bill got nowhere. At one point in the fruitless debate, Clemenceau asked the Assembly: "But surely you do not want to besiege

Paris?"[59] That, in fact, was exactly what they wanted. Clemenceau resigned his seat in the Assembly. On March 26, the *Comite* held its own municipal elections, defying the Assembly. The revolutionaries were swept into office and the moderates—Clemenceau among them—were trounced. The new government was now officially the "Commune," and Clemenceau's mayoralty was at an end.

It is probably fortunate for Clemenceau that he was not in Paris during the "bloody week" of May 21–28, when Thiers retook the city and the *communards* took out their vengeance on their hostages, followed by the army taking out its vengeance on the *communards*. Never having joined the Commune—as had his former friends Blanqui, Delescluze, Louise Michel and others—he was viewed with suspicion by them, and would remain so for years. He was also viewed with suspicion from the right as having been too close to the Commune. Had he been in Paris that week (he was back in L'Aubraie with Mary), it is very possible that he would have been killed by one side or the other.

The Third Republic was proclaimed by Jules Favre and Lèon Gambetta on September 4, 1870. It lasted until July 10, 1940, when it collapsed under the third German invasion of France. During its seventy years, France had no less than *sixty* governments. That is not to say that France during that period had sixty prime ministers. Some, including Clemenceau, served as prime minister more than once. Charles de Freycinet headed up four ministries, Aristide Briand six. The longest of Briand's governments lasted eighteen months; the shortest, two months. The 1877 government of the "moderate monarchist" Gaetan de Rochebonet lasted all of twenty days. Clemenceau's two ministries were outliers in that both lasted more than two years. There are a number of reasons for this revolving door of governments. For one, France had no political parties as we now know them. In the latter part of the 19th century, a political party was little more than a grouping around an individual or a platform. There was little or no party discipline; politicians could, if they wished, join more than one grouping at a time, or none, and could come and go as they pleased. There were no local party organizations to speak of. And for the last two decades of the 19th century one man—Georges Clemenceau—kept his hand on the revolving door, and kept pushing.

Another reason for the fragility of French ministries lay in the nature of its parliamentary system. In the Third Republic power resided in the Chamber of Deputies. If a deputy rose and posed an *interpellation*—a question—to a minister, and the response was deemed by the majority unsatisfactory, the government could fall. Ministers feared the voters less than they feared their fellow deputies.

A final reason for the instability of the Third Republic, at least in its early days, was that there was by no means a consensus that France should be a republic. The declaration of a republic on the steps of the Hôtel de Ville was just that—a declaration. The February, 1871 elections had resulted in a huge conservative majority, and most of the conservatives were monarchists ready to snuff out the republic in its infancy. By-elections held in July, 1871 showed that the February elections were the result of war-time conditions. Republicans won 99 of 114 open seats, but that still left a conservative majority wishing to restore the monarchy. And as France had no constitution—and would not have one until 1875—there was nothing that officially made France a republic.

In September, 1873, *two years early*, France made the final payment of the indemnities required by the Treaty of Frankfort, and the last German troops left French soil. Bismarck's expectation that the indemnities would cripple France for fifty years proved to be woefully optimistic. Thiers' conservative government began the process of reforming French public education and the banking system. He began the reformation of the army, ending the practice of substitutes. Now Bismarck saw in France a country that had not only recovered, but was rebounding nicely. To his undying consternation, France was still a great power. What was worse, although the Treaty of Frankfort had imposed what was assumed would be a crushing financial burden, it had imposed no limit on French arms. What was still worse, France was, in many quarters, a nation thirsting for *revanche* over the lost provinces.

Yet another event that did not please Bismarck was the accession of the monarchist MacMahon to the presidency in 1873. It is ironic that Bismarck and Clemenceau both favored a republican France, but for very different reasons. Bismarck assumed that the threat of the spread of French republicanism throughout Europe would make France a pariah among the monarchies of Europe, particularly in Moscow and Vienna. And so keeping France isolated and weak became the centerpiece of Bismarck's foreign policy. In that year, Bismarck was the driving force behind the "Three Emperor's League" of Germany, Russia and Austria-Hungary, whose sole purpose was to isolate France. As Bismarck said in1874: "We wish to keep the peace, but if the French so order their preparations that in five years they will be ready and determined to strike, then in three years we shall begin the war."[60]

France and Germany did not go to war in 1875, and we can never know with certainty how close the two countries came. What is certain is that in the "War-in-Sight" crisis of that year, Bismarck's bullying nearly tipped France and Germany—and perhaps most of Europe—into war. In March of 1875, a rumor spread in Germany that the French war office was trying to purchase large quantities of horses. The rumor was false, but was taken so seriously in Berlin that an Imperial decree was issued forbidding the export of horses. On March 10, the French National Assembly enacted the "Law of the Fourth Battalions," as part of the overall reform of the French military. Henceforth, each French regiment would have four—not three—battalions. Berlin immediately perceived this statute as preparation for the much-feared *revanche*. Even the aging Emperor Wilhelm expressed his fear that France was preparing for war. In fact, this statute resulted in only a minor increase in French army strength; at the same time, the number companies in each battalion was reduced from six to four.

Almost immediately, the German press began to denounce the "Law of the Fourth Battalions." But what set off the crisis was an article in the April 8 edition of the influential *Berliner Post* under the headline "*Ist der Krieg in Sicht?*" ("Is War in Sight?") No one on either side of the Rhine doubted that this article represented the thinking of the Iron Chancellor himself. Just to be sure, the April 11 edition of *Norddeutsche Allegemeine* made the same point, and the April 12 edition of *Preussische Jahrbücher* went even further, commenting that: "When the moment shall have arrived for us to place before France the choice between disarmament and war, rests with the Chancellor and Moltke to determine."[61] With that, the French ambassador to Berlin, Viscount Elie de Gontaut-Biron appeared before the German Foreign Secretary, Bernard von Bülow. He assured von Bülow that the rumors regarding the purchases of horses were false, and that France had no intention of preparing for war. Bülow accepted Gontaut-Biron's assurances, and both concluded the meeting with a feeling that the matter was closed. It was not, because Bismarck would not let it. On April 21, Gontaut found himself seated at a dinner at the British embassy beside Joseph von Radowitz, Jr., Berlin's ambassador to Moscow. Radowitz was so close a confidante of Bismarck that anything Radowitz said could be assumed to come from the Chancellor himself, and this evening Radowitz delivered of himself Germany's doctrine of "preventive war": "We can reassure ourselves for the present, but for the future we can hardly cease to be anxious. How long does the present last? When does the future begin? It is equally difficult to say."[62] He conceded that France would one day seek to recover the lost provinces: "But if revenge is the inmost thought of France—and it cannot be otherwise—why wait to attack her until she has recovered her strength and contracted her alliances? You must agree that from a political, from a philosophical, even from a Christian point of view, these deductions are well grounded and these preoccupations are fitted to guide the policy of Germany."[63]

With this, one diplomat's indiscretion became another diplomat's opportunity. When France's Foreign Minister, the Duc Decazes, read Gontaut's report of the meeting, he ordered that its contents be circulated to all of his ambassadors in Europe, with instructions they circulate it to all of the foreign courts to which they were posted, with specific instructions that they point out the report as evidence of German intentions. The one foreign actor whom Decazes was most interested in enlisting was Tsar Alexander II. The Tsar had recently indicated to the French ambassador, Gen. Adolphe Le Flo, that he opposed Germany's bullying of France ("The interests of our two countries are common, and if…you should some day be seriously threatened, you would know of it very quickly…you would know of it from me."[64]) Now, knowing that the Tsar would soon travel to Berlin to meet his uncle, Kaiser Wilhelm, Decazes upped the ante: He ordered Gontaut to request that the Tsar cover his protection "with his sword."

At this point, Bismarck could have let the matter drop. He did the opposite. He had his ambassadors throughout Europe circulate Berlin's apprehension that the increase in French military strength could signify only France's preparation for war. As ever, von Moltke was blunt: "[W]e ought not to wait until France is ready, but our duty is to anticipate war."[65] But the sabre-rattling proved to be counterproductive, as it all got back to the Tsar. On May 3, Le Flo carried Decazes' letter to the Tsar requesting protection "with his sword" to the aged Russian Chancellor, Prince Gorchakov. He also brought for delivery to the Tsar a file documenting German belligerency. Gorchakov agreed to deliver the letter and the file to the Tsar. On May 5, the Tsar granted Le Flo an audience.

"You ask me," said the Tsar, "to engage to draw the sword for you. No, I shall not draw it, nor will you either; we shall manage without that. I am going to Berlin, and I promise you to put an end to the matter."[66] Moreover, the Tsar committed his government to seeking the support of Austria *and England* against Germany. This at a time when Russia, Austria-Hungary and Germany were allied in the admittedly flimsy "Three Emperor's League."

Alexander II had given his word that he would support France in his forthcoming meeting with his uncle Kaiser Wilhelm, but it was an open question if he would actually do it. But Decazes was not finished. Just as Bismarck could use the press to further his ends, so could Decazes. His instrument was the London *Times* and its Paris correspondent, Henri de Blowitz. London awoke on May 6 to an article titled "A French 'Scare.'" In it, Blowitz laid out the German "preventive war" theory as laid out in Radowitz' table talk: "Germany is troubled by the knowledge of only having half crushed her enemy, and of being able to defend herself only by sleeping with one eye open. What today promptly executed would cost only an insignificant sacrifice, two years hence would cost oceans of blood shed for the sake of uncertain victories.[67] He went on to note that "Peace or war is about to depend on the interview of the German and Russian Emperors."[68]

One of Decazes' purposes in instigating the *Times* article was to involve the British to the same extent as he had the Tsar (the other purpose being to buck up the Tsar himself) and in this respect the *Times* article succeeded spectacularly. On May 8, the British Foreign Secretary, Lord Derby, assured the French *charge d'affaires* that: "Such an aggression would arouse in Europe universal indignation; and this sentiment would be nowhere stronger than in England…You may rest assured that the [British] government will not fail in its duty."[69] Now Derby was fully engaged. On the same day, he sent a circular to all of his ambassadors, with instructions that they use their best efforts to end the Franco-German "misunderstanding." The result was that Britain and Russia each had the tacit assurance that, if matters truly came to a head, each would not be acting alone. Now all that remained was for the Tsar to actually communicate Russia's support of France to Wilhelm.

On May 10, the Tsar and his party—Bismarck included—arrived in Berlin. Prior to the meeting of the two emperors, Britain's ambassador to Berlin, Lord Odo Russell, met with Bismarck. He delivered Derby's forceful statement of May 8. Bismarck retreated, claiming that France had nothing to worry about, to which Russell replied: "Then why all these observations you have charged your agents to make to the cabinets where they are accredited, calling attention to the French armaments, the danger they present, and the necessity of opposing them?"[70] To which Bismarck had no answer.

Russell took his leave of Bismarck and was hardly out the door when he met Prince Gorchakov on his way in. Gorchakov seized Russell by the arm and now the two of them marched in to meet Bismarck, Russell for the second time. Russell stayed long enough to hear the elderly Gorchakov's opening: "My dear Bismarck, now don't get nervous. You have in you two Bismarck's—one that is really you that I like, and the other a nervous and excitable Bismarck."[71] With that, Russell advised Bismarck that his government concurred with everything Gorchakov was about to say, and left. The next day, Gorchakov advised Gontaut that he had received received Bismarck's assurances of Germany's peaceful intentions. Wilhelm shared the Tsar's desire for peace. What is significant is that Wilhelm disavowed the doctrine of preventive war. Following their meeting, the Tsar repeated to Le Flo his previous promise to warn France if a similar crisis were again to arise, adding: "We have common interests and we ought to remain united."[72]

The actual meeting between the two emperors was something of an anti-climax. And with that, the "War-in-Sight" scare was over. We cannot know why Bismarck chose this time to foment what turned out to be a diplomatic embarrassment for Germany. It was not caused (as Bismarck later claimed) by a diplomat (Radowitz) who had difficulty holding his wine. It may have been a clumsy attempt by Bismarck to force France to cease its rearmament. It may have been an attempt by Bismarck to reopen the Treaty of Frankfort. What is more likely is that it was intended to be a warning to France not to develop pretensions towards renewed great power status. At worst, it may have been Bismarck's attempt to lay the groundwork for another war. If so, Decazes must be credited with having kept the peace, at least for another thirty-nine years.

Georges Clemenceau never forgot the "War-in-Sight" scare. In 1911, during a Senate debate on a proposed treaty with Germany over Morocco, he reminded his auditors of the German policy of "preventive war." He took them back to the fateful British embassy dinner conversation between Gontaut and Radowitz. Relying on Gontaut's memoirs, he quoted Radowitz: "[We have an interest, we Germans, in not allowing [France] to recover, to grow stronger, and to regain the force which she would use against us; we have reason for rendering her incapable, from now on, of injuring us."[73] Clemenceau characterized the "preventive war" policy thusly: "[I]t is the method which consists in dispatching the wounded on the field of battle. Because the sword is broken in a man's hand, because he lies prone, let us kill him off, for he might become an enemy later."[74]

Anyone standing at the rostrum of the National Assembly between 1871 and 1875, facing the deputies, who were arranged in benches according to their politics, would have noticed that more than half (approximately 60%) of the deputies were "rightists" of one stripe or another, either legitimists, Orleanists, or a few diehard Bonapartists, most of whom hailed from Corsica, Napoleon I's birthplace. Casting one's gaze leftward from the rightists, one would next see a collection of "Republicans" a term that does not derive from the republic proclaimed on September 4, 1870; it refers to the *First* republic proclaimed in 1789 that arose out of the French Revolution. To many deputies—and their fellow Frenchmen who called themselves Republicans—the First Republic was something of a cult. To them, the First Republic represented not only the hopes of the French, but of all of mankind, and to them France was entrusted with bringing to fruition all of mankind's hopes for freedom and justice. Thus, when Clemenceau served as mayor of Montmartre, he argued that his goal of separating the domain of law from the domain of religious belief was a goal "in accordance with the traditions of the French Revolution."[75] When Clemenceau ran for the Chamber of Deputies in 1876, he announced his program as being "the completion of the great renovation of 1789 that has been abandoned by the French bourgeoisie."[76] Occupying the Republican benches closest to the right were the conservative republicans. Thiers was their leader ("the Republic will be conservative or it will not survive"[77]) until his resignation in 1873. They included an increasing number of former monarchists who had moved to the left and who had come to accept that France would be a republic. Thus Thiers in 1872: "It [the Republic] exists. It is the legal government of the country; to replace it would be a revolution and the most dangerous kind of revolution."[78]

Casting one's gaze further to the left, one would see the *moderate* Republicans. They believed in incremental reform, which would occur only at the opportune time. The Republicans to their left accused them of being *opportunists*, but they adopted the label as their own. To the Opportunists' left were the Radical republicans, or Radical Socialist Republicans, the faction to which Clemenceau would adhere throughout his legislative and ministerial career. They differed from the Opportunists in their devotion to the separation of church and state and to their passion for amnesty for the *communards*. Approximately 30% of the deputies were Republicans, and approximately a third of them were Radicals. Seated farthest to the left were the Socialists of one stripe or another, comprising approximately 10% of the deputies. In varying degrees, they believed in violent revolution and in collectivization.

If the same person had returned to the chamber between 1876 and 1881, he or she would have immediately noticed that the number of deputies (in what was now known as the *Chamber of Deputies* after the constitution of 1875) on the right had shrunk to slightly more than a third, and that the number of deputies calling themselves Republicans had grown to more than a majority, with slight increases in the number of Socialists. What would not have been apparent was the shift in many of the individual deputies. Many of the former monarchists accepted the fact of the republic and moved to the left. But such men as Lèon Gambetta, formerly the symbol and fact of resistance in 1870, moved rightward, becoming the leader of the Opportunists.[79] Gambetta, it turned out, was nothing if not a pragmatist. He realized (as Clemenceau early in his career did not) that many of the planks in the Republican platform—notably separation of Church and state and amnesty for the communards—were not feasible is long as a large minority of the Chamber, and the constituents they represented, were monarchists, and that to push too hard would endanger the fledgling Republic.[80] So Gambetta, much to Clemenceau's frustration, practiced moderation, biding his time.

It is not possible to state with certainty where the fifteen-year-old Georges Clemenceau was or what he was doing on December 28, 1856. We know that he was living in Nantes with his family, attending the local *lycée*. As this day was a Sunday, he did not attend school, and he certainly did not attend church. He may have gone hunting or riding or gone on a long walk with his father. The family would have gathered for their Sunday meal, and Dr. Benjamin might have peppered young Georges with questions about his lessons. In the evening, Georges might have read a portion of *Robinson Crusoe* or *Uncle Tom's Cabin*.

What we do know is that on that day—December 28, 1856—in Staunton, Virginia, Thomas Woodrow Wilson was born. We also know that his and Georges Clemenceau's paths would cross, and by it the arc of the twentieth century would be altered. But that was still many decades away.

2

DESTROYER OF MINISTRIES

Speak of it never; think of it always.

—Lèon Gambetta, on *La revanche*

Between 1871, when he lost his seat in the National Assembly, and 1876, when he regained it, Georges Clemenceau took almost no part in French national affairs. He set up a small, two-room medical clinic at No. 3, rue de Trois-Freres in the Montmartre, and there, on Wednesdays and Sundays between 9–11 A.M., he practiced medicine. He lived in a small flat at 15 rue de Miromesnil in the 8th *arrondissement* and walked to the clinic twice weekly. His patients were mostly the poor, of which there was no shortage in the Montmartre. The illnesses and maladies he treated were mostly the results of their mean conditions. Like his father, he made little money from his medical practice. But the combination of medical doctor two mornings per week and municipal councilor the balance of his time was an ideal way to make himself known.

In April, 1871, the new National Assembly give Paris permission to elect a municipal council comprised of eighty members, four from each *arrondissement*. In August, Clemenceau was elected to the Paris Municipal Council from Montmartre, in the 18th *arrondissement*. The Council had little actual power; the police power and control of Paris' finances resided in the prefect of the Seine, controlled by the Assembly. So Clemenceau busied himself with local matters, concentrating on the field he then knew best, public health. In November, 1875, he was elected president of the Council.

The commune may have been crushed, but the recriminations against the *communards* went unabated. By the thousands they continued to be tried and exiled to New Caledonia. In November, 1981, he argued before a military commission on their behalf, arguing that they had acted out of patriotic motives, believing that they were resisting the German peace terms. His words fell on deaf ears.

In 1875 three laws were enacted that, in the aggregate, became the French constitution. The Third Republic had been declared on September 4, 1871, but its organization was completely ad hoc. Everyone on all sides of the political spectrum realized that sooner or later something more substantial would have to be put in writing. In 1875 it was, but it was the work of a majority of rightists and monarchists, the rightists who remembered and feared a repeat of the *commune* and the monarchists who secretly (and often openly) desired to crush the Republic and speed the return of a king.

In order to assure that there would not be too much democracy, the new constitution provided for a bicameral legislature, a Chamber of Deputies elected by universal male suffrage (women could not vote until 1945) and a Senate, which was not. Intended as a brake against the popular will, a fourth of the senators were elected *for life*. The others were elected to nine-year terms. None of the the Senators were directly elected; each was elected by special electoral colleges whose members were chosen by local worthies. The new constitution provided for a president, but he was also not directly elected. When a vacancy occurred, the new president was chosen (for a seven-year term) by the Chamber of Deputies and the Senate, sitting as a National Assembly, with each deputy and senator having one vote. If the president and the Senate agreed, they could dissolve the Chamber of Deputies and call for new elections. On May 16,1877, President Patrice MacMahon did just that (in what became known as the *seize mai*), but the backlash against him was so great (and ultimately ended his career) that this presidential power was never again exercised. The constitution did give the president two significant powers: the power over peace and war, and the power to name the prime minister. But the power to *name* a prime minister did not mean he would have him; the Chamber of Deputies had to approve his selection. Judges were not elected; the president appointed them.

The 1875 constitution was crafted to assure that the notables retained ultimate power, since no law could be enacted unless it had the consent of a majority of the deputies and the senators. Clemenceau would rail against this Constitution for the next two decades, demanding that it be reformed or scrapped, despite the fact that, as the years went by, Republicans would wrest control of the Senate and Clemenceau himself would become a senator.

Clemenceau's career on the national stage began on February 20, 1876, when he won a seat to the Chamber of Deputies from the Clingancourt section of the Montmartre, a district he would represent for the next thirteen years. He left the voters with no doubt as to where he stood. He was a Radical Republican, devoted to "the completion of the great renovation of 1789 that has been abandoned by the French bourgeoisie."[1] His program did not lack in specifics. Speaking at the Cirque Fernando, a local hall where he would give many of his major speeches in the coming years, he outlined his program. He wanted the separation of church and state, accompanied by free and obligatory primary education, and the expulsion of the Jesuits from the schools. At that time, more than half of French children were taught in church schools. Although France had a constitution, it had no equivalent of the American Bill of Rights. Clemenceau demanded freedom of speech, press and assembly, the election of judges and the elimination of the death penalty. He wanted an income tax, an inheritance tax, and truly compulsory military service. And of course, he demanded amnesty for the *communards*.[2]

He won easily. The Republicans swept to a majority in the Chamber of Deputies, winning 367 of 532 seats. In his election address, he told his constituents: "The conservative Republicans ask for the minimum Republic…We ask for the maximum. We, the Radical Republicans, want the Republic for its natural consequences—the great and fruitful social reforms it brings with it."[3] But not all Republicans were *radicals*; Clemenceau and his fellow radicals were a minority of all of the Republicans and a tiny minority of the Chamber as a whole. The "right," which included monarchists such as President MacMahon, and conservative republicans, controlled the Senate.

Clemenceau was now thirty-five. He closed his medical office following his election. His career as a medical doctor was now over. On March 12, the radicals caucused in Victor Hugo's home. They decided to introduce bills in the Chamber and the Senate calling for a total amnesty for the communards. Victor Hugo introduced the bill in the Senate. Eighty-two year-old Francois-Vincent Raspail, a veteran of the 1848 revolution and a hero to the radicals, introduced the bill in the Chamber. Clemenceau's career as an orator began on May 16, when he rose in the Chamber to plead what he must have known to be the hopeless cause of amnesty for the condemned of the commune.

Clemenceau was not and would never be an eloquent orator; he did not have a powerful voice. He made his career by his choice of words and the way he marshalled his facts. A not unbiased observer, Camille Pelletan, who would be his editor at *La Justice*, observed: "If you want to know the man, go and listen to him at the tribune. No ornaments, save from time to time a biting line, a word struck with a punch. No concern to round out a sentence, to make a phrase sing… [His] word is naked, tempered and sharpened like a foil; his speeches resemble a fencing match; they riddle the opponent with direct lunges."[4] Another friendly observer, Louis Andrieux, one of Clemenceau's editors at *La Travail* during their student days, was present on the day of Clemenceau's maiden address. Years later he wrote: "I can still see Clemenceau standing in the tribune while he enlarged upon his argument in curt, simple sentences…without any bombastic and oratorical show, but accurate, neat and to the point."[5]

At the time of the speech, there were 5,496 condemned communards. Of these 3,609 had ben deported, 240 were serving sentences at hard labor, and 1,647 were in solitary confinement. Upwards of 100,000 had fled the country to avoid imprisonment.[6] Clemenceau began his case for amnesty with a review of recent French history. He referred to "February 2" the date in 1851 when Louis-Napoleon crushed the Second Republic with the coup that brought with it the Second Empire. "Has there ever been an insurrection more criminal than that?…Has there ever been one less excusable, less justified?" He then asked why this crime was never "amnestied?" "Because it was successful!" He then turned to the recent war itself. "Who," he asked, "prepared for war and prepared us for defeat, and declared war under pretexts which they today cannot here produce, and which they have never tried to produce." He was interrupted with applause, but only from his fellow deputies from the left. He reminded his fellow deputies of Marshal Bazaine, who had surrendered his entire army at Metz without a fight, "who committed treason to his country, who delivered up his entire army to the enemy…who was condemned to death, but who now walks freely through all of the capitals of Europe." And then: "I ask you why all of this severity to one side, and all this indulgence to the other?"

He pleaded with the deputies to consider the conditions under which the commune arose. There was the siege, and all of the privations that it brought. There was also the feeling that the people of Paris had felt betrayed by a government too eager to capitulate. "You will never find an insurrection with less premeditation, or one where human wishes had less impact on events." He urged the deputies to offer amnesty as a way of binding the country so as to avoid future insurrections. The issue was not just theoretical; it was also personal. His mentor of student days Louis Blanqui was still in prison. His Montmartre friend Louise Michel was languishing in exile in Noumea in New Caledonia, receiving small cash gifts from Clemenceau to ease her suffering. "Do you believe," he asked, "that by leaving men in Noumea you avoid the danger of new insurrections? The danger will not be there; it will be in our streets, our homes, our cities."[7]

When he rose to speak, he was a freshman deputy. When he sat down, he was the leader of the radicals. As expected, the bills failed by wide margins in the Chamber and

the Senate, having attracted no support from the monarchist right. But the bill in the
Chamber also failed to garner the support of the Opportunists, and in particular their
leader, Léon Gambetta. The man who had founded the Republic, who had at his peril
escaped the siege in a balloon so as to form an army and who embodied the resistance
to the invaders, was now firmly in the moderate center.

A bill for partial amnesty was introduced in 1879. It would exclude from amnesty
all of the condemned considered "enemies of society." Clemenceau mocked this half
step in the Chamber: "M. le duc de Broglie (a former prime minister) is an enemy of
society in the eyes of M. de Baudry d' Asson (a monarchist deputy), and I hold M. de
Baudry d'Asson to be an enemy of society. We are thirty-six million 'enemies of society'
who are condemned to live in the same society."[8] The partial amnesty passed, and those
in exile were reduced to approximately a thousand. Full amnesty did not come until
the next year, and when it did Gambetta supported it. Louise Michel, who had been
exiled in 1873, did not return until 1880. She had been offered an earlier pardon, but
refused to accept it until every communard was freed. When she returned, Clemenceau
was standing on the station platform to greet her.[9]

Clemenceau was now the leader of the radical left, and there he stayed. In 1879,
Clemenceau formally broke with Gambetta, and took his radical followers with him.
In that year, the Republican anthem, *La Marseillaise,* was adopted as France's national
anthem; July 14 was proclaimed as a national holiday.

Any Parisian in 1880 wishing to buy a daily newspaper had upwards of *seventy* from
which to choose. Most were four to six pages and had small circulations. They carried
little hard news but lots of commentary. Most were the mouthpieces of a politician
or faction, catering to a faithful following. Léon Gambetta's house organ was *La
Republique Francaise.* Jules Grévy, the President from 1879–1887, had *La Paix.* The
leading liberal outlet was still *Le Temps,* with whom Clemenceau had corresponded
from New York years before. In November, 1879, Clemenceau approached Auguste
Scheurer-Kestner. He wanted to start a newspaper of republican ideas "a little more
advanced" than Gambetta's paper.[10]

On January 16, 1880, *La Justice* was born. The seed capital for *La Justice* came
from Clemenceau's father, who sold a parcel of land to raise the cash. Other members
of Clemenceau's family contributed, as did Scheurer-Kestner. He also received a stake
from one Cornelius Herz, a shadowy investor who would land Clemenceau in more
trouble than Herz's investment was worth. By December, 1886, *La Justice* would feel

constrained to announce in its pages that Herz was no longer a shareholder in *La Justice*, his shares having been bought out in April, 1885.

La Justice had modest offices at 10, rue du Faubourg in the Montmartre that it shared with *Le Temps*. *La Justice* accepted no advertising and had no regular subscribers. It did attract ten thousand daily readers, but it never turned a profit and Clemenceau constantly scrounged for loans and gifts. Clemenceau gave himself the title of "political director," at an annual salary of 30,000 francs (approximately $6,000). But he did very little actual writing, most of which was done by the editor-in-chief, Camille Pelletan. Clemenceau had a large office, but was usually present only during the evening. Gustave Geffroy, an acquaintance of Manet, Monet and Renoir, was the art critic. Alexandre Millerand, a future prime minister, served on the staff, as did Charles Longuet, Karl Marx's son-in-law, now taking a second turn under Clemenceau, having served on the staff of *La Travail* during their student days. Stephen Pichon, age twenty-three in 1880, would ghost-write many of Clemenceau's articles. He would later serve as Clemenceau's foreign minister and accompany Clemenceau to the Peace Conference in 1919. Clemenceau would make his mark as an orator, not as a writer. He said that he had a fear of blank paper.

The lead article on the first day of publication, headed "To our Readers," stated the new newspaper's intentions: "We have no need for long explanations. We know who we are. What we want can be taken in one word: The Republic."[11] A long article on the front page was headed "La Justice." It began: "Justice, a little word, the greatest of them all this side of kindness. A word that man cannot hear without feeling better… The great formula of the Revolution, Liberty, Equality, Fraternity, which contain in these three words all the rights of man, all the social reforms, all of the precepts of morality, can be resumed in a still briefer formula, Justice."[12] It continued: "Justice! It is the new doctrine that must destroy the old dogmas; it is the truth and the right, the light and the force of conscience. The golden key to the future…"[13] *La Justice* also carried this small item that first day: "Various official papers affirm the news that the German government intends to ask the Reichstag for credits to increase the artillery of the army of the German Empire."[14]

Clemenceau founded *La Justice* in the midst of a thaw in French-German relations. After the "War in Sight" scare, neither Paris nor Berlin wished for war. Bismarck's goals, as ever, were more subtle. Following France's surprisingly rapid recovery from the war and the early repayment of the indemnities, Bismarck sought to isolate France diplomatically from the rest of Europe. He did this by concluding treaties with other powers that excluded France, and by encouraging the rise of French republicanism, in the belief that a republican France would be anathema to the crowned heads of

Europe, particularly the tsar in Moscow and the kaiser in Vienna. He also openly encouraged and aided France's colonial expansion into Africa and southeast Asia. This policy was cynical, but not secret. He made no attempt to hide his belief that a France that was preoccupied elsewhere might not think too hard about Alsace and Lorraine, once confiding to the French ambassador: "I hope to reach the point where you will forgive Sedan as you have forgiven Waterloo. Renounce the Rhine, and I will help you to secure everywhere else the satisfactions you desire."[15]

Clemenceau opposed French colonial expansion for the same reason that Bismarck fostered it. Clemenceau feared that colonial expansion was a diversion of French resources which would weaken France militarily if war with Germany ever came. He would always urge that France focus on "the blue line of the Vosges" behind which lay the eternal menace—Germany.[16] He also feared that colonial expansion was a German trap; that expanding into Africa and Asia would place France at loggerheads with other European powers, further diverting France from Germany. His fears proved prescient. France would repeatedly clash with England in Egypt. After France snatched Tunisia in 1881, Italy, unable to stop an incursion into what it believed to be in its sphere of influence, joined the alliance with Germany and Austria-Hungary, further isolating France. Clemenceau also saw in colonial expansion a profit motive: "One begins with the missionary, follows up with the soldiers, and ends up with the bankers."[17]

In his attempt to divert French consciousness from Alsace-Lorraine, Bismarck had a perfect partner in Jules Ferry, the Opportunist prime minister from September, 1880 to November, 1881 (and again from February 1883 to April, 1885), and the man who would be Clemenceau's principal *bete noire* throughout this period. Just as Bismarck wished France would forget Alsace and Lorraine, Ferry wished it too. In a telling exchange with the arch-*revanchist* Paul Déroulède, Ferry asked Déroulède: "Must we hypnotise ourselves with the lost provinces, and should we not take compensations elsewhere?" To which Déroulède replied: "That is just the point. I have lost two children, and you offer me twenty domestics."[18]

Jules Ferry (1832–1893) began his career as a journalist in the Second Empire. A man of "strong views and strong character,"[19] he was, like Clemenceau, a devotee of Auguste Comte's "positivist" philosophy. "My aim," he said, "is to organize humanity without God or King."[20] Like Clemenceau, he had refused a church wedding. Unlike Clemenceau, he was slow on his feet, and twice it would be his undoing at Clemenceau's hands. In September, 1880, Ferry was made minister of public instruction, and he would make the most of it in his brief (fourteen-month) tenure. When Ferry took office, a majority of French children were taught in church schools and/or taught by lay brothers or nuns. All that was required for a brother or nun to teach in a state-supported school was a "letter of obedience" from the local cleric. To Republicans of all stripes, this was particularly galling. Not only did the Republicans believe that French children were receiving a poor education, they also believed (correctly) that the children were imbibing monarchist, anti-republican views. hey feared that if another generation of French children was taught in church schools, the Republic might founder. There was no greater issue in Republican minds than reform of French education.

Ferry's principal target was the Jesuits. There were other teaching orders, but it was for the Jesuits that Ferry directed his greatest wrath: "[I]t is from them that we wish to tear away the soul of the youth of France."[21] He proposed a statute requiring all "unauthorized religious orders" to disband. When the Senate—still very much in the grip of conservatives—failed to pass it, he accomplished the same end by means of a decree giving them three months to disband. When the Jesuits refused, he ordered them exiled. In 1880, the first *lycee* for girls was opened. He also opened state-run normal schools, which became the source of lay teachers. In 1881, Ferry pushed through the first law mandating compulsory primary education. The next year, after he became prime minister, free primary education was established. Ferry pushed through a law that required all teachers to pass a state exam; a majority of the clerical teachers passed. All of these statutes were enacted over the opposition of the Church and their followers in the Chamber. But most important to the Republicans was the *laicization* of the syllabus, to exclude religious teaching in state-supported schools. But none of this was enough for Clemenceau, who called Ferry's education reforms little more than "removing of the furniture from the Capuchins."[22] Indeed, Church brothers and nuns could still teach in state schools. They were not banned from the schools until 1886.

Moritz Szeps (1835–1902) was a Viennese journalist and the editor of *Neues Wiener Tagblatt*, the leading liberal daily in Vienna. He was also a confidant of liberal-leaning Crown Prince Rudolf, the son of Emperor Franz Joseph I and the heir to the Austro-Hungarian throne. Rudolf never acceded to the throne. Despondent over a failing marriage and his father's demand that he end his relationship with his mistress, Rudolf took his life in 1889, at the age of thirty-one. Szeps and his daughter, Berta Szeps-Zuckerkandl, were also close to Clemenceau. In 1882, Berta's sister Sophie married Clemenceau's younger brother Paul, and the two families were thereafter united by marriage.

Szeps' first interview with Clemenceau occurred on May 1, 1880, shortly before he founded *La Justice*. He noted that Clemenceau was "medium-sized, supple, has short black hair with a few streaks of grey, moustache is still quite dark, olive complexion, black and lively eyes, talks quickly but distinctly, light baritone voice. Carelessly dressed, he had the obvious nervousness of a very busy man."[23] There were two things on Clemenceau's mind that day. The first was his constant frustration with the temporizing of the Opportunists. There was then no law guaranteeing freedom of assembly or freedom of the press. "The present government believes what previous governments have believed–that it is not strong enough to permit freedom of meetings and freedom of the press. To uphold the government two great liberties must be withheld, liberties without which no real liberty is possible."[24] The second thing on Clemenceau's mind that day was Germany. "[I] do know what France ought to do against Bismarck. Do you remember how the Prussians managed to take Paris? They didn't move until we had exhausted our provisions, and then we had to surrender. That is the way we ought to treat Bismarck. Remain quiet. Bismarck is surrounded by hundreds of difficulties, which will repeat themselves and increase, until from these difficulties real danger will develop. If Bismarck is not alive then, his successor will be, and I have the confident hope that we shall be able to take back that which is ours and which can never cease to be ours. That is my prediction of the course of the future."[25] He continued: "I am informed about certain political combinations who want Bismarck to give us back Metz and Lorraine, while on the other hand the German provinces of Austria should be joined in a new German Bund. Bismarck's power would be increased by this. Metz and Lorraine would be worthless to us unless Alsace were included. But even if they give us both, we must consider carefully whether Austria should be dismembered in this way. It might be better to avoid this and wait for the time when Alsace-Lorraine will be returned to us. Or even to make war to prevent the German provinces in Austria from being joined to Germany."[26]

Clemenceau's antipathy to Jules Ferry stemmed from the days of the commune, when Ferry supported Thiers' unsuccessful attempt to seize the guns of Montmartre. But the issue that divided them most was Ferry's policy of colonial expansion, and Clemenceau's opposition to it.

France had colonial outposts before Ferry assumed office, in Algeria and Senegal in Africa and another in "cochinchina," which was the southern third of present-day Vietnam, with its capital at Saigon. Ferry's stated reasons for wanting more colonies were that with other European nations becoming more protectionist, France needed sources of raw materials for French industries and outlets for its exports. A practical reason for colonial expansion was to give French army officers something to do, as many of them were languishing of boredom. But the principal reason may have been psychological:

Ferry believed that France needed to do something assuage the humiliation of Sedan. A war with Germany was out of the question, but news of victories in far-off places would be good for France and better for the Republicans.

Ferry had another rationale for colonies, akin to the British "white man's burden." Ferry said that "The European nations have a superior duty of civilization towards the native peoples…that the superior races have rights over inferior races…France must carry everywhere she can her language, her customs, her flag, her arms, her genius."[27] Clemenceau later skewered this argument: "The Chinese, an inferior race!…[W[hen Chinese diplomats are at grips with certain European diplomats…they cut a pretty good figure; if you consult the diplomatic records of certain peoples you'll find documents which prove that the yellow race from the standpoint of business skills—the conduct of infinitely delicate operations—is in no way inferior to those who are in too much of a hurry to proclaim their supremacy."[28]

And so Ferry set his sights on—Tunisia! On March 31, 1881, the Ferry government announced that a nomadic tribe based in Tunisia had crossed the border into Algeria, threatening France's colony there. Ferry, in his request for credits to fund the expedition, stated that "the government of the Republic does not seek conquests;" that it intended to do nothing more than punish the marauding Kroumirs.[29] This was the pretext for the government's incursion into Tunisia. It was patently specious, with wags in Paris suggesting that the government would provide a reward to anyone who could find a Kroumir. As Clemenceau would later delight in pointing out, the proof that the Kroumirs were a fig leaf for the real purpose of the expedition was that French forces, once they crossed the border into Tunisia, headed straight for the palace of the local prince, the Bey. The army commander was given authority to enter into a treaty with the dissolute and bankrupt Bey, a treaty that Ferry's government had prepared in advance and which lacked only the Bey's signature. The Treaty of Bardo (the Bey's summer palace) was concluded on May 12, which the Chamber of Deputies ratified on May 23. In exchange for being allowed to keep his throne, the Bey ceded authority over all foreign affairs and most internal affairs to France. Tunisia was now a French protectorate. Bismarck publicly supported the policy, and Ferry expressed his gratitude for Bismarck's support.[30] Bismarck added that he hoped that one day France would realize that German friendship was more valuable to France than the million inhabitants of Alsace-Lorraine.[31]

That is where matters might have ended, except that fighting broke out among the Tunisian tribes, and it appeared that the army would have to fight a prolonged—and expensive—war in the north African desert. The rebellion continued, with heavy losses, and the public began to suspect that the operation was benefitting speculators, not France. All of this occurred in the midst of French elections. The results were a huge victory for the Republicans, who obtained an outright majority in the Chamber of Deputies for the first time. But Gambetta's followers fared better than the more conservative Ferry (Clemenceau won re-election handily) and it became clear that Ferry's days were numbered.

Clemenceau challenged Ferry's Tunisia policy in the Chamber. He delighted in pointing out that the request for credits was titled: "Operations on the Border of Tunisia" but the first thing that the army did was head straight for the walls of Bardo.[32] Ferry appealed to the patriotism of the deputies, asserting that dissention at home was the real enemy of French interests abroad. To which Clemenceau rejoined: "Patriotism does not consist in pronouncing excited phrases about the grandeur of *La Patrie*: true patriotism consists in saying that today we want the truth."[33] Not only had Ferry started a shooting war and presented the Chamber with a *fait accompli*, but Ferry had violated the Constitution: "The prime minister thinks he can close the affair by saying: 'We have not declared war.' But that is precisely our grievance. You have not declared war, but you have made it."[34]

A majority of the Chamber wanted Ferry out, but many deputies—Gambetta included—were not at all opposed to France gaining another colony. Gambetta proposed a compromise: The Chamber would express its approval of the Treaty of Bardo, but would at the same time record a vote of no confidence against Ferry. The compromise carried by a vote of 355–68. The next day, November 14, 1881, four days after having been skewered by Clemenceau, the revolving door swung again, and Ferry resigned. It was the beginning of Clemenceau's reputation as the "destroyer of ministries" (although the election returns had destroyed Ferry as much as Clemenceau's oratory) and it would not be the last time he and Ferry would lock horns over colonies.

Ferry was out and Gambetta in, and France kept her protectorate in Tunisia. The détente with Germany continued. Clemenceau's opposition to colonies would always be a minority position, with most Frenchmen taking pride in France's overseas possessions as a sign of French greatness, or at least a sign of French recovery. By the beginning of the First World War France would have the world's second largest colonial empire, second only to Great Britain's.

The revolving door swung quickly for Gambetta. He ministry lasted all of ten weeks, foundering on questions of constitutional reform. By January 30, 1882, he was out. It would prove to be the end of his career. Shortly before the elections, Gambetta sat for an interview with Moritz Szeps. During the course of a wide-ranging *tour d'horizon*, he advised Szeps: "If we ever had a war with Germany and we were victorious we would not commit the folly of asking for a war indemnity of many billions and create an economic breakdown such as Germany created in France."[35] He would not live to see how wrong his prophesy would prove to be. On the last day of 1882, he accidently shot himself in the arm. The gunshot wound didn't kill him, but the appendicitis did. He was forty-four.

In 1882, France fell into a depression from which it would not fully recover until the end of the century. Everything that the politicians said and did during this period must be filtered through the prism of the economic misery that afflicted every sector of French society. The depression was world-wide, having begun in the United States with the "Panic of 1873," which lasted until 1879. Nations were affected at different times and in differing degrees of severity. France, whose economy had grown at a steady 3% per annum from 1847 to 1859, grew not at all between 1882 and 1892.[36]

It began relatively late in France, with the crash of the Paris stock market—the *bourse*—in January, 1882. The most spectacular collapse was that of *Union Générale*. A relative newcomer (founded in 1878) it was created as a business venture for the Catholic political right, monarchists and Church members. Its shareholders included bishops, archbishops, and Cardinal Jacobini, the pope's personal secretary.[37] Its founder, Eugène Bontoux (1820–1905) a devout Catholic, stated that it was his purpose to "unite the financial strength of Catholics…which [now] is entirely in the hands of adversaries of their faith and their interests."[38] Everyone understood that "adversaries of their faith" meant Jews and Protestants. Bontoux investing in everything, including Russian factories, Roman tramways, Romanian natural gas fields, and French breweries,[39] spending investors' money as fast as he could rake it in. In 1879, a share of *Union Générale* could be had for five hundred francs. By 1881, that share could be sold for three thousand francs. Then the price leveled off; then it crashed. When it did, the disaster touched all of France, from the well-to-do down to domestic servants. On the day it closed, they lined the street in front of *Union Générale*'s offices in the vain hope of retrieving some of their money. *Le Figaro* reported: "The despair of these people who have lost everything is pitiable to contemplate. Numbers of priests were among them, and many women, weeping bitterly."[40] Bontoux was arrested, charged with having attracted investors the old-fashioned way: by cooking the bank's books. He was sentenced to five years in prison, but escaped to Spain to avoid his sentence. Predictably, he took no responsibility for the bank's collapse, blaming instead the Jews and the Freemasons who, he believed, wished to kill off a competitor.

What came to be called the "Long Depression" was in France a period of price deflation. It did not hit all industries equally. The wine growers were hit the hardest; the depression coincided with the "French Wine Blight," which destroyed 40% of French grape vines and is estimated to have cost France twice what it paid to Germany in indemnities. The misery that the depression caused resulted in many Frenchmen losing patience with the endless ministerial revolving door. As only Republicans came and went, the public would naturally blame the Republicans. There would be a reckoning.

The revolving door swung a few more times, and by February, 1883, Ferry was back in, (his predecessor had lasted all of twenty-three days) and the rage for colonies intensified. In 1881, a French naval officer, Pierre de Brazza, explored the Congo River basin and founded what is now Brazzaville, the capital of the Republic of Congo. In 1883, France conquered the island of Madagascar, and the next year laid claim to what is now Guinea.

During Ferry's first ministry, France had established a protectorate over conchinchina, the southern third of present-day Vietnam. The northern two-thirds consisted of Annam, and the northern part of Annam was Tonkin, with its capital at Hanoi. It was a tempting target. Not only were there merchants in Hanoi in need of protection, but if the French could control Tonkin it would facilitate trade with China without the need to go through Chinese port cities. In April, 1882, the French naval commandant, Henri Riviére, acting completely on his own, stormed Hanoi. The Chinese indicated that they would not turn a blind eye to Tonkin falling under the French. Riviére should have been cashiered for his actions—he expected to be—but once the revolving door swung Ferry was back in and Riviére was saved. But not for long. A year-long war broke out between the French and Chinese-backed "Black Flag" guerrillas. At the Battle of the Paper Bridge, Riviére and some of his fellow officers were killed.

Ferry dug in. He made it clear to the Chinese that he expected Tonkin to fall under French control. A 10,000-man Tonkin Expeditionary Force was formed. In order to raise and equip such an army Ferry needed money, and in order to raise the money he needed the consent of the Chamber of Deputies. Ferry's strategy was to ask for the credits piecemeal, making it difficult for the Chamber to deny any particular request. Of course, once the troops were on the ground, the army could not be left unprotected. When deputies had the temerity to inquire into the military situation, Ferry responded that to provide details would undercut his negotiations with the Chinese and the Vietnamese. The military operations were successful, and in May, 1884, France and China entered into the Tientsin Accord, wherein China recognized a French protectorate over Annam and Tonkin. [At the same time, France obtained a similar concession from the King of Cambodia.] The Tientsin Accord called for the Chinese to leave Tonkin, and when they were slow to do so, a nasty (but largely hidden) war broke out between France and China that would last another year.[41] After the Chinese ambushed French forces at the village of Bac-Lé in June 1884, resulting in the deaths of eighteen French soldiers, Ferry demanded an apology and an indemnity of two hundred million francs, which the Chinese refused, offering to pay an indemnity of three and a half million francs, which Ferry spurned.[42] Ferry doubled down again. He ordered a naval blockade of the island of Formosa, as a "pledge" against Chinese withdrawal from Tonkin.

Clemenceau rose in the Chamber on November 22 in opposition to yet another of Ferry's requests for credits to fight the war. He delivered his sharpest criticism of Ferry's colonial policy to date. The *détente* with Bismarck that had begun during Ferry's first ministry was blossoming into a rosy *entente*. In September, 1884, Ferry's minister of war, General Campenon, observed to a German officer that his government desired a *rapprochement* with Germany. His counterpart replied that this would be possible only if France would finally come to grips with the Treaty of Frankfurt that ended the Franco-Prussian War. To which Campenon replied: "That is what I am always telling my colleagues…We should no longer weakly occupy ourselves with the past, but should reckon with the present. With such an alliance France would at one blow regain her standing."[43]

Clemenceau was familiar with this thinking, and was alarmed by it. He began on that November day by noting that "Nowhere is French diplomacy found to be easier than in relations with Berlin," that "in the interests of peace, it is proposed to make [France] forget [its] losses and grievances of 1870, and to resolve to restore between France and Germany… a common interest, and the recognition of services rendered by a powerful neighbor [who]…kindly, without demands, never effects the airs of a protector."[44] "This work," he noted, "is today almost a *fait accompli.*" "But," he added, "to complete this *rapprochement*…there must have been a great change in the direction of French policy." With remarkable prescience, he observed that "[T]he policy of expansion and colonial conquest adopted by France since 1880… necessarily puts [France] in conflict with England, who considers the right of colonization as her privilege and her monopoly." He noted that at the recently-concluded London Conference on Egyptian finances, England had rejected French claims for indemnities rising out of rioting in Alexandria. "[T]he friendship of John Bull consists of deceiving France"… The ill will of Germany will be returned by the perfidy of Albion… If our neighbors think only of their interests, we should do the same." Clemenceau continued by noting that anyone who enters upon a colonial policy cannot "do any act but with the consent of the one who is, in Europe, the ruler of peace and war." Clemenceau wished, "as much as any of you, for a policy of good harmony and good relations with all of our neighbors. But there is one thing we must safeguard over all; it is our independence." "Gentlemen," he added, "Prince Bismarck is a dangerous enemy, but is perhaps a more dangerous friend." At this point he digressed and became somewhat philosophical: "Perhaps we were in greater pain in peace than in war. In war, there was the common effort to defeat the invader. After the defeat, the common feeling of recovery by work, by disinterest, by sacrifice. The dignity of defeat was intact because the right stayed intact…" However, "[I]n peace: the uncertainty of the future, the instability, the feeling that peace is capricious and impossible to predict…the irritation, the divisions, the helplessness, the awakened appetites: the neighbor takes, or wants to take; the sense of morality is weakened, right is sacrificed, national policy is distorted." Closer to the question at hand, he noted: "I know that we will seize Tonkin. I know that our valiant soldiers will be victors over the Chinese everywhere they meet them…But it is more than about Tonkin at this moment, the question is greater: it is about France…." "And now," he concluded, "the question that is posed before us is this: Is it peace or war?…I know, I am sure, that today peace is possible on the basis of the Treaty of Tientsin." Noting that the Chinese had offered an indemnity of three and a half million francs—which Ferry had rejected—he mocked the foolishness of the operation: "We fight for an indemnity of 80 millions, of which we subtract 3-1/2 millions, that is to say an indemnity of 76-1/2 millions. We engage in a deplorable commercial operation, since we spend 150 million to derive 76-1/2 million." "Yes, gentlemen, if you want peace today, you can have it." [45]

Five days later, Clemenceau was back. He again chided Ferry for failing to accept the provisions of the Treaty of Tientsin, which he called "a true miracle," because "the Chinese handed over three Tonkin provinces that you had not conquered…and offered you three and a half million, and you refused it! It is an aberration; a folly. You had that day everything you had a right to expect…You found that an indemnity of three and a half million was not sufficient. Why? There is no amount that can be paid for French blood spilled." Looking straight at Ferry, he stated that "The men who are dying at Le-Baq, they who die heroically in combat in Tonkin, they die by your mistakes. The blood spilled, the millions spent…it is your work and yours alone, since in refusing an honorable peace you have decreed a useless war."[46] But his words went unheeded, yet again. The previous day, Ferry informed the Chamber: "You will once more have patience. You will not only vote these credits, but also the forty-three millions of the next half-year; and you will patriotically insure the possession of this magnificent colony—a corollary, as it were, to our colony in Cochin-China."[47] There was little chance that the Chamber would deny the resources needed to sustain troops in the field. The Chamber voted the credits.

The war continued. It did not go well. The French found themselves fighting against not only the Black Flag guerrillas, but Chinese army regulars. By March, 1885, France had

35,000 men in Tonkin, under the command of Gen Louis Brière de l'Isle, a Martiniquais who had been captured at Sedan and who had risen rapidly in the Far East.[48] They fought continuously; even the victories proved costly. As the fighting dragged on, Ferry was required to ask for more credits. In February, one of Brière de l'Isle's commanders, Gen. Oscar de Négrier, captured Lang Son, ten miles from the Chinese border. De Négrier established an outpost at Dong Dang, right on the border, and on March 22 his troops crossed into China. Two days later he found himself locked in combat with what appeared to be the entire Imperial Army. He fell back on Lang Son, wiring Brière de l'Isle: "All the wounded have been transferred to Lang Son. Our losses stand at about two hundred killed and wounded.[49] De Négrier was himself wounded, and was replaced by Lieutenant-Colonel Paul-Gustave Herbinger, who, it quickly became obvious to all of the officers serving under him, was completely out of his depth.

On Saturday, March 28, Ferry advised the Chamber (which *La Justice* was delighted to reprint the following Monday): "He [Brière de l'Isle] is certain that, at present, General de Négrier has…the forces necessary to hold Lang-Son. He is certain that he has acquired full possession of the Tonkinese border and that we are in the best position to retreat if we wish to…Not only Lang-Son is being protected, but the entire line from Chu to Lang-Son is strongly occupied by our troops."[50]

Herbinger would surely have wondered what war Ferry was referring to had he heard those words, but at that time he was busy retreating, for the Chinese had chosen this very day to attack Lang Son. On the evening of March 28, Brière de l'Isle authored the telegram that would bring down Ferry's government: "I announce with sorrow that General de Négrier, gravely wounded, has been forced to evacuate Lang Son. The Chinese, advancing in great masses and in three columns, have attacked with an impetuosity our forward positions of Kilua. Colonel Herbinger, before this great numerical superiority and exhausted of ammunition, informs me that he has been obliged to retreat to Dong Son and Cho Moi. I am concentrating all my means of action on the outlets of Chu and of Kep. The enemy continues to increase on the [Red River]. Whatever happens, I hope to be able to defend the whole Delta. I ask the government to send me fresh reinforcements as soon as possible."[51]

In fact, Herbinger's position was not nearly as bleak as the telegram suggested, nor was de Négrier "gravely" wounded; he was only slightly wounded, and he recovered quickly, as a later telegram made clear. But the damage had been done. Paris was in a frenzy. By Monday, March 30, *Le Figaro* led with the headline "A Disaster." The next day's *Le Petit Journal* led with "The Invasion of the Barbarians." Every newspaper plastered Brière de l'Isle's telegram on its front page. By 2:00 PM, two to three thousand people were milling about in front of the Chamber of Deputies.[52]

When Jules Ferry entered the Chamber that day, he knew that his government was finished. He at least tried to salvage his policy: "The Lang Son rebuff must be retrieved and avenged. It is essential not merely for the possession of Tonkin and the future of our Indo-Chinese establishments, but for our honour all over the world."[53] Not for the last time would a powerful nation be asked to continue a failed policy in Indo-China because withdrawal would affect its "honour." In order to distance himself from the policy, he asked that the Chamber vote an additional 200 million francs ($40 million) in credits, but not to consider it to be a vote of confidence in his ministry.

Clemenceau rose. With Ferry looking directly at him, he began: "I have not come here to reply to M. Ferry…. All debate is at an end between us. We do not want to hear you anymore. We have no further desire to discuss with you the great interests of the country…We do not know you any longer; we do not wish to know you any more. On what you have said and done up to this time I wish today to throw the veil of oblivion. *It is not ministers I have before me, these are the accused.*"[54] A voice was heard: "So get off the ministers' bench."[55]

Ferry made the mistake of smiling at Clemenceau, and it caused a sensation. A deputy interrupted: "There is an indignation which cannot be suppressed. M. Jules Ferry, the president of the Council, was laughing." Clemenceau continued: "Yes, persons accused of high treason, on whom, if there be any principle of justice in France, the hand of the law will descend before long." Another interrupted: "I can state that M. Jules Ferry is still laughing."[56] Still another deputy shouted out: "They are not laughing in Tonkin, Mr. Prime minister. The country must know that you are laughing."[57]

The worst for Ferry came when he left the Chamber. He walked stoically through the ugly crowd, to the cries of "*A bas Ferry!*" "*A bas Le Chinois.*" "*Into the river with him.*" The ministry of the man who many considered the most talented politician in France was over. Clemenceau held no such opinion of Ferry. Reminiscing forty-four years later, he told his secretary, Jean Martet: "[I]n the matter of intelligence he was sub-normal, unable to do anything, not even put two words together."[58] More substantively: "You cannot have any idea of the stupidity, the incompetence, which ruled these undertakings…When Ferry pushed us toward Tonkin, he diverted us from the one thing it was imperative that we should heed and fear—Germany."[59]

In the end, the French navy soon successfully blockaded China. A new Tientsin Accord was signed implementing the original treaty. The Chinese recognized Tonkin as a French protectorate, but no indemnity was paid. The Sino-French War was over. With it ended—at least for now—France's desire for overseas expansion. Also gone with Ferry was the *entente* with Bismarck. The jeering crowds outside the Chamber had come to accept what Clemenceau had told the Chamber the prior year, that France could not "do any act but with the consent of the one who is, in Europe, the ruler of peace and war." When they realized that no colony could be had without Bismarck's approval it became clear that colonies alone could not expiate the humiliation of Sedan; that truckling for *rapprochement* with Bismarck was itself a humiliation. So France would no longer look overseas, it would look to "the blue line of the Vosges," the eastern border separating France from Germany.

The revolving door that swung Ferry out swung Henri Brisson in, but all agreed that Brisson was merely a placeholder, pending the elections scheduled for October. Since 1876, Clemenceau had represented the Montmartre in the Chamber, but in 1885 he chose to run as a candidate from both Montmartre and the town of Draguignan in the department of the Var, in the southeast of France. There are a number of plausible explanations for the decision. He had made speaking trips to the area on a number of occasions, had befriended the mayor of Toulon, Henri Dutasta, and found the area congenial, which was heavily agricultural but staunchly republican. More importantly, the republicans in Paris were splintering into numerous subgroups and factions, just at a time when the rightists and monarchists were uniting into a conservative front. It is also possible that Clemenceau feared opposition from his *left*. He believed in social reform and called himself a "socialist," but not for a moment was he opposed to private property. In 1885, the Socialists would get their first deputy elected. Clemenceau may have seen the handwriting on the wall. He was elected from both Montmartre and the Var, and chose to represent the Var. It would be his political home for the rest of his career.

In July, Clemenceau was making a campaign speech in Bordeaux, focusing on the usual republican issues of electoral reform and universal suffrage, when he was interrupted by a voice in the crowd: "What about Alsace-Lorraine?" He didn't miss a beat: "We have nothing to hide. We do not wish to unleash a war in Europe, but if a war is unleashed on us, we will accept it. But there is a greater *revanche* than a military *revanche*, it is the *revanche* of a republic who, by the example of the revival that it shows to the nations, by the wisdom with which it conducts itself, by the development of its political, economic and social institutions…that justice will be rendered to the people of France." He continued: "But since you have awakened the memory, let me say that the duty of the French government is to safeguard above all the dignity of its independence…I mean by that it must maintain resolve…against those who are the masters of Europe…and their fantasies." He noted that "today peace is made, yet we retain 35,000 men in the Orient, while we did not have more than 25,000 in time of war, and if we are challenged, perhaps you will return to those who gave us these poor counsels and repeat to them the words the interrupter spoke a little while ago: "What about Alsace-Lorraine?"[60]

The republicans suffered a defeat at the polls, with the former Legitimists, Orleanists, Bonapartists and other rightists now united in a Conservative front. They wisely resisted calling for a kingly restoration, even though a restoration was what many Conservatives still longed for. They ran a clever campaign. In wheat-growing regions they promised to raise the price of wheat. In industrial regions they promised to lower the price of necessities. In some regions they were protectionists; in others they were free traders.[61] It worked. Conservatives of all stripes doubled their seats in the Chamber. A combination of the effects of the depression, the now-discredited colonial policy and a weariness with the revolving door contributed to the republican defeat. That the Opportunists under Ferry had instituted numerous reforms including expansion of freedom of the press, legalization of trade unions and the secularization of education was forgotten. But the defeat contained a silver lining for the radicals. Before the election, the Opportunists could form a government and choose a cabinet without their help. Now, the Opportunists would need to turn to the radicals and their leader Clemenceau to form a government. The man chosen was Charles de Freycinet, Gambetta's right-hand man in the desperate days after Sedan when Gambetta formed an army in the vain hope of breaking the siege of Paris. This would be de Freycinet's third turn as prime minister, and the second time he would succeed Ferry.

Clemenceau's input in the formation of de Freycinet's ministry was in the man he nominated to be Minister of War. His choice would not only call into question his judgment but would for a brief moment imperil the very existence of republican government in France.

It is not that General Georges-Ernest-Jean-Marie Boulanger (1837–1891) and Clemenceau had nothing in common. Both grew up in Nantes, and had even attended the same *lycee*. Boulanger's father had been persecuted by the Second Empire, as had Benjamin Clemenceau. Clemenceau must have appreciated that Boulanger did not attend mass. But that is where the similarities end. The great French diplomat Paul Cambon said that it was hard to imagine what attracted Clemenceau to Boulanger, as "Boulanger read little and knew little."[62] Before the de Freycinet cabinet was formed, Clemenceau told Moritz Szeps' daughter that he was "rather fond" of Boulanger, that he was a "*charmeur*," a "good speaker" who "wins everyone's heart," and that he hoped de Freycinet would appoint Boulanger as Minister of War.[63] If Clemenceau couldn't see through Boulanger, others did. One of Boulanger's fellow officers called Boulanger "the greatest theatrical genius of all time…Whether he is giving an order or receiving a wound, all the attention is focused on him. Assemble a hundred generals and he is the only one who gets noticed.[64] Ferry called him a "shameless demagogue."[65] Clemenceau's great friend Auguste Scheurer-Kestner wrote that Clemenceau knew "perfectly well" that Boulanger was "quite without intellectual value," and lacked "moral sense."[66] Those who came to know Boulanger—even those who supported him—came to know that he was an unprincipled chameleon who agreed with everyone he met.

Minister of War was considered an apolitical appointment, and by tradition was filled by a general. The belief was unanimous that Clemenceau pushed de Freycinet into taking Boulanger. He did not have to push very hard. With Clemenceau's nominee in office, de Freycinet felt that he had inoculated himself from Clemenceau and the radicals and might even ensure himself of Clemenceau's support. With Boulanger by his side, the revolving door would not swing. When someone warned de Freycinet of the danger of having a man like Boulanger in his cabinet, he replied: "Do not be uneasy. I have an eye on him."[67]

On January 7, 1886, de Freycinet formed his government. On the very next day, Boulanger went to work. He issued an "Order of the Day" to all officers and enlisted men, calling for discipline and promising to continue the work of reforming the army that had begun before the war. On that same day, he began replacing upper-echelon war ministry personnel with his own acquaintances. Curiously, he established a press office in the war ministry, which had never felt the need to issue press releases. He quickly began to institute changes that while minor were intended to improve the soldiers' morale. He improved the quality of their food. He allowed them to grow beards. Noncommissioned officers would be allowed to live with their wives in the towns where they were stationed. In a move surely designed to burnish his republican credentials, he proposed to end the exemption from military service of men studying for the priesthood. (The measure was adopted in 1889.) He wanted to abolish promotion based on seniority. The proposal didn't pass, but it further endeared him to the radicals.

With *détente* with Germany now dead, Boulanger had no objection to being called "General Revanche." One admirer wrote to him: "Save us from the abyss…Lead our legions to glory…Guide our two sisters Alsace and Lorraine back home with your strong hand."[68] But no one counseled a military *revanche* more openly than Paul Déroulède (1846–1914). Captured at Sedan at the age of twenty-four, he escaped to fight *against* the commune. He published a series of popular patriotic poems, *Chants du Soldat*. In 1882 he formed the *Ligue des patriotes*, which had one purpose: *revanche*. He claimed that it had 300,000 members. It may not have had a third of that, but whatever their numbers, they made themselves known at annual war commemorations. They stressed physical fitness and rifle practice on the German model. Déroulède would have nothing to do with *entente*, and by 1885 was calling Ferry an ally of Bismarck. He believed that what France had lost by war she could regain only by war. In the 1885 elections he ran for a Paris seat, and won with 100,000 votes. Boulanger was his man. He wrote to Boulanger: "Some people believe the wounds in our flanks caused by the loss of Alsace-Lorraine have healed. You have reopened these wounds. You have deepened them. You have bored into them with glowing iron. You have caused them to bleed anew and prevented them from healing."[69]

If the French longed for a man on horseback, Boulanger would be that man. The Bastille Day festivities had been relatively low-key affairs prior to 1886, then being a *republican* celebration, which many French conservatives had little interest in observing. Boulanger changed that. He moved the celebration to the Longchamps racetrack in the Bois de Boulogne. Fifteen thousand soldiers, many festooned in their colonial garb, paraded past the cheering spectators, with Boulanger, on his newly-purchased black steed (he named it "Tunis") in the lead. No one—including de Freycinet and President Grévy—could fail to notice that Boulanger received the loudest cheers.

Across the Rhine, Bismarck noticed the rise of Boulanger, and used it to his advantage. The German press began calling Boulanger "General Revanche," in an attempt to scare the German parliament into approving a seven-year military appropriation. When Bismarck received only a three-year appropriation, he prorogued parliament and called for new elections. Bismarck warned France's ambassador to Berlin: "If Boulanger becomes premier or president of the republic, it means war."[70] A month before the German elections, Bismarck massed seventy-two thousand reservists for military exercises *in Alsace-Lorraine*. In response, Boulanger—without informing his government—ordered materials for the construction of military installations in French Lorraine. When word of this reached Bismarck, he demanded an explanation from de Freycinet, who, of course, knew nothing of it. Again without consulting his government, Boulanger drafted an order for maneuvers only a few kilometers from where the Germans were training. When President Grévy learned of it, he confronted Boulanger: "Don't you realize that this would mean war?" Boulanger replied: "I am ready," to which Grévy coolly replied that if war came between Germany and an unprepared France, Boulanger would have to fight it on the Marne, not the Saar.[71] The French constitution gave the president few powers, but the power over peace and war was one of them. When Boulanger threatened to resign if the order was not approved, Grévy called his bluff, and no French troops were sent to the border. Calm was restored only after the German elections in February, 1887. The results were favorable to Bismarck, who got his seven-year military appropriation.

Soon after Boulanger assumed office, he began building an extensive network of spies. Among them was one Guillaume Schnaebelé, an Alsatian-born *commissaire spéciale* (a police inspector), who had his own network of spies along the Alsatian border. On April 20, 1887, in response to an invitation from a German border official, Schnaebelé crossed the border into Germany, whereupon he was promptly arrested and hauled off to jail in Leipzig. Boulanger pressed for mobilization, which Grévy refused. In the negotiations that followed (which did not include Boulanger) de Freycinet pressed the case that since Schnaebelé had been *invited* over the border, it was the equivalent of a diplomatic safe conduct. Bismarck agreed, and ten days after his capture Schnaebelé was released. The Schnaebelé "Affair" was over. But the man who emerged with his reputation enhanced was Boulanger. In the public mind, someone—Boulanger—had finally stood up to Bismarck with success.

But by now Clemenceau as well as the Opportunists were becoming alarmed at Boulanger's recklessness. When the government of René Goblet fell in May, 1887 (having replaced de Freycinet, who was ousted the prior December) Boulanger went with him. Moderates in both the Chamber and the Senate made it clear to Goblet's successor, Maurice Rouvier, that re-appointing Boulanger was out of the question. Rouvier's accession to the premiership was significant for Clemenceau and the radicals, in that Rouvier formed a coalition with the center and the *right*; the radicals were excluded. Rouvier appointed Boulanger as commander of the 13th Army Corps in Clermont-Ferrand, in central France. Although it wasn't New Caledonia, it was far enough from Paris that they thought they were done with him. They were mistaken. On July 8, the day he was scheduled to depart for oblivion from the Gare de Lyon, a crowd estimated at three thousand surrounded his hotel. Newspapers loyal to him published the intended route and the time of his arrival at the station. The Paris chief of police estimated that there were twenty thousand cheering partisans at the station. They walked on the tracks, and for two hours would not let Boulanger's train depart. When he was finally able to depart with the aid of the chief of police, the angry crowd dispersed to cries of "Down with Grévy," and "To the Elysée."[72] If this had been a moment where Boulanger could have mounted a *coup de'etat*, he had let it pass.

Three days later, Clemenceau referred to his former protegé in the Chamber as a man whose "popularity has come too quickly to someone who liked noise too much, or who, to speak more equitably, did not avoid it enough.[73] But if Clemenceau thought he was done with Boulanger, he too was mistaken.

If there is one thing that Boulanger wanted, it was his former position as minister of war. Having been forsaken by the left, Boulanger turned to the right. In January, 1888, Boulanger (who was, of course, still in uniform) met secretly in Switzerland with

Prince Jerome Napoleon, a grand nephew of Napoleon I, advising the prince that he was considering going into politics. The prince promised him financial support. Boulanger hooked up with a Bonapartist journalist, Georges Thiébaud, who saw in Boulanger a "new Napoleon," who devised a brilliant strategy. At that time, candidates for the Chamber were permitted to run from multiple constituencies (just as Clemenceau had run from Montmartre and the Var), and constituencies could have multiple representatives. Boulanger would run in by-elections all over France. If he won, he would immediately resign, and stand for office in the next by-election. The result would be a national plebiscite on Boulanger.

Boulanger's appeal to the monarchist right was obvious: They would use him in a last-ditch attempt to overthrow the republic and effect a restoration. Boulanger was not a monarchist (at bottom, he believed in nothing) but he professed a belief in a strong executive. Sensing the electorate's weariness with the revolving door, Boulanger made as his platform the revision of the constitution in favor of a powerful executive. Already hugely popular following the Schnaebelé incident, his message would resonate.

In March, 1888, *La Justice* reported that on three occasions Boulanger had left his post without permission, which was then prohibited. President Sadi Carnot dismissed him from the army. Rather than deter Boulanger, it freed him to actively and openly engage in politics. The very next month, he ran in a by-election in the Nord. He ran a modern campaign, with posters, playing cards and song sheets distributed by the thousands to an electorate that included many illiterate peasants. The money for the effort came from the right, notably the three million francs he received from the Duchesse d' Uzès, the heiress to a wine-making fortune, and an additional three million from the Comte de Paris.[74] He lied to the voters about his role in the recent confrontation with Germany: "If I wanted war, I would be a fool; if I did not prepare for it, I would be a wretch."[75] He had no real ideas, instead making himself the vessel for every discontent across the political spectrum, from socialists (Louise Michel supported him) to monarchists. Be it discontent with the continued depression, discontent with a parliament that had proved to be incapable of easing its pain, or the continued sense of inferiority vis-à-vis Germany, he had the answer: revise the constitution to provide for a powerful, independent executive. He trounced his Opportunist rival, receiving 173,000 votes to the opponent's 76,000.

In August, he ran in three by-elections *in a single day*, winning them all, the Duchesse d' Uzès contributing 500,000 francs for this day alone. Her money was well-spent: At rallies, newsboys were hired to initiate cheers, at twenty-five centimes per cheer.[76] But these by-elections were side shows. Nationwide elections were scheduled for September, 1889. The plan was to sweep the 1889 elections and obtain a mandate for a constitutional revision that the monarchists hoped would be the final step in the overthrow of the republic and the restoration of the monarchy.

On January 27, 1889, Boulanger ran in a Paris by-election. It was one thing for Boulanger to trounce his rivals in rural precincts; Paris was the beating heart of the Republic. It was here that Léon Gambetta had proclaimed the Republic three days after Sedan. It was the city that had held out when most of the rest of France had collapsed. But in a campaign that had cost his backers 400,000 francs, Boulanger garnered 244,000 votes, his republican opponent 162,000 and a socialist 16,000. It was a stunning victory. He won even in Clemenceau's working-class Montmartre. It was clear that, at the polls at least, Boulanger could not be stopped. Friedrich Engels best summed up the results: "To put it mildly, Paris has, at least temporarily, abdicated as a revolutionary city."[77]

On that night, a legend was born. We know for certain that Boulanger and his inner circle (including Paul Déroulède) repaired to Durand's restaurant on the Place Madelaine to celebrate the victory. A crowd gathered outside the restaurant singing *La Marseillaise* and Boulangist songs. If there would ever be a moment for a *coup d'etat*, this was it. Clemenceau himself feared a coup, at this moment nervously asking a former *communard* what life was like in New Caledonia.[78] Before midnight, Boulanger excused himself from the restaurant and went to consult with his mistress, Madame Marguerite de Bonnemains. Apparently, when he returned he had decided that there would be no coup that night or any night, allegedly stating: "I am certain that I shall win the victory by parliamentary methods."[79] He then departed, Déroulède apparently on his heels desperately trying to change his mind. The final coda: At five minutes past midnight, Georges Thiébaud looked at his watch, and said: "*Boulangisme est en baisse*" ("Boulangism is falling").

Did Boulanger forsake an opportunity that a Hitler or a Mussolini would surely have grabbed had either stood in Boulanger's boots? There may be more myth to the story than legend. The notion that Boulanger considered a coup, then dithered, opting to spend the night in the arms of his mistress rather than the Elysee Palace, is a notion fostered by a few unreliable memoirs, including Déroulède's. If Boulanger was to be stopped and the republic saved, it would not come at the ballot box. Different means would be required. And at almost exactly that moment, one man stepped forward and set himself with the task of destroying Gen. Georges Boulanger.

Ernest Constans (1833-1913) had lately been France's governor-general of Indo-China. On February 22, 1889—less than a month after Boulanger's Paris victory—he was appointed minister of the interior. He immediately banned all public demonstrations in Paris. There would be no more marching crowds singing Boulanger songs. Then, less than three weeks after assuming office, Constans had his prosecutor announce that Paul Déroulède's *Ligue des patriotes* would be prosecuted for the offence being a "secret organization." The charge was patently absurd; the *Ligue* was among the least secret organizations in France. Nonetheless, Déroulède and two others were hauled before a High Court of the Senate. Déroulède was able to prove that all *Ligue* meetings were open to all. There being absolutely no evidence that the *Ligue* was a secret society, they were acquitted. They were, however, fined 100 francs for running an *unauthorized* organization.

But Déroulède was not the man that Constans was after. Constans had an arrest warrant prepared against Boulanger, charging him with "plotting against the state," an equally specious charge. Before serving the warrant, Constans allowed one of Boulanger's friends to "accidently" see the warrant. Word got back to Boulanger, and on April 1, 1889, Boulanger, in a disguise, with Madame de Bonnemains at his side, fled to Brussels. He too was tried before a High Court of the Senate. After a one-week trial that featured little evidence to prove the charge but which included a sufficient amount of dirt impugning Boulanger's character and morals, he was convicted and sentenced to exile.

But even this might not have been enough to seal Boulanger's fate. If Boulanger had succeeded by running in multiple districts, the obvious expedient would be to outlaw the practice, which is exactly what parliament did. In the September, 1889 elections, Boulanger would run for one seat, not all over France. The Boulangists did poorly in the 1889 elections, and the danger of a Boulangist takeover passed. It is difficult to say whether Boulanger's absence from the campaign, or the change in the election laws, or a realization that France really did not want or need a man on horseback, finally cooled the electorate to the general. In exile, Boulanger changed horses once again, now becoming a left-wing radical. It didn't matter. The real love of Boulanger's life was Madame de Bonnemains. She contracted consumption and died on July 16, 1891. On October 10, 1891, *Le Petit Journal* featured a full-color cover portrait of Boulanger standing on Madame de Bonnemains' grave. His left hand is perched on her gravestone. In his right he holds a large revolver, pressed against his right temple, no doubt at the instant before he pulled the trigger and ended his life.

On March 9, 1888, Kaiser Wilhelm I died at the age of ninety. He was succeeded by his son, Frederick III, 56. Frederick was considered something of a "liberal" (these things are relative) and hopes for him were high. He contracted cancer of the larynx, and died on June 15, having reigned for ninety-nine days. He was succeeded by his son, Wilhelm II, 29. Wilhelm had been born with a left arm six inches shorter than his right. In photos of Wilhelm, his left arm is either hidden or shown on the hilt of a sword or leaning on the horn of a saddle. At best, Wilhelm II was erratic. At worst, he was insane. When he assumed the throne, Bismarck had to convince his new sovereign not to go to war with Russia, that even if Germany prevailed, it would result in yet another neighbor pledging *revanche*. In 1890, Wilhelm II dismissed Bismarck from office. Wilhelm II believed that France was a "born mortal enemy."[80]

The definitive history of the building of the Panama Canal is told by David McCullough in *The Path Between the Seas*.[81] The story of France's quest—and ultimate failure—to build the canal is principally the story of one man: Ferdinand de Lesseps. Born in 1805, he was sixty-four when he completed the Suez Canal in 1869. De Lesseps was less an engineer than he was an entrepreneur. In fact, he was more of a salesman than anything else. But the Suez Canal—his canal—would become the pride of France, at a time when pride was very much needed, as its completion was followed the very next year by Sedan, occupation, the commune and reparations. Ferdinand de Lesseps became the toast of France.

De Lesseps once encountered a man on a train who did not recognize him. When asked his occupation, de Lesseps replied: "isthmuses." And so, de Lesseps set out to build a canal through the isthmus of Panama. It would be, like Suez, a sea level canal. Just as he had cut through the Egyptian desert, he would cut his way straight through the Panamanian jungle. There were doubters right from the start; engineers who knew that the isthmus of Panama had the most inhospitable climate *in the world*. It had malaria, it had yellow fever, it had earthquakes, but worst of all it had the raging Chagres River, which during the rainy season (which lasted eight months) could rise thirty feet in a few *hours*. For a canal to be built, the Chagres would have to be rerouted. The rain brought mudslides which could (and would) wipe away months of digging in an afternoon. They advised de Lesseps to build a canal that was a series of locks. He would have none of it. A canal that hoisted up ships and plopped them down was not his way of doing things. It was not manly; it was not *French*.

In March, 1881, *the Compagnie Universelle du Canal Interoceanique* was incorporated. De Lesseps estimated that the canal would cost 658,000,000 francs (approximately $132 million) and take eight years to build. The company offered to sell 1,200,000 shares at five hundred francs ($100.00) per share. This at a time when the average French worker earned five hundred francs *in a year*. The entire subscription was sold out in three days to 100,000 separate subscribers, making it the most widely held business in France. It meant that people by the thousands emptied their savings and mortgaged their homes and farms get in on the ground floor. Of course, they were putting their faith not in the engineers in Panama; their faith was in Ferdinand de Lesseps.

Digging began on January 20, 1882. Of all of the things that were unanticipated, including the mortality rate from yellow fever, the most serious was the extent to which de Lesseps had underestimated the sheer amount of dirt that had to be moved. Because of the mudslides, the canal had to be wider and the slope of the sides gentler than first planned. Excavating more dirt meant the cost had to be revised, which meant that the initial subscription would not come close to covering the cost of construction. To make matters worse, not all of the money went towards actual construction. Far from it. Commissions to the stock dealers (and later, bond sellers) had to be paid. Newspapers were paid for "publicity," which is a genteel way of saying their support was bought.

So the company floated bonds. Of course, not all of the money raised went towards construction. Interest had to be paid on the debt, and commissions were owed. But the public continued to place its faith in de Lesseps, the man who had built the Suez Canal. By the spring of 1885, some journalists began to question whether the canal could be completed as promised. In April of that year, the entire port city of Colon, on the Atlantic side of the isthmus, burned to the ground. Having promised to complete the canal in eight years, only ten percent had been completed by 1885. The price of the company's stock had fallen below its five hundred francs per share initial offering price, and was falling. That more journalists did not question the entire operation resulted from them having been paid for "publicity."

By 1887, de Lessups was running out of money, despite a series of conventional debt offerings. The company's stock had fallen to 287 francs per share. So de Lesseps began thinking about issuing "lottery-bonds," i.e. bonds with lottery tickets stapled to them. A purchaser was promised his interest, but he also had the prospect of winning a large cash prize if his number came up. De Lesseps' problem with lottery-bonds was that he needed the consent of the legislature to sell them. In March, 1888, several deputies introduced a bill to permit de Lesseps to sell the lottery-bonds. At the same time, the company tried yet another conventional bond offering. It was a fiasco, with only a third of the bonds having been sold. De Lesseps' only chance of survival was lottery-bonds. On April 28, the Chamber approved the issuance of the lottery-bonds by a wide margin; on June 5, the Senate approved. The law went into effect on June 8, authorizing the issuance of up to 720,000,000 francs in lottery-bonds, an amount greater than the initial stock offering. McCullough noted "The intensity of feeling for and against the company was enormous. Throughout France people talked of little else."[82]

The lottery-bond issue was a bust. Only 2,000,000 francs in bonds were sold to 350,000 investors. But after commissions and a required reserve for interest and cash prizes on the lottery, the company netted only one million francs, not nearly enough to complete the canal. But now there were an additional 350,000 people whose life savings—and whose lives—were invested in the canal. When the company tried to sell the remaining lottery-bonds on better terms it failed to raise the minimum required to complete the offering. With that, de Lesseps was out of tricks. On December, 14, 1888, the company went into receivership, and was liquidated in February, 1889. On May 15, the liquidator ordered work on the canal halted. De Lesseps, now eighty-four, took to his bed. Perhaps the most surprising thing about the collapse of the the *Compagnie Universelle* is what did not happen next. There were no riots in the streets. No one called for the government to resign. The hundreds of thousands who lost everything in the canal accept their fate. Nothing happened.

Until 1892. Edouard Drumont was a "journalist" only in the broadest sense. The horse he rode was antisemitism. His newspaper was *La Libre Parole*, and every crackpot antisemitic theory ever concocted found its way into this rag. Drumont believed (or so he alleged) that every woe and disaster that had befallen France—including the war with Prussia—was the handiwork of Jews, particularly the supposed cabal of international Jewish bankers. Everything, according to Drumont, could be traced to the Rothschilds and their cohorts.

La Libre Parole began publishing articles to the effect that members of the Chamber and the Senate had been bribed to approve the lottery-bonds. Drumont named no names, but asserted that there were as many as twenty legislators on the take. The articles were specific enough about the inner workings of the *Compagnie Universelle* that it became clear that Drumont had a source who had worked within the company. Drumont's source turned out to be Baron Jacques de Reinach, an Italian-born and French-naturalized nobleman who had been *Compagnie Universelle*'s financial agent since 1885. De Reinach was also a Jew. Was it possible that Drumont's source was a Jew? It was. De Reinach apparently agreed to act as Drumont's source on the promise that he himself would not be implicated. As the company's financial agent, it was he who was charged with making the payments to the newspapers for "publicity." But, it turned out, he was also the disbursing agent for payments to deputies to secure their support for the lottery-loan. And when it all came out, it was learned that he had disbursed almost a million francs to Cornelius Herz for distribution to Republican legislators. *That* Cornelius Herz. The one who had invested heavily in *La Justice*, owning half of the newspaper. The one who Clemenceau had found it expedient to buy out of *La Justice* in 1885 and announce in its pages that he had done so. The same man who was so close to Clemenceau that when Clemenceau traveled to Marseilles during a cholera outbreak and feared he might not return, he named Herz as the executor of his estate. Herz had been made a member of the Legion of Honor; Clemenceau denied helping him get it. And what must have thrilled Edouard Drumont to his bones was that Herz, like de Reinach, was also a Jew.

We now know that Cornelius Herz was blackmailing de Reinach. We do not know what was the secret Herz held over de Reinach, other than the obvious fact that de Reinach was the company's paymaster of bribes. We also know that on November 20, 1892, Maurice Rouvier, a former prime minister and current minister of finance, asked Clemenceau to accompany him and de Reinach to a meeting at Herz' home. Rouvier knew that he was one of the deputies that de Reinach had bribed. When Rouvier and de Reinach arrived at Herz' home, Clemenceau was already there. The meeting was very brief, with Herz stating that he was powerless to keep the enfolding scandal out of the newspapers. According to Clemenceau, when de Reinach and Clemenceau left Herz' home, de Reinach said to Clemenceau "I am lost." Clemenceau later said that "I saw a man struck to death, but I did not know why he was lost."[83]

The next day—November 21, 1892—was one of the busier days in French history. In the morning, the public prosecutor issued warrants for the arrest of Ferdinand de Lesseps, his son Charles, (who had been active in the company) and others. Later that morning, the body of Jacques de Reinach was found, an apparent suicide. He was quickly buried. A week later, the Chamber ordered his body exhumed. When the prime minister, Emile Loubet, expressed his reluctance to order the autopsy, his government fell. The autopsy was inconclusive, and the exact cause of death was never determined. But when Cornelius Herz learned of de Reinach's death on the morning of the twenty-first, he fled the country for London, where he remained.

Later that day, Jules Delahaye, a Boulangist deputy (Boulanger was dead, but there were forty Boulangist deputies in the Chamber) rose to speak. He was forty-one. He had black slicked hair, a full black waxed moustache and a spade beard. He had collaborated with Drumont and La Parole Libre, but whether he was doing Drumont's bidding on this day is unclear. No sooner did he begin to speak than he caused a sensation. He began by saying that he had come to the Chamber that day to fulfill "a great duty of social salubrity." He then said that he "quite well knew all the hundred or so corrupt deputies before him."[84] The London Times correspondent reported that it caused an "anarchic negation of Parliamentary decorum."[85] They began yelling "The names! The names!" He coolly responded that "If you wish for them, vote the inquiry." He got his way. The Chamber voted to appoint a commission with full power "to shed light on the allegations preferred at the tribune with reference to Panama affairs."[86]

In the end, the commission produced little. But on December 19 a banker admitted to the public prosecutor that he still had in his possession twenty-six check stubs in de Reinach's handwriting, stubs that represented payments that de Reinach had made to ministers, one of whom was Rouvier. He defended himself in the Chamber not by denying that de Reinach had bribed him (that was impossible) but by excusing his conduct as a way of defending the Republic. Since neither he nor the government had the funds to defend the Republic, he required an outside source of funding. Rouvier's defense is plausible if not excusable. If a deputy did not have an outside source of wealth, he was a poor man. At any time, fifty or more deputies had their salaries attached by creditors. Anyone wishing to bribe a deputy did not need to exert himself.

The commission did, however, call Clemenceau to testify, and they zeroed in on Clemenceau's dealings with Herz. He explained that Herz had been a "silent partner" in *La Justice* and that Herz' investment had lost him two hundred thousand francs, with Clemenceau having lost fifty thousand.[87] That afternoon Clemenceau, for what must have been the first time in his career, found himself on the defensive in the Chamber. When Clemenceau asserted that he had never recommended Herz for a decoration, a deputy interrupted: "He won't come back from England to contradict you." Clemenceau lamely rejoined: "Consult the dossiers. You won't find my signature there, and no minister can say that I verbally recommended M. Cornelius Herz to him for a decoration."[88]

But worse was to come. Much worse. On December 20 that unreconciled Boulangist, Paul Déroulède, mounted the rostrum. Innocently enough, he posed an *interpellation*, asking what was being done to rescind Herz's admission to the Legion of Honor. But that was just the hook for his larger purpose: "Without patronage and without a patron the little German Jew could not have made such strides on the road to honors. He could not, in a few years, have so completely and brilliantly left the gutter... He needed a presenter, an ambassador, to open all of the doors to everyone, above all the political people. He needed a more indulgent and devoted friend who could open up, as equals, with the ministers, the directors of the newspapers, and even, I know, with General Boulanger."[89] "But," he continued, now looked directly at Clemenceau, "this devoted one, this tireless intermediary so active and so dangerous, you know him, his name is on all your lips. Yet not one of you will say it, because he has three things that you dread: his sword, his pistol and his tongue...I will say it: M. Clemenceau."

He then told of a half-forgotten 1885 meeting that he had had with Herz. In the telling, a deputy whom Déroulède did not know approached Déroulède with the suggestion that there was a man who wished to speak with him. A meeting was arranged for the same day. The meeting was brief. Herz said that he had already given four hundred thousand francs to Clemenceau, and that "if the day comes where you need money, you can find me."[90]

He then asked: "What passed between this foreigner and this politician so that there could be no trace of any interchange of good offices? Did one give all and the other nothing? Would this German without an interest, without an object, without a view to gaining anything, have piled up all these repeated and redoubled payments? Whom will you get to believe that, M. Clemenceau?" "We must ask ourselves whether what he expected, if not demanded of you was not precisely the overthrow of these ministries, all these attacks on all men in power, all the trouble caused by you and your great talent in all the affairs of this country and in Parliament…It is to destruction that you have dedicated your efforts."[91]

The charge was absurd, but effective. The inference was that the little "German Jew" (who was not a German and who had been born in France) was an agent for Germany and that Clemenceau was his willing partner. In fact, the Ferry ministries that Clemenceau had helped in ousting were doing Bismarck's work, and that the *détente* with Germany ended only when the last Ferry ministry was ousted.

Clemenceau rose to respond. He said that he was surprised and hence unprepared. He admitted that Herz had been an investor in *La Justice* but asserted that many others had been as well. He denied that he had recommended Herz for the Legion of Honor. He tried to defend the absent Herz, noting that Herz was not a German, but that he had become a naturalized American citizen, having represented his country at the Paris Electrical Congress, and that he had served France in the Prussian war, not as a soldier but as a doctor. But as to the main charge that Herz had used Clemenceau to gain influence, Clemenceau was adamant: "You have said that I have brought to these benches a foreign influence of which I have been the agent; that I have been a traitor to my country, a traitor to my patrimony; that I was guided, influenced and subject to this foreign influence; that I have, by my parliamentary acts, sought to bring disorder and disruption to my country. This is the accusation that you have brought to the tribune. I have responded to all the other points with as much calm and coolness as possible. There is only one other response to make: *M. Paul Déroulède, you have lied.*"[92] The stenographer noted that when he returned to his seat, he was greeted with "hearty congratulations from his friends."

There can be but one result when one deputy accuses the other of being a liar. The duel took place two days hence at the St. Ouen race course, a short walk north of Clemenceau's old Clignancourt constituency. This duel was not intended to be for show; Clemenceau did not know if he would survive it, and gave instructions to an aide in the event he did not. The duel was to be fought with pistols at twenty-five paces, with each combatant firing from where he stood.

Clemenceau and his seconds arrived at 2:35 P.M, slightly after Déroulède. He remained in his carriage. A huge crowd gathered, estimated in the hundreds. The seconds marked off the dueling ground in the middle of the main race course. They had agreed that each would fire three shots. A second would yell "one, two, three," and each would be required to fire before hearing "three." By 3:05 P.M. they were at their places. Déroulède was hatless; Clemenceau wore a top hat. A second yelled "one, two, three." They both fired, and both missed. The cry was repeated; they both missed again. For a third time the cry went out, and again they both missed.[93] They shook hands and headed back to Paris. What actually happened is open to debate. Déroulède may have examined his coat following the duel, thinking he had been hit. Déroulède's final shot may have actually hit Clemenceau's revolver.

But there was a loser, and it was Clemenceau, and not only on the dueling ground. Before Déroulède made his accusations, wild as they were, Clemenceau had been the unchallenged ruler of the Chamber. His oratory had been a weapon that they had feared. He could and did bring down ministers. Now, he had been challenged. He would not be the same again.

Parliamentary elections were scheduled for the summer of 1893. Having changed the rules in order to topple Boulanger, Clemenceau now had to live with them. He could run in only one district, and that was the Var. The Boulangists were ready. The plan was to encourage as many candidates as they could drum up to oppose him, in the hope of denying Clemenceau a majority on the first ballot. Without a majority, he would be forced into a runoff, where they would concentrate their resources on the candidate who had fared the best.

The campaign was conducted in small towns and villages, to an electorate that was not amenable to outsiders. The forces against Clemenceau included Ernest Judet, the editor of *Le Petit Journal*. One particularly effective issue featured a cartoon showing Clemenceau in top hat and tails on the opera stage, juggling sacks of British pounds. No one could miss its meaning: Clemenceau was a paid agent of the British, doing their bidding. Of course, it didn't help that Clemenceau was known to speak English and had visited London many times.

A Boulangist deputy, Lucien Millevoye, announced in the Chamber that he had documents proving that Clemenceau was on the British payroll. When he was required to actually produce the documents, they were such obvious forgeries that he was laughed out of the Chamber. Clemenceau brought a libel suit and won, but the damage had been done.

The campaign became ugly. He was heckled, the hecklers yelling "Cornelius Herz" and "oh yes, oh yes," in English, mocking his supposed English ties. His carriage was stoned. Fights broke out at his rallies, causing more than one to be canceled. To make matters worse, he contracted dysentery. The principal opponent was a local nonentity, Joseph Jourdan. He may have been colorless, but he was local. A disaffected radical was also entered, as was a socialist. In the balloting on August 20, Clemenceau received 6,679 votes; Jourdan received 4,705. But the radical received 1034 and the socialist 1717. Shy of a majority, Clemenceau was forced into a runoff. The socialist threw his support to Jourdan. On the second round, Jourdan won with a plurality of nine hundred votes out of 18,000 cast.

And so, at least for now, his political career, which had begun sixteen years earlier with his spirited plea for amnesty for the *communards*, which had defended the ideals of the Republic at every turn, which had warned of the dangers of foreign conquests and *détente* with Bismarck, was over. As he entered his carriage and headed for Paris, he could not know if it was merely the end of a chapter or simply the end.

3

ON THE OUTSIDE LOOKING IN

It is impossible to understand the man apart from his religious faith.

—Arthur S. Link

In 1560, John Knox (1513[?]-1572) founded the Presbyterian Church of Scotland—the *kirk*. Its founding document was the Scottish (or "Scots") Confession of Faith, which, according to legend, Knox drafted in four days. In that year, the Scottish parliament made the *kirk* the official church of Scotland.

The Confession of Faith is a summary of Scots reformist beliefs. One of its central features provides that man, having sinned against God, is powerless to effect his own redemption by good works or by faith. Rather, God determined, even before the creation of the world, who shall be saved (the "Elect") and who shall suffer the damnation that every person, through Adam's fall, deserves. This Calvinist doctrine has come to be known as "predestination." The Confession of Faith was the guiding statement of faith of the Presbyterian Church of Scotland until it was replaced (but not superseded) in 1647 by the Westminster Confession of Faith, which is a clearer expression of the doctrine of predestination. It provides that: "All those whom God has predestined unto life, and those only, He is pleased, in His appointed time, effectively to call, by His Word and Spirit, out of that state of sin and death…" However, "Others, not elected, although they may be called by the ministry of the Word, and may have some common operations of the Spirit, yet they never truly come unto Christ, and therefore cannot be saved…"

A true believer in this doctrine knows that there is nothing he can do, by way of good works, or faith, or prayer, or by confession, to undo what God determined eons ago. Indeed, he knows that he has done nothing to deserve being part of the Elect. But he also knows that God, in His infinite good, would never allow a sinner to come into grace. He knows, deep in his heart, whether he is—or is not—part of the Elect. It is no wonder that true believers appear stern, and dour: They know that one misstep can be the proof that the miscreant is not—and cannot be—part of the Elect. The doctrine of predestination is softened somewhat by the *covenant of grace*, being a covenant that God entered into with mankind. Under it, those who live according to God's rule lead moral lives and will be saved. But the covenant of grace is reserved only for the Elect; one cannot earn it. Believers spend their lives doing good works as proof that they are part of the Elect.

The Westminster Confession came into being near the end of the English Civil War (1642-1649). As early as 1625, King Charles I had sought to impose his will on the Presbyterian Church of Scotland. It was partly about money (there was all that church property in Scotland, not to mention the tithes) but it was also about doctrine. Although not a Catholic, Charles was married to one. In 1637, Charles sought to impose a new liturgy on Scotland, making it conform to the English church. He vehicle was a new *Book of Common Prayer*, which many Scots violently opposed. On February 28, 1638, a group of the most dedicated opponents met in the courtyard of Greyfriars Kirk in Edinburgh, and there they signed the *National Covenant,* which had previously been drafted by two of their number. The Covenant pledged that the signers—the *covenanters*—would defend the true religion against innovation. The Covenant listed specific acts that offended them, most of which smacked of "popery." They pledged to lead lives that showed they were in covenant with God. Covenanters were not opposed to Charles' right to rule, only his right to rule their church. The National Covenant was truly national: It was circulated throughout Scotland. Thousands signed, some with their blood. When, in 1639, Charles attempted to crush the covenanters by force, he was defeated by a covenanters' army. When civil war broke out between Charles and Parliament, the covenants sided with Parliament. The *Solemn League and Covenant* (1643) was a treaty between the covenanters and Parliament. In exchange for a guarantee that Parliament would accept the *kirk* as the national religion of Scotland, the covenanters agreed to send an army south of the border in aid of Parliament in his struggle with Charles. Late in life, Woodrow Wilson would remark: "The stern Covenanter tradition that is behind me sends many as echo down the years.[1] The words "stern" and "covenanter" are often used together. Wilson's brother-in-law once remarked of Wilson: "The idea of an all-merciful God was, I believe to him, a piece of soft sentimentality."[2]

From time out of mind there arose a Glasgow-based line of Presbyterian divines—the Wodrows. If any of them actually signed the *National Covenant*, it was Robert Wodrow, born in 1600. His son, James Wodrow (1637-1707), was a Glasgow professor of divinity. James' son, Robert Wodrow (1679-1734), was a parish minister and historian who wrote *The History of the Sufferings of the Church of Scotland from the Restoration to the Revolution*. Robert sired sixteen children, one of whom was John Wodrow (1765-1837), a ruling elder of the Church of Scotland. One of John Wodrow's seven children was Rev. Thomas Wodrow (1793-1877).

Thomas Wodrow would be the last of the Wodrow divines to reside in Scotland. In 1820 he moved to Carlisle, England, changing the spelling of his name to *Woodrow*, to conform to the English pronunciation. He preached at the Independent Church in Carlisle, but by 1835 he, his wife and eight children were on the move again, this time for New York. One month after they arrived, the wife died. He preached briefly in Canada before settling in Chillicothe, Ohio in 1838. One of those children (there would be four more by a second wife) was James, born in 1828, who became a distinguished scholar and minister. He studied at Harvard, graduated *summa cum laude* from the University of Heidelberg, was ordained as a Presbyterian minister in 1859, and settled in as a teacher at the Columbia (S.C.) Theological Seminary, shortly after Charles Darwin published *On the Origin of Species*. James Woodrow was unable to keep his favorable opinion of evolution to himself. In 1886, he was hauled before the Augusta, Georgia Presbytery, accused of being a heretic. His defense was the commonsense notion that "God's work and God's word cannot contradict each other."[3] He was acquitted, but the Atlanta Synod overturned the acquittal. He was removed from the faculty of the Augusta Presbytery, but never actually defrocked. He went on to become the president of South Carolina College.

One of James Woodrow's older sisters was Janet, born in 1826 and forever known as "Jessie." In 1847, Jessie was attending the Female Seminary in Steubenville, Ohio. According to family legend, one day she happened by the home of one James Wilson. In the garden, raking leaves, was his son, Joseph Ruggles Wilson, age 25. James Wilson was born in Ulster in 1787. In 1808 he boarded a ship and landed in Philadelphia. In that same year he married Anne Adams, also from Ulster. They probably met on the crossing. No sooner had James set foot in Philadelphia than he apprenticed himself in the printing trade, working for William Duane on the *Philadelphia Aurora*, the house organ of the Republicans and Thomas Jefferson. When Duane, a lawyer, politician and future secretary of the treasury, decided he had had enough of publishing, he turned the paper over to young James.[4] In 1812, James decided he had had enough of *Aurora*, and began scouting about for a good location to start his own paper. He moved to Steubenville, Ohio, where he bought the ailing *Western Herald*. He became the director of a bank, and did not let the lack of any legal education stand in the way of his becoming a county judge.

Joseph Wilson was the youngest of James Wilson's twelve children, and by far the most brilliant. He graduated first in his class from Jefferson College, Canonsburg, Pennsylvania. In 1846, he obtained a bachelor's degree in divinity from Princeton Theological University (which is not Princeton University), was licensed to preach in 1848 and was ordained a minister by the Presbytery of Ohio in 1849. Shortly thereafter, he marred Jessie Woodrow, the girl he met as she walked past his father's home. Jessie's father, Rev. Thomas Woodrow, performed the ceremony.

Joseph Wilson then turned south, where he would remain for the rest of his life. In 1851, he obtained a professorship at Hampden-Sydney College in Virginia. In 1855, he was appointed pastor of the First Presbyterian Church of Staunton, Virginia. He was born for the pulpit. He was strikingly handsome, his most prominent features being his pronounced cheekbones. He brought his depth of scholarship to his sermons. At a time when the local clergyman was among the more respected men in the community, he leveraged his position into considerable fame and power. After only two years in Staunton, he was appointed pastor of the First Presbyterian Church of Augusta, Georgia, where he would remain for the next thirteen years. By this time, there were three small children in tow; a fourth would arrive in 1867.

Augusta, Georgia had sixteen thousand residents in 1858, half of whom were colored. The Presbyterians stood atop the social hierarchy. The congregation provided Rev. Wilson with a manse across the street from the church, and a stable for his horse. They were not wealthy, but they lived comfortably on Rev. Wilson's $4,000 annual salary. Their meals were prepared and served by a slave, but there is no evidence that Joseph Wilson was a slave owner. He probably followed the custom of "borrowing" a slave from a parishioner. But considering that this was ante-bellum Georgia, there is little likelihood that the Wilsons paid her.

Although relatively new to the South, Joseph Wilson supported the Confederacy, serving briefly as an army chaplain. Augusta had been spared Sherman's march (legend has it that Sherman had a girlfriend in the town), and was the home of the United States Arsenal. Rev. Wilson once dismissed Sunday services early so that the entire congregation could repair to the Arsenal to assist in cartridge rolling in preparation for an impending battle.[5]

Joseph Wilson believed that the affairs of the world are governed by God's moral law. Man, the church and society each have a prescribed place within the divine scheme for the world's governance. Above all, this presupposes a stratified society, where everyone has a place. The roles of men and women were defined; slavery was accepted. In May, 1858, he delivered a sermon on the role of the sexes: "the one ruling at the head, the other subject to that head." The woman's place was in the home, "away from the rush and storm of life."[6]

Many American Protestant churches were rent by the slavery question, and the Presbyterians were no exception. Southern Presbyterians broke off from the national church, forming the Presbyterian Church of the Confederate States of America. The organizing meeting took place in Rev. Wilson's church. By 1862, Rev. Wilson was the Permanent Clerk of the PCCSA, a position he would hold for the next thirty-seven years. Even before the PCCSA was formed, a number of Southern Presbyterians asked Rev. Wilson to formulate the Southern position on slavery. He did so gladly. The result was his most famous sermon, "Mutual Relation of the Masters and Slaves as Taught in the Bible," which he delivered on January 6, 1861, three months before Fort Sumter. The sermon was printed and widely distributed throughout the South, and became the official PCCSA position on the biblical authority for slavery. His authority was Leviticus 25:44: "Both thy bondman and thy bondwoman which you shalt have, shall be of the heathen that are round about you...they shall be your bondmen forever."[7] And since slavery confirmed God's order, the threat to the institution of slavery was a threat to God's will. He did add that since masters acted as God's agents, masters were required to treat their slaves with compassion, just as slaves were required to obey their masters. Two weeks after delivering his sermon, Georgia seceded.

Seated in the fourth pew on the day Rev. Wilson delivered this sermon, as he did twice-weekly every week during his childhood, absorbing with the rest of the congregation the power of Rev. Wilson's words and the majesty of his oratory was Rev. Wilson's third child and only son, five-year-old "Tommy," Thomas Woodrow Wilson.

Woodrow Wilson was the twenty-seventh man to ascend to the presidency of the United States. Unlike Adams and Jefferson before him, he had fathered no great revolution. Unlike Washington, Grant, Theodore Roosevelt and others, he had not led men to victory in battle. He was neither a legislator, nor a diplomat nor a jurist, and except for a few months in which he attempted to practice law, he spent more than forty years in academia, either as a student, a teacher or as an administrator. His path to the presidency was unique: It was fueled entirely by his extraordinary intellect, an intellect that powered his pen and, more than anything, his voice. More than any man before or since, he propelled himself to fame and power by means of hundreds of after-dinner speeches, commencement addresses, garden club chats and classroom seminars.

The power of his oratory was so great that complete strangers within the sound of his voice (years before the advent of mass communications) would leave convinced of the brilliance of the man and the soundness of his beliefs. First by hundreds, then by thousands, then by millions, they would come away certain that he, more than any other man, should be and was destined to be president of the United States. Over time, Wilson himself became convinced that he could sway any audience at any time and at any place. Only at the end, when he needed it the most, did his oratorical gifts fail him, and then spectacularly.

But no one would predict this of the little Tommy Wilson who sat mesmerized by his father's sermons, for the nine-year-old Tommy could not recognize his letters, and was eleven or twelve before he would learn to read. Living in a small town in post-bellum Georgia, there was little the Wilsons could do for Tommy except buy him glasses, which helped him not at all.[8] Only many decades later did some practitioners come to believe that young Tommy had suffered from a stroke of the type that has no effect upon a person's ability to speak but impairs the ability to read.[9] Wilson was always a slow reader, and overcame this disability through prodigious effort. The issue of the cause of his slow learning is important. Later in adulthood, and then later as president, Wilson was often in poor health and would suffer debilitating strokes.

Tommy Wilson could not read, so his father read to him and to his two older sisters, mostly Scott, Dickens and English poets. Rev. Wilson was stern in his beliefs, but he was not humorless. He had a quick wit and a lifelong addiction to puns.[10] When Tommy was a child, father and son would play riotous games of tag. Later, they would play chess and billiards, but not cards, which Rev. Wilson considered the work of the devil. The family prayed together every day, with the entire family kneeling as Rev. Wilson prayed aloud in his deep bass voice. On Sunday nights, they would gather around the piano and sing hymns.

Rev. Wilson may have been lax about Tommy's formal education, but right from the start he was strict about speech. If Tommy said something that Rev. Wilson felt was muddled or indistinct, he would stop his young son. "What do you mean by that?" he would ask. Then Tommy would explain himself, using more distinct language. "Then why don't you say so?" Rev. Wilson would demand.[11] Late in life, Wilson would remember: "As a young boy…at the age of four or five, I was taught to think about what I was going to say, and then I was required to say it correctly. Before I was grown, it became a habit."[12] Young Tommy saw the results of his father's teachings. He heard his father's sermons twice-weekly. He saw how his father could both instruct and dominate his audience. Years later Wilson wrote: "I wish that I could believe that I had inherited the rarest gift of making great truths attractive in the telling and of inspiring with great purposes by sheer force of eloquence or by the gentle stresses of persuasion."[13] He may not have inherited it, but he would surely develop it.

In 1870, when Tommy was thirteen, Rev. Wilson accepted a teaching position at the Columbia Theological Seminary in Columbia, South Carolina. Shortly thereafter, he was appointed pastor of the First Presbyterian Church. Tommy was enrolled in a private school of fifty boys run by Charles H. Barnwell, who was the only teacher. He taught Latin, Greek and all the other subjects. The monthly tuition was seven or eight dollars. Due to his late start, Tommy was a poor student. Only in his senior year did he begin to receive decent grades.

In 1873, when he was sixteen, Tommy formally joined the Presbyterian Church. Later in life, he would call the Bible the "Magna Carta of the human soul."[14] He read the Bible daily, and would wear out Bibles from constant use. He prayed on his knees, said grace before every meal, and throughout his life referred to Sunday as the Sabbath. His grandfather, Rev. Thomas Woodrow, now in his late seventies, would often visit, and grill him on the Westminster Shorter Catechism:

> "Question 16: Did all mankind fall in Adam's first transgression?"
>
> "Answer 16: The covenant being made with Adam, not for himself, but for his posterity, all mankind, descending from him by ordinary generation, sinned in him, and fell with him, in his first transgression."

Rev. Wilson's ambition was for Tommy to become a minister. He was hoping against hope. From a very early age, Tommy decided he would enter politics. As early as sixteen, he hung a portrait of William Gladstone on his bedroom wall. When a cousin asked who the man was, he replied: "That is Gladstone, the greatest statesman that ever lived. I intend to be a statesman too."[15]

Also in 1873, Wilson enrolled in Davidson College, Charlotte, North Carolina, then a very small (107 students) Presbyterian school. He was a mediocre student, but here he began to exhibit patterns that would continue throughout his schooling. He joined the debating society, which debated such question as: "Was the introduction of slavery into the United States beneficial to the human race?" and "Was the death of Lincoln beneficial to the South?"[16] He began giving speeches. Only sixteen when he entered, he was terribly homesick, and probably depressed. He wrote in a journal he briefly kept: "It is sad when looking over my past life to see how few of those seventeen years I have spent in the fear of God, and how much time I have spent in the service of the Devil...if God will give me the grace I will try to serve him from this time on, and will endeavor to attain nearer and nearer to perfection."[17] He left Davidson in

June, 1874, never to return. His friendlier biographers ascribe the cause to "intestinal" ailments. He remained at home for fifteen months.

In September, 1875, Wilson enrolled in Princeton, University as a freshman, then known as the College of New Jersey. When he arrived, it was a cross between a country college and a boarding school. It had five hundred undergraduates and eight graduate fellows. Of the twenty-seven faculty members, eleven were Presbyterian ministers, as were fourteen of the fifteen trustees. Twenty percent of Wilson's class of 1879 became ministers.[18] The level of instruction was very low, the teachers being little more than indigent candidates of the Presbyterian ministry. They were charged with keeping discipline, a hopeless task. Hazing was so rampant that one student shot another in thee leg with a revolver. The man who set himself out to change all this was its president, Dr. James McCosh (1811-1894), a Scots-born Presbyterian minister and friend of Rev. Wilson. McCosh began hiring instructors based on their scholarship rather than their piety. Shortly before Wilson arrived, McCosh had banned the fraternities. All this was opposed by many of the trustees.

Wilson's first friend at Princeton was Robert McCarter. He remembered Wilson being a normal boy, perhaps quieter and more thoughtful than most. Others remembered him being "detached," "quiet," "aloof," and "thoughtful." Wilson agreed. He wrote a fellow classmate that "I, perhaps, am colder and more reserved than most of those who are fortunate enough to have been born in our beloved South."[19] McCarter also remembered him as being "quite a Secessionist." But he was also a joiner. He debated, played baseball and was elected by his classmates to various offices. He organized the Liberal Debating Club and wrote its constitution, a practice he would repeat time and again. Membership was limited to the class of '79. He modeled it after the British House of Commons. It had a "secretary of state" who introduced "bills" to be debated. If a bill did not carry, the secretary of state would be forced to resign, similar to the actual House of Commons. McCarter remembered a debate that went so much against the South that Wilson couldn't stand it, and left the room.[20]

Wilson became a leading member of Whig Hall, a Princeton literary and debating society. He was elected its speaker, a position once held by Princeton's most illustrious undergraduate, James Madison. His classmates remembered him excelling in debate and extemporaneous speaking. He gave a speech at Whig Hall in his sophomore year that ended: "Work is the keystone of a perfect life. Work and trust in God."[21]

Wilson began honing a peaking style that he would use throughout his career. He rejected the bombastic, declamatory style then prevalent, in favor of a more conversational style. Years later he would write his wife: "Oratory is not declamation, not of swelling tones and excited delivery, but the art of persuasion, the art of putting things so as to appeal irresistibly to an audience…"[22] Wilson also possessed the most extraordinary ability to paint word pictures, even of places and events Wilson himself had not witnessed. When he described for his undergraduates the signing of the Scottish National Covenant in the courtyard of Greyfriars Kirk in 1638, his students decades later could recall it vividly, as if they had been there. And although he was born and raised in the South, he never spoke with a Southern accent.

In the fall of 1877, during his sophomore year, Wilson delivered his first major speech, which was later printed in Princeton's literary bimonthly, the *Nassau Literary Magazine*. Of all things, he chose for his first effort a biographical sketch of Bismarck, who the twenty-year-old Wilson much admired. Wilson began: We may…estimate his merits without the hatred of the Austrian, the fear-begotten bitterness of the Frenchman or the prejudice of the Englishman to warp our judgment.[23] Referring to Bismarck's military campaigns, Wilson described the war with Austria-Hungary as "a campaign of almost unrivaled brilliancy and rapidity, then brought proud France to the feet of Prussia, exposing the 'misunderstood incapacity' of Napoleon and adding to the smiling fields of Alsace and Lorraine to the already powerful kingdom…"[24] Wilson marveled at Bismarck's "keenness of insight, clearness of judgment and promptness of decision…who, by mere genius and force of character, has attained the proudest position in all Europe…" He concludes that Prussia will not soon find another Bismarck."[25] Wilson was not unmindful of Bismarck's "bad faith" and "occasional breach of honor." He was willing to let Bismarck's ends justify his means. He admired Bismarck as a man never disabled by indecisiveness. More than anything else, Bismarck was a man of action.

In October, 1878, Wilson wrote "William Earl Chatham," a biographical sketch of William Pitt the Elder. The essay earned him $20 when published in the *Nassau Literary Magazine*. As with Bismarck, it was Pitt's forcefulness that Wilson admired most: "His mind was strong and clear, his will was unswerving, his convictions were uncompromising, his imagination was powerful enough to invest all plans of national policy with a poetic charm, his confidence in himself was implicit, his love of country was real and intense."[26] Of course, he was describing what he, at age twenty-one, modeled for himself. In "William Earl Chatham," Wilson showed off his bravura writing style, beginning the essay with a description of Pitt's statue: "Beneath Westminster Abbey's arched roof, with commanding mien, haughty features, and gesture of authority, stands the statue of Chatham."[27] Reading this, one might assume that the author had actually seen this statue which, of course, he had not.

At this time, Wilson read Walter Bagehot's *The English Constitution*, first published in England in 1867. Bagehot (1826-1877) was businessman, journalist and for many years the editor-in-chief of *The Economist*. To this day, the *Economist*'s weekly column on British political affairs in titled "Bagehot." *The English Constitution* is Bagehot's greatest work. In it, he describes not only the legal relations between Parliament and Crown, but the actual workings of the British government. Bagehot believed that Britain's "cabinet government," wherein each cabinet secretary is a member of Parliament and answerable to it, was superior to the American system. Bagehot believed that the British system produced the best men and that the American system tended to produce corruption. Wilson was profoundly influenced by *The English Constitution*, both in its conclusions and as a work of scholarship. He would return to it time and again.

In his junior year, Wilson was elected managing editor of the school newspaper, *The Princetonian*. It concerned itself mainly with matters of interest to the students, such as Princeton's baseball and football teams. But in one editorial ("Our Course in History") he opined on what he believed was the poor selection of available history courses: "It surely cannot be that the College places little value on historical study. The lawyer, the minister, the physician, the business man, each and all need to be acquainted with its teachings."[28] This was an early harbinger of the struggles over academic reform Wilson would have with Princeton's trustees decades later.

In early 1879, Wilson wrote "Cabinet Government in the United States," in which Wilson, till an undergraduate, proposed a complete revision of the American framework of government. In it, Wilson described the problem, and posited the solution. The problem, as Wilson saw it, was that the government operated not as intended by the framers, but by the standing committees of the House of Representatives, whose deliberations were secret. "Great measures of legislation are discussed and determined, not conspicuously in public session of the people's representatives, but in the unapproachable privacy of committee rooms...."[29] [W]e hail an adjournment of Congress as a temporary immunity from danger."[30] Throughout Wilson's life, he would return to what he considered the greatest evil of government: secrecy. "Nothing can be more obvious than the fact that the very life of free, popular institutions is dependent upon their breathing air of thorough, exhaustive and open discussion..."[31]

His solution was to amend the Constitution so that Congress would function along the lines of the British House of Commons. Specifically, the president would select his cabinet from elected members of Congress, who would continue to serve in Congress. These cabinet members would initiate legislation, would be answerable to Congress, and would be forced to resign if their policies failed. The key to the system's success would be *debate*: "Party trickery, legislative jobbery, are deprived of the very air they breathe—the air of secrecy, of concealment…debate is the essential function of a popular representative body…"[32] As in a British-type system, Wilson averred, appropriations would be based upon national needs, and not upon secret legislative dealmaking and logrolling. He concluded: "The most despotic of Governments under the control of wise statesmen is preference to the freest ruled by demagogues."[33] There was, of course, no chance that any of Wilson's recommendations would ever be enacted. What is remarkable is the self-assurance and confidence that this college senior displayed. It would be his style for life.

"Cabinet Government in the United States" would be published in the August, 1879 issue of *International Review*. The man who accepted it for publication was its twenty-nine-year-old co-editor, Henry Cabot Lodge. Forty years later, as Senator Henry Cabot Lodge, their paths would cross again.

In September, 1879, Wilson completed "Self-Government in France," an article for which he never found a publisher. Wilson begins: "We ought to understand the French, but we do not."[34] But he accuses the French of having a "violent, ill-controlled humor," and that "the grain of the ordinary French mind seems to run at right angles to the law, and parallel with every dangerous extreme. It has become habituated to heroic remedies. Quick amputation of an offending limb has been preferred to the tedium of nursing."[35] He compares England's history to France, and finds France wanting. "England has long since learned to govern themselves…Frenchmen were still unexperienced in the exercise of liberty, and knew only alternatively to obey and to overthrow."[36] Reviewing the current scene, he criticizes the Assembly for "hampering" Adolphe Thiers in the suppression of the commune. He claims—without evidence—that the Assembly forced Thiers from office and replaced him with MacMahon, "through whom they hoped to gather the reins of absolute power into their own itching palms." He does not, however, credit the Republicans for resisting MacMahon (in the *seize Mai* crisis), noting that "the Republic may at last to have become an actuality."[37] The fact that Wilson had not yet visited France and may not yet have met a Frenchman did not get in the way of Wilson's confident style.

One of Wilson's closest friends at Princeton was Charles A. Talcott. In their senior year, Wilson and Talcott formed a "solemn covenant" that they would "use all our powers and passions for the work of establishing the principles we held in common; that we would acquire knowledge that we might have power, and that we would drill ourselves in the arts of persuasion, but especially in oratory."[38] Both kept the bargain. Talcott went on to serve as mayor of Utica, New York, and represented Utica in Congress.

In 1883, Wilson wrote Ellen Axson, then his fiancée: "The profession I chose was politics; the profession I entered was the law. I entered the one because I thought it would lead to the other."[39] It did not, and his experience in the practice of law was the most unqualified failure of his career.

Wilson entered the University of Virginia at Charlottesville in October, 1879. It was very different from Princeton. The course work was rigorous, requiring long hours of study, with little time for extracurricula. All of the law courses were taught by two professors, one of whom was John Barbee Minor, one of the pre-eminent legal scholars of the nineteenth century. Wilson, who entered law school with his mind filled with the renovation of Congress along the lines of the British House of Commons, now found a curriculum comprised of third-party contracts, remainder interests and *in rem* jurisdiction to be a terrible bore. Early in 1880 he wrote Charles Talcott: "This excellent thing, the law, gets as monotonous as that other immortal article of food, Hash, when served with such endless frequency."[40]

He did find time to join, and lead, Virginia's only functioning debating club, the Jefferson Society. Continuing a practice he began at Princeton, he rewrote the constitution, inserting a provision that no one could be required to debate a position contrary to his convictions. The Jefferson Society held an annual debate contest, awarding a prize to the winner. Wilson finished second, beaten by fellow Virginian William Cabell Bruce. He took the defeat hard: "Bruce beat me on this, but I will bet him in life, for I am a worker, and he is not."[41] Wilson would be proven right, but it was a near thing. Bruce went on to forge a successful legal career in Baltimore, served one term as a senator from Maryland, and later won a Pulitzer Prize for his biography of Benjamin Franklin.

In his first year at Virginia, Wilson delivered a well-received speech to the Jefferson Society. His subject was John Bright (1811-1889), a British Liberal who served in the House of Commons for forty-six years. Bright was one of Wilson's early heroes. Bright was a free-trader, responsible for the repeal of the Corn Laws, the protectionist tariffs on imported wheat. Bright also opposed the Confederacy. Speaking to a room full of Southerners, Wilson said: "I yield to no one in precedence in love for the South. But because I love the South, I rejoice in the failure of the Confederacy."[42] Wilson's rationale was that the Confederacy, had it prevailed, could never have competed with the North. "The perpetuation of slavery would, beyond all question, have wrecked our agricultural and commercial interests...We cannot conceal from ourselves the fact that slavery was enervating to our Southern society and exhausting our Southern energies."[43] Wilson did not state that slavery was wrong, just that it was harmful to the South. Wilson knew that his father would hear of the speech (it was published in the March, 1880 issue of the *University of Virginia Magazine*) and may have tiptoed around the issue so as not to offend him.

Wilson admired Bright's oratory as much as he did his politics: "[Bright's voice] is described by those who have heard him speak as for the most part calm and measured in its tones, but with peculiar vibrations of unspeakable power, answering to the movements of scorn, indignation, pathos or pity that stir his thoughts.[44] John Bright was the man who Wilson wished to become.

During that year, Wilson fell in love with a first cousin, Harriet Woodrow, then a student at Augusta Female Seminary in Staunton, Virginia. He missed so many classes in courting her that for a time he was in danger of being expelled. She summarily rejected his suit. He took it hard.

In December, 1880, three months into his senior year, he abruptly left law school. The cause may have been "dyspepsia." It may also have resulted from an argument of unknown cause he had had with John Minor. Whatever the cause, he left so abruptly that he left his books and trunk behind. While at home, he continued to practice elocution, aided by a chart of gestures, writing to Harriet Woodrow: "I intend to spare no trouble in gaining complete command of my voice in reading and speaking."[45] He continued to study law on his own, and continued reading political theory. Having taught himself a form of shorthand years before, he now bought a typewriter and learned how to type. Virginia did award him a law degree.

Wilson's political beliefs at this time defy categorization. He was a free trader. He was a "sound money" man as opposed to "bimetallism" who, despite being a Democrat, did not support Bryan's "free coinage of silver" campaign in 1896. His political heroes were Hamilton and Webster, not Jefferson, who Wilson believed was "not a thorough American because of the strain of French philosophy that permeated and weakened all his thought."[46] He opposed giving the vote to freed slaves: "We object to their votes because their *minds* are dark…they are ignorant, uneducated and incompetent to form an enlightened opinion on any of the public questions which they may be called upon to decide at the polls."[47]

Having graduated from law school, it was now time to set out on the legal career that was intended to be the springboard to his political career. Wilson consulted his father, and they agreed that the most promising place to begin a law practice was Atlanta, which was then a city of 48,000 with all of 143 lawyers. In January, 1882, Wilson received a letter from Edward Renick, a fellow classmate at Virginia who Wilson had never met. Renick advised Wilson that he had leased an office in downtown Atlanta, and offered to share expenses. Wilson's share would amount to $4.50 per month. Renick noted that they could also get a servant for $0.50 to $0.75 per *month*. Wilson agreed, and with that, Renick and Wilson was formed. Wilson began referring to himself as "Woodrow Wilson," the name he would use for the rest of his life. They agreed to divide the work according to their interests. Renick would do the office work and Wilson would be the "barrister" arguing cases in court.

There was no work to divide. They had no connections, and no means of attracting business. Others might slowly build a practice by glad-handing the local babbitts at chamber of commerce dinners, but that was not for Wilson. He wrote a friend that he was "buried in humdrum life down here in slow, ignorant, uninteresting Georgia," adding: "The philosophical study of the law—which must be a pleasure to any thoughtful man—is very different from its scheming and haggling practice.[48] But more than anything else, he simply hated practicing law, and never viewed it as anything other than a steppingstone to politics. As early as August, 1882, two months before he was admitted to the Georgia bar, he wrote to his mother that he was depressed by the outlook for his legal career. His father, who was subsidizing his son to the tune of fifty dollars per month, advised him to keep at it. "I am at last fully admitted to the bar, and have just enough business to keep me in spirits.[49] But there is no evidence that in its very short existence Renick & Wilson collected any fees, and Wilson probably never actually appeared in court. In the spring of 1883 Renick & Wilson dissolved. They parted amicably. Renick abandoned the practice shortly after Wilson left. He found a position in Washington as legal secretary to the first comptroller of the treasury.

His months as a practicing lawyer had one great benefit. While representing his mother on an estate matter, it brought him to Rome, Georgia. There he met Ellen Axson, the daughter of the local Presbyterian minister. She was twenty-two, he twenty-six. They became engaged shortly thereafter, and married in 1885. She was his alter ego, helper, confidante and best friend until her death thirty years later. She bore him three daughters, but not wishing her children to be considered Northerners, she returned to the South for the births of her first two children. Their collected love letters fill volumes.

It was at this time that Wilson changed the course of his life. He realized that he would never achieve a political career via the practice of law. If he were to fulfill his "covenant" with Charles Talcott, if he would "use [his] powers and passions for the work of establishing the principles [they] held in common," if he would put his oratorical skills to use, it would not come from working on the inside. He would use his skills to exert influence as an outside observer of the political scene. He had already achieved a modicum of success with "Cabinet Government in the United States." It would be in academia, if anywhere, where he would make his mark.

In the second half of the nineteenth century, if a scholar wished to engage in serious postgraduate work, he or she would have to travel to Europe to study in the great universities of England or Germany. Baltimore's John Hopkins University was founded in 1876 to change that. By September, 1883, when Woodrow Wilson entered, it had only three hundred students, 174 of whom were graduate students. In order to attract the best students from the United States and abroad, Johns Hopkins offered $500 per year fellowships and free tuition. Wilson applied for a fellowship, didn't get one, but enrolled anyway, his father once again supporting him.

Johns Hopkins originated the *seminary* system. Instead of lecturers reading to students, students did their own independent research, which they then presented to—and were critiqued by—their professor and their fellow students, seated around large seminar tables. For example, in April, 1884, the "Historical and Political Science" seminary debated the Blair Common School Bill, which was the brainchild of Sen. Henry W. Blair, a New Hampshire Republican. If enacted (it never was) the bill would have appropriated $77 million for educational purposes, to be distributed among the states in proportion to the percentage of illiterates in each state. Since the South had the highest percentage of illiterates, it would receive the most money, which was the purpose of the bill. Three students spoke in favor of the bill; one—Wilson—spoke against, arguing that the bill was both inexpedient and unconstitutional, that the matter of primary and secondary education should be left entirely to the states. One of the three who argued in favor was John Dewey, then studying for a Ph. D. Dewey went on to become one of the nation's leading educational reformers.[50]

Wilson quickly became a favorite of his fellow students and professors. He joined the Matriculate Society, the undergraduate literary and forensic club. Following a pattern, he rewrote its constitution, reorganizing it around the lines of the British House of Commons. The Matriculate Society now had a "government" that could be supported or turned out following a debate.

He was by now an accomplished public speaker. A fellow student remembered his "easy affability of manner…a voice of peculiar charm…it was clear, penetrating and flexible; its modulations fell on the ear like some distant chime of bells."[51] He wrote to Ellen Axson, then his fianceé, that he had a power over men collectively that he did not have singly, that he felt "intoxicated" by public speaking, and could not sleep afterwards,[52] noting the "absolute joy in facing and conquering a hostile audience… or thawing out a cold one."[53]

During his first year at Johns Hopkins, Wilson began writing *Congressional Government*, his first and perhaps his greatest book. His theme was the same as his earlier essay, "Cabinet Government in the United States," being the defects in the American system of government. Wilson was writing at a time when the public's perception of its government was at a low ebb. For twenty years, five weak and ineffective presidents—Johnson, Grant, Hayes, Garfield and now Arthur—had succeeded themselves. Wilson posited that the cause of presidential weakness was that all power lay in the hands of the standing committees of the House of Representatives, committees that acted in secret. The policies that emerged were not Republican policies or Democratic policies, since members of both parties sat on each committee, but were the result of deal-making and log rolling. The worst defect of government by standing committees was the lack of accountability. He contrasted this system with the British, where the minority party had no power. If a particular policy failed, everyone knew whose fault it was, and the responsible minister—or the responsible government—resigned. Wilson also decried what he felt was the decline of the states relative to the federal government, asking: "Who does not feel…that it is more dangerous to molest a mail-carrier than to knock down a policeman?"[54]

Wilson decried that there was a great parliamentary leader in England (Gladstone) and a great parliamentary leader in Germany (Bismarck) but none in the United States. This was personal for Wilson. It meant that, unlike Gladstone in England, a man in America could not rise to prominence solely by means of his oratory.

In *Congressional Government*, Wilson, then only twenty-eight, anticipated Theodore Roosevelt's presidency, arguing that, as a result of Congressional inaction, there were pressing problems, such as the regulation of giant corporations and the restraint of monopolies. He anticipated the creation of the Federal Reserve, predicting "the perfection of fiscal arrangements…that currently are not subject to federal control but which will require it as the country expands."[55]

Wilson was not modest about his abilities as a stylist. He wrote to Ellen: "I have imagined a style clear, bold, fresh and facile; a style flexible but always strong, capable of light touches and heavy blows.[56] He did not disappoint. Here is a part of his description of the House of Representatives: "[E]ach member has a roomy desk and an easy revolving chair; where broad aisles spread and stretch themselves; where ample, soft-carpeted areas lie about the spacious desks of the Speaker and clerks…an immense capacious chamber, disposing its great dimensions freely beneath the great level lacunar ceiling through whose glass panels the full light of day pours in."[57] In reading these words, the reader might assume that the author had actually seen the House chamber. He had not, despite his being only forty-seven miles away as he wrote.

Wilson began reading early chapters of *Congressional Government* to his fellow seminarians. One student remembered: "We had about the ablest and maturest paper ever read there."[58] Johns Hopkins, which had denied Wilson a fellowship when he first applied, awarded him one for his second year. Houghton Mifflin published the book in January, 1885. It was an immediate success. It was favorably reviewed in the *Nation* and the *New York Times*, although the *Times* called his writing style "involved and clumsy." The *New York Tribune* was less charitable. Picking up on Wilson's claim that "our generation...has serious doubts about the superiority of our own institutions as compared with the systems of Europe." The *Tribune* reviewer responded: "This is quite wrong. Our generation has no such absurd feeling."[59] Nevertheless, by 1900 *Congressional Government* had gone through fifteen editions. It is still in print.

Shortly after *Congressional Government* was published, Wilson penned an extraordinarily self-revealing letter to Ellen Axson. Despite the favorable reception of the book, Wilson expressed his "deep regret" that he had been "shut out from my heart's first primary ambition and purpose, which is to take an active, if possible a leading part in public life, and strike out for myself, if I had the ability, a *statesman's* career." He continued: "I have a strong instinct for leadership, an unmistakably oratorical temperament and the keenest possible delight in affairs; and it has required very constant and stringent schooling to content me with the sober methods of the scholar and the man of letters."[60] He would bear the frustrating feeling being an outsider for many years.

Wilson had entered Johns Hopkins as a complete unknown. He left self-assured and well-known, at least within academia. But he was twenty-nine, was engaged and was eager to marry, and wished no longer to rely on his father's largesse. More than anything, what he now needed was a job.

In 1885, the year Woodrow Wilson left Johns Hopkins, the Society of Friends—the Quakers—founded Bryn Mawr College for the purpose of educating women. The first day that it opened was the first day of Wilson's teaching career. He was one of nine professors, and the only one without a doctorate or who had studied abroad. He was poorly paid, but he had just married, and his first child, daughter Margaret, would arrive in April, 1886. A second daughter, Jessie, would arrive in August, 1887. His family life was blissful; his professional life was not.

The first dean of Bryn Mawr was Dr. Martha Carey Thomas (1857-1935). Her life's work was to prove that women could be educated to the same levels of scholarship as were men. Her relationship with Wilson was testy, in large part because Wilson did not believe in women's education, and could not conceal his condescension. He wrote a friend: "I find that teaching women relaxes my mental muscle."[61] He said that his students dutifully wrote down every word he said, even the jokes he told. But his students remembered his lectures, using such words as "spellbound," and "inspiring," as would his students wherever he taught. As he had at Johns Hopkins, he organized a Bryn Mawr "House of Commons."

Wilson taught English and French history concurrently, which afforded his students a unique ability to compare the two systems of government. Also while at Bryn Mawr, Wilson gave an annual lecture on the study of history. One of those lectures ended with a little homily on "the value of discussion." In it he expresses the beliefs that would one day find their full expression in the idea for the League of Nations. His lecture notes survive: "There is a modern tendency to decry discussion, under the contemptuous name of 'talk;' but talk which concerns itself with principles cannot be too much encouraged. (1) It means the substitution of reason for force, and thus of order for anarchy. It creates a disposition to hear both sides and to yield to the voice of the majority. (2) It offers prizes to intelligence by bringing all of the faculties into active play. (3) It develops that type of intellect which is the highest of all, namely the 'speculative intellect'—by conditioning success on the better argument, on the use of the faculties. (4) Its detective processes discover the truth. (5) It begets tolerance, a very modern product. (6) It turns the old vigour of the race, which once went to produce eager, restless, oftentimes rash action, into channels of clear creative thought, and so produces that calmness without sluggishness and that deliberation without weakness, that 'animated moderation' in action which the uncivilized man knows nothing of, but which is the perfect flower of social growth."[62]

So there it was. One day men would gather to "hear both sides," which would beget "tolerance." They would substitute "reason for force, and thus of order for anarchy." It would be like the British House of Commons, where men like Gladstone dominated through the power of their oratory. Wilson had two graduate fellows at Bryn Mawr. He told one of them, Lucy Maynard Salmon, that if the American political system were like the British, he could have entered Parliament and risen to the top.[63]

In March, 1886, Wilson saw Congress for the first time, as a tourist. In that month, he delivered a speech to the Princeton Alumni Club of New York. The topic he chose was "The College and the Government." It was a disaster. It was overly long and too serious for the occasion. He was frequently interrupted, and audience members left as he spoke. Worse was to come when he sat down. The prominent railroad lawyer and future senator, Chauncey Depew, rose and mocked his earnestness. It was the only time in his career that he was laughed at, and it was a terrible blow to a man who hoped to use his voice to further his career.[64] He was long in overcoming the evening, and he would never again misread an audience so badly. Shortly after the speech, he tried to get a job in government as an assistant secretary of state. Nothing came of it.[65]

In April, 1886, Wilson signed a contract with the Boston publisher D.C. Heath to write a textbook outlining the forms of world government. He hated the idea of writing a textbook, but not the idea of the extra income. It took him three years to write *"The State: Elements of Historical and Practical Politics."* Much of the source material was in German. He and Ellen wore out dictionaries translating the German. In it, Wilson is mildly critical of the French Chamber of Deputies, not because it did not have the "cabinet government" that Wilson so much admired, but that it had too much of it. "The power of interpellation has been so indiscriminately and unwisely used in France as seriously to discredit her system of cabinet government...[T]he system no doubt awaits for its successful operation the formation of two national parties, capable of organizing for government instead of merely for rivalry."[66] He continues: "France is staggering under that most burdensome, that most intolerable of all forms of government, *government by mass meeting*" [Italics in the original].[67] Referring to the rise of General Boulanger: "It is this state of affairs which has...seemed on at least one notable occasion to create an opportunity for another return to some sort of dictatorship.[68]

Wilson's teaching schedule at Bryn Mawr left him plenty of time to read and write, and he did so prodigiously. In addition to grinding out "The State," he authored two of his most important scholarly articles, the first of which was "Of the Study of Politics," which appeared in the March, 1887 *New Princeton Review*. In it Wilson argues that politics cannot be learned from books alone, but from observing politicians in action. The article must be read as a self-rebuke, or at least as evidence that he was eager to get out of Bryn Mawr. He notes that "Bagehot and de Toqueville were not merely students, but also *men of the world*, for whom the only acceptable philosophy of politics was the generalization from actual daily observation of men and things [Italics in the original]."[69] What Wilson wants is for the "man of the world" and the "man of books" to be merged into the student of politics, asking "was not John Stuart Mill the better student for having served the East India Company and sat in the House of Commons."[70] He asserts that the student of politics "must frequent the street, the counting-house, the drawing room, the club house, the administrative offices, the halls—yes, and the lobbies—of legislatures."[71] He concludes that "In order really to know anything about government, you must *see it alive* [Italics in the original]."[72]

Only Wilson himself could have known the personal bitterness that underlay this article. Wilson had only recently sought a position—any position—in government, only to be rebuffed. Rather than "see" government "alive," he was teaching girls in rural Pennsylvania, and hating every minute of it.

The second essay, "Of the Study of Administration," published in the June, 1887 *Political Science Quarterly* has been called the seminal work on the study of government administration. Wilson published the article just at the time when the issue that was roiling the nation was civil service reform, i.e. the elimination of the "spoils" system under which the winning political party tossed out all of the adherents of the losing party. Wilson begins the article by asking: "Why... have we just begun purifying a civil service which was rotten fully fifty years ago?"[73] He notes the present "poisonous atmosphere of city government, the crooked secrets of state administration, the confusion, sinecurism and corruption ever and again discovered at the bureaux at Washington,"[74] and says that as government naturally expands, "It is getting harder to *run* a constitution than to frame one [Italics in the original]."[75] He adds that once a nation is done with the business of making a constitution, it is difficult to go on to the next step of creating a skilled, economical administration. Instead, countries keep trying to improve themselves by amending their constitutions: "There seems to be no end of tinkering of constitutions... We go on criticizing when we ought to be creating.[76] Wilson suggests that we should learn administration from the Europeans, even those that are not democratic.

The principal problem in effecting change in a democracy, Wilson argues, is public opinion. A ruler must first get the public's attention—no easy task—and then mold the public in the direction the ruler wishes. The difficulty is that "The bulk of mankind is highly unphilosophical, and nowadays the bulk of mankind votes...And where is this unphilosophical bulk of mankind more multifarious than in the United States?" To know the public mind in the United States, a ruler must know not only of the "older stocks" of Americans, but also "of Irishmen, of Germans, of negroes...."[77] The article is instructive not only as a call for the study of public administration, but as an insight into the thirty-one-year-old Wilson's mind. He was beginning to think about what it would take to attain public office.

Just at that time, Wilson signed a three-year contract with Bryn Mawr. He was promoted from "associate" to "associate professor," and his salary was *increased* to $2,000 per year. But when in June, 1888 he was offered a professorship at Wesleyan University in Middletown, Connecticut, he jumped at the opportunity; it meant teaching *men.* There was, however, the matter of the contract Wilson had recently concluded with Bryn Mawr. Lawyers were consulted, litigation was threatened, but in the end Bryn Mawr let him go. He did not depart on the best of terms.

Wesleyan University in 1888 had only 215 undergraduates, only fifteen of whom were women. There were only five graduate students. They were all carefully screened, as were their professors. The endowed chair that Wilson occupied had been vacant for three years prior to his appointment, and would remain vacant for five years after he left. The education that Wilson's students received was far more rigorous than the education he had received at Princeton. As he had at Bryn Mawr, he taught English and French history concurrently.

Wilson loved teaching the men at Wesleyan, thoroughly preparing every lecture. And they loved him back. Years later they remembered being held in rapt attention by him. "He…talked to us in the most informal, jolly way, yet with absolute clearness and sureness."[78] He had an…air of academic aristocracy" that "gave an impression of having arrived, of mastery.[79] But they also remembered him as being stubborn, one remarking that "He was distinctly not open-minded on any subject that he was interested in….He could freeze you if you crossed him. That we all knew."[80] Just as he had at Johns Hopkins and at Bryn Mawr, he founded a debating society modeled on the British House of Commons. It did not survive after he left.

Wilson was now writing and lecturing feverishly, augmenting his income by speaking on the Chautauqua circuit, then in its heyday. He was becoming well-known. He became a little industry, reworking the lectures into published articles, then re-fashioning the articles into different lectures tailored to fit each audience. Someone asked him how often he could give the same re-worked lecture before he could no longer use it. He replied: "I don't know yet." Beginning in February, 1888, he gave twenty-five lectures per year on administration at Johns Hopkins, a practice he continued until 1898. What with lectures in Providence, Hartford, Boston and elsewhere, in addition to the bi-monthly lectures in Baltimore, he was constantly on the move. He was universally well-received. He never read his lectures, speaking extemporaneously from notes he kept on index cards. A Johns Hopkins student remembered: "He was not stiff or formal; he was almost conversational in tone….But he made no concessions; there was no play to the gallery whatever…He used simple forms of speech—that was one reason for his lucidity; there was nothing he said that we did not understand."[81] It was exactly the style he would employ running for president.

Early in his tenure at Wesleyan, Wilson was asked to review the recently-published *The American Commonwealth* by James Bryce, a leading British Liberal statesman. Bryce had traveled to America frequently, retracing de Tocqueville's travels, with the intent of updating de Tocqueville. Wilson's review, which appeared in the March, 1889 *Political Science Quarterly*, reveals that Wilson—then thirty-three—had arrived as a first-class political thinker and stylist.

Wilson began the review: "This is a great work, worthy of the heartiest praise."[82] He continues: "[H]e has written a book invaluable to students of comparative politics—

invaluable because of its fullness, its accuracy, its candor…its sage, balance of political judgment."[83] It is not an accident that Wilson agrees with Bryce in Bryce's conclusion that the American separation of powers makes for "slipshod, haphazard, unskilled and hasty legislation."[84] Echoing his own *Congressional Government*, Wilson laments that due to the absence of cabinet secretaries in the American Congress—as there are government ministers in the House of Commons—"we remain for long periods of embarrassment without any solution of some of the simplest problems that await legislation."[85] Writing in 1889, America had just completed almost a generation of weak and ineffective presidents. Wilson warns: "America is now sauntering through her resources and through the mazes of her policies with nonchalance; but presently there will come a time when she will be surprised to find herself grown old—a country crowded, strained and perplexed—when she will be obliged to fall back upon her conservatism, obliged to pull herself together, adopt a regimen of life, husband her resources, concentrate her strength, steady her methods, sober her views, restrict her vagaries, trust her best, not her average members."[86]

But Wilson also knew that he would not likely be among those "best…members." He laments that in the British system, a man like Bryce could be both a scholar and a legislator. "He has breathed the air of practical politics…he is so familiar with the machinery of government at home as to be able to perceive at once the most characteristic differences, as well as the real resemblances, between political arrangements in England and the United States."[87]

Wilson remained at Wesleyan for only two years. Much as he loved teaching there, as much as the love was reciprocated by the students and the faculty, and as much as he and his family were comfortable in Middletown, Wesleyan lacked one thing: It was not Princeton, and Princeton was Wilson's spiritual home. And so a number of Wilson's 1879 classmates, chief among them Robert Bridges, then an editor at Charles Scribner's Sons, worked behind the scenes to secure a position for Wilson at Princeton. Wilson did not assist in the effort, but he was aware of it. Princeton appointed him professor of jurisprudence and political economy. Wilson hated teaching economics. Princeton's president, Francis L. Patton, a Presbyterian minister who had been impressed by *Congressional Government*, assured him that after two years he would be relieved of the burden of economics. Not everyone was pleased by the appointment, one trustee predicting: "He is a Southerner and will make trouble."[88] He arrived in September, 1890, already well-known and with a solid reputation. He would remain for the next twenty years. He would make trouble, but not because he was a Southerner.

No sooner had he arrived than he began to hit the lecture trail. His fee was $100, but he waived the fee when lecturing to charitable groups or before such audiences as the Princeton Ladies Club. In November, 1890, he addressed the Connecticut Valley Economic Association of Springfield, Massachusetts, on "The Evils of Democracy." He must have startled his audience when he reminded them that "The Constitution is not by intention democratic. It has been made so by subsequent changes—by presidential nominating conventions and by the widening of the franchise."[89] He announced that he was opposed to the direct election of senators. (The Seventeenth Amendment, which provided for direct election, was not ratified until 1913.) He first delivered his address "Democracy" in 1891, and would continue to deliver it to audiences far and wide throughout the 1890's. Continuing his "Evils of Democracy" theme, he expressed his displeasure at the broadening of the franchise. He wanted, he claimed a "free nation—a people not self-directed but directed by the boldest, most prevalent minds…A free nation loves a bold man. It uses slaves only for lack of better men, because the work *must somehow be done*." [Italics in the original.][90]

Wilson was also opposed to women's suffrage, but was honest about: "I do not believe in it, but I never argue against it, as there are no logical arguments against it."[91] Wilson's heart was, as ever, in the British House of Commons, where a small group of learned men made policy.

Wilson was a very popular lecturer at Princeton, with many of his students later becoming ardent political supporters. One alumnus remembered: "Young men were seized with the thrill of expectancy when he entered to begin a lecture."[92] Another later recalled the vividness with which he described the signing of the National Covenant in Greyfriars churchyard in 1638. "His enthusiasm was contagious…"[93] They would see him as he pedaled his bicycle to class, the tails of his coat flapping in the breeze. For a time he was an assistant coach of a very bad Princeton football team. (The team caption was Edgar Allen Poe.) The senior class voted him the most popular lecturer every year between 1896 and 1903. He continued lecturing at Johns Hopkins, popular as ever.

He quickly became involved in Princeton affairs beyond his own classroom. A schism arose between the younger faculty members who pressed President Patton to modernize the curriculum and the teaching methods, and the older ones who resisted change. Wilson, still in his thirties, became a champion of the younger faculty. He had been at Princeton barely six months when, addressing the Princeton Club of New York, he stated that Princeton was "in a very critical condition," that "unless there is a rapid progression there would certainly be a retrogression," With an eye on Harvard and Yale, Wilson pressed for a law school and additional professorships in political economy and history.

In 1892, Wilson was offered the presidency of the University of Illinois, at an annual salary of $6,000. He considered it, but was dissuaded by his fellow Princeton alumni, principally the industrialist Cyrus McCormick, then a Princeton trustee. McCormick advised that Illinois, then an agricultural college, was "little more than a high school,"[94] and that the high salary meant that it would be Wilson's responsibility to wheedle every dime of increased funding out of the Illinois legislature. Without even visiting the Urbana, Illinois campus, he wisely chose to remain where he was.

By 1895, the money he was making on the lecture circuit exceeded his salary. He was building a house in Princeton, in part with borrowed money, the debt secured by some of Ellen's inheritance. He was lecturing to repay the debt. He signed up with the Brooklyn Institute of Arts & Sciences to deliver six lectures on "Leaders of Political Thought" for $250, between October 10 and November 22. As soon as those lectures were completed, he signed with the American Society for the Extension of University Training, to deliver the same series of lectures in Lancaster, Pennsylvania, between November 20 and January 10, 1896. In the spring he addressed meetings of the Princeton and Virginia alumni and delivered the commencement addresses at Wellesley College and Oberlin College in Ohio. At Wellesley, his topic was "Political Liberty," and he could not resist a dig at the French: "It [Liberty] is a difficult thing to speculate about, and to enjoy liberty. The nations who have enjoyed liberty have not speculated about it. In France they have said most about liberty and know it the least."[95] In one of his Lancaster lectures, he amused his audience with another jibe at the French. "It is a little difficult for people of other nations to appreciate a Frenchman; they are too expressively humorous…The French writer has a way of playing with his subjects which does not meet with general approval for foreigners."[96] There is no record of Wilson actually having met a Frenchman prior to uttering these remarks. It is certain that he had not yet traveled abroad.

His topic for the Oberlin commencement was "Leaders of Men," an address he first gave in 1889 and would give repeatedly throughout the 1890's.[97] He begins by again returning to his theme in "The Study of Politics," viz., the distinction between "men who lead in action" and those who "lead in silent thought." He defends the role of the thinker. "A book is often quite as quickening a trumpet as any made in brass and sounded in the field." Wilson concedes the obvious: "The men who act stand nearer to the mass of men than do the men who write," and he is reconciled to this: "He [the scholar] may be back of the leaders, but he is not the leader….Not many of the multitudes who crowd about him buy his books. But, if the few who can understand read and are convinced, will not his thought finally leaven the mass?" He now realizes there is no place for "literary" men in the arena: "Imagine Thackeray leading the House of Commons, or Mr. Lowell on the stump. How comically would their very genius defeat them." The leader of men is not a literary man: "[T]he whole question with him is a question of the application of force. There are men to be moved; how shall he move them?…Men are as clay in the hands of the consummate leader."

According to Wilson, no one personified the distinction between the literary man and the leader of men better than Edmund Burke, who proved that literary brilliance was not enough. Although his life was spent in Parliament, with "eloquence he poured forth there…as deathless as our literature," Burke had little ability to effect legislation: "How noble a figure in the history of English politics: how large a man; how commanding a mind; and yet how ineffectual in the work of bringing men to turn their faces as he would have them, toward the high purposes he had in view.…His power was literary, not forensic. He was no leader of men. He was an organizer of thought, but not of party politics." Burke's thoughts "penetrate the mind and possess the heart of the quiet student.…But his are not thoughts to be shouted over."

So how does a leader of men lead? Bordering on the cynical, Wilson advises that "Men are not led by being told what they do not know. *Persuasion* is a force, *but not information*; and persuasion is accomplished by creeping into the confidence of those you lead. Their confidence is not gained by preaching new thoughts to them. It is gained by qualities which they can recognize at first sight by arguments which they can assimilate at once…" He advises the successful politician not to get too far ahead of the public: "[N]o reform may succeed for which the major thought of the nation is not prepared…the instructed few may not be safe leaders except insofar as they have communicated their instruction to the many—except insofar as they have transmuted their thought into a common, popular thought." He advises that on occasion a politician must dumb it down: "It will not do to incarnate too many ideas at a time if you are to be universally understood and numerously followed." Wilson realizes that this may be a prescription for demagoguery, and attempts to draw a distinction between the demagogue and the statesman: "The one [the demagogue] adjusts his sails to the breeze of the day; the other makes plans to ripen with slow progress of the years. While the one solicitously watches the capricious changes of the weather, the other diligently sows the grains on their season. The one ministers to himself, the other to the race."

Wilson concludes "Leaders of Men" by counseling *compromise*, which is astounding in light of his conduct as president: "A wide sympathy and tolerance is needed in dealing with men, and uncompromising men cannot lead…There is and must be in politics a sort of pervasive sense of compromise, an abiding consciousness of the fact that in the general growth and progress of affairs no absolute initiative for any one man, but that each must both give and take." Wilson would forget every one of these words, but that was years away.

"Leaders of Men" at least had some meat on the bones. Most of his lectures were light entertainments. Speaking to the New Jersey Historical Society in Newark on May 16, (his topic being "The Course of American History") he said: "Our roughened race, embrowned in the sun, hardened in manner by a course of life rife with change and danger, loving the rude woods and the crack of the rifle, living to begin something new every day, striking with the broad and open hand, delicate in nothing but the touch of the trigger, leaving cities in its track as if by accident rather than design, settling again to the steady ways of a fixed life only when it must; such was the American people whose achievement it was to be to take possession of their continent from end to end ere their national government was a century old."[98]

Everywhere he spoke, his lectures were well-received by both his audiences and whatever local newspapers that reported them. But Franklin William Hooper, who headed the Brooklyn Institute of Arts & Sciences, was not pleased, writing Wilson: "[T]he lectures were different from what I expected they would be. They are in my judgment addressed to a more popular audience than I hoped they would be. We desire particularly to emphasize the instructive element in our work rather than the attractive or popular or entertaining element."[99] There is no record of Wilson's response, but it must have stung.

In 1893, the nation was beset by what was then called a "panic," but what really was a depression that lasted until 1897. At its height, the unemployment rate may have reached 18% (this before accurate statistical measurement). Farmers lost their farms due to falling prices for wheat and cotton. Banks failed by the hundreds, at a time when there was no deposit insurance. In April, 1894, the coal miners went on strike. The worst of it may have been in May, 1894, when four thousand workers at the Pullman Company (the manufacturer of railroad sleeping cars) went on strike to protest a *reduction* in wages. On June 26, the head of the Amalgamated Railway Union, Eugene V. Debs, called on all of his ARU railroad workers to boycott any train that included a Pullman car. By June 30, 125,000 railway workers had walked off the job, and the nation's railroads were crippled. The *New York Times* opined that the strike and boycott "has assumed the proportions of the greatest battle between labor and capital that has ever been inaugurated in the United States."[100]

If one had attended every one of Woodrow Wilson's lectures in the decade of the 1890's, but had read no newspapers or magazines, that person would not have heard of the Panic of 1893 and would have learned nothing of the issues then roiling the nation and the world, for Wilson spoke nary a word of any of it. It is reported, however, that during his July 31, 1894 address in Denver on "The Origin and Derivation of Political Liberty," Wilson did mention that he had spoken to the locomotive engineer on the way into town, and that the engineer had advised Wilson that he was opposed to strikes, because "in a strike everybody was so mad that they couldn't settle anything."[101]

By the spring of 1896, the pace of the work was becoming too much. Wilson began missing lectures. His friends began to notice his appearance, and advised him to take a vacation. He took their advice. He planned for himself a leisurely bicycle trip through Scotland and England. He was scheduled to sail for Glasgow on the *S.S. Ethiopia* on May 30. On or about May 27, he suffered his first stroke. He lost the ability to use his right hand, and he experienced pain in his right arm and numbness in the tips of his fingers. He did not cancel the trip. He wrote remarkably legible letters to Ellen with his left hand. The stroke did not affect his ability to bicycle many miles every day, and he enjoyed himself immensely, and returned invigorated and refreshed. But the weakness in his right arm persisted for many months.

By October Wilson had recovered sufficiently to give the most important address of his life to date. Eighteen ninety-six was the year of Princeton's sesquicentennial, and President Patton pulled out all of the stops in the planning of the celebration. He gave Dean Andrew Fleming West a $20,000 budget for the event. Prominent educators from across America and Europe were invited. The three-day event featured numerous addresses, alumni dinners, a parade attended by President Cleveland, a football game (Princeton defeated Virginia, 48-0), bands and fireworks. On the first day of the celebration, October 20, President Patten announced that after 150 years, "The College of New Jersey" would henceforth officially be known as "Princeton University." But the keynote came the next day, Wilson's speech on "Princeton in the Nation's Service."

As Wilson approached the podium, the members of the class of '79 stood and cheered one of their own. Wilson knew the audience he faced, as he always did. The presidential election was a fortnight away. It might be McKinley, but it might be "The Great Commoner," "The Boy Orator of the Platte," William Jennings Bryan, and there was hardly a soul in the audience—Cleveland included—not terrified of Bryan. Wilson's address was steeped in Burkean conservatism. After a lengthy review of Princeton's truly glorious past, he got to the heart of the matter: "We are in danger to lose our memory and become infantile in every generation. That is the real menace under which we cower everywhere in this time of change. The Old World trembles to see its proletariat in the saddle: we are dismayed to find ourselves growing no older, always as young as the information of our most numerous voters."[102] Echoing Burke, he said: "[I]f you will look you have the law of conservatism disclosed, it is the law of progress. But not all change is progress, not all growth is the manifestation of life....The growth that is a manifestation of life is equable, draws its springs gently out of the old fountains of strength, builds upon old tissue, covers the old airs that have blown upon it time out of mind in the past. Colleges must surely to be the best nurseries of such life, the best schools of the progress which conserves." Wilson's prescription is to steep college students with the classics, the literature that has withstood the test of time. "In America, especially, we run perpetually this risk of newness...The men whom Madison led in the making of the Constitution were men who regarded the past. They had flung off from the mother country, not to get a new liberty but to preserve an old, not to break a Constitution but to keep it."[103] He reserved his greatest antipathy not for science, but for the overuse of the scientific method: "I have no laboratory but the world of books and men in which I live; but I am much mistaken if the scientific spirit of the age is not doing us a great disservice, working in us a certain great degeneracy. Science has bred in us a spirit of experiment and a contempt for the past. It has made us credulous of quick improvement, hopeful of discovering panaceas, confident of success in every new thing."[104]

He was repeatedly interrupted by applause. When he finished, the class of '79 led the cheering. The address was a huge success, reported upon favorably and at length in the *New York Times* and the *Philadelphia Inquirer*. More importantly, it was reported that one aspiring candidate for Princeton's presidency (if and when President Patton retired) was heard muttering that there were now no candidates for the position other than Wilson.[105]

There is no end of the ironies of that day. None of the alumni or undergraduates cheering Wilson could have imagined that this man would develop ideas for Princeton's future that would be hateful to them. Wilson could not have imagined that his principal opponent would be one of the men seated on the dais—Dean West himself—or that President Cleveland would enjoy himself so much that day that he would retire to Princeton, become a trustee of the university, and become one of Dean West's principal allies in the struggle with Wilson.

"J'ACCUSE"

Truth is on the march, and nothing will stop it.

—Émile Zola

On March 18, 1890, thirty-one-year-old Kaiser Wilhelm II dismissed seventy-four-year-old Otto von Bismarck as the German Chancellor, Wilhelm believing he could conduct foreign policy just as well as Bismarck. Since the end of the Franco-Prussian War, Bismarck had deftly kept all of the contending European powers at arms-length, in an uneasy peace, but at peace nonetheless. He tied Austria-Hungary to Germany, kept France diplomatically isolated, and sought to assure that Russia did not feel isolated. All that was now about to change.

One of Bismarck's handiworks was a secret "Reinsurance Treaty" between Germany and Russia, which required each of them to remain neutral if the other were attacked by a third party. No sooner did Wilhelm dismiss Bismarck that he let the Reinsurance Treaty lapse. The result was what Bismarck had feared. Russia now felt isolated, as did France. The two began looking towards each other. The result was an 1892 military convention between France and Russia that bound each to assist the other if attacked by one or more of the signatories to the Triple Alliance: Germany, Austria-Hungary and Italy. In 1894 the military convention became a formal alliance. It ended France's diplomatic isolation and gave France some protection in the event of another German invasion.

Soon after taking control of German foreign policy, Wilhelm decided that a thaw in Franco-German relations was possible. The attempt at *détente* began when Wilhelm told visiting French elder statesman and former prime minister Jules Simon: "Your army has made great progress and is ready. If it were engaged in single combat with the German army no one could forecast the result of the struggle. Therefore I should regard as a madman or a criminal whoever stirred up the peoples to make war."[1] The organizers of a Berlin art exhibit invited French artists to participate. France reciprocated, making a German physicist, Hermann von Helmholtz, a member of the Legion of Honour.

All this went up in smoke with the February, 1891, visit to Paris by Wilhelm's widowed mother, Empress Frederick. Billed as an unofficial shopping trip, the visit had wide publicity; she was followed wherever she went. Tactlessly, she visited Versailles, the site of Germany's 1871 unification. She also visited the ruins of the Chateau Saint-Cloud, destroyed by Germany during the war. The perceived insult resulted in noisy demonstrations fomented by Paul Déroulède and his *Ligue des Patriotes*. The demonstrations caused the *Kölnische Zeitung* to editorialize: "The French have a right to think of revenge but they have no right to injure the feelings of the head of the Empire and his mother by insults that only could be expected by scoundrels."[2] Déroulède sent a letter to the Paris press: "Our [the Ligue des Patriotes] object has been achieved. The check to the Prussian is complete and French dignity is saved."[3] Déroulède was correct; his object had been achieved. French artists withdrew from the forthcoming Berlin art exhibition. Empress Frederick left Paris by train, without incident, but it took 500 *gendarmes* at the Gare du Nord to assure that this was so. The German ambassador advised Alexandre Ribot, the French foreign minister, that this had been Germany's "final attempt to conciliate France." Moreover, the incident had the collateral effect of complicating France's relations with England. Empress Frederick was not only Wilhelm's mother; she was also Queen Victoria's daughter.

By 1893, the Third French Republic was anything but an unqualified success. From its founding on September 4, 1801, the revolving door had swung twenty-five governments in and out. In 1882, the *Union Generale* had collapsed, taking with it the life savings of thousands. In 1887 came the news that Daniel Wilson, President Grevy's son-in-law, had been peddling decorations from within the Elysee Palace. Then came Panama; then came Boulanger. And all of this in the context of a depressed economy. It was easy for many Frenchman to conclude that the Republic was a cesspool of corruption controlled by a syndicate of Jews. If anyone doubted it, Edouard Drumont was delighted to provide the evidence of Jewish perfidy in *La Libre Parole*. He was not alone. The Archbishop of

Bordeaux warned his parishioners that the blight killing French vineyards was God's retribution for their allowing France to come under the influence of the "usurers."

If there was one institution that was close to the heart of almost every Frenchman, the institution that appeared to be above the partisanship and the corruption, it was the army. The army was the Republic's unqualified success. Beginning in 1872, the National Assembly (the forerunner to the Chamber of Deputies before the 1875 constitution) enacted a conscription bill that eliminated a wealthy man's ability to avoid service by buying a substitute. France modernized its army. If it didn't have the money it borrowed heavily, floating bonds. Between 1871 and 1900 France roughly matched Germany in military spending; their armies were roughly the same size. But it came at a price for France. France had a stagnant population; Germany was growing. The result was that by 1900, in order to maintain parity with Germany, France had 14 men for every 1000 under arms; Germany only 11.[4]

The most significant improvement came in 1874, when France created a general staff within the ministry of war, modeled after Germany's. It was divided into personnel, intelligence, operations and training and logistics divisions, all devoted to the planning and execution of military maneuvers. It is said that before 1870, "war in the French army was not something that you prepared for, but rather something that one fought when it came along."[5] That had all changed. The general staff was now considered France's *L'Arche Sainte*, the "Holy Ark."

In 1876, France created the *Ecole Supérieure de guerre*, France's equivalent of the United States Army War College. Admission was strictly by merit. Neither money, lineage, nor connections could get an undeserving officer in. Every year the top twelve graduates were posted to the general staff. The identity of the top twelve graduates was determined solely on the basis of the average of each student-officer's test scores. Once again, neither influence nor aristocratic status was of any help to an officer whose grades did not measure up. It was by this method that, on April 21, 1890, Captain Alfred Dreyfus learned that he had finished ninth in his class and thus would be assigned as a *stagiaire*, a trainee, to the general staff. He received the news on the same day that he married his bride, Lucie. Born in 1859, Dreyfus was Alsatian. Under the Treaty of Frankfort, his family was given the choice of remaining in their home in Mulhouse and becoming German citizens, or emigrating to France. The entire family opted for France, with the exception of two brothers who stayed behind to operate the family textile business.

Alfred Dreyfus was not a typical French junior officer. He was married and would soon have two children. He was highly dedicated and patriotic. A graduate of the competitive *Ecole Polytechnique*, he was an artillery specialist. He was very wealthy. He was also a Jew, which explains, in part, why he was not very well-liked among his fellow officers. His reviews from his superior officers noted that he had a tinny, emotionless voice, not the voice of command. He was the first Jew ever posted to the general staff. But if he would ever need someone up the chain of command to look out for him, to protect him, that person did not exist. He would be alone.

Marie Bastian was a *femme de ménage*—a cleaning lady—in the German embassy in Paris. She swept the offices, she washed down the stairs, she lit the fires, and each night she emptied the waste basket from under the desk of the military attaché, Colonel Maximilien von Schwartzkoppen. She emptied the basket, but she did not discard the contents, for Marie Bastian was a spy in the employ of the innocuously-named "Statistical Section" of France's general staff. She swept the crumpled-up contents of Colonel Schwartzkoppen's waste basket into paper bags, and once or twice a month— always after hours—she made the short walk from the embassy to the Basilique Sainte-Clotilde. There, in the chapel, in exchange for a fistful of cash, she delivered the bags to Maj. Hubert-Joseph Henry, the second-in-command of the Statistical Section.

The Statistical Section had been created in 1876, and its principal function was counterintelligence, which included disinformation, i.e. creating fake documents which would be fed to known spies. It was never a big operation, with only five officers and four aides in 1894.[6] It was notoriously slipshod. One of its officers once sold an unused strongbox. When the buyer opened it, he discovered a trove of secret documents which, fortunately, he immediately returned.[7]

Maj. Henry, 48, was a semi-literate peasant. He had started in the enlisted ranks, served with distinction in North Africa and Indo-China, and was made an officer in 1877. He was thick-set, with close-cropped hair, and resembled a bulldog. He spoke no foreign languages and his French revealed his peasant origins. Marie Bastian was only one of a number of lowlifes he dealt with in the demimonde of espionage, but she was the most productive. Her nightly foray through Colonel Schwartzkoppen's waste basket became known as the "ordinary route," and it had already uncovered a lively espionage correspondence between Colonel Schwartzkoppen and his counterpart in the Italian embassy, Col. Alessandro Panizzardi.

Maj. Henry's boss, the head of the Statistical Section, was Col. Nicholas Sandherr, 48. He was born in Mulhouse, in Alsace, the same town that Dreyfus hailed from. He was a graduate of Saint Cyr, the French West Point. The Statistical Section reported directly to the Vice Chief of Staff, which in 1894 was in the person of Gen. Charles-

Arthur Gonse, 56. Gonse, also a graduate of Saint Cyr, was a life-long friend of the senior military officer of the French army, its chief of staff, Gen. Raoul le Mouton de Boisdeffre.

Boisdeffre, 56, was one of the most respected military officers of his time. A cavalry officer in the Franco-Prussian War, he had risen quickly. He had served as military attaché in Russia in 1879, and developed a keen interest in Russian military affairs. Recently, he had been the principal architect and negotiator of the alliance with Russia. He was "dignified, industrious, quietly persistent, everywhere respected."[8] He embodied the French people's reverence for their army.

If Boisdeffre had a nominal superior officer, it was the minister of war himself, Gen. Auguste Mercier, 60. He had been captured near Metz in 1870. One of the officers who had served under Mercier said that once an idea was set in Mercier's mind "he could neither withdraw it nor undo it."[9] He had been appointed minister of war in December, 1893, and his tenure had not been a happy one. A series of minor blunders had put him on shaky ground, and by the summer of 1894 he feared that he might be replaced.

These five men: Henry, Sandherr, Gonse, Boisdeffre and Mercier (there would be others later) would combine negligence, idiocy and outright criminality to soon convict an innocent man of treason and later set in train a series of events that would threaten to tear France apart. But that was in the future on the evening of September 26, 1894, when Maj. Henry, seated at his desk at home, upended one of Marie Bastian's paper bags. He noticed that one of the papers, a partially-torn onion skin, was not written in German; it was in French. It was unsigned and undated. It began: "Without news indicating that you wish to see me, nevertheless, sir, I send you some interesting information:" It then listed five numbered items, all of a technical military nature, including: "1. A note on the hydraulic buffer of the 120 and the way in which this gun behaves…" It concluded with: "I am just off to manoeuvres." This cover letter, essentially a list, came to be known as the *bordereau*. When Henry saw it, his heart must have stopped. It revealed to him that not only was there a spy in the army, but that the spy was actively divulging secrets to the Germans. Later, when an aide translated it for him, he realized that this spy had, or was prepared to, reveal the secrets of the new French 120mm cannon. At just that moment, the Statistical Section was working to spread *false* information about the 120.

On a prior occasion, Marie Bastian's trove had uncovered a letter from Schwartzkoppen to Colonel Panizzardi that read in part: "Enclosed are twelve detail maps of Nice that the Scoundrel D. ["…la canaille D…"] left with me for you…" Could it be that "the scoundrel D" was also the author of the bordereau? Henry immediately showed the bordereau to Col. Sandherr. Copies of it were circulated to every command in the army. With luck, someone might recognize the traitor's handwriting. No one did.

On October 6, one of the general staff officers, a Lt. Col. Aboville, had an idea. Since the bordereau mentioned military matters dealing with different branches of the service, the traitor was most likely a *stagiaire*, since stagiaires were rotated among the different commands. Narrow the search to the stagiaires, he advised, and the traitor would be found. The search immediately turned up Col. Alfred Dreyfus. They compared his handwriting to the bordereau. They seemed *similar*, if not exact. Dreyfus might be the traitor.

By the evening of that same day—October 6—the matter of the bordereau had gone up the chain of command as far as Gen. Boisdeffre. He appointed his cousin, Maj. Mercier du Paty de Clam, 41, an amateur "graphologist," to compare Dreyfus' handwriting to the bordereau, and to oversee the matter. Paty also thought the handwriting was close enough to warrant a further investigation.

Matters were now moving very quickly, but all in secret, the public completely unaware of events. On October 8, Boisdeffre briefed Mercier. On October 10, Mercier briefed France's president, Jean Casimir-Perier, and the prime minister, Charles Dupuy, falsely advising them that a traitor had been uncovered. He did not mention Dreyfus' name. The next day, Mercier briefed the entire cabinet, telling them that he knew the identity of the traitor, but again not mentioning his name. Mercier, his position in the government shaky, could well have used the quick identification and cashiering of an officer spying for the Germans. But more than one cabinet officer urged caution. The foreign minister, Gabriel Hanotaux, suggested that publicly identifying the traitor might complicate relations with Germany, in light of the fact that his identity had been unearthed by the French having their own spy rummaging through the German embassy's trash.

On that same day—October 11—the general staff hired a professional handwriting expert, Alfred Gobert, an employee of the Bank of France, to compare Dreyfus' handwriting with the bordereau. Gobert would not report his findings until Saturday, October 13. But also on October 11 Mercier ordered Vice Chief of Staff Gonse to "get more evidence" on Dreyfus. On Friday, October 12, still without the benefit of Gobert's report, Mercier ordered Boisdeffre to order du Paty to arrest Dreyfus on Monday, October 15.

On Saturday, October 13, Gobert reported his findings. He opined that whereas the bordereau might have been authored by Dreyfus, it might also have been the work of *any other person*. At which point Gobert's findings were completely ignored. Gonse hired another consultant who was not even an amateur graphologist, who concluded that Dreyfus was the author of the bordereau.

On Monday, Paty had Dreyfus arrested and hauled into the Cherche-Midi military prison. He was held incommunicado, and was not advised of the charges. His wife was advised that it would be best for her husband if she kept quiet. For the next twelve days, Paty did everything to get Dreyfus to confess. He shined lights in his eyes. He forced Dreyfus to take dictation in the middle of the night and in odd postures. He cut up a copy of the bordereau and mixed the pieces with cut up pieces of Dreyfus' handwriting. Dreyfus picked out his own handwriting every time. Nothing worked. They ransacked Dreyfus home in search of—something. Nothing turned up. All the while, Dreyfus proclaimed his innocence, of what he was not sure.

Finally, on October 27, Paty reported to Boisdeffre, with Henry and Sandherr present. He advised Boisdeffre that Dreyfus had not confessed, that the searches of Dreyfus' home and elsewhere had turned up nothing, and that if they charged Dreyfus he might be acquitted. Boisdeffre replied: "We have gone too far to be able to retreat. Dreyfus is a swine who deserves the firing squad. Get on with your work without worrying about the consequences, and don't sulk."[10] What is more important about this meeting is that Henry, the peasant soldier, found himself in the presence of the greatest soldier of his day, and whether or not Boisdeffre knew it or intended it, Henry had received his orders that day, and as a good soldier, would carry them out.

Up until October 28 everything had been conducted in secret. Mercier and Boisdeffre could have dropped the investigation, they could have sent Dreyfus to Algeria or Indo-China, they could have kept looking for the real traitor, and no one in France would have been the wiser. Mercier would have been acutely embarrassed and might have lost his ministry, but it would have ended there. That all ended on the morning of October 29, when Edouard Drumont's *La Libre Parole* asked: "Is it true that an extremely important arrest has taken place by military order?"[11] We will never know Drumont's source. It has been suggested that it was Henry.[12]

Now the pressure to dig up more evidence linking Dreyfus to the crime became intense. And so Henry, whose duties included creating misinformation, began forging documents, including a report of Dreyfus' "gambling" and "womanizing." Henry and Sandherr were convinced of Dreyfus' guilt; they saw nothing wrong in supplementing the evidence to prove it. News of the arrest, and the identity of the accused, was seeping out.

On October 29, Paty gave his final report to Boisdeffre and Mercier. Paty believed that Dreyfus was guilty, but warned that there might not be enough evidence to convict him. By October 31 everyone in Paris knew that a Jew named Dreyfus had been accused of high treason. Mercier now knew that if Dreyfus were acquitted he would be finished, not only as minister of war but in the army. There was now no turning back.

On October 31, Dreyfus' older brother Mathieu hurried to Paris and began organizing his brother's defense. He was certain of Alfred's innocence, and assumed that it was a case of mistaken identity that could be cleared up. He could not know that he was setting out on a journey that would consume his life for the next five years. He engaged one of the most eminent lawyers in Paris, the Catholic Edgar Demange. When Demange first saw the government's file on Dreyfus, he told Mathieu: "If Captain Dreyfus were not Jewish he would not be in the Cherche-Midi."

On November 3, Mercier addressed the cabinet. He advised his fellow ministers that Dreyfus was guilty. They approved an indictment, accusing Dreyfus of having "delivered to a foreign power a certain number of confidential documents relating to national defense, thus enabling them to undertake a war with France."[13] The only "evidence" they had was the bordereau, and the handwriting experts were divided as to its author.

The German ambassador to France, Count Georg Münster, was not amused by any of this. He, Schwartzkoppen and Dreyfus himself shared one thing in common: the absolute certainty that Dreyfus was not in the employ of the German embassy. In late November, he filed the first of a number of official protests with the French foreign office: "No official or officer in my Embassy has ever had any relations of any kind with Captain Dreyfus."[14] There was no chance that this protest would be responded to. Marie Bastian was still emptying Schwartzkoppen's waste basket, every night.

In mid-December, president Casimir-Perier was engaged in conversation with Gen. Félix-Gaston Saussier, the military governor of Paris and the man designated to actually lead the troops in the event of war with Germany. Saussier told his president: "Dreyfus is not guilty. That fool Mercier has put his finger in his own eye again." "Then why," he was asked, "is the Commander in Chief having Dreyfus court-martialed?" "That's exactly what I asked him, and he said that the report of the examining officer did not permit him to act otherwise, and besides, it did not matter, because the court-martial will decide."[15] Like most Frenchmen, Gen. Saussier firmly believed that a panel of French officers would not—could not—convict an innocent man.

The court-martial began on December 19. The judges were seven army officers, one colonel, one lieutenant-colonel, three majors and two captains. The first thing they did, over lawyer Demange's objection, was vote to conduct the trial in secret. There would be no stenographic record, or record of any kind, of the proceeding, other than the recollections of the participants and the witnesses. From the start, it did not go well for the prosecution. Maj. Henry made for a bad witness. Gen. Gonse was called to discredit M. Gobert, the Bank of France handwriting expert who had refused to opine that the bordereau was in Dreyfus' handwriting. To counter Gobert, the prosecution summoned one Alphonse Bertillon, who was not a handwriting expert, but who had devised a method of identifying criminals by the size of their heads. Bertillon testified that Dreyfus had written the bordereau by *forging his own signature.* Paty did no better. He testified that when, during his interrogation of Dreyfus, he required him to take dictation, his hand trembled. When presented with the document that Dreyfus had been required to write, Paty had to admit that there was no sign of trembling. He then changed his testimony. The fact that Dreyfus could undergo the interrogation so coolly proved he was guilty.

Seeing how badly it was going, Henry asked to be recalled. Over Demange's vigorous objection, Henry testified that months before he had received warnings from "a man of honour" that there was a traitor in their midst and then, very dramatically, he pointed to Dreyfus: "And there is the traitor." It was, of course, classic hearsay, and there is little chance that a civilian court anywhere, even in France, would have received such testimony. Demange demanded that Henry reveal his informant's identity. Henry refused: "There are secrets in an officer's head which even his cap mustn't know."[16] But the presiding officer fell for it, asking Henry to swear "on his honour" that Henry's unnamed informant had identified Dreyfus. "I swear it," he replied.

But the prosecution was still uncertain of a conviction. And so, after all the evidence was in, Mercier, Sandherr and Henry gave the judges a file of "evidence" that Dreyfus' defense did not see and of which it was not aware. The entire contents of the "secret dossier" are unknown to this day, but they certainly included the forged "biographical sketch" of Dreyfus pointing to his "gambling" and "womanizing," and the note from Schwartzkoppen to Panizzardi referring to the plans of military installations in Nice that "that scoundrel D has given me for you." Just to make certain that they got the point, Paty advised the judges, in secret, that he believed that "D" was Dreyfus. After the trial, Mercier retrieved the secret dossier. He burned the biographical sketch and ordered Sandherr to disperse the other documents within the Statistical Section's files. That order was never obeyed.

The court-martial lasted all of three days. On December 22, the judges met in secret, then announced their unanimous verdict of guilty. Dreyfus was sentenced to life imprisonment and deportation. There would be a degradation ceremony. It was the maximum possible penalty. He was spared the death penalty only because his was considered an exempt "political crime." Demange said to Dreyfus: "Your condemnation is the greatest crime of the century."[17] He was mistaken. The century was not yet over; worse was still to come.

When Georges Clemenceau was defeated in the August, 1893 elections, he returned to Paris with less than nothing. Having lost his seat, he lost his salary. He was heavily in debt, and *La Justice*, never a money-maker, was failing. His medical career was long over. He moved to a smaller flat on the rue Franklin that would be his home, office and headquarters for the rest of his life. He sold some of his Manets, Pissarros and Rafaellis. He returned to *La Justice*, but now, of necessity, he turned to journalism. No longer able to afford ghost writers, he began to write to support himself. He wrote eight articles a month for *La Dépeche de Toulouse*. He wrote about anything that came to mind. He wasn't very good. He had not yet found his voice.

The first article Clemenceau penned dealing with Dreyfus—there would be hundreds more—appeared on December 25, 1894, three days after the verdict. Titled simply "The Traitor," he began: "Unanimously, the court-martial has declared Captain Alfred Dreyfus guilty of treason. The crime is so appalling that one wants to doubt it until the last moment…How could a human being make himself so dishonorable, that one cannot wait to spit out the disgust."[18] Clemenceau accepted the need for a closed trial, agreeing with the presiding officer: "There are interests greater than the interests of the person." He was so offended by the act of treason that his only objection was with the sentence. Like most Republicans, he was opposed to the death penalty. But he also believed that the greatest penalty should be reserved for the greatest of crimes, treason. He noted that the day before, a young, frightened soldier had been court-martialed for breaking objects in the barracks. He continued: "At the hearing he throws his hat at the government commissioner. Death. And for the man who helped the enemy in the invasion of the country…who opened the road to new fires…to the thieves of territory, to the torturers of the fatherland, a peaceful life, with all the pleasures of coconut farming. There has never been been anything so revolting." Clemenceau was very mistaken regarding the "peaceful life" that Dreyfus faced.

The ceremonial degradation took place on the morning of January 5, 1895, at the *Ecole Militaire*. Five thousand soldiers, representing regiments from throughout Paris, were assembled, covering three sides of the parade ground. Outside the iron gates, an angry mob formed, screaming for Dreyfus' neck. Dreyfus was marched onto the parade ground behind a regimental officer, stiff and unbending, eyes forward, a bit flushed but with no sign of loss of composure. The *New York Times* correspondent opined that "Generally, 99 of every 100 men who are thus degraded weep like children, but Dreyfus was firm throughout."[19] Many saw Dreyfus' demeanor as proof of his guilt. Dreyfus was then stopped and forced to face the officer, who read a statement: "Dreyfus, you are unworthy to carry arms. In the name of the people of France, we degrade you." He then took Dreyfus' sword, broke it over his knee, and cast the pieces on the ground. He then ripped the epaulets and buttons from Dreyfus' uniform, and flung them to the ground. To the sound of drums marking time, he was marched past every one of the assembled soldiers.

It had taken all of four minutes. But it wasn't over. As he was marched out Dreyfus began shouting: "You have degraded an innocent man. I swear that I am innocent. Vive la France." When he marched past the members of the press he yelled: "I declare that I am innocent." "Tell the whole of France that I am innocent." But his pleas only incensed the crowd: "*A mort le traitre*"—"Death to the traitor."

Col. Sandherr was present at the degradation. He observed that "…this race [the Jews] has neither patriotism, nor honor, nor pride. For centuries they have done nothing but betray."[20] Also present—outside the gates—was Theodor Herzl, 34, then working as a journalist for Vienna's *Neue Freie Presse*. Although he believed Dreyfus to be guilty, the murderous crowd convinced him that only in a Jewish state could Jews be free from persecution. Two years later, he convened the First Zionist Congress in Basel, Switzerland, and would devote the rest of his life to the concept of a Jewish state in Palestine.

Dreyfus was shipped to île du Diable—Devil's Island—a bleak rock off the coast of French Guiana. He was its only prisoner. A small hut was built for him, into which the guards could constantly watch him, but who were not permitted to speak to him. He lost weight. Some of his teeth fell out. He lost the power of speech. He was permitted to send and receive mail, but it was heavily censored. He would be completely oblivious of the five-year drama of which he would be the central character and which would draw the attention of the world. They expected that Devil's Island would kill him. To his own surprise, it did not.

There would later be scores, then hundreds, of *Dreyfusards*, the people who would demand justice for Dreyfus. But in the beginning there was only his brother Mathieu and his wife Lucie. Mathieu's only hope was to keep the flame alive, so that France would not forget a traitor who had been discovered, charged, convicted and sentenced. He hired a young Jewish journalist, Bernard Lazare, who had written a history of anti-Semitism, to write a series of articles denouncing the trial. Mathieu caught a small break when, shortly after the degradation, the revolving door revolved again, and the government of prime minister Charles Dupuy fell. Out with Dupuy went his minister of war, Gen. Mercier. Mathieu caught a bigger break in July, 1895, when Col. Sandherr, terminally ill with paralysis probably resulting from syphilis, was forced to resign as the head of the Statistical Section. He was replaced by Col. Georges Picquart, 40. If nothing else, the cast of characters was changing.

Georges Picquart was a highly-decorated infantry officer, having served with distinction in Indo-China. He loved music, was fluent in German, English and Spanish, and by 1886 was the youngest lieutenant-colonel in the army. He had taught at the *Ecole Superieure de guerre*, where one of his students had been Dreyfus. Dreyfus was attracted to Picquart and tried to befriend him, but the attraction wasn't mutual. He had been posted as an observer to Dreyfus' trial and, having been aware of the secret dossier that the judges had seen (without having seen it himself) he was convinced of Dreyfus' guilt. During a meeting with Boisdeffre, Boisdeffre remarked to him: "Of course the case is closed, but there is one aspect of it that haunts me. What motive…could Dreyfus have had for the treachery? The man had everything, wealth, a satisfactory family situation, a responsible position in the army. What could have induced him to betray his country?"[21]

It was bound to happen. Since Dreyfus was not the traitor, and since Marie Bastian was still emptying Col. Schwartzkoppen's waste basket every night, there was every possibility that, if the real spy were brazen enough, more evidence linking Col. Schwartzkoppen to the real spy would fall into Mme. Bastian's hands. And in March, 1896, a full fourteen months following Dreyfus' conviction, it did. It was a draft of a letter that someone in the German embassy had written:

> "Sir, I await above all a more detailed explanation than the one you gave me the other day on the question at issue. Consequently, I ask that you give it to me in writing so that I may judge whether I should continue my relations with the firm of R. or not. C."

The letter was addressed to "Commandant Esterhazy, 27, rue de la Bienfaisance." The letter was on blue paper of the type used for intra-post office communications via pneumatic tube. It became known as the *petit bleu*. Although its author has never been identified, Col. Schwartzkoppen later confirmed that it emanated from his office.

When Picquart stared at the *petit bleu*, he did not conclude that this Commandant Esterhazy—and not Dreyfus—was the traitor. Instead, he believed that he might have a *second* spy on his hands. And so, for the next four months, he told no one of the *petit bleu*. But he did launch a discreet investigation into this man Esterhazy. Picquart learned that Esterhazy was deeply in debt, a petty thief and confidence man who, although married, was living with a common prostitute. In short, Esterhazy was everything Dreyfus was not. He also had the perfect profile for someone motivated to sell military secrets. But Picquart also learned that Esterhazy was a close friend of Maurice Weil, an influential retired officer who has close to Gen. Saussier, the military governor of Paris (Saussier was the lover of Mme. Weil). Unlike Dreyfus, who had stood alone, if Esterhazy were charged, he would have friends in high places. On more than one occasion, Esterhazy was spotted entering the German embassy. A double agent advised Picquart that Esterhazy might be a spy. Still, Picquart, mindful that the general staff had moved too quickly to charge Dreyfus, did nothing.

The bordereau had been discovered by the Statistical Section almost two years prior, but Esterhazy was still walking the streets. That fact may have emboldened Esterhazy. In August, 1896, Esterhazy tried to get himself posted to the war ministry, probably in order to get closer to secret documents he might then sell. The new minister of war, Gen. Jean-Baptiste Billot, forwarded Esterhazy's letters of candidacy to none other than Picquart. When Picquart saw the handwriting, it appeared very familiar to him. He compared the letters to the bordereau. The handwriting was identical. Picquart now knew what only Col. Schwartkoppen and Esterhazy himself knew, that Dreyfus had been sent to Devil's Island for another man's crime and that Esterhazy was an active spy in the French army. Had there been any military justice in France, Dreyfus' release from Devil's Island would have been delayed only for as long as it might take to obtain a court order and communicate the order to his jailers. But there was no military justice in France, Dreyfus' ordeal would continue, and the "Dreyfus Affaire" was just beginning.

Starting in mid-September, 1896, the high command of the General Staff began a cover-up of their participation in Dreyfus' court-martial. If Mathieu could produce some new evidence pointing to his brother's innocence, he might be able to force a new trial. But if Dreyfus was innocent, it meant that seven army officers had wrongly condemned a fellow officer. The high command now knew that not only was Dreyfus innocent, but that he had been convicted based on evidence his defense had not seen, and which itself was fraudulent. If Dreyfus was innocent, they were guilty.

Picquart brought his findings to Gonse. Rather than start the process of bringing the real traitor to justice, Gonse, to Picquart's amazement, replied: "What does it matter to you if this Jew stays on Devil's Island. If you don't tell anyone, no one will know." Picquart couldn't believe his ears. "General," he replied, "what you have said is

abominable. I don't know what I will do, but I will not take this secret to the grave."[22]
Picquart then wrote to Gonse, presciently advising him that delaying the release of
Dreyfus and the arrest of Esterhazy could result in a crisis, "a harmful, useless crisis,
which could be avoided by doing justice in time."[23]

On September 16, 1896, the newspaper *l'Eclair* broke a story under the head "How
Dreyfus' Guilt was Proven." The story recounted how the judges had received "the
scoundrel D" letter that Schwartzkoppen had sent to Panizzardi. But *l'Eclair* incorrectly
reported that the letter read "the scoundrel Dreyfus." But now the word was out that the
judges had violated their own procedures, receiving evidence hidden from the defense.
On September 20, Lucie Dreyfus petitioned the Chamber of Deputies, demanding a
new trial, based on *l'Eclair's* article. The petition was denied.

Picquart told Boisdeffre that he believed Dreyfus was innocent and that Esterhazy
was the spy. Boisdeffre would have none of it. He told Picquart that the bordereau and
the *petit bleu* were two separate matters, which was nonsensical in light of the fact that
Picquart had the proof that Esterhazy was the author of the bordereau. But what this
colloquy proved to Boideffre was that Picquart was a loose cannon who was probably
the source for the *l'Éclair* article, and who could upset the applecart if he kept poking
around. Gonse and Boisdeffre began suspecting that Picquart might be colluding
with Mathieu. In this, they were mistaken. Mathieu was unaware that Picquart had
identified the author of the bordereau. But in the hope that someone would recognize
the handwriting, Mathieu had posters of the bordereau plastered all over Paris, and
even reproduced it in booklet form. Gonse and Boisdeffre knew they had to get rid
of Picquart. They told told him he was being reassigned. He was to inspect military
installations—in North Africa.

On November 10, the newspaper *Le Matin* was the first to publish a photo of the
bordereau. Gonse believed Picquart had leaked it, and had minister of war Billot order
Picquart to leave Paris within forty-eight hours. By the end of the month, he was posted
to Tunisia. Named as his replacement as head of the Statistical Section was Maj. Henry.
But all this had the effect Mathieu had hoped for. Almost two years after his brother's
conviction, the matter was not forgotten, and some people, even if they believed Dreyfus
was guilty, began to believe that the trial had been conducted improperly.

Some time in November, 1896, Maj. Henry cranked up his forgery machine
and produced his masterpiece. In what purported to be a letter from Panizzardi to
Schwartzkoppen, he had Panizzardi write:

> "My dear friend: I have read that a deputy is going to raise questions about
> Dreyfus. If new explanations are asked for in Rome I will say that I never

had contact with this Jew. That is understood. If you are asked, say the same, because nobody must ever know what took place with him. Alexandrine."

"Alexandrine" was the pseudonym Panizzardi commonly used when communicating with Schwartzkoppen. This forgery later became known as the *faux Henry*. Henry showed his masterwork to Gonse and Boisdeffre, bypassing Picquart. Its principal purpose was to bolster minister of war Billot's confidence in Dreyfus' guilt, as it would anyone who read it. It is unknown if Gonse and/or Boisdeffre ordered Henry to craft the *faux Henry*, or whether he did it on his own, knowing what his superiors wanted and needed. In any case, it served its purpose. Billot became an unknowing but active co-conspirator in working to prevent a new trial. Nor was Henry finished. He now began creating forgeries directed against Picquart.

Now that the bordereau was in the public domain, Mathieu engaged handwriting experts from all over Europe to compare Alfred's handwriting to the copy of the bordereau as printed in *Le Matin*. They concluded that Alfred was not the author. Now the ranks of the *Dreyfusards* began to swell. They included Senator Arthur Ranc, an old friend of Clemenceau's from the days of the commune, who had seconded for him in more than one of his many duels, and Joseph Reinach, a Jewish deputy and nephew of the Baron de Reinach of Panama infamy, and the Vice President of the Senate, Auguste Scheurer-Kestner.

Scheurer-Kestner. Clemenceau's oldest friend. The man whose sister-in-law Clemenceau had so ardently and unsuccessfully courted during his student days. The wealthy Alsatian, born in the same city as Dreyfus, now sixty-six, had been one of the original investors in *La Justice*. He was now considered the conscience of the Senate. In early 1897, Mathieu went to Scheurer-Kestner to enlist his aid. He listened, but offered no help. He had no reason to believe Dreyfus innocent, even though he was troubled at what appeared a motiveless crime. He promised he would keep his eyes and ears open, nothing more.

In the spring of 1897, Picquart obtained leave and returned to Paris. Fearing that he was now the general staff's target—fearing even that he might be killed—he engaged a Paris lawyer, Louis Leblois. He told Leblois everything. He told him of the secret dossier that Mercier had given the judges, of Esterhazy's authorship of the bordereau, of Esterhazy's shady past, Gonse's and Boisdeffre cover-up, everything. He gave Leblois a letter addressed to the president of the Republic to be opened only in the event of

Picquart's death. But being still under military discipline, he swore Leblois to secrecy, prohibiting Leblois from sharing what he had divulged with Mathieu.

On July 13, 1897, Leblois could hold the truth no longer. He visited Scheurer-Kestner, and, without revealing the identity of his client, told him everything. Scheurer-Kestner came away convinced not only that the trial had been a sham, but that Dreyfus was innocent. The next day, at the Bastille Day festivities at the Longchamps racetrack, Scheurer-Kestner told his fellow senators that he believed Dreyfus was innocent. Soon all of Paris knew of his belief. Now Scheurer-Kestner joined the ranks of those who were daily vilified in *La Libre Parole* and the rest of the anti-Dreyfusard press as being a paid German agent and part of the Jewish "syndicate" out to defame the army and obtain the release of the traitor. The stories were fed to *La Libre Parole* and the others by Henry, Paty and by Esterhazy himself.

By the autumn of 1897, it became clear to Gonse and Henry that their loose cannon was not Picquart, but Esterhazy. If he made a false move, the entire cover-up might unravel. And so they joined forces with Esterhazy, a spy for the Germans willing to betray his country and their army, in order to keep one of their wrongly-convicted officers on Devil's Island. Gonse ordered Paty: "If Commandant Esterhazy, not being warned, resorted to some reproachful act, there could result the greatest harm for the country and for certain army chiefs."[24] And so Henry and Paty met secretly with Esterhazy, Paty wearing a false beard, to coordinate strategy. Esterhazy became active in his own defense, his brazenness knowing no bounds. He wrote to the new president of the Republic, Felix Faure, making veiled threats to embarrass certain people with documents in his possession if he were not protected. In another letter to Faure he threatened to reveal a document which, if revealed, would "force France to humiliate herself or go to war."[25] His specific threats might have been baseless, but Esterhazy held a power over all of them: He could expose the cover-up.

On October 19, 1897, a new morning newspaper, *L'Aurore* (the "Dawn") appeared for the first time in Paris. Its editor-in-chief was the journalist Ernest Vaughan. With the help of some Belgian investors, he created *L'Aurore* as a vehicle for Clemenceau. *La Justice* limped along with a few more issues, but was essentially finished. *L'Aurore* would be Clemenceau's vehicle for the next two years, writing hundreds of articles on the "Dreyfus Affaire" alone, articles that when compiled fill seven volumes.

Throughout this period Henry kept his forgery machine busy. Mme. Bastian's nightly foray into Schwartzkoppen's waste basket had previously yielded a note from

Panizzardi to Schwartzkoppen, that read: "P brought me many interesting things." Henry changed the "P" to a "D."

On October 30, Scheurer-Kestner met with minister of war Billot, urging him to reopen the case. Billot refused, citing the *faux Henry*, the incontrovertible proof that Dreyfus was the spy. They did, however, agree to keep in touch. News of the meeting leaked out, and it created a firestorm in the anti-Semitic, nationalist press. They now claimed that Scheurer-Kestner was a paid German agent. The stories were planted by Henry, Paty, and Esterhazy himself.

A few days after the first appearance of *L'Aurore*, Clemenceau encountered old friend Arthur Ranc on the street. The conversation turned to the articles Bernard Lazare had written in defense of Dreyfus. Clemenceau remarked that "we all like his talent, but we've insisted that he leave us in peace with his Dreyfus affair." "What?" replied Ranc, "you don't know that Dreyfus is innocent?" "What are you telling me?" "The truth," said Ranc. "Scheurer-Kestner has the proof. Go and see him, he'll show you." Clemenceau replied: "If that is so, it is the greatest crime of the century."[26]

Clemenceau's first article on the Dreyfus case in almost two years appeared on the morning of November 1. He wrote it the previous day, after his chance encounter with Arthur Ranc, but before he visited Scheurer-Kestner. Headed "L'Affaire Dreyfus," he was obviously conflicted. He began: "Is it not possible to be finished with this story? Dreyfus has been judged by his peers, and declared guilty. We must hold that the judgment is valid until further notice." But, he conceded, "[C]ertain documents of the trial have been withheld…in the highest interest of France." He also noted that the expertise of the handwriting experts had elsewhere been discounted. Moreover, "[B]ecause Dreyfus is a Jew…a protracted anti-Semitic campaign has created on the part of French opinion a violent prejudice against the people from whom Jesus came…. The good faith of the judges cannot be questioned." However, he is quick to add, "men are fallible." He related what Arthur Ranc had told him: "[W]e are told that Scheurer-Kestner possesses irrefutable proofs of Dreyfus' innocence…Scheurer-Kestner is not a man to be taken lightly. If he has something to say, let him speak, without further delay. He concluded: "I ask that we be finished with Dreyfus. If out of all this noise nothing is to come out, let the traitor return to the scornful pity of silence."[27]

Clemenceau was silent for one whole day. On November 1 he met with Scheurer-Kestner. His article of the next morning, headed "Again the Dreyfus Affair," begins with Clemenceau noting that he had met Scheurer-Kestner "who I have not seen for many months, and who has never spoken to me about Dreyfus"…."I found his attitude so clear, his words so resolute, and his confidence so deep…that he has exploded the truth, that I was not able to defend the impression I was suffering from." Clemenceau did not know the source of Scheurer-Kestner's knowledge because Scheurer-Kestner refused to tell him. But Clemenceau mentioned that "chance put him on the trail that he has followed....Today he declared without reticence that he knew the truth, the whole truth, and that he would say it. Dreyfus is, according to him, the victim of an appalling judicial error. If the fact is proven, we cannot but shudder at the thought of the unspeakable tortures inflicted on this unfortunate man. But it must be proven."

He concluded: "I did not ask Scheurer-Kestner for the shocking proof that he was declaring. I simply said that if there are significant presumptions of error, the trial must be reopened."[28] Clemenceau was not yet a committed Dreyfusard, but he was inching closer.

Some time in early to mid-November, a stock broker named deCastro was strolling along the Seine. He saw one of the posters of the bordereau that Mathieu had put up in the hope that someone would recognize the handwriting. Castro did. He bought one of the pamphlets of the bordereau that Mathieu had printed up, took it home, and went through his files. Sure enough, the handwriting matched that of one of his clients, Commandant Esterhazy. Someone got deCastro in touch with Mathieu, and deCastro told Mathieu that it was his client, Esterhazy, who had authored the bordereau. When Mathieu heard this news, he did not wait to find a hansom cab. He *ran* to Scheurer-Kestner's home, pounded on the door, and exclaimed to the startled Scheurer-Kestner: "I'm going to tell you the name of the traitor. It's Esterhazy." "Yes," replied Scheurer-Kestner, "that's him."[29]

On November 15, Mathieu wrote a letter to minister of war Billot, denouncing Esterhazy as the traitor. He stated the obvious. Esterhazy's handwriting matched the bordereau, and the evidence on which Dreyfus had been convicted was the bordereau. Finally, after almost two years, Mathieu got results. Billot asked Gen. Saussier to open an investigation *into Esterhazy*. Saussier in turn appointed Brig. Gen Georges-Gabriel de Pellieux, 55, to head the investigation. Pellieux was also a graduate of Saint Cyr, had seen action in the Franco-Prussian war, had served in Algeria and Tunisia, and had been elected to the Legion of Honour. His role now was akin to an American prosecutor conducting a grand jury investigation. He could take testimony, charge (or not charge) a defendant with a crime, but he could not convict. As de Pellieux was not a lawyer, Judge Paul Jules Bertulus, was appointed to assist him.

On the next day, November 16, the news of of Mathieu's denunciation of Esterhazy was all over Paris. "The bombshell has burst," reported one foreign ministry observer.[30] Now there were two sides, the Dreyfusards who demanded a retrial for Dreyfus, whose home in the press became *l'Aurore*, and the anti-Dreyfusard nationalists whose champions in the press were Edouard Drumont's anti-Semitic *La Libre Parole* and the Roman Catholic *La Croix*. The issue no longer was solely whether or not Dreyfus was innocent. France now became divided over the army. If Dreyfus was innocent, seven army officers had wrongly convicted an innocent man. If the verdict were overturned, would the army be weakened in the face of the enemy, as the anti-Dreyfusards claimed? Indeed, the issue was even deeper than the army. To many, such as Clemenceau, the issue was the Republic itself, which many nationalists had never fully accepted. The Dreyfus case was not dividing France, but it was deepening and exposing the fissures that had been there since September 4, 1870, the day the Republic was created.

Gen. Pellieux was no impartial investigator. His heart was with the army. His investigation was a farce. He heard testimony from all of the principals, including Esterhazy and Picquart. Based largely on the *faux Henry*, Pellieux determined that there was not sufficient evidence to charge Esterhazy. As for the bordereau itself, Pellieux refused to consider it, holding that it was a *chose jugée*—a thing already decided—and hence could not be revisited.

By now, Esterhazy was becoming a public figure, one who felt he had nothing to fear because he was being protected by the general staff. Esterhazy was, however, indebted to a former mistress, a Madame de Boulancy, who, unable to collect on the debt, decided that this was the perfect time to wreak her revenge. She had a stash of old love letters that Esterhazy had written her, ones that would reveal the character of this man. She gave them to her lawyer, with instructions to make sure that they received the widest possible publicity. On the morning of November 28, all of Paris read excerpts from the letters, the most infamous one revealing the depths of his hatred for the French: "These people [the French] aren't worth the cartridges it would take to kill them…and if one night I should be told that I serving as a captain of Uhlans [Polish cavalry officers] should die massacring the French I should be entirely happy…"[31] Another letter read: "I would not harm a puppy, but I would kill 100,000 Frenchmen with pleasure…What sorry figures they would cut in the red sun of battle if Paris were taken by storm and left at the mercy of 100,000 drunken and plundering soldiers. This is the feast I dream of."[32]

Henceforth, Clemenceau referred to Esterhazy as "the Uhlan Esterhazy" or simply as "the Uhlan."

Esterhazy's defenders now had to prove that not only was the bordereau a forgery, i.e. that someone—perhaps Dreyfus himself—had forged Esterhazy's handwriting, but that the Uhlan letters were forgeries too. Not a problem. Paty found three handwriting experts who were willing to swear that the bordereau and the "Uhlan letters" were all forgeries. The nationalist press assured its readers that it was all the handiwork of the Jewish syndicate out to frame Esterhazy and free Dreyfus. When Pellieux confronted Mme. de Boulancy, he chided her on having insulted the army.

By late November, Clemenceau was becoming convinced that the army was covering up for Esterhazy. He would no longer accept the army's assurances that certain documents which proved Dreyfus' guilt were too sensitive for the public to see, asking "[I]t would be enough to produce them now and put an end to this sad affair… If Gen. de Boisdeffre has the proof that the commandant [Esterhazy] is the victim of an odious plot, he does not have the right to 'serve' us the documentary proof."[33] He was also suspicious of minister of war Billot's refusal to allow Picquart to return from Tunisia: "We are told that colonel Picquart will have to be exiled for having spoken too much…[I]t is not because he has spoken, but because it is feared that he will speak."[34] He repeated the warning that Picquart first gave Boisdeffre: "The army cannot be responsible for the crime of any traitor. The only thing that can harm it in this affair is the inexplicable attitude of some army chiefs."[35]

As expected, Pellieux left everything unchanged. Esterhazy still walked the streets, confident as ever, mindful of the grip he had over the general staff. Dreyfus languished on Devil's Island, oblivious of everything. Henry was promoted to lieutenant-colonel, rewarded for a job well done. On December 4, the prime minister, Jules Méline (coincidentally, a fellow editor with Clemenceau of La Travail from student days) armed with Pellieux' findings, announced in the Chamber of Deputies that "There is no Dreyfus Affair. There is none at present and there will be no Dreyfus Affair."[36] They then passed a bill expressing respect for the 1894 verdict and scorning the "ringleaders of the odious campaign to trouble the public mind."[37]

The next day, in an article headed *Bafouillage* ("gibberish"), Clemenceau ridiculed the Chamber's actions, asserting that only "fools think that it was an attack on the French army to demand the indictment of the Uhlan Esterhazy," adding that "when we have been forced by public opinion to open an inquiry against the French officer who was to invade France at the head of the Uhlans, we spared the wretch."…"Let him [Gen. Billot] tell us if he can why he searched colonel Picquart's home, a witness whose whole life has been honor, while no search was made—even for the sake of form—of the Uhlan who dishonored his uniform by his infamous letters."[38] "[W]hy the law… stops impotently before this man who can with impunity cast the worst outrages on his brothers in arms…without anyone getting up to denounce him."[39] He concluded *Bafouillage*: "You will delay the light; you will not extinguish it."[40]

Esterhazy was so confident that he now demanded that *he* be court-martialed, in order to clear his name. The general staff acquiesced, either fearing to cross Esterhazy or convinced that an acquittal of Esterhazy would finally put the Dreyfus case to rest. For Boisdeffre, Gonse and Mercier (no longer minister of war but still in uniform), it would prove to be a terrible mistake.

The court-martial began, and ended, on January 10, 1898, in the same military courtroom on the Rue Cherche-Midi in which Dreyfus had been tried. The judges were all military officers. Before it began, Clemenceau took Picquart aside and reminded him of his oath not to take the knowledge of Dreyfus' innocence to the grave. Picquart told him not to worry.[41] Picquart testified, as did Esterhazy, very calmly. Esterhazy's lawyer spoke for five hours. The judges took *three minutes* to acquit. The public was invited to hear the verdict the next day. When it was announced, the mobs yelled "Long live Esterhazy!" "Long live the army!" "Death to the Jews!" On the same day, Picquart was arrested, charged with passing state secrets to the lawyer, Leblois. He would serve part of his imprisonment in solitary confinement.

But the court-martial had had one salutary effect. The Dreyfus affair, which could have died following Pellieux's investigation, was still alive.

In December, 1897, Émile Zola, 57, was one of the most prominent writers in the world, his novels being translated into many languages. He was wealthy, but not universally respected, many being offended by his realistic portrayal of the seamy side of life, one newspaper calling his novels "a mass of filth which should be handled with a forceps."[42] He was in Italy finishing a novel, and had paid little attention to the Dreyfus court-martial, other than to be offended by the anti-Semitic ravings of the crowd at Dreyfus' degradation. He was growing weary of novel-writing.

In the fall of 1897, he was introduced to Leblois, Picquart's lawyer, who told him everything. Leblois sent him to Scheurer-Kestner, who showed him the proof. Zola saw the dramatic aspects of the story, but mostly he was incensed by the manifest injustice. Then came the acquittal of Esterhazy and the arrest of Picquart. He signed on with the centrist *Le Figaro* to write a series of articles. In an article under the head "The Syndicate," he observed that the treason that so distressed France was not Dreyfus' supposed treason, or any future treason. It was the belief in a supposed past treason: "[W]e are so overwhelmed by the ancient defeat [in the Franco-Prussian War], in the obstinate idea that only by treason could we have been defeated." He ended the article by admitting what the anti-Semites claimed, that he was a member of a Dreyfusard "syndicate," "a syndicate to campaign until truth is done, until justice is rendered, against all obstacles even if years of struggle are still required. That syndicate! Yes! I'm in it, and I hope that all good people of France will be."[43]

The anti-Dreyfusards roared back. They launched a campaign against *Le Figaro* so forcefully that Zola's articles were discontinued and the editor fired. *Le Figaro* dropped out of the Dreyfusard ranks, never to return. Zola was now without a platform. Then on January 11, 1898, Esterhazy was acquitted. The acquittal incensed Zola as Dreyfus' conviction never did. Intending to write a pamphlet, he wrote through the night and into the next day. Then he changed his mind about the pamphlet. On the evening of January 12 he showed up at *L'Aurore*'s office. In his hand was an "Open Letter to the President of the French Republic." By the next morning it would be the most famous letter-to-the-editor in history.

We do not know who was present at *L'Aurore* that night. Clemenceau and Ernest Vaughan certainly were. Scheurer-Kestner was not. Zola read the missive aloud. When he was done, Clemenceau is said to have offered one correction: "I don't like the title, Zola. It doesn't have enough bite."[44] Clemenceau suggested that "Open Letter to the President of the French Republic" be the sub-head, and that the title be "J'Accuse." So it was.

Addressed to president Felix Faure, J'Accuse got right to the point:

> "...what filth this wretched Dreyfus affair has cast on your name...your reign. A court martial, under orders, has just dared to acquit this character, Esterhazy, the supreme insult to all truth and all justice." And now the image of France is sullied by this filth, and History shall record that it was under your Presidency that this crime against society was committed. Knowing your integrity, I am convinced that you do not know the truth...But to whom if not you...shall I reveal the vile baseness of those who are guilty?"

Zola named Paty as the centerpiece of the whole affair, the man who "invented Dreyfus the traitor, the one who orchestrated the whole affair and made it his own." Zola never mentioned Henry or his forgeries. He could not; Zola was unaware of him. He mentioned the now-deceased Col. Sandherr, but also the very much alive Gens. Mercier, Gonse and even the previously untouchable Boisdeffre "who appears to have yielded to his own religious bigotry."

He then reviewed Dreyfus' trial, the centerpiece of which was "that idiot bordereau," and how "Generals Mercier, de Boisdeffre and Gonse became so ensnared in this falsehood that they would later feel to impose it as holy and indisputable truth...."

Having set it all in motion merely by carelessness and lack of intelligence, they seem at worst to have given in to the religious bias of their milieu and the prejudices of their class. In the end, they allowed stupidity to prevail."

He mocked how flimsy was the indictment: "Is it possible a man has been found guilty on the strength of it? Dreyfus speaks several languages, does he? This is a crime. Not one compromising paper was found in his home. A crime. He occasionally pays a visit to the region he hails from. A crime. He is a hard-working man, eager to know everything. A crime. He does not get flustered. A crime. He does get flustered? A crime."

He mocked the secrecy of the trial: "Could these things be true, these unspeakable acts, these deeds sodangerous that they must be carefully hidden behind closed doors to keep Europe from going up in flames? No. They were nothing but demented fabrications of Major du Paty de Clam, a coverup of the most preposterous fantasies imaginable." The sole evidence being the bordereau, the general staff had to concoct some other evidence "a secret document, that like God, could not be shown, but which explained everything, and was invisible, unknowable and incontrovertible.... "I deny the existence of that document. With all my strength, I deny it...A document concerning national defense that could not be produced without sparking an immediate declaration of war tomorrow? No. No. It is a lie, all the more odious and cynical in that its perpetrators are getting off free without even admitting it."

He then focused on Picquart and Esterhazy, noting that Picquart had succeeded Sandherr, who then came into possession of the *petit bleu*, the telegram addressed to Esterhazy. "Picquart conducted his investigation, and concluded that Esterhazy was the author of the bordereau....Lt. Col. Picquart carried out his duty as an honest man. He kept insisting to his superiors in the name of justice. He begged them, telling them how impolitic it was to temporize in the face of the terrible storm that was brewing and that would break when the truth became known....But no! The crime had been committed and the General Staff could no longer admit to it. And so Lt. Colonel Picquart was sent away on official duty....A retrial would mean that this whole extraordinary saga, so extravagant, so tragic, with its denouement on Devil's Island, would fall apart....It came down, once again, to the General Staff protecting itself, not wanting to admit its crime, an abomination that has been growing by the minute.... General de Boisdeffre, then General Gonse, and finally General Billot himself were all pulled into the effort...Dreyfus' innocence would make the War Office collapse under the weight of publiccontempt."

"J'Accuse,"—4,000 words—occupied the entire front page of *L'Aurore*, and three columns of the next. Only at the end did Zola make the formal accusations:

"I accuse Lt. Col. du Paty de Clam of being the diabolical creator of this miscarriage of justice—unknowingly, I am willing to believe—and of defending this sorry deed, over the last three years, by all manner of bizarre and evil machinations."

"I accuse General Mercier of complicity, at least by mental weakness, in one of the greatest inequities of the century."

"I accuse General Billot of having held in his hands absolute proof of Dreyfus' innocence and concealing it, thereby making himself guilty of crimes against mankind and justice, as a political expedient and a way for the compromised General Staff to save itself."

"I accuse General de Boisdeffre and General Gonse of complicity in the same crime, the former, no doubt, out of religious prejudice, the latter perhaps out of that esprit de corps that has transformed the War Office into an unassailable holy ark."

He accused others as well, including Pellieux and the judges at Esterhazy's court-martial who "on orders," committed "the judicial crime of acquitting a guilty man with full knowledge of his guilt."

He concluded by lighting a fuse: "In making these allegations I am aware that I am making myself liable to articles 30 and 31 of the July 29, 1881 law on the press making libel a punishable offense. I expose myself to that risk voluntarily....Let them dare, then, to bring me before a court of law and investigate in the full light of day! "I am waiting."

The new *L'Aurore* had a small circulation. But on the morning of January 13, 1898, 300,000 copies were sold. More than that read it. People bought the paper and then stopped in their tracks to read it. They passed the pages from reader to reader. It caused a sensation. There were anti-Jewish riots throughout France. Small towns that had no Jews saw mobs screaming "Death to the Jews." Jews were assaulted on the streets. Synagogues were stoned; Jewish shops were burned, often with the complicity, if not the indulgence, of the police. There was an anti-Jewish pogrom in Algiers, where two people were killed and 500 rioters arrested.[45] A mob attacked Zola's home, shouting "Into the Seine! Throw Zola into the Seine." Effigies of Zola and Clemenceau were hung from lampposts, which must have delighted Clemenceau.[46] The nationalist press accused Zola of having received "bags of gold" from the "Jewish syndicate." A former minister of war, François Claude de Barail, 77, summed up the feeling of the army, the anti-Dreyfusards and a substantial portion of French public opinion when he declared that the misfortune of a single individual could not be compared with the "national calamity which would result from a slur cast on the honor of the army."[47]

In an article penned on January 17, Clemenceau put in print what most Frenchmen were thinking: "What does it mean to me that Dreyfus was judged well or poorly? Between a Jew and the army one cannot hesitate." He supplied the answer: "There is no salvation other than respect for justice for all." He reminded his readers of the imbecility of the army officers who had perpetrated the injustice: "What will be the price, in the future, of our submission to these worthy successors of Metz and Sedan?"[48]

The sun had not set on "J'Accuse" before prime minister Méline, at the insistence of the Chamber of Deputies, decided to bring the charges that Zola had dared them to bring. But after consulting with the army, Méline decided that the charge would be very narrow. It would be a civil trial with a jury, as Zola had hoped, but the only libel Zola would be accused of was Zola's assertion that the judges at the Esterhazy court martial had been *ordered* to acquit Esterhazy. For good measure, one of *L'Aurore*'s sub-editors, Alexandre Perrenx, was also accused of libel.

The trial began on February 7 in the Palais de Justice in the Ile de Cite. Zola, Clemenceau and the lawyers had to pass through mobs yelling "Down with Zola! Down with the crook!" Zola was represented by Fernand Labori, 37, who had already built a solid reputation as a trial lawyer. Perrenx was represented by Clemenceau's younger brother (by twenty years), Albert. Clemenceau had requested, and received, permission to assist his brother, and so this doctor-turned-journalist was part of the legal team. When Clemenceau stood to speak, the crowd shouted "Cornelius Herz." The judge did little to stop them.

Before the trial opened, Gonse, through an intermediary, let Picquart know that if he stayed loyal to the army in his testimony, his career would not be ruined. Picquart replied that he would do his best to reconcile his duty as a soldier with his duty as a witness, which was not the answer Gonse wanted. As it was a jury trial, the witnesses played to the jury. Gen. Mercier: "We have not the right to reopen the 1894 trial. But if we had to return to it, and I were asked my word as a soldier, I would swear once more that Dreyfus was a traitor and was rightly and legally convicted."[49] Pellieux read the *faux Henry* to the jury, Henry's masterpiece, directly linking Dreyfus to Schwartzkoppen. He read it, but since it was still considered a state secret, no one was permitted to see it.

But the army's star witness was Boisdeffre himself. Tall and erect in his bemedaled uniform, this most revered officer in France's most respected institution faced the jury: "[I]n 1894 there was no doubt in my mind about the guilt of Captain Dreyfus. Innumerable pieces of evidence have since come to us have made my certainty unshakable." Then Boisdeffre challenged the jury, demanding that they "must trust the military officers who testify, whose duty it is to preserve the nation. If not, the officers will resign *en bloc* from the army."[50] So there it was. If the civilian jury did not trust the word of the army officers, they would all quit, and leave the nation defenseless in the face of the Germans.

When the public prosecutor demanded proof that the army had ordered the judges at the Esterhazy court-martial to acquit, Leblois responded that they had just seen it *again*. Boisdeffre had just ordered the jury to convict, on pain of the officer corps resigning *en masse*.

Zola's team had agreed that Clemenceau would deliver the closing argument. He had never been a brilliant orator. He had made his reputation in the Chamber of Deputies through his choice of words and the force of his logic. But he had not spoken in public in years. "The principle of civilian society is liberty and justice, while that of the military is obedience, discipline and order," he said, "but the army is no longer a professional army. It is the people's army. It must embodythe same principles as does the nation. If the civilian society in its anxiety over national defense fell into the slavery of the military, then the soil perhaps could be defended, but morally the nation would be lost. By forfeiting the principles of justice and liberty, we would give up what, to the entire world, has been the glory and honor of France....There is no civilian honor and military honor; there is only honor for all." He pointed to a large portrait of Christ on the cross on the wall behind the judge. "Look there, gentlemen of the jury. You see Christ on the cross. There you see the adjudged case. The picture hangs behind the judge, that he should not be embarrassed by its sight. It should hang rather in front of the judges, that they should have it before their eyes as they pass sentence, to see the example of a miscarriage of justice, that our civilization holds to be the shame of mankind....We destroyed the Bastille and every July 14 we dance in the streets to commemorate the destruction of this monument to the reasons of state. Yet, deep inside, a Bastille remains as long as we are able to accept injustice. In making your decision, there is only one danger to beware; that you do not abandon the cause of justice which you represent. You will not do this. You will uphold civilian law above all prejudices. You will leave unstained the treasure of liberty and justice that we have acquired. Free of racial and religious prejudice, you will render inestimable service to France if you

suppress the beginnings of a religious war that threatens to dishonor our country...
Gentlemen, we represent the law, tolerance, the traditions of the French spirit. We
defend the army."[51] He now had almost to scream to be heard above the derisive howls
of the crowd: "Yes, it is we, it is we who are the defenders of the army when we [are]
call[ed] upon to drive Esterhazy out of it. The conscious or unconscious enemies of the
army are those who propose to cashier Picquart and retain Esterhazy. Gentlemen of
the jury, a general has come here to talk to you about your children. Tell me which of
them would you like to find yourself in Esterhazy's battalion? Tell me, would you hand
over your sons to this officer to lead against the enemy? The very question is enough.
Who does not know the answer before it is given? Gentlemen of the jury, I have done.
We have passed through terrible experiences in this century. We have known glory
and disaster in every form, we are even at this moment face to face with the unknown.
Fears and hopes encompass us around. Grasp the opportunity as we ourselves have
grasped it. Be masters of your own destinies. A people sitting in judgment on itself is
a noble thing. A stirring scene is also a people deciding on its own future. Your task,
gentlemen of the jury, is to pronounce a verdict less upon us than upon yourselves.
We are appearing before you. You will appear before history."[52]

It took the jury only 35 minutes to find Zola and Perrenx guilty of having libeled
the army, four of the twelve dissenting. They were given the maximum allowable
penalty, a year in prison for Zola and four months for Perrenx, plus a 3000 franc fine
for each. Clemenceau considered it a blessing. He feared the mob would have killed
them if the jury had acquitted.

The next morning, the *Berliner Tageblatt* couldn't resist: "Yesterday the French
army won its first victory since 1870-1871."[53] Queen Victoria wrote her grandson,
Kaiser Wilhelm, asking him, confidentially, if Dreyfus had been in his service. He
replied, "no."[54]

After the trial, Clemenceau wrote an article dripping with vitriol, headed "Winners
and Losers." In the ranks of the winners he counted Méline and Billot, who had
succeeded in covering up a violation of the law. The Church and the monarchists
were also winners. Esterhazy was a winner. The losers were, of course, Zola, but "the
future will weigh in the balance whether the results are happy or unhappy." Picquart
was also a loser, who "will be chased out of the army while Esterhazy parades under
the friendly regard of our generals."[55] Finally, France was a loser, in this perversion of
justice: "de Boisdeffre put his sword on the Code of Law, daring anyone to touch it.
The jury has declared that it does not dare to touch it."[56]

In May, 1898, elections to the Chamber of Deputies were held. They were a disaster for the Dreyfusards. Anyone associated with them lost his seat. Worse, that arch-anti-Semite, Drumont, won a seat, as did Paul Déroulède. But the overall makeup of the Chamber did not change. The Republicans remained in control. But Méline was out as prime minister, and his minister of war, Gen. Billot, went with him. Godefroy Cavaignac, 45, became minister of war. He would serve in that office for all of nine weeks, but what a nine weeks it was.

Unlike Billot and Mercier before him, Cavaignac was not a general. A graduate of the *Ecole Polytehnique*, he was a civil engineer. Like Billot, he believed in Dreyfus' guilt, but he decided that a new strategy was needed to finally put the Dreyfus affair to rest. He decided to abandon the strategy of relying on "reasons of state" to keep key documents hidden. His would be a strategy of openness. He addressed the Chamber of Deputies, affirming his belief in Dreyfus' guilt, but also averred that "No reason of public security, however high, could ever persuade me to keep an innocent man in jail."[57] He made no mention of the illegality of Dreyfus' trial. To prove Dreyfus' guilt, he read from three key documents from the ministry of war's file. All were forgeries, the work of Henry. He read from the *faux Henry*, asserting confidently that "I rest upon the material authenticity and upon the moral authenticity of this document."[58] The Chamber was so impressed by this performance that they voted that it be published and placarded throughout France. So it was. Soon every one of the 35,000 *mairies*—mayor's offices—throughout France was festooned with a placard in which Cavaignac swore to the authenticity of the *faux Henry*.

Two days later, the new prime minister, Henri Brisson, received an open letter from Picquart:

> "I have not yet been allowed an opportunity of explaining myself freely on the subject of the secret documents by which Captain Dreyfus's guilt is alleged to have been established. The minister of war having quoted at the tribune of the Chamber of Deputies three of these documents, I consider it my duty to inform you that I am in a position to prove, before any competent tribunal, that the two documents dated 1894 cannot possibly apply to Dreyfus, and that the one dated 1896 [the *faux* Henry] has all the marks of a forgery. It will thus appear manifest that the good faith of the minister of war has been imposed upon, and that the same is true also of all those who believed in the value of the two former documents and in the authenticity of the last one."[59]

The Dreyfus Affair never proceeded in a straight line. There were byways and detours that occasionally lead to something and often were dead ends. In mid-July, Judge Paul Bertulus, the civilian lawyer appointed to assist Pellieux, decided to keep investigating. The telegrams that Henry had forged to impugn Picquart intrigued him. He called Henry into his office, believing that Henry might be Esterhazy's accomplice. Out of the blue, Bertulus asked Henry: "Is Esterhazy the author of the bordereau?" At this, Henry burst into tears, and through his tears replied: "The honor of the army above all! Do not insist! Do not insist!"[60] Henry then stood up, kissed Bertulus on the mouth, and ran out. Bertulus came away from the meeting believing that the general staff knew that Esterhazy was guilty and that Henry had helped protect him.

Cavaignac followed through on his stated policy of openness. He ordered that the ministry of war's entire Dreyfus file be examined. What had started out as a thin file when Picquart first saw it was now a massive 1,500 pages, the result of Henry having larded it with irrelevant documents in the hope of throwing off the trail anyone who decided to dig into it. The thankless task went to a Captain Louis Cuignet. He started on August 1 and worked every day and into the night, reading every document in the massive file. Late in the evening of August 13 he came across the *faux Henry*. For some reason, he held the paper to the light. That is when he noticed that the lines on the top of the page were a slightly different color than the lines on the bottom, and the spacing was also different. Cuignet could see that someone had glued two pieces of paper together. The sentence on the bottom, the sentence that incriminated Dreyfus, was on paper different from the innocuous writing on the top. Cuignet knew that the document in his hands was a forgery.

Cuignet told Cavaignac, and Cavaignac told Gonse and Boisdeffre. Henry was on leave. They decided not to call him back, as it might tip him off. They waited until he returned on August 30, when Cavaignac called Henry into his office. Gonse and Boisdeffre were present. Henry was presented the evidence of the *faux Henry*. At first, he denied it. "I want you to give me an explanation," demanded Cavaignac. "I cannot," said Henry, "what I did I did for the good of the country." Cavaignac grilled Henry for an hour. "Tell everything," pressed Cavaignac, "you received in 1896 a letter of no importance. You suppressed the letter and forged another instead."[61] Finally, exhausted, Henry replied, "Yes."

Boisdeffre, whose entire life had been the army, who had entered Saint Cyr before the war with Prussia, who had served in the war as a cavalry major, who had been the leading force in forging France's alliance with Russia, who had for five years served as the head of the eneral staff, now sat down at a desk and wrote:

"My dear Minister:

"I have acquired proof that my trust in Colonel Henry, chief of the Intelligence Service, was unjustified. That trust was absolute and led me to the mistake of declaring a document to be genuine which was not, and of presenting it to you as such. In this situation I must ask you to relieve me of my duties."[62]

Cavaignac immediately ordered Henry's arrest. He was taken to the prison in the Mont Valérian fortress. Next morning, they discovered Henry's body in a pool of blood. He had slit his throat with a razor. Two days later, *La Croix*, the mouthpiece of the Roman Catholic Assumptionist order, editorialized that Henry had been murdered by the Jews in order to silence him. Esterhazy fled to London.

The morning after Henry's body was discovered, Clemenceau penned an article titled "Totally Collapsed." Picking up on Zola's famous assertion that "truth is on the march," he taunted the "gentlemen of the false patriotism" that "the truth is on the march, and it has arrived." He could not resist a poke at Caviagnac: "Here is M. Cavaignac, the minister imposed by the Esterhazyistes. It is to him we owe this work. I feel, for my part, a special pleasure in thanking him." Of the general staff: "[T]hese same men wanted to hear nothing, and pretended that in denouncing the treason of the Uhlan we offended the army." Of Paty and Henry: "Two forgers on the general staff." Of Henry: "A head of the intelligence bureau. We have chosen this one because he does not know a foreign language. There is some reason to believe that he does not know French." Of the Chamber of Deputies, "who came to be convinced that a man could be convicted of a crime outside of the safeguards of the law." But there was one question that Clemenceau posed that he could not answer: "Why did Colonel Henry do the forgery? What interest could he have in maintaining an innocent man in prison?...For what purpose? Who did it profit? Inspired, pushed, aided by whom? Who will answer?"[63]

On September 5, Cavaignac followed de Boisdeffre out the door. It is by now impossible for anyone to seriously maintain that Dreyfus was the author of the bordereau, *including Esterhazy*. From the safety of London, Esterhazy at long last admitted that he had penned the bordereau. His explanation: He had had actually been working with the Statistical Section. Under orders from Sandherr and Henry, he had authored the bordereau in order to confuse the Germans. As Sandherr and Henry were now both dead, they could not contradict his story.

With the knowledge that Dreyfus had not written the bordereau, and with the further knowledge that Dreyfus had been convicted based on evidence that had been shielded from the defense, one would assume that Dreyfus' release would now be a formality. Yet Dreyfus would have to suffer for more than another year.

Prime minister Henri Brisson convinced his cabinet that a review of Dreyfus' court-martial was now inevitable. They agreed to recommend the case to the Criminal Chamber of the *Cour de Cassation*, roughly equivalent to an American court of appeals. The fourteen judges of the Criminal Chamber began their work, in secret, in late October, 1898. In early November, 1898, Brisson's government fell. The new prime minister was Charles Dupuy, who had been the prime minister when Dreyfus was first arrested. His was the sixth government to hold office during the Dreyfus affair. It would not be the last.

The fourteen judges interviewed witnesses. They read documents. They took their time. By February, 1899, they were still at it. Then, just before they were about to conclude their work and announce their decision, the Chamber of Deputies enacted a statute that removed the case from them. It was determined that all of the judges of the Cour de Cassation—all forty-six of them—including the civil judges, must hear the case. And so they had to start all over again.

In February, 1899, president Felix Faure, 60, the man to whom Zola had addressed *J'Accuse*, was found dead late one afternoon in the arms of his lover. He had suffered a stroke. Faure had opposed a re-trial for Dreyfus, and his death was a blow for the anti-Dreyfusards. (Clemenceau wrote: "Felix Faure has just died. That does not mean there is one less man in France."[64]) Worse for the anti-Dreyfusards was the election of his successor, Emile Loubet, who favored a new trial. The nationalist press called Loubet's election "a victory for Jewish treason."

In March, the full Cour de Cassation began its review of Dreyfus' court-martial. They had a number of options. Of course, they could have upheld the verdict. They also could have held that the court-martial was so tainted that no retrial was possible, in which event Dreyfus would have been immediately freed. They also could have ordered a new court-martial. Unlike an American court of appeals, the forty-six judges were permitted to hear new evidence. At long last, these judges demanded, and finally received the general staff's Dreyfus file. It was so lacking in evidence inculpating Dreyfus that one of the judges asked if they had actually received the entire file. One of the handwriting experts at Dreyfus' court-martial changed his opinion as to whether Dreyfus had authored the bordereau after he was shown copies of Esterhazy's handwriting on documents found after Esterhazy's home was searched. Boisdeffre and Mercier both testified, refusing to admit or deny that the "canaille d" document had been given to the judges at the court-martial. So the court assumed from their silence that the judges at the court-martial had received this document in secret.

On June 3, 1899, Mathieu Dreyfus' tireless work of the last 4-1/2 years came to fruition: "The court hereby rescinds and annuls the verdict rendered...against Alfred Dreyfus, and sends the accused before the Court-Martial of Rennes." The decision was based on two facts that were obvious at least from the day that Picquart first matched Esterhazy's handwriting with the bordereau, or the day that deCastro matched Esterhazy's handwriting with the bordereau. The first fact was that Dreyfus did not write the bordereau. The second fact was that the "canaille D" letter did not refer to Dreyfus, and had never been produced in evidence at his court-martial.

But justice had not yet triumphed. Dreyfus was not yet free; he would be court-martialed again. But Esterhazy having admitted that he wrote the bordereau, and without any other evidence, how could Dreyfus possibly by convicted?

Two days later, on June 5, 1899, Dreyfus' warden entered his cell, and handed Dreyfus a cable:

> "In consequence of the decision of the high court of appeal, Captain Dreyfus has ceased to be subject to the rules for deportees...and is again permitted to wear military uniform...the guard is to be dismissed and Dreyfus released from criminal custody. The cruiser *Sfax* sails today from Fort-de-France to return Dreyfus to France."[65]

Years later, Dreyfus wrote that he was so stunned by this cable that he feared he would not survive it. He could not stop weeping. For the past two years, he had not so much as seen the ocean. Now he was headed home. Five French governments had come and gone in his absence. His name was on the lips and in the consciousness of any person within reach of a newspaper throughout the civilized world. He was oblivious to all of it. Soon he would learn it all.

On the day after the Cour de Cassation's decision was announced, a riot broke out at the Auteuil racetrack. A nobleman, Baron Fernand Chevreau de Christiani, attacked president Loubet with his cane. Fifty people, many of them noblemen, were arrested. The following week, there was a Republican counterdemonstration at the same racetrack. There were scuffles with the police. On June 9, the charges against Picquart for forging the *petit bleu* were dropped and he was released from prison. Unlike all of the other officers on the general staff who were tainted by Dreyfus, he emerged with his honor intact. On June 12, Charles Dupuy's government collapsed.

Ten days later, Pierre Waldeck-Rousseau, 53, became prime minister, forming a "government of republican defense." For the first time, Socialists were invited into the cabinet. His ministry would last three years, and would result in the left-right alignment that Clemenceau had been urging for twenty years. Waldeck-Rousseau seriously wished to get France over the Dreyfus affair. He pushed through a general amnesty of all of the Dreyfus players *except Dreyfus*. This was at the urging of Dreyfus' lawyers, who wanted the complete vindication that an acquittal would provide. The amnesty spared Zola from a year in prison, but it also spared Boisdeffre, Gonse, Mercier, Paty and others from prosecution. On June 30, Dreyfus arrived back in France, gaunt and speechless after years of enforced silence. He was allowed to meet with Lucie, but only with a guard present.

The Rennes court-martial began on August 7, 1899. The Cour de Cassation chose Rennes for the simple reason that it was not Paris, and that Dreyfus could be easily transported there. No one could seriously maintain that Dreyfus was guilty. Before the trial began, the Catholic *La Croix* editorialized: "The question is not whether this wretch is guilty or innocent, but whether or not the Jews and the Protestants—this vanguard of Germany, England and their allies—are to rule our country."[66] The judges were seven military officers. Dreyfus' first court-martial lasted three days; this one would last five weeks. Dreyfus was represented by the quiet, courtly Demange, who had represented Dreyfus at the first court-martial, and young, fiery Fernand Labori, who had represented Zola. Neither Clemenceau nor Zola attended the trial, in the hope that their absence might calm the passions. They were hoping against hope. A week into the trial, someone shot Labori in the back as he entered the courthouse. The assailant escaped and was never found. Labori recovered. Two weeks into the trial, an anti-Dreyfus riot broke out in Paris. Some five thousand demonstrators, whipped up by the nationalist press, attacked the police.

The trial began. There was an audible gasp from the spectators when Dreyfus entered the courtroom. What they saw was an emaciated old man who was all of thirty-nine. He rose, slowly, and addressed the judges: "I say again that I am innocent, as I always said it, as I cried out in 1894. For five years I have said that, my colonel, now I say it again for the honor of my name and that of my children. I am innocent, my colonel."[67]

From August 7 through August 10, the judges met in closed session to consider the entire dossier. Then they heard testimony. Mercier testified that he gave the secret documents to the judges in the first court-martial because a war would have erupted if the documents had been made public. It was a lie. Boisdeffre and Gonse testified that Dreyfus was Esterhazy's partner in treason. They both lied. Alphonse Bertillon, the amateur graphologist who had testified at the first court-martial that Dreyfus had forged his own handwriting on the bordereau, held to that story again, despite the fact that Esterhazy had already admitted that he had written the bordereau.

On September 9, the judges met to consider the evidence. It took them all of one hour to conclude, by a vote of five to two, that Dreyfus was guilty—*with extenuating circumstances*. His sentence was reduced to *ten years*. The judges were not required to state—and never did state—what the "extenuating circumstances" were. They didn't need to. Everyone understood what the "extenuating circumstances" were. It was that Dreyfus was innocent. He was innocent, but if they had declared him innocent, it would have meant that the army had been guilty, and no military court was prepared to do that.

The day after the verdict, Clemenceau dipped his pen in vitriol, and didn't let up for a week. "A verdict with extenuating circumstances?" he asked. "Since when are there extenuating circumstances for treason?"[68] "The extenuating circumstances belong not to the accused but to the judges who in fact voted extenuating circumstances for themselves. The vote is nothing but a confession that they struck a deal between discipline and their consciences."[69] On September 13, in an article headed "To Action,": "A country that bases its honor on acquitting a criminal and attacking an innocent may call itself a republic…may have a parliament, city councils, ministers, judges, hospitals and theaters, all of the external facades of civilization; it may construct railroads, conquer territories…make use of electricity and the telephone…all this will be but dust in the storms to come. Without firm foundations in thought, without the moral cement of right and justice, no society can prevail."[70]

He opposed the amnesty as bitterly as he mocked the verdict. In his own version of *J'Accuse*, he reviewed the crimes of those who now could never be prosecuted: "Mercier obtained the 1894 verdict by forgeries. He destroyed the state document which accused him. He attempted to introduce…a new forgery into the secret file. He gave false testimony…All that now does not count…Honor to crime…This is the Republic of France. Meline and Billot knowingly used the forgery. Meline lied to the Chamber, saying he did not know of the *faux Henry* until it was revealed publicly….Full and complete amnesty. The forgers did not forge. The liars did not lie. Scoundrels are brave people. This is the Republic of France. Fifteen forgeries without known authors. How many forgers for fifteen forgeries? We'll never know. These men prefer not to be known. This is the Republic of France. Boisdeffre was the head of the General Staff of the army of France. The General Staff furnished the false beard and the blue eyeglasses for night meetings in cemeteries and under bridges, to conspire with a traitor on the best way to deceive justice and save the informant of Germany...The traitor is a patriot, and the patriots are traitors. This is the Republic of France."[71]

Mathieu knew that his brother would not survive another six months in prison, much less ten years. The issue thus became whether to ask for a presidential pardon. Waldeck-Rousseau wanted a pardon as much as anyone. In fact, he wanted it as quickly as possible, as a sign that the pardon was a rejection of the Rennes verdict. But a pardon would mean that Dreyfus would not be exonerated; it could be seen as an admission of guilt. Mathieu raced back to Paris. In a meeting that included Jean Jaurès, the rising Socialist leader, and Alexandre Millerand, 40, a former associate of Clemenceau at *La Justice* and now the newly-appointed minister of commerce, and Clemenceau himself, they weighed the pros and cons of a pardon. Initially, the only one opposed was Clemenceau. He knew that if the pardon were seen as an admission of guilt, everything he and others had worked for over two years would go up in smoke. But he also knew that rejecting the pardon was a death sentence for Dreyfus. For some reason, Mathieu insisted that the decision be unanimous. Finally, Clemenceau agreed. "All right," he said. "If I were the brother, I would accept." On September 19, the President of the Republic, Émile Loubet, signed the pardon. On the same day, Auguste Scheurer-Kestner died.

Two days later, Dreyfus left the Rennes prison in the middle of the night, so as to avoid hostile crowds. He and Mathieu traveled to the home of their sister, just north of Avignon. That same day, *L'Aurore* carried a short note from Dreyfus (drafted by Jean Jaurès) on its front page:

"The government of the Republic has granted me my liberty. It is nothing to me without my honor. Starting today, I will continue to pursue the repair of the frightful judicial error of which I am still the victim. I want France to know by a final judgment that I am innocent. My heart will know no rest until not one Frenchman is left who holds me responsible for a crime that was committed by someone else."

The army needed to save face. On September 21, the new minister of war Gaston de Gallifet, ordered that a statement be read to every French soldier:

"The incident is closed. The military judges, surrounded by the respect of all, have rendered their verdict with complete independence. Without any reservation, we bow to their decision. We also bow to the sentiment of profound pity that has guided the president of the republic."[72]

In July, 1906, the Cour de Cassation overturned the Rennes court-martial. It had taken almost twelve years, but Captain Alfred Dreyfus had finally obtained the vindication of his honor. But by then, few people cared. There was a ceremony in the courtyard of the *Ecole Militaire*, the site of his degradation in 1895. There were no screaming crowds outside the gates as he was decorated with the insignia of a chevalier of the Legion of Honour. Picquart was present. Someone shouted "Long live Picquart," to which Picquart replied "No. Long live Dreyfus." To which Dreyfus replied: "No. Long live the Republic. Long live truth."[73]

Also in 1906, Picquart was reinstated in the army and promoted to brigadier-general. In October of that year, Clemenceau became the prime minister of France. He named Picquart as his minister of war.

Maximilien von Schwartzkoppen returned to Germany. He fought on the Russian front. In December, 1916, as he lay on his deathbed, in his wife's hearing, he proclaimed Captain Alfred Dreyfus' innocence.

In November, 1918, on the eve of the Armistice, the Allies victorious, the congratulations poured in to prime minister Clemenceau. There was one letter he took pains to preserve:

"Dear Mr. President:

"I wanted to let the flood of congratulations which you received on your birthday go by before sending you my own on the occasion. I am not forgetful of the past and I have a faithful memory. But what I want to express to you today is the sentiment which we all hold on this march to victory, a sentiment which has led our soldiers to bestow on you the very charming nickname of "Father of Victory."

"Please accept this expression of my loyal devotion.

Alfred Dreyfus"

In December, 1899, Clemenceau left *L'Aurore*. The reasons are unclear. He had a falling out with one of the editors, Urbain Gohier, whose anti-Semitism was exceeded only by his antimilitarism. He may also have refused to take a cut in pay from the struggling newspaper. He still wrote twice-weekly for *La Dépêche de Toulouse*, but throughout the year 1900 he had no platform in Paris. Early in 1901 he founded a weekly, *Le Bloc*. It was less a newspaper than a 15-20 page weekly pamphlet of his own ideas. Each page had only two columns. There were no illustrations, and little advertising. The intended audience was the Republicans and the intellectuals who had found their voice in the Dreyfus affair. *Le Bloc* covered the theater and the arts, but a majority of the coverage was national affairs.[74] Clemenceau was still bitter over the amnesty, and his bitterness only deepened when, in January 1900, Gen. Mercier was elected to the Senate.

Turning to foreign affairs, he was, as always, opposed to France's colonial adventures. He opposed France's participation in a coalition of nations formed to suppress the "Boxer Rebellion," a nationalist uprising in China, believing, as always, that French treasure was being expended to support missionaries. He wrote on the Franco-Russian alliance, giving it grudging support. He held that the alliance was the inevitable consequence of the annexation of Alsace-Lorraine by Germany, which no power could undo, as England was following a policy of "splendid isolation," noting: "There is no other combination possible to counterbalance the Triple Alliance."[75] But he noted that the alliance was a contradiction, since the two countries were, in his opinion, fighting an economic war: "Russia is closed to our commerce but is open to Germany's."[76] The only advantage of the alliance, he believed, was the maintenance of peace.

He noted a thaw in Franco-German relations: "Certainly the signs of rapprochement are visible. Rapprochements are made on the sporting level and we have seen French capital emigrate to Germany."[77] He noted that Wilhelm had suppressed "Sedan Day," a semi-official holiday commemorating Prussia's victory in 1870. But for Clemenceau, there remained "only one difficulty: Alsace-Lorraine, which he termed "French lands despite German soldiers." He differed from the Socialist Jean Jaurés, who was willing to move on: "It would be a duty of our children to give their blood, if it were necessary, to remake the dismembered nation."[78]

Early in 1902, one of the "life" senators died. Under an 1884 law, his successor would not be a life senator, but would represent a constituency. The identity of that constituency was drawn by lot, and Clemenceau's former constituency, the Var, won. A delegation of Republicans from the Var—headed by the mayor of Dreguignan—visited Clemenceau and pressed him to run for the open seat. He declined. For twenty-five years Clemenceau had railed against the Senate—with its life senators—as a monarchist bulwark against democracy. But the Senate had held up fairly well in the Dreyfus affair, and age (he was now sixty-one) had mellowed him. But he still declined. Then he was visited by his printer, who gave Clemenceau a dose of reality. *Le Bloc* was no more successful than *La Justice*, and was not likely to survive. His opinions would carry less and less force with each year as he stayed on the sidelines. There was also the matter of the 9,000 franc annual salary of a senator. His brother Albert, his daughter Madelaine and his secretary all urged him to run. He telephoned the delegation, still in Paris. He had changed his mind. He was in.

Clemenceau inserted a note in the March 25, 1902 issue of *Le Bloc*, advising his readers that he was suspending publication in order to travel to the Var to campaign, which might have caused some consternation to those readers who had paid for a two-year subscription in advance. *Le Bloc* would never appear again.

Clemenceau had been a Radical Republican from the start, but in his absence the Republicans had formed their own party, *Le Party Républicain Radical et Radical-Socialiste*, and he was not of it. His former ghostwriter at *La Justice*, Camille Pelletan, was a rising star in the party and would soon have a portfolio in the cabinet. So Clemenceau ran without a party. He easily defeated a moderate Republican and a Socialist.

So he was back after all. He had assumed that he had left his life as a legislator behind. Having railed against the Senate for years and having written against it as recently as 1896, he must have felt a certain sense of irony when he entered the chamber for the first time. He would not, however, be a senator for long.

5

....

WELSH TRIBUNE

He alone displayed courage when everybody else was knocking about at the knees.

—Winston Churchill

O f the three men who met and negotiated the Treaty of Versailles, two had loving, nurturing and supportive fathers. David Lloyd George's father died when he was sixteen-months old. Of the three, two had university educations. Lloyd George's formal schooling ended when he was fourteen. Of the three, two were raised in households that, while not wealthy, were comfortable. Lloyd George grew up in genteel poverty, where every shilling was husbanded against the day when there might be no shillings.

He was not as poor as he later claimed (for political effect) to have been. He never starved and he never wore rags. But he never ate fresh meat and his greatest luxury was *half* an egg on Sunday morning.[1] But unlike most men, who remember their childhoods with at least a tinge of fondness, he called his childhood "the most unpleasant season of my life," averring years later that "I'd never go through it again at any price."[2]

It is somewhat ironic that the man who more than any other statesman became identified with Wales (he was the first and only British prime minister for whom English was the second language) was not born there. His father, William George, a schoolmaster and sometime farmer, lived with his wife Elizabeth in Manchester, in England. In 1864, at the age of forty-three, William George died, leaving his widow with a few sticks of furniture and little else. Her brother, Richard Lloyd, rushed to Manchester and retrieved her, bringing her and young David back to his home in the rural village of Llanystumdwy in North Wales (Welsh for "the church at the bend of the Dwyfor River"). David Lloyd George would spend the first sixteen years of his life in Llanystumdwy.

Richard Lloyd (known within the family as "Uncle Lloyd") was a part-time cobbler and part-time preacher. He never married, devoting himself to rearing his sister's children. His favorite was David. Uncle Lloyd would forever be a source of encouragement, support and love for David, and David reciprocated the love. Decades later, when David became prime minister, Uncle Lloyd remarked "The man is greater than his office."[3]

David's veneration of Uncle Lloyd is the source of the confusion regarding David's name that has bedeviled librarians and newspaper editors ever since. He was christened "David Lloyd George," *Dafydd* in Welsh, the name his brother used throughout David's life. To honor his uncle, some time during his late teens David changed his name without changing any of his names. "Lloyd" ceased to be his middle name, and became part of his new surname, "Lloyd George." His father's surname had been "George," his brother's surname remained "George," but David's surname would henceforth be "Lloyd George." When he married, his wife was Margaret Lloyd George. He never hyphenated his surname, a fact that the House of Commons immediately brushed aside, always referring to him in reports of debates as "Mr. Lloyd-George." When he became a peer in 1945, he was "Earl Lloyd-George of Dwyfor."

The one overarching fact that formed David's early life was that Wales was then in the grip of the established Church of Wales (part and parcel of the Church of England) and that the George family were "Nonconformists," as were a majority of the Welsh, most of whom were Calvinistic Methodists. The Georges were Disciples of Christ, a Baptist offshoot, who believed that preachers should not be compensated, following the example of the Apostle Paul. The Established Church was an ally of the local squirearchy, the often-absent landlords (some of whom could not speak Welsh) and both were allied with the Tories—the Conservative Party. It was said that the Church of England was little more than the Conservative Party at prayer. Loosening the grip of the official Church from Welsh society—*disestablishment*—would become Lloyd George's principal goal for much of his early life.

David entered the local school in Llanystumdwy before his fourth birthday. It was a "National" school; a public school supported by the government, but in fact an arm of the Church of England, whose catechism and practices were mandatory and where the speaking of Welsh was forbidden. Most of the students came from Nonconformist families.

In 1867, when David was four years old, Parliament loosened the voting requirements. Many rural tenant-farmers and small shopkeepers who previously could not vote now could for the first time. What Parliament failed to do was to provide them a secret ballot. In 1868, in the first election where they could vote, those tenants brave enough to vote did so with their landlords looking over their shoulders. They voted for the Liberals and their great leader, William Gladstone, the man who the young Woodrow Wilson so admired. With Gladstone triumphant, the squires retaliated—the very next day. They evicted their tenants. Young David saw pregnant and nursing mothers thrown into the streets. He saw families forced to take refuge from the elements in hayricks for want of a roof over their heads. He remembered fellow students suddenly forced to leave school: "I knew the reason why they left—because the great squire of the parish had turned their fathers out of their homes purely because they dared to vote for the Liberal candidate. It is my first memory of politics."[4] Thus was born his lifelong hatred of landlords, inherited wealth and all of the influence it brought, and his devotion to land reform. "Never shall I forget the harrowing narratives I heard when a mere boy—told thousands of times—of excessive rents and goading oppressions."[5]

The few people who remembered little David recall him being bookish—always with a satchel of books under his arm—and slightly aloof. When he was fourteen his schooling ended; there was no "high school." The best option for a bright child was to apprentice as a student-teacher (he was offered the position), but that would have required him to become a member of the Church of England. It was out of the question. His mother told him that she would rather see him working in one of the local quarries than denounce his religion. The other option open to other bright children—apprenticeship in the clergy—was also foreclosed to David. The Disciples of Christ did not pay their ministers.

In October, 1877, with the assistance of a local solicitor, David's mother secured for him an apprenticeship to become a law clerk with Breeze, Jones and Casson, a firm of solicitors located in Portmadog, six miles east of Llanystumdwy. And so, at fourteen, David George went to work. The practice of law in Great Britain was then—and is still today—bifurcated between the solicitors who meet the clients, draft the contracts and deeds and negotiate the deals, and the barristers who plead the solicitor's clients' cases in court. As an apprentice law clerk in a firm of solicitors, young David collected rents and fire insurance premiums, and handled all of the minutia of real estate. For a bright child who caught on quickly, there was no better education. The solicitors in the firm were all ardent and active Liberals, as became David.

Shortly after David signed on with Breeze, Jones and Casson, Uncle Lloyd's cobbler business failed. The family moved to the larger town of Criccieth, less than two miles east, and slid further down the economic scale. Until David (and later his younger brother William) were able to support his mother and uncle, they survived on odd jobs, boarders and borrowing. When the family left Llanystumdwy, David wrote in his diary: "Left Llanystumdwy without a feeling of regret, remorse or longing."[6]

When David was sixteen, Uncle Lloyd paid Breeze, Jones and Casson the £180 in fees and taxes necessary for David to become a law *clerk*. For the family, it was a huge sum, and may have left them almost penniless. At that time, he recorded his life's goals in his diary:

> "Q. Your chief ambition?
>
> A.   To promote myself by honest endeavor to do benefit to others."
>
> Q. The Aim in Life.
>
> A.   1. to develop my manhood
>
>   2. to do good
>
>   3. to seek truth
>
>   4. to bring truths to benefit our fellows.
>
> Q. Your idea of Happiness.
>
> A.   To perceive my own efforts succeed."[7]

David's idea of seeking truth would never include any kind of religious belief or observance. We do not know if he believed in an afterlife, or judgment, or whether he prayed.[8] As an adult, he confided to a friend that "If an angel came down from Heaven to demand it I could not write down what my religious convictions are." Once as a young backbencher in the House of Commons he wrote his wife that he would be taking a Sunday morning boat ride up the Thames to Kew Gardens rather than attend church services. In a return letter, she scolded him for it. His response: "There is a great deal of difference between the temptation to leave your work for the pleasure of being cramped up in a suffocating. malodorous chapel listening to some superstitious rot I had heard thousands of times before and on the other hand the temptation to have a pleasant ride on the river in the fresh air with a terminus at one of the loveliest gardens in Europe."[9]

The one Baptist teaching he did believe in was temperance. But he was never a teetotaler. His *bete noire* was not drink, it was drunkenness, and all the social evils that came with it. He would for years be the bane of Welsh tavern owners—*publicans*—who he believed preyed upon their neighbors. As early as eighteen, he began speaking at temperance meetings and at Disciples of Christ congregations. He was an effective speaker, right from the start.

His first known foray into political journalism came on November 5, 1880, when *The North Wales Express* published a long rambling letter denouncing Lord Salisbury, one of the Tory giants, which he signed as "Brutus." In local Parliamentary elections a local landlord (a Tory, of course) ran against a Liberal. He began the letter by asserting that a member of the squirearchy could not represent the people. Exhibiting an early lack of respect for his elders (he was then only seventeen), the letter concludes:

"Toryism has not been barren of statesmen—real and not charlatan—statesmen who prized the honour of England above the interests of party, who really hated oppression and demonstrated their detestation of it, not by pleading immunity from condign punishment for the instigation of foul and atrocious crimes, but by the laudable assistance which they rendered in the name of England to weak nationalities in their desperate struggles for liberty—for freedom from the yoke of human despots—for very existence. By so much was the Canning of ancient Toryism superior, nobler than the Salisbury of modern conservatism."[10]

Lloyd George and Salisbury would cross swords later, in person.

It is likely that he began to consider a career in politics as early as 1881, when he was eighteen. He joined the local debating societies. By the time he was twenty, he was well-known as a public speaker throughout North Wales. Had his goal been a successful career as a solicitor representing landlords and businessmen, he would not have staked out the left-wing positions that he did. Looking ahead, he wrote in his diary that if he were to achieve renown, it would depend entirely on "what forces of pluck and industry I can muster."[11] He did not lack industry, juggling his apprenticeship, his legal studies and his public speaking. Just as Woodrow Wilson intended his law practice as merely a steppingstone to politics, so did Lloyd George have no intention of spending his life as a local solicitor.

In 1881 he saw London for the first time, in order to take (and pass) the Intermediate Law Examination. He was back in April, 1884, to take (and pass) his final exam. The family was now so stretched that money had to be borrowed to enable David to make the trip. While in London he managed to get a ticket to the Strangers' Gallery of the House of Commons, and there saw for the first time the man they affectionately called the "G.O.M." (the "Great Old Man")—Prime Minister William Ewart Gladstone. He was then seventy-four, speaking in favor of the Franchise Bill, a proposal to extend voting rights throughout the United Kingdom. Shortly after hearing him Lloyd George wrote: "I can well remember the painful silence that fell upon the crowded Tory benches when the speech was over. It was as if they had been prostrated by a series of shocks from a powerful electric battery."[12]

Having passed his final exams, he was now a full-fledged solicitor. Breeze, Jones and Casson offered him a position as an assistant solicitor at a salary of one pound *per week* plus a commission on all new business he brought to the firm. And so, in early 1885, he opened up his own office, in the back parlor of his mother's home in Criccieth. He was twenty-two.

Not for many years would David Lloyd George concern himself with foreign affairs or even national affairs that did not touch upon the concerns of the Welsh. From the beginning, he became the tribune of the Welsh common man. There were many issues, but they all reduced themselves to the grip that the squirearchy and its ally, the established Church of England, had on the people of Wales. First, there was the issue of *disestablishmentarianism*, the official connection between the government and the Church of England (and its cousin, the Church of Wales), that prevented little David from becoming a teacher's assistant in a public school unless he swore allegiance to the official Church. Closely related was the issue of *endowment*, the use of public funds to support the clergy of the official Church. Closely related to endowment was the issue of the *tithe*, in reality a property tax on land that went directly to support the established clergy. In theory, the tax fell on the landowner. In practice, the landowners, often absent, always Tory, passed the burden of the tithe on to their tenants in the form of increased rents. Lloyd George was speaking on the issue in 1886 when he was interrupted by a local Church of England clergyman: "Why should you (the audience) listen to this little attorney? If you go to his office you'll pay six (shillings) and eightpence for him to speak a word to you." Lloyd George immediately responded: "The reverend gentleman is right when he says I'm a lawyer...If you don't come to see me I shan't ask you to pay me anything. But for this man, whether you go to hear his sermon or not, you will have to pay *him* just the same."[13]

In fact, disestablishment and disendowment were not Lloyd George's big issues. Land reform was his primary concern. The squires evicted their tenants following the 1868 election because they could; the tenants had no rights. If the tenants were guaranteed long leases, if they had the right to be compensated for improvements they made to their leaseholds, and if there were local land courts to hear their grievances, the squires would no longer be able to burden their tenants with the tithes. All that could be achieved with what was Lloyd George's real goal, *home rule* for Wales, with a local legislature enacting local laws free of obstruction from London. It was all very audacious, and had no support at all from the Liberal Party in Parliament, much less from the Tories. But as he said in 1885: "Humdrum Liberalism won't win elections."

In 1886, when he was all of twenty-three, he decided he would run for Parliament, assuming there would be no election for another three years. He set down in his diary his plan for success:

> "There are two or three impressions I must be careful to make...1st and foremost that I am a good speaker. 2ndly that I am a sound and thorough politician. 3rdly that I can afford to attend to parliamentary duties. To succeed in the first I must avail myself of every opportunity to speak in public so as to perfect myself & attain some reputation as a speaker. To succeed in the 2nd point I must put into those speeches good sound matter well-arranged so as to catch the ear of the intelligent...I must also write political articles on Welsh politics so as to show my mastery of them. To attain the 3rd reputation I must (1) attend to my business well so as to build up a good practice (2) practice economy so as to accumulate some matter of wealth (3) get all my cases well advertised (4) subscribe judiciously."[14]

In 1887, David's younger brother William George (no "Lloyd George" for him) was himself admitted to the bar as a solicitor. They formed "Lloyd George and George." Lloyd George, as he grew more famous, attracted the clients; William provided the services. The firm was very successful, and soon had offices throughout North Wales. By 1888, the George family's days of poverty were behind them. Lloyd George could not have had a political career but for Lloyd George and George. His half share of the legal fees sustained him, even when, as a member of Parliament, he contributed little or no legal work.

In setting forth what he felt was required to get to Parliament, Lloyd George ignored the element of luck, but it may have been luck, as much as anything, that landed him there, for in 1888 there appeared on his desk what became known as the Llanfrothen Burial Case, which would make him a hero to many in Wales and well-known to all. The instant he got the case, he saw the possibilities.

Llanfrothen is a village lying ten miles east of Criccieth. Some time in 1864, a Mr. and Mrs. Owen donated a parcel of land that was used to enlarge the churchyard at the Established Church in Llanfrothen. In 1880 Parliament enacted a law that required that burials be conducted under the rites and in accordance with the wishes of the deceased and their families, regardless of denomination. This incensed the bigoted Llanfrothen rector, Richard Jones, who simply refused to bury anyone who would not agree to have the service conducted by himself under the rites of the Church of England. After Mr. Owen died, he had Mrs. Owen reconvey the parcel into a trust of which none other than Rector Jones was the trustee, this time with the express proviso that no burial be conducted in the donated parcel except by Church of England rites. When a local Nonconformist quarryman, Robert Roberts, lay dying, he asked that he be buried beside his daughter in the churchyard annex (the donated parcel) under Noncomformist rites. Rector Jones refused, and locked the churchyard. The family sought Lloyd George's counsel. He advised that they break into the churchyard at night, which they did. They conducted a Nonconformist burial service. Rector Jones refused to admit defeat. He sued the family, who were defended by Lloyd George.

The facts were not in dispute. The legal issue was whether the original 1864 conveyance was valid, in which case the later conveyance to the trust was a legal "nullity." Lloyd George tried the case to a jury. They ruled that the original deed was valid, so that the subsequent deed conveyed nothing. The local judge overturned the jury verdict. In late December, 1888, the case was argued before two appeals court judges in London, who restored the jury verdict. The case received national attention. The local newspapers in Wales reported the proceedings verbatim.

Was it luck, or was it a set-up? Early in the case, he was quoted as saying "I see in Llanfrothen the chance to strike a mortal blow against the Church of England."[15] Did the dying Robert Roberts seek out Lloyd George, or did Lloyd George root about for someone willing to challenge the established Church? In any event, he was now famous. Two weeks after he won the case, he secured the Liberal Party nomination for Parliament from the Caernarvon District. His platform was simple: "I am a Welsh Nationalist first and a Liberal afterwards."[16]

Eighteen eighty-eight was a very busy year for David Lloyd George. On January 24, he married Margaret (Maggie) Owen, whom he had known since childhood. It was a long and difficult courtship for him. Her parents were devout Methodists, unsure if they wanted their daughter to marry into a household of Baptists. He made it clear to her that his political career came first: "I am prepared to thrust even love itself under the wheels of my Juggernaut, if it obstructs the way."[17] The "Juggernaut" was his political career. They would have five children, Richard in 1889, Mair Eluned ("Mary Ellen") in 1890, Olwen (a daughter) in 1892, Gwilym (a son) in 1894, and Megan in 1902. Maggie was his constant support and conscience throughout their marriage. There were difficult times, especially during the Boer War, when most of their neighbors supported the government and Lloyd George did not. They were often separated. He quickly grew bored with Criccieth; she hated the noise and grime of London, visiting as little as she could. They remained married until Maggie's death in 1941. But from 1912 on she had to share him with Megan's temporary governess, Frances Stevenson, who remained his mistress until Maggie's death.

In early January, 1888, Lloyd George launched what would be a short-lived weekly Welsh-language newspaper, *Udgorn Rhyddid,* ("Trumpet of Freedom"). In its first issue, he wrote: "The place of greatest need is where men are suffering under the greatest pressure: amidst the workers, labourers and farmers. It is an odd fact about all reforms that they are brought about by persons outside the sufferers themselves..."[18] Of course, he considered himself one of those persons.

Lloyd George obtained the Liberal nomination for Parliament in 1888; he did not expect to have to campaign for the office until 1891, when parliamentary elections throughout the United Kingdom would be held. The interval would give him time to become better known and to build up a war chest. All that was thrown into a cocked hat when the Tory M.P. for Caernarvon Boroughs, one Edmund Sweetenham, Q.C., suddenly died. Lloyd George would not be running for office for the first time in 1891 with all of the other candidates. He would be running in a bye-election in April, 1890.

It promised to be an uphill fight. The main issue for the Liberals and their revered leader, William Gladstone, was Home Rule for Ireland, an issue that did not resonate in rural Wales. Although Wales itself was very Liberal, Caernarvon Boroughs was split; Sweetenham himself had carried the district in 1886 by only two hundred votes. Of the 30,000 people who lived in the district, only 4,628 were eligible to vote. Of the six boroughs in the district, the two most populous were Caernarvon, which was Welsh-speaking, Nonconformist and Liberal, and Bangor, which was English-speaking, Church of England, and Conservative. The least populous borough was his home, Criccieth.

With little money, he campaigned tirelessly, on foot, knocking on doors that were opened by astonished residents who had never seen a candidate for Parliament at their doorsteps. Fortune shined on him, yet again. The sudden death of their incumbent meant that the Tories had little time to find a replacement. They settled on a local squire, Hugh John Ellis-Nanney, already twice-defeated for Parliament, a candidate so diffident that he did not speak in public. He opposed disestablishment, opposed the disendowment of the Church of England, and opposed Home Rule for Ireland, an issue that meant little to Lloyd George but much to the Catholic voters in the district.

True to custom, the Tories distributed free blankets and coal to the poor, which had less effect in an April bye-election than it would during the winter. Lloyd George constantly reminded his audiences who his opponent was: "a capital representative of his Party; he was of the aristocracy, a landlord, and a moneyed gentleman..."[19]

But more than anything, the audiences in rural Wales were learning what a generation of Englishmen would soon discover, that this rather short, mustachioed, slightly rumpled young man was the most galvanizing public speaker they would ever hear. During the campaign, the Tories sent one of their agents to attend one of his speeches, to learn what this young man was all about. He reported back: "I attended Lloyd George's meeting at Caernarvon this evening, and under the sway of his marvelous oratorical powers the audience was electrified beyond anything I have ever witnessed in the whole course of my life. Strong men broke down with emotion, while those who have hitherto been neutral and even indifferent were swept off their feet with the whirlwind of his eloquence. A man who can make so thrilling and overpowering an appeal to the emotions is absolutely invincible in Wales, and for that reason I feel compelled to warn you that in my opinion the seat is lost to our party."[20]

One of his biographers heard him speak, noting that Lloyd George could "charm a bird off a tree...If he was eloquent in English, he was positively mesmeric in Welsh."[21]

Balloting took place in the district on April 10, 1890. After two recounts, the results were announced. Lloyd George had received 1963 votes, Ellis-Nanney 1945. He had won by 18 votes. If ten Welshmen had gone the other way, Lloyd George's career, which would take him to 10 Downing Street and then to an earldom, might never have happened. Some said that had the fishing fleet not been at sea on April 10, he would have lost. The day after the election, he told a cheering crowd that the victory had been a hard one, all of the landlords being opposed to him. They would continue to oppose him, and he them, throughout his career.

By April 17 he was in London, in the chamber of the House of Commons. He took the oath, signed the roll, and was greeted by the speaker. He would sit in one of the opposition benches, the Liberals having lost the 1886 general election. The G.O.M.— Gladstone—was still their leader, and Home Rule for Ireland his big issue. It was not David Lloyd George's big issue. There would be conflicts.

On that day, Woodrow Wilson, then thirty-three, was lecturing at Wesleyan University in Middletown, Connecticut. Wilson considered the British House of Commons the greatest political institution man had ever devised, and William Gladstone its greatest statesman. But Wilson had given up on a career in the arena, resigning himself to life in the academy, purveying whatever influence he could from the sidelines. One of the thinkers that Wilson admired most, James Bryce, the author of *The American Commonwealth*, was then also a Liberal backbencher, seated alongside Lloyd George. One of the perquisites of being a Liberal member of Parliament was membership in the National Liberal Club, founded by Gladstone as a place to provide facilities for Liberal Party members, where Lloyd George would rub elbows with the likes of George Bernard Shaw and H.G. Wells. Beginning on that day, David Lloyd George would begin to live the life that Woodrow Wilson wished to live—ached to live—but could not. He was twenty-seven-years old.

Dod's Parliamentary Companion is an annual guidebook to each member of Parliament. The members are free to describe themselves in *Dod's* as they please. In 1890, Lloyd George described himself as a "Welsh Nationalist," supporting "Home Rule" (for Ireland), "Temperance," "disestablishment," and "other items in the programme of the Advanced Liberal Party." Anyone reading *Dod's* might assume that the new and very young backbencher would take his place as an unassuming follower of Gladstone, ready to follow the commands of the party whips.

Lloyd George first spoke in public as a Member of Parliament exactly a month after he arrived, at the Metropolitan Tabernacle, a large Baptist church in London. He spoke exclusively on the evils of the Church of England in Wales. He decried the apparent increase in Church of England membership in Wales, claiming that it was the result of enforced proselytization. Speaking from personal experience, he pointed out that if a child wished to better himself by becoming a student-teacher, he could do so only by joining the Established Church: "I am here to denounce it as the greatest curse which ever afflicted little Wales." One Conservative Welsh newspaper commented: "After his speech at the Metropolitan Tabernacle no one will for a moment think of accusing him of being too moderate, too polite, too gentlemanly."[22] He was more fulsome in his own praise, writing to Maggie: "Not a man moved whilst I spoke. They were all attention. The cheering and laughter which greeted my remarks drove me on from point to point."[23]

On May 29, a group a local Welsh Methodists took what was essentially a sight-seeing trip to Hawarden Castle, William Gladstone's home in northeast Wales. The Liberals were then out of power, but Gladstone, then eighty-one, having already served as prime minister three times, was still very much the leader of the Liberals in Parliament. Gladstone was in residence that day, and Lloyd George was in the crowd. Gladstone's overriding concern was Irish Home Rule, which was not the overriding concern of the Welsh Noncomformists in his audience. And so Gladstone urged his followers to be patient. Referring to the most recent (1886) elections, he said: "[T]he battle was fought very much upon the great Irish issue, but you are perfectly aware that in fighting the battle of Ireland you are also fighting the battle of Wales…" He stressed that once the issue of Ireland had been resolved, the local claims of Wales and Scotland could be more easily addressed. He then paid Lloyd George a public compliment: "[Y] ou returned a much larger Liberal majority in Wales, and you have now, I rejoice to say, added to that majority at Carnarvon."[24]

Following Gladstone's speech, a number of the more influential members of the delegation were invited to meet the G.O.M. personally, and at that moment, the greatest Liberal statesman of the nineteenth century first met the man who would become the greatest Liberal statesman of the twentieth. Gladstone was exactly three times Lloyd George's age. He had grown accustomed to deference. The meeting did not go well. Lloyd George hectored Gladstone to promise to put Welsh disestablishment on the legislative calendar. Gladstone, a practicing member of the Church of England, was evasive. Lloyd George, who on that date had all of six weeks experience in Parliament and who had not yet made his maiden speech, pressed the G.O.M., who was not accustomed to being pressed. Gladstone then snubbed Lloyd George, remarking "Well, go on agitating and no doubt in time disestablishment will come."[25] Lloyd George left the encounter feeling humiliated.[26]

One of the first issues confronting Lloyd George was the tithe, the tax on land that the landlords passed on to their tenants in the form of higher rents. Right from the start he showed his independent streak. With crop prices low and land values declining, the landlords now had difficulty passing the tax to their tenants. A bill ("The Rent Charge Recovery Bill") was proposed (never enacted) to lower the tithe, which most Liberals instinctively supported. Not Lloyd George. Looking far ahead, he anticipated the day when the tithe would no longer land in the pockets of the clergy of the Established Church, but would go to support local schools and other government services. With that in mind, he wanted to keep the tithe as *high* as possible. Members of the House of Commons then (and still today) did not vote by raising their hands. They voted by *division;* they left the chamber and lined up to be counted in either the Liberal or Conservative lobbies. Young Lloyd George rose from his seat and crossed over to the other side of the chamber to line up with the Tories. Mindful that he had just won election by an eighteen-vote margin, he defended his action in a letter to the *Carnarvon Herald*: "[W]ho would benefit from this enormous remission [the lowering of the tax]? The landlords, and they alone. I have yet to learn that it is a part of the duty of a Radical MP to enrich our great land monopolists at the expense of impoverishing the educational resources of the nation."[27] One Tory newspaper commented on his vote that it was "eloquent portent that Welsh thralldom to Mr. Gladstone is about to end."[28] The Rent Charge Recovery Bill was far from the last time he would cross the G.O.M.

He said of Gladstone: "[He] would sit and shake his head at us…and glare at us with a fierce eye—oh! How fierce when you are fighting him.[29] Years later he said of Gladstone: "I did not like him much. He hated Noncomformists and Welsh Noncomformists in particular, and he had no real sympathy for the working classes." But he also said that Gladstone was "far and away the best parliamentary speaker I have ever heard."[30]

When Lloyd George had been a member of Parliament for less than four months a routine bill came up to authorize some very small expenses to support what he called "the peacockism of royalty." These included £438 for the installation of Prince Henry of Prussia as a Knight of the Garter, and £180 for the funeral of the Duchess of Cambridge. Most of his fellow Liberals (and all of the Tories) were willing to allow for these incidentals, but not Lloyd George, and in opposing them he had a field day. With respect to the £438 for Prince Henry of Prussia: "I object to this Vote, not on account of the amount, but on account of the principle involved…Fees paid on the installation of his Royal Highness Prince Henry of Prussia as a Knight of the Garter I wish to point out that that dignity is, as a general rule, granted for some signal service rendered to this country; but what service has Prince Henry of Prussia ever rendered to this country? He has not yet rendered any service to his own country, to say nothing of service to Great Britain."[31]

With respect to the £180 to cover the funeral expenses of the Duchess of Cambridge, he pointed out that "[T]he family of the Duke of Cambridge has from first to last received something like £3,000,000 out of the Exchequer. I think it is positively monstrous that we should be paying these sums for what is absolutely worthless to this country, when there is so much suffering, so much absolute penury and want among our working classes.[32] One member was so exasperated by this that he offered to pay the £180 out of his own pocket. The Queen learned of Lloyd George's remarks relative to the Duchess of Cambridge. She was not amused. She complained to the prime minister.[33]

Five days later, Parliament adjourned. During his four months as a member, Lloyd George had built a reputation as a renegade. During those four months, he had seen little of Criccieth. The trip home was tedious, and he was learning to like the lights of London.

Lloyd George spent as much time as he could in 1891 campaigning, knowing that nationwide elections were coming, ever-mindful of his eighteen-vote victory. In a typical speech in October, he ridiculed the Established Church, asking his audience to compare St. Peter to the current Church of England curates: "Can you imagine him living in a stately mansion with a host of menials ministering to his luxuries? Can you fancy him drawing a salary large enough to keep the temple going for months—and all this with the poor rolling in misery at the very gates of the palace?"[34]

The centerpiece of Gladstone's agenda was Home Rule for Ireland. Lloyd George supported it only as a convenience, i.e. only as it furthered the cause of *Welsh* Home Rule. Gladstone, Church of England to the bone, never supported disestablishment in Wales, giving it lip service to the extent needed to keep Welsh Liberals in the fold. In 1890, the cause of Irish Home Rule suffered when its principal organizer and tribune, Charles Stewart Parnell, 40, the leader of the Irish Parliamentary Party, was caught up in an ugly divorce case that included testimony of bedroom windows, fire escapes and disguises. He was named as the co-respondent in a case brought by Captain William O'Shea, a fellow Irish M.P., against his wife, Katherine. Parnell's assurances to his followers that he would be exonerated proved overly optimistic. The evidence revealed that Parnell and Katherine O'Shea's affair had not been a fleeting one; it had produced three children. This was too much for many Liberals, especially the Welsh Noncomformists for whom adultery was anathema. When Parnell refused to resign as the leader of the Irish, his party split into Parnell and anti-Parnell factions. Parnell died of pneumonia in October, 1891, but the damage to the cause of Irish Home Rule had been done. Gladstone (and Lloyd George) did not abandon the cause of Irish Home Rule, but they entered the 1892 elections wounded.

The Tories sensed that they could recover the seat that Lloyd George had so narrowly snatched from them in the bye-election. They nominated an existing MP, Sir John Puleston, a far more substantial candidate than the hapless Ellis-Nanney, who, unlike Ellis-Nanney, at least spoke Welsh. But Puleston had his own baggage: He had converted to the Church of England, and he opposed disestablishment. He campaigned on Lloyd George's youth ("Was he [Puleston] not a member of Parliament when Lloyd George was still at school?").[35] Puleston also alleged that Lloyd George's shenanigans during his first sitting in Parliament had resulted in his own party leader—Gladstone— opposing him. Thus caused Lloyd George's campaign to send the G.O.M. a letter, asking Gladstone for a public endorsement. They received in return a less than whole-hearted cable of support, Gladstone stating that were he "an elector for Carnarvon Boroughs I should vote against Sir J. Puleston and in favor of Mr. Lloyd George."[36]

The balloting was conducted on July 8, 1892, and the results were announced two days later. Lloyd George had received 2,154 votes to Puleston's 1958, a margin of 196. Lloyd George had bettered his eighteen-vote bye-election margin, but his margin of victory was the narrowest of any Liberal in North Wales. Wales was still solidly Liberal, sending thirty-one members to Parliament, all but three of whom were Liberals. But the vote was close throughout Great Britain. The Liberals won 270 seats, the Conservatives

268. The Liberal Unionists, a party that had broken off from Gladstone over Irish Home Rule, garnered forty-seven seats. The guiding light of the Liberal Unionists was the Birmingham businessman Joseph Chamberlain, 56, who would later cross swords with Lloyd George over Chamberlain's colonial policies. (Chamberlain's son, Neville, would infamously declare that he had achieved "peace in our time" after meeting with Hitler in Munich in 1938). The Irish Parliamentary Party won eighty-one seats. The results meant that if the Welsh Liberals voted as a bloc, they could threaten to unseat a Liberal government. *The North Wales Express* editorialized: "the return of Mr. Lloyd George is not only a warning to the Tories that Wales is in earnest, but notice to the English Liberals that they must be in earnest too."[37] Lloyd George himself echoed the warning: "[T]he Welsh members want nothing for themselves, but they must get something for their little country, and I don't think they will support a Liberal ministry—I care not how illustrious the Minister who leads it—unless he pledges to concede to Wales those great measures of reform upon which Wales has set its heart."[38] No one doubted that the "illustrious" minister to whom he referred was the G.O.M. himself.

There was a little-noticed omen in the 1892 balloting, one that would later prove to be ruinous to the Liberals. In that year, the Labour Party would send its first member, Keir Hardie, a socialist and pacifist, to Parliament. But that was in the future. The Liberals were now back in power, with Gladstone taking his fourth turn as prime minister, dependent for his survival on the support of the Irish Parliamentary Party and the Welsh Liberals.

Lloyd George—now thirty-one—was back as a Liberal backbencher. Prior to 1911, MP's received no salary whatever unless they were also cabinet ministers, which Lloyd George was not and, as long as Gladstone was prime minister, had little prospect of becoming. In 1894, he reported his *annual* income as £338, the equivalent of £24,870 ($32,157) today.[39] (In 2017, the annual salary of a member of the United States House of Representatives was $174,000.) Most of Lloyd George's income came from the firm of Lloyd George and George. Without his brother's constant devotion to their law practice, Lloyd George could not have maintained a political career.

In the 1893 session of Parliament, Gladstone promised the Welsh Liberals that the disestablishment of the Church in Wales would be a priority on the legislative calendar *next* year. Eighteen ninety-three would prove to be Gladstone's last try at his signature cause, Home Rule for Ireland. Marshalling all of his energies, Gladstone managed to get The Second Home Rule Bill narrowly passed in the House of Commons. But prior to 1911, the House of Lords had the ability to veto legislation passed in the Commons, which the Conservatives who controlled the Lords promptly and overwhelmingly did. It was the end (for now) of Home Rule for Ireland, and of the political career of William Gladstone. In January, 1894, Gladstone—now eighty-four—retired.

Gladstone was succeeded (briefly) as prime minister by the Earl of Rosebury, 46. As a peer, Lord Rosebury could not set foot in the House of Commons. The Liberals' leader in the Commons was Sir William Harcourt, 67, then the Chancellor of the Exchequer. Rosebury was as cool to Irish Home Rule as Gladstone had been ardent, and every bit as cool to Welsh disestablishment as Gladstone had been. Although Rosebury formally endorsed Irish Home Rule, his endorsement was so lukewarm that it alienated the Irish MP's who the Liberals relied upon for their slim majority.

In March, 1894, Lloyd George and a number of other Welsh Liberal MP's went to William Harcourt demanding that Welsh disestablishment be placed on the legislative calendar and passed in this session. Lloyd George felt that he had a commitment from Gladstone and Harcourt from the last session to put the issue on the calendar next year, and next year was now. Yet when Rosebury brought up yet another Irish-favored bill (The Evicted Tenants Bill, designed to redress Irish tenants' grievances, which was also killed in the House of Lords), Lloyd George and his fellow Welsh Liberals felt that they had been had. The result was the April, 1894, "Revolt of the Four," consisting of Lloyd George and three other Welsh Liberals. The "revolt" consisting of the four renouncing their allegiance to the Liberals. They did so in a letter to the Liberal Party whips, advising them that because they felt they had been "trifled with," "circulars in regard to division need no longer be sent to them."[40] In other words, on those occasions when party discipline on a forthcoming vote (a "division") was demanded, the party whips need not bother advising them of it.

The "revolt," such as it was, had no chance of succeeding, since only four of the thirty-five Welsh Liberal MP's took part. But the revolt was popular in Wales, and for Lloyd George, that is what mattered. Lloyd George sensed that the Rosebury government was doomed; there was no point in being too closely associated with it. The "Revolt of the Four" was the beginning of Lloyd George's campaign to form a separate Welsh political party, similar to the Irish Parliamentary Party. Later that summer, he pushed the formation of the *Cymru Fydd* ("Young Wales") *League*, a purely political organization formed for the purpose of advancing Welsh political aims. He hoped that *Cymru Fydd* would be the instrument that would lead to a united Welsh party of the House of Commons, on the Irish model. But he got nowhere, primarily because the idea was opposed by Welsh Liberal MP's from *South* Wales. The split over *Cymru Fidd* manifested the divisions between North Wales and South Wales. North Wales was more rural, less populous, and less wealthy than South Wales, but overrepresented in the House of Commons. Liberal PM's from South Wales feared that a united Welsh party would be dominated by North Wales, and their leader, Lloyd George.

In early 1895, Lord Rosebury did bring up the "Established Church (Wales) Bill." Had it passed, it would have ended the Church of England as the established church in Wales, and would have eliminated most, but not all, of the Church's holdings and income in Wales. As Lloyd George had predicted when he first opposed the lowering of the tithe, the tithe income would now be administered by county councils, for public purposes. A split developed between North and South Wales over the allocation of tithe income. If the income were distributed based upon the land from whence the tithe was derived (which Lloyd George favored), it would have favored the less populous North; if it were distributed on a per capita basis, it would have favored the more populous South. The debate became heated. In the event, the Established Church (Wales) Bill met the same fate as Irish Home Rule: It was killed in the House of Lords. Not until 1914 (after the Lords' power to veto legislation had been curtailed) was the Church disestablished in Wales.

In June, 1895, Lord Rosebury's government, which had a majority of only seven seats, collapsed over a minor issue. The Conservative leader, Lord Salisbury (the man who the seventeen-year-old Lloyd George had skewered in his first letter-to-the editor) became prime minister for the third time and immediately called for elections. Not everyone agreed with Lloyd George's call for a united Welsh party; not everyone supported *Cymru Fydd*. But as luck would have it, the Tories nominated as his opponent none other than Ellis-Nanney, who would now be making his fourth run at a seat from Carnarvon Boroughs. When the results of the July 20 balloting were announced, they revealed 2,265 votes for Lloyd George and 2,071 for Ellis-Nanney, a margin only two votes shy of Lloyd George's victory margin over Sir John Puleston. Lloyd George couldn't resist noting that, at that rate, it would take the Tories 550 years to wrest the seat from him.[41]

But the elections were a disaster for the Liberals, who lost 100 seats throughout the country, including six in Wales. The Liberals would be out of power for the next ten years. It spelled the end, for the time being, of Irish Home Rule and Welsh disestablishment. For the next few years, Lloyd George would remain a backbencher powerless to effect events. But he was tireless. Still only in his early thirties, he was everywhere, speaking on any subject that was current and peaked his interest, whether it was the working conditions of women in laundries, fighting government subsidies for church schools, railing against the fees charged inventors by the patent office, or opposing the appointment of a Chief Inspector of Schools in Wales who could not speak Welsh. During the 1896 session, he opposed the Agricultural Land Rating Bill, a Tory effort to lower the taxes on agricultural landlords. Any legislation designed to aid landlords was bound to raise his ire. The ostensible purpose of the bill was to assist agriculture, then in a depression. Under the bill the treasury would subsidize localities for the loss of agricultural tax revenues. Lloyd George saw it instead as a bailout for the wealthy at the expense of the taxpayers. When the bill came to a vote (i.e., a "division") Lloyd George and three other MP's refused to "divide;" they refused to leave the chamber, and were forcibly removed by the Sergeant at Arms. Lloyd George was suspended from the House of Commons for a week, but he was a hero in Wales. He was now one of the leaders of the opposition, and beginning to be mentioned as a possible minister, should the Liberals regain power. In the 1898 session, he opposed the creation of a Roman Catholic university in Ireland (the proposal was withdrawn.) He opposed appropriating £750,000 in tax relief to Irish landlords ("...we ought to protest against a sum of £750,000 when we cannot find the money for old age pensions in this country...")[42] He also supported a bill to provide for teachers' colleges free from sectarian control. This at the same time that similar legislation was being considered in France.

Throughout these years, he earned not a shilling as a member of Parliament. His successful campaign against Ellis-Nanney cost £400, which Lloyd-George did not have. The debt was underwritten by *eighty* supporters. In 1897, he formed a London law firm with fellow Liberal Arthur Rhys Roberts, but his main income still came from Lloyd George and George.

Then, in 1899, Lloyd George, then thirty-three, took the political gamble of his life. In that year, the British Empire went to war against the *Boers*, the Dutch-descended farmers in South Africa. Most of Great Britain sided with their "tommies."[*] Lloyd George risked his career and on more than one occasion his life in his instinctive, visceral and consistent opposition to the war.

Following the defeat of Napoleon, Great Britain seized the entire area of the Cape of Good Hope from the Dutch. In 1815, there were 27,000 "Cape Dutch" settlors in what is now South Africa. They spoke Afrikaans, a mixture of Dutch, Flemish and German.

---

[*]   The nickname for the common British soldier immortalized in a Rudyard Kipling poem:

> "For it's Tommy this, an' Tommy that
> an' 'Chuck him out, the brute'
> But it's 'Saviour of 'is country'
> When the guns begin to shoot."

These *Afrikaners* belonged to the Dutch Reformed Church, believed in racial purity, and were fiercely independent. They had grown accustomed to being neglected by the Dutch, which was to their liking. They outnumbered the English-speaking whites, but the Afrikaners and the English-speakers together were outnumbered by the black tribes. More than anything, the Afrikaners wished to be left alone. The British were not in the habit of leaving their colonial subjects alone.

South Africa was then four separate states. Cape Colony, to the west, with its capital at Cape Town, was predominantly English-speaking. To the north and east of Cape Colony lay Orange Free State, and north and east of it lay Transvaal, with its capital at Pretoria. Both were Afrikaner-controlled. Natal, south of Transvaal, with a large Zulu population, was annexed by the British in 1844.

The Afrikaners first became uncomfortable with British rule when, in 1827, the British made English the official language of Cape Colony. In 1833, the British outlawed slavery throughout the Empire. Parliament set aside a fund to compensate the slave-owners, but the Afrikaner farmers—the *Boers*—who had summarily lost their principal asset, their slaves, felt the compensation insufficient. Liberal British governments also had notions about fair treatment for the indigenous blacks. And so, in 1834, thousands of Cape Colony Afrikaner farmers, deciding they had had enough of British interference in their lives, entered upon the "Great Trek," packing bag and baggage, sheep and cattle, and migrating in covered wagons east across the Orange River to Orange Free State and Transvaal in the hope of better land and freedom from the British. Among them was a twelve-year old boy, Paul Kruger. These *trekboers* became part of Afrikaner legend.

In the 1850's the British granted local autonomy to Orange Free State and Transvaal; Cape Colony was granted autonomy in 1872. In 1869 Louis Napoleon completed the Suez Canal, and the relative importance of the Cape to the British Navy and British commercial interests declined. But the *trekboers* and their descendants did not thrive in their new lands. Drought and cattle disease decimated their farms, and by 1877 the Transvaal government was completely bankrupt. Worse, Transvaal was threatened by Zulu tribes operating out of Natal. In 1877, the British annexed Transvaal outright. By 1879, the British army had suppressed the Zulus, apparently for good. Unfortunately, this eliminated the rationale for British domination, and the Afrikaners wanted their country back. On February 27, 1881, the 627 troops under Maj. Gen. Sir George Pomeroy Colley found themselves atop Majuba Hill near the Natal-Transvaal border. Colley was reasonably certain that the local Transvaal militia facing him could never take the hill. He was mistaken. Although the foe turned out to be mostly farm boys, they were excellent marksmen, and in the brief fighting that followed, more than half of Colley's men were casualties before Colley did the unthinkable: He raised a white flag. The Boers had lost all of one man. Following the battle, the Gladstone government was pleased to restore autonomy to Transvaal, now named the South African Republic. But to Conservatives, the surrender at Majuba Hill was a humiliation they could not forget. It had to be avenged.

Fate was not kind to a people who wished only to be left alone. In 1884, gold was discovered at Witwatersrand, west of present-day Pretoria. It was, in fact, the largest gold deposit in the world. Miners began flooding into the gold fields by the thousands. Most of them were British, but they came from everywhere, and within little more than a decade they outnumbered the Boers by more than two to one. To the Boers, they were *Uitlanders*, literally, "outsiders," not intended as a term of flattery. Theirs was not the Bible; it was *The Cape Times*.

A year prior to the gold strike, Paul Kruger ("Oom Paul," or "uncle Paul") was elected president of the South African Republic, declaring that "God's Word" would be the basis of his rule.[43] David Lloyd George had left school at fourteen; Kruger's formal education ended when he was ten. The difference is that Lloyd George kept reading and learning; "Oom" Paul did not. As president, he was once required to dedicate a synagogue. He did so as follows: "In the name of the Lord Jesus Christ, I dedicate this building open."[44] Kruger was uneducated, but he was by no means stupid. He realized that if the Uitlanders were given voting rights equal to the Boers, they would soon control the country. And so he imposed a *fourteen-year* waiting period before any immigrant could vote. When someone suggested that the voting requirement be relaxed, he pointed to the Transvaal flag outside his office: "You see that flag, if I grant the franchise I may as well pull it down."[45]

Kruger saw that real money could be made from the mining companies. They all needed dynamite. Kruger made sure they could buy it only from the government-controlled monopoly. The miners also needed to transport the ore. This they could do only on the government-controlled railway. In short order, 90% of Kruger's government's revenues came from the miners.[46] As Kruger's government became richer, the combination of high fees and no franchise resulted in the classic "taxation without representation" grievance. Kruger and his government were becoming more than an annoyance to the Uitlanders. Something had to be done.

The man who would try was Cecil John Rhodes (1853-1902). Born in Hertfordshire, just north of London, he emigrated to Cape Colony when he was seventeen for reasons of health. He got himself elected to the Cape Colony parliament when he was twenty-seven (the same age that Lloyd George entered the British parliament.) By 1890, he was president of the Cape Colony. Along the way, he became fabulously wealthy in the diamond business. His Chartered Company became a semi-autonomous empire, controlling what was then Rhodesia and Southern Rhodesia, today's Zambia and Zimbabwe. He had his own police force.

Rhodes' and Kruger's goals were precisely incompatible. Kruger wanted a united South Africa, ruled by the Afrikaners, free from interference from London. Rhodes believed in the supremacy of the Anglo-Saxon race everywhere. He wanted a united South Africa ruled by the whites, free from interference from London. Rhodes had a kindred spirit in Joseph Chamberlain, the Birmingham industrialist-turned-politician who headed the Liberal Unionists. When Salisbury formed a government following the 1895 elections with the help of the Liberal Unionists, he offered Chamberlain the choice of any cabinet post except foreign secretary. Chamberlain chose Secretary of State for the Colonies. Chamberlain made no bones about his policies: "I believe that the British race is the greatest of the governing races that the world has ever seen."[47] He also said that: "It is not enough to occupy the great spaces of the world's surfaces unless you can make the best of them. It is the duty of the landlord to develop his estate."[48] David Lloyd George hated landlords.

Rhodes decided that he would end his Kruger problem in the most direct manner possible: He would simply overthrow Kruger's government by force. Not having a large enough army at his disposal to accomplish this goal, he decided that a small force would invade the Transvaal, where the local Uitlanders, alerted to the invasion, would rise up, join forces with raiders, and overthrow Kruger. The concept was similar to the Bay of Pigs invasion of 1961, which was also dependent for its success on an uprising by the locals.

The man Rhodes selected to carry out the raid was Leander Starr Jameson, 42, a Scottish-born physician and one of Rhodes' closest and most dedicated aides. Jameson had hoped to recruit 1,500 volunteers from Rhodes' police forces and from other sources. He attracted barely 500, but decided to proceed anyway. On Sunday, December 29, 1895, Jameson and his men were bivouacked at Pitsani, in the Transvaal, waiting for the go-ahead from Rhodes to attack Johannnesburg, almost 200 miles to the east. He also awaited word from the Uitlander leaders that the uprising was ready. Neither came, but Jameson was eager to go, telling all within earshot that he would "kick the Boers all round the Transvaal." In order to assure secrecy, Jameson planned to cut the telegraph wire to Pretoria. The soldier he sent to cut the wire mistook a fence wire for the telegraph wire, and cut it. By Tuesday everyone as far away as London and as close as Johannesburg knew that the raiders were on their way. Jameson never made it to Johannesburg. By Thursday, January 2, 1896, Jameson and his exhausted men were stopped at Doornkop, just west of Johannesburg, by a larger force. Realizing that there would be no Uitlander uprising, Jameson gave up. Kruger turned him over to the

British, who jailed him for fifteen months. Even before Jameson reached Doornkop, Joseph Chamberlain read the handwriting on the wall, and distanced himself and the Colonial Office from the raiders.

Rhodes was forced to resign as president of Cape Colony as a result of the raid. Chamberlain denied any prior knowledge of the raid. A House of Commons inquiry into the raid was inconclusive. Rhodes scoffed at the whole thing, telling Sir William Harcourt, the leader of the Liberals in the House of Commons, that "Nobody is going to name a country after you."[49] Lloyd George paid scant attention to the raid. He noted, in one speech, that "a small republic, with an army the size of a small principality, has been able to defy the power of Great Britain."[50] He wrote to Maggie: "The government have had a snub from old Kruger the Boer and Chamberlain has met his first reverse as a Minister."[51]

One man who did notice the raid was Kaiser Wilhelm, who cabled Kruger on January 3: "I express to you my sincere congratulations that without calling on the aid of friendly Powers you and your people, by your own energy against the armed bands which have broken into your country as disturbers of the peace, have succeeded in re-establishing peace, and defending the independence of the country against attacks from without."[52] No one in England misunderstood the reference to "friendly Powers." It could refer only to Germany.

War did not break out between Kruger's government and the British Empire following the Jameson Raid, and might not have erupted at all had Joseph Chamberlain not upped the ante. In April, 1897, Chamberlain appointed Sir Alfred Milner, 44, an Oxford-educated Tory, as Governor of Cape Colony and High Commissioner of South Africa. Milner believed in the inherent superiority of the British just as much as Chamberlain did. To him, it was "a great game between ourselves and Transvaal for the mastery of South Africa," with the goal of "uniting South Africa as a British State."[53]

In February, 1898, Kruger was re-elected as president of the South African Republic, and began to exhibit signs of conciliation. He offered to give the franchise to all foreigners resident for seven years, retroactive to the date of each person's arrival. It meant, of course, that in only seven years, the entire issue of the franchise would resolve itself. Milner rejected it. Milner met with Kruger in May, 1899. At that summit, Milner demanded the *immediate* franchise for all Uitlanders, also demanding that English be the language of the Transvaal parliament and that Britain have the right to veto any law enacted by Kruger's government, demands that Milner knew Kruger could never accept. Kruger looked Milner in the eye and put into words what everyone knew: "It is our country that you want."[54] Both countries moved slowly but inexorably to war. In August, 1899, Britain, which had had only 10,000 troops in the Cape, dispatched an additional 50,000 and posted them on the Transvaal frontier.

Lloyd George was vacationing in western Canada that September. He wrote his brother that he felt that war was now "inevitable," and that "The prospect oppresses me with a deep sense of horror. If I have the courage I shall protest with all the vehemence at my command against the outrage which is perpetrated in the name of human freedom."[55] The South African Republic declared war on October 11, followed immediately by Orange Free State. Lloyd George hurriedly departed Canada on the same day.

Why did Lloyd George oppose a war that most of his constituents, let alone the British people as a whole, and even many in his own party, supported? Why was he so outspoken when he was so against the tide, risking his successful career? For one, he was revolted by the hypocrisy. He knew that the issue of voting rights for the Uitlanders was a smokescreen for a land grab by the likes of Cecil Rhodes. Secondly, he thought little of the Uitlanders themselves, ("They prefer to lounge about the hotels of Cape Town, while English homes are made desolate on their behalf.")[56] He despised the Unionists and their leader, Joseph Chamberlain. More importantly, he knew that the cost of war would divert funds needed at home ("I know of nothing that arrests progress like war.")[57]

None of these reasons explain his deep loathing for this war. But Lloyd George himself gave the answer in a speech on the floor of the House of Commons toward the end of the conflict. In 1868, when he was only five years old, he had witnessed the wholesale eviction of tenants from their homes following the Liberal election victory. He never forgot the sight of nursing mothers thrown into the street. He remembered his now-homeless classmates forced to leave school. He carried his hatred of landlords through life, and in the Boer War, he saw these scenes repeated, with the British Empire acting as the landlord. Speaking on March 20, 1902, he likened the war to "a lord of the manor evicting a squatter on the fringe of his estate. For the lord of the manor it was simply a question of that particular croft…We see here a squatter on the fringe of our Empire. He is very troublesome, he poaches and destroys our game, and is a great nuisance and we have determined to evict him." It is very different for the squatter: "He and his ancestors had been there from time immemorial, and he was fighting for his home…" For the lord of the manor, the extent he would prosecute the squatter was a matter of "expenditures and difficulties;" but "it would be a different thing if you were fighting for freedom and independence."[58] So there it was. The British Empire—the lord of the manor—seeking to evict the Boers, a helpless tenant. He could not possibly have supported this war.

Shortly after the fighting began, Lloyd George was speaking in Carmarthen, in South Wales. He held back nothing. "Why do I object to war?" he asked. "Nothing arrested progress like war." Employing a metaphor he would use repeatedly, he stated that "There was not a lyddite shell that burst on the African hills which did not carry away an old age pension." He said that the war was a "fight against a little country whose population was less than that of Carmarthenshire." [He was correct if one did not include the *black* population of South Africa, who were forgotten by all.[59]] He received "loud laughter," from his audience when he said that "It was cowardice to trample upon the Boers, and it was not to be wondered that no country in Europe said a good word for us *except the Turks*." But he received only "slight applause" when he said that he "... would be recreant before God and man if at this first opportunity..." he did not enter a protest against what he considered an infamy. "And here I do it tonight, even if I leave Carmarthen tomorrow without a friend." The *Evening Express* reporter noted that his remarks were "perceptibly against the feeling of the thinking portion of the audience."[60]

The war began with the Boers attacking Cape Colony and Natal. Their strategy was to hope for a quick victory, knowing that time was not on their side. In mid- October, the town of Mafeking, on the border with the Bechuanaland Protectorate (now Botswana), was besieged. The town of Ladysmith, in Natal, was also besieged, as was the mining town of Kimberly, with Cecil Rhodes in it. Repeated attempts to relieve the Ladysmith siege by troops under the inept Gen. Sir Redvers Buller failed, and earned Buller the sobriquet "Reverse" Buller. October 30, 1899 became "Mournful Monday," to commemorate a British defeat north of Ladysmith in which thirty Empire soldiers were killed and 800 taken prisoner. Among the captives was the twenty-four-year-old correspondent for the *Morning Post,* Winston Churchill.

Matters improved for the British with the demotion of Bullers and his replacement by Field Marshal Lord Frederick Sleigh Roberts, a/k/a "Bobs," a veteran of India, Afghanistan and most of Britain's other wars of the nineteenth century. Lord Roberts arrived on December 23, 1899 and set to work. He now had 170,000 troops at his disposal, the largest overseas expedition in British history to date, fighting some 30,000 Boers. By March, 1900, he had captured the Orange Free State capital of Bloemfontein. He then set out to capture all of Transvaal. On May 18, he broke through and lifted the siege of Mafeking. On May 31 he captured Johannesburg and on June 5 Pretoria fell. "Oom Paul" Kruger fled the country for Holland, never to return. Except for the work of mopping up, it appeared that the war was over. In December, Lord Roberts, feeling that his work was done, turned his command over to Lord Herbert Kitchener, and returned to London, a national hero. Queen Victoria made him an earl and a knight of the Order of the Garter. Patriotic feeling ran very high. The editor of a *socialist* newspaper wrote: "My whole heart is with the British troops...when England is at war I am English. I have no politics and no party. I am English."[61]

The people supported the "tommies;" Lloyd George opposed the war and everything about it. In February, 1900, he asked, on the floor of the House of Commons, "How many workmen in this country realize that the wages earned by the miners in Transvaal were four times as high as at home?" He also noted that the Transvaal miners had an eight-hour day, something not yet guaranteed to British workers.[62] He again mocked the idea that the war was over voting rights for the Uitlanders: "I do not believe the war has any connection with the franchise. It is a question of forty-five percent dividends..."[63]

He was fast becoming one of the most hated politicians in Great Britain. Following a speech in Glasgow in March, he wrote his brother: "Have just arrived from Glasgow alive and unhurt—a tumultuous experience—the worst public meeting row I have ever witnessed—10,000 people trying to break in to the meeting—surging, struggling, fighting, yelling, howling like savages..."[64] Worse came next month in Bangor, in North Wales. He needed a police escort to enter the hall. He spoke to the accompaniment of breaking glass from the windows breaking all around him, smashed by local youths demonstrating against him. He did manage to make himself heard: "Four thousand men dead and £60,000,000 spent to dig their graves....The money which might have been spent to provide 300,000 workmen's cottages given to dig graves in South Africa and to fill them with the flower of five nations."[65] He reminded his audience that there was free speech in Transvaal, "freer than in Bangor tonight."[66]

After Pretoria fell, when most of Great Britain felt that the war was over, the Tories decided that there was no better time to call an election. This would be a "khaki election," the name for any British election in which war is the issue. Lloyd George was resigned to the possibility that he might lose his seat as a result of his opposition to the war.

Parliament dissolved on September 17, 1900, in order that the members might campaign. An hour before it did, Lloyd George launched his bitterest—and most personal—attack on Joseph Chamberlain. On the floor of the House of Commons, he accused Chamberlain of having profited personally from the war through Kynoch's & Co., a Birmingham ammunition manufacturer of which his brother was chairman. The extensive contracts that Kynochs had with the war department were not necessarily awarded to the lowest bidder, and the ammunition delivered was not necessarily of the highest quality. Chamberlain, seething with anger, rose and gave a weak defense. "My brother is chairman of Kynochs. That is perfectly true, but I have never discussed the matter with my brother...[I]t is a gross abuse to attack a public man through his relatives, for whom he is not responsible."[67] On the campaign trail, Lloyd George did mention another armaments firm, Hoskins & Co, of which Chamberlain was not a shareholder, but of which all of Chamberlain's relatives, including Chamberlain's wife, were shareholders. Lloyd George introduced an amendment which would have required the Queen to personally approve all government contracts in which ministers had an interest. The amendment failed, as Lloyd George knew it would, and with that the House adjourned.

Once again fortune smiled on Lloyd George in the man the Tories ran against him. This time it was a retired army colonel, one Henry Platt, no more adept at campaigning that had been Ellis-Nanney. Of course, the Tories tried to make Lloyd George's opposition to the war the issue. A Platt leaflet gave four reasons to vote for Platt:

"1. BECAUSE he champions the rights of his own country.
2. BECAUSE he supports a Government which has given us good laws and better trade.
3. BECAUSE he will not allow the Blood and Treasure spent in the South African War to be sacrificed in vain.
4. BECAUSE his opponent has been on the enemy's side throughout the War, and has insulted the Generals and Soldiers of the Queen."[68]

Of the four reasons given to vote for Platt, three accused Lloyd George of treason. On the campaign trial, Lloyd George admitted that two out of three of his constituents did not agree with him on the issue of the war, but he said, it was an MP's duty to give his constituents honest advice, not to tell them exactly what they wanted to hear.

Enough of Lloyd George's constituents agreed with him to re-elect him, with 2,412 votes to Platt's 2,116. But the overall result was a resounding approval of the war. The Tories under Salisbury won 335 seats and Chamberlain's Liberal Unionists won sixty-seven, for a working majority of 402. The Liberals, now under the leadership of Sir Henry Campbell-Bannerman, won 183 seats. But Wales remained a Liberal bastion, awarding twenty-seven of its thirty-four seats to the Liberals.

The war in South Africa was not over. Defeated by overwhelming forces in the field, the Boers resorted to guerilla warfare. Lord Kitchener decided that the best way to defeat the guerillas was to deny them their bases of operations. Farms, fields, even entire villages were put to the torch. The homeless noncombatants, i.e. the elderly, the wives and the children of the Boer fighters were herded into concentration camps. The conditions in the camps were appalling, and they began to die by the thousands of disease (measles, influenza, typhoid, malaria) and malnutrition. Their suffering was used by the British as a military weapon. Wives and children of Boer fighters were placed on half-rations, but restored to full rations if their fighting husbands and fathers turned themselves in. As Lloyd George pointed out on the floor of the House of Commons, this policy gave the Boer fighters the option of watching their families starve if they continued fighting. The Liberal leader, Sir Henry Campbell-Bannerman, initially a lukewarm supporter of the war, decided he had had enough, asking: "When is a war not a war? When it is carried on by methods of barbarism in South Africa."[69] A *third* of the inmates in the camps died. The death rate among the children was *fifty percent*. By the war's end, 25,000 had died in the camps.

Safely re-elected, Lloyd George continued to flay the government. Speaking in Liverpool in November, 1900, he read a letter from a British officer: "We are disgusted with this job we have been put to—the pillaging of cattle, the burning of farms, and the turning of widows and children out in the veldt to starve." He asserted that the government was "engaged in a war the most hopeless of all wars—a war to destroy a nation...In attempting this impossible task we are making foes of this country in every land under the sun."[70]

He continued to speak out against the war throughout 1901. As the war dragged on, as the news of the concentration camps began to filter in with the casualty lists, his message began getting through. In a speech in Birkenhead he attacked Chamberlain's imperial policies. He noted that the countries within the Empire that were closest to Britain, such as Australia, were the freest. "We ought to give freedom everywhere— freedom in Canada...in Africa, in Wales, and in India. We will never govern India as it ought to be governed until we have given it freedom."[71] These sentiments were anathema to Chamberlain. He called people like Lloyd George "little Englanders."

Lloyd George had placed himself in danger before, but nothing approached the reception he received in Chamberlain's home base, Birmingham, on December 18, 1901. Lloyd George had accepted an invitation the previous summer from the local Liberal Association. It was to have been a meeting closed to all but the members of the Association. But the two pro-Chamberlain newspapers, *The Birmingham Daily Mail* and the *Birmingham Daily Post*, both editorialized that his appearance would spark a riot, thus encouraging it. He managed to arrive in the town unnoticed, and somehow managed his way into the hall. But between 30,000 and 200,000 supporters of the war surrounded the hall, with, as Lloyd George later put it, "intent to kill me."[72] There was no way to keep the rioters out. Soon they rushed the stage, armed with anything lethal they could find: sticks, bricks, knives, hammers. Every window in the hall was shattered, and the hall's glass dome began to give way. Just before the rioters could get their hands on him, a squadron of police hidden under the stage surged forward and confronted the rioters. The Chief Constable advised him that the only way he would get out of the hall alive was to disguise himself as a policeman. Ruefully, he complied. Two people, one of them a policeman, died in the riot. Forty were hurt.[73]

And then, to everyone's surprise, the war ended. The Boers had been defeated militarily and were ruined economically, but the British were exhausted. In The Treaty of Vereeniging entered into on May 31, 1902, the Boers received very favorable terms. The Boers who had taken up arms against the British Empire received a general amnesty. Afrikaans, the language of the Boers, could be taught in their schools. Great Britain even promised to give the Boers £3 million to rebuild their country. The Boers agreed to British *sovereignty*, but Transvaal and Orange Free State obtained a guarantee of *autonomy*. The blacks, coloureds and Asians, the majority in South Africa, got nothing.

The acceptance of British "sovereignty" meant nothing. By 1910, all four of the South African states, including Cape Colony and Natal, were united into a Union of South Africa, dominated by the Afrikaners. They would rule South Africa for most of the twentieth century, until 1994, when Nelson Mandela and his African National Congress would oust them for good. If, as Lord Milner believed, it had all been a "great game" to see who would control a united South Africa—the British or the Boers—the British had lost the game.

The Boer War made David Lloyd George a statesman respected for his foresight and his courage. But he would have to wait, with the rest of his fellow Liberals, before he could assume real power. Great Britain had gained nothing from the war except the approbrium of the civilized world. Worse, watchful eyes in Berlin and elsewhere noticed the inept generalship and the poor leadership. They saw how a ragtag band of farmers had held the British Empire at bay for three years. It was a lesson they would not forget.

Many years later, Lloyd George told his friend Lucy Masterman, herself a Liberal politician, diarist and author "On the Day of Judgment when I shall have to answer for my sins—and God knows I have enough to answer for—I shall say only one thing: 'Sir, I was pro-Boer' and they will let me in."[74]

6

EMBATTLED ACADEMIC

His friends loved him and his enemies hated him for the same reason,
namely his uncompromising adherence to his ideals.

—Edwin Grant Conklin

On June 9, 1902, nine days after the Treaty of Vereeniging ended the Boer War and one day prior to the day that Georges Clemenceau entered the French *Senat*, Woodrow Wilson became the thirteenth president of Princeton University.

Earlier that day, Francis Landey Patton had abruptly resigned as president. His fourteen-year reign had been one of drift and inactivity. Patton believed that the approximately twelve hundred undergraduates were incapable of serious study, and so felt no need to raise academic standards. Many came directly from the elite eastern boarding schools—Lawrenceville, St. Paul's, Andover and others. "Princeton is a rich man's college," he said, "It is better to have come and loafed than never to have come at all."[1] He boasted that he was the head of the finest country club in America.[2] There was hazing (one student was shot) and little discipline; Patton did not believe in it.

At its sesquicentennial in 1896, Princeton had renamed itself a "university," but in the six succeeding years under Patton it had made no progress toward that end. It had no law school and no medical school. Its graduate school consisted of approximately forty graduate students, with no place to house them. Princeton in 1902, far from being a "university," was a sleepy country college held in low esteem by the rest of academia.

In 1900, in order to assure that there might one day actually be a graduate school, Princeton's trustees named Andrew Fleming West, a professor of Latin, as the dean of the almost-non-existent graduate school. He was to report directly to the trustees, circumventing the drowsy president Patton. West was given complete authority over admissions, fellowships and curricula. Graduate students paid their tuition directly to his bursar's office. But West's independent little fiefdom would present a problem when there was a president of Princeton more activist than Patton and jealous of his authority.

By 1902, the trustees and faculty—including Prof. Wilson—were in open revolt against Patton. Wilson had said that "Our president does not bother us by having a mistaken policy, he daunts us by having no will or policy at all."[3] But it was West who led the revolt. Patton saw the handwriting on the wall. He knew that if he did not resign, he would be ousted. Rather than fight, he secured for himself a satisfactory golden parachute (and the presidency of the Princeton Theological Seminary) and resigned. He recommended Wilson as his successor. That same day, the twenty-six trustees of Princeton University, disregarding their own bylaws that required them to wait at least one day, unanimously elected Wilson as president. He was the first president in Princeton's 156-year history who was not a Presbyterian minister. The *New York Times* editorialized: "The new president is a man of distinction. His political writings have already made him well known to the country as a man capable of clean straightforward thinking upon the problems of government, while his career as an educator testifies to his fitness for the new responsibility."[4]

He got to work. Armed with a secret power granted by the trustees to fire any professor he wanted gone, including tenured professors, he began to wield the ax. Lazy professors (one would regularly dismiss his class after thirty minutes), professors who could not teach, professors whose courses were not exacting enough, were asked to resign. To replace them, he began hiring professors, often raiding the faculties of other universities for talent. The first Catholic and the first Jewish faculty members were hired under Wilson. The fact that he did not have the authority to hire any professor without the consent of the trustees did not stand in his way; he simply arrogated the authority to himself, and the trustees acquiesced. He tightened entrance requirements. Wilson himself had been admitted to Princeton on little more than his father's acquaintance with President McCosh. Beginning in 1904, high school seniors (including those at the elite prep schools) had to take an entrance exam that included English, Latin, math, Greek and either French or German, the only concession being that advanced math could be substituted for Greek.[5] As a result, the dropout rate among freshmen declined.

He changed the curriculum, which under Patton had been a chaos of elective courses. Under Wilson, freshmen had no electives, sophomores few. Juniors and seniors were guided in the electives they were permitted to take. They could not be too focused, but they had to have a focus. He weeded out the "snap" or "gut" courses that lazy upperclassmen elected, although one of the notoriously easy courses was the one taught by Wilson himself. He reorganized the university into separate departments, hiring young department heads, and delegated to them the authority to fire deadwood professors. Some things did not change. No women and no blacks were admitted during his presidency. Mandatory chapel attendance remained mandatory.

Wilson was formally installed as president on the morning of October 25, 1902, in the 900-seat Romanesque Alexander Hall, built to house the annual commencement exercises. Every seat was filled. The presidents and deans of scores of colleges and universities marched in two-by-two, resplendent in their academic robes, Harvard in crimson, Oxford in scarlet, Yale in blue, and, of course, all those from Princeton in orange and black. The guests included ex-President Grover Cleveland, now a resident of Princeton and a trustee, Booker T. Washington, Mark Twain with his shock of white hair, Thomas B. Reed, ex-speaker of the House of Representatives, William Dean Howells, J. Pierpont Morgan and Robert T. Lincoln, son of the late president. Wilson was introduced, and the audience rose as one, cheered for eight minutes, ignoring Wilson's appeals for them to stop.

Wilson spoke that day of "Princeton for the Nation's Service." He insisted that it is the duty of American universities to prepare well-rounded, liberally-educated men, not technocrats. These men should be more than "excellent servants of a trade or skilled practitioners of a profession." They should have "elasticity of faculty and breadth of vision."[6] Tucked in the speech was a mention of his intention to build a graduate college. He was specific as to *where* it was to be built: "We shall build it, not apart, but as nearly as may be at the very heart, the geographical heart, of the university..."[7] There were powerful men seated about him who would oppose that vision.

One anonymous attendee commented on Wilson's speech: "He spoke without the slightest effort in a voice as clear as any bell. Both his enunciation and pronunciation were perfection...I was delighted with the man and the speech." He could not remember, however, exactly what Wilson had said.[8]

There was one man in the audience who *The New York Times* did not list among the dignitaries, and who probably went unnoticed by most of the attendees. He was Col. George Brinton McClellan Harvey, the forty-two-year-old journalist and owner of the *North American Review* and editor of *Harper's Weekly*. (The "Col." was an honorific bestowed upon him by a former governor of New Jersey.) He had no connection with Princeton and was there that day as the guest of a friend. When Wilson finished speaking, Harvey thought to himself that this man could be president…of the United States. That night, he read everything that Wilson had ever published, not finishing until past midnight. More than anyone other than Wilson himself, Harvey would be responsible for making the idea of a Wilson presidency a reality.

Three days prior to his formal inauguration, Wilson delivered his first written report to the trustees. It did not make for pleasant reading. Wilson reported that the condition of Princeton was "critical," that it was effectively broke, relying on annual subsidies from wealthy alumni to stay afloat. The faculty was overworked and underpaid. The departments of biology, history and economics were particularly weak. The "lecture" system, by which students attended lectures in large lecture halls, taking notes, and then regurgitating those notes on final exams, had "failed," especially in the social sciences. Princeton, which in its first 150 years had amassed an endowment of $3 million, now needed $6 million. If Princeton was to be the university that it had advertised itself to be since 1896, it needed to build a graduate school, a law school, a school of electrical engineering and a museum of natural history. To do that would take an *additional* $6 million. "Without these things," he wrote, "we are not doing honestly what we advertise in our catalogue."[9]

Early in his administration, someone asked Wilson how many students there were at Princeton. "About ten percent," he replied. He now proposed to fix the failed lecture system, in which students "slept, poked each other, or fidgeted until the instructor called on them," in an atmosphere that was "torpor mixed with terror."[10] Wilson believed that the lecture system treated the students like "thoughtless boys performing tasks." He wanted to transform them into "thinking men," and in a December, 1902 speech in New York to the Princeton alumni, he laid out his vision to achieve that end.

Wilson proposed a tutorial system, soon to be renamed the *preceptorial* system, where young scholars—*preceptors*—would guide the studies of the undergraduates in their charge. A typical course that now required three weekly hours of lecture would henceforth be two hours of lecture and one hour of informal conference with the preceptor. The preceptors would be the "companions and coaches and guides of the men's reading."[11] They would not give exams or grade their charges, which their professors would continue to do. The preceptors would provide reading lists to encourage further reading, all with the goal of having the students *educate themselves*. Wilson told the alumni that night, "[N]o man is a man who receives his knowledge by instruction from somebody else…a man is a man who receives his instruction by his own efforts and inquiries."[12] The preceptorial system was intended to be one of "reading, comparing, reflecting; not cramming, but daily, methodical study."[13] He added that if he could find fifty qualified preceptors he could transform Princeton into "a place where there are men doing thinking, men who are conversing about the things of thought, men who are eager and interested in the things of thought..." When he said that he did not believe that Princeton students should work all the time, there were shouts of "Right! Good!" from the alumni. But he quickly added: "I am not going to propose that we compel the undergraduates to work all the time, but I am going to propose that we want to make the undergraduates want to work all the time."[14]

Wilson once remarked that he would rather have just one scholarly student enrolled than a thousand regular men.[15] The ideal student that Wilson proposed to forge through the preceptorial system was, of course, "Tommy" Wilson himself, the undergraduate who educated himself, who read prodigiously on his own, keeping detailed reading lists, who complained that there were not enough history classes offered, and who published scholarly articles while still an upperclassman. If Princeton hired fifty preceptors, it would double Princeton's faculty. And for a university whose endowment was only $3 million, Wilson advised the alumni that to hire and pay the preceptors, he would need $2.25 million. This produced whistles from the alumni, each of whom knew that he proposed to get the money from them. "And then, gentlemen, in order to do these other things which I have dreamed of, we shall need a great deal more than two million and a quarter."[16]

Wilson was able to hire the fifty preceptors. He found young men scattered through academia, and invited them to visit Princeton. One of the preceptors Wilson hired was Yale English professor Robert K. Root, who years later remembered: "Before five minutes had passed I knew I was in the presence of a very great man...Had Woodrow Wilson asked me to go with him and work under him while he inaugurated a new university in Kamchatka or Senegambia I would have said 'yes' without further question."[17] Another preceptor Wilson recruited, political scientist Edward S. Corwin, remembered his interview, Wilson being "cordial with a touch of reserve but not of condescension; his utterance was singularly beautiful and imparted distinction to his words."[18] Corwin would spend the next forty-one years at Princeton.

There was no opposition to the preceptorial system from the trustees or the faculty. Even Dean West, who knew that the preceptorial system would delay the construction of the graduate college, supported the plan. By 1906, Wilson's vision was in operation, the *New York Evening Post* commenting that Wilson "has ruined what was universally agreed to be the most agreeable and aristocratic country club in America by transforming it into an institution of learning."[19] But in practice the vision was flawed. One undergraduate complained that as a result of the preceptorial system Princeton was not the place it used to be, that "men were actually talking about their studies…" but most of the criticisms came from the preceptors themselves. In order to adequately guide each student, each preceptor had to read everything that each student might read, amounting to thousands of pages. Truly motivated students who might wish to pursue graduate studies chafed under the system; it did not allow for sufficient specialization. The "minimum" reading list that preceptors gave to their students quickly became the "maximum" list. The library did not see a substantial increase in the books undergraduates were checking out, indicating that the system did not encourage independent reading. Most importantly, the system whereby preceptors could not grade their students simply did not work. The system was modified; preceptors could test and grade their students. But they ceased to be their "guides" and "friends" and became their adversaries.

In 1917, the Princeton faculty appointed a committee of its own to study the preceptorial system. Its report, "Twelve Years of the Preceptorial Method of Instruction" was generally favorable. Prior to the inauguration of the system, lecturers and students "were to all intents and purposes strangers to one another."[20] Before the inauguration of the system, a student could pass most courses by cramming the night before the final exam. Under the preceptorial system, students were required to actually read Shakespeare, rather than listen to a professor lecture about Shakespeare. One alumnus summed it up: "I would exchange nothing else that I got out of Princeton for the mental hunger I got—and retain—from those informal preceptorial hours in professors' libraries."[21]

The doubling of the faculty reduced the teacher-student ratio which, if nothing else, improved the quality of education at Princeton. In one form or another, the system was copied by scores of other colleges and universities. Wilson's preceptorial vision, albeit flawed, may have been his greatest achievement at Princeton.

Wilson was a favorite of the students throughout his tenure at Princeton. He was open and accessible. His course in Jurisprudence and Politics was so popular that it had to be moved to a larger auditorium to accommodate the juniors and seniors who elected it. But an incident occurred in the fall of 1904 that dented his popularity, and revealed the fiber of the man the students were dealing with.

Princeton provided its president with a residence, "Prospect," which in the early part of the twentieth century abutted a large open field. By 1904, a trolley line connecting Trenton to Princeton had been completed. Tourists could now easily day-trip to and from Trenton. To Wilson's horror, couples were using the field behind Prospect for "necking." (Wilson's three daughters were then 19, 18 and 16). During the summer of 1904, Wilson had a permanent iron fence built around Prospect. When the students returned from summer vacation on September 24, they immediately realized that Wilson's fence ran down one side of their beloved, elm tree-lined McCosh Walk, which to this day remains one of the lovelier walkways in all of academia.

The fence became an immediate sensation on campus. The more the students talked, the more they talked of tearing it down. Edward H. Hilliard was then the editor-in-chief of The *Daily Princetonian.22* He believed that a statement from the much-respected Wilson was all that was needed to defuse the situation. He requested and was granted an interview with Wilson. He asked if Wilson would make a statement explaining the need for the fence. To his surprise, Wilson refused, saying words to the effect that when a man is right, he needed no explanation. During the night of September 30, students tore down huge sections of the fence. (One of whom may have been Eugene O'Neill, then (briefly) a Princeton undergraduate.) Wilson ordered the sections replaced. Saturday, October 8, was the day of the annual Senior Parade, where every senior marched in costume. Some dressed as tramps, some as frogs, one dressed as Carrie Nation, and, in full view of president Wilson, ten seniors dressed as—the fence! Each was in black gown, black mask, with a long pointed black hat. They were chained together, and formed a square, representing the entire square fence. They carried a sign: "Picket Lane, formerly McCosh Walk." In their midst they wheeled a cart, and in the cart was a live pig. Legend has it that the pig carried a sign: "Hogging the Campus."

Eventually the portion of the fence abutting McCosh Walk came down, with the face-saving announcement that the Grounds and Buildings Committee had constructed the fence without Wilson's knowledge. The incident would have been forgotten if Wilson had made a conciliatory statement. But he could not. When a man is right, he needs no explanation. The ten seniors dressed as the fence had hurt Wilson, and the hurt did not heal. Many years later, one of Wilson's daughters was introduced to Norman Thomas, the great Socialist leader. He mentioned in passing that he had graduated Princeton in 1905. "Oh," she replied, "that was the class that was so cruel to father."

George Brinton McClellan Harvey (1864-1928) was born in the tiny town of Peacham, Vermont. At eighteen, he got a job as a cub reporter for the *Springfield Republican*.

By the age of twenty-six, he was the insurance commissioner of New Jersey. While in New Jersey, he dabbled in politics, rounding up support for Grover Cleveland. At twenty-eight, he was the managing editor of Joseph Pulitzer's *New York World*. Along the way, he saw the future in urban street railways, invested heavily, and made a large enough fortune to buy the influential *North American Review*. In 1901, he bought *Harper's Weekly*. In October, 1902, he was seated in Alexander Hall when he decided that the new president of Princeton could be the next president of the United States.

He did nothing to achieve that goal (not even informing Wilson of the goal) until the evening of February 3, 1906. That night, Wilson was the guest of honor at the Lotos Club in Manhattan, a social club of journalists, artists and business people. Wilson made his usual well-received remarks. When he finished, Harvey rose from his seat. He had prepared his extended toast to Wilson, which included:

> "One who reads understandingly the record of his country as set down by him (Wilson) cannot fail to be impressed with the belief that he is by instinct a statesman. The complete grasp of fundamentals, the seemingly unconscious application of primary truths to changing conditions, the breadth of thought and reason manifested on the pages of his books..."

> "If one could be found who should unite in his personality, in addition to these qualities, the instinct of true statesmanship, as the effect of early environment and the no less valuable capacity of practical application as the result of subsequent endeavors in another field, the ideal would be at hand. Such a man it is my firm belief, and I venture earnestly to insist, is to be found in Woodrow Wilson of Virginia and New Jersey."

> "As one of a considerable number of Democrats who have become tired of voting Republican tickets, it is with a sense almost of rapture that I contemplate even the remotest possibility of casting a ballot for the president of Princeton University to become President of the United States."[23]

Later that evening, Wilson penned a short note of thanks to Harvey: "It was most delightful to have such thoughts uttered about me, whether they were deserved or not, and I thank you with all my heart."[24]

Harvey had just begun. He put Wilson on the cover of the March 10, 1906 issue of *Harper's Weekly*, reprinted his Lotos Club remarks, and wrote an editorial on why Wilson would make a good president. The April and May, 1906 issues quoted favorable newspaper comment from across the country regarding Wilson's "candidacy." The influential *Literary Digest* of April 14 quoted Harvey calling Wilson a statesman of "...breadth, depth and exceptional sagacity; an idealist who, at the same time, shall be exceptionally sane, " adding: "Is it not a fact that all Northern Democrats, all Independents, and many large-minded Republicans are convinced that the time has come to make a Southern man Chief Magistrate?"[25]

At that time, it was assumed that the Republican candidate in 1908 would be President Roosevelt, who was eligible for another term. It was also likely that William Jennings Bryan, who firmly controlled his party, would be able to resist anyone's attempt to wrest the Democratic nomination from him. Although professing no interest in seeking the presidency, Wilson was not hiding either. On April 16, Wilson was the keynote speaker at the annual Democratic Jefferson Day dinner in New York. Ostensibly speaking on Jefferson, he outlined where he stood politically, which was to the right of Roosevelt and Bryan: "[W]e shall reject, as we would reject poison itself, the prescriptions of Socialism...Thomas Jefferson's creed was a creed of individualism, not of Socialism."[26] Distancing himself from Roosevelt: "What are we struggling for now? To curb the power of corporations because we do not believe in corporations? No, I think not..."[27] Contrary to Roosevelt's aggressive regulation of trusts, Wilson believed that men who Roosevelt termed "the malefactors of great wealth" should be prosecuted, but the corporations themselves should not be regulated: "[W]e do not need more laws, but we do need laws which shall find the men."[28] He would return to this theme again and again in the next two years. As always, the speech was repeatedly interrupted by applause. The mayor of New York, George McClellan, later sent Wilson a note: "It was the clearest and most forceful and eloquent oration that it has been my good fortune to hear in many a day."[29]

On May 28, 1906, Wilson awoke completely blind in his left eye, and his right hand was numb. His close friend, Prof. John Grier Hibben, took him to Philadelphia, where he was examined by an ophthalmologist, Dr. George de Schweinitz, who found that the blindness had been caused by the bursting of a blood vessel in his eye. His vision returned, but his eye would be permanently impaired.[30] We now know that Wilson had suffered another stroke. He would suffer yet another in December, 1907, manifested by numbness in his shoulder and arm.

We cannot know with any degree of certainty if and to what extent these strokes affected Wilson's personality, his conduct or his abilities. Dean West believed that Wilson's hostility towards him spiked immediately after the 1906 stroke. Prof. William

Magie also believed that Wilson changed markedly after 1906.[31] We do know that in the spring on 1906 Wilson was at the height of his popularity, considered Princeton's principal asset. We also know that Wilson's defeats as president—largely self-inflicted—occurred after 1906.

In the last decade of the nineteenth century and the first decade of the twentieth there arose at Princeton a number of upperclass eating clubs. Unlike college fraternities (president McCosh had banned fraternities at Princeton decades earlier), they served mainly as dining facilities; students could not room there. They had billiard rooms, lounges and capacious porches where members could luxuriate. Like many college fraternities, they were exclusive; a student needed to prove that he was socially acceptable to be admitted. The clubhouses, one more opulent than the next, stood like fortresses along Prospect Avenue: "Colonial," "Tiger Inn," and others on one side, "Quadrangle," "Ivy," "Cottage," and "Cap & Gown" on the other. Every June, during Commencement, returning alumni would be feted by their clubs, and alumni and upperclassmen would toast those lucky sophomores who had been tapped for admission. (Freshmen were not permitted to so much as set foot on Prospect Avenue.) By 1906, there were thirteen clubs (eight of which were less than twelve years old), and three-fourths of Princeton upperclassmen belonged to one or another. Many of the unlucky "unclubbables" who had not been selected considered the stigma to be so great that they withdrew from Princeton entirely. Sophomore clubs (known as "hat lines" for their distinctive hat bands) were formed for the sole purpose of moving their entire membership into one club or another. Freshman clubs were formed for the purpose of getting their members into the sophomore "hat lines." By 1906, almost everyone at Princeton—including the members of the eating clubs themselves—realized that the situation was completely out of control and cried out for reform.

As did their president. On December 13, 1906, Wilson submitted a "Supplementary Report"[32] to the Princeton trustees. He reviewed the current situation, noting that getting into a particular club was consuming many of the students. Wilson reminded the trustees that the democratic spirit that had prevailed when he and the trustees were undergraduates was being killed by the eating clubs. Worst, the eating clubs were "hostile to the spirit of study, incompatible with the principles of a true republic of letters and of learning." They were "a menace to the right guidance of our university growth."

The remedy that Wilson suggested was to abolish them. In their place, the students would live together in "colleges," along the lines of the colleges at Oxford and Cambridge. Each college would consist not only of a dining hall, but of a number of contiguous dormitories. A "master" would reside with the students, as would one or two of their bachelor preceptors, who would take their meals with the students. Each of the current eating clubs would meld into the different colleges. This presented a problem. The eating clubs owned their facilities. Integrating them into the new system would mean forcing them to either sell or cede them to the university. The "colleges" quickly became known as "quadrangles." Wilson's proposal became known as the "Quad Plan."

The trustees designated a committee of seven trustees to consider Wilson's plan; Wilson was its chairman. One of the trustees on the committee was Moses Taylor Pyne. Pyne, 51, was the largest benefactor in Princeton's history. Having inherited a fortune, he made it his life's work to promote Princeton, his alma mater. In 1884, at the age of twenty-eight, he had become a Princeton trustee. Unlike most trustees, he resided in Princeton. He was an honorary member of twelve of the eating clubs lining Prospect Avenue.

Shortly after the December 13 meeting, President Cleveland, a trustee but not a member of the committee appointed to study the proposal, voiced his concern that implementing the Quad Plan would delay the construction of the Graduate College. Dean West felt the same. It was not a good omen. After the meeting, Wilson sailed off to Bermuda for a month's vacation.

On June 10, 1907, the committee submitted its "Report on the Social Coordination of the University"[33] to the trustees. Wilson had written the report himself, on his typewriter. He began his report by asserting that an "immediate" solution was necessary for the "health and progress" of Princeton, and the only solution was the Quad Plan. At length, he reviewed the evils of the eating clubs, the principal evil being that it cut the freshmen off from the sophomores and both from the upperclassmen. He reminded the trustees that students who failed to be admitted to any club often left the university in disgrace: "About one-third are left out of the elections; and their lot is little less than deplorable." The report concludes that the only way to correct these evils is: "the grouping of the undergraduates in residential quadrangles, each with its common room for intercourse and diversion, and its resident master and preceptors; where members of all four classes shall be associated in a sort of family life, not merely as neighbors in the dormitories but also as comrades at meals and in many daily activities."[34] The report ended with a proposed resolution of the Board: "Your Committee, therefore, recommend that the President of the University be authorized to take such steps as may seem wisest for maturing the general plan, and for seeking the cooperation and counsel of the upper-class clubs in its elaboration; and that this Committee be continued to consult with the President from time to time as the matter may take shape and as he may require further counsel and advice, and to mature detailed plans for the future consideration of this Board so soon as such plans can be perfected by common counsel among all concerned."[35]

After submitting the written report, Wilson rose from his seat and addressed the twenty-five trustees present. Standing to address his listeners was not unusual for Wilson. On occasion, even when addressing only three or four listeners in his private study, he would stand to address them. He began: "I have never had occasion, I probably never shall have occasion to lay a more important matter before you than the proposal contained in this report; and, full as that report is, I feel justified in detaining you to add some explanatory matter of my own."[36] He continued: "I have long foreseen the necessity of…drawing the undergraduates together in genuinely residential groups in direct association with members of the Faculty, as an indispensable accompaniment and completion of the preceptorial system and all of the other measures we have taken to quicken and mature the intellectual life of the University."[37] By the time Wilson sat down, more than one of the trustees believed that Wilson had delivered the speech of his life. They agreed, by a vote of 24-1, with President Cleveland joining the majority, to adopt the proposal. But what, exactly, had they agreed to? Had they agreed, as Wilson believed, to the Quad Plan, with only the details left to be filled in by Wilson, or had the trustees consented only to allow Wilson to proceed to develop a more definite plan, which Wilson would later submit to the trustees for their approval?

The trustees' meeting coincided with Commencement Week, when many of the New York-area alumni returned to Princeton, many of them to be feted by their eating clubs. It was just then that Wilson sent a circular to the eating clubs informing them that they would have to give up and become part of the quad system. The result was a firestorm of protest from the alumni. One alumnus wrote: "The autocratic manner in which the plan has been proposed has deeply hurt the feelings of the most loyal and devoted body of college alumni in America."[38] Another alumnus wrote that he had spoken to over a hundred alumni, none of whom supported the plan: "If you believe that any considerable body of the alumni, residing in or about the large cities is with you, you are greatly mistaken."[39] Yet another asked: "May I ask why this revolutionary scheme was suddenly and without warning sprung upon Princeton? It may be that the ideas of the Alumni are of little worth…I am confirmed in my original opinion that the adoption of the plan will be the destruction of Princeton."[40] Wilson had to admit that there had not been a "flood of commendatory letters" from the alumni.[41] Some of the alumni offered compromises, such as requiring the eating clubs to admit sophomores, or requiring the clubs to admit all applicants, or having the university create an all-university club. Moses Taylor Pyne suggested a small, experimental quad. Wilson rejected that too. It was all or nothing—now. "I can find no substitute," wrote Wilson.[42]

Wilson dug in, rejecting every proposed compromise. He wrote his friend and fellow classmate, the philanthropist Cleveland Dodge: "The fight is on, and I regard it, not as a fight for the development but as a fight for the restoration of Princeton. My heart is in it more than anything else, because it is a scheme of salvation."[43] Wilson's brother-in-law, Stockton Axson, then a professor at Princeton, later wrote that he had never seen Wilson "more stiffly bent and insistent on a project; he thought he might resign if it were not put through…he could not be interested in merely being the titular head of a college formed on lines which he could not believe in…"[44] Wilson's later press secretary and most loving biographer, Ray Stannard Baker, wrote of the quad fight: "Opposition was a challenge to battle, to be engaged with all the doggedness and zest of his Covenanter forbears."[45] "Opposition did not deter him; it convinced him."[46]

In taking the quad plan to the trustees, Wilson had failed to enlist—or even consult—the faculty. He sought to correct this error when, on September 26, 1907, Wilson chaired a meeting of the faculty called to discuss the Quad Plan. He was, as usual, at his oratorical best: "I beg of you to follow me in this hazardous but splendid adventure."[47] A motion, written by Wilson, was presented supporting the Quad Plan. Just then, Prof. Henry Van Dyke presented his motion, which merely called for the faculty to investigate the social conditions of the University with the view to promoting the "unity, democracy and scholarly life of the undergraduates." Wilson, in the chair, asked if anyone seconded Van Dyke's motion. Wilson purportedly turned pale when his great friend, Prof. John Grier Hibben, rose and seconded the motion. "Do I understand that Professor Hibben seconds the motion?" "I do, Mr. President," he replied.[48] The faculty voted to support the Quad Plan, 80 to 23. Forty-nine of the eighty votes in favor came from the preceptors.

But the damage had been done. "Jack" Hibben had been Wilson's closest friend in the world. Hibben was a Presbyterian minister who, like, Wilson, was of Scots descent. The Wilsons and the Hibbens socialized together frequently. When Wilson awoke blind in his left eye, it had been Jack Hibben that he turned to to take him to the ophthalmologist in Philadelphia. That friendship was now ended, forever. When Wilson later resigned as president of Princeton, the man chosen to succeed him was none other than Jack Hibben. Of course, Wilson was invited to Hibben's inauguration. He declined.

John Grier Hibben was not the only faculty member who opposed the Quad Plan. Dean West wrote Wilson of his opposition not only to the merits of the plan but of the arbitrary manner in which Wilson had pushed it: "If the spirit of Princeton is to be killed, I have little interest in the details of the funeral."[49] West was very close to Grover Cleveland, and Cleveland was becoming uneasy about the Quad Plan. But nothing was more detrimental to Wilson's hopes for the Quad Plan than the opposition of Moses Taylor Pyne, who came to believe that the plan was "Utopian." On October 17, with only one trustee dissenting, the trustees, having heard the howls of the alumni, voted to rescind their June 10 resolution supporting the Quad Plan.

After the defeat, Wilson considered resigning. He thought he might go back to Virginia to practice law. He drafted a letter of resignation, but never sent it.

Throughout the fight over the Quad Plan, George Harvey continued to harbor hopes that Wilson might be the Democrats' nominee in 1908. Harvey's job was made difficult because no one knew what Wilson believed. In August, 1907, Harvey urged Wilson to outline his political beliefs. Wilson did so in a "Credo." In it he made clear that he was the conservative antithesis of the activist in the White House, Theodore Roosevelt. He believed that the "great trusts and combinations" were necessary as the "most convenient and efficient instrumentalities of modern business." To the extent that these trusts produced evils, the evils could not be remedied through direct regulation. He wrote that there was a danger to "governing the people overmuch [which] are sure in the long run to slacken the energy of private enterprise."[50] Astoundingly, he wrote that "The Constitution guarantees to every man the right to sell his labor to whom he pleases for such price as he is willing to accept."[51] Of course, this view would render unconstitutional any attempt by the federal government to enact minimum wage laws or to otherwise regulate working conditions and wages. The "Credo" was music to the ears of Col. Harvey and his business friends everywhere.

In late November, 1907, Wilson granted an extended interview to a reporter for the *New York Times Magazine*, who visited him at his home in Princeton. The article that followed, "Dr. Woodrow Wilson Defines Material Issues" featured a portrait of Wilson on the cover of the magazine. The *Times* reporter was very much taken by Wilson, "as he sat in his office chair, erect, alert, alive in every degree of a man's best conception of republican ideals."[52] Far from "defining" "material issues," Wilson fed the reporter a large helping of empty platitudes and clichés: "Morality is a tremendous force in the impetus of American prosperity, and it is due to this impulse of the American people that we are passing through a crisis, a struggle for its supremacy in the affairs of the nation." And: "We are a people with a gift of foresight, but we have fallen into a bad habit of making rash promises, not because we make these promises fraudulently, but because we have a mania for quick results."

Wilson insisted that he was not running for any public office, and lest readers might assume that he was running for office, he refused to state his opinions on any particular issue. But he did venture that he had "specific objections" to Bryan, "political propositions in his platform that I consider absurd," but he refused to specify which "political propositions," lest his intentions be misinterpreted. "No matter how humble my prospects, I should still be accused of political intention if I went into these matters." He could not resist taking a swipe at Roosevelt: "I am told that he no sooner thinks that he talks, which is a miracle not wholly in accord with an educational theory of forming an opinion."

The quad fight now over, Wilson hit the speaking trail. In Nashville in November, he told his audience that what the country needed was "disinterested leadership—leadership of men who do not represent particular interests of any kind...who can be trusted to act only upon knowledge after sufficient investigation make them definite and sure of their object." The next morning's *Nashville Tennessean* described Wilson as "today a more or less receptive candidate for a presidential nomination, which he is not going to get."[53]

Speaking in Indianapolis in December, he explicitly distanced himself from Roosevelt. He said that he did not trust either the Republican party, "to which I do not belong," or the Democratic Party, "to which I suppose I belong but would like to be allowed to trust."[54] Aiming directly at Roosevelt, he stated: "A great political party is trying to fool the people of the United States with a perfectly futile program of reform," adding, "there has never been a country so drunk with confidence in legislation as in this country. When we want anything all we think we have to do is go into the legislative halls and get a bill passed." The country was then in one of its periodic recessions ("The Panic of 1907"). Wilson blamed it on Roosevelt and "the aggressive attitude of legislation toward the railroads that made it impossible for them to borrow money."[55] He blamed the Interstate Commerce Commission, created for the purpose of equalizing railroad rates, with having "done much to impede the progress of transportation." In August, an Illinois federal judge, Kenesaw M. Landis (later to be the first commissioner of baseball), fined Standard Oil of Indiana $29,240,000 (the largest criminal fine in history) after a jury had found it guilty of paying illegal kickbacks. Wilson counseled Standard Oil not to pay it, on the ground that if it did so it would remove the money from circulation, thus hurting the economy.

Neither Wilson nor anyone else could deny Bryan the Democratic nomination in 1908. Col. Harvey went to Denver, the site of the convention, to drum up support. Wilson was vacationing at the time in Scotland. Harvey told Wilson to stay near a telegraph, just in case. So Wilson decamped himself in Edinburgh. Wilson wrote that he felt silly waiting for a call that he knew would never come.

Andrew Fleming West (1853-1943) and Woodrow Wilson were alike in many ways. Both were the sons of Presbyterian ministers. Both were Princeton alumni. Both believed in a classical education; they knew little and cared less for science. Both had traveled to Oxford and Cambridge, and both had fallen in love with the Gothic architecture and the enclosed quadrangles "full of quiet chambers, secluded ancient courts, and gardens shut away from intrusion…for those who would learn and be with their own thoughts."[56] They shared a total devotion to Princeton.

But they were different men. West was not a distinguished scholar. He had written a Latin grammar text for high school students, and had served as the principal of a New Jersey high school. The doctorate Princeton had awarded him was an *honorary* degree. West and Wilson had first crossed swords in 1897, when both were still Princeton professors. Wilson pressed hard for the hiring of the historian Frederick Jackson Turner, whose essay "The Significance of the Frontier in American History" had caused a sensation among historians. West opposed Turner, on the ground that Turner was a Unitarian. President Patton, who preferred to hire Princeton alumni and their relatives, sided with West. Turner would teach for twenty years at Wisconsin and twelve at Harvard.

They were different temperamentally. Wilson did not make friends easily. Due in large part to the fact that West's wife had been institutionalized with mental illness, West led a bachelor's life. He socialized constantly, made friends quickly, and maintained his friendships. When in 1896 Patton decided to pull out all the stops in planning the sesquicentennial celebration, Patton turned to West. The three-day extravaganza that West mounted was a brilliant success. It so charmed Grover Cleveland, then about to leave office, that he decided to retire to Princeton. West found him a house near the campus, which Cleveland named "Westland." In 1900, the trustees appointed West as dean of the graduate school, with complete authority over its operations. Cleveland was elected a university trustee, and later became chairman of the trustees' committee on the graduate school. West and Cleveland were now an alliance.

West was dean of a graduate school that still had no place to house its students. West was not shy about what the graduate college, once built, would look like: oak interiors, vaulted ceiling, Gothic windows: "Every evening the entire college is to dine in hall, the students seated at two or three long tables running lengthwise, and the professors and visitors at the high table under the western window."[57] West admitted that he believed that the "cultural" side of a man's character was as important as the intellectual side, and the "cultural" side could best be fostered by a "club-like" atmosphere.[58] That atmosphere, West came to believe, could best be achieved by a graduate college physically apart from the undergraduates and their crazy antics. West may have forgotten that in Wilson's inaugural address he had made specific reference to the construction of a graduate college within the campus, with the specific goal of having the graduates interact with the undergraduates. If West had forgotten, Wilson had not.

In the fall of 1906, West was offered the presidency of the Massachusetts Institute of Technology, an offer that included a substantial increase in pay. On one level, West was a curious choice, since he knew nothing about science or technology. On the practical level, it was brilliant. West was a prodigious fundraiser. (The undergraduates nicknamed him "Andy three millions West" in honor of his fundraising abilities.) He made the offer public. On October 16, at a meeting in Cleveland's home in which Wilson was present, West stated his reasons for considering the offer. He had been made the dean of the graduate school in 1900, but there was no graduate school. West and Cleveland both believed that when Wilson announced the Quad Plan, he had reneged on a promise to give the graduate college precedence. West said that he did not want to be identified with a failing effort. But there was more. Facing Wilson, West said "I have not hit it off with you."[59] When Wilson pressed him for details, West spent the next half hour detailing all of the slights that West felt Wilson had inflicted on him. According to West, Wilson could only respond: "I am bound to say you have a remarkable memory."[60]

The next day, at Wilson's insistence, Princeton's trustees passed a resolution asking West to stay. The resolution also stated: "The Board has particularly counted upon him to put into operation the Graduate College which it has planned." West now thought that his plan for the graduate college had been approved. He declined MIT's offer. Asking Andrew Fleming West to stay on at Princeton would prove to be the biggest mistake Wilson would make at Princeton. West's idea for a graduate college composed of gentlemen removed from the Princeton campus was incompatible with Wilson's democratic ideals.

The beginning of Wilson's undoing as the president of Princeton occurred in January, 1907, when a $250,000 bequest to Princeton from Josephine Thomson Swann was announced. Mrs. Swann's will specified that the bequest was to build The John R. Thomson Graduate College, in memory of her late husband, and that the college was to be built "on the grounds" of the Princeton campus. On the face of it, Wilson had won. If Princeton wished to build the graduate college with Mrs. Swann's money, it would have to be situated "on the grounds" of Princeton, and not on some locale remote from the rest of Princeton. West seemed to accept this. Architects were engaged, and plans were drawn, for a graduate college on Prospect Avenue, an easy walk from Wilson's home.

But West was not finished. Years before, when West had been teaching school in Cincinnati, he had befriended William Cooper Procter (1862-1934), the heir to half of Procter & Gamble, the manufacturers of Ivory Soap. In May, 1909, West (*not* Wilson) received a letter from Procter, in which Procter offered $500,000 to build a graduate college, provided that an additional $500,000 be raised from other sources by May, 1910. Procter's letter stated: "I have visited the proposed site at Prospect…it is not suitable for such a College…[T]his offer is made upon the further understanding that some other site be chosen, which shall be satisfactory to me."[61]

West soon made it clear where was the site "satisfactory" to him. Approximately one mile southwest of the Princeton campus lay a series of golf links, which remains to this day as the Springdale Golf Course. The site of the clubhouse, west of the golf links themselves, was perfect for Procter. And for West. There, with Procter's money, West would build his dream of a graduate college, where gentlemen would congregate for dinner beneath the cathedral ceiling as the organ intoned Latin hymns, far removed from the raucous undergraduates. The graduate college would also have a great Gothic tower in honor of Grover Cleveland, who had died in 1908.

But what of Mrs. Swann's bequest, which specified that *her* bequest be limited to the construction of a graduate college "on the grounds" of Princeton? It so happened that in 1904, after Mrs. Swann's will was drawn but before her death, Princeton had acquired the golf links! Did Swann's proposed site qualify as being "on the grounds"? The attorneys for the executors of Mrs. Swann's will were consulted, and they concluded that Mrs. Swann's will did permit construction on the golf links, now "on the grounds" of Princeton. There was nothing that prevented the use of Mrs. Swann's bequest *and* Procter's gift to build the graduate college on the golf links. Woodrow Wilson opposed it. He believed that West's idea for a graduate college would make it nothing more than a "great big upper class club."[62] He believed that using the Swann bequest to build on the golf links would violate the spirit, if not the letter, of her will. The fight was on. He wrote his friend Mary Peck that he was a "Scots-Irishman who will not be conquered."[63]

Just as with the fight over the Quad Plan, the fight over the graduate college caught the attention of the alumni, who were, by and large, incredulous that this was even an issue, which one alumnus characterized as "Where shall we build a boardinghouse for graduates?" One alumnus, reflecting the views of most, wrote in the *Princeton Alumni Weekly*: "I have no opinion on the site question…and cannot understand how such a tempest has been raised over it."[64] They directed their ire at Wilson. Ominously, another alumnus wrote: "[i]f this tendency to 'look a gift horse in the mouth' is not immediately and permanently suppressed, the list of the benefactors of Princeton in the future will be a very small one."[65]

On October 20, Wilson met with Procter, in an attempt to win him over. Procter remained adamant; it was the golf links or nothing. On the next day, Princeton's trustees voted 14-10 to accept Procter's offer. One of the trustees voting in favor was Moses Taylor Pyne.

In late December, Wilson met with Procter again in New York. This time, Wilson offered a "compromise." He suggested that Princeton erect two graduate colleges, one with Mrs. Swann's bequest on the Princeton campus, and the other with Procter's gift on the golf links. It was an absurd proposal, with no chance of being accepted. On December 22, seated in the train station following his meeting with Procter, Wilson penned a letter to "Momo" Pyne. He wrote that the acceptance of the Procter offer had taken control of the university out of his hands. He ended the letter: "I seem to have come to the end."[66] Pyne returned his letter immediately, urging Wilson to stay calm. But in a letter dated Christmas Day, Wilson responded to Pyne: "I cannot accede to the acceptance of gifts upon terms which take the educational policy of the University out of the hands of the Trustees and Faculty and permit it to be determined by those who give the money."[67] Of course, Wilson was concerned about *his* loss of control, not that of the trustees or the faculty. He concluded the letter by saying that the trustees had to choose between him and Procter's money. If they accepted the gift, he would resign. They could decide at the next regularly scheduled meeting of the board, January 13, 1910.

That day proved to be Wilson's worst at Princeton. He entered the meeting with a resolution he had drafted for the board, a resolution rejecting Procter's offer. But before he could present it, Pyne read a letter from Procter. In it, Procter stated that he would accept Wilson's "compromise" to build two graduate colleges, one on the golf links and one on the campus. Wilson was stunned. The *location* of the graduate college was not the issue, he said, and he blurted out: "If the graduate school is based on proper ideals, our faculty can make a success of it anywhere in Mercer County."[68] Now it was the trustees' turn to be stunned. If the location was not the issue, why had he opposed accepting Procter's gift? Wilson backtracked. He pulled out a copy of West's 1902 promotional book for the graduate college: "*Proposed Graduate College of Princeton University.*" "There, gentlemen, in that book is the real reason why the Procter gift must be declined. The book contains Professor West's ideals for the Graduate School. They are his personal ideals; they are not the ideals of Princeton University, and they are radically wrong. The fundamental difficulty with Mr. Procter's offer is that it is specifically intended to carry out the ideals of the book. A graduate school based on these ideals cannot succeed."[69] To which one of the trustees simply asked Wilson why, if the book was so contrary to Princeton's ideals, had Wilson written a highly commendatory preface to the book? Wilson lamely replied that he had written the preface before he had actually seen the book.

It got worse. One of the trustees asked why the compromise that Wilson himself had proposed was objectionable? Wilson replied that the compromise had been a mistake, and that "[T]he faculty…convinced me that the plan was impracticable and unwise."[70] If that were true, a trustee asked, why had he written to Pyne on December 25 that his compromise had the "hearty concurrence" of the faculty? He had no answer. The meeting ended inconclusively. A committee was appointed to attempt to meet with Procter. But January 13 was the end of Wilson's friendship with Pyne.

On February 6, at Pyne's urging, Procter withdrew his offer completely. One alumnus wrote for many in the pages of the *Princeton Alumni Weekly*: "The reason why Princeton is in peril is because there is in the mind of President Wilson an ideal conception for a University in Utopia which he is trying to materialize in Princeton," and that as a result of the withdrawal of Procter's offer, it left "Princeton bereft, through the unreason and Quixotic obstinacy of one man, of a complete Graduate School."[71] Pyne also urged West to resign as dean of the graduate school. Pyne was now working to force Wilson's resignation, which would be followed by Procter renewing his offer and the trustees reappointing West as dean.[72]

On February 14, Wilson sailed for Bermuda, and did not return until March 9. Usually, the easy-going pace and the soft breezes of Bermuda enabled Wilson to think clearly. He always returned from Bermuda refreshed and invigorated. But no one could have anticipated the speech that Wilson delivered on April 16.

He spoke extemporaneously to the Pittsburgh alumni, who must have thought they were listening to Bryan or Eugene Debs. Smarting from the fact that five of the six Presbyterian ministers on Princeton's board of trustees had opposed him on the graduate school fight, Wilson lashed out against all Protestant churches: "[They] are serving the classes and not the masses of the people…They serve certain strata, certain uplifted strata, but they are not serving the men whose need is dire. The churches have more regard for their pew rents than for men's souls…The colleges in this country are in the same danger. They are looking to the support of the classes; looking to the support of wealth; they are not looking to the service of the people at large…Where does the strength of the nation come from? From the conspicuous classes? Not at all. It comes from the great masses of the unknown, of the unrecognized men, whose powers are being developed by struggle, who will form their opinions as they progress in that struggle, and who will emerge with opinions which must rule." He then tied this to the graduate college struggle: "Will America tolerate the seclusion of graduate students? Will America tolerate the idea of having graduate students set apart?…Seclude a man, separate him from the rough and tumble of college life, from the contacts of every sort and condition of men, and you have done a thing which America will brand with its contemptuous disapproval." He concluded that America's political parties "are going to pieces," and that if America "loses her self-possession America will stagger like France through the field of blood before she again finds peace and prosperity under the leadership of men who understand their needs."[73] One attendee thought that Wilson looked "despondent and ill."[74]

Within a few short years, it would become apparent that the Pittsburgh speech marked a turning point in Wilson's intellectual life. To a degree that perhaps even Wilson himself did not then realize, his defeat of the Quad Plan and his imminent defeat in the graduate college struggle—defeats at the hands of wealth and privilege—had radicalized him. He was beginning to see for himself what life in America was really like.

But for now Wilson realized that the speech had been a disaster, telling friends that it had been a "stupid blunder." He wrote a letter to the *New York Evening Post* that was reprinted in the *Princeton Alumni Weekly*: "Sir: I do not need to tell you that the reports of my recent address in Pittsburgh have, by piecemeal quotation, conveyed an entirely false impression."[75] Wilson failed to mention in his letter that he had reviewed and edited the text of the speech before it was printed.

Ever since July 1, 1909, Andrew Fleming West had held a trump card, but he couldn't play that trump until May 18, 1910, the day that Isaac C. Wyman, a wealthy octogenarian, died in Salem, Massachusetts. Wyman had graduated from Princeton in 1848. Wyman's father had fought with General Washington at the Battle of Princeton, on the same grounds that Procter's proposed graduate college stood. When Wyman's will—dated July 1, 1909—was read, it was revealed that Wyman, a lifelong bachelor, had bequeathed the bulk of his entire estate, which it was assumed might top out at $10 million, for the purpose of building a graduate college at Princeton University. The will did not specify the site of the graduate college. It didn't need to. The will gave complete discretion over the disposition of the bequest to Wyman's two named executors, John M. Raymond, Esq., the attorney who had drafted the will, and…Andrew Fleming West. Raymond had drafted the will, but the man who convinced Wyman to make the bequest was "Andy three millions West."

And with that, the fight over the location of the graduate college was over. When Wilson heard of Wyman's bequest, he remarked to Ellen: "We've beaten the living, but we can't fight the dead. The game's up."[76] On June 6, Procter renewed his offer, which was immediately accepted. Wilson agreed to accept the gift, on the ground that so much money was now available for additional fellowships and professorships, that it didn't matter where the graduate college was located. The Wyman bequest, the Swann bequest and Procter's gift all went towards construction of the graduate college on the grounds of the golf course. Completed in 1913, the ornate Gothic structure features the 173-foot Cleveland Tower. Later, a road was cut making it easier for students to walk from the graduate college to the main campus. A student taking that short walk today might wonder what the fuss was all about.

Just as Wilson's presidency at Princeton was disintegrating, his political prospects were brightening. After Col. Harvey failed to get the 1908 presidential nomination for Wilson, he determined that the best way to wrest the 1912 nomination would be for Wilson to be elected governor of New Jersey in 1910.

The path to the Democratic nomination led through the biggest New Jersey boss, James Smith, Jr. (1851-1927). Smith was the archetype of the nineteenth century urban political boss. Starting out as a clerk in his father's grocery, he entered politics as a local alderman, rising to become the boss of Essex County (Newark). He later acquired the *New Jersey Northern Star* and the *Evening Star.* He branched out into leather manufacturing and banking. He had served one term as a United States Senator from 1893 to 1899, but had declined to run for a second term. He now contemplated returning to the Senate. Charming and accessible, seated at the front desk of the Federal Trust Company in Newark, he was always ready to do a favor.[77] It is said that there was never a day when he did not attend a funeral.[78]

In January, 1910, Harvey invited Smith to lunch. Both knew that after many years of Republican corruption and mismanagement, 1910 promised to be a big year for the Democrats. If the right man were nominated, one who could win enough votes from Republicans and independents, he could carry New Jersey by a wide-enough margin to sweep other Democrats into the legislature, which could assure that Smith could return to the Senate. (In 1910, United States senators were still appointed by their state legislatures; the Nineteenth Amendment, mandating the direct election of senators, was not ratified until 1913.) Smith, who had sent three sons to Princeton, was casually acquainted with Wilson. Smith told Harvey that there were other potential candidates for the nomination, but that he would consider Wilson and get back to him.[79] Smith sounded out Democratic leaders throughout the state and the nation, and reported back to Harvey that he was fully on board for Wilson.

There was, of course, the matter of convincing Wilson, who was then in the throes of the graduate college fight, to run for governor. Some time in early February, Col.

and Mrs. Harvey were the overnight guests of the Wilsons. The next morning Harvey and Wilson discussed the possibility of Wilson running for governor. According to Harvey, he said to Wilson: "It all resolves to this: If I can handle the matter so that the nomination for governor shall be tendered to you on a silver platter, without you turning a hand to obtain it, and without any requirement or suggestion of any pledge whatsoever, what do you think would be your attitude?"[80]

At this, according to Harvey, Wilson walked up and down the floor for a few minutes in deep thought. One must wonder what Wilson was thinking as he paced the floor for those few minutes. He was fifty-three-years old. From his days as an undergraduate he had yearned to get into the fray. He had studied law and had tried lawyering as the means to a political career, and it had failed. He had attempted to get a job in the government, and all his attempts had failed. All of the decades of teaching and writing and lecturing had been from the sidelines; he could never set foot in the arena. And now, just as his presidency of Princeton was collapsing, he was being offered the nomination for governor, *on a silver platter*.

Again according to Harvey, Wilson finally replied: "If the nomination for governor should come to me that way, I should regard it as my duty to give the matter very serious consideration."[81] Harvey reported the meeting to Smith. Smith deemed Wilson's response to be satisfactory. But Smith was not the only Democratic boss that had be brought around. Robert ("Little Bob") Davis (1848-1911) was the boss of Hudson County (Jersey City). Davis was no reformer, but the young mayor of Jersey City, H. Otto Wittpenn, was. Wittpenn had his eyes on the Democratic nomination for governor. The last thing that Davis wanted was this reformer, who he knew he could never control, as governor. Wilson was a man he might be able to control. After years of vying for control of New Jersey Democratic politics, Smith and Davis now agreed to bury the hatchet. Both were in for Wilson.

One matter that surely gave Smith and Davis pause was whether the unknown Wilson, once elected, could be counted on not to turn against the organization. In May, 1908, Wilson had authored an article in Harvey's *North American Review* sure to please any political boss. In *The States and the Federal Government*, Wilson wrote that the voters "must of necessity leave the selection [of candidates] to a few persons who, from one motive or another, volunteer to make a business of it. They are the political bosses and managers whom the people obey and affect to despise. Under a system of innumerable nominations they are indispensable."[82] But now that they were about to hand Wilson the nomination, Smith wanted further assurances. Through a friend, Smith asked Wilson if he were elected, "[You] would not set about fighting and breaking down the existing Democratic organization and replacing it with one of your own."[83]

Wilson responded to Smith's friend: "I would be perfectly willing to assure Mr. Smith that I would not, if elected governor, set about 'fighting and breaking down the existing Democratic organization and replacing it with one of my own.' The last thing I should think of would be building up a machine of my own. So long as the existing Democratic organization was willing to work with thoroughness and heartiness for such policies as would re-establish the reputation of the State and the credit of the Democratic Party in serving the State, I should deem myself inexcusable for antagonizing it, so long as I was left absolutely free in the matter of measures and men."[84] Smith indicated that Wilson's response was "entirely satisfactory."

Wilson was troubled that if he resigned as Princeton's president so soon after the graduate college debacle, it would be seen as him resigning in a fit of pique. So in late June he wrote to a group of Princeton trustees who had sided with him throughout the quad fight and the graduate college fight, asking their opinion. Trustee David B. Jones responded: "All four [trustees] unreservedly [are] in the opinion that no obligation whatever exists on your part, either to any individual supporter or to the University as a whole, which should deter you in following your inclination."[85] It is difficult to imagine Wilson *not* running for governor if the response had not been positive.

Wilson made his decision to run public on July 15, 1910, in an open letter to the *Trenton True American* and the *Newark Evening News*. He announced he was running by announcing that he was *not* running. He said he would not be a candidate (the nomination had been offered "on a silver platter") and would do nothing to seek the nomination, but that "it would be an affectation and discourtesy on my part to ignore the matter any longer," and if "a decided majority of the thoughtful Democrats of the State "believed that he should accept the nomination," he would deem it his duty "as well as an honor and a privilege, to do so." In the interim, he did not wish to be drawn away from his duties at Princeton.[86]

It was a brilliant strategy. A few days later, a reporter for the *Trenton True American*, who introduced Wilson to his readers as a "prospective Governor of New Jersey and President of the United States," tried to pin Wilson down on the issues. Wilson refused, saying that to do so would make him sound like he was seeking the office.[87] One of the issues favored by most progressive Democrats was the direct election of senators. Privately, Wilson told Harvey that he was opposed to it, as was Harvey himself.[88] The other issues near and dear to New Jersey Democrats was the creation of a state commission to regulate public utilities and direct primaries for the election of state officers. Wilson was silent on all these issues.

Otto Wittpenn was not Wilson's only opponent for the nomination. Frank S. Katzenbach, very popular with the rank-and-file, a former candidate for governor and also a progressive, considered running again. Katzenbach hailed from Mercer County, Wilson's home, and if Wilson were to lose his home county, it would prove embarrassing. Yet another progressive, State Senator George Silzer, also decided to run. These were all progressives. Wilson was being postured by his opponents as the candidate of the bosses. Wilson's old speeches denouncing organized labor came back to haunt him. "Union Labor Stand Committed to Work for Wilson's Defeat" reported the *Trenton Evening Times*.[89] Wilson remained mum. On August 5, the *Trenton Evening Times* headlined: "Wilson Will Not Discuss Issues,"..."Says to Talk Now Would Suggest He is Seeking Democratic Nomination."

In 1910, Democratic nominees were chosen by means of primary elections for the selection of delegates to the state convention. At the convention, the elected delegates chose the nominee. In the September 13 primaries, the Smith machine in Newark and the Davis machine in Jersey City turned out huge majorities for Wilson. To Wilson's chagrin, Katzenbach trounced him in Mercer County. The convention opened the next day at the Taylor Opera House in Trenton. Far from presenting Wilson with the nomination "on a silver platter," it was a donnybrook. At one point, Harvey feared that the convention might be stampeded for Katzenbach. But Smith and Davis had the delegates. Wilson won the nomination on the first ballot with 747.5 votes, to 373 for Katzenbach, 210 for Silzer and 76.5 for Wittpenn. In accordance with tradition, a motion was made and carried to make the nomination unanimous. The convention secretary intoned: "We have just received word that Mr. Wilson, the candidate for the governorship *and the next president of the United States*, has received word of his nomination, has left Princeton, and is now on his way to the convention."[90]

Wilson had spent the morning playing golf. When he mounted the podium to give his acceptance speech, he was still wearing his golf jacket. He was unaware that the nomination had not been handed to him on a silver platter, and had been the result of a bruising fight. He then did what he did best, what he had trained to do since he was a teenager standing before a mirror, what he had done hundreds of times before. There was not the slightest hint of the typical political bombast in his speech. An unknown quantity to most of them, he spoke calmly, as if to each of them: "As you know, I did not seek this nomination. It has come to me absolutely unsolicited, with the consequence that I shall enter upon the duties of the office of Governor, if elected, with absolutely no pledges of any kind to prevent me from serving the people of the State with singleness of purpose. Not only have no pledges of any kind been given, but none have been proposed or desired."[91]

Not a word of it was true, as Smith and Harvey well knew. But the effect of the words upon the audience was electric. For the first time, he came out in favor of a public service commission to regulate utilities. If he failed to make any mention of the direct election of senators, it probably went unnoticed. He concluded his short speech: "We are witnessing a renaissance of public spirit, a reawakening of sober public opinion, a revival of the power of the people, the beginning of an age of thoughtful reconstruction that makes our thought hark back to the great age in which democracy was set up in America. With the new age we shall show a new spirit. We shall serve justice and candor and all things that make for right. Is not our own ancient party the party disciplined and made ready for the great task? Shall we not forget ourselves in making it the instrument of righteousness for the State and for the Nation?"

They couldn't get enough of it. "Go on, go on," they shouted.[92] But he was finished. They mobbed him. The police had to form a square around him to escort him from the hall. Men who had fought his nomination became converts on the spot. Smith predicted he would win by 25,000 votes.

The Republicans nominated Vivian M. Lewis (1869-1950), the commissioner of banking and insurance. The Republicans were split between conservatives and "New Idea" progressives. Lewis announced he would be a passive governor, a "constitutional governor," and would not try to pressure the legislature. Wilson knew that if he could peel off the "New Idea" Republicans, he would win.

Wilson told Harvey that shaking hands and kissing babies was not his style. They agreed that Wilson would do what he did best; he would give one speech each evening in each of New Jersey's twenty-one counties. At first, Wilson attempted to continue the pre-convention strategy of being as vague as possible, but he was criticized for it. He discarded the strategy. Speaking in Newark on September 30, Wilson came out strongly in favor of state control of corporations, in favor of primary elections for state offices, and, contrary to his private assurances to Harvey, he came out in favor of the direct election of United States senators. Using words that could have been written by Bryan, he said: "What has made us strong? The toil of millions of men, the toil of men who do not boast, who are inconspicuous, but who live their lives humbly from day to day, and this great body of workers, this great body of toilers, constitute the might of America."[93]

Speaking in Trenton on October 3, he railed against secrecy in government, saying that it was the root of political corruption: "Publicity is one of the purifying elements in politics. The best thing you can do with anything that is crooked is to lift it up where people can see that it is crooked, and then it will either straighten itself out or disappear…it is a System that I object to, *and a System I will do everything in my power to break up.*"[94] Wilson was now all in on the side of the progressives. The criticisms he had made of organized labor? That was just some constructive advice one gives as a friend. On October 15, speaking in Asbury Park, with Smith and Harvey in the audience, he explicitly reneged on the promise he had made that if elected he would leave their cherished party organization intact: "Do you want entangled leaders, or do you want disentangled leaders? Do you want leaders with a countless number of commitments, or do you want leaders with no commitments at all?"[95]

Smith had already contributed $50,000 of his own money to the campaign. As he sat there, he consoled himself with the thought that Wilson's attack on his political machine was just campaign rhetoric. One wonders what went through Harvey's mind as he heard these words. Since 1906, he had thrown all of his energies and the services of his publications to getting Wilson nominated, assuming that he and his conservative friends could control Wilson once he was elected. By Harvey's own account, he had read everything that Wilson had written on the day that he first heard Wilson in 1902. If he had truly read everything, he would have read Wilson's loving essay on Bismarck, written when Wilson was a Princeton sophomore. Had he read that article, he would have realized that more than anything else, Wilson admired strength and despised weakness. Harvey would have realized that to both Bismarck and Wilson ethics meant little in the pursuit of power. Just as Wilson could easily accommodate himself to Bismarck's doctoring of the "Ems Telegram" in order to induce France to declare war on Prussia, he could break his promise not to smash the New Jersey Democratic machine. But for Harvey, Smith and the other Democratic bosses, it was too late.

Wilson was tireless. The strategy of one speech per night was discarded. On October 27, he gave three speeches in three cities. There was no "stump" speech. He scribbled notes on a sheet of paper, then spoke extemporaneously, as flawlessly as if every speech had been painstakingly prepared. Now firmly aligned with the progressives, Otto Wittpenn and Frank Katzenbach supported him. The Democrats were united.

On November 8, 1910, Wilson awaited the election returns at his home in Princeton. It was a big night for the Democrats everywhere. The House of Representatives would have a Democratic majority for the first time in eighteen years. In New Jersey, Smith's machine in Essex County and Davis' machine in Hudson County turned out huge majorities. Smith's prediction that Wilson would defeat Lewis by 25,000 votes proved to be conservative. Wilson defeated Lewis by 49,000 votes.

While still a senior at Princeton, Wilson had entered into a "solemn covenant" with fellow senior Charles Talcott, in which they mutually agreed that they would use "all our powers and passions for the work of establishing the principles we [hold] in common; that we [will] acquire knowledge that we might have power; and that we [will] drill ourselves in the arts of persuasion, but especially in oratory, that we might have facility in leading others into our ways of thinking and enlisting them in our purposes."[96] Now, thirty-one years later, Wilson had fulfilled his end of the "solemn covenant." On the same night that Wilson was elected governor of New Jersey, Charles Talcott was elected to the United States House of Representatives from his home town of Utica, New York, fulfilling his end of the covenant. But a seat in the House of Representatives was the highest office Charles Talcott would ever achieve. For Woodrow Wilson, the governor's mansion in Trenton was a mere way-station to the ultimate prize, a prize that was now within his grasp.

Wilson's parents, Joseph Wilson and
Jessie Woodrow

Wilson and Ellen Axson

The "Iron Chancellor" Otto von Bismarck

The "GOM"—The Great Old Man—William E. Gladstone

Jules Ferry

Clemenceau by
Eduard Manet

Lloyd George as a
young backbencher

Clemenceau juggling
British pounds, as a
tool of the British

7

THE FIRST COP IN FRANCE

Anti-clerical, anti-monarchist, anti-communist, anti-German, and in all this he represented the dominant spirit in France.

—Winston Churchill

He was sixty in June, 1902, when he entered the ornate Senate chamber in the Palais-Luxembourg for the first time, occupying the chair once used by Victor Hugo. His hair was gone; his moustache had turned gray. He was (as he called himself) an "old beginner." He was, as a result of the Dreyfus affair, the most celebrated, if not the most well-loved, Republican in France. But he had no chance of becoming a minister. France's president, Émile Loubet, despised Clemenceau, ("As long as I am at the Elysee, Clemenceau will not be a minister"[1]), and Loubet's term would not expire until 1906. But in June, 1903, the new owners of *L'Aurore* invited him back as editor-in-chief. He didn't need a ministry; he had his pen.

Since the beginning of the Third Republic in 1870, France had had no real political parties. At best, there were temporary, floating coalitions around the politician of the moment. But in his absence, political parties had formed. The old coalition of radicals that had supported Clemenceau in the past was now the *Parti Republicain Radical et Radical Socialistes*. It had other leaders, including his old ghostwriter at *La Justice*, Camille Pelleton. Clemenceau never joined it, or any political party.

Shortly after Clemenceau entered the Senate, Émile Combes (1835–1921), a Freemason who had once studied for the priesthood, became prime minister. Combes ("the little Father") made no bones about the purpose of his ministry, which was to break the back of the Catholic Church in France. In 1801, Napoleon had entered into an agreement—a *concordat*—with Pope Pius VII that had made the Church the official religion of France. The state paid the salaries of the clergy, and appointed the bishops. Combes set out to change all that, to effect a total separation of church and state in France. It was what Clemenceau had been pushing for since the first days of the Republic. The 1902 elections had been good for the Republicans, shifting the center of gravity in the Chamber of Deputies decidedly to the left. A coalition of radical and socialist parties, the *bloc des gauches*, had a majority. Combes could now achieve what Clemenceau had only dreamed of.

Combes began in October, 1902, with a law closing most of the Catholic monastic orders. In Clemenceau's maiden speech in the Senate, he supported it. He was a life-long atheist, but his ideas on the state's relation to religion were nuanced: "Governments can do nothing against beliefs. Religions have been seen to rise; religions have died out. Never has a religion been seen to die under the actions of governments…We do not wish to destroy a single belief…but we wish and we are able to destroy everything that pertains to the Roman government."[2] More important was a 1904 law banning members of religious orders from teaching in public schools. Clemenceau supported that too. But when Combes proposed a law banning all Church schools, Clemenceau vigorously opposed it in the Senate, holding that a unified educational system was a "negation of liberty."[3] "I oppose the omnipotence of the lay state because I see in it a tyranny…Because I am the enemy of Kings, Emperors and Popes, I am the enemy of the omnipotent state."[4] The purpose of the Revolution their fathers had made was to win freedom, not to change one master for another: "We have guillotined the King; long live the State-King! We have dethroned the Pope; long live the State-Pope! We are casting out God, as these gentlemen on the right say; long live the State-God."[5]

He summed up his stand: "If there were ever a conflict between the Republic and liberty, the Republic would be on the wrong side and I should choose liberty."[6] The measure to ban all Church schools was defeated.

When Combes formed his cabinet, his most unfortunate selection turned out to be his selection as minister of war, Gen. Louis André (1838-1913). Every bit as anti-clerical as Combes, André set about to root out all of the clerical influences in the army. But how to do it, he asked himself: "To attain my goal, my first preoccupation was to seek out among the anonymous and silent mass of officers, those whose republican sentiments could single them out for attention…How did one recognize them?"[7] How indeed.

What he did was to establish a network of spies among his fellow Masons throughout France. The spies were charged with determining just how Catholic an army officer was. If the officer was seen attending church with his family, he received a demerit. If his wife took his children to a Church-run school, he received more demerits. Worst of all was the bachelor officer who regularly attended church by himself. All of these infractions were duly noted on file cards ("*affiches*") that were forwarded to André. In short order, André had thousands of file cards, and was using them to determine which officers were promoted, and which were not.

With thousands of file cards floating around, the inevitable happened. In late 1904, someone within André's ministry offered to sell a few file cards, which fell into the hands of one Gustave Guyot de Villeneuve, a right-wing deputy. De Villeneuve promptly rose in the Chamber of Deputies and began reading the file cards, setting off the *affaire des affiches*. At the revelation, André was unapologetic: "How otherwise, given the inertia of the high command, could I have accomplished my task?" However, André did acknowledge that the revelation had deprived him of his "moral authority," and resigned.

Many on the French left did not wish for Combes to follow André out the door, for fear that his downfall might split the *bloc des gauches* and pave the way for a more conservative prime minister. Not Clemenceau. He saw the *affaire des affiches* as the mirror image of the Dreyfus affair, only with the "secret files" this time in the hands of the left, rather than the right: "What was the Dreyfus affair," he wrote in *L'Aurore*, "if not the more scandalous secret file of the Jesuits, with all of its train of files of turpitude?… It is up to us to ensure that the evil cease immediately, both on the clerical side and the anti-clerical side. For that, I have only one way: the repression of wrong-doing in whatever camp it may have been committed."[8]

The *affaire* set off a firestorm throughout France. Army officers challenged the Masons who had spied on them to duels. Masonic lawyers who had spied were disbarred. Students demanded the ouster of professors who had spied. Regiments where some officers had spied on others were torn apart. By late January, 1905, the revolving door swung again, and Combes resigned, the victim of André and his *affiches*.

Combes had been more fortunate in his minister of foreign affairs. Having no interest in anything but his anti-clericalism, and having especially no interest in foreign affairs (except to sever diplomatic relations with the Vatican) Combes left the conduct of foreign affairs in the capable hands of Theophile Delcassé (1852-1923), who, although he spoke no foreign languages, would serve as foreign minister through six governments from 1898 until 1905, longer than any prior foreign minister since the creation of the Third Republic, leaving a lasting mark on France's relations with Germany and the rest of Europe.

Delcassé was born and raised in the foothills of the Pyrenees. He was nineteen when France went down to defeat in 1871, and the Treaty of Frankfort, which ripped Alsace-Lorraine from France, enraged him. His hero was Gambetta. A mediocre student, he first thought he might become a lawyer, but then found himself when he landed a junior position on Gambetta's paper, *La Republique Francaise.* He was soon scouring the Chamber of Deputies looking for stories, and found that his real interest was foreign affairs. He was a strong supporter of Ferry's colonial policies, even after Ferry's humiliating fall, largely at Clemenceau's hands. Like Ferry, he dreamed of a French colonial empire stretching from Morocco and Tunisia on the Mediterranean to the Congo. But nothing surpassed Alsace-Lorraine in his thoughts. One Russian foreign minister called Delcassé a "maniac," for whom "everything is subordinated to the idea of *Revanche.* He sees only Strasbourg without thinking of the superior interests of Europe."[9]

Delcassé married a wealthy widow when he was thirty-five, which freed him to pursue a political career. In 1889 he was elected to the Chamber from his home department of Ariege in southern France. By 1894 he was colonial administrator, and foreign minister by 1898. When he arrived at the Quai d'Orsay, then and now the Paris headquarters of the foreign ministry, he said "I do not wish to leave this desk without having established an *entente* with England."[10] He arrived at exactly the moment that France almost came to war with Great Britain over a dusty town in the Sudan then called Fashoda. Just as France was attempting to complete an uninterrupted string of colonies running west to east in Africa, Great Britain was completing its uninterrupted string of colonies running north to south from Cairo to Cape Town. The two goals were incompatible. When a much larger army under Lord Kitchener encountered a much smaller French garrison at Fashoda, the two countries almost fulfilled Bismarck's dream of having France and Great Britain come to blows over colonies. The British were willing to fight over Sudan, which they considered the gateway to the Upper Nile. Ever the realist, Delcassé decided that France was in no position to fight. ("We have arguments down there, and they have soldiers.") Advising the Chamber of Deputies that "a conflict would have involved sacrifices disproportionate to the object," he convinced the Chamber that France must swallow the humiliation and withdraw.[11] Many blamed Delcassé for Fashoda, but he had acted only to salvage a situation created by his predecessors. Clemenceau supported the comedown at Fashoda, writing that "France cannot think of throwing herself into war for the possession of some African marshes while the German is encamped in Metz and Strasbourg."[12]

Fashoda aside, Clemenceau truly despised Delcassé, which is somewhat surprising considering that for both of them, their orientation would always be "the blue line of the Vosges," the lost provinces. They had their differences. Delcassé coveted France's 1892 alliance with Russia; it was France's only alliance. Clemenceau never placed much faith in Russia's friendship, and when, on January 22, 1905, ("Bloody Sunday") Czar Nicholas' troops fired on unarmed demonstrators peacefully gathered before the St. Petersburg Winter Palace, killing and wounding hundreds, including women and children, Delcassé tried to soft-pedal the affair, in fear that criticism would damage the alliance. Clemenceau would have none of it, writing in *L'Aurore*: "Nothing can excuse M. Delcassé for having attempted to justify the massacre in the face of humanity's world-wide condemnation. This misguided man is still beglamoured by his visits to St. Petersburg."[13]

The antipathy may simply have been personal. Delcassé was short, with close-cropped hair. He wore a pince-nez. He had a self-assured air, and he affected a speaking style of a professor instructing a class of not-so-bright students. Clemenceau called him "our small bore Metternich." His hatred may have hardened when Clemenceau asked Delcassé to find an ambassadorship for a close friend, Delcassé brushed the request aside, saying that he had no openings.

Clemenceau had to watch as Delcassé went from success to success. In 1902, Delcassé was successful in prying Italy loose from its alliance with Germany and Austria-Hungary. In exchange for giving Italy a free hand in Tripoli, Italy agreed to give France a free hand in Morocco. He entered into an agreement with Spain settling France's differences with Spain over Morocco. But his greatest achievement was the "Anglo-French Agreement of 1904," which soon became known as the "Entente Cordiale."

Relations between Britain and France had been strained throughout the 1890's. In 1882, Britain took control of Egypt, and it continued to rankle in Paris. The two countries tangled over colonies in West Africa and Siam. Then there was Fashoda. When France split apart over Dreyfus, the British press was decidedly—and vocally—Dreyfusard. When Britain went to war with the Boers, the French press, reflecting French public opinion, was almost unanimous in support of the Boers. But the "South African War" showed the British how isolated they were. With Germany now building a navy to rival its own, the era of "splendid isolation" was coming to an end. It ended with Delcassé's skillful negotiation of the "Anglo-French Agreement of 1904," under which Britain agreed to give France a free hand in Morocco, in exchange for France finally acceding to British hegemony in Egypt. In so doing, Delcassé gave up almost nothing, since France had no influence over Egyptian affairs. The agreement was strictly *diplomatic*; neither side pledged to provide military assistance to the other. But soon after the agreement was signed, British and French military and naval advisors began meeting in secret for the purpose of coordinating their efforts in case either side was attacked. The agreement ended France's diplomatic isolation that Bismarck had so skillfully imposed since 1871. As with the agreements he had entered into with Spain and Italy regarding Morocco, Delcassé was careful to notify the German foreign office that he had concluded these agreements, and to advise them that German commercial interests in Morocco would be unaffected by them. Germany's response to France's *entente* with Great Britain was anodyne. Chancellor Bernhard von Bülow commented that Germany's interests in Morocco were only commercial, and that the *entente* did not imperil these rights. Kaiser Wilhelm echoed the sentiment.

But Delcassé's long-standing antipathy to Germany got the better of him, and he overplayed his hand. He set out to make Morocco a French *protectorate*, in much the same fashion that Ferry had made a protectorate of Tunisia. But unlike Ferry, Delcassé was determined to accomplish his end without using force. His would be a policy of *"penetration pacifique"* ("peaceful penetration"). Under *penetration pacifique,* Delcassé began instituting certain "reforms" regarding the policing of Morocco. He insisted on spreading the French language in Morocco, and increasing French economic power within Morocco. He did not consult with Germany. All this ran counter to the Madrid Convention of 1880—of which France and Germany both were signatories—that guaranteed the independence of the Sultan, Abd-al-Aziz. If France was to make changes to the Sultan's status, Germany had a right to be consulted.

Von Bülow then had a change of heart. He determined that Delcassé's overreach in Morocco might just be the occasion to weaken France's new *entente* with Great Britain. Von Bülow advised Kaiser Wilhelm that a visit by His Majesty might just be the thing to both shore up the Sultan and "embarrass M. Delcassé, thwart his plans, and benefit our economic interests in Morocco."[14] And so, on March 31, 1905, Kaiser Wilhelm interrupted his Mediterranean cruise, landed in Tangier, rode around on a white horse, and met with the French *charge d'affairs*, advising him that Germany considered the Sultan the independent ruler of Morocco. He then addressed Tangier's small German colony gathered for the occasion: "The Empire has great and growing interests in Morocco. Commerce can only progress if all the powers are considered to have equal rights under the sovereignty of the Sultan and respect the independence of the country. My visit is in recognition of that independence…It is to the Sultan in his capacity of independent sovereign that I pay my visit today"[15] He said that no country was predominant in Morocco, advising his German auditors to "form square and keep shoulder to shoulder."[16] His *coup de Tanger* had lasted all of two hours.

The visit inflamed public opinion on both sides of the Rhine, and Wilhelm proceeded to fan the flames: "I hope the events now in progress will keep the attention of our nation awake and strengthen its courage. I hope we shall find ourselves united if it becomes necessary to intervene in world politics."[17] Von Bülow, echoing his sovereign, demanded that an international conference be convened to settle all of the conflicting Moroccan claims. The Sultan also demanded a conference. Wilhelm's two-hour jaunt through the streets of Tangier was now the "First Moroccan Crisis." Never a proponent of colonial expansion, Clemenceau urged calm: "We have certain explanations to ask of Germany. Nothing is simpler than to ask for them, since we are certain in advance that the conversation will be most courteous and that an understanding is inevitable."[18] He had no confidence in his old *bete noire*, Delcassé. Writing within a week of Wilhelm's *coup de Tanger*: "[Delcassé] …might make, perhaps, an excellent undersecretary or minister of agriculture. He is not a minister of foreign affairs."[19]

When the Combes government collapsed over the *affaire des affiches*, Combes was replaced by his minister of finance, Maurice Rouvier, the former prime minister who had barely escaped the Panama scandal, and who, like Delcassé, was a disciple of Gambetta, but who, unlike Combes, was unwilling to give Delcassé a free hand in running foreign affairs. German sabre-rattling was also beginning to unnerve the Chamber of Deputies which, like Clemenceau, was unwilling to risk war over Morocco. On April 19, Delcassé was hammered in the Chamber by both the left and the right for failing to advise von Bülow of his intentions in Morocco. No one rose to defend Delcassè except Rouvier, who felt that if Delcassé were ousted his government would fall with him. Rouvier promised the Chamber that he would supervise French foreign policy. Delcassé went to president Loubet and asked to resign. Loubet begged him to reconsider, as did Rouvier. Delcassé withdrew his resignation, but Rouvier, not Delcassé, was now running France's affairs vis-à-vis Germany and Morocco.

On April 26, Rouvier met with the German ambassador, Prince Hugo von Radolin. He told von Radolin that "We will do everything that is possible to give you the explanations and satisfaction that you desire." But he didn't stop there. He advised von Radolin that the French people liked the Germans more than they liked the British, and that while a few French politicians still caviled about *revanche,* it was only "foolish prating," and that France should resign herself to the situation. Von Radolin replied that an international conference would be the best way to defuse the crisis. When word of Rouvier's remarks got back to Delcassé, he exploded, calling Rouvier a "traitor." Delcassé correctly characterized Rouvier's remarks as: "I don't give a damn about Alsace-Lorraine. Do you want me to sacrifice Delcassé?"[20] Delcassé's head was exactly what von Bülow wanted, von Radolin insisting that Germany could not remain indifferent to Delcassé's "intimidation and violence." Initially, Rouvier refused, wondering aloud: "I cannot cause Delcassé to fall just because Germany frowns. I should be reproached always—always."[21]

Delcassé's fate was sealed by events not in Tangier or Paris but in the Sea of Japan. Since early 1904, Russia–France's only ally—had been fighting a losing land and sea war against the Empire of Japan. On May 25, 1905, a month after Rouvier's meeting with von Radolin, Japan smashed the Russian fleet at the Battle of Tsushima Strait. It would soon lead to a negotiated settlement brokered by President Roosevelt. But for now France's 1894 alliance with Russia became a worthless scrap of paper. France's army, still not fully recovered from the Dreyfus affair and reeling from the *affaire des affiches*, was anything but prepared for war with Germany. And the Sultan and the German chancellor were demanding an international conference.

Delcassé met with Rouvier's cabinet on June 6. He insisted that France remain firm against Germany. He advised that France reject an international conference on Morocco, that yielding on this point would expose France's weakness. As for the threat of war with Germany, he insisted that Germany was bluffing. But he was alone. He resigned.

Clemenceau could not conceal his delight at Delcassé's misfortune. Writing the very next day in *L'Aurore*, in an article headed "The Ouster," he said that, at bottom, Delcassé had committed only one fault, which was to accept the position of foreign minister in the first place. More seriously, he reminded his readers that, in order to effect his policies in Morocco, Delcassé had duly advised the governments of Great Britain, Spain and Italy, but had failed to advise Germany or the Sultan: "Let us take advantage of the new lesson given us, after so many others, and we will not be exposed to awakening in fears of war, like those which are fortunately dissipated today." As for Delcassé, "He was haunted by the great idea of his regime, the conquest of Morocco, just as the conquest of Mexico haunted...Napoleon III."[22]

Delcassé was out as foreign minister (Rouvier elected to keep that portfolio for himself) but Delcassé was not gone; he still held his seat in the Chamber. Clemenceau had not seen the last of Theophile Delcassè.

It was sometime during this period that Clemenceau earned the nickname "The Tiger" (*"Le Tigre"*) that would stick for life. The origins are murky, and the claimants are numerous. The best claim to authorship belongs to Emile Buré, then one of Clemenceau's staff writers at *L'Aurore*. Clemenceau would arrive at the office during the evening, often terrorizing the staff. Once, when hearing Clemenceau's footsteps on the stairs, Buré shouted: "Look out! Here comes the Tiger!"[23]

When the Combes government fell over the *affaire des affiches*, the job of enacting and implementing the separation of church and state in France ("*laïcité*") fell to Rouvier. But the "Law on the Separation of the Churches and State" was the handiwork of a young (43) Nantes lawyer and socialist, Aristide Briand, who would go on to serve in various capacities, often as prime minister, for the next quarter-century, and cap his career with a Nobel Peace Prize. But for now he set himself to the task of completing what Jules Ferry had begun when Ferry banned religious instruction in French public schools. Under the 1905 Separation Law, "freedom of conscience" and "the free exercise of religion" were guaranteed. The radical change was that "The Republic does not guarantee, pay, or subsidize any religious sect." In abolishing Napoleon's *concordat* with the Vatican, France would no longer pay the salaries of priests or subsidize religious orders.

It was the manner in which the Separation Law was to be administered that caused the explosion. Church real estate had always been the property of the state (and thus exempt from taxation) but henceforth all church property, and every franc dropped into every collection box, would revert to the state, to be administered by *associations culturelles*, i.e. associations run by laymen, not priests and bishops. And in order to determine exactly what property had fallen into the hands of the state, every candlestick, crozier and miter of every church, presbytery and rectory in France, from *Notre Dame* to the smallest village parsonage, had to be *inventoried*. Soon, state inventory officers bearing ledger books were knocking on church doors demanding entry.

As could be expected, the result was a firestorm, the fire being fanned by Pope Pius X, who denounced not only the inventories but the entire Separation Law. The inventories were seen, with some justification, as the first step towards the expropriation of the Church's assets. Throughout France, the locals fought the law in the only way they could, by blocking the inventories. At one church in Coucouron in southern France, hundreds of men armed with guns and hatchets and well-provisioned with food and ammunition locked themselves inside their church. In Saint M'hervé, a hundred miles north of Nantes, Clemenceau's home town, the registration official was seriously wounded by demonstrators armed with cudgels, iron bars and pitchforks. At Abeele, on the Belgian border, forty armed men were posted on the church roof, ready to shoot anyone entering.[24] In one church, they dissuaded the inventory agent from entering by chaining a bear to the door. The inventory agents were confronted by sullen, hostile churchgoers everywhere.

And with that, Maurice Rouvier's government collapsed.

Rouvier's government fell on March 12, 1906, in the middle of the international conference on Morocco convened at Chancellor von Bülow's insistence. If Rouvier had thought that ousting Delcassé would cool von Bülow's ardor for an international conference, he was mistaken. Just as Declassé had overplayed his hand in trying to make Morocco a French protectorate behind Germany's back, von Bülow now overplayed his hand. After Decassé's ouster, Rouvier sought to negotiate a bilateral treaty with Germany delineating the two countries' rights in Morocco, just as Delcassé had done in 1902 with Italy, in 1904 with Spain, and, most notably in 1904 with Great Britain under the *entente cordiale*. But von Bülow wasn't buying, calculating that if an international conference were summoned at which Great Britain failed to support France's claims in Morocco, it would destroy the *entente*. In the face of a strident press campaign in Germany against France, and a belligerent Kaiser Wilhelm, Rouvier agreed to the conference.

It opened on January 16, 1906 in Algeciras, Spain. Thirteen nations, including the United States, Austria-Hungary, Russia and (at Germany's insistence) the Sultan, attended. The principal topic on the agenda was which country (or countries) would police Morocco's ports. The power to police was understood to be tantamount to sovereignty. From the start, the conference was a disaster for von Bülow's negotiators. Contrary to their expectations, President Roosevelt, who favored an "open door" policy in China, was unwilling to provide similar support in Morocco. Russia, smarting from their defeat at the hands of Japan, felt the need to strengthen its ties with France, and supported France's policing claims. Most importantly, France received the solid support of the British, in the person of the very new foreign secretary, Sir Edward Grey. Grey, who would serve as foreign secretary for the next eleven years, came in with the new Liberal administration of Sir Henry Campbell-Bannerman. The French negotiators knew that they could count on the support of the Conservatives; they were unsure what support they might receive from the Liberals. They need not have worried. Grey considered Britain's *entente* with France "very new and untried," and was determined to see it strengthened. He was unwilling to give France a blank check, but strongly intimated to his German counterparts, privately, that in the event Germany tried to use force to settle her claims over Morocco, British public opinion would demand that Great Britain provide military support to France.[25]

The Act of Algeciras was signed on April 7, 1906. France gained little, since it had held most of the Moroccan policing rights before the conference, and Germany lost little. (Germany was ceded a voice in the running of the Moroccan state bank.) But if, as has been suggested, Germany had no interest in Morocco other than as a means of driving a wedge between Great Britain and France, the conference was a disaster for German diplomacy. The conference was seen in Germany (and elsewhere) as a humiliation for Germany. Great Britain had stood behind France and had strengthened the *entente cordiale*. France's ties with Russia were strengthened as well. No nation had sided with Germany at the conference except Austria-Hungary. The week after the conference closed *L'Aurore* editorialized that "The conference and its results leave us nothing but satisfaction."[26]

Clemenceau did not sign *L'Aurore*'s editorial; he was no longer with the paper, having just entered the government as the minister of the interior. Three weeks before Rouvier's government collapsed, Èmile Loubet's seven-year term as president of France expired. Loubet had sworn that Clemenceau would not be a minister as long as he was president, and Loubet was now gone. His successor, Armand Fallières, harbored no ill feelings for Clemenceau, and the way was now open for Clemenceau, then sixty-four, to enter the government for the first time. Parliamentary elections were scheduled for May; the next government would be a placeholder, filling the void until the voters determined the political stripe of the new Chamber of Deputies. The man selected to succeed Rouvier until after the election was sixty-five-year-old Ferdinand Sarrien, a man who can charitably be described as "colorless." When Clemenceau heard that Fallières had asked Sarrien to form a government, he exclaimed: "*ca rien?*" ("That nothing?").

As the most celebrated Republican in France, it was assumed that, whatever portfolio Clemenceau accepted, Clemenceau would be Sarrien's co-equal in governing France. But which portfolio? Sarrien had reserved foreign affairs for Léon Bourgeois. Clemenceau could not be given the justice portfolio because he was not a lawyer, and he couldn't be named minister of finance because, by Clemenceau's own admission, he knew nothing of finance. No matter; the post Clemenceau coveted was minister of the interior. Administering the Separation Law would fall to him. A story made the rounds, and has been so often repeated that it might be true. According to legend, shortly before taking office Sarrien invited the prospective ministers to his home. When Clemenceau arrived, Sarrien, referring to the buffet table, asked Clemenceau: "What would you like?" to which Clemenceau is alleged to have responded: "*Interior.*" And that is the post he received. On March 14, 1906, he was appointed minister of the interior, thirty-five years after he first entered the old National Assembly. It was said that he had destroyed nineteen ministries. He had replied: "only one, they were all the same." Now, for the first time, he would need to prove that he could not just destroy a government, but govern.

On February 26, 1906, one of the last days of Clemenceau's tenure as editor-in-chief, *L'Aurore* carried a small item summarizing the political make-up of Alsace. It noted that there were German functionaries in Alsace who were seeking to Germanize that province. But, the paper reported, the reverse was happening; the Germans were becoming French. Of these German functionaries, *L'Aurore* concluded: "*Their children speak Alsatian; their grandchildren will speak French.*"[27]

If Clemenceau ever regretted taking on the interior ministry, there is no record of it, but he could be excused if he did.

On the morning of Saturday, March 10, 1906, the very day that Sarrien met with Clemenceau and others to form his cabinet, what would turn out to be the worst mine disaster in Europe in the twentieth century occurred in the Pas-de-Calais *department,* approximately 140 miles north of Paris. The coal mining operations there were so extensive that miners entered the pits from different towns and villages—Courrières, Méricourt, Sallaumines, Billy-Montigny, Lens—some of which were ten miles distant from the next town—and worked together underground in the interconnected pits. That morning, 1,800 miners entered the pits. Between 6:30 a.m. and 7 a.m., the miners first heard a roaring sound, then a crackling, then the explosion, so violent that men who were descending the shafts in cages were hurled into the air, the roofs of the pits having been blown off. Men trapped underground were asphyxiated, or burned to death, or crushed by the collapsing pits. Twelve hundred never made it out alive. Rescue operations—later recovery operations—were hindered by explosions in the mines days after the initial explosion.

The immediate result was fury. A disaster of this magnitude could occur, the miners and their families believed, only if the mine owners had been negligent, had ignored the safety of the miners. And so they called a strike. No one would enter the mines until *something was done.* Thirty-two thousand miners walked out.

The labor movement in France had grown apace with the rise of international socialism. Jean Jaurès had first entered the Chamber of Deputies, as a Socialist deputy, in 1895. But the movement was split in France and throughout Europe, as it was in the United States, between those who wished to work within the system to improve working conditions, and those who wished to overthrow bourgeois capitalism altogether. In the United States, the rejectionists were the International Workers of the World ("IWW"). In France, they were the *confederation generale du travail* ("CGT")—the General Confederation of Labor. Their weapon was the general strike. The CGT was opposed in the French mines by the Union of Miners, headed in the Pas-de-Calais by Émile

Basly (1854-1928), who not only headed the local union but who represented the district in the Chamber and who was the mayor of Lens. He was an old acquaintance of Clemenceau.

On Saturday, March 17, three days after he assumed office as minister of the interior, Clemenceau visited the striking miners. He took the 9 a.m. train to Arras, then got into a car for Lens. He first met with Basly. He told Basly that he wished to meet with the CGT. Basly advised against it. The mood was ugly and Clemenceau was unarmed. He rejected Basly's advice. He went on foot, alone, down a side street, to the "House of the People," an inn that the miners used as their headquarters. He met first with the CGT leaders, then he addressed the striking miners, who received him "coolly."[28] "I am not here to take part in your meeting. I have come simply as a representative of the government of the republic, charged to respect the rights of everyone, and to say that you have the right to strike, and that this right will not be disputed. We intend that the law will be respected by all, both by the president of the republic and by the most modest worker." He was there to advise them that the government would not use force to break their strike. But the promise was conditional: "We do not intend to interfere with your claims, but simply to warn against excess. You have the right to strike, but also the duty to respect those who do not think as you do, above all to respect property, because on the day when you have destroyed the mines, what will become of the mine workers?" He urged them to "Stay calm. You have not seen soldiers in the streets…I beg you, respect the freedom of everyone…If you do not want the soldiers, stay calm…Give to France a great example, because this is the first time that the government does not send troops against a strike. Show that you are men deserving of liberty, and that, as we, you want to strive towards a system of social justice that we all have in our hearts."[29] The miners applauded, but there were also cries of *"vive la greve"* ("Long live the strike.") He then got into his car, and drove off to meet the miners of Billy-Montigny, where a hundred miners had lost their lives.

The next day, Sunday, he met again with Basly and with the representatives of the mining companies, who were headed by former prime minister and president Jean Casimir-Perier. They announced that despite their not being obligated to do so, but in light of the general suffering, they were granting a 10% wage increase to all below-ground employees, and a 5% increase to those who worked above-ground.[30] But violence erupted the next day, and Eugène Étienne, the new minister of war, advised Clemenceau that there weren't sufficient police to guard the mines. So Clemenceau, despite his promise to the miners, called out the army: 20,000 troops, one for every two strikers. It earned him the moniker that he himself would adopt: *le premier flic de France* ("the first cop in France.") It was March 18. Clemenceau could not help noticing that it was exactly thirty-five years from the day that the Paris *commune* had erupted in the Montmartre, with him in the middle between the rioters and Thiers' troops. He later called this day "some of the abominable hours of my life."[31]

The troops arrived, and the miners tried to halt the troop trains. There were injuries; a trooper was killed. The head of the local branch of the CGT, twenty-seven-year-old Benoit Broutchoux, got into a scuffle with the police, and was arrested. He spent two months in jail. Scabs were brought in. The miners captured three of them, and paraded them through the streets of Lens bearing placards: "We are dupes; we are false brothers." Clemenceau later secured their release.

On March 20, Clemenceau decided that the confrontations with priests and parishioners barricading themselves in their churches all over France had gone far enough. Advising the Senate that "counting church candlesticks was not worth a human life," he suspended the inventories.[32]

The electrical engineers went on strike. The Paris "Metro" stopped running. Clemenceau was seated at his desk when the lights went out. He ordered the Army engineers into service, and the strike fizzled.

On March 25, Basly called for a referendum on whether to continue the strike. With no income and no strike fund, the miners were getting hungry. They voted on March 28, 32,000 to 18,000 to continue the strike. But if abstentions were counted, those voting to continue the strike were in a minority. In late April, Clemenceau returned to Lens, met with Basly, and interviewed some of the strikers as to whether they wished to continue the strike. The answers were equivocal. He met again with the CGT leaders, again warning against violence: "You are behind a barricade and I am in front of it; your means of action is disorder; my duty is to keep order. My role, therefore, is contrary to your efforts."[33]

The CGT called for a May 1 nationwide general strike. Clemenceau called out the army—50,000 troops in Paris alone—to assure the strike would be peaceful. He ordered the arrest of two CGT leaders before the strike. There were strikes that day, (more than 100,000 strikers in Paris alone) but the general strike was nowhere near to being complete, with many workers—including miners—ignoring it. Clemenceau estimated that 90% of those who did strike did so in fear of the other 10%.[34] He also voiced his belief that the "reactionaries" had hoped that the soldiers would fire on the strikers, in the hope of creating a "revolt" against the Republicans.[35] By then, the miners' strike in the Pas-de-Calais had petered out.

On May 6, parliamentary elections were held throughout France. The radical left gained seats, mostly at the expense of the right, which lost sixty seats. The Socialists added a few seats. The Republic was safer than it had ever been.

When the new Chamber of Deputies convened in June after the elections, Jean Jaurès rose in the Chamber to lambaste Clemenceau for his handling of the strikes. It sparked a debate between Jaurès and Clemenceau that lasted a week, and was remembered as one of the last acts in a "golden age" of oratory. Clemenceau and Jaurès had worked together in the Dreyfus case, they had both long opposed the power of the Church and supported the Separation Law. Jaurès had an enormous capacity for work. He was "always fresh, always in good spirits, always ready to contribute wit and vivacity to any company in which he found himself."[36] But they were very different men. Clemenceau was sixty-four, Jaurès forty-six. They looked different: Jaurès was short, stout and bearded; Clemenceau leaner. They spoke differently: Jaurès was the more theatrical, employing long rounded sentences delivered in a deep, lyrical baritone. Clemenceau, as always, was high-pitched, punching out pungent, witty, sarcastic mots. But more than anything, they were poles apart in their beliefs: Jaurès, the committed Socialist, convinced that the force of history decreed that one day all property would be collectivized, supporting the syndicalist program of the C.G.T. Clemenceau, the reformer, but devoted to the notion of the sanctity of private property. Jaurès, committed to the class struggle; Clemenceau denying that there was such a thing.

Jaurès and Clemenceau both believed that each was the true heir of the French Revolution. Referring to his use of force in the miners' strike, Clemenceau averred: "My efforts were those of a Minister of the Interior doing his duty"[37] referring to himself as "but a fallible man groping towards obscurity...like all of you."[38] Jaurès pounced: "There are moments in history when men must choose sides. One hundred years ago, when the Great Revolution broke out...they dared; they knew that the old world was crumbling, and they had to sweep away the debris to launch a new society...We are now at such a moment and you are offering empty phrases, partial solutions, hesitation. You have fallen behind the will of the people." Against Jaurès' collectivism, Clemenceau defended the rights of the individual: "I have taken my part, as you well know, against you and your ideas, and for a society based on justice, liberty and the sovereignty of the individual, a society which emanated from the French Revolution itself."[39] "The Socialist principle is the abandonment of the individual."[40] "The French Revolution, with its ideal of the rights of man, had aimed at results exactly the opposite of those desired by the Socialists."[41]

The immediate issues that divided them were Clemenceau's use of force during the strikes, and particularly his support of the use of strike breakers. Jaurès charged that Clemenceau had used excessive force. He also charged that allowing men to fill the jobs that strikers had quit was a form of strikebreaking. Jaurès said that the conditions of the workers were difficult enough without them having to confront others "hurling themselves against labour's effort to emancipate itself, and, whether by weakness or an excess of misery, lending support to their oppressors."[42] Clemenceau replied: "I believe that all men who need to work and find work have a right to work. I believe that society and the public powers have the duty to assure him the exercise of that right."[43] With respect to the charge that he had used excessive force: "I am accused of being prejudiced in favor of order, and I am willing to admit it."[44] He said that all of the dead and injured were among the troops, not the strikers. He said that he had photos of workers' houses that had been pillaged by strikers. "The working class was not…[made up of] the miserable wretches who pillaged and destroyed the homes of fellow-miners whose only crime was their refusal to strike." He then turned to Jaurès: "I challenge M. Jaurès to say what he would do under such circumstances as I have had to face."[45] Jaurès did not respond. "By not replying," said Clemenceau, "you have replied."

Although not expressed in this debate, there was one overriding reason Clemenceau despised the Socialists: their pacifism. He knew that if the Socialists ever came to power, it would spell the end of the dream of the recapture of the lost provinces.

Clemenceau had served as minister of the interior for only six months when Ferdinand Sarrien resigned, citing ill-health. There was no cabinet crisis. Clemenceau had essentially been Sarrien's co-prime minister; it was inevitable that Clemenceau would be his successor. And so, on October 21, 1906, at an age when most men still alive were well into retirement, Clemenceau, who had recently celebrated his sixty-fifth birthday, was invited to the Elysèe Palace and asked by President Fallières to form a government.

He told a friend that he wanted in his cabinet "only my own men,"[46] and that is what he set out to get. He appointed his old associate at *La Justice*, Stephen Pichon, as foreign minister. Pichon would later serve at Clemenceau's side at the Peace Conference. But for now he was content to do Clemenceau's bidding; both knew that Clemenceau intended to be his own foreign minister. He tapped as minister of finance the young (43) and brilliant Joseph Caillaux. As minister of war he chose Gen. Georges Picquart, the man persecuted by the army during the Dreyfus affair. His appointment came only three months after his reinstatement in the army, and was taken by the army as in insult, which it was intended to be. Picquart turned out to be a poor administrator, and Clemenceau came to regret the choice. His cabinet included two moderate Socialists: Briand as minister of education and public worship, and René Viviani in the new post of minister of labor and social insurance. He kept the interior ministry for himself. All of them were relatively young; five would go on to become prime minister.

Labor unrest would dog his government. One of the first issues he had to confront was whether the increasingly militant public workers would be allowed to form unions. He was not opposed, but he prohibited public workers such as the teachers and the postal workers from joining the CGT, on the sensible ground that government workers could not join an organization dedicated to overthrowing the state, a move that provoked Jaurès' ire. With respect to the CGT itself, which represented two thousand trade unions comprising 200,000 members, Clemenceau was caught in the middle. Many deputies (including Delcassé) wanted it banned outright. Clemenceau was opposed, arguing that if it were banned, it would reconstitute itself the next day "under a halo of persecution," as a martyr.[47]

One of the most serious labor conflicts occurred in June, 1907, involving the wine growers of southern France. In the two preceding years, these wine producers, most of them owners (or tenants) on small plots of land, had seen prices plummet as much as 80% as a result of overproduction and, they claimed, cheap imports from Algeria. They also complained of unfair competition; that some of the competing wine was "fraudulent," i.e. watered. They began protesting, the protests led by a former actor (and small wine grower himself), Marcelin Albert, who had the ability to whip up a crowd, some carrying placards reading "Death to Clemenceau." The CGT took up the cause of the wine growers. The protests turned violent. Five were killed, and Clemenceau called out the army. One of the units called out to suppress the violence was the 17th Infantry Regiment, a locally-recruited unit. When these soldiers refused to fire on their neighbors, a full-scale mutiny of the army loomed. Clemenceau transferred the 17th to Tunisia. In the Chamber, Jaurés blamed Clemenceau for the rioting, alleging that Clemenceau had fomented it in order to suppress it. Albert, in hiding from the police, caught a train to Paris and asked to see Clemenceau. On June 23, the meeting took place, Clemenceau meeting Albert in his capacity as minister of the interior. Clemenceau scolded Albert, blaming him for the violence, at which point Albert burst into tears, saying through his tears that he had not meant any harm. He asked Albert to return home, promising to do all he could to alleviate the economic crisis. Before Albert left, Clemenceau asked him if he had the train fare to return home. When Albert replied that he did not, Clemenceau reached into his pocket and gave it to him.[48] But when news of Clemenceau's largesse, and Albert's acceptance of it, reached Albert's followers, his effectiveness ended. In any event, wine prices recovered in late 1907, Clemenceau rammed through legislation curbing watered wine and limiting production, and soon the crisis was over.

There were strikes throughout his ministry, many peaceful; some not. When they turned violent (or threatened to do so), he did not hesitate to call out the army. In June,

1908, a strike of the sandpit workers in Seine-et-Oise, a Paris suburb, turned violent; six died. Ten thousand strikers turned out for the funerals. There were cries of "Death to Clemenceau."[49] The next month, a strike of construction workers in Villeneuve-Saint-Georges, another Paris suburb, left four dead in clashes with the army. When the Paris postal workers struck in 1909, he sent in troops to replace them. The strike, and Clemenceau's actions in response, produced another debate in the Chamber between Clemenceau and Jaurès. Clemenceau defended himself, saying that he would not give his approval to anarchy. Jaurès responded that Clemenceau was "anarchy crowned." Clemenceau replied that he was willing to defend his program of "social reform and legal order against revolutionaries."[50] His government prevailed on a vote of confidence by a wide margin. On the whole, the public supported their "first cop in France." He preserved order.

Clemenceau pressed for a number of much-needed reforms. Caillaux introduced legislation for a progressive income tax. It passed in the Chamber of Deputies, but died in the more conservative Senate. He called for a ten-hour work day, old age pensions, and workers' compensation. All of these measures eventually became law, but not while Clemenceau was prime minister. A law granting to women the right to control their own property was enacted in 1907, and a Railway Pension Law was enacted in 1909, providing pensions to all railroad workers, but women were not granted the right to vote. Clemenceau opposed it, citing their general adherence to Catholicism.[51] Women in France did not receive the franchise until 1945.

Foreign affairs concerned Clemenceau more than anything; he was as his own foreign minister. After Russia's defeat at the hands of Japan, France's alliance with Russia was of questionable value. It was the 1904 *entente cordiale*, the diplomatic alliance with Great Britain which did not require either party to come to the aid of the other in case of war, that Clemenceau was eager to strengthen.

In April, 1907, Clemenceau's British opposite number, Prime Minister Henry Campbell-Bannerman visited Paris. Clemenceau wanted a commitment that Great Britain would come to France's aid in case it was attacked by Germany, and this was exactly what Campbell-Bannerman was unwilling to give. At a meeting at the British Embassy, Clemenceau told Campbell-Bannerman that he was alarmed by the decline in British military spending. Campbell-Bannerman responded that the cuts were made for budgetary reasons. Clemenceau replied: "I could economize on the price of my shoes and catch pneumonia, but that would not be economy."[52] Something of a contretemps emerged from this meeting. Clemenceau thought he heard Campbell-Bannerman say that under no circumstances would British public opinion permit the dispatch of British troops for joint action with France. Campbell-Bannerman later denied having said it. But in a letter from King Edward to Charles Hardinge, the under-secretary of the foreign office, the King confirmed Clemenceau's version of the meeting.[53]

Later that summer, Eugène Étienne, Sarrien's minister of war and now a member of the Chamber of Deputies, was received by Kaiser Wilhelm. Wilhelm surprised him by offering France an alliance with Germany. Étienne turned the offer aside, on the sensible ground that French public opinion was not ready for it. Clemenceau concurred, advising that a move in the direction of Germany would imperil France's relations with Great Britain and Russia.

A year after Campbell-Bannerman's visit to Paris, Clemenceau was in London for Campbell-Bannerman's funeral. He met with Foreign Minister Grey, and again received no assurance of British aid in the event of attack, Grey advising Clemenceau to look to Russia for help in the event of attack.

Every summer, Clemenceau took a couple of weeks' vacation at the spa in Karlsbad, which was then in Austria and is now in the Czech Republic. In August, 1908, King Edward invited Clemenceau to meet him at the king's retreat at Marienbad, a short drive south of Karlsbad. Clemenceau delivered to the king a number of warnings, and the king was impressed. Clemenceau bluntly told the king that the British army was a "play-thing," reminded the King that Napoleon was brought down at Waterloo, not Trafalgar,[54] and, echoing what he had told Campbell-Bannerman, asked that Great Britain increase the size of its army by 250,000 to 500,000 men. Clemenceau predicted that if a war ever broke out between Great Britain and Germany, Germany would invade Great Britain through France, adding: "I am convinced that our position will be one of extreme danger until England has an army worthy of its name."[55] After the meeting, the king wrote: "Clemenceau is a true friend of his own country and of ours."[56]

Shortly before meeting the king, Clemenceau was introduced by a friend, the Irish journalist T.P. O'Connor, to the British Chancellor of the Exchequer, David Lloyd George, who had stopped over following a semi-official trip to Berlin. Clemenceau and Lloyd George had never met before, and there is no record that they had ever corresponded. Their meeting lasted five minutes. Afterwards, O'Connor thought that Lloyd George was "immediately impressed" by Clemenceau,[57] but writing years later Lloyd George recalled: "Had I never seen him again, I should have recalled him as a powerful but disagreeable and rather bad-tempered old savage."[58] Clemenceau's opinion of Lloyd George was worse, writing immediately afterwards to foreign minister Pichon that Lloyd George's ignorance of the political state of the peoples of Europe and America was "phenomenal." During his interview with the king, Clemenceau informed His Majesty that "Some of your public men are appallingly ignorant."[59]

On September 25, 1908, *L'Aurore*, in a one-sentence insert, noted that the minister of war had nominated a general "Fauche" to head the Army War College. They misspelled his name. He was general Ferdinand Jean Marie Foch, and on November 11, 1918, as a Marshal of France, he would accept the German request for an armistice ending the First World War.

When one considers Clemenceau's antipathy to the occupiers of Alsace-Lorraine, it may come as a surprise that Clemenceau's term as prime minister was marked by the most pacific period of Franco-German relations before the First World War. It should not surprise. Never a believer in colonial adventures, Clemenceau was not about to stir up trouble over colonies, and unlike Combes with his Delcassé, Clemenceau inserted the conciliatory Pichon as his minister of foreign affairs, and watched him closely. He transferred his great diplomat, Jules Cambon, from Madrid to Berlin; Cambon was also a conciliator. Moreover, Clemenceau understood the relative military strengths of France and Germany. Russia's disastrous war with Japan had temporarily sidelined Russia as an effective ally. Clemenceau knew that Britain's small—and declining—army would be of little help in a land conflict. A war with Germany would imperial the Republic. He was a realist. Shortly before the Algeciras conference over Morocco he wrote a friend: "[I]n my opinion the situation in Europe is such that a great armed conflict appears to me to be inevitable at some date which I can in no way predict, and our duty is to prepare for the worst."[60]

His policy was tested in July, 1907, and once again (and not for the last time) the issue was Morocco. On July 30, nine Europeans were murdered in Casablanca. The Algeciras Convention gave France and Spain joint policing rights, and Clemenceau could have used the incident as an excuse to beef up France's military and naval strength there. He insisted on treading lightly, writing Pichon from Karlsbad: "[If] we furnish the slightest pretext and [foreign minister] Bülow can pretend to believe that we have exceeded the prescriptions of Algeciras, you will witness a brutal turnaround,"[61] admonishing Pichon not to "trust Germany too much, which I think can turn against us," and specifically warning him not to make the same mistake as Delcassé, who was "willing to believe she [Germany] would not make war on us…"

Soon after Jules Cambon took up his post in Berlin in April, 1907, he began picking up hints that Germany was willing to improve relations over Morocco. In early 1909, von Bülow took the initiative, proposing an agreement whereby France would recognize Germany's economic equality in Morocco, in exchange for Germany's conceding France's political pre-eminence there. Pinchon was receptive, and secret negotiations, conducted by Cambon, ensued. In February, 1909, the agreement was concluded. It represented the only bilateral agreement of any kind entered into between France and Germany throughout the history of the Third Republic. Clemenceau walked a tightrope with respect to this agreement; his British allies were suspicious regarding the secrecy in which the negotiations were conducted. The Russians viewed the agreement as freeing Germany's hands, and for a period relations between France and Russia cooled. But French public opinion welcomed the lessening of tensions between these two constant adversaries.

On March 12, 1907, the battleship *Iéna* exploded while undergoing repairs at the Toulon drydock. The explosion was caused by an ammunition propellant that had become unstable with age. One hundred eighteen sailors and two civilians were killed. There then ensued a series of smaller naval accidents in 1908, and the minister of marine, Gaston Thomson, resigned. Clemenceau replaced him with Alfred Picard, an apolitical professional engineer. But in 1909 the Chamber of Deputies created a commission to examine the administration of the navy. The commission was created at the initiative of deputy Theophile Delcassé. The man appointed to head the commission was Delcassé. When Delcassé's commission submitted its report, it was highly critical of the navy's organization, procurement and shipbuilding.

Late in the evening of July 20, 1909, the Chamber of Deputies convened to consider Delcassé's report. The Chamber was scheduled to conclude its sitting for summer recess in a couple of days. Of the 563 members of the Chamber, 175 were absent, many having sailed for a conference in Stockholm, others having departed early for summer vacation. Considering the lateness of the hour, the public galleries were empty. On the table was Delcassé's motion to censure the government for its handling of the navy. Delcassé was present, as was Clemenceau, seated on the front bench with the rest of his cabinet. Everyone expected Delcassé's motion to go down to defeat.

Picard spoke first. He was conciliatory. He had been minister of marine for only ten months. He said that he had instituted many of the reforms in the administration of the navy that the commission had suggested, but defended the navy's overall readiness. Then

Delcassé rose. When he did, Clemenceau said, in a voice loud enough for everyone to hear, "What's that gentleman's name?"[62] Delcassé stared at Clemenceau, seated directly before him on the front bench. He accused Clemenceau of *criminally* washing his hands of all personal responsibility for the naval mishaps. He said that since the government had failed to do its duty, it was now time for the Chamber to do its duty. Clemenceau then rose to speak, and committed a terrible breach of parliamentary etiquette. Rather than address the issue at hand, he attacked Delcassé personally: "M. Delcassé forgets that he was a cabinet minister. He would do well to apply to himself the excellent advice which he has been so good as to give to the head of the government. That would be all the more to the point, as he was then mastering in his mind the vast schemes of European policies which were destined to carry us to Algeciras."[63] This was met with "loud protests." But Clemenceau continued: "Recall that moment, and tell me whether it is admissible that the man who brought us to Algeciras should taint ministers with carelessness and negligence in the preparation of the national defense."

Delcassé mounted the tribune in response. His face flushed with emotion, he responded: "Nothing in my past, nothing in my present can cause me any embarrassment." Looking directly at Clemenceau, he said that he could almost hear Clemenceau's famous 1885 remark to Ferry in the Chamber: "Go! We do not wish to deal with you anymore in the great interests of the nation." But now it would be different. Unlike Ferry, he would not slink away in shame. He rattled off his accomplishments: an agreement with Spain, an agreement with Italy, the mediation of the Spanish-American War, seven permanent treaties of arbitration, and, of course, the *entente* with Great Britain. He sat down to "loud and prolonged cheers."

Clemenceau rose to face what was now a hostile Chamber. He repeated the accusation: "M. Delcassé has taken a great deal of trouble not to reply to the only question which I put to him—namely, you were minister and you followed a policy which was bound to carry us to one of the greatest humiliations." The Chamber erupted. Palms slapped at desks. There were shouts of "Resign." When the room quieted, Clemenceau continued: "You led us, M. Delcassé, within a hairs breath of war and you did nothing to prepare for such a policy by taking military precautions...I have not humiliated France; M. Delcassé humiliated her."

The Chamber rose to vote on what was now a vote of confidence on Clemenceau's ministry. A new rule barring proxy voting meant that the 175 deputies sailing to Stockholm or on early vacation could not vote. As the deputies filed out to vote, one deputy, remarking on Clemenceau's opening remark ("What's that gentleman's name?") yelled out: *"His name is Delcassé!"*

By a vote was 212 to 176, Clemenceau's ministry fell. It came so suddenly and unexpectedly that when Clemenceau went to the Elysée Palace to formally tender his resignation to president Fallières, the president, who had been at dinner, did not know that the government had fallen. One deputy remarked after the vote: "M. Clemenceau did not fall; he plunged out of office." He had been prime minister for thirty-three months, the second-longest ministry in the history of the Third Republic. Some said that his ouster was so self-inflicted that he must have planned it, an unprovable theory. But there is no doubt that he was relieved that it was over. The night of his defeat he had dinner with the great composers Gabriel Fauré and Claude Debussy. The next day he wrote a friend: "I'm in the full joy of deliverance."[64] A few days later, he headed off to Karlsbad for his summer vacation. He was sixty-eight. He had diabetes, and he was tired. He could now contemplate a well-deserved retirement of travel, of reading, of spending time with his great friend Claude Monet. A long life in the arena that had begun as the embattled mayor of Montmartre during the *commune* was now finally over.

Or so he thought.

8

MINISTER FROM WALES

*If the Boer War had made Lloyd George notorious, the Education Bill
made him famous.*

—Malcolm Thomson

When David Lloyd George was a boy growing up in Llanystumbdwy, in North Wales, he attended the only primary school available, the one paid for by the state but run by the Established Church of England. He was forced to study its catechism. If he had wished to continue his education past primary school, he could do so only as a "pupil-teacher," but to do so he would have had to pledge his allegiance to the Church of England. His mother, a devout Baptist, would never have consented. There was no high school available. And so, when he was fourteen years old, his formal education ended. He was apprenticed to a firm of solicitors.

A quarter-century later he sat in the House of Commons, but nothing had changed. There were still eight thousand parishes in Great Britain like Llanystumbdwy where there was no alternative to the church-run school. One million Nonconformist children attended schools outside of their faith. Secondary school was still not only not mandatory, it was mostly unavailable. There were only 125,000 children in secondary schools of any kind in all of Great Britain, and only 25,000 of these in state-run schools.

In December, 1900, one T.B. Cockerton, an auditor for the London Local Government Board, performed an audit on some art classes offered to the public.

He compared the expenditure to the exact wording of the Education Act of 1870, the statute governing public education, and determined that any public money devoted to any instruction post-primary school was unauthorized by the statute and hence illegal...*ultra vires*! On the day after the "Cockerton Judgment," at the dawn of the twentieth century, public secondary education in Great Britain was not only rare, it was illegal. The government appealed the "Cockerton Judgment," and in April, 1901, the government lost. The government obtained a one-year stay of Cockerton's ruling, but something had to be done.

The House of Commons was then controlled—as it had been since 1896—by a coalition of Conservatives under the leadership of the elderly Lord Salisbury (and his nephew Arthur Balfour) and the Liberal Unionists led by Lloyd George's nemesis, the Birmingham screw manufacturer Joseph Chamberlain. In March, 1902, shortly before the stay of the enforcement of the Cockerton Judgment would expire, Balfour, then the Tory leader in the House of Commons, introduced the Education Bill of 1902.

Education in Great Britain was then controlled by a crazy-quilt of thousands of local school boards, dispensing public funds directly to "voluntary," i.e. church-run schools. Balfour's Education Bill proposed to eliminate these boards in favor of "local education associations" ("LEAs"). Education would be funded in large part by local property taxes (the "rates"). The LEAs would set the rates and disburse the tax revenues. But the LEAs would themselves be controlled by the local prelates who ran the schools. The Education Bill would overturn the Cockerton Judgment, permitting tax revenues to be used for secondary education. But each locality would have to tax itself to build a high school. If a parish was too poor and its tax base too low, there would still be no public high school, a fact of little concern to the Tory toffs who sent their sons to Eton and Harrow.[1] Moreover, the Education Bill did nothing to alleviate the worst feature of British education, the eight thousand parishes where the only school available was a church-run school. Worst of all, public tax revenues would be used for religious instruction by teachers hired by the local clergy who controlled the schools.

When Lloyd George, seated in one of the back benches in the House chamber, first heard the reading of the Bill, he supported it, writing Margaret: "Llanystumbdwy School will now be under the County Council & a very great improvement it is."[2] He failed to notice what all of his Welsh Nonconformist neighbors realized immediately, that the Education Bill meant that they would be taxed to pay for church schools teaching catechism by teachers selected by clergymen. The outcry was loud and immediate. Lloyd George soon realized where the parade was headed, and quickly jumped in front to lead it.

If Lloyd George was conflicted about the Education Bill, it is because he knew, as well as anyone, how deficient was British education. He compared British education to its fast-growing competitors, the United States and Germany, and found Britain's wanting. Worse, the deficiency fell mostly on the poor. "The rich man can afford to be ignorant; the poor man cannot," adding that he would rather entrust the country's future to "an educated, thoughtful people than I would to men who have got three years' of catechism from the parsons." Noting that in America a "rail splitter" had become president, "I had rather have the religion which, in America, brings the millionaire's son, side by side, to learn in the same school with the carpenter's son.[3]

He had no choice but to oppose the Education Bill. He had stood alone against the government during the Boer War, but at least then there were fellow Liberals who shared his conviction. This was different; opposition to the bill by Welsh Nonconformists was fierce and unanimous. The bill was also opposed by millions of Nonconformists in England; by opposing the bill, he would become their champion as well. "If he had unduly prevaricated on this issue," his nephew wrote, "he would have suffered political catastrophe."[4]

He soon began speaking against the bill in the House of Commons. He could distill the opposition into a single sentence: "If anyone prefers the Catechism to the Bible, he had better teach it at his own expense."[5] Or this: "In some cases a man might even have to pay to have his own child taught that his father was a heretic and sinner in not attending the Catholic Church or in not recognizing its doctrines."[6] He ranged all over England and Wales, speaking more than anyone against the Bill. The diffident leader of the Liberal opposition, Campbell-Bannerman, was nowhere to be heard, and Lloyd George quickly became the *de facto* leader of the Liberals opposing the bill. On the stump, as only he could, he had his listeners imagine a Church of England-run school interviewing for a new teacher. The first applicant has a brilliant academic resumé, years of teaching experience and excellent references, but he is a Nonconformist; he is turned away. The second applicant was a poor student, has few references and little experience, but he can play the church organ. He is hired! "We talk of improving our education in order to get abreast of Switzerland and Germany and the United States," he told the House of Commons, and yet, with this Bill, "for the sake of teaching dogmas to children who cannot understand them we, in the midst of our difficulties and the rocks that surround us, we propose to put the chaplain on the bridge of the ship. It is a mad proposal."[7]

On May 31, 1902, the Treaty of Vereeniging was signed, ending the Boer War. The Liberals had been badly split over the war, with many English Nonconformists supporting the Tory government. But the Education Bill now united them, and Lloyd

George was their leader. As the fight over the bill dragged on, Lloyd George proposed an amendment to the effect that an LEA could withhold payment for the upkeep of a church school whose managers had not sufficiently maintained the school. Balfour let the amendment pass. He would regret it.

With the Tories and the Liberal Unionists holding a solid majority, there was no chance that the Education Bill could be defeated. The Irish Parliamentary Party, which had united with the Liberals for Irish Home Rule, deserted the Liberals; the bill would benefit the overwhelmingly Catholic-run schools in Ireland. And the Lords, most of whom were Tory and Church of England, approved the Bill. It became law on December 10, 1902. But the fight was not over, and it was his opposition *after* the bill became the Education Law that made Lloyd George famous. English Nonconformists proposed to oppose the law through passive resistance. If they were powerless in running a church-run school, they would simply withhold that portion of their taxes that went to maintain the school. ("Without our say, no pay" was the slogan). They staged one of the largest protests in memory in London's Hyde Park. At least 250,000 people turned out to hear speeches denouncing the Education Act. Passive resistance was the rage throughout England.

But not in Wales. Lloyd George had a better idea. He saw that withholding taxes that had been legally assessed would never work. The portion of each person's tax bill that went to operate the local school was simply too small to matter. It was also patently illegal, and the nonpayment of taxes, even a small portion of the tax bill, could result in the *distraint*—the seizure—of a man's property. "My advice is," he said, "let us capture the enemy's artillery and turn his guns against him."[8] A property owner could not be liable for nonpayment of tax the local government had never assessed it. He proposed that the local county councils (the LEAs in Wales) delegate to a Welsh central board the power to assess taxes for local schools. Using the amendment that he had slipped passed Balfour as a hook, the central board would withhold funds from any church school that had fallen into disrepair until the managers of the school brought the school up to standard. He knew that many of the church schools, chronically starved of funds, were in terrible shape. The scheme was a fig-leaf for flouting the Law, as Lloyd George well knew. Most (but not all) of the Welsh county councils, popularly elected and in the hands of Nonconformists, went along, refusing to provide funds to church schools that needed repairs. Wales was now in open revolt against the government, and Lloyd George was their leader. "No control; no cash" he told a cheering crowd.

He may not have counted on Arthur Balfour's response. In April, 1904, Balfour used his solid majority in the House to enact the Default Bill, which Lloyd George quickly dubbed the "Coercion of Wales Bill." This law empowered the central board of education to pay funds from the treasury directly to church schools, withholding a like amount from the funds that otherwise would be paid to the recalcitrant locality. Suddenly, teachers in Wales became nervous; they wondered if and how they would be paid. They might even be terminated. Lloyd George now saw, as only he could, that he had climbed too far out on a limb. He continued to make fiery speeches on the stump, but behind the scenes, he sought a compromise. His best hope, he knew, was a change in government, one that would not enforce the Default Bill. This was no idle hope. The Tories and their Liberal Unionist allies had held power since 1896. They had been responsible for the disastrous war against the Boers, and all of the Nonconformists were united against them in opposition to the Education Law. A big Liberal sweep was in the offing.

Lloyd George was not present in Hyde Park on the day of the huge protest rally against the Education Law. He was in Cambridge that day, speaking on the issue of "tariff reform."

Free trade had been Holy Writ for Liberals for decades. Two of Woodrow Wilson's great Liberal boyhood heroes, John Bright and Richard Cobden, had spearheaded the Anti-Corn Law League in the 1840's in the fight to repeal the tariffs that had kept food prices high and the working class poor. Free trade is what made a Liberal a Liberal, and Lloyd George had been a free-trader his entire life ("Protection is never a cure, but always a curse," he had said).[9] It thus caused a sensation when Joseph Chamberlain, Balfour's Secretary of State for the Colonies, leader of the Liberal Unionists, former Liberal and one-time hero of Lloyd George, announced in a speech in Birmingham on May 15, 1903 a proposal for "tariff reform." The idea was simple: Free trade would be replaced by a system of "imperial preference." Britain and its dominions—notably Canada and Australia—would enter into a free trade pact with Great Britain at the expense of all of its other principal trading partners, notably the United States and Germany. The scheme would increase much-needed revenues from increased tariffs, and, most importantly, would strengthen the bonds of the British Empire. "I believe in a British Empire," Chamberlain said, "in an Empire which, although it should be its first duty to cultivate friendships with all nations of the world, should yet, even if alone, be self-sustaining and self-sufficient, and able to maintain itself against the competition of its rivals."[10]

A week later, Lloyd George was in Cambridge, skewering Chamberlain on tariff reform. Just as every leading economist then (and now) realized that protectionism was an economic illusion, Lloyd George realized it too, and walked his audience through a careful explanation of why. He noted that Britain was an exporting nation, whose annual exports exceeded its imports by £250 million, and that *three-fourths* of Britain's foreign trade came from countries outside of the British Empire. Moreover, Britain benefitted from trade in which it was neither a buyer or a seller; a majority of the world's trade was conducted in British bottoms. Britain's merchant marine flourished under a system of free trade. He concluded: "It is the duty of every man who loved his country to use his whole intelligence, conviction and energy to fight this proposal to the very last."[11]

Five days later, he was on the floor of the House of Commons, confronting Joseph Chamberlain directly. It was here that he exposed tariff reform's greatest weakness: If American and German imports of wheat would be subject to tax, local producers would be free to raise their prices. Chamberlain was forced to concede it: "If you are to give a preference to the Colonies—I do not say that you are—you must put a tax on food. I make the Honourable Gentleman opposite a present of that."[12] The "Honourable Gentleman opposite" was Lloyd George. So there it was. "Tariff reform" was a food tax; a tax that would fall on every worker and benefit every producer.

One of Lloyd George's Conservative supporters, who joined Lloyd George that day in opposing Chamberlain, was one of the newest MP's, Winston Churchill. Churchill had been even younger than Lloyd George had been when he entered the House of Commons, winning a seat from Oldham in 1900 when he was only twenty-five. He ran as a Conservative mostly out of instinct; his grandfather, the Duke of Marlborough, and his father, Lord Randolph Churchill, had both served in Parliament as Conservatives. But the conservatism of Lord Salisbury and his nephew, the new Prime Minister Arthur Balfour, began to chafe. Initially, Balfour was noncommittal on tariff reform. Later, he came out in favor. Churchill was every bit the free trader that Lloyd George was, and a few weeks after Chamberlain announced for tariff reform Churchill co-founded the Free Food League, a group of Tory and Unionist MP's dedicated to opposing tariff reform. Churchill's days in the Conservative Party were numbered.

In December, 1903, the Oldham Conservative Association informed Churchill that it would not support him in his next campaign for re-election. He began consulting with Liberal leaders, who found Churchill a vacancy in a Liberal stronghold in Manchester. On May 31, 1904, Churchill made the break complete. He entered the House chamber, and stopped momentarily at the Bar, a painted white stripe on the floor directly opposite the Speaker. The members from the ruling party are seated to the Speaker's right; the members of the opposition to the Speaker's left. He stepped forward, bowed to the Speaker, and made a turn to his *right*, to the Liberal benches, and took a seat, the same seat that his father Randolph Churchill had occupied when he, as a Conservative, was in opposition. He sat beside Lloyd George.[13]

Lloyd George and Churchill were very different in background, but much alike in temperament. Lloyd George was born in a cottage in Manchester, Churchill at his ancestral home, Blenheim Palace. Lloyd George had felt privation first-hand and sided with the poor and the working class by instinct; Churchill learned it by reading and through the eyes of his working class nanny, Mrs. Everest, whom he called "Woom." But more than anything, they became and would remain close friends despite their difference in age (Lloyd George was twelve years older) because they loved each other's company. Each knew that they were both smarter and wittier than anyone else. They would grow apart, but that would be many years distant.

Winston Churchill took being expelled by the Oldham Conservative Association in stride; he could see which way the political winds were blowing. The Tories and their Liberal Unionist allies had fostered the South African War and the Education Law on the British people, and they now proposed to increase the price of bread. A huge Liberal election sweep was in the offing.

On December 4, 1905, Arthur Balfour and his government resigned. King Edward made it known that his choice to succeed Balfour was the Liberal leader, Sir Henry Campbell-Bannerman. This despite Campbell-Bannerman's now infamous reaction to the South African War. ("When is a war not a war? When it is carried on by methods of barbarism in South Africa.")

Henry Campbell-Bannerman had been born Henry Campbell in Glasgow in 1836, the son of a successful draper. He became Campbell-Bannerman after a wealthy uncle, Henry Bannerman, made him a huge bequest in his will, contingent on his changing his name to Campbell-Bannerman. He did, and hated the "horrid" name ever since, inviting one and all to call him "C-B". And so "C-B" it was. Educated at the University of Glasgow and Cambridge, he was fluent in French, German and Italian. First elected to the House of Commons in 1868, he rose quickly (more quickly than Lloyd George) becoming Financial Secretary to the War Office after only three years. He was a "homely, round-faced podgy little man,"[14] He was a disciple of Gladstone, strong on free trade, Irish Home Rule, fiscal economy and social reforms when necessary. He had a gruff, no-nonsense air. He had served as a minister since 1886, but in 1905 he was sixty-eight and not in good health. Before taking office, a cabal of senior Liberals that included Sir Edward Grey (but not Lloyd George) tried to kick him upstairs by proposing that he accept a peerage and enter the House of Lords. The cabal failed. "C-B" became Prime Minister.

Despite Grey's role in the cabal, Campbell-Bannerman named him Foreign Secretary. He appointed Herbert Henry ("H.H.") Asquith as Chancellor of the Exchequer and Woodrow Wilson's friend and mentor, James Bryce, the author of *The American Commonwealth*, as Chief Secretary for Ireland. Churchill, only five years in the House, became Undersecretary for the Colonies, a sub-cabinet position. And he named Lloyd George as president of the board of trade. It was a smart choice. He had led the fight against Chamberlain's South African War, he was popular with English Nonconformists as a result of the Education Law fight, he was leading the fight against tariff reform and being Welsh he gave the Cabinet geographical balance. At forty-two, he was the youngest member of the Cabinet, and the first native Welshman ever to serve as a minister. He would serve in the Cabinet, in one capacity or another, for the next seventeen years. His career as a backbencher was over. The open question was whether the Welsh terrier who could thunder invective on the stump and from the back benches could now actually run a government ministry.

Balfour had resigned, but he had not dissolved Parliament. Five days after taking office, Campbell-Bannerman did, and a nationwide election campaign was on. Campbell-Bannerman was ready for it: "This reckless, criminal escapade of Joe's [Chamberlain] is the greatest event of our time...it is like disputing the Law of Gravitation. All the old war horses about me are snorting with excitement. We are in for a great time."[15]

On December 11, 1905 Lloyd George's appointment as President of the board of trade was made official when he received the seals of office at Buckingham Palace ("King very gracious," he wrote Margaret). On that day, his life changed forever. For the first time, he would receive a salary (£2,000 per year, the equivalent of more than £200,000 today). His financial reliance on the law practices in Criccieth and London was over, and he would soon sever those ties. (On the day of his appointment, he was overdrawn by £400 at his bank.) For the first time, he would be entitled to a private room in the House of Commons, ironically the one that had been occupied by Joseph Chamberlain. He would sit on the front bench in the House, and henceforth be addressed, by fellow Liberals and opposition members alike, as the *Right Honourable* gentleman.

The board of trade was a hodgepodge ministry dealing with most aspects of commercial business. It oversaw bankruptcy, merchant shipping, the registration of patents and trademarks, and the regulation of railways and other public utilities. It mediated labor disputes, and advised the Foreign Office with respect to commercial negotiations with foreign governments. The "board" of which Lloyd George was "president" had long since ceased to exist. Yet, during his ministry, he still went through the motions of taking actions at a meeting of a "board" at which he was the only member present. He had a budget of £270,000 and a staff of a thousand.[16]

The election campaign opened in January, 1906. Lloyd George was everywhere, campaigning not only for himself but for younger Liberal candidates, always ready to sacrifice a weekend for a few speeches. He was tireless; "He lives longer in one day than most men do in a month."[17] His wit never deserted him. Once on the stump he said that "we shall have Home Rule for Ireland and for England and for Scotland and for Wales." A heckler shouted: "And for Hell." "Quite right," Lloyd George retorted, "I like to hear a man stand up for his own country."[18]

The Liberal victory that everyone predicted was even larger than expected. The Tories and their Liberal Unionist allies lost over two hundred seats, giving the Liberals their largest working majority in the House of Commons since 1832. The number of MP's who were not Church of England doubled. Even Arthur Balfour lost his seat. (He was returned a few weeks later from a safe seat in a bye-election.) Lloyd George easily won re-election. His original eighteen-vote margin was now 1,224; he would never again be seriously challenged at the polls. The Education Law now became a dead letter, at least in Wales, as Lloyd George had hoped. The new Liberal government would not enforce the Default Law. But thirty new MP's were from the newly-formed Labour Party. The Liberals espoused the same causes as Labour; they stood for the same programs. But almost all of the Liberals in the House were university trained, they socialized with their Tory friends, and were as middle-class as Lloyd George and Churchill. They were all British gentlemen; there was not a laborer in their ranks. Lloyd George saw the danger that Labour presented to the Liberals. He knew that if the Liberals did not soon deal with the needs of the workers, the workingmen of Great Britain would desert the Liberals for Labour, which, of course, is exactly what they did.

"What can I do for commerce?" he said when he took over the board of trade.[19] It turned out that there was plenty he could do for commerce, to the surprise of many business leaders who expected the worst from the Welsh firebrand. They would learn (perhaps as even Lloyd George himself would learn) that it was not the rich that he despised, it was the *idle* rich; the landlords. He had no economic theory. He never read Marx, but read and reread *Les Miserables*. It turned out that he liked and admired businessmen, especially those who had risen from humble beginnings. Far from being antagonistic, he was conciliatory. Before he introduced a bill in the House, he consulted with all of the groups interested in the bill, so that when the bill was presented it had already won the approval of the interested groups; the House was presented with a *fait accompli*. He had no ideology; he was a pragmatist.

One of the first answers to "What can I do for commerce?" was the Merchant Shipping Bill of 1906. For years, British merchant shippers had chafed under a weight limit (the "load line") of the cargo they carried. The load line was a safety measure designed to eliminate overloaded and hence unstable ships that too-often capsized ("coffin ships"), and all-too-often were over-insured. But foreign shippers were not subject to the limit, and domestic shippers felt they could not compete. Lloyd George consulted with the shipowners (much to their surprise and delight) and the unions. The result was a bill that relaxed the load line, but which was made applicable to foreign ships in British ports. The bill was larded with many worker safety and comfort features, such as the requirement that each vessel carry a certified cook, and a requirement that if a seaman was discharged in a foreign port, he would be repatriated at the shipowner's expense. When the Merchant Shipping Bill was introduced in the House, it was another *fait accompli*. Lloyd George emerged from the negotiations with a reputation of being both knowledgeable and easy to work with. Another answer to "What can I do for commerce?" involved patents. In 1906, almost half the patents in Great Britain were issued to foreigners who often did not use their patents in Great Britain, and who often took out a patent solely to stifle competition. Lloyd George changed the law, allowing the government to revoke a patent if it was not used in Great Britain. When not crafting legislation, he was busy mediating labor disputes, mooting a ferry service between Dover and Calais, modernizing the collection of business statistics, and broadening an international network of commercial attachés.

Few people possess the skill-set necessary to be a successful mediator; the ability to craft and then lead opposing parties to a resolution. In September, 1907, the members of one of two competing railroad unions, the Amalgamated Society of Railway Servants ("ASRS") voted overwhelmingly to authorize a nationwide rail strike, demanding the railroads recognize their union. In the days before air travel, when automobiles were still rare, a rail strike would have been calamitous. But the managers of the railroads refused to recognize the union, or even to bargain. It fell to Lloyd George to mediate the dispute. The most significant thing he did was to insist that he meet with the railroad managers and the ASRS *separately*. He shuttled between them; they never faced each other. When meeting with the railroad managers, he threatened them with a bill that would have required mandatory arbitration of all labor disputes. ("Conciliation first but failing that the steamroller," he wrote his brother.[20]) When the *Daily Mail* editorialized demanding compulsory arbitration, no one knew that Lloyd George was behind the editorial. When he learned from the head of the ASRS that the union would not insist on formal recognition as long as their demands were met, he pocketed that datum, withholding it from the railway managers. Shortly before midnight on November 6, after weeks of shuttling between them, they reached a tentative agreement. But before they signed, the railroad managers wished to consult with their shareholders and the union leaders wished to consult with their members. Lloyd George refused, insisting to both sides that the deal would collapse unless they signed *right now*. Each side came in and signed, each agreeing to terms with the board of trade, not with each other. They had never met face-to-face. In the final agreement, the union was not formally recognized, but the railroads agreed to set up "boards of conciliation and arbitration." The railroads agreed to meet with representatives from the ranks of their current employees, who, technically, did not have to be union officials. In the end, the ASRS gained little, the nation avoided a rail strike, and Lloyd George was a hero.

The next day, the liberal *Manchester Guardian* editorialized that "The settlement of the Railway Dispute is really an astonishing triumph for the President of the Board of Trade…Mr. Lloyd George has contrived to extract a treaty of peace which not merely averts the present danger, but puts future industrial disputes on the railways in a fair way for quiet settlement."[21]

It was a greater tribute that the conservative *Times* predicted: "Mr. Lloyd George has very probably enhanced his political reputation and his personal prestige by his successful treatment of the railway dispute," noting that the task had called for "capacity and for courage, as well as for the tact and patience essential in the reconciliation of opposing interests."[22] The Prime Minister wrote the King: "The country was so largely indebted for so blessed a conclusion to the knowledge, skill, astuteness and tact, of the President of the Board of Trade."[23]

Three weeks after Lloyd George settled the railway dispute, tragedy struck. His daughter, Mair Elunid ("Mary Ellen") died of peritonitis following an appendectomy. She was seventeen, a bright, beautiful high school student, and clearly she was his favorite. She was a talented musician, and he loved to sing Welsh hymns accompanied by her. He would try to assuage the pain by burying himself in work, but the wound truly would never heal.

Campbell-Bannerman's health continued to decline, and on April 1, 1908, he resigned. He chose as his successor, the man Campbell-Bannerman considered "the greatest gentleman I have ever met" his chancellor of the exchequer, Herbert Henry Asquith, 55. On April 8, Asquith (who insisted on being called "HH") accepted the seals of office and became prime minister. But he had to travel to France to do it. King Edward refused to interrupt his Biarritz vacation, and so Asquith had to travel there to "kiss hands." Two weeks later, Campbell-Bannerman died.

Asquith could have stayed on as his own chancellor of the exchequer; Gladstone had done so when he became prime minister. Instead, he elevated Lloyd George to the exchequer, who now, at forty-five, became the second most powerful man in Great Britain. He became the first solicitor to serve as chancellor, and would be chancellor for seven years, longer than any man in a hundred years. His appointment meant that Asquith and Lloyd George would now be neighbors; the chancellor of the exchequer resides at No. 11 Downing Street. (Unlike No. 10, which is the Prime Minister's office and residence, No. 11 is only a residence, a fact that Margaret much appreciated.) They would be neighbors, they would meet in Cabinet, but they would never socialize, and never become friends. They were very different men, despite both being Nonconformists from modest backgrounds. Asquith had been, and still was, an imperialist who had supported the South African War; Lloyd George had risen to fame in his lonely opposition. But it was Asquith, not Lloyd George (who divided his time with the Education Bill fight) who led the Liberals against tariff reform. Asquith was highly educated (Baillol College, Oxford) urbane and reserved. Lloyd George, high on champagne, would sing musical comedy choruses in a hotel dining room, who could not pay his hotel bill because he had lost his checkbook and could not remember the name of his bank. To Asquith, Lloyd George was a "Welsh peasant."[24]

Asquith named Lloyd George as chancellor in large part because Lloyd George had been the only Liberal minister who could point to any success. Campbell-Bannerman's attempt at a revised education law had been so mangled by the House of Lords that he withdrew it. A Licensing Bill, designed to reduce the number of public houses, which had passed the House, was summarily rejected by the Lords, as was a Coal Miner's Eight Hours bill. In 1907, Britain fell into recession. Tariff reform, an issue that had never died, was revived. The Liberals began losing bye-elections. Worse, they were losing seats to Labour candidates.

The Chancellor runs the British treasury department, controlling the finances of other departments, collecting the revenue, and formulating the budget. Lloyd George quickly found that the hide-bound treasury bureaucracy was not nearly as much to his liking as had been the board of trade. These bureaucrats liked to write reports; he didn't much want to read them. He preferred to absorb information in face-to-face conferences; they had never experienced that. He wanted to initiate new policies, as he had at the board of trade. Their instinct was to keep expenditures as low as possible. The Treasury clerks dubbed him "The Welsh Goat." The name stuck.

When, in 1907, Georges Clemenceau had pressed Campbell-Bannerman to increase the size of the British army, claiming that its army was not worthy of a great nation, he knew that Great Britain relied on its navy for its defense and for the control of the Empire. He also knew that Britain was actually reducing its army expenditures, and he knew why. Britain had just launched *HMS Dreadnought*, the largest, fastest and most powerful battleship in the world. With a revolutionary steam turbine engine, it could speed at twenty-one knots, outrunning any other ship. Its decks bristled with ten twelve-inch guns, throwing more firepower at greater range than any other ship. But it had cost £2,000,000. Worse, in rendering the ships of every other nation obsolete, it also rendered every other ship in the British fleet obsolete, so that after *HMS Dreadnought* was launched, Great Britain's naval advantage over Germany was exactly *one ship*, an advantage that would be completely erased the moment Germany launched its own *Dreadnought*-class battleship, which it was sure to do. The launching of *HMS Dreadnought* thus set off a fierce, and ferociously expensive, arms race with Germany.

HMS Dreadnought had been the brainchild of Britain's tempestuous, charismatic First Sea Lord, Adm. John Arbuthnot ("Jacky") Fisher (1841-1920), a man who "rushed through life from one seething, volcanic controversy to the next."[25] "We could sleep soundly in our beds because of the invincibility of our navy," he said, and he and his vocal supporters demanded the funds for eight Dreadnoughts. ("We want eight and we won't wait," they chanted.) Asquith's civilian first lord of the admiralty, Reginald McKenna, wanted six. Lloyd George (and Churchill, who had succeeded Lloyd George at the board of trade) wanted no more than four, knowing that no matter how many Britain built, Germany would likely match it in a futile escalation. In the end, something of a compromise was reached. Four Dreadnoughts (as this new class of battleships was called) were budgeted for 1909, and an additional four for 1910. Each would cost £2,000,000 and it would fall to the chancellor of the exchequer to find the money. Forty percent of Britain's annual tax revenues already went to the military.

The Dreadnoughts would have to fight for revenues with "old age pensions," the British term for retirement security. Old age pensions had been a Liberal goal for years; Lloyd George had lamented during the South African War that every shell that exploded on a Transvaal hillside carried with it an old age pension. But during the ten years that the Tories held power before the Liberal sweep in 1906, there was no chance that old age pensions could pass the House of Commons. When he was chancellor,

Asquith had formulated a bill to provide for old age pensions. It was now up to Lloyd George to get it passed.

The Old Age Pensions Act provided a very modest retirement benefit. Limited to retirees over seventy who had worked continuously their *entire lives*, the benefit was five shillings per week ($36.83 in 2017 dollars), and no one who had an income above £31, 10s per year ($4,640 in 2017 dollars) was eligible. The benefit was deliberately modest, so that people would be encouraged to save for retirement. But unlike American Social Security, the Old Age Pensions Act was entirely non-contributory. Neither the worker nor his employer contributed to it; the benefits were paid entirely from the budget. Another difference: No checks were mailed. Retirees had to queue up weekly at the post office for their payment, and for years they said they were going to pick up their "lloyd george." When Lloyd George became chancellor, he was surprised to learn that his predecessor had conducted no actuarial studies to determine what the Old Age Pensions Act might cost. The Act took effect on August 1, 1908, the government having guessed at an annual cost of £6 million to £6.5 million (three Dreadnoughts). By March, 1910, the annual cost was £8.5 million (four Dreadnoughts), with no end in sight. That was when Lloyd George made an honest, if imprudent, admission: "I have got to rob somebody's hen-roost next year. I am on the lookout which will be the easiest to get and where I will be the least punished, and where I will get the most eggs, and not only that, but where they can be the most easily spared."[26]

The Old Age Pensions Act passed in the House of Commons because the Liberals and their Labour allies had the votes. It passed the House of Lords not because a majority of the Lords favored it (they did not) but because of tradition. The Lords freely and often mangled, diluted, or simply rejected anything and everything that the House of Commons threw at them, but not since 1660 had the Lords rejected a "money" bill, i.e. anything dealing directly with taxation and spending. Nothing in writing prevented their doing so; Great Britain has no written constitution.

During his years at the board of trade, and through most of his years running the treasury, Lloyd George dealt exclusively with domestic matters; he had no writ with respect to foreign affairs. But the need to fill a £16 million annual shortfall in his budget changed that. In July, 1908, he appeared before the London meeting of the International Peace Congress, and he devoted his speech to Great Britain's relations with Germany. He stressed that since Great Britain and Germany were active trading partners, there was no reason the two nations should be hostile, and certainly no reason they should arm themselves for war: "They buy about thirty millions of goods from us. Well, really, when a man comes into your shop like this, you don't knock him down with a cannon-ball....It really seems incredible when you begin to reflect upon it that it should be necessary in the 20th century of the Christian Era to hold a meeting in a civilized country to protect against the expenditure of 400 millions a year upon preparing for one nation to kill another." More to the point: "For fear of each other (Great Britain and Germany) we are arming and rushing into the very quarrel we are afraid if."[27] His speech was well-received, but not by the twenty-or so members of the Women's Social and Political Union, who heckled him repeatedly. These were the "suffragettes," and they were now disrupting his speeches regularly. They were ejected from the hall "screaming and protesting." The foreign secretary, Sir Edward Grey, was also not impressed by Lloyd George's performance, fearing that a clamor for rapprochement with Germany would do nothing but endanger the *ententes* with France and Russia.

Speeches to peace groups were not going to reduce an arm's race, and so the next month he was off to Berlin, on his first foray into foreign policy as chancellor. The ostensible purpose of his visit was to study Germany's advanced social safety net that had been instituted by Bismarck. He did meet with German officials, and did impress them with the alacrity in which he grasped the German system ("The German officials say they never met such a quick-witted man," noted the *Manchester Guardian*.[28]) But old-age pensions and health insurance were not the real purpose of his trip. Along the way, he gave an interview to Vienna's *Neue Freie Presse*, proposing an understanding between Great Britain and Germany for the purpose of reducing naval expenditures, so that both countries could concentrate on social reforms. He did not suggest that it could be done immediately, but that something needed to be done to dissipate the mutual misunderstanding between the two countries: "We must work for the conclusion of an entente between England and Germany in order that we may be able to devote ourselves wholly to the tasks of peace, of progress and social reform...there must be an end to the evil game of setting England and Germany upon each other like two dogs."[29]

He hoped to meet with Kaiser Wilhelm or at least with Chancellor von Bülow, but neither would agree to meet. Instead, he met for dinner with Theobald von Bethmann Hollweg, soon to be the German chancellor, but then the vice chancellor, whose writ included Germany's social programs. During the dinner, Bethmann Hollweg, apparently lubricated by a few large tankards of beer, gave Lloyd George an earful. He decried what he felt was the growing hostility of England, France and Russia towards Germany, and the "iron ring" that these nations were pressing around Germany. He began shouting: "An iron ring," he repeated, "England is embracing France. She is making friends with Russia. But it is not that you love each other; it is that you hate—hate—hate Germany."

In his beer-fueled rant, he even mocked Bavaria, noting that every Prussian would give his life for the kaiser, but not so the luke-warm Bavarians.[30]

Lloyd George's trip to Berlin was a flop, to say the least. (It was on his way home that he had his first encounter with Clemenceau at Carlsbad, with Clemenceau later opining to King Edward how ill-informed he felt Lloyd George was). When the French press got wind of the *Neue Freie Presse* interview, it at least took comfort that Lloyd George, as the *finance* minister, could not conclude any formal agreements. When King Edward himself learned of it, he was outraged, wondering why the prime minister allowed Lloyd George to involve himself in matters of "which he know[s] nothing."[31] Nothing came of the trip, but he still had a £16 million annual deficit to fill. And how he proposed to do that would soon change the British class system, and the manner in which Great Britain is governed, forever.

In May, 1908, barely one month into office as chancellor, Lloyd George circulated a memo to the Cabinet. In it he advised Prime Minister Asquith and his fellow ministers that if the government was to pay for new Dreadnoughts and fund old-age pensions, new tax revenues needed to be found. In August, 1908, the Old-Age Pensions Law went into effect. The government's estimate (hope) claims would be modest, since only those retirees who had worked their entire lives, but who had also not earned very much, would be eligible, was proven to be a chimera; annual claims were exceeding £10 million. For 1909, four Dreadnoughts, at £2 million per, had been promised.

It was not until Budget Day, April 29, 1909, that both houses of Parliament and the rest of the world learned how Lloyd George promised to pay for military spending and social programs. "Budget Day" in Great Britain is both a substantive and a ceremonial event, analogous to the president's annual State of the Union address. In the months preceding the speech, the treasury gathers from the various departments their own budget estimates, and allocates projected revenues. A Finance Bill is drafted, and presented to the Cabinet for their review and revision. On the day before the chancellor delivers his Budget Day Speech, the chancellor presents the budget to the King, who, as a constitutional monarch, has no power to reject or modify it. The next day, the chancellor walks from 11 Downing Street to Parliament, carrying the speech in an ancient red box. The rule against liquor on the floor of the House of Commons is waived this day; the chancellor may refresh himself as he pleases. When he is finished, the House begins to debate the Finance Bill. When the finished bill finally passes the House of Commons, it is sent to the Lords. They are technically free to reject it, but they had not done so since 1660.

Lloyd George rose to speak that day at 3:10 P.M., and did not finish until after 8:00 P.M. He read every word of the typescript he held in his hands. Never adept with numbers, he read many passages obviously not comprehending what he was reading. By the consensus of all present—friend and opponent alike—it was the worst speech he ever gave. Some said that it was the worst speech they had ever heard in the House. That night, he admitted that the speech had been a "thorough flop." But it was the substance that mattered, and the substance was revolutionary. He proposed that Great Britain do something that had never been tried before. Rather than merely collect taxes to meet expenses, for the first time Great Britain would tax one class—the rich—for the express purpose of aiding another—the working class. An otherwise dismal address contained one notable turn of phrase: "This is a war Budget. It is for raising money to wage implacable war against poverty and squalidness. I cannot help hoping and believing that before this generation has passed away we shall have advanced a great step towards that good time when poverty and human degradation (which always follows in its camp) will be as remote to the people of this country as the wolves which once infested its forests."[32]

He proposed a 10% increase in the income tax, and a "supertax" on annual incomes in excess of £5,000. There were only 10,000 taxpayers in Great Britain subject to the supertax, but it was the first income tax targeted solely at the rich. He proposed a one-third increase in inheritance taxes. There would be excise taxes on liquor and tobacco aimed at reducing consumption, and increase license fees on pubs, aimed at reducing their number. He even proposed the first gasoline tax targeted at improving roads, a tax that would fall only on those wealthy enough to own a motorcar. But that was only the beginning. The man who as a child watched helplessly as the landlords drove nursing mothers from their little cottages now proposed a series of taxes aimed directly at the landowners. There would be a 20% tax on the "unearned increment" in land, i.e. the increase in the value of land not caused directly by the improvements made by the landowner, to be collected when the land was sold or passed to an heir. For the first time, there would be a tax on the value of undeveloped land, a tax on the enhanced value of terminated leases, and a tax on mineral royalties. The worst feature, at least from the standpoint of the landowners, was that in order to effect the collection of these taxes, a nationwide re-evaluation of land would take place, valuing land at its current highest and best use, rather than its historical value. In truth, the land taxes did not promise to produce nearly as much revenue as the income taxes, but the land taxes fell most heavily on the landed peers in the House of Lords, who as everyone knew, had not rejected a "money" bill since 1660.

The opposition to what became known as the "People's Budget" was immediate. A Budget Protest League was formed, and a thousand people showed up for one of its first meetings, the hall sporting a banner: "We protest against the budget in the name of democracy, liberty and justice." No group opposed the budget louder than the Tariff Reform League, fully aware that if the budget passed, it spelled the end of protectionism and "imperial preference." No longer would the revenues generated by tariffs be needed; the new taxes would also save free trade. The man who headed the opposition in the House was the Tory leader, Arthur Balfour. Balfour, a man who Lord Randolph Churchill had described as "a person in easy circumstances who was very content with himself and who was extremely surprised that not all the world was equally contented as him,"[33] who believed in his heart that the Tories should by right govern Great Britain, whether they were in power or not, opposed the budget on the ground that it was an assault on the landed aristocracy, which it was.[34] One peer called the budget "Socialism and Collectivism." The head of the dockers' union termed this a "libel on Socialism."[35] Another peer termed it "not a Budget but a revolution." Quickly there was talk that the Lords might break more than 250 years of precedent and reject the budget. At the very least, they might butcher it. Churchill immediately scotched the idea: "No amendments, no excision, no modifying or mutilating will be agreed by us."[36]

Many budget bills fly through the House. The debate on the 1909 budget consumed seventy-two days. Many sessions went through the night. The usual summer recess was canceled. Before it was over, the members voted ("divided") on various aspects of the budget 554 times. It fell to the chancellor to answer every question and engage in every debate throughout the seventy-two days. The Liberals' Irish allies opposed the taxes on liquor and tobacco, but the broad outlines of the budget that Lloyd George proposed on Budget Day finally passed on November 4, 1908.

If the Budget Day Speech was Lloyd George's worst ever, he considered his July 30 speech defending the People's Budget his very best. He spoke in the Limehouse district of East London, at the "Edinburgh Castle," a former pub converted to a temperance hall. Four thousand people heard the speech, including Churchill's wife, Clementine. He was in rare form.

He began by noting that the wealthy had clamored for Dreadnoughts, and had agreed to pay for them. But now, "we are spending the money, but they won't pay. What has happened since to alter their tone? Simply that we have sent them the bill." And then: "Somebody has got to pay; and then these gentlemen say: 'Perfectly true; somebody has got to pay but we would rather that somebody were somebody else.' We started building; we wanted money to pay for the building; so we sent the hat round. We sent it round amongst the workmen and winders of Derbyshire and Yorkshire, the weavers in High Peak and the Scotsmen of Dumfries who, like all their countrymen, know the value of money. They all dropped in their coppers. We went round Belgravia; [a tony London district]; and there has been such a howl ever since that it has completely deafened us." He leveled his fire directly at the wealthy: "There are so many in the country blessed by Providence with great wealth, and if there are amongst them men who grudge out of their riches a fair contribution towards the less fortunate of their fellow countrymen they are very shabby rich men." The taxes that the People's Budget would produce would "bring forth fruit," by improving the security of the country: "The provision for the aged and deserving poor—it was time it was done. It is rather a shame for a rich country like ours, probably the richest in the world, if not the richest the world has ever seen, that it should allow those who have toiled all their days to end in penury and possibly starvation...We are raising money to pay for the new road, aye, and to widen it, so that 200,000 paupers will be able to join in the march."

He focused on the land taxes: "[I]t is perfectly clear that the one part of the Budget that attracts all the hostility and animosity is that part which deals with the taxation of land." Taxation was (and is) a difficult, abstruse subject. He simplified it. He pointed to acreage between the Lea and the Thames that had once been a useless marsh, not fit even for agriculture. But as Great Britain's trade expanded geometrically (thanks, he noted, to free trade) the useless marsh became the Port of London. People came to work at the port by the thousands, and they all needed housing. "That was the opportunity of the owners of the marsh. All that land became valuable building land." Land that had rented for £2 or £3 an acre was recently selling for upwards of £8,000 an acre. "Who created that increment?" he asked. "Was it the landlord? Was it his energy?" It was "purely the combined efforts of all the people who engaged in the trade and commerce of the Port of London—trader, merchant, shipowner, dock labourer, workman, everybody except the landlord." But "thanks to a munificent Tory Government" the landlord was paying taxes based on undeveloped agricultural land, not even at a valuation of £2 or £3. "We mean to value all the land in the kingdom," he said. "In the future those landlords will have to contribute to the taxation of the country on the basis of the real value."[37]

After walking his audience through all of the land tax provisions, he concluded: "We are placing burdens on the broadest shoulders. Why should I put burdens on the people? I am one of the children of the people. I was brought up amongst them. I know their trials; and God forbid that I should add one grain of trouble to the anxieties they bear with such patience and fortitude. When the Prime Minister did me the honour of inviting me to take charge of the National Exchequer at a time of great difficulty, I made up my mind, in framing the Budget which was in front of me, that at any rate no cupboard should be barer, no lot would be harder. By that test I challenge them to judge the Budget."

After the speech, Asquith met with the king, who was not pleased. Asquith found him in a "state of great agitation and annoyance" at the Limehouse speech, which he found to be "a menace to property and a Socialistic spirit,"[38] "calculated to set class against class and to inflame the passions of the working and lower classes against people who happened to be the owners of property."[39] As a result of the speech, Balfour determined that the Lords would not amend the budget, they would reject it, and on November 30 they did just that, overwhelmingly. But they framed the veto as being only "suspensory," pending a general election in which the people would vote on the issue of the budget. Three days later, Asquith introduced a motion in the House: "an action of the House of Lords in refusing to pass into law the financial provisions made by the House for the service of the year is a breach of the constitution and a usurpation of the rights of the Commons."[40] It passed, 349 to 134, with the support of the Irish Parliamentary Party. In exchange, Asquith promised to renew the dormant fight for Irish Home Rule. After the vote, Asquith *prorogued* (i.e. suspended) Parliament; he did not dissolve it. After the rejection, Lloyd George said of the Lords: "At last, with all their cunning, their greed has overborne their craft,[41]...we have got them at last. And we do not mean to let them go until all the accounts have been settled."[42] The election campaign was on.

The focus shifted. The issue became more than the People's Budget, but the Lords themselves. Prior to the Lords' rejection of the Budget, Lloyd George delivered a speech in Newcastle in which he flayed the Lords as never before: "A fully equipped duke costs as much to keep up as two Dreadnoughts (laughter), and are just as great a terror (renewed laughter), and they last longer (more laughter)...Who ordained that a few should have the land of Britain as a perquisite; who made 10,000 people owners of the soil, and the rest of us trespassers in the land of our birth?"[43] No law could pass the House of Lords eliminating or curbing its veto power without its own consent, which, of course, the Lords would never give. Asquith had only one card he could play. He could stock the House of Lords with enough new Liberal peers—five hundred of them—that the suddenly enlarged Lords would vote to curb its own powers. New peers are nominated by the prime minister and approved by the king. The king usually approves a new peer as a matter of course, but five hundred of them at once for the purpose of neutering the Lords was another matter. Asquith went to King Edward and laid out the plan. The king advised Asquith that he would agree only following a second election for the specific purpose of eliminating the powers of the Lords.

The first election was held between January 14 and February 10, 1910. Lloyd George and Churchill campaigned tirelessly, constantly heckled by suffragettes, one of whom locked herself (and Lloyd George) in Lloyd George's car. Ninety-two percent of those eligible voted, but only 58% of adult males (and no women) were eligible. The results were a disappointment for the Liberals. They emerged with slightly more MP's than the Tories and their Unionist allies. They held a working majority only with the help of the Labour and Irish Parliamentary Party MP's. The balloting proved that their huge 1906 victory did not reflect a permanent change in British attitudes, but instead reflected the voters' revulsion with the Boer War, which was receding into the past. On April 27, Asquith moved the budget in the House of Commons, and it passed. The following day, the Lords acceded to the people's will; they passed it too.

King Edward had given Asquith his assurance that he would agree to create five hundred new peers following a second election. But on May 6, 1910, King Edward, 68, died. Asquith then had to obtain the same "hypothetical understanding" from the new king, George V, which he duly received. King George agreed to create as many new peers as were needed to disarm the Lords, if that represented the will of the people. A second election (the last election before the First World War), conducted between December 3–9, 1910, on the Parliament Bill, produced the same results as the prior election. The Parliament Bill enacted into law what had been only tradition: The Lords could delay money bills for only one month, effectively eliminating their veto. They could delay all other bills for no longer than two years (later reduced to one year).

The Lords now had a very unpleasant choice. They could vote to eliminate their own powers, becoming a pleasant social club empowered to carry on debates, or they could reject the Parliament Bill and find themselves seated beside hundreds of new Liberal peers. On August 10, 1911, by a vote of 131-114, with hundreds of peers either not present or abstaining, the Lords chose to neuter themselves. The 114 peers who made a last ditch stand for the prerogatives of inherited wealth became known as the "Ditchers." The conservative *Times* editorialized "They have done what they felt was their duty, they have satisfied their consciences and died in the ditch." And with that, what the *Times* called "the great Constitutional drama of our time" was over.[44]

On June 22, 1911, Edward VII's son, George V, was crowned at Westminster Abbey. To facilitate their viewing of the coronation, a grandstand had been erected which was reserved for the peers, their wives, and their guests. As Lloyd George, the chancellor of the exchequer, paraded past them, they booed him lustily. He left no record of how much he relished that moment. One can only imagine.

9

THE NEW PROGRESSIVE

You shall not crucify mankind upon a cross of gold"

—William Jennings Bryan

The Civil War ended, and America boomed. The amount of coal the miners took from the earth quadrupled. The miles of railroad track laid quintupled. By 1900, America's gross domestic product, the measure of all goods and services produced, led the world, greater than Great Britain, greater than France, even greater than Germany.[1] Between 1870 and 1900, the population doubled. The city of Chicago, a sleepy village of thirty thousand in 1850, counted one million by 1890. Between 1890 and 1910, it doubled again. Midwestern cities such as St. Louis, Cleveland and Milwaukee all experienced similar explosive rates of growth.[2] And if a man was dissatisfied with his prospects in New York or Boston or anywhere else, he could pick himself up and move West. The American frontier, with free land for the taking, was still wide open.

But not everyone benefitted from boom. Between 1865 and the end of the century, the wheat and corn that American farmers produced more than doubled but American farmers experienced a *deflation* in the prices they received for their crops, in part caused by rising competition from Canada, Argentina, Australia and elsewhere, and in part from advances in technology that increased every farmer's output. A farmer's debt that could be repaid with the equivalent of 1,000 bushels of wheat in 1865 required 3,000 bushels in 1895.[3] Even after prices began to rise after 1896, the farmers had plenty to complain about: the predatory prices the railroads charged to transport their crops, the tight credit demanded from the banks, and the prices the grain elevator combines charged to store their crops. They wanted the railroads regulated and relief from their debts. They also wanted the tariffs lowered. The tariffs increased the prices on all of the manufactured items the farmers had to buy, but depressed the prices of their exports. They were angry, and in 1900 38% of the labor force was farmers.

The big boom ended for almost everyone in 1893. They called it a "panic" ("The Panic of 1893") but it was a depression. Speculation in railroad stocks caused two large railroads, the Philadelphia & Reading and the Northern Pacific, to fail. Banks that had invested in the railroads ceased lending, and when the big Eastern banks stopped lending the smaller Western banks dependent on them began failing. At a time when there was no deposit insurance, five hundred banks failed. Then the stock market crashed. By the time the "Panic" was over—four years later—16,000 businesses had failed. By the end of 1893, at a time when there was no unemployment insurance, 18% of Americans were out of work. The president through all of this was Grover Cleveland, a Democrat. He believed in sound money and did nothing to alleviate the suffering. The Democrats became known as the "Party of Depression."

People began to notice that the new American prosperity was spread very unevenly. Between 1860 and 1900, the wealthiest one percent of Americans owned 51% of all U.S. property; the bottom 44% owned slightly more than one percent. Americans spent all that they earned on food, clothing and rent; three-fourths of Americans had no savings whatever. The first American to ask why in a land of growing prosperity there was also rising poverty was the journalist and economist Henry George (1839-1897). In 1879 he self-published *Progress and Poverty*. In more than five hundred pages of ringing prose, he answered the question he posed. He claimed that as wealth naturally accreted to landowners in the form of rent paid to them, the landowners grew richer as the renters became poorer. His solution was a "single tax" i.e. a confiscatory tax on rents. If this tax were enacted, he claimed, it would eliminate the need for tariffs and all other taxes. George also suggested that the practice of awarding franchises for public utilities such as railroads and streetcars be terminated, since they were essentially giveaways of public land for private use.

Progress and Poverty caused a sensation and made George famous. By 1900, it had sold three million copies in a country of only eighty-three million, and spread around the world. David Lloyd George read it, as did Leo Tolstoy, Dr. Sun-Yat Sen, Albert Einstein and Woodrow Wilson. His idea for a "single tax" never caught on, but the publication of *Progress and Poverty* is generally credited with launching the Progressive Era. George dabbled in politics, running for mayor of New York in 1886 as a fringe-party candidate. He came in second, but he did edge out the Republican candidate, twenty-eight-year-old Theodore Roosevelt.

One of the many influenced by Henry George was the Danish-born journalist Jacob Riis (1849-1914). What George could describe only in words Riis, in *How the Other Half Lives*, published in 1880, showed his readers in pictures. Capitalizing on advances in flash photography, Riis roamed the slums of New York capturing images of the poor, later writing "The sights I saw there gripped my heart until I felt that I must tell of them, or burst, or turn anarchist, or something."[4] He specialized in children: children in rags huddled together in dingy hovels; children toiling in sweatshops; children bearing impossible loads in the garment district. Theodore Roosevelt, then New York's commissioner of civil service, read it. He left a card in Riis' newspaper office noting that he had read it and that he "had come to help." Roosevelt knew that Riis had exposed to New Yorkers of his class conditions they could not have imagined. Riis and Roosevelt became friends for life.

The Populist movement had preceded the Progressive Era. The Progressives were a broad-based national movement; the Populists never succeeded in expanding out of their agrarian base and never appealed to urban workers. The Progressives had a large agenda of economic and political reforms. The principal Populist goal, above everything else, was relief for the farmer. The Populists advocated an income tax to replace the protective tariff and pressed for regulation of the railroads, but their one all-important issue was the "money issue," which to the Populists meant going off the gold standard in favor of "bimetallism," or, in the parlance of the day, the "free coinage of silver." The treasury had adopted a strict gold standard only in 1873. In 1890, Congress provided some liquidity based on silver, with the passage of the Silver Purchase Act, which required the treasury to redeem certain government notes in gold or silver. Congress repealed it only three years later. The Populist nostrum was simple: If all money had to be backed in gold, all debts had to be paid in gold or in currency backed by gold. If, however, the government allowed a farmer's debts to be paid in silver, and if the treasury printed currency backed by silver, the farmer could repay his debts with cheaper money. Of course, coining silver would inflate—cheapen—the currency, but inflation always aids debtors at the expense of creditors. The free coinage of silver may have been the answer to the prayers of every farmer burdened by a mountain of debt, but it struck terror in the hearts not just of lenders but to middle-class merchants and professionals in the cities and towns who saw the free coinage of silver as wrecking the economy, the cancellation of our trade agreements and perhaps the end of civilization as we know it.

The Populists formed a political party in 1891 and ran a candidate for president (former congressman James Weaver of Iowa) in 1892, on a platform of free coinage of silver, a graduated income tax and government ownership of the railroads. Weaver polled only 8.5% of the vote, but won Colorado, Idaho, Kansas, Nevada and North Dakota outright.

The apogee of the Populist movement arrived on July 9, 1896, on the third day of the Democratic national convention in Chicago, in the person of William Jennings Bryan (1860-1925). Born and raised in Illinois, he became a lawyer and practiced in Jacksonville, Illinois. In 1887, when he was only twenty-seven, he and his wife decamped for Lincoln, Nebraska. The next year, he campaigned effectively for Cleveland. He was a natural orator, powerfully built, physically attractive, with a deep baritone voice. At a time before microphones, when listeners beyond the first few rows needed to strain to hear, Bryan could reach the balconies. He was a classic extrovert, numbering his friends in the thousands. He loved crowds, and they loved him. He was deeply religious, and in his adult life probably read no book except the Bible. He claimed that "a good democratic speech is so much like a sermon that you can hardly tell the difference between them."[5] In 1890, he defeated a Republican incumbent for Congress, running on a platform of free coinage of silver, a graduated income tax, federal insurance of bank deposits and federal protection of workers' right to strike. He ran for the Senate in 1894 but was swamped in the Republican deluge of that year. He then traveled the world, studying the welfare states of Great Britain and Germany, ranging as far as Japan and Russia, where he met Tolstoy. He was a true believer in Jeffersonian values, in agrarian virtue and the evil inherent in the cities and in modernization. Woodrow Wilson summed him up: "[T]he man has no brains."[6]

The Democratic convention in 1896 was unusual in that it was less a contest between men as it was a contest of policy. The issue was the "money issue." Would the party stick by Cleveland's hard money policies, or would it veer off into bimetallism? With the nation in the third year of a depression, and with Cleveland being held responsible, there was no chance that Cleveland would be nominated for a third term. Thus, when Bryan mounted the speaker's platform it was in the throes of a fight over the party platform.

There are no sound recordings of Bryan's speech. It is believed that he spoke for approximately twenty minutes. He began by noting that "[T]his is not a contest among persons. The humblest citizen in all the land when clad in the armor of a righteous cause is stronger than all the hosts of error that they can bring. I come to speak to you in defense of a cause as holy as the cause of liberty—the cause of humanity."[7] Actually, the cause he had come to defend was bimetallism, as he soon made clear. "When you come before us and tell us that we shall disturb your business interests, we reply that you have disturbed our business interests by your action. We say to you that you have made too limited in its application the definition of a businessman. The man who is employed for wages is as much a businessman as his employer. The attorney in a country town is as much a businessman as the corporation counsel in a great metropolis. The merchant at the crossroads store is as much a businessman as the merchant of New York. The farmer who goes forth in the morning and toils all day, begins in the spring and toils all summer, and by the application of brain and muscle to the natural resources of this country creates wealth, is as much a businessman as the man who goes upon the Board of Trade and bets upon the price of grain."

His plea was a plea for the farmers: "[M]y friends, we say not one word against those who live upon the Atlantic Coast; but those hardy pioneers who braved all the dangers of the wilderness, who had made the desert blossom as the rose—those pioneers away out there, rearing their children near to nature's heart, where they can mingle their voices with the voices of the birds—out there where they have erected schoolhouses for the education of their children and churches where they praise their Creator, and cemeteries where sleep the ashes of their dead—are as deserving of the consideration of this party as any people in this country." He pleaded for a federal income tax, and for tariff reform, but he said that the "paramount" issue was the money issue: "[W]hen we have restored the money of the Constitution [i.e. gold *and* silver] all other necessary reforms will be possible, and that until that is done there is no reform that can be accomplished."..."[M]y friends, it is simply a question that we shall decide upon which side shall the Democratic Party fight. Upon the side of the idle holders of idle capital, or upon the side of the struggling masses?"..."There are two ideas of government. There are those who believe that if you just legislate to make the well-to-do prosperous, that their prosperity will leak through on those below. The Democratic idea has been that if you legislate to make the masses prosperous their prosperity will find its way up and through every class that rests upon it."

And near the end: "You come to us and tell us that the great cities are in favor of the gold standard. I tell you that the great cities rest upon the broad and fertile prairies. Burn down your cities and leave your farms, and your cities will spring up again as if by magic. But destroy our farms and the grass will grow in the streets of every city in the country." He then stepped back from the rostrum. He stood straight up. "Having behind us the commercial interests and the laboring interests and the toiling masses, we shall answer their demands for a gold standard by saying to them..." He lifted up his arms and pointed to his temples: "you shall not press down upon the brow of labor this crown of thorns." He then extended his arms, in the pose of the Crucifixion: "*You shall not crucify mankind upon a cross of gold.*"

Silence. He dismounted the rostrum, walked to his seat in the Nebraska delegation, and sat down. Silence. Then the auditorium erupted "as one great burst of artillery" in what observers recall was total delirium. Men cheered, wept, threw their hats and coats into the air. Bryan was nominated for president the next day. He became the "Peerless Leader" of the Democrats; the "Great Commoner." But his nomination divided the Democracy (as the Democrats were then also called). A splinter party of "Gold Democrats" opposed to bimetallism nominated Illinois senator John M. Palmer for president. Woodrow Wilson, a Democrat his entire life, and tens of thousands of other Democrats terrified of free coinage of silver, deserted Bryan and voted for Palmer. The Republicans nominated safe, sane, hard money former Ohio governor William McKinley. Businessmen who had never contributed to a political party dug deep; the Republicans outspent the Democrats ten to one. Bryan crisscrossed the country; McKinley campaigned from his front porch. America was in the third year of a depression blamed on the Democrats. Bryan held the "Solid South" and a few Western states, but McKinley took the rest.

Bryan was the leader of the party. In 1900 he ran against McKinley again, and lost again. But before McKinley was renominated New York Republicans pleaded to have their obstreperous Governor, Theodore Roosevelt, nominated for vice president, in order to get him out of the way. When he heard of the plan, Ohio senator Marcus Hanna warned: "Don't any of you realize there's only one life between this madman and the presidency?"[8] They nominated Roosevelt anyway. The next year, after McKinley stepped in the way of an anarchist's bullet, Hanna could only bemoan: "Now look! That damned cowboy is president of the United States."[9] Bryan and the Progressives lost control of the party in 1904, but regained it in 1908, losing again. But after losing the presidency for the third time, Bryan was still only forty-eight, and he was still the leader of the party.

The Progressive Era was just rolling into high gear after Bryan's first defeat. The cause of reform was taken up by others. Underlying the Progressive movement was the belief that the people had the power of *reason*; that if evil was exposed, the people would respond positively, and would act. The Progressives believed in progress. One of the first among them was Robert M. La Follette, (1855-1925) a Wisconsin Republican. In 1900 he was elected governor of Wisconsin, bent on reform. At a time when United States senators were selected by their state legislators, and the state legislators were appointed by party bosses in league with corporations, La Follette pressed for the popular election of senators. (The Seventeenth Amendment, providing for the popular election of senators, became effective only in 1913). In order to loosen the grip of machine-backed state legislators, La Follette backed the election of state legislators through primaries. In order to further weaken the bosses, La Follette backed the *initiative, referendum and recall*. With the initiative, citizens could propose and enact reform legislation opposed by the moneyed interests. With the referendum, state legislatures would be required to obtain the approval of voters before enacting certain legislation, and with the recall, voters could terminate corrupt officials before their terms ended. In addition to political reform, La Follette pressed for a progressive federal income tax to replace the protective tariff, legislation to curb the rate-making powers of the railroads, the right of workers to strike, worker's compensation and conservation of natural resources. In 1905, he nominated himself to the United States Senate, where he served until his death in 1925. While in the Senate, he was the leading voice for reform. His journal *La Follette's Weekly Magazine*, which he began in 1909, became a sounding-board for Progressives.

For some, the Progressive movement was a religious movement. The *Social Gospel* movement was premised on the notion that social justice and Christianity were synonymous. Emphasizing Christ's concern for the poor, the Social Gospel doctrine posed the question: "What would Jesus do?" The answer for some came in the settlement house movement. In 1889, Jane Addams, the daughter of an Illinois bank president, co-founded Hull House in Chicago. In 1893, Lillian Wald, then only twenty-two, founded the Henry Street Settlement on the Lower East Side of New York. By 1910, there were four hundred settlement houses providing health care, education and a broad range of social services to the urban poor at a time when government provided little or none.

On September 14, 1901, Theodore Roosevelt became president of the United States. He became known as the "trust buster," but no presidential moniker is less apt, and Roosevelt himself denied the label. His goal was not to bust the great industrial combines (the "trusts") but to regulate them. In his first message to Congress, he wrote that "combination and concentration...should be, not prohibited, but supervised and within reasonable limits controlled...Corporations engaged in interstate commerce should be regulated if they are found to exercise a license working to the public injury."[10] Shortly after he became president, he intervened in the anthracite coal strike in eastern Pennsylvania, forcing the mine owners to accept arbitration. In that year, he brought suit to block the merger of several railroads into the Northern Securities Company. In 1904, the Supreme Court ruled in his favor. During his presidency, he would sue Standard

Oil, American Tobacco and the Sugar Trust. He would be the first conservationist president. But on election night in 1904 he made what would prove to be his biggest mistake: He blurted out a pledge that he would not run for president ever again.

Despite all of La Follette's efforts, it was journalists as much as politicians that kept the Progressive flame burning. Beginning in 1903, S.S. McClure, the proprietor of *McClure's* magazine, began publishing investigative articles, some of which were later compiled into best-selling books. In 1904, Ida M. Tarbell published *The History of the Standard Oil Company*, which began as a series of articles in *McClure's*. She unearthed documents from Standard Oil's files, and conducted interviews with former Standard Oil executives. In painstaking detail, in nineteen installments, she documented how John D. Rockefeller had crushed rival oil producers, first in Cleveland and then nationwide, by means of secret deals with railroads that provided discounts to Rockefeller and that gouged his competitors, forcing his competitors to sell out. For Tarbell, the issue was personal. One of the small Cleveland oil producers that Rockefeller had driven out of business was her father, Frank Tarbell. In 1906, Lincoln Steffens published *The Shame of the Cities*, which had also begun as a series of articles in *McClure's*. Steffens focused on the rampant corruption in some of the largest cities, his purpose being to "sound for the civic pride of an apparently shameless citizenship."[11] He reported that a St. Louis grand jury found that not a single local ordinance could be enacted in St. Louis unless the legislators had been paid off by those interested in the legislation. He reported that in Minneapolis, the police were so corrupt that when they determined that the kickbacks they received from the madams who operated the local brothels were insufficient, they suggested that the madams *expand* their operations. They suggested candy stores. So it came to pass that while children were buying candy in the front, prostitution under the protection of the police was being conducted in the back. But Steffens reserved his greatest scorn for Philadelphia, which he termed the most corrupt city in America. The voting lists were kept by the local assessor, and the assessor was an employee of the local boss. He pointed to the experience of a man who went to vote on election day only to be informed that he had already voted—twice!

In 1906, freelance journalist David Graham Phillips published *The Treason of the Senate*, an exposé of the corrupt connection between United States senators and the railroads that appointed them. He focused on Nelson W. Aldrich, a Rhode Island Republican who was credited with controlling the Senate, and New York senator Chauncey Depew, who began his career as a railroad lawyer.

A twenty-eight-year-old Socialist, Upton Sinclair, published *The Jungle*, which in searing and often sickening detail documented the conditions in which immigrants in Chicago labored in the meatpacking houses, including the scene in which a worker actually fell into a rendering vat. No book had a more immediate effect. Roosevelt read it, invited Sinclair to lunch, and within three months he had enacted the Pure Food and Drug Act and the Meat Inspection Act. Intended to foster the socialist ideal, Sinclair lamented that: "I aimed at the public's heart and by accident I hit it in the stomach."

Roosevelt coined a term for McClure, Steffens, Tarbell, Sinclair, Phillips and their ilk. He called them "muckrakers." He did not mean it as a compliment, but they took it as such. Woodrow Wilson claimed that no one followed the writings of the muckrakers more intensely than he.[12]

The Progressive Era crested in 1910. Aided by a 1907-1908 recession, on election night in 1910 the Democrats took control of the House of Representatives for the first time since 1892. The new speaker was Champ Clark of Missouri, an early Progressive who had supported Bryan and free silver. He replaced "Uncle" Joe Cannon, who had thwarted reform legislation for years. New York elected its first Democratic governor in sixteen years. Normally Republican states such as Massachusetts, Connecticut and Ohio all elected Democratic governors. New York Senator Chauncey Depew, the subject of one of David Graham Phillips' profiles in *The Treason of the Senate*, retired. In Milwaukee, two Socialists were elected to the House. Former president (they now called him "Colonel") Roosevelt opined: "[T]he Democrats whipped the Republicans to a frazzle and put them over the ropes..."[13] The Colonel lost his home district, Oyster Bay, New York, to the Democrats, by sixty votes. To everyone's surprise, solidly Republican New Jersey was caught up in the Democratic tsunami. The New Jersey Assembly now had a Democratic majority. In the New Jersey Senate, the Republicans maintained a slight majority, but enough of them were "New Idea" Progressives so that the entire legislature was controlled by Progressives. And Woodrow Wilson rode the tide and became the governor of New Jersey.

Wilson had been a conservative his entire life. While still a professor at Princeton, he had penned a five-volume history of the United States from the conservative point of view. He praised President Cleveland's suppression of the 1894 Pullman Railway Strike, and mocked the Populists. Of the Fifteenth Amendment, which gave freed slaves the right to vote, he wrote: "The dominance of the negroes in the South was to be made a principle of the very Constitution of the Union."[14] Of Reconstruction: "The white men of the South were aroused by the mere instinct of self-preservation, to rid themselves, by means fair or foul, of the intolerable burden of governments sustained by the votes of ignorant negroes and conducted in the interest of adventurers." Of the Ku Klux Klan: "It became the chief object of the night-riding comrades to silence or drive from the country the mischief-makers of the reconstruction regime, whether black or white."[15] He had harsh words for the Italian and Polish immigrants, a fact that would come back to haunt him when he ran for president. As for organized labor, he had told a Princeton graduating class that the chief object of labor unions was to keep production standards as low as possible. In August, 1907, when Col. Harvey, harboring a hope that he might secure the 1908 Democratic nomination for the then-unknown Wilson, asked Wilson to pen a "Credo" setting forth his views, Wilson wrote: "The Constitution guarantees to every man the right to sell his labor to whom he pleases for such price as he is willing to accept."[16] Of the trusts, he believed that the "great trusts and combinations" were necessary as "the most convenient and efficient instrumentalities of modern business," and counseled against any legislation to curb them. In his speeches, he fell back on the bromide that punishing predatory corporations was akin to punishing a car following an auto accident. The Interstate Commerce Commission had been created for the express purpose of curbing the predatory rate-making powers of the railroads. Wilson opined that the ICC was impeding the progress of transportation. As for the political bosses, Wilson wrote in Harvey's *North American Review*, as recently as May, 1908, that they were "indispensable," and that voters "must of necessity leave the selection [of candidates] to a few persons, who, from one motive or another, volunteer to make a business of it."[17] As recently as 1907, he had been on record as opposing the initiative, the referendum and the recall. At the start of his campaign for governor, he opposed direct primaries for state offices, then changed his mind. As for the direct election of United States senators, Wilson assured Harvey he was against it.

But then, late in his Princeton presidency, Wilson received a bracing dose of real life. In the "Quad Plan" fight and in the fight over the graduate college, Wilson had been defeated by money and privilege. Right had not prevailed; money and the power money brought had prevailed. If, as he claimed, he had been closely following the writings of the muckrakers, they must have had some effect. He was questioning the beliefs of a lifetime. Slowly and imperceptibly–even to Wilson himself–he had been radicalized. But the bosses had made him governor; he owed his nomination and his election to them. And the first test of Wilson the new Progressive governor would come even before he was inaugurated.

In 1910, United States senators—including New Jersey's two senators—were still selected by their respective legislatures. But with the spirit of reform in the air, New

Jersey in 1910 instituted a non-binding primary (a "beauty contest") to determine the majority party's selection for senator. It may have been non-binding, but the winner would be the choice of the people. If the New Jersey Democratic party was serious about reform, it would accede to the will of the people. The primary was scheduled for September 13, 1910.

No one believed that the Democrats had a chance of capturing the legislature in November. The winner of the Democratic primary would have won nothing. Former senator and Newark boss James E. Smith, Jr., who may or may not have wanted to return to the Senate, did not bother to enter the primary. Democrats rooted about for a candidate to act as the sacrificial lamb. They found him in James E. Martine, the "Farmer Orator," a man who had spent the better part of the preceding forty years running for every possible office in New Jersey, losing every time, a man described as "a lovable character and his own torch-light procession."[18] He had become so much of a joke that this time, even Martine had to be coaxed into running. He pleaded: "I am now married to a good woman, and it isn't fair to her for me to permit myself to be regarded as a political buffoon."[19] But he relented, and agreed to run. Martine was backed by the Progressives. He was opposed by one Frank M. McDermott, a former Newark attorney ("former" in that he had already been disbarred) of questionable reputation. On primary day, Martine trounced McDermott. He was now the Democratic party's choice for United States senator.

Shortly after being elected governor and the Democrats taking control of the legislature, Wilson told James Kerney, the editor of the *Trenton Evening Times*, that he did not think Martine was qualified to be a United States senator, and was opposed to the legislature electing him, the will of the people notwithstanding. (During this same meeting, Wilson advised Kerney that he read no New Jersey newspapers, having time only for the *New York Post*.) Then boss Smith changed his mind, deciding that he should be New Jersey's next senator, the will of the people be damned. Wilson met with Smith urging him not to run, telling Smith that the people wanted some new, untried man in the Senate. Wilson admitted to Smith that the preference primary had been a farce, and that perhaps some compromise candidate could be agreed upon.

Wilson had a problem. If he opposed Smith and Smith was able to win the balloting in the legislature without Wilson's support, Smith would have his revenge and set about destroying Wilson's governorship in its infancy and perhaps his chance at the presidency. Wilson could choose to stay above the fray, taking the position that, as governor, whoever became senator was none of his concern. But that would tarnish–perhaps destroy–whatever Progressive credentials he had, again perhaps ending any hopes of the presidency.

It was during this period that Wilson met Joseph Patrick Tumulty (1879-1954) a young lawyer and politician. Born and raised in Jersey City, Tumulty (pronounced TUM-ulty) claimed that he learned politics sitting around the barrels at the general store. He paraded, handed out fliers and did other odd jobs for Robert Davis' Democratic machine. He saw with his own eyes what Lincoln Steffens wrote about: He once saw boss Davis drawing up election results a few days *before* an election. He attended tiny St. Peter's College in Jersey City, clerked in a local law firm, and was admitted to the bar in 1902. He supported Bryan, and backed the full Progressive agenda: direct election of senators, direct primaries, the initiative, referendum and recall, regulation of public utilities, and protection of a worker's right to strike. For these reasons, he initially did not support Wilson's run for governor, believing that Wilson was a tool of the bosses. But he was in the hall when Wilson delivered his acceptance speech, and like so many others, was completely won over. During the campaign, Tumulty was warming up a crowd in West Hoboken when Wilson entered the hall, unnoticed. He saw Tumulty enthrall the crowd with Irish dialect stories. Immediately afterward, Wilson asked Tumulty to join the campaign, and Tumulty accepted.[20] He would become Wilson's private secretary and closest aide during Wilson's term as governor and throughout his presidency.

Shortly after winning the election, Wilson visited Tumulty in his Jersey City law office, seeking his advice, as yet undecided if he should back Martine for the Senate or stay out of the race. Tumulty was unequivocal. He advised Wilson that he had to back Martine. Martine's fitness for the office was not the issue; Martine was the people's choice. Years later Tumulty wrote that he advised Wilson: "The action you take will have far-reaching effect upon our party's fortunes and no one can calculate the effect it will undoubtedly have on your own political future…This is really the first step to the Presidency."[21] As Wilson left Tumulty's office, he asked Tumulty if he thought he could defeat the powerful Newark boss. Tumulty advised him that he could.

Wilson then received a letter from Judge John W. Wescott, a leader of the New Jersey Progressives who, like Tumulty, had opposed Wilson for governor. Wescott warned Wilson that if the legislature elected Smith "his election will prove a bargain and sale, the office going to the highest bidder." Also, Smith's election would prove that "Dr. Wilson is controlled by the same interests and methods that control Mr. Smith… Dr. Wilson, so far as his usefulness in American regeneration is concerned, would be a negative quality and quantity…"[22] Wilson would later name Wescott as New Jersey's attorney-general, and he would twice nominate Wilson for president.

On November 15, Wilson wrote a "Parsonal [*sic*] and Confidential" letter to Col. Harvey. It is possible that the letter was not intended to be "Confidential" at all; that

Wilson wanted Harvey to show the letter to Smith. He wrote: "I am very anxious about the question of the senatorship. If not handled right, it will destroy every fortunate impression of the campaign and open my administration with a split party. I have learned to have a very high opinion of Senator Smith. I have very little doubt that, if he were sent to the Senate he would acquit himself with honour and do a great deal to correct the impressions of his former term." Echoing Tumulty and Judge Wescott's advice, Wilson wrote: "It is a national as well as a State question. If the independent Republicans who in this State voted for me are not to be attracted to us they will assuredly turn again, in desperation, to Mr. Roosevelt, and the chance of a generation will be lost to the Democracy..."[23]

Smith may or may not have received the letter. He certainly never got the message. On November 19, he decided to run for the Senate. Wilson now opposed him, as fully as if he had opposed Smith and everything he stood for his entire life. Of course, the Newark machine backed Smith. Wilson visited Jersey City boss Robert Davis, urging him not to back Smith. Davis said he had given Smith his word, and would not renege. But he also said that the Hudson County legislators beholden to his machine could vote as they wished. Wilson met with all of them individually. His pitch to each of them was that the principle of direct election of senators required that they support Martine. On December 6, Wilson traveled to Smith's home in Newark. As reported by Tumulty, Wilson pleaded with Smith to withdraw from the race, suggesting a compromise candidate, arguing that "Senator, you have it in your power to become instantly the biggest man in the state."[24] Also according to Tumulty, Smith refused, and the meeting ended with both men realizing that "a state of war" existed between them. Two days later, Wilson issued a "Statement on the Senatorship" to the press. It noted that: "[F]orty eight thousand Democratic voters, a majority of the whole number who voted in the primaries, declared their preference for Mr. Martine, of Union County. For me, that vote is conclusive...It is clearly the duty of every Democratic legislator, who would keep faith with the law of the State and with the avowed principles of his party, to vote for Mr. Martine.[25] A week later, Smith formally announced his candidacy. Wilson vowed to defeat him "if it takes every ounce of strength out of me."[26]

Wilson's *volte-face* on direct primaries caused him some embarrassment. He granted an interview to the *New York Evening World*, stating that support for Martine was "the absolute moral obligation which the Democratic party was bound to carry out if it kept faith with the people."[27] "But," the *Evening World* reporter inquired, "did you not go to Mr. Smith two days before you announced your opposition to him and suggest a compromise candidate?" The *Evening World* reported Wilson replied that that was "before he had a full knowledge of his duty or of the men." The next day,

Wilson repudiated the story, issuing a statement in which he said that the report was a perversion of what he had told the reporter.[28]

Wilson made the senatorial campaign an issue of people rule versus boss rule. In late December he issued a statement to the press stating that Smith "has assumed that he and the other gentlemen not elected to the legislature by the people would have the same control over the action of the houses that is understood to have been exercised by the so-called Board of Guardians of the Republican party in recent years...The issue is plain. If Mr. Smith is sent back to the United States Senate, the Democratic Party and the state itself is once more delivered into the hands of the very influences from which it had struggled to set itself free."[29] He met with a group of New Jersey legislators who had previously pledged their support to Smith. He advised them that they could in good conscience break their pledges to Smith in that he had fraudulently induced their support; Smith had initially said that he would not run. No one seemed to notice the *non sequitur*. One legislator reported of the meeting: "He is a great man and talked to us as a father would."[30]

It was a bruising battle. The Smith forces spread a rumor that Wilson was anti-Catholic. Speaking in Jersey City on January 5, twelve days before Wilson's own inaugural as governor, he singled out for praise three of his supporters on the platform, one of whom was Joseph Tumulty. All three were Roman Catholics. Wilson reminded his audience that Smith represented a corrupt system, the alliance of big business and politics, and that Martine "represents an opportunity of the people of New Jersey to say whether they believe in the popular choice of United States Senators, or do not believe in it."[31] Of course, only a few short weeks prior to this Wilson had assured Col. Harvey that he himself did not believe in it, but no matter. He stated that in electing Martine "[Y]ou will have achieved, in view of the whole country, one of the most important and decisive triumphs for popular government that has been achieved in our day." He continued: "I have heard a great many men hope for compromise. God defend us against compromise."[32]

On January 24, 1911, in a combined caucus of the Democratic members of the New Jersey Senate and the New Jersey Assembly, James E. Martine, the "Farmer Orator," easily defeated Smith. It assured that the legislature, now controlled by the Democrats, would elect Martine as its next United States Senator. He would be the last New Jersey senator so elected; in 1913, the Seventeenth Amendment was ratified. The real victor was Wilson. He had not only defeated the New Jersey Democratic machine, but he had established himself as one of the leading Progressives in America. They were talking about him for president.

Wilson had no intention of being a passive governor. He knew that all eyes were now on him. For example, in his Lincoln, Nebraska weekly, *The Commoner*, Bryan noted that Wilson's candidacy had been fostered by the bosses, but "Undoubtedly Governor Wilson knows more about practical politics today than he did when James Smith, Jr. and the other New Jersey corporationists gave him the gubernatorial nomination and held before his eyes the tempting hope for the Presidency. He knows that many crimes are committed in the name of conservatism."[33] If Wilson was to use his victory as a springboard to the White House, he would have to make good on his Progressive promise.

Wilson had a solid Democratic legislature to work with. Forty-two of the sixty members of the Assembly were Democrats. The Republicans held a slim 12-9 majority in the Senate, but enough of the Republicans were "New Idea" Progressives to give Wilson a working majority in the Senate as well. The Smith machine was defeated, but it was not dead. Smith himself had been elected to the Assembly, and eleven of the forty-two members of the Assembly were Essex County Democrats under Smith's control. The Democratic state chairman, James R. Nugent, was Smith's nephew.

Before Joseph Tumulty and the other New Jersey Progressives came around to Wilson, they had a legislative agenda they wanted enacted that included direct primary elections for state offices, a corrupt practices law that included limits on campaign contributions and the full disclosure of contributions, the regulation of public utilities, and a worker's compensation law. Within four months of taking office, every item of the agenda had been enacted, but not without some difficulty. The bill for direct party primary elections for all state elected officials was bitterly opposed by the regular Democratic machine. In one infamous incident, during the course of a meeting with chairman Nugent in Wilson's office, Nugent accused Wilson of using patronage to get votes. According to both Wilson's and Nugent's accounts of the meeting, Wilson responded, "Good afternoon, Mr. Nugent," motioning to the door. Nugent then shouted that Wilson was no gentleman and that he had always thought that he was no gentleman, to which Wilson shot back, "Good afternoon, Mr. Nugent."[34] A cartoon depicting Nugent being physically booted out the door by Wilson did not harm Wilson's reputation. Nugent made the mistake of publicly calling Wilson "an ingrate and a liar."[35] He was replaced as party chairman. The enactment of the primary elections law drew national attention. The law regulating public utilities was one of the most advanced in the nation. A commission was established with the power to set rates, and the railways' property was subject to fair taxation. Wilson had some difficulty with the worker's compensation law; organized labor thought that the bill did not go far enough. Wilson personally intervened and negotiated a compromise. Prior to its enactment a worker injured on the job could not sue a negligent employer, based on the age-old theories that the worker had "assumed the risk" or that the accident had been caused by a "fellow servant." The law that Wilson passed assured that a worker injured on the job would be compensated, without the necessity of proving that the employer had been at fault.

By this time, Wilson had convinced himself that not only was he a true Progressive, but that he had been one all along. We can be confident in this by his letters to his great friend, Mary Peck. Wilson may have dissembled to the New Jersey bosses. Like every politician in a democracy, he shaded the truth on the platform. But in his letters to Mary Peck he spoke from the heart, never imagining that anyone other than Mary Peck herself would read them. In an April 23, 1911 letter following the just-concluded legislative session, he boasted that "I got everything I strove for,–and more besides: all four of the great acts I had set my heart on."[36] In a letter the next month, he wrote: "I am *not* conservative. I am a radical.[37] [His italics.] Commenting on the presidential campaign that lay ahead, he wrote: "The forces of greed and the forces of justice and humanity are about to grapple for a bout in which men will spend all the life that is in them. God grant that I may have strength enough to count, to tip the balance in the unequal and tremendous struggle."[38]

Wilson may have come very late to the Progressive cause, and his conversion was still incomplete, but he was no hypocrite. The losing battles he had fought as president of Princeton had radicalized him. He was a changed man as he started on the road to the presidency.

Wilson's early backers convinced him that in order to achieve the Democratic nomination he would need to get the support of western delegates, and to do that he should make a swing through the West. His early supporters included Walter Hines Page, the editor of *World's Week*, whom Wilson had befriended while still a lawyer in Atlanta, William F. McCombs, a New York lawyer who had been one of Wilson's students at Princeton, and, of course, Col. Harvey. They all assumed that Wilson's principal opponent for the nomination would be Champ Clark, the Speaker of the House. James Beauchamp ("Champ") Clark (1850-1921) was a Missouri lawyer who had first been elected to the House in 1892, and by 1908 had risen to be minority leader. When the Democrats swept the House in 1910, they elected him Speaker. An earlier and more consistent Progressive than Wilson, he had been an early supporter of Bryan, "free silver" and all. Like Wilson, he opposed the protective tariff. His fellow Democrats in the House supported him, as did many of the city and state Democratic machines. Wilson had nothing to offer the big-city and state bosses, all of whom remembered what he had done to James Smith, Jr. Another possible contender was Oscar Underwood (1862-1929), a Birmingham lawyer who had risen to become the House Majority Leader. He would be formidable if he could break out of his southern base. And then there was that great unknown, thrice-defeated William Jennings Bryan, but still the titular head of the party.

Wilson set out to do what he had always done best, speak in public. He would cover nine thousand miles in eight months. Starting on March 10, 1911, he appeared in Atlanta on the same platform as President Taft. Taft was well-received, but the next day's *Atlanta Constitution* called Wilson's speech a "masterpiece." "He handled his subject with marvelous ease, and with the grace of one who has himself well in hand. His oratory was striking, his logic convincing, and his summary was masterful."[39]

The next day, Wilson hurried back to Princeton. Bryan was scheduled to speak at the Princeton Theological Seminary, which Wilson's father had attended. They met at the Princeton Inn and had a pleasant meeting. What did not emerge was an endorsement from Bryan. They met again on April 5, on the same platform in Burlington, New Jersey. Bryan publicly praised Wilson's work "as one of the greatest influences for public advancement in all the East...I am glad to stand on this same platform with him, and of his constituents here there is none more anxious to do him honor than I."[40] He had come close, but there was still no formal endorsement.

On April 29 he spoke in Norfolk, the *Virginian-Pilot* opining that "The boldness, the directness, the incisiveness, the fearlessness and the force of the...words crashed at times through the throng like a series of thunderbolt jolts."[41] He told an interviewer from the Norfolk *Landmark* that he favored the popular election of United States Senators and the initiative, referendum and recall (but not the recall of judges).[42] On May 5th he was in Kansas City, in Denver on the 7th, and in Los Angeles on the 13th. While in Denver his topic was the Bible, tying the Bible to reform. He wrote Mary Peck: "This traveling and speaking is strenuous business, but it actually seems to refresh and revive me after the long, anxious trying grind of Trenton."[43] He was genuinely surprised at the reception he was getting, writing Mary Peck: "I am astonished to find how much everybody knew about me beforehand and how careful, how eagerly cordial, they are. They seem really to think of me as one of the leaders of the country, to whom the people, and men of all sorts, must look for successful and enlightened and determined leadership."[44] He was well received in Los Angeles, telling the non-partisan City Club that "[T]he Democratic party as a whole is naturally progressive and that it is easier, through the instrumentality of that party, to accomplish the new purposes of the day than through...the Republican party." He came out in favor of the initiative, referendum and recall, in favor of direct primaries, and against the protective tariff, saying tariffs had become a means of favoritism for certain businessmen.[45] But while in very progressive California he was dogged by his views on female suffrage. In a 1911 letter he had written that he was "strongly" against it.[46] Now, he dodged the issue, saying the issue was up to each state to decide.

On May 18 he was in Portland. Oregon had been a Progressive leader, having already enacted the initiative, referendum and recall. Wilson praised them: "You have broken the machine. You have substituted yourselves for the machine."[47] The *Oregon Daily Journal* editorialized that Wilson had been "Terse, analytical, epigrammatic, his force was in the facts and the masterful logic of their presentation."[48] McKee Barclay, a political writer for the *Baltimore Sun* traveling with the Wilson party wrote: "Contact with Gov. Wilson is a liberal education in itself. He is pure gold. He keenly comprehends, he educates, he leads, and the people of the nation are looking toward him."[49]

While Wilson was out West the Supreme Court decided *Standard Oil of New Jersey v. United States of America*, holding that Standard Oil had violated the Sherman Anti-Trust Act of 1890, and was engaged in the *unreasonable* restraint of trade, ordering that Standard Oil be broken up into thirty-four regional companies. But in doing so, the Justices adopted a *rule of reason*, a rule first enunciated by President Taft when he was a circuit judge, to the effect that the Sherman Act was violated only when a defendant engaged in an *unreasonable* restraint of trade. Taft, of course, hailed the court's decision. La Follette, Bryan and other Progressives blasted it. Wilson opposed it for a different reason: He claimed that breaking up Standard Oil would have no effect; the pieces would be worth more than the whole. He was right; the aggregate value of John D. Rockefeller's holdings *increased*.

On May 24 he was in St. Paul, speaking to yet another group of local boosters. But in a speech reminiscent of his infamous address to the Pittsburgh alumni, he gave them an earful: "Every time I am told that this is a representative gathering. But what are you representative of? You are representative of the success of men in various lines in St. Paul, representative of leadership. You are men who have arrived or are arriving. But where did you come from? Where are all the men who have been left behind in this race for life? There is a great deal more in life than a little company of well-fed men like this."[50]

He then swung east, Chapel Hill, North Carolina on May 30, Columbia, South Carolina on June 2, and Harrisburg, Pennsylvania on June 15. It was in Harrisburg that he went too far, possibly because he was speaking on the same platform as Champ Clark, who was mounting his own run for the nomination. Wilson spoke on banking reform, then a hot topic, of which he knew absolutely nothing. The nation needed some form of central bank empowered, if the need arose, to pump liquidity into the economy. Nelson W. Aldrich, the archconservative Rhode Island Republican, had introduced the "Aldrich Plan" in the Senate, which would have created a board of private bankers empowered to issue government debt. It was akin to, but different from, the Federal Reserve Act that was enacted shortly after Wilson became president. Roosevelt and Bryan both denounced the Aldrich Plan, on the ground that it concentrated too much power in the hands of private bankers. Wilson denounced it too. "The great monopoly in this country is the money monopoly…Now, a money monopoly exists. It must be destroyed."[51] He continued that the control of credit was dangerously concentrated, and that the growth of the nation was in the hands of a few men. The speech was picked up by the wire services and widely distributed in the next morning's newspapers. To many conservative Democrats, this sounded eerily like Bryan. When George Harvey had stood up at the Lotos Club in 1906 and proposed Wilson for president, it was in large part because he saw in Wilson the Democratic antidote to Bryan.

Later in the year Wilson received a long letter from William Garrott Brown, a sometime editorial writer for Col. Harvey's *Harper's Weekly*, who was then bedridden with the tuberculosis that would shortly take his life. Brown was an ardent Progressive and Wilson supporter, but he let Wilson have it: "In Cleveland's day, our hopes were wrecked by the free-silver blunder, and we feel that the party's greatest weakness and danger is still its proneness to go wrong on questions of finance. There is not a Democrat in Congress of proved competence to deal with such questions, and the country is full of men ready to appeal to prejudice and ignorance, to class and section, when such questions come up…Don't, we beg of you,–I will be old-fashioned and *implore* you—don't throw away what Cleveland kept, what Roosevelt lost—the confidence of men of your class."[52] Wilson responded to Brown's letter: "I know perfectly well that I went off half cocked about the Aldrich matter. I so thoroughly distrust him that it was incredible to me that anything bearing his signature could be other than a scheme to put us more completely in the hands from those whose domination we are trying to escape." He promised Brown that "I intend to go more thoroughly into this matter before saying anything about it…"[53]

At this time, Wilson authorized the creation of a publicity bureau for the sole purpose of promoting his candidacy. It soon had a mailing list of forty thousand names, which included anyone who had ever been active in Democratic politics. From its offices at 42 Broadway in New York, the office sent out reprints of Wilson's speeches and favorable editorials. Later, a branch was opened in Washington, D.C. for the purpose of sending material directly to eight hundred daily and two thousand weekly newspapers. Wilson appointed a campaign manager, his former student, William F. McCombs.

In February, 1911, Col. Harvey received a letter from another ersatz "Colonel," the Texan Edward M. House. House touted his relationship with Bryan, who had been House's neighbor years' prior when Bryan briefly lived in Austin. House reminded Harvey of the importance of Bryan's support if Wilson were to secure the nomination. Harvey forwarded the letter to Wilson (as House expected Harvey to do) with a cover letter saying that House was "an exceptionally able man, well-to-do financially and, I think, sound politically."[54]

Edward Mandell House (1858-1938), born in Houston, was the son of a wealthy cotton trader. He twice failed the Yale entrance exam, then enrolled at Cornell where he fared poorly. He dropped out in 1880 following his father's death. An inheritance provided him with a $25,000 annuity that allowed him to devote himself to Texas politics. He relocated to Austin, and in 1892, then only thirty-four, he successfully managed the gubernatorial campaign of James W. Hogg, who gratefully bestowed upon him the "Colonel" honorific. In the next ten years, he successfully managed the campaigns of and served as advisor to three more Texas governors. He determined from the start to always work behind the scenes. He declined all offers of public office; he never asked for anything for himself. "He seems to be in constant and delightful agreement with his auditor," wrote the editor William Allen White, "[H]e is never servile, but always serving; gentle without being soft, exceedingly courteous with the most unbending dignity. He is forever punctuating one's sentences with 'that's true... that's true.'"[55] He was a Progressive Democrat. Being Bryan's next-door neighbor didn't alter House's opinion of Bryan, that Bryan "feels that his ideas are God-given and are not susceptible to the mutability of those of the ordinary human being."[56] House began to tire of Texas politics shortly after the turn of the century, hoping to employ his talents on a national scale. In the summer of 1910, House began looking about for a presidential candidate to back. At Bryan's suggestion, House came to New York to meet with Mayor William J. Gaynor. House was impressed with Gaynor, and suggested that Gaynor run for governor of New York as a stepping-stone to the presidency. Gaynor wasn't interested. House then decided that the man who had the best prospect to be the Democratic nominee in 1912 would be Woodrow Wilson.

In October, 1911, House wrote to Wilson: "We have so many mutual friends that I feel that I need no introduction to you."[57] Wilson was scheduled to speak at the Texas State Fair in Dallas at the end of the month. House wrote Wilson that a rumor making the rounds in Texas that Wilson had never voted for Bryan needed to be dealt with. Wilson replied, advising House that in 1896 he had voted for the "Gold Democrat," Senator John Palmer, solely because he, like many Democrats, differed from Bryan on the "free-silver" issue. He also advised House that he had voted for

Bryan in 1900 and 1908, and that he had voted for Judge Alton B. Parker, the Democrat who Roosevelt defeated in 1904. House immediately sent a telegram to Texas Senator Charles Culberson, the leader of the Texas Progressives: "Governor Woodrow Wilson informs me that he voted for…both William Jennings Bryan and Judge Parker, and that he never at any time supported a republican ticket."[58] The issue blew over and Wilson was well-received in Texas.

In early November, Wilson and House met for the first time in House's apartment in New York. After the meeting, House wrote: "We talked and talked. We knew each other for congenial souls at the very beginning…we agreed about everything." They had a second meeting a few days later, House writing in his diary: "I never met a man whose thought ran so identical to mine."[59] After meeting Wilson a few more times that winter, House asked Wilson if Wilson realized "that we had known one another for so short a time," to which Wilson replied "My dear friend, we have known each other always."[60] House would become Wilson's closest advisor, despite the fact that their face-to-face meetings were few. House would serve as Wilson's principal foreign policy advisor throughout the First World War and at the Peace Conference.

In November, 1911, a *contretemps* arose that nearly sank Wilson's candidacy. The fact that Wilson had turned on the New Jersey bosses who had lifted him from obscurity and was now running as a Progressive did not cool George Harvey's desire to see his candidate become President. Starting with the November 11, 1911 issue of *Harper's Weekly*, Harvey put "For President Woodrow Wilson" above the masthead of every issue. On December 7, Wilson met at the Manhattan Club with Harvey and Henry Watterson, 71, the owner of the *Louisville Courier-Journal* who was an early Wilson supporter but who saw himself as something of a father figure to Harvey. As the meeting was breaking up, Harvey matter-of-factly asked Wilson if he thought that such outspoken support coming from a well-known plutocrat might hurt Wilson. Wilson casually replied that yes, he had been hearing that Harvey's support might be hurting him with voters in the West. Harvey then replied: "Then I will simply sing low."[61] The December 9 issue was the last to feature the "For President Woodrow Wilson" banner.

This was the beginning of the supposed Wilson-Harvey "break up." After the meeting, Wilson relayed its substance to Tumulty, who suggested that Wilson might have inadvertently offended Harvey.[62] Wilson then penned an apology to Harvey: "A long time after that interview with you and Marse Henry at the Manhattan Club it came over me that when (at the close of the interview) you asked me that question about the 'Weekly' I answered it simply as a matter of fact, and of business, and said never a word of my sincere gratitude to you for all your generous support, or of my hope that it might be continued. Forgive me, and forget my manners!"[63] Harvey's reply was equally gracious: "[T]here is no particle of personal rancor or resentment left in me. And I beg you to believe that I have not said one word to anybody of criticism of you….I *have* to print a word of explanation to the *Weekly*'s readers, but it will be the briefest possible.[64] The "word of explanation" that Harvey printed on the first page of the January 20, 1912 issue of *Harper's Weekly* stated, in part: "The name of Woodrow Wilson as our candidate for President was taken down from the head of these columns in response to a statement made to us directly by Gov. Wilson, to the effect that our support was affecting his candidacy injuriously….The only course left open to us, in simple fairness to Mr. Wilson, no less than in consideration of our own self-respect was to cease to advocate his nomination."[65] This notice failed to mention the key element, that it was Harvey himself who asked Wilson if he had been hurting him, and that Wilson had answered him truthfully.

If Wilson and Harvey were willing to let the matter rest, "Marse" Henry Watterson, who would not let a real or imagined insult go unchallenged, was not. The meeting was leaked to the press and was widely, and incorrectly, reported by the Hearst press, then supporting Clark. Typical was the San Francisco *Examiner*, which reported on page 1 that Wilson had said to Harvey: "Harvey, the time has come when your advocacy of my candidacy for president is doing me more harm than good and I want you to stop it." To which Harvey was incorrectly reported to have replied: "You shall have my full and open support or none at all."[66] Everywhere that the story appeared, Wilson was made to appear an ingrate, having turned his back on the man who made him governor of New Jersey. Wilson's principal biographers believe that an actual "break" did occur. Arthur S. Link believed that Harvey's courteous reply to Wilson's letter of apology was disingenuous, and that Harvey had conspired with Watterson to spread the story of Wilson's supposed ingratitude. Ray Stannard Baker wrote that Harvey shifted his support to Clark. There is no evidence for any of this. If Harvey had truly chosen to back another candidate, he chose a strange way to evidence it. He was the publisher of both *Harper's Weekly* and *The North American Review*. In neither journal was a kind word spoken for any of Wilson's opponents throughout the campaign. When Wilson finally wrested the nomination from Clark, Harvey put Wilson on the cover of *Harper's Weekly*, reminding its readers that the *Weekly* had predicted Wilson's election as far back as 1906. What was assumed to be the "break" with Wilson was what Harvey had promised to Wilson: he would "sing low" for the duration of the campaign.

January 8, 1912 was the night of the Jackson Day dinner, the unofficial kickoff of the presidential campaign. Upwards of a thousand Democrats gathered at the Raleigh Hotel in Washington, D.C. The principal candidates vying for the nomination, Wilson, Clark and Underwood, were there, as was the boss of Tammany Hall, Charlie Murphy, William Randolph Hearst and George Harvey. Bryan was also present. By the end of 1911 Wilson had come full circle and was now considered the leading Progressive. That night, he told his fellow Democrats: "Our government has for many years...been controlled in the interest of business....Being Democrats, believing the private control of business by comparatively small groups of men, the same groups that have come virtually to control the government to be fatal to the best interests of the country, how are we to translate our principles into effective action? He answered his own question: "We shall insist upon absolutely divorcing political action from the control of the great moneyed interests when it comes to nominations and elections and the choice of public policy."[67] At the close of his remarks, Wilson and Bryan toasted each other. Afterwards, Bryan's followers in the audience passed the word that Wilson was acceptable to them, regardless of what Wilson might have said of the Peerless Leader in the past.

In early February, Wilson appeared at a Philadelphia dinner hosted by the Association of Periodical Publishers. George Harvey was present, seated at a small table. Most of the attendees assumed there had been a "break" between him and Wilson. Wilson began his remarks with a perfect-pitch jibe at himself: "I used to be afraid that they [the publishers] would not publish what I offered them, but now I am afraid they will."[68] He spoke against the protective tariff and in favor of direct elections: "Nobody has a more profound and reverent belief in representative government than I have, but I haven't the least sentiment or regard for government that is not representative."[69] He was repeatedly interrupted by applause. Robert La Follette was also one of the invited speakers. He arrived late and worn out. Apparently distressed over his daughter's serious illness, he gave a rambling and incoherent speech. Whatever hope he had of winning the Republican nomination in 1912 died that night. He issued a statement: "If a Democrat is to be elected the next President of the United States, I hope it will be Woodrow Wilson."[70] Wilson spent the rest of February campaigning in Kentucky, New Hampshire, Kansas, Tennessee and Iowa. Speaking in Des Moines, he came out in favor of the direct election of United States senators, which surely made George Harvey wince. Only recently had Wilson assured Harvey that he was opposed to people voting for senators.

With the campaign in full swing, someone in William Randolph Hearst's employ decided to pull a copy of Wilson's *A History of the American People* off the shelf. It was not Wilson's even-handed treatment of the Ku Klux Klan or his distaste for the Fifteenth

Amendment that caught their eye. It was Wilson's praise of Cleveland's suppression of the 1894 American Railway Strike, his contempt for agrarian radicals and, what proved to be most embarrassing to Wilson, his opinions of Polish, Italian and Hungarian immigrants, whom he compared unfavorably to prior waves of immigration from Great Britain and France: "[N]ow there came multitudes of men of the lowest class from the south of Italy and men of the meaner sort out of Hungary and Poland, men out of the ranks where there was neither skill nor energy nor any initiative of quick intelligence; and they came in numbers which increased from year to year, as if the countries of the south of Europe were disburdening themselves of the more sordid and hapless elements of their population, the men whose standards of life and of work were such as American workmen had never dreamed of hitherto."[71] Worse, he compared these immigrants unfavorably to the more recent Chinese immigrants, who were "more to be desired." Wilson lamely tried to explain that he meant to describe only those foreigners who had immigrated, often against their will, and not to all Italians, Poles or Hungarians. But it cost him in the large cities and, ironically, in the South, not because he had disrespected Italians, Poles and Hungarians, but because he had compared white people unfavorably to Asians.

The primary season got under way in April. Wilson soon learned that cheers and applause do not always translate into votes, and that the support of a big-city machine on election day can be at least as important as a well-received speech. Under the Democratic rules then in effect, a candidate needed two-thirds of the delegates to the national convention to be the nominee. On April 9, Clark trounced Wilson in the Illinois primary. On April 13, Wilson won the Pennsylvania Democratic primary. Four days later, Clark swept Nebraska. Bryan thus became a nominal Clark delegate, but he was still officially neutral between Clark and Wilson. People began to wonder. Was Bryan secretly hoping for a deadlocked convention in order to emerge as a compromise candidate for yet the fourth time? On April 30, Oscar Underwood crushed Wilson in the Florida primary. ("Buried! Wilson Boom Laid to Rest in Florida" screamed the *Atlanta Constitution* on its front page.[72]) In a front-page editorial, the *Atlanta Constitution* urged its readers to support Underwood in the Georgia primary: "For the first time since Appomattox, the south has a full-fledged and undeniable opportunity to send one of its sons to the White House."[73] The next day, Underwood won the primary, sweeping 75% of Georgia's counties. But Underwood's appeal was limited to the South; he could win the nomination only as a compromise candidate. In late April, Wilson won the primaries in Delaware and Oregon. At its convention, Colorado instructed its delegates to vote for Clark, but only as long as Clark remained a candidate or Clark released them. On May 13, Clark won in Wyoming and the next day Clark, heavily supported by Hearst, took California. The next day, Wilson won in South Carolina; Michigan, not bound by a "unit" rule, split. On May 23, Underwood won in Virginia. On May 28, with Edward M. House's help, the Texas convention went for Wilson. In New York, every delegate to the convention was hand-picked by Tammany Hall boss Charlie Murphy. Murphy took the entire delegation—ninety delegates—into the convention uncommitted. And so it went, state after state. By the end of May, Wilson's publicity operation at 42 Broadway was completely broke. At the Republican convention in Chicago, Taft was renominated. Roosevelt and his supporters bolted and formed the "Progressive party," known to all as the "Bull Moose."

The Democrats gathered in Baltimore's steamy Convention Hall on June 25. Seven hundred twenty-nine delegates were needed to achieve the two-thirds supermajority for the nomination. Judge John W. Wescott, who early in 1911 had warned Wilson that he had to support Martine for the Senate, nominated Wilson, calling him the "ultimate Democrat, the genius of liberty and the very incarnation of progress."[74] After the first ballot, Clark had 440-1/2 delegates, Wilson 324, Underwood 117-1/2, and Ohio's favorite son, Governor Judson Harmon, 148. Clark was comfortably ahead, but far short of the two-thirds he needed. There was also that eminence seated in the Nebraska delegation: William Jennings Bryan.

According to the custom of the day, Wilson and the other candidates avoided the convention. Wilson, his family and Tumulty were at the governor's summer cottage at Sea Girt, connected to the convention by telephone and Western Union. Wilson's floor lieutenants were the volatile but effective William F. McCombs, F.P. Stockbridge, handling publicity, Congressman A. Mitchell Palmer (who would later become Wilson's Attorney-General), and William Gibbs McAdoo. McAdoo, 49, was a Tennessee lawyer who had moved to New York in 1892. He headed the Hudson & Manhattan Railroad, the company that had built the tube train connecting New York and New Jersey (today, the "PATH" train) and which would later build the Holland Tunnel. He was a brilliant organizer. Later in the campaign, when McCombs took a leave of absence due to poor health, McAdoo became the campaign chairman. By 1914, he would be Wilson's Secretary of the Treasury and son-in-law; he married Wilson's youngest daughter, Eleanor.

The candidates' strengths remained relatively fixed for the next nine ballots. On the tenth ballot, Tammany boss Charlie Murphy voted all of New York's ninety delegates for Clark. It gave Clark 556 delegates, a majority, but not the two-thirds needed for the nomination. But the Democrats had a tradition: Once a candidate obtained a majority, his opponents would concede and the remaining delegates would switch to him. Not since 1844 had a candidate who had achieved a majority failed to be nominated. When Tumulty saw the news come over the wire that Clark had a majority, he later wrote that "I almost collapsed at the news."[75] When Tumulty relayed the news to Wilson, Wilson telephoned McCombs in Baltimore. Tumulty heard Wilson say into the telephone "So you think it is hopeless?" When Wilson ended the call, Tumulty saw that Ellen was in tears. She said: "My dear Woodrow, I am sorry, indeed, that you have failed." Wilson, who had thrown body and soul into the race for more than a year, who had worn himself out traveling thousands of miles, but who was the embodiment of Presbyterian predestination theology, met the news with perfect equanimity: "My dear, of course I am disappointed, but we must not complain. We must be sportsmen. After all, it is God's will, and I feel that a great load has been lifted from my shoulders."[76]

Wilson composed a message to be sent to McCombs, congratulating Clark. According to Tumulty, it was Tumulty himself who convinced Wilson not to send it. In any event, the unstable McCombs took it upon himself to deliver a concession to Clark. Then, according to separate accounts from Tumulty and Stockbridge, Roger C. Sullivan, the boss of the Illinois Democrats who favored Wilson and feared Bryan in equal measure, heard of what McCombs was about to do, rushed over to McCombs and shouted: "Damn you, don't do that! Sit steady in the boat."[77] The congratulatory message to Clark was never sent. Without Sullivan's intercession Clark would have been the nominee, might have become the next president, and Wilson would have faded into the obscurity reserved for Clark. Such as this is history made.

Even with his majority, there was no stampede to Clark. Then, during the fourteenth ballot, the Nebraska delegation was "polled," i.e. each member of the delegation was asked to state his preference publicity. It came to Bryan, who despised Charlie Murphy, Tammany Hall and big-city machines. The loathing was mutual. Bryan announced that he would withhold his support for Clark as long as Murphy and the New York delegation supported Clark. However, if Murphy withdrew his support for Clark and switched to Wilson, Bryan would withdraw his support for Wilson. He sat down. By promising to oppose any candidate Murphy backed, Bryan had effectively deadlocked the convention. Was a deadlocked convention Bryan's secret goal all along?

Clark's support began to erode as Wilson's increased. After the twenty-sixth ballot, Clark had slipped from 556 delegates to 463-1/2; Wilson had inched up to 407-1/2. Underwood was still in the race, with 112-1/2. Murphy and the New York delegation were still firm for Clark. Illinois was still for Clark because he had won its primary. But Roger Sullivan, the Illinois boss, was for Wilson. On June 30, a Sunday, the exhausted delegates recessed. When they reconvened on Monday, Iowa switched from Clark to

Wilson. Indiana, which had supported its favorite son, Governor Thomas R. Marshall, threw in with Wilson. Vermont, Wyoming and Michigan followed. Wilson now led Clark for the first time, but was short a majority. After the forty-second ballot, Wilson had six hundred delegates, still short. That's when Roger Sullivan decided to throw the entire Illinois delegation to Wilson. It still left Wilson short of the magic number of 729. But with further erosion of Clark's support, Wilson went over the top on the forty-sixth ballot.

The final matter for the exhausted delegates was the selection of a candidate for vice president. Wilson wanted Oscar Underwood, who declined. Wilson's lieutenants strongly suggested Indiana's Governor Marshall. "But he is a very small caliber man," complained Wilson.[78] But, they advised, he was from the mid-West, which would be a battle ground. Wilson had left explicit instructions that no promises would be made in his name; he made it clear that he had no intention of buying the nomination. McCombs pressed for Marshall, and Wilson relented. He failed to inform Wilson that he had promised Marshall the vice presidency in exchange for Indiana's delegates.

Wilson formally "accepted" the nomination from the front porch of the governor's summer cottage at Sea Girt on August 8, 1912. People picnicked on the spacious lawn. Men sold sandwiches and popcorn, and the crowd ate as Wilson spoke.

The entire presidential campaign had dealt exclusively with domestic affairs: the tariff, women's suffrage, the direct election of senators, the trusts. No candidate had uttered a word about foreign affairs for the simple reason that what was going on beyond America's borders was of no concern to most voters. America's recent short war with Spain was receding in memory; America was still cosseted by two oceans. The world outside was very far away. In his acceptance speech, which was far from his best work, he methodically reviewed all of the planks in the Democratic platform, all but one of which dealt with domestic matters. Near the end of his address, he came to the one plank in the platform that touched on foreign affairs: the Philippines, which had been grabbed from Spain following the war. He said: "In dealing with the Philippines we should not allow ourselves to stand upon any mere point of pride, as if, in order to keep our countenance in the family of nations, it were necessary for us to make the same blunders as other nations have made. We are not the owners of the Philippine Islands. We hold them in trust for the people who live in them. They are theirs, for the uses of their life. We are not even their partners. It is our duty, as trustees, to make whatever arrangement of government will be most serviceable to their freedom and development. Here, again, we are to set up the rule of justice and of right."[79]

Woodrow Wilson, David Lloyd George and Georges Clemenceau were very different men, but they shared one belief. Whether it was the Philippines for Wilson, South Africa for Lloyd George or Indo-China for Clemenceau, each was opposed to his own country's foreign adventures.

It was clear to both Wilson and Roosevelt that the race was a two-man race between them. Roosevelt ran against Wilson, not Wilson and Taft. Wilson ran against Roosevelt, not Roosevelt and Taft. While on the stump, someone yelled at Roosevelt: "Tell us about Taft!" Roosevelt replied: I never discuss dead issues."[80] Taft sensed his own futility; he did not campaign. Wilson predicted, correctly, that Taft would finish third. (A fourth candidate, Eugene V. Debs, ran on the Socialist Party ticket.)

The main issues in the campaign were the tariff and control of the trusts. In 1912, everyone was a Progressive, even Taft, who could point to a credible record of trust-busting. The Progressive Party platform acknowledged that large monopolies were here to stay: "The concentration of modern business, in some degree, is both inevitable and necessary for national and international business efficiency." Their proposed solution was "a strong Federal, administrative commission of high standing, which shall maintain permanent active supervision over industrial corporations engaged in interstate commerce." Roosevelt slapped a label on this, the "New Nationalism." The Democratic platform (largely the work of Bryan) proclaimed that: "A private monopoly is indefensible and intolerable. We therefore favor the rigorous enforcement of the criminal as well as the civil law of trusts…and demand the enactment of such additional legislation as may be necessary to make it impossible for a private monopoly to exist in the United States." For years, Wilson had been peddling the notion that individuals, not corporations, were the root of the problem, and that suing a corporation for the actions of its directors was akin to suing a car following a traffic accident. Now Wilson had to admit that he was a blank slate on the issue. Fortunately for Wilson, he was able to enlist the best tutor in the land, the Kentucky-born Boston lawyer, Louis Dembitz Brandeis (1856-1941), an acknowledged expert in trade regulation. Shortly after accepting the nomination, Wilson invited Brandeis to Sea Girt for the first of many meetings. Wilson was, as always, a quick study. Brandeis convinced Wilson that what needed to be regulated was not the trusts but competition itself; that it was government's role to ensure that small entrepreneurs could grow larger without being crushed by the depredations of larger competitors. As Wilson summarized in on the stump: "The big fellow cannot put the little fellow out of business."[81]This too got its own label, the "New Freedom."

It is doubtful that most voters were able to draw fine distinctions between "New Nationalism" and "New Freedom." What probably mattered more to many voters was that Roosevelt had made a promise not to run for a second term, and had reneged on his promise. The public had tired of both Taft and Roosevelt, and Wilson was fresh air.

On November 5, 1912, the people voted. Wilson was expected to take the Solid South. He also swept the mid-West, save Michigan. He won forty states to Roosevelt's six. Taft won Vermont and Nevada. Wilson garnered 41.8% of the vote, Roosevelt 27.4% and Taft, finishing third as Wilson predicted, won 23.2%. Debs pulled in more than 901,000 votes, or 6%, a remarkable showing for an underfinanced candidate. In the end, however, Wilson polled fewer votes than Bryan had in any of Bryan's three losing campaigns. A conventional wisdom has arisen since 1912 that Wilson won only because Roosevelt created a three-cornered race. That is unlikely. Roosevelt probably drew at least as many votes from Wilson as he drew from Taft. It is equally plausible that Taft's presence in the race cost Roosevelt the election.

When young "Tommy" Wilson was sixteen, he tacked a photo of William Gladstone to his bedroom wall, telling his cousin: "That is Gladstone, the greatest statesman that ever lived. I intend to be a statesman too." But for the next thirty years, his ambition had been stymied. He was a student until he was thirty, a college teacher and administrator until he was fifty-four. Then, in February, 1910, George B. McClellan Harvey offered him the governorship of New Jersey "on a silver platter." Now, a scant thirty-three months later, he was the president-elect of the United States.

He had hoped that in his first term as president, he would be able to concentrate on domestic matters; he hoped that foreign affairs would not intrude. He knew, of course, that he could not control the world outside. Fate would not accommodate his desire. He would need to deal with the world outside America's borders sooner than he had hoped or planned.

10

WAR CLOUDS

*The lamps are going out all over Europe; we shall not see them lit again
in our lifetime.*

—Sir Edward Grey

In July, 1909, when he was ousted as prime minister, Georges Clemenceau was sixty-eight years old. He was not in good health. A liver disorder gave him a yellowish appearance. He had diabetes. His prostate was hurting. He was glad to be out, writing: "I am in the full joy of deliverance. No more people to see. No more demands. Nothing more but freedom."[1] A friend recalled that he had "never witnessed an outburst of joy so sincere, so gleeful."[2] He was still a member of the Senate, but that required only as much of his time as he was willing to give.

He bought and furnished a house in Bernouville, a two-hour drive north of Paris. It was a short drive from Giverny, the home of his great friend and contemporary Claude Monet (Monet was ten months older), and the two visited each other often. But Clemenceau never stayed in Bernouville for more than a few days, always returning to his home, office and base of operations on the rue Franklin.

The month after his ouster he took his annual holiday at Karlsbad. There he met his old friend, Berta Szeps. As usual, he brought with him bags and suitcases filled with newspapers. He was in great spirits. "Now I will become a journalist again," he laughed, "Now I am free once more. Now I can laugh and swear at other people's stupidities again, instead of perpetuating stupidities myself."[3] The day after he arrived King Edward invited him to lunch at Marienbad, and Clemenceau invited Berta Szeps to accompany him on the short drive. She reported that he was worried. In 1908, while Clemenceau was still prime minister, Austria, seeing that the Ottoman Empire was weak and growing weaker, had annexed Bosnia-Herzegovina. (Also noting the Ottoman's weakness, Bulgaria had proclaimed its independence.) Austria's takeover of Bosnia-Herzegovina thwarted Serbia's own designs; its quest for a "Greater Serbia" uniting all Slavs was no secret. Clemenceau and Edward met privately. After the meeting, Clemenceau reported to Berta Szeps that the two had commiserated over Austria's rash move into the Balkans: "It was a bad mistake for Francis Joseph and Aerenthal (the Austrian foreign minister) to hide their plan for the annexation of Bosnia and Herzegovina; and one day that mistake will revenge itself…[T]oday one thing has become quite clear to me—in order to rule the east, Austria has lost the west." Clemenceau also warned Edward of the sad state of the British Army. Edward could only concur.[4]

In April, 1910, Clemenceau met the touring ex-President Roosevelt at the Foreign Ministry. TR was not the first American president Clemenceau had met; he had interviewed General Grant at Army headquarters shortly after the Civil War ended.

In June, 1910, Clemenceau was off on a lecture tour of South America, at the invitation of the *Alliance Francaise*. He was apparently their third choice, after the Czech violinist Jan Kubelik and Jean Jaurès. His fee was apparently large enough to free him of his debts forever, and his audiences got what they paid for. He gave eight lectures on "Democracy" in Buenos Aires, Montevideo, Rio de Janeiro and smaller cities, advising his auditors: "Have the courage to act, the courage to debate. Do not be afraid of making enemies. If you have none, it is because you have done nothing. You wanted democracy. You have written it into your laws. Live it."[5] He admitted that he had changed his mind about the French Senate. Having reviled it in his youth as a monarchical vestige, he now opined that he favored bicameral legislatures. He was feted by heads of state and local dignitaries, toured the local sights, and thoroughly enjoyed himself, not returning until late October. Upon his return, he wrote a charming little travelogue, *South America Today*.

He was seventy. He was slowing down. He feared that Austria might set off a war by its Balkan incursion. But the next flashpoint was not in the Balkans. It was, once again, Morocco.

The First Moroccan Crisis had ended in 1906 in what all sides considered a French diplomatic victory and a German humiliation. In the face of German threats and posturing (the kaiser's two-hour ride on horseback through the streets of Tangier), Great Britain had stood by France. German Chancellor von Bülow's attempt to weaken the Triple Entente ended with Britain's ties to France stronger than ever. At the Algeciras Conference, France was ceded the primary political role in Morocco, subject to the commercial rights of all nations, including Germany. The Act of Algeciras was strengthened in 1909. Germany conceded the "special interests of France in Morocco," and "resolved not to thwart those interests." In return, France promised to safeguard the principle of economic equality and "consequently not to obstruct German commercial and industrial interests in the country." What these two agreements did *not* give France was a protectorate over Morocco.

Early in 1911 a civil war broke out between the always-broke sultan, Mulai Hafid, headquartered in Fez, and his brother, who claimed himself as sultan. The French consul in Fez cabled Paris that the European community in Fez was threatened with a massacre. On April 19, the French government announced that, in response to the sultan's "appeal," France would send a column of troops to Fez to relieve the surrounded sultan. This alarmed Bethmann Hollweg, the German chancellor, who warned the French ambassador, Jules Cambon, that Germany did not believe any Europeans were in danger in Fez, and that the action was a pretext to extend French influence. "You know German opinion on Morocco, and I must take it into account. If you go to Fez, you will stay there, and then the whole Moroccan question will be raised, which I wish at all costs to avoid."[6] France did not heed the warning, and did send the troops. A column was marched 183 miles inland from Casablanca, and the siege was lifted on May 21.

France was far from blameless in this matter. It appears that the troops were dispatched to Fez *before* the sultan's "appeal" for relief. In doing so, France violated the spirit, if not the text, of the Act of Algeciras by seeking to dominate the sultan, which altered the Moroccan *status quo*. Germany rightly felt squeezed by France's unilateral action. But it was now the turn of German Foreign Minister Alfred von Kiderlen-Wächter in what was now the Second Moroccan Crisis, to overplay his hand, just as von Bülow had done in 1905. When Jules Cambon advised Kiderlen that the troops would depart Fez as soon as the civilians were rescued, Kiderein replied: "If French troops remain in Fez so that the sultan rules only with the aid of French bayonets, Germany will regard the Act of Algeciras as no longer in force and will resume complete liberty of action."[7] Kiderlen decided that if France could present Germany with a *fait accompli* in northern Morocco, Germany would present France with a *fait accompli* in southern Morocco. If Kiderlen could manage to partition Morocco, he could trade southern Morocco back to the French in exchange for "compensation" somewhere else.

To accomplish this end, Kiderlen needed an excuse similar to France's in Fez, viz. that *German* personnel were endangered in southern Morocco. It is here that the Second Moroccan Crisis takes on comic-opera overtones. Unfortunately for Kiderlen, Germany had no personnel or assets of any kind in southern Morocco in need of protection. Kiderlen circulated among German industrialists a petition in which they were requested to ask the government to protect their commercial interests in southern Morocco, of which there were none. Not a problem. Kiderlen decided to use old-fashioned gunboat diplomacy to partition Morocco. Sending a warship to Morocco required the kaiser's consent, who was hesitant to grant it. Eventually the kaiser relented. Kiderlen then had all of his ambassadors deliver a message to their host governments: "Some German firms established in the south of Morocco, notably at Agadir and in the vicinity, have been alarmed by a certain ferment which has shown itself among the local tribes…These firms have applied to the Imperial Government for protection for the lives of their employees and their property. At their request, the Imperial Government has decided to send a warship to the port of Agadir, to lend help and assistance, in case of need, to its subjects and employees, as well as to protect the important German interests in the territory in question."[8]

On July 1, 1911, the German gunboat *Panther*, heading north after a voyage around the cape, docked off of Agadir. The next day, the larger cruiser *Berlin* arrived, both with the mission of rescuing Germans. Of course, there were no Germans in Agadir in need of rescue, but Kiderlen had planned for this. He found a German national, a Herr Wilburg, who had been stationed in Mogodor, some seventy-five miles north of Agadir, and dispatched Wilburg to Agadir, to act as the "rescued" German. Wilburg scurried to Agadir as fast as he could, but arrived in Agadir to be rescued three days *after* the *Panther* dropped anchor. He was reduced to running along the shoreline waving his arms to attract the attention of his "rescuers." He was "rescued" on July 5.

Just at this time another French government fell, but not for the usual reasons. The prime minister, Ernest Monis, was seriously injured while watching the start of a Paris-to-Madrid air race; one of the planes crashed into the crowd. He was forced to resign. In his place stepped Finance Minister Joseph Caillaux, who had served as Clemenceau's finance minister. Caillaux chose as his foreign minister Justin de Selves, a local politician with no foreign policy experience. It was a signal that Caillaux planned to act as his own foreign minister. Caillaux's accommodationist tendencies towards Germany were well known.

The one thing that Kiderlen had not considered when he sent the *Panther* to Morocco was the reaction in London. On July 4, shortly after the *Panther* arrived off the coast of Agadir, Foreign Secretary Sir Edward Grey dispatched a letter to the

German ambassador, Count Metternich, advising that Great Britain had an interest in the future of Morocco. Just as during the First Moroccan Crisis, Grey felt that the Entente with France would be weakened if Britain did not back up France. Under the Entente, Britain was required to lend France diplomatic—not military—support. A message needed to be delivered to both stiffen the resolve of the French and show Kiderlen that the British were serious. The message would be delivered by an unlikely source: the chancellor of the exchequer, David Lloyd George.

Grey's warning to Metternich went unanswered for the next seventeen days. Lloyd George later wrote that he felt that the failure to respond might mean that Kiderlen was unaware that Britain took her Entente obligations seriously, that "we were drifting clumsily toward war."⁹ Lloyd George was scheduled to address a bankers' meeting at London's Mansion House on the evening of the twenty-first. As chancellor of the exchequer, he had no writ in foreign policy. So he cleared the idea of a public warning to the Germans with both Grey and Prime Minister Asquith, both of whom gave him the go-ahead. Most of the speech dealt with economic matters of concern mostly to the assembled bankers. But then Lloyd George changed the subject: "I would make great sacrifices to preserve peace. I conceive that nothing would justify a disturbance of international good will except questions of the gravest national moment. But if a situation were forced upon us in which peace could only be preserved by the surrender of the great and beneficent position Britain has won by centuries of heroism and achievement, by allowing Britain to be treated, where her interests were vitally affected, as if she were of no account in the Cabinet of Nations, then I say emphatically that peace at that price would be a humiliation intolerable for a great country like ours to endure."¹⁰

What made the speech so effective was its source: Lloyd George had rightly been considered a Germanophile, one always seeking to improve British-German relations. But if Lloyd George was threatening war over Morocco, it meant that the entire British political spectrum shared his views. Moreover, since the speech was delivered by a cabinet officer having no official role in foreign affairs, the German foreign office assumed—incorrectly—that the speech had actually been written by Grey and/or Asquith. Years later, Grey wrote that it was the Mansion House speech that changed everything. Before the speech, Kiderlen deprecated the chances that Britain would interfere on France's behalf. After the speech, he could not be sure if pressing the issue in Morocco might lead to a war with France, Britain and perhaps the third party to the Entente, Russia. "It was my opinion then," Grey wrote years later, "and it is so still, that the speech had much to do with preserving the peace in 1911."¹¹

The immediate effect of the speech was to moderate Kiderlen's approach. On July 24, Metternich met with Grey, their first meeting since Grey's warning letter. Metternich advised Grey that no German troops had landed in Agadir and that none would. He added that Germany had no territorial intentions in Morocco, had no intention of establishing a naval base there, and sought only compensation for France's tearing up the Act of Algeciras. But in a meeting the next day, Metternich hedged. He said that Lloyd George's speech had hardened German public opinion, and that whatever Metternich had said the day before was to be treated as confidential. But on the next day—armed with new instructions from Kiderlen—Metternich changed course again, advising that Grey could release for publication what he had said on the twenty-fourth.

Henceforth, negotiations would be conducted directly between Kiderlen and Jules Cambon, the only issue being what "compensation" Germany would receive in exchange for a French protectorate over Morocco. The negotiations were hampered by colonial hardliners in Paris and Berlin. Initially, Kiderlen sought all of what is today the French Congo. France, stiffened by British support, refused. The negotiations dragged on until October. In the final agreement, France achieved its protectorate over Morocco (although the word "protectorate" was diplomatically omitted). Germany received a slice of worthless land from France's colony in the Congo, which it added to its colony in Cameroon (and which it lost following the First World War). Grey later recorded: "The end was almost a fiasco for Germany; out of this mountain of German-made crisis came a mouse of colonial territory in Africa. France was left with her prestige intact and free of the Morocco thumbscrews."[12] The Second Moroccan Crisis was considered a German failure, as was the first. The German chancellor, Bethmann Hollweg, tried to defend the agreement in the Reichstag, saying: "We drew up a program and carried it out." His statement was met by peals of derisive laughter.[13]

There was one thing that Jules Cambon did not—could not—know during the months that he was negotiating the agreement to end the Second Moroccan Crisis: He was not the only person negotiating on France's behalf. It would soon be revealed that behind Cambon's back the prime minister, Joseph Caillaux, was negotiating with the Germans himself.

The treaty that Jules Cambon negotiated with Kiderlen required legislative approval. As word was leaking out that Caillaux had been secretly negotiating with the Germans, the Senate appointed a commission of inquiry. One of the senators appointed was Clemenceau. The fateful day came on January 9, 1912. Testifying before the commission,

Caillaux, on his word of honor, denied that he had secretly dealt with Germany over Morocco. Clemenceau then turned to Caillaux's foreign minister, Justin de Selves. He asked de Selves if he could confirm Caillaux's testimony. De Selves replied: "I have regard for the truth, and also for the correct attitude commanded by my function; I ask not to be allowed to reply to that question."[14] A recess was called. De Selves resigned. Unable to find a replacement, Caillaux himself resigned as prime minister on January 21. Clemenceau, who decades before had earned the sobriquet of "destroyer of ministries" as a member of the Chamber of Deputies, had now felled his first as a senator. It eventuated that Caillaux had begun negotiating with the Germans even before the Germans sent the *Panther* to Agadir, while still the minister of finance in the Monis government. Worse, some of those conducting the negotiations on Caillaux's behalf had financial interests in the Congo. Still worse, they were negotiating not with officials of the German foreign office, but with German secret agents.

The irony was that most of France was delighted with the outcome: France had traded worthless, undeveloped land in central Africa for complete control over Morocco. The treaty was certain to win approval in both chambers. But it would do so over the strong objection of Georges Clemenceau.

Clemenceau's misgivings about colonial adventures were of long standing and were widely known. He had driven Jules Ferry from office over France's adventure in Indo-China. He had ridiculed France's incursion into Tunisia. But he was in the minority; most of France, even his fellow Republicans, felt pride in France's expanding African empire. The fact that France had almost gone to war with Great Britain at Fashoda over the Sudan was now largely forgotten. And so, when Clemenceau mounted the tribune on February 12, 1912, shortly after the Caillaux government had fallen, it was to oppose the treaty granting France a protectorate over Morocco, a battle he knew was lost. But before he yielded the floor he would not only state his reasons for opposing the treaty; he would state—as never before—his beliefs respecting the fundamental differences between modern Germany and the Third Republic.

He began by conceding a fact that he need not have conceded, that France had to send troops to Fez to rescue the European community. If Caillaux had withdrawn the troops after the threat was lifted, he could have supported the treaty. But easing the threat was not enough for Caillaux; he wanted more: "The tempter" brought Caillaux "...up to the mountain and told him: 'The protectorate of Morocco is there.' It was dazzled before his eyes; he was struck by the greatness of his work that destiny brought him...the idea of giving France a great empire that went from the Atlantic to Sirte."[15]

Clemenceau's principal objection was not to the terms of the treaty, but the manner in which it came about: France had negotiated "under the guns of Agadir." He quoted Count Bernsdorff, the German ambassador to the United States, who admitted, rather undiplomatically, that the "negotiations [were] conducted under the moral pressure of sending the *Panther* to Agadir."[16] Clemenceau warned that it was a delusion to believe that now that France had its protectorate over Morocco, France was finished with Germany in Morocco. Quite the contrary. Just as Germany had used the threat of war to slice off a piece of France's African empire, Germany would do so again. To prove his point, he quoted at length from an article by a Herr Daniels in a German scholarly magazine, *Preussiches Jahrbuch* ("Prussian Yearbook"), in which the author praised Kiderlen and the benefits of the treaty to Germany: "As long as Germany is not determined to plunge into an interminable series of wars, she must content herself with gleanings in colonial dominions...We should be happy every time we have a chance to acquire a piece of territory in foreign lands."[17].... "If they [the French] persuaded themselves that they are free forever from German intervention in Morocco, a painful awakening will be inevitably assured to our amiable neighbors. The Moroccan treaty creates in the North African empire a state of things far more favorable to us than that offered by the Act of Algeciras or by the Franco-German agreement of 1909."[18] Under the treaty, France would be required to use armed force to pacify a country in part for the commercial benefit of Germany. The author predicts that: "A few years from now there will have arisen plenty of subjects for dispute, created by the non-application or the sophistical interpretation of the Moroccan treaty...So much the better!...[O]ur diplomacy will then be forceful enough to oblige the French who are impatiently demanding a freer and freer hand in Morocco, to cede to us new territories from their rich equatorial domain..."[19] The article concludes: "The war with France, which our superpatriots desire to-day, can always be had as the result of a later stage of the Moroccan question."[20]

For Clemenceau, the dispatch of the *Panther* to Agadir was just the latest in a long line of German moves against France, and would not be the last. He began his exegesis by reminding his auditors that "I broach this subject without being troubled by what I am about to say, because there is no feeling in my heart, no hatred, to use the exact word, toward the German people." But in comparing the Germans to the French he noted that "The German, so far as I can judge, is above all else enamored of force, and he rarely neglects an opportunity to say so; but where he differs from the Latin is in the fact that his first thought is to employ that force."[21] Germany gained her unity by force, by blood and iron. She desired this unity so much...that she intends to use it. She wants to scatter through the world an enormous surplus of population. She therefore finds herself led, by a destiny which is impossible for her to escape, to bring to bear upon her neighbors such pressure as to make them grant her, at the very least, the economic favors that she needs."[22] But using words that later would ring with irony, he reminded his listeners that following the war "Germany took from us…an indemnity of five billions, and in so doing robbed us of our vital energy. It is the modern form of ancient slavery. In older days warriors took possession of men, to make them work and enjoy the fruit of their toil. Now the method is changed; the victors force the vanquished to pay them perpetual tribute. That is what was done. We are free, we are left in our country, we can work, but each year we are losing the interest of the sum we paid."[23] He remarked that the "ebb and flow of conflicts on the banks of the Rhine" would finally cease only when there appeared "a conqueror superior to his conquest, a victor who will be a hero in moderation." He admitted that "Napoleon was not such a conqueror," but neither was Bismarck.[24]

The French, he averred, are very different: "We have a Latin manner, we like display and flourishes of glory, but at heart we are not bad fellows; there is proof enough of it in the way our soldiers were received in the capitals of Europe which they traversed."[25] "The French people [are] a people of idealism, critical in spirit, restive under discipline, given to wars and revolutions. Its character is ill fitted for continuous action. Indeed, the French people have flights of enthusiasm that are magnificent, but, as the poet says, it is sometimes necessary to measure the height of the flight by the depth of the fall."[26]

He asked the senators to "let your minds go back to the time" of the founding of the Republic: "The foreign war, the invasion, and the Assembly, formed to make peace, which would impose monarchy on the Republic; the revolts of the Commune, Paris in flames, a reaction under way in the heart of the Assembly directing the Republic which meant to destroy the Republic, struggles following one another without end."[27] Out of this rose "the party for the Republic, gaining the confidence of the country, molding a public mind now reasserting itself and endeavoring from this moment, not only to repair the military forces of France but to recreate France herself, from the beginning, in her spirit, for her future."[28] The rebuilding of France "had to be undertaken from the foundation, from the one foundation that is unshakable, namely, the heart of every citizen…but the thing that needed to be done first was…to make citizens, and it was necessary to create them…We are still struggling with the great work; we hope to carry it to success."[29]

He was proud of the Republic. "The work that we have done must not be judged by what is visible, but by the ideas and the sentiments that we have implanted in the hearts of all French citizens. Since the French Revolution democracy has found its way around the world. There is now a parliament in China, in Turkey; the German people have gained universal suffrage and a Reichstag on the battlefields of France…. When we look back over the events…of forty years…we have availed for something, that indeed a great work has been accomplished"[30]....Gentlemen, it must be evident that the French people have never shown a less aggressive mood than today. Why? Because they understand that in order to develop their principles, in order to live their full life, they have only to invoke the right of all peoples so to live."[31] In order for the principles of the Republic to succeed, what France needed more than anything was peace. But time and again since the birth of the Republic, Clemenceau reminded the Senate, Germany had threatened France with war. For those in his audience too young to remember, he reviewed the history of the 1875 "War in Sight" scare, the Schnaebele affair, and repeated threats over Morocco. "Yes...it is just this right of all peoples so to live their life which has been denied to us by Germany since the day of our defeat."[32]

He was near the end. He could have continued but his prostate was hurting. "In all good faith we want peace; we want because we have need of it to rebuild our country. But in spite of all, if war is imposed on us, we shall not be found wanting." (The Senate stenographer reported "Loud applause from all sides.") He continued: "This is the trouble between Germany and us: Germany believes that the logical result of her victory is domination, and we do not believe that the logical result of our defeat is vassalage." (More "Loud applause from all sides.") And then: "We are pacifists, or rather we are pacific. We do not subscribe to the terms of abdication and the surrender of our rights as our neighbors have drawn them up. We are heirs of a noble history and we mean to preserve the tradition....The dead have created the living; the living will remain faithful to the dead."[33]

Shortly after the speech, Clemenceau had his prostate removed, then a risky and dangerous operation. Years later he would quip that there are two useless things one can do without. One is the prostate, the other is the president of France.

Neither Clemenceau nor anyone else could then foresee it, but Austria's 1908 annexation of Bosnia-Herzegovina had set a long fuse that would cause an explosion in 1914. Everyone now saw how tenuous was the Ottoman Empire's grip on its holdings in Europe. In September, 1911, Italy invaded the Ottoman provinces in North Africa that would later comprise modern Libya, including Tripoli. The war lasted until October, 1912. England and the other powers stayed out, giving Italy a free hand. Before the "Tripolitanian War" ended, Serbia, Montenegro, Bulgaria and Greece—seeing how weak the Ottomans were—formed the "Balkan League," the goal of which was to evict the Ottomans from Macedonia and divvy up the spoils. Greece also had the goal of evicting the Ottomans from Crete. The war broke out on October 17, 1912, the *New York Times* reporting the next day that: "Five states are at war, three kings are at the front, and a million men are in arms. The greatest conflict that Europe has known since the Franco-Prussian War has opened under conditions which make the struggle likely to be one of the blood-thirstiest in modern history."[34] By May, 1913, the Balkan League had defeated the Ottomans. It was officially ended with the Treaty of London, brokered by Sir Edward Grey. It had remained a local war. France did not want to see the Ottomans collapse, fearful of the Muslim reaction in its North African territories. Russia felt kinship with their Slav co-religionists, but stayed out, still not fully recovered from its defeat at the hands of Japan.

No sooner had what became known as the "First Balkan War" ended than the members of the Balkan League fell out among themselves. Bulgaria believed that it had not received a sufficient share of the Macedonian spoils, and declared war on its former Balkan League partners and the Ottoman Empire. Rumania joined the fray against Bulgaria. Bulgaria was quickly defeated (in the "Second Balkan War') and gave up its share of Macedonia. The big winner to emerge from both Balkan wars was Serbia, doubling in size and seeing its ancient dream of a "Greater Serbia"—the unification of all Serbs residing everywhere—coming closer to realization. The loser was Austria-Hungary, which now had to contend with a growing and aggressive Serbia smarting over the annexation of Bosnia-Herzegovina. The mistake of the great powers was in believing that these local conflicts could always be settled by convening yet another conference of diplomats and that if war did break out, it could be kept local.

Forcing Joseph Caillaux from office proved to be a bittersweet victory for Clemenceau. Caillaux was succeeded by the Lorraine lawyer Raymond Poincaré (1860-1934), a man whom Clemenceau loathed, whom he felt was a stiff, witless pedant. The loathing was mutual; Poincare despised Clemenceau's wit. Clemenceau actually supported Poincare's accession to the office, simply to block Delcassé, who he disliked even more than Poincaré. In early 1913, Poincaré decided that he wished to be president of the Republic. Tradition had it that the office would be occupied by weaklings (hence Clemenceau's likening it to the prostate gland); Poincaré set out to change that. Poincaré defeated another candidate supported by Clemenceau. There was now no chance that Clemenceau could return to government as long as Poincaré was president. At least for now.

When Poincaré became president he was succeeded by Aristide Briand, now taking his third turn as prime minister. Briand's government would last less than two months, but during that interval Briand submitted to the Chamber of Deputies the "Three-Year Law," extending the required military service of all draftees from two years to three.

In 1905, the required length of service had been *reduced* from three years to two, representing the only victory that the Dreyfusards had achieved over the army. Clemenceau had supported the reduction. But it soon became obvious that demography had caught up with France. In 1870, the population of France and Germany was roughly equal. By 1913, however, Germany boasted a population of sixty-seven million; France's population had *declined* to 41.5 million, the result of German mothers producing babies at a far faster rate than their French counterparts. The German birth rate was 27.6 children per 100,000; the French rate was only 19.1 children per 100,000. France's population was now lower than that of the United Kingdom, Russia and Austria-Hungary, and Italy was closing the gap.[35] France was drafting every available man to the colors, but it still wasn't enough. The only way for France to keep pace was to extend the time of required service, especially in light of Germany's own 1913 Army Bill, which provided for huge increases in funding for all branches of the German army and navy, which increased the size of the army by 170,000 troops. No one supported the French Three Year Law more than Clemenceau. No sooner had Briand introduced the law than there were demonstrations throughout France in opposition, led by men like Caillaux and Jaurès. In 1913, France was still largely agricultural. Removing a man from his farm for three years would cause real hardship, especially since few people foresaw a major war on the horizon. The Three-Year Law would roil French politics right up to the start of the First World War.

In May, 1913, Clemenceau became a journalist again. On May 5, *L'Homme Libre* ("The Free Man") first appeared. It remains unknown who Clemenceau's backers were. The four-page daily had a sports section, covered the arts, (Gustave Geffroy, who was with him at *La Justice*, was back) contained a little news and carried some advertising. But it was principally a vehicle for the opinions of its "Editor-in-Chief," Clemenceau. Every day—seven days a week—he wrote a 1000 to 2000-word front page editorial. He wrote in the early morning at the horseshoe desk in the rue Franklin, furiously dipping his pen into the inkwell (he disdained fountain pens). A messenger delivered his scripts to *L'Homme Libre*'s offices, and Clemenceau arrived in the early evening to review the finished proofs. *L'Homme Libre* had a circulation of only a few thousand, but it was required reading for France's politicians.

For his first editorial ("A Difficult Hour") France's readiness and the Three-Year Law were on his mind, and would remain his principal focus for the next year. "The obligation to provide for the necessities of an armed peace such as Germany is forcing on us entails an increase in troop levels, not in order to maintain an old routine such as magnificently led us to disaster, but for a methodical plan of military education and preparation with a view to a superior efficiency."[36] Three days later, in an editorial titled simply "The Three-Year Law," he compared Germany's and France's forces. He claimed that as a result of Germany's Army Bill, German troop strength, which had been 622,000 in 1905, would increase to more than 827,000 by 1915, and that those troops would be better trained. The increase would serve to supplement every unit; to give a third battalion to regiments that had had only two, to increase the number of companies in every battalion, etc. The Germans had improved their heavy artillery, cavalry, railroads, and all forms of communications, all of which had been "disastrously neglected by the French general staff.... Germany will be able to put on the line, in time of war, an army in the first shock of war, younger and better trained....In the presence of such a great effort, how could we remain inactive?" In sum, France needed to find an additional 150,000 men "simply to put ourselves at the level of the German effort."[37]

The next day, in "Blood and Money," he railed against the difficulty in finding additional troops to defend France when there were sixty thousand French troops in Morocco. He mocked the folly of trying to pacify a "colony without colonists," noting that French soldiers were being killed and wounded in Morocco at the rate of fifty a week trying to suppress tribal conflicts, in part for the purpose of safeguarding German industry in Morocco. "Today," he wrote, "if all the French soldiers were in metropolitan France, it would take only a slight reform to cope with the difficulties of the day, without resorting to a three-year law." There was no chance that he would vote against the Three-Year Law, but he concluded: "I would like to be assured, before voting a three-year service claimed by the continental defense, that we do not take advantage of it to throw the extra French soldiers into the monster devouring adventures."[38] When war loomed with Germany the following year, all of the soldiers stationed in North Africa were quickly called home.

On May 21, as the Senate was debating the Three-Year Law, Clemenceau headed his column "For National Defense," writing: "The thing that too many people among us will not yet understand is that Germany, organized primarily for the exercise of military domination, could not, even if she would—and certainly she has no appearance of desiring to—escape the fate of a growing passion for war"....Under the pretext of guaranteeing herself against our aggression, she will only continue her programs of super-armament up to the day that she considers propitious for destroying us. For one must be willfully blind not to see that her rage for domination, the explosion of which will one day shake the whole continent of Europe, commits her to a policy of the extermination of France"....Those who saw 1870-71 can no longer let slip a single opportunity, however small, to avoid a return of those terrible days, the horror of which could only be increased a hundredfold." He ended by quoting the words of an unnamed veteran of 1870: "Service for five years would be absurd. Yet I should vote for it if the government asked it of me, for I do not wish to reproach myself on my death-bed with having contributed, even in part, to a catastrophe from which France would never recover."[39]

A debate opened in the German Reichstag on Alsace-Lorraine. Specifically, the amount of press freedom the Germans would permit in those provinces. It sparked Clemenceau's June 3 column, "The Question of Alsace-Lorraine," in which he asked: "The Germans proclaim that there is no question of Alsace-Lorraine. In that case, how comes it that for them it is a permanent subject of discussion?" Clemenceau's answer was that Alsace-Lorraine was haunting the German conscience: "[T]he question of Alsace-Lorraine flourishes, not in the flowery fields of diplomacy, but in a nook from which no German police force could uproot it—I mean in the inviolable refuge of the human conscience." He claimed that: "[W]e cannot talk with a German without his questioning eyes seeming to say to us 'I hope you do not think about it anymore.' As for him, he must think about it since, as I said before, he speaks of it all the time, and this makes more alive than ever the question he would like to go away." He likened the Germans to Lady Macbeth: "If [she] had given herself a pair of gloves, no one would have seen the little red spot, but she would have known that there was blood, which was too much for her peace of mind." He concluded, "[T]he fate of a land can be decided, for a time, upon the battlefield, but not the mastery of souls, which escape the might of the sword."[40]

On June 6, the Chamber of Deputies took up the Three-Year Law. The Socialists and many left-wing radicals strongly opposed it. Two days later, in an editorial headed "A Question of Existence," Clemenceau warned that if the law were defeated, "we must without delay renounce our independence and go beg on bended knee for 'the friendship' of Germany....I wonder, indeed, why we are bent on preserving just enough military power to attract the shock of German thunderbolts, to see ourselves again carved in pieces, slashed up, ground down, despoiled of our goods, our dignity, our reason for existence, falling to the lowest depths of servitude, and crowning the deeds of our great ancestors with an ignoble surrender of ourselves." He conceded the hardship to a family whose breadwinner would be removed for three years, but "This workman does not wish to become German, I assure you. He clings to his home and his country with all that is in him. If he had been able to foresee, before the war of 1870, what danger threatened him, he would have lavished the sacrifices without counting them and from the financial point of view only—subordinated here—he would have made a wise transaction."[41]

The debate dragged on in the Chamber. Finally, on July 18, it narrowly passed. In the Senate, where the members were older and more of them, like Clemenceau, had memories of 1870, the law passed with ease on August 7. But the increase in army strength was yet only hypothetical. Funds had to be appropriated for the army, and an election loomed. The fight was far from over.

On October 28, 1913, a twenty-year-old German second lieutenant, Gunter von Forstner, was addressing his troops in the town of Zabern (now known as Saverne) in Alsace. He referred to the locals as *Wackes*, a term for Alsatians so derogatory that German army regulations prohibited its use. The locals did not hear of the incident until November 6, when two local newspapers reported it. Worse than the initial insult was von Forstner's "punishment," six days of house arrest. The German attitude was made manifest when a German sergeant-major and eight privates were placed under military arrest for the more serious crime of giving military secrets to the press. Forstner himself was reassigned.[42] A French journalist and politician, Paul de Cassagnac, challenged von Forstner to a duel. The traditional means of challenge (dropping a glove), being unavailable to him, de Cassagnac issued the challenge by means of a registered letter, which von Forstner returned unopened.[43] On November 28, a huge crowd assembled in front of the Zabern army barracks. The protesters were given an order to disperse. They refused. Between twenty-five and thirty people were arrested. They were kept in a cellar overnight, were turned over to the civilian authorities the next morning, and released. But martial law was imposed throughout southern Alsace. Sentries with loaded rifles and fixed bayonets patrolled Zabern.[44]

What to do about Zabern made it to the Reichstag. There was considerable opposition to the manner in which the military had handled Zabern. Chancellor Bethmann Hollweg threatened to resign unless some concessions were made, which placed the issue in the hands of the kaiser. He ordered the 95th Infantry Regiment—von Forstner's regiment—out of Zabern.[45] It was the end of the "Zabern Affair."

Clemenceau did not weigh in on the Zabern affair until January, 1914: "I do not know why there has been so much talk about the Zabern affair. What is there that can astonish those who know the German rule?…Germany took Alsace-Lorraine away from us, with five billions to defray the expenses of original establishment, and the first of thanks was that the conquered country must be Germanized by any and all means…. Immigration and shrewd policies, these were the two methods that seemed surest to inculcate in French heads a love of Teutonism."[46] Clemenceau was prescient. In May, the German authorities in Alsace-Lorraine announced that the residency permits for

French citizens residing there, which they had routinely renewed annually, would no longer be renewed.[47]

At the same time that Clemenceau was writing about the Zabern Affair, former chancellor Bernhard von Bülow published his memoir, *Imperial Germany*, in which he opined: "It seems to me weakness to entertain the hope of a real and sincere reconciliation with France, so long as we have no intention of giving up Alsace-Lorraine. And there is no such intention in Germany."[48]

France went to the polls on April 26 and again on May 10. The Socialists, who held not a single seat in the Chamber of Deputies before 1885, went from 12% to 16%, and they opposed the Three-Year Law. In his May 14 editorial ("Bargaining for Life") Clemenceau wrote: "When we reopen, since we must, the discussion of the three-year service, I wish that every Frenchman might be possessed, first of all, with this idea: that if the conflict comes about for which all the German race is madly preparing, our defeat would mean the final enslaving of our people, the very termination of our history. This is where we stand, and since we stand here, it would be the height of crime to leave to evil fortune any chance of which our foresight might deprive her. I am quite willing to give too much for national defense. I decline the right to give less than is necessary, however little."[49] Clemenceau also correctly predicted that should war break out, the German Socialists would not unite with their fellow Socialists west of the Rhine (as Jean Jaurès hoped), but would support the German military.[50]

No one—Clemenceau included—could realize it at the time, but the twentieth century took a dramatic turn on the morning June 28, 1914, when the heir to the Hapsburg throne of Austria-Hungary, the Archduke Franz Ferdinand, was assassinated by a young Serb in the Bosnian town of Sarajevo. Franz Ferdinand, Emperor Franz Joseph's nephew, was the immediate heir only by virtue of Franz Joseph's only son, Crown Prince Rudolph, having committed suicide in 1889 as a result of Franz Joseph's refusal to grant thirty-one-year-old Rudolph a divorce so that Rudolph could marry his mistress, and Franz Joseph's brother, Archduke Karl, having died in 1896. The assassination was in revenge for Austria's 1908 annexation of Bosnia-Herzegovina. The irony was that Franz Ferdinand, unlike his senescent uncle, was willing to grant the Serbs within the empire a greater degree of autonomy, not because he was a liberal (he was anything but) but because he realized that the rise of nationalism had to be contained or it might overwhelm his polyglot empire. But it was not to be. The assassins, encouraged and supplied by the Serbian "Unification or Death" movement, (commonly known as the "Black Hand") threw a bomb under the open car in which the Archduke was riding en route to a reception at the city hall. The bomb caused numerous injuries, but left the Archduke and his wife unscathed. Franz Ferdinand insisted on altering his schedule to console the wounded in hospital. On his return, his driver took a wrong turn, stopping just in front of the amazed Gavrilo Princip, one of the plotters, who proceeded to empty his pistol into the Archduke and his wife. The Archduke's last words were "Don't die, Sophie. Live for the children." She did not.

Europe was stunned by the killings, but not particularly concerned. There had been wars and crises in the Balkans in the recent past. They came and went, and did not overly trouble the great powers. But time would reveal that this crisis was different; the assassination of the heir to the Austrian throne by a Serb was considered an existential threat in Vienna. If Serbia, now enhanced and emboldened by the two Balkan Wars, was not punished for this act, the Hapsburg dynasty and Austria-Hungary itself might be doomed. When Kaiser Wilhelm foolishly granted to his Austrian ally a "blank check" to do with Serbia as it pleased, there would be no turning back.

Clemenceau first wrote of the assassination on July 1. He too could not foresee the events to come, and he reacted philosophically to the murders. His sympathies lay with the Serbs, who he considered an underdog oppressed by a mighty empire. "The temptation to violence remains the first of our animal impulses. There will probably be more of the beast than the angel in our earthly condition."[51] Turning to the Balkans, he asked: "What is the 'Serb Idea,' or 'Pan-Serbism' as it is called?…The aspiration for a 'Greater Serbia' is not dissimilar to the ambition for a 'Greater England' or a 'Greater Germany.' We cannot be astonished by the tumult of Pan-Serbism when masses of Serbs turn their eyes toward Belgrade from which they await the magical gesture which will deliver them from the evils of conquest." He noted that in Bosnia-Herzegovina, 590,000 Muslims and 760,000 Orthodox Serbs now found themselves in Catholic Austria (there being only 360,000 Catholics in Bosnia-Herzegovina), and that in the Empire "[T]he development of Catholic influence is the predominant interest…," while "Muslims and Serbs live in permanent discontent." To those who would rebuke the violence of the assassin, he reminded his readers that the conquest of Bosnia-Herzegovina was a daily, ongoing "violence," and that "It is only one of the innumerable manifestations of human weakness, indulgent to the strong, ferocious to the isolated."[52] He concluded that with Franz Ferdinand gone, "the person of Franz Joseph is the guarantor of peace." In this he would prove to be tragically mistaken.

The assassination set in motion what has become known as the "July Crisis," the increasingly frantic efforts of the great powers to avert a war between Austria-Hungary and Serbia and, failing that, to contain the conflict. Not until the last week in July did the crisis attract the attention of the public.

On July 13, the French Senate received the report of a senate commission, headed by Senator Charles Humbert, into the state of readiness of the French army. The report was devastating. Guns lacked sufficient ammunition; the defensive forts were defective. French artillery was rapidly falling behind its German counterpart. The 1911 Italian war in Libya had shown that ground forces could be attacked by air, yet there was absolutely no provision for defense against air attack. And if a war broke out, the army lacked *two million* pairs of boots. The minister of war, Adolphe Messimy, admitted that Humbert's conclusions were correct, but only as exceptions to the rule. Beyond that, Messimy said he could not respond immediately. Clemenceau was on his feet: "The country has a right to know how its money has been spent; we must have an immediate reply." Moving a resolution to have an immediate explanation from the government, he said: "There are moments when all of us assume our responsibilities. Never since 1870 have I taken part in such disastrous proceedings as today. You must reply, it is necessary for the Army, Parliament and the country. Things cannot be allowed to slide. Today we must cry a halt…The truth must be known." It was agreed that the debate would be continued the next day, July 14—Bastille Day—a national holiday.[53]

The next day, the debate continued. Messimy admitted that all that could have been done had not been done. It became known that between 1900 and 1913, German military spending had outpaced France by two to one. The minister of war would make annual funding requests to the minister of finance, who would slash them. In 1913, the minister of war had requested the equivalent of £20 million pounds, and had received £1.2 million.[54] During the debate, Messimy unfortunately claimed that *moral force* would outweigh all other forms of preparedness, to which Clemenceau shouted out: "Then let them buy cross-bows."[55] It was agreed that the minister of war would deliver a final report…in October!

From July 15 until July 23, Clemenceau, unaware of the calamity in the making in the Balkans, devoted his daily column exclusively to the Humbert report. In his July 15 column ("Neither Defended nor Governed") he wrote: We will not, we cannot, undergo the same trial a second time. It is not enough to be heroes. We must be victors."[56]

On July 23, Austria delivered an ultimatum to Serbia. Austria's demands were brutal: Serbia had to permit Austrian officials to enter upon Serbian soil to investigate into the assassination. Serbia would be required to dismiss from the army and government all those deemed by Austria to have hostile sympathies, with the names provided by Austria. Serbia would be required to suppress all nationalist organizations. Anti-Austrian references had to be removed from all Serbian schoolbooks. The demands went on and on. As Austria well knew, to accept the demands meant the end of Serbia's sovereignty; the ultimatum, drafted with Berlin's assistance, was meant to be rejected. Serbia had forty-eight hours to accept, or find itself at war with Austria.

Austria delayed the delivery of the ultimatum by an hour so as to be sure that President Poincaré and his prime minister, René Viviani, (who was also his own foreign minister) were safely at sea on their way to St. Petersburg, a visit they had planned to shore up France's alliance with Russia, strained by the two Balkan wars. For the next week, the week, as it eventuated, before war erupted, France was without a government.

Clemenceau turned his attention to the crisis on July 24, the day after the ultimatum was delivered but before it expired. In a column headed simply ("The Austrian Ultimatum") he predicted that Serbia would try to open discussions, but that "The tone of the ultimatum makes me fear that it will be unsuccessful." As to the ultimatum itself, he concluded that Serbia could not possibly accept it, that it represented the choice of "abdication or death." He assumed (correctly) that Austria would not have issued such an ultimatum unless it had the full concurrence of the kaiser. He assumed further that Germany and Austria both considered, and were willing to accept, the consequence of a general war in which Russia would stand alongside its fellow Slavs. But "Russian preparation is behind schedule....As is ours. Add to that, in our particular case we find ourselves without a government. M. Poincaré sails, with M. Viviani, and their cruising will keep them away from us for a whole week; the statesmen have not very well chosen their moment....Europe was not at rest when they embarked. They could have predicted it, but they did not." He mused that "Never since 1870 was Europe so close to the shock of war, the extent of which cannot be measured....I would ask, as soon as possible, for a friendly intervention from Europe, if I knew what Europe is, and where it can meet."[57] As he wrote, Serbia mobilized.

Clemenceau was now focused on the Balkans; the rest of Paris was not.

Mme. Henriette Raynouard was already married when she met Joseph Caillaux, then the prime minister. He too was married. They became lovers, divorced their respective spouses, and married. Caillaux was the *bete noire* of the Paris daily *Le Figaro*, and its editor, Gaston Calmette. Calmette engaged in a long and ceaseless campaign against Caillaux, accusing him of any number of financial improprieties and insider trading bordering on treason. Calmette came into possession of a number of letters Caillaux had written to Henriette while still married to his first wife. Henriette had returned the letters to Caillaux, but these had been stolen from Caillaux's desk. In one of the letters Caillaux advised Henriette that he would have to wait six months before obtaining a divorce; that he could not undergo a divorce during an election campaign. Someone advised Henriette that Calmette planned to publish the letters in the March 17 edition of *Le Figaro*. On March 16 Henriette entered the offices of *Le Figaro* asking to speak to Calmette. Incredibly, she was granted an audience. The fashionably dressed Mme. Caillaux sported a fur muff. Upon entering Calmette's office she withdrew a revolver from the muff and emptied it into Calmette, who died six hours later. She declined a police paddy wagon, insisting upon been driven from the crime scene by her chauffeur.

Her murder trial opened on July 20 in the Palais de Justice, the courtroom packed, with crowds outside shouting cheers or epithets at Caillaux. The trial was the front-page feature story in every Paris newspaper. They carried transcripts of the daily testimony. The newspapers did report daily on the comings and goings of Poincaré and Viviani as they were feted by the tsar in the Russian capital. But as to the Balkans, nobody cared. When war did come to France, it would come, to most, as a complete surprise.

Events were now moving faster than Clemenceau could comment on them. On July 25, Austria-Hungary, deeming Serbia's response it the ultimatum unsatisfactory, broke diplomatic relations and mobilized. Poincaré and Viviani, having left St. Petersburg, were en route to Stockholm. Clemenceau, in a column headed "Without Government," opined that "[T]he Triple Entente, without firm diplomacy, without common views other than fears…has permitted the opponent to choose the will, the day and the hour of aggression….France has no official way to decide, to act. If Messrs. Poincaré and Viviani give their opinions from Stockholm to St. Petersburg, it is without consulting the ministers, without knowing the whole of the dispatches received by the Quai d'Orsay (the French foreign office). In the general jolt of Europe, we are without direction, without recourse, without a voice, without will. We are a country abandoned by its government—a supreme temptation, for the aggressor, to push things to the bottom."[58]

On July 26, France canceled all military leaves, and recalled home all of its troops in Morocco. The next day, Austrian troops crossed the border into Serbia. In the House of Commons, Sir Edward Grey proposed that the four powers not directly involved in the conflict, Germany, France, Great Britain and Italy, convene in London at an attempt at mediation. France, Great Britain and Italy readily agreed; the kaiser remained silent.

On July 28, Austria declared war on Serbia. In Paris, the case against Mme. Caillaux went to the jury. They deliberated for fifty minutes. She faced the jurors dressed in an evening gown. They acquitted her, holding that it was a "crime of passion." From the rear of the courtroom were heard cries of "Assassin!" and "Murderess!" Thousands rioted in the streets protesting both the verdict and the husband. The next day, Austria occupied Belgrade. Russia mobilized 1.2 million men, which represented only a *partial* mobilization. In Brussels, Jean Jaurès attended a conference of international Socialists denouncing the war.

On July 30, Kaiser Wilhelm demanded that Russia halt its mobilization; if it failed to do so, Germany would mobilize all of its forces. The Russian foreign minister, Sazanov, replied that the mobilization could not be halted. Seated at the horseshoe desk in the rue Franklin, Clemenceau penned his daily column, headed "At the Edge of a Chasm." "Every civilized country," he wrote, "knows whence the aggression came. Every civilized country knows from which side came the diplomatic interventions for peace, and which side resisted it. The German Emperor interposed his resistance from the first day to prevent Russia, the protector of the Slav people, intervening in favor of Serbia, threatened with being crushed....And when Russia, taking legitimate precautions, in response to Austrian mobilization, resolves to mobilize a very weak part of its troops, Wilhelm II came to declare to the tsar that, if he had the audacity to defend himself, all of Europe would be set aflame."[59] Clemenceau made one prediction that proved to be remarkably prescient: Austria would have a difficult time with Serbia: "It [Serbia] has a disadvantage in numbers but that was also the case of Japan against Russia in Manchuria. The Serb soldier is among the best in Europe, and if it is true, as it appears from the result of the Balkan Wars, Serbia can put 400,00 well-trained men in the line, the Austrian army, perhaps badly informed about the worth of its adversary, could soon find out who she's talking to....Everyone has already remarked that Austria has not seen combat since 1866 at Sadowa, while the Serb soldier is still hot from a difficult war, in the middle of winter, where he surprised allies and adversaries by his endurance and ardor. It is a big mistake to underestimate the enemy."[60]

In the early evening of the following day, Jean Jaurès, just returned from Brussels, was seated in the Café du Croissant in the rue Montmartre. A young man entered the café and asked the maître d' to point out M. Jaurès, who graciously complied. The young man approached the table and began firing wildly. Most of the shots missed, but one struck Jaurès in the head, killing him. The man said he killed Jaurès because of Jaurès' opposition to the Three-Year Law. Clemenceau wrote of his erstwhile adversary: "It was the fate of

Jaurès to preach the brotherhood of nations and to believe with such unswerving faith in this noble conception that he was not daunted by the brutal reality of the facts."[61]

In Moscow, the tsar ordered full mobilization. In Berlin, the kaiser announced that a "state of war" existed between Germany and Russia.

The next day, August 1, Germany formally declared war on Russia. France ordered a general mobilization. In the Paris streets a crowd of five thousand marched at 2:00 A.M., singing the *Marseillaise* and shouting "On to Berlin." It was the same cry heard at the outbreak of the war with Prussia in 1870. Clemenceau penned a long article that day ("On the Eve of Action") beginning: "It is the hour of grave decision. For France, indeed, the question is one of life or death." "In 1871," he wrote, "we were vanquished, dismembered, all but annihilated. Bled to the last drops, we endeavored to regain our life, and for forty years we have continued, well or ill, to maintain our existence. But that very existence is a crime in the eyes of our conquerors, who believed they had finished with us forever....The civilized world must bear witness for us that these forty years we have been a force for peace on the continent of Europe." He pleaded for unity: "In this work we must set aside at this moment all considerations of party....Today there must not be two Frenchmen who hate each other. It is time that we knew the joy of loving each other." And he placed the blame for the conflict on the shoulders of one man, Kaiser Wilhelm: "Intoxicated with power, the German Emperor, who leads his blinded people to exploits whose outcome no one can foresee, is dealing without excuse and as though haunted by the example of the barbaric invasions, the most cruel blow against all that is the pride of civilization. He wishes to finish with France, with England, with Russia, not realizing that you can never finish with peoples that you can neither wipe out nor assimilate."[62]

Events were now moving faster than Clemenceau could comment on them. On August 2, Russia invaded Germany, Germany quickly conquered Luxemburg and marched on France through Luxemburg. On August 3, Great Britain mobilized its fleet, Austria-Hungary bombarded Belgrade but, as Clemenceau predicted, was meeting fierce resistance from the Serbs. Germany declared war on France.

The following day, as Germany marched on Belgium, as Great Britain mobilized its army and President Wilson proclaimed America's strict neutrality, Clemenceau sat at the horseshoe desk and wrote an editorial simply titled "We Must Win": "Wilhelm II has willed it....And now to arms, all of us! I have seen weeping among those who cannot go first. Everyone's turn will come. There will not be a child of this land who will not have a part in the enormous struggle. To die is nothing. We must win. And for that we need all men's power. The weakest will have his share of glory. There come times, in the lives of peoples, when there passes over them a tempest of heroic action."[63]

It was August 4, 1914.

LAST DAYS OF PEACE

Lloyd George is not immune to the microbe of Germanophobia.

—C.P. Scott

In 1909, as part of the "People's Budget," David Lloyd George announced that the Liberal government contemplated legislation for the amelioration of a British worker's "sickness, invalidity and unemployment." But not until the enactment of the Parliament Act of 1911, which effectively neutered the House of Lords, did any such legislation have a chance of passage. But now that the Lords were in check, the path was clear.

Lloyd George rose in the House of Commons on May 4, 1911 and, in a two-hour address, introduced the National Insurance Bill, Great Britain's system of *compulsory* health insurance. As he had in the past, the bill was as close to a finished product as he could make it before he introduced it, having consulted and compromised with the doctors, the insurance carriers and the "friendly societies," the fraternal orders and mutual benefit societies throughout Great Britain that provided insurance to their members.

The bill was intended to "relieve untold misery in myriads of homes—misery which is undeserved."[1] Under the Bill, all workers earning under £160 *per year* were required to contribute four pence* per week (three pence for working women) to a

---

* Prior to the United Kingdom "going decimal" in 1971, there were twelve pence in a shilling and twenty shillings in a pound.

central fund. The employer contributed three pence, and the government contributed two, which gave rise to the catch-phrase Lloyd George used to sell the Bill: "Nine pence for four pence." (In 1911, anyone earning less than £160 pounds per year was exempt from income taxes; it was considered the dividing line between the working and middle class.) If a worker became ill, injured or disabled for any reason, he or she was entitled to receive ten shillings per week for the first thirteen weeks (seven shillings, six pence for women) and five shillings per week for the next thirteen weeks. If the worker had contributed into the plan for more than two years, and if the sickness or injury persisted beyond twenty-six weeks, the worker was entitled to receive five shillings per week indefinitely, but only until age seventy, when the Old Age Pensions law kicked in. Moreover, the ill or injured worker could visit any doctor he or she chose from an approved list, at no cost. Special benefits for the treatment of tuberculosis were provided and, heeding the pressure of women's groups, Lloyd George included a flat thirty shilling maternity benefit to the wives of workers enrolled in the plan. The Bill included Great Britain's first unemployment benefit, but only for those engaged in seven industries deemed "seasonal," such as construction and shipbuilding.

Every worker was included, including taxi drivers and domestic servants, which prompted a letter to the *Times* from one angry toff who warned that requiring him to contribute three pence per week for each of his servants would require him to dismiss them, which in turn resulted in Lloyd George remarking that if the Bill passed one might see signs posted on Belgravia (a tony section of London) townhouses advising that Lady would not be receiving visitors today because she was doing the laundry.

The Bill covered all workers, but only the workers, not their spouses or children, nor were the unemployed covered. But in a nation of forty-four million, it covered fourteen million. At first, the Bill was opposed by the doctors, but Lloyd George brought them around. In order to assure the support of the "friendly societies," and the trade unions, the plan was administered by them. In order to assure the support of the insurance companies, the Bill provided no widows pensions, no life insurance, and no burial insurance, all of which they sold to workers. In 1911 Great Britain, a man might end his life with little more than the threadbare clothes on his back, but a decent sendoff was considered essential. The Socialist leader Keir Hardie and many others in the Labour Party opposed the Bill on the ground that workers had to contribute to it. They wanted the health insurance to be free, paid for by more progressive taxation.

But it was the workers themselves who opposed the Bill the loudest. The benefit was over the horizon; the weekly contribution (roughly equal to a pint of beer) was right now, and it was felt. In bye-elections all over Great Britain after the Bill was enacted, the Liberals were clobbered. When King George gave his "royal assent" signing the Bill into law on December 16, 1911, Lloyd George advised the House of Commons that "This is not a perfect bill, but then this is not a perfect world."[2] The National Insurance Act would be his last triumph as chancellor of the exchequer.

It was during this period that Frances Stevenson entered Lloyd George's life. She was twenty-three, he forty-six. Coincidentally, she had been a classmate of his daughter, Mair. She was now a teacher, and he needed a tutor in French and music for his youngest daughter, Megan. She was immediately attracted to him. He soon offered her the post of private secretary *on his terms*. Both understood exactly what that meant, that she would become his mistress. He made it clear that he would never divorce Margaret. Indeed, he never lost his attachment, if not love, for Margaret. But Margaret's life would always be in Criccieth and his would be in London. Frances Stevenson gave her life to him, knowing she would never have a traditional marriage or children. She would remain his secretary and mistress until Margaret died in 1943, after fifty-five years of marriage. Only then were she and Lloyd George married.

Lloyd George's early and lonely opposition to the South African War had earned for him in the public mind a reputation as a pacifist. His unsuccessful attempt to seek an accommodation with Germany enhanced that reputation. Thus, his bellicose speech at the Mansion House in July 1911 during the Agadir crisis landed him in trouble with his former pro-Boer allies. The Mansion House address did not reflect a change in his thinking; he was never a pacifist. As he advised a friend: "People think that because I was pro-Boer I am anti-war in general. I am not against war a bit…I am all for peace but I am not going to be jack-booted by anybody."[3] After the Agadir crisis ended, he told the Tory leader, Arthur Balfour, that he was certain that Germany wanted war, and that it would be best to have it out sooner rather than later.[4] But when war appeared imminent in late July and early August of 1914, he backtracked.

Prior to his Mansion House address, Lloyd George had been kept out of the loop on foreign affairs. But after the speech Prime Minister Asquith appointed him (and Churchill) to a foreign affairs subcommittee of the Committee of Imperial Defense, the body charged with coordinating military strategy for the Empire. It permitted him, for the first time, to see Foreign Office correspondence. It was then that he learned of the ongoing military and naval planning between the British and French general staffs. Gen. Sir Henry Wilson, the Director of Military Operations, employing a large map and a long pointer, briefed him on plans to land four to six divisions on the continent in the event of an invasion of France. Gen. Wilson found Lloyd George "quite in favor of war now" and in favor of conscription.[5]

Lloyd George spent the latter half of 1912 and part of 1913 embroiled in a scandal of his own making that threatened his career and caused permanent damage to his reputation.

In 1911 the government decided to build a chain of world-wide wireless radio stations. When completed, it would provide enhanced security and cohesion to the Empire. The experts were unanimous that the Marconi Company, a British firm, was the only candidate qualified to build the stations. In March, 1912, Herbert Samuel, the postmaster-general, accepted Marconi's tender to build the stations. The contract was subject to Parliamentary approval.

Marconi Company owned 50% of its American subsidiary, Marconi of America. The subsidiary would play no part in the construction or operation of the wireless stations. The managing director of British Marconi was Godfrey Isaacs, who was also a director of Marconi of America. Godfrey Isaacs' brother was Rufus Isaacs, a barrister and the attorney-general in the Asquith cabinet. Rufus Isaacs and Lloyd George were more than casual friends. In 1909 Rufus Isaacs had successfully represented Lloyd George when Lloyd George sued the newspaper *People* for libel after that newspaper alleged that Lloyd George was the co-respondent in a divorce case. As attorney-general, he had assisted Lloyd George in the preparation of the National Insurance Bill. Herbert Samuel and the brothers Isaacs were all Jews. As with the Panama scandal that had interrupted Clemenceau's career, what became known as the "Marconi Scandal" was also tinged with anti-Semitism.

In early April, 1912, Marconi of America was preparing a public offering of its shares. Rufus Isaacs had privately acquired ten thousand shares, for which he had paid £2 per share, before the offering was to open in London on April 19. On the night of April 14-15 *RMS Titanic* hit an iceberg. As passengers were loaded into lifeboats, *Titanic* sent out wireless radio messages alerting ships to their locations. Seven hundred survivors were pulled out of the icy waters of the North Atlantic and were taken to the Cunard line pier in New York. Among those standing on the pier to greet them was none other than Guglielmo Marconi himself, helpfully advising a *New York Times* reporter that without the aid of the ship's wireless telegraphy, no one would have survived. It assured the success of Marconi of America's impending stock offering.

Rufus Isaacs offered to sell some of his shares to his friend Lloyd George at the price he had paid for them. He appears to have no motive other than to help a friend. Lloyd George bought a thousand of Rufus Isaacs' shares. He wanted to buy more, writing Margaret on April 15: "So you have only £50 to spare. Very well. I will invest that for you. Sorry you have no more available as I think it is quite a good thing I have got."[6] Lloyd George acquired his shares on April 17. Marconi of America went public in London on April 19, and closed at £4 per share. Lloyd George sold his shares the next day, having doubled his investment in three days. There the matter lay.

On August 7, Herbert Samuel introduced the contract with British Marconi in Parliament for its approval. The next day, an anti-Semitic publication, *Eye-Witness*, alleged that the letting of the contract was the result of insider trading, failing to make a distinction between British Marconi and Marconi of America. Soon thereafter, another anti-Semitic publication, *Outlook*, repeated the story, this time naming Lloyd George as well as Samuel (who had not profited from the sale of Marconi of America shares) and Godfrey and Rufus Isaacs. As a result of these allegations, with the Tories smelling blood, Asquith felt he needed to appoint a select committee to investigate the letting of the Marconi contract.

Lloyd George sank into a depression. His son recalled that "He would get very absent-minded, and wander away in the middle of a conversation. He would sit and brood for hours. Mother once found him sitting alone in the dark in his room, miserable as a beaten child."[7] Neither encouraging letters from supporters in Wales, golf outings with friends nor the comfort of Frances Stevenson seemed to help. He had committed no crime, nor had he violated any rule, but he and Rufus Isaacs were about to make matters worse. When Parliament convened on October 11 to debate the establishment of the Marconi Select Committee, Rufus Isaacs rose and delivered these very carefully chosen words: "Never from the beginning…have I had one single transaction with the shares of *that company*. I am not only speaking for myself, but also speaking on behalf, I know, of my right hon. friends the Postmaster-General and the Chancellor of the Exchequer, who in some way or other, in some of the articles, have been brought into this matter."[8] In referring to "that company," Isaacs meant—and everyone present understood him to mean—British Marconi. As such, his statement was literally true. Of course, he had failed to mention that he and Lloyd George had profited from the purchase and sale of shares of Marconi of America. He had dissembled in the House of Commons, and Lloyd George, by his silence, had dissembled with him. A select committee (the "Spicer Committee," after its chairman, Sir Albert Spicer) was appointed.

Six months later, on February 14, 1913, the Paris daily *Le Matin* ran a story accusing Lloyd George, Isaacs and Samuel of insider trading. Isaacs and Samuel sued for libel. *Le Matin* published a retraction. But knowing that the truth would out, Isaacs' and Samuel's lawyers did not drop the lawsuit; they used it to set the record straight in what they hoped would be the most innocuous way: In open court, they admitted that Lloyd

George and Isaacs had indeed acquired shares in Marconi of America. But in so doing, Isaacs' lawyers admitted a further fact that proved embarrassing that the man—the chancellor of the exchequer—is supposed to know a little something of finance. They revealed that after Lloyd George had sold his shares in Marconi of America, he had used the profits to buy more shares. When the price dropped, it eventuated that Lloyd George had actually lost money on his flyer in Marconi of America. None of Lloyd George's friends were surprised; they knew how indifferent he was to money matters.

Lloyd George appeared before the Spicer Committee on March 28, 1913, in a hearing room in the House of Commons packed with spectators. He had aged. He was leaner and grayer; he needed spectacles to read. But when the inquiry turned to his personal finances, he took to the offensive. He mocked the rumors that he had enriched himself in the stock market or that he owned a villa in France. He had carried a briefcase into the hearing. At the appropriate moment, he upended its contents onto the table. Out tumbled the little pass books and bank statements. "There is my great fortune!" he exclaimed. "My total investments bring in about £400 per year. That is my great fortune....That is all I could leave if I went down."[9] He invited the commissioners to examine not only his assets, but those of his wife and his brother as well.[10] The committee had a Liberal majority, which exonerated him. The Tory commissioners issued a minority report, which did not.

Much more serious was the June 18, 1913 debate in the House of Commons on the motion to censure him and Rufus Isaacs. Had the motion passed, it could have ended his career. "I have spent most of my active life in the service of the House," he said, "and I should be deeply aggrieved indeed if the House of Commons thought...that I had been lacking frankness and openness in my dealings with them."[11] He conceded that the purchase of the shares had been unwise: "I do not care whether you use the word 'judicious' or 'wise' or 'discreet'...I accept any of them. It was not...."If you will, I acted thoughtlessly, I acted carelessly, I acted mistakenly, but I acted innocently, I acted openly and I acted honestly. That is why I, with confidence, place myself in the hands of...Members of all parts of this great assembly."[12] The censure motion was defeated, 346 to 268. Only three Liberals voted against him, but there were a number of Liberal abstentions. Most importantly, he had Asquith's support, who spoke in his favor, knowing that his government might fall if he were to lose Lloyd George and Isaacs, two of his most brilliant ministers. Asquith admitted that Lloyd George may not have "fully observed" the "rules of prudence."[13] The lasting effect of the "Marconi Scandal" was the level of mistrust it engendered, particularly in the older Liberals. That mistrust might have prevented Lloyd George from ever becoming prime minister. But like so much else, the war changed all that.

Lloyd George had the ability to focus all of his intelligence and energies on issues that interested him, but not all of the issues that interested his fellow Liberals or his fellow Welshmen interested him. He had long since lost interest in the disestablishment of the Church of Wales, even though he could, when called upon, deliver a rousing speech in its favor. He had never been an ardent supporter of Home Rule for Ireland, viewing the issue as a means to achieve greater autonomy for Wales ("Home Rule all Round"). But the one issue that continued to excite him from his days as a young backbencher was that of agricultural reform. Now that the House of Lords had been neutered, the path was open for him to finally do something. He would be fighting a lonely battle.

No sooner had the Parliament Act been enacted than he raised the issue at a 1911 meeting of the National Liberal Federation: "The most urgent need of Britain today is the regeneration of rural Britain. You will not do that without complete reform of the land laws."[14] He told a friend that "I feel that the land and the agricultural labourer are the root of the whole social evil," by which he meant the neglect of the former and the exploitation of the latter.[15] In January, 1913, he told the National Liberal Club: "Foremost among the tasks of Liberalism in the near future is the regeneration of rural life and the emancipation of the land in this country from the paralyzing grip of a rusty, effete and unprofitable system. Land is the greatest, and most essential, of our national assets."[16]

He set up an unofficial and privately funded "Land Enquiry Committee" to look into the state of British agriculture. The Committee issued its first report in October 1913. It concluded that British agriculture was in decline. Farm laborers were subsisting on starvation wages, living as tenants in cottages unfit for human habitation, from which they could be evicted on a week's notice. Disease among farm laborers was high. Young people left the farms for the cities as early as they could. The land itself was under-cultivated, left wild and increasingly used by the squires for "country sports" such as fox hunting. As proof, Lloyd George noted that the number of gamekeepers in Great Britain had increased from nine thousand in 1851 to twenty-three thousand in 1911. The Committee recommended the establishment of land courts to adjudicate against unfair wages and unfair evictions of rural tenants.

Lloyd George formally kicked off the land campaign with a speech in Bedford, north of London, on October 11, 1913. For almost two hours he railed against the privileged landowners. He spoke of the "hopeless, underfed, landless drudge" working the soil: "This country has got to choose between the power of the landlord and the prosperity of the labourer," noting that "one-third of the land of England belongs to the House of Lords, asking "Isn't it time these things should be put an end to?"[17] But when he was almost finished, a heckler interrupted: "What is the remedy, sir?"[18] The heckler was disappointed. The speech was long on the grievances, but Lloyd George had not yet worked out the specifics; there were no remedies.

Lloyd George's Bedford speech (there were actually two in Bedford that day) produced little enthusiasm for land reform, both within the government and among the voters. A poor tenant farmer might support a proposal to curb the power of the landowner to evict him, and would surely support a proposal to ensure that the landowner could not confiscate the improvements the tenant farmer had made, but if the government could acquire unproductive land, that could result in the acquisition of *his* land. The land campaign held little appeal to city dwellers; Lloyd George made no attempt to convince urban voters that improving British agriculture helped them. Although Asquith supported the land campaign, he got no support from Asquith's cabinet, many of whom, although Liberals, were also landowners. His stock was now also at a low ebb; he had launched the land campaign shortly after the conclusion of the Marconi scandal. The electorate was becoming distracted by the issue of Irish Home Rule. But perhaps the primary reason for the failure of the land campaign was that Lloyd George himself became distracted. He was required to spend the early months of 1914 in a fight with Winston Churchill over funding for the British navy.

Winston Churchill became the first lord of the admiralty (the civilian head of the British navy) in October, 1911. As with everything he did throughout his life, Churchill immediately threw all his energies into the navy, touring installations, crawling through the engine rooms of *Dreadnaughts*, and hectoring admirals. He became the navy's greatest advocate. It was thus inevitable that he would come into conflict with the chancellor of the exchequer, charged with preparing the budget and raising the revenue to fund a Liberal government still committed by instinct and tradition to fiscal prudence.

It had for some time been British policy that Britain's North Sea fleet would always be sixty percent larger than the German North Sea fleet. Churchill was committed to this ratio. But as Germany increased the size of its fleet, maintaining the ratio became expensive. In February, 1912, at the urging of Lloyd George and Churchill, Foreign Secretary Sir Edward Grey secretly dispatched Secretary of State for War R.B. Haldane to Berlin with a mission: to slow down the naval arms race. Haldane proposed a naval holiday. Kaiser Wilhelm would agree on the condition that Britain remain neutral in the event Germany went to war with France, a condition that Britain had to reject. Haldane's mission ended in failure.

But with the Agadir crisis fading into history, British-German relations were relatively cordial in 1912. In July, Lloyd George was back at the Mansion House again addressing the British bankers, but with a very different message: "I am glad to be able to feel that the disturbing element in our foreign relations has been settled—that great question which has always been rather an irritant and a menace to the relations of the Great Powers…the question of Morocco….There is nothing that rankles. All the parties are pleased at the settlement, and that means that the era of goodwill has begun."[19]

When the Balkans blew up in 1912 (and again in 1913) and both Balkan wars remained local without involving the great powers, Lloyd George, like many others, became overconfident. That is when Winston Churchill announced that for the fiscal year 1914-1915, he needed an appropriation for the navy of £50 million, an expenditure which would include four new *Dreadnaughts*. Churchill was fully committed to the 60% superiority ratio. On January 1, 1914, Lloyd George submitted to an interview with the *Daily Chronicle* newspaper. In it he said that neither political party would be able to lower the burden of taxation "unless there is a real effort made to reduce the overwhelming extravagance of our expenditure on armaments." He recommended that the time was ripe for a reduction in the navy's budget because "our relations with Germany are infinitely more friendly than they have been in years…Under the circumstances, it seems to me that we can afford to just quietly…maintain the superiority we possess at present without making feverish efforts to increase it any further. The Navy is now, according to all impartial testimony, at the height of its efficiency. If we maintain that standard no one can complain, but if we went on spending and swelling its strength, we should wantonly provoke other nations."[20] He concluded by noting that Germany's principal focus was not on sea power, but in maintaining her land army on the continent.[21]

His speech caused no end of angst in France. Clemenceau did not comment himself, leaving it to one of his young editors at *L'Homme Libre*, François Albert, to comment: "The Chancellor of the Exchequer thinks that the growing maritime armaments give him a lot of trouble, when he has to balance his budget. This is a worry he shares with the finance ministers of the great nations. He hopes that an entente between the nations will permit him to cut down on the credits that his national defense colleagues demand. We can only join him in wishing for this golden age. But now…he seems to see that Germany is ready to talk with England to hasten the advent of this new era. And, best of all, he develops the motives likely to legitimize this hope…Germany, contented power, threatened especially by France, has to take precautions only on land. Why would they search for such a long time to rival England at sea? Common sense invites him to limit his efforts. We would not reasonably want to exercise his supremacy in all domains. No less reasonably, England should stop wanting to provoke Germany by the search for a disproportionate superiority."[22]

Unlike his 1911 Mansion House speech, Lloyd George had failed to clear the interview with either Asquith or Grey, and Grey was furious after reading a newspaper account of the interview. In a January 20 meeting with Asquith, first Churchill, then Lloyd George, threatened to resign. Asquith reminded them that if either resigned he would dissolve the government, which neither of them wished. After the meeting, Asquith wrote his wife: "LG squeezing in one direction and Winston in the other. Neither of them wants to go, and in an odd sort of way they are really fond of one another."[23] In the end, Churchill won his battle with Lloyd George over the 1914-1915 naval budget. Asquith backed him.

Just as France was distracted by the Caillaux scandal in the run-up to the First World War, Great Britain in the summer of 1914 was distracted by the issue of Home Rule for Ireland. By then, the issue was not whether Ireland would receive a measure of autonomy with respect to its purely local matters; most members of the House of Commons agreed that it should. The issue was the fate of Ulster, the counties in northern Ireland with Protestant majorities whose citizens would not countenance being ruled from Dublin. But to Dubliners, excluding Ulster (and keeping it part of the United Kingdom) meant the partition of their country. Home Rule for Ireland had been part of the Liberal creed since Gladstone, but only with the enactment of the Parliament Act of 1911 did Home Rule become something more than a symbolic issue. The Lords could delay, but they could no longer block, autonomy for Ireland.

In February, 1912, Lloyd George proposed in cabinet a Home Rule bill that excluded Ulster. He had little interest in Home Rule; in his years as chancellor of the exchequer, he had not once set foot in Ireland. He wanted only for the issue to go away, so that the Liberal government could concentrate on other things. In April, Asquith introduced a Home Rule Bill that made no provision for the exclusion of Ulster. As it wound its way through both houses of Parliament, it became clear that Home Rule without taking the needs of Ulster into account would not work; a compromise was needed.

That Ulster had to be addressed became clear on the morning of September 28 in Belfast's City Hall. The Ulster Solemn League and Covenant had been placed on a small table draped in a Union Jack. The "Ulster Covenant," as it came to be known, pledged each signer to "defeat the present conspiracy to set up a Home Rule Parliament in Ireland," and that in the event "of such a Parliament being forced upon us, we further solemnly mutually pledge ourselves to refuse to recognize its authority." At exactly noon, the first to step forward was the leader of the Irish Unionists, Sir Edward Carson, who signed with a silver pen. Other dignitaries, including clerics, the lord mayor of Belfast and his councilors in their robes of office, and military officers, followed him to the table. Some signed with their blood. Before the ceremony had ended, almost five hundred thousand men and women had signed. They had made their point.[24]

In November, 1913, Lloyd George proposed a compromise in cabinet, in which Ireland would be granted Home Rule, but the Ulster counties would be excluded for six years, after which Ulster would become subject to rule from Dublin, unless a successor government—which everyone meant would be the Tories—would keep Ulster out permanently. Asquith's cabinet agreed, but neither the Ulster Unionists nor the Irish in Dublin did, and the plan died. Sir Edward Carson derided Lloyd George's plan as "A sentence of death with a six-year stay of execution."

By March, 1914, Ireland was arming and headed towards civil war. The Ulster Volunteers had been formed to block Home Rule by force, if necessary. In Dublin, the Irish Volunteers formed to secure Home Rule. On March 9 Asquith introduced a provision almost identical to the one Lloyd George had floated the previous November. Sir Edward Carson again opposed it, demanding Ulster's permanent exclusion from Irish Home Rule. As a Home Rule Bill appeared close to enactment, the Ulster Volunteers armed themselves. A rumor spread in Belfast that a warrant had been issued for the arrest of Sir Edward Carson. The Ulster Volunteers took up positions to prevent his arrest, by force if necessary. On March 20, in what became known as the "Curragh Mutiny," a number of regular army officers threatened to resign if called upon to take up arms against them; many officers resided in or had family in Ulster. The immediate crisis eased without bloodshed, but the result was that it emboldened the Unionists and convinced the Irish Nationalists that they could not count on the support of the British army.

King George involved himself in an attempt to mediate, and in late July he commanded a conference of all parties. By then, the only issue was how many of the Ulster counties would be excluded from Home Rule, and for how long. The difficulty was that in only five of the nine counties and boroughs comprising Ulster was there a Protestant majority, and in two of those counties—Londonderry and Armagh—only by a slim majority. County Tyrone, Ulster's wealthiest county, was only 44% Protestant. The nine Ulster counties accounted for 80% of Ireland's tax revenues, leaving Ireland with a huge shortfall were all nine counties excluded. Asquith and Lloyd George attended for the government. Bonar Law, the Tory leader, represented the opposition. Sir Edward Carson represented the Ulster Unionists and John Redmond the Irish Nationalists. The conference convened at Buckingham Palace on July 21 with a plea from the king for conciliation. They conferred each day for a few hours.

During the conference, on July 23, Lloyd George addressed the House of Commons
in defense of the naval budget. He opined that: "I am firmly of opinion that armaments
will be arrested only when the great financial interests of the world begin to realize
what menace they are to capital, to property, to industry, and to the prosperity of the
world, and I think they are beginning to realize it." Making reference to Germany, he
continued: "Take a neighbor of ours whom we were very concerned about a few years
ago. The relations are very much better. There is nothing of the snarling which we used
to hear, especially in the press of the two great empires. The feeling is better altogether.
They begin to realize that they can co-operate for common ends, and that the points of
co-operation are greater and more important than the points of possible difference. All
that is typical." His remarks were met with "ministerial cheers."[25] That same day, Austria
issued its ultimatum to Serbia. Also on July 23, the *Guardian* newspaper editorialized
that "Vienna is notoriously the most jumpy capital in Europe, and the talk about war
between Austria and Serbia is surely not to be taken very seriously."[26] The next day,
after three days of desultory talks, the king's conference on Ireland ended in failure.
Two days later, British Army troops fired on Irish Volunteers who were attempting
to smuggle weapons into Dublin, killing three. It meant that Irish Nationalists in the
House of Commons would vote against any measure that permanently excluded any
of the Ulster counties from Home Rule, and that any hope of compromise was dead.

When Lloyd George first heard of Franz Ferdinand's assassination, he said "This means
war." He meant a war between Austria and Serbia, which he assumed Edward Grey
would resolve without the participation of the great powers, as he had after the outbreak
of the First Balkan War.[27] It was not until July 24, the day after the Austrian ultimatum
and after Lloyd George's optimistic speech in the House of Commons, that Edward
Grey warned the cabinet that the Austrian ultimatum meant that a serious crisis was
developing in the Balkans. But, according to Lloyd George's recollection, even Grey was
"hopeful that the conversations which were proceeding between Austria and Russia
might lead to a pacific settlement. We separated upon that assurance."[28] They were all
focused on Ireland, then on the brink of civil war.

On July 27, Edward Grey addressed the House of Commons on the situation in
the Balkans for the first time. He now called it "grave," a "crisis." He advised the House
that he had asked the other three non-belligerent powers, Germany, France and Italy,
to meet with him in an attempt to resolve the crisis, and that he had asked Austria and
Russia to halt mobilizations until the conference had concluded, warning that: "[T]
he moment the dispute ceases to be one between Austria-Hungary and Servia and

becomes one to which another Great Power is involved, it can but end in the greatest catastrophe that has ever befallen the Continent of Europe at one blow..."[29] The German chancellor, Bethmann Hollweg, rejected the idea of a conference.

Lloyd George dashed off a note to Margaret: "Crisis upon crisis. Ireland is serious but Austria-Serbia is pandemonium let loose. I am off to Cabinet to consider both."[30] Asquith's cabinet contained a few hawks, notably Churchill and Grey. Asquith himself could be considered a hawk. But the cabinet also contained pacifists who would not countenance Great Britain entering a continental war under any circumstances, including Sir John Simon, the attorney-general, John Burns, the president of the board of trade, and John Morley, the lord president of the council. The man in the middle was Lloyd George himself. He told the journalist C.P. Scott that there "could be no question of our taking part in any way in the first instance," that [he] "knew of no minister who would be in favor of it..." but that "a difficult question would arise if the German fleet were attacking French towns on the other side of the channel..."[31] A further "difficulty" was the 1839 Treaty of London, to which Great Britain, Germany, Russia and the German federation all were signatories, and which guaranteed the independence of Belgium, and which obligated Great Britain to protect Belgian neutrality. If Germany invaded Belgium en route to France, what then?

The next day, Lloyd George, still hopeful, wrote Margaret: "War trembling in the balance. No one can tell what will or will not happen. I still believe peace can be preserved. The Great Powers will hesitate before they plunge their countries into the hell of war."[32]

On Friday, July 31, Grey sent a request to France and Germany that each honor Belgian neutrality. France agreed immediately; Germany evaded. Asquith's cabinet was now meeting in almost continuous session. Lloyd George spent the extended weekend of July 31 to Monday, August 3 at 11 Downing Street with Frances Stevenson. Years later, she recalled the weekend: "L.G.'s mind was made up from the first, that he knew we would have to go in, and that the invasion of Belgium was, to be cynical, a heaven-sent excuse for supporting a declaration of war."[33] But only Grey and Churchill were committed to going to war even if Germany did not violate Belgium's neutrality.

On Saturday, August 1, Lloyd George met with Sir Walter Cunliffe, the governor of the Bank of England, who advised Lloyd George that "the City," i.e. the financial and commercial powers in London, was totally against Great Britain entering the war.[34] During that day's cabinet meeting, Churchill passed a note to Lloyd George: "I am most profoundly anxious that our long co-operation may not be severed. Remember your part in Agadir. I implore you to come and bring your mighty aid to the discharge of our duty. Afterwards, by participating, we can regulate the settlement and prevent a renewal of the 1870 conditions."[35] Asquith wrote in his diary: "Winston very bellicose and demanding immediate mobilization." He added that Grey would resign if the cabinet adopted the position of the pacifists to stay out in all events, and that "Lloyd George all for peace, is more sensible and statesmanlike for keeping the position still open."[36] That same day, Germany declared war on Russia.

On Sunday, August 2, Germany invaded Luxemburg and demanded that Belgium grant her free passage through Belgium in order to invade France. Belgium was given twelve hours to respond. Crowds were forming on the streets, Lloyd George recalling that "we could hear the hum of this surging mass from the cabinet chamber."[37] During the meeting (the first of that day), it was agreed that a substantial violation of Belgian neutrality would be unacceptable. But it was also agreed that Germany would be advised that Great Britain would not enter the war if Belgium's neutrality were honored and if the German fleet did not fire on the French Channel ports. Edward Grey reminded the cabinet that France had shifted its fleet to the Mediterranean, abandoning the Channel ports, in reliance on British guarantees. He advised that he would resign if Britain did not come to the aid of France, whether or not Belgian neutrality were violated. Two of the pacifists, John Burns and John Morley, resigned. But they were the only two. It meant that Asquith's government would not fall if he led the country into war.

That evening, Lloyd George met over dinner with Sir John Simon, Ramsay MacDonald (the future prime minister) and Liberal politician Charles Masterman at the home of the newspaper owner Sir Charles Riddell. A large war map detailing the positions of the opposing forces covered the table. During the meeting, Lloyd George advised the others that he would resign if Great Britain entered the war despite Germany honoring Belgian neutrality and not attacking the French coast. Riddell recounted that he and Masterman disagreed, with Riddell stating: "Whether the Entente was a mistake or not, we must act up to our word, both express and implied." Lloyd George called Masterman and Riddell "jingoes."[38]

On Monday morning, the cabinet met again. Now they learned of Germany's ultimatum to Belgium. They received a telegram from Albert, King of the Belgians, pleading for support: "I make a supreme appeal to the diplomatic intervention of your Majesty's Government to safeguard the integrity of Belgium."[39] Lloyd George now crossed the Rubicon. He persuaded Sir John Simon, who had brought a letter of resignation to the meeting, not to resign. He dashed off another letter to Margaret: "I am moving through a nightmare world these days. I have fought hard for peace & succeeded so far in keeping the Cabinet out of it but I am driven to the conclusion that if the small nationality of Belgium is attacked by Germany all my traditions & even prejudices will be engaged on the side of war. I am filled with horror at the prospect. I am more than horrified that I should ever appear to have a share in it but I must bear my share of the ghastly burden though it scorches my flesh to do so."[40]

Later that day, Asquith and his cabinet repaired to Parliament to hear Edward Grey address the House of Commons. As he entered, Lloyd George was cheered by a crowd waving Union Jacks and singing *God Save the King* and the *Marseillaise*. "This is not my crowd," he said, "I never want to be cheered by a war crowd."[41] He sat slumped in his seat as Grey put the case for entering the war: "I am authorized to announce that if the German fleet comes into the Channel or through the North Sea to undertake hostile operations against the French coasts or shipping, the British fleet will give all the protection in its power." He reported that he had recently received the ultimatum that Germany had delivered to Belgium, demanding passage through Belgium as the price for peace. "[T]here is the more serious consideration—becoming more serious every hour—there is the question of the neutrality of Belgium." He made the case that it was in Great Britain's interest that Belgian neutrality not be violated, and that France not be crushed by Germany. "If in a crisis like this, from those obligations of honour and interest as regards the Belgian Treaty, I doubt whether, whatever material force we might have at the end, it would not be of very much value in face of the respect we should have lost."[42]

Germany declared war on France.

The next morning, the cabinet met and sent an ultimatum to Berlin. Germany had until midnight (11:00 P.M. in London) to provide Great Britain with assurances of German withdrawal from Belgium. If none were received, Great Britain and Germany would be at war. "We felt," wrote Lloyd George, "it was the stroke of doom."[43] They sat around the cabinet table and waited. Then they heard Big Ben chime eleven times. King George, Queen Mary and the Prince of Wales appeared on the balcony of Buckingham Palace as a throng of thirty thousand below sang *God Save the King.*" Sir Edward Grey looked out and saw the lamps going out all over Europe. Great Britain was at war.

It was August 4, 1914.

12

AMATEURS

I will back the amateur against the professional every time, because the professional does it out of the book and the amateur does it with his eyes open...He knows so little about it that he is fool enough to try the right thing.

—Woodrow Wilson

"God ordained that I should be the next President of the United States," he told William F. McCombs, the chairman of the Democratic National Committee, shortly after the election.[1]

But what kind of president would he be? A passive executor, like his predecessor, Taft, and the string of weak presidents from Lincoln to Roosevelt, or like TR himself and quickly seize the reins of power? Anyone who had read or heard his *Leaders of Men* lectures, or who had read his undergraduate essay praising Bismarck, or who had followed his term as New Jersey's governor, knew the answer. Woodrow Wilson believed in men who acted, who were not afraid to use power. He despised weakness. The populist wave that had brought him to the presidency had also swept in sixty-one additional Democrats in the House (who now held a 291-134 majority, plus nine Progressives), and three additional senators, where the Democrats now enjoyed a 53-42 edge. The fact the Wilson himself was a minority president, elected with only 41% of the vote, disturbed him not in the least. With these solid majorities, he was ready to govern, and the Democrats, who had been out of power for sixteen years, were ready for him to lead.

Wilson's first order of business, as with every president, was filling the cabinet. Wilson's principal advisor and confidante now was Col. House. "You are the only person in the world with whom I can discuss everything," he had told House,[2] and Wilson and House met frequently before the March 4, 1913 inauguration to round out the cabinet. No one was tapped without House's approval, and a few, like Postmaster-General Albert S. Burleson, only at House's urging. The first and most important issue was what to do with William Jennings Bryan, still a leader of the Progressive wing of the party, with millions of followers. Wilson's opinion of Bryan was well known ("The man has no brains") but leaving him out could split the party. House pushed Bryan as a "political necessity." Even before the election, Wilson had asked Albert Burleson what to do with Bryan. Burleson's reply: "Make him secretary of state."[3] House counseled that it would be better to have Bryan in the administration that outside it, calling it a "political necessity."[4] The only dissenter was Mrs. Wilson. She predicted that a split with Bryan was inevitable and that when it came it would split the party. But Wilson believed that he and Bryan would "work well in harness."[5] In the end, she was proven right. Wilson probably knew that it did not matter who he named as secretary of state. He planned to make his own policy, and planned to use outsiders like House to execute it.

It also did not matter to Wilson that Bryan was a lifelong pacifist, ready to renounce force altogether in international relations, on record that "I believe that this nation could stand before the world today and tell the world that it did not believe in war, that it did not believe that it was the right way to settle disputes, that it had no disputes that it was not willing to submit to the judgment of the world."[6] Wilson met with Bryan in his office in Trenton and offered him the State Department. Bryan accepted, but raised one condition. A committed teetotaler, he asked that he be allowed not to serve liquor at diplomatic functions. Wilson said this would present no problem, and Bryan became secretary of state.[7]

Prior to the enactment of the National Defense Act of 1947, which created the Department of Defense headed by the secretary of defense, the secretary of war was the civilian head of the Army, and the secretary of the navy headed the Navy. Wilson chose Josephus Daniels, the editor of the *Raleigh News & Observer*, to head up the navy department. Daniels had actively supported Wilson during the 1912 campaign. He turned out to be an able secretary, and served for Wilson's full two terms, although he irked the officers by banning liquor from their shipboard mess. He was aided by his very able assistant secretary, Franklin D. Roosevelt.

Wilson had more difficulty finding a secretary of war. Four days prior to the inauguration, Wilson met with Rep. A. Mitchell Palmer, a Pennsylvania Democrat who had supported Wilson at the Baltimore convention, and offered him the Army post. To Wilson's surprise, Palmer declined, on the ground that he was a Quaker. Wilson then telephoned his secretary, Joseph Tumulty, asking for suggestions. Tumulty opined that there should be at least one New Jersey man in the cabinet. According to Tumulty's account, the two batted around a few names, deciding on none. Tumulty then advised Wilson that he would think about it and get back to Wilson. Tumulty then went home, took a copy of the New Jersey *Lawyers' Diary* off the shelf, and began searching for names. He hit upon Lindley Garrison, a well-respected New Jersey judge, but who had never served in the Army. Wilson had met Garrison only once, but could not recall him. When Wilson offered him the post of secretary of war, Garrison was stunned. But three days later he was on his way to Washington D.C. as the secretary of war.[8] Once in office, the Army brass loved Garrison; he gave them free rein to do as they pleased. He did not, however, get along with Wilson: "[E]ach considered himself superior to the other in knowledge and character," and Garrison was not shy about letting Wilson know it.[9] Wilson decided to replace Garrison as early as June, 1915, and by February, 1916, he was out.

Wilson offered the Treasury to William Gibbs McAdoo, who by 1913 was part of the family circle. McAdoo readily accepted. In 1914 he married Wilson's youngest daughter, Eleanor.

Wilson nominated James C. McReynolds to be attorney-general, but McReynolds was not Wilson's first choice. Wilson preferred his mentor and friend, Louis D. Brandeis. Progressives such as Bryan and Sen. Robert La Follette were ardent in their support for Brandeis, but the business community hated and feared him. House also opposed him, and finally Wilson relented, convinced that Brandeis was simply too controversial. He chose McReynolds instead. McReynolds was an extraordinarily disagreeable man, hating blacks, Jews and women in equal measure. He soon got into a row with McAdoo over control of the construction of a new building for the Department of Justice. Partly to get rid of him, Wilson used McReynolds to fill a vacancy to the Supreme Court in 1915. But fate played a trick on McReynolds: The next year, Wilson nominated Brandeis to be the first Jew to sit on the court. For years, McReynolds refused to so much acknowledge Brandeis' presence. But the legend that the court for years could not get its annual group photo taken because McReynolds would not sit with a Jew is probably false. McReynolds refused to sit for the group photo simply because he felt it was unnecessary during those years when the makeup of the court had not changed.

It was a good omen: The sun burst through the clouds shortly before Wilson took the oath of office on March 4, 1913 as the twenty-eighth president of the United States. The largest inaugural crowd ever—estimated at 100,000—witnessed Chief Justice Edward White, a former Confederate soldier, administer the oath.

Wilson began his inaugural address by citing the many material things that made life in America great. But then he changed his tone: "But the evil has come with the good, and much fine gold has been corroded. With riches has come inexcusable waste. We have squandered a great part of what we might have used, and have not stopped to conserve the exceeding bounty of nature without which our genius for enterprise would have been worthless and impotent, scorning to be careful, shamefully prodigal as well as admirably efficient. We have been proud of our industrial achievements, but we have not hitherto stopped thoughtfully enough to count the human cost, the cost of lives snuffed out, of energies overtaxed and broken, the fearful physical and spiritual cost to the men and women and children upon whom the dead weight and burden of it all has fallen pitilessly the years through." He was frequently interrupted by applause. He continued: "At last a vision has been vouchsafed us of our life as a whole. We see the bad with the good, the debased and decadent with the sound and vital. With this vision we approach new affairs. Our duty is to cleanse, to reconsider, to restore, to correct the evil without impairing the good, to purify and humanize every process of our common life without weakening or sentimentalizing it." He mentioned in passing some legislative priorities, such as banking and currency reform and reform of the nation's tariffs, "which cuts us off from our proper part in the commerce of the world, violates the principles of taxation, and makes the government a facile instrument in the hands of private interests." He concluded: "This is not a day of triumph; it is a day of dedication. Here muster, not the forces of party, but the forces of humanity. Men's hearts wait upon us, men's lives hang in the balance; men's hopes call upon us to say what we will do. Who shall live up to the great trust? Who dares fail to try? I summon all honest men, all patriotic, all forward-looking men, to my side. God helping me, I will not fail them, if they will but counsel and sustain me."[10]

The first thing that William Jennings Bryan set out to do as secretary of state was to rip out the corps of Western Hemisphere professional diplomats at its roots. He fired *every* American ambassador to South and Central America, all of whom spoke the local language, and set out to replace them with party hacks and others to whom favors were owed. An example: In Costa Rica, Bryan replaced Lewis Einstein, a thirty-six-year-old career diplomat, with Edward J. Hale, a seventy-four-year-old civil war veteran with no diplomatic experience but who had supported Wilson in the campaign. Wilson supported Bryan in this, writing former Harvard president Charles Eliot: "We find that those who have been occupying the legations and embassies have been habituated to a point of view which is very different, indeed, from the point of view of the present administration. They have had the material interests of individuals in the United States very much more in mind than the moral and public considerations which it seems to us ought to control. They have been so bred in a different school that we have found, in several instances, that it was difficult for them to comprehend our point of view and purposes."[11]

Bryan's cavalier attitude toward diplomacy was a direct result of his foreign policy, which was framed by his pacifism. Shortly after assuming office, he addressed the International Peace Conference: "I am a believer in peace, I am proud to be connected with an administration that is an advocate and exponent of peace....[A]s the world moves forward in intelligence it must move toward peace. But there is another force, a force that is even greater. It is the moral progress of the world....There is more altruism on this earth than this earth has previously known...No nation shall go beyond us in its advocacy for peace or in its work for peace." He noted, also, that since the United States was a nation of immigrants who had ties to other nations, this would prevent us from going to war with other nations.[12] Toward this end, Bryan set out to enter into bilateral "cooling off" treaties with as many nations as he could line up. Under each treaty, both nations agreed to six-month cooling off periods, during which their disputes were submitted to international commissions, before they could go to war. Within a year, he had entered into twenty-nine such treaties, twenty of which were ratified, including treaties with Great Britain and France. At each signing ceremony, he handed out paperweights which were miniature plowshares, which had been forged from an old army sword.

Bryan and Wilson's foreign policy has been succinctly summarized one of Wilson's principal biographers, Arthur S. Link, and is worth quoting in full: "Wilson and Bryan assumed that moral force controlled the relations of powers, that reason would prevail over ignorance and passion in the formulation of public opinion, and that men and nations everywhere were automatically progressing toward an orderly and righteous international society. If these assumptions were true, then a combination of Christian love and moral suasion would suffice to solve all international problems."[13]

Bryan's naiveté quickly became apparent. James Bryce, Great Britain's ambassador to the United States, wrote Foreign Secretary Edward Grey shortly after Bryan assumed office, that Bryan had "absolutely no knowledge of that kind of work [i.e., foreign affairs]...and evidently feels the difficulties which his want of experience places in his way."[14] Mexico soon became a primary concern for the new administration. When Assistant Secretary Francis Huntington Wilson, a career diplomat and Taft holdover, was briefing Bryan, he mentioned the Mexican revolutionary Pascual Orozco. Bryan confused him with the Orinoco, a river in Venezuela.[15]

On the day he became president, Wilson first met Dr. Cary T. Grayson, a thirty-five-year-old navy surgeon who had been Taft's (and before him Roosevelt's) White House physician. Wilson, who had three daughters but no sons, quickly warmed to this fellow Virginian. They golfed together almost daily, went on long afternoon drives and to the theater. The last words that Ellen Wilson uttered before she died were to Grayson ("Doctor, if I go away, promise me you will take good care of my husband."[16]) He was by Wilson's side throughout the Peace Conference in 1919. Years after both he and Wilson had died, the extent to which Grayson had hidden Wilson's physical ailments from public view finally came to light.[17]

Bryan and Wilson's first foreign policy test came six days after the inauguration, when three American bankers, Willard Straight and Henry Davison of Morgan & Company, and Paul Warburg of Kuhn, Loeb & Company, called on Bryan. These bankers represented the American participation in a consortium of six nations (the others being Great Britain, Germany, France, Russia and Japan) that had agreed to make a substantial loan to the new Chinese republic, then in desperate need of financing following the overthrow of the emperor. The terms of the loan were harsh. It would be secured by Chinese tax receipts and administered by the foreign lenders to assure prompt payment. While the loan was outstanding, the Chinese were prohibited from borrowing elsewhere. The bankers were in Bryan's office seeking the new administration's consent to the loan, which was odd, since they had already received the go-ahead from the Taft administration, and did not need any additional approval. Yet they were there, and Bryan promised he would raise the matter, in cabinet, with Wilson.

The cabinet met two days later. According to Navy Secretary Daniels, Bryan was "luminous" in his opposition to the loan, and Wilson agreed, "clear in his conviction that we could not…effect the loan, and that we ought to help China in some better way. It was decided that the President should draw up a statement to be presented at the next meeting of the cabinet."[18] Wilson issued the statement six days later: "The administration has declined [the] request because it did not approve the conditions of the loan or the implications of responsibility on our own part which it was plainly told would be involved in the request....The conditions include not only the pledging of particular taxes, some of them antiquated and burdensome, to secure the loan, but also the administration of those taxes by foreign agents. The responsibility on the part of our government implied in the encouragement of the loan thus secured and administered is plain enough and is obnoxious to the principles upon which the government of our people rest....Our interests are those of the open door—a door of friendship and mutual advantage. This is the only door we care to enter."[19] At the next cabinet meeting Wilson advised his secretaries: "I feel so keenly the desire to help China that I prefer to err in the line of helping that country than otherwise. If we had entered into the loan with other powers we would have got nothing but mere influence in China and lost the proud position which America secured when Secretary Hay stood for the open door in China after the Boxer Uprising."[20]

But in unilaterally quashing the loan, Wilson had violated the agreement with the other five powers, which required them to act concurrently. He had also failed to notify anyone in his own State Department. Assistant Secretary Francis Huntington Wilson (the same who had explained the difference between Orozco and Orinoco to Bryan) read of it only in the newspapers, and promptly resigned. Germany's ambassador wrote Chancellor Bethmann Hollweg: "[T]hey have little understanding in America of the formalities of international exchanges, and we must constantly remember that the only consistency in the diplomacy of the United States lies in its surprises, which it always offers to the world."[21]

Why had the bankers sought Wilson's consent to the loan when they had already received it from Taft? It turns out that they had developed second thoughts about a large loan to a shaky government, and wanted out. But rather than simply withdraw, they opted to have the administration pull the plug for them, avoiding the responsibility. They assumed, correctly, that Bryan and Wilson would object on moral grounds. They had played the new administration from the start, and Wilson and Bryan were never the wiser.

Ever since the conclusion of the brief war with Spain in 1898, the principal foreign policy focus of the United States had not been China, or Asia, or even Europe. It was Latin America. The Panama Canal was nearing completion, and its security became a paramount issue. Roosevelt's policy toward the nations of the hemisphere was nothing if not muscular. He had fomented a "revolution" in Colombia for the purpose of wrenching the Panamanian isthmus from that country, creating the nation of Panama. In what became known as the "Roosevelt Corollary," he added muscle to the Monroe Doctrine, asserting that the United States reserved the right to intervene militarily in a Latin

American country if the United States deemed that that country was "unstable" and/ or could not meet its international obligations. Under Taft, and his secretary of state, the industrialist (founder of United States Steel) Philander Knox, the United States encouraged investment in Latin America for the purpose of increasing our economic and political influence. The express term for this policy was "dollar diplomacy."

Wilson and Bryan were in office for less than a fortnight when they determined to expressly repudiate "dollar diplomacy." In a statement to the press drafted by Wilson himself, the policy that would govern the new administration was announced: "One of the chief objects of my administration will be to cultivate the friendship and deserve the confidence of our sister republics of Central and South America, and to promote in every proper and honorable way the interests that are common to the peoples of the two continents....We hold, as I am sure all thoughtful leaders of republican government everywhere hold, that just government rests always upon the consent of the governed, and that there can be no freedom without order based upon law and upon the public conscience and approval. We shall look to make these principles the basis of mutual intercourse, respect and helpfulness between our sister republics and ourselves....We can have no sympathy with those who seek to seize the power of government to advance their own personal interests or ambition. We are the friends of peace, but we know that there can be no lasting or stable peace in such circumstances. As friends, therefore, we shall prefer those who act in the interest of peace and honor, who protect private rights and respect the restraints of constitutional provision. Mutual respect seems to us the indispensable foundation of friendship between states, as between individuals.... The United States has nothing to seek in Central and South America except the lasting interests of the peoples of the two continents, the security of governments intended for the people and for no special group or interest, and the development of personal and trade relationships between the two continents which shall be redound to the profit and advantage of both and interfere with the rights and liberties of neither."[22]

The new policy would be tested very quickly, and very close to home.

In 1911, the eighty-one year old president of Mexico, Porfirio Diaz, who had served as president since 1876, was overthrown by a collection of reformers and revolutionaries, one of whom was Francisco I. Madero, who was installed as president following what was generally considered a fair election. But by 1913, Madero had become widely unpopular. His supporters were corrupt and he had become oppressive. Worst of all, he was unable to maintain order, the one thing Diaz had been succeeded in doing. The American ambassador, Henry Lane Wilson, a Republican holdover, publicly despised

Madero, calling him a "lunatic." On February 9, 1913, at the start of what became known as *La Decena Tragica*—the "Ten Tragic Days"–Gen. Felix Diaz, ex-President Diaz' nephew, attempted a coup. Madero sent Gen. Victoriano Huerta, 63, to crush Diaz. Instead, Huerta joined forces with Diaz. The next day, fighting broke out in Mexico City between pro- and anti-Madero forces. Ambassador Wilson demanded that Madero restore order for the safety of the large American community in Mexico City. Wilson now became instrumental in pushing Madero out, counseling him to resign, which Madero refused to do. But by February 17, the coup, now led by Huerta, succeeded, and Madero and his vice president, José Suárez, were captured and marched to the penitentiary. The next day, Huerta cabled President Taft: "I have the honor to inform you that I have overthrown the government. The forces are with me, and from now on peace and prosperity will reign."[23] Huerta also announced that: "Authorized by the Senate, I have assumed the executive power, the president and his cabinet being prisoners."[24]

In order to give his takeover the patina of legitimacy, Huerta then forced Madera and Vice President Suarez to resign at gunpoint. Next in line was the foreign minister, Pedro Lascuráin, who, with the offices of president and vice president now vacant, became the acting president. He then appointed Huerta as interior minister, and in what may have been the shortest presidency ever, Lascuráin resigned, and Huerta moved into the presidency as the next in line. On February 21, Huerta met with Ambassador Wilson at the American Embassy. The next day, Madero and Suárez were murdered. Ten days later, Woodrow Wilson was inaugurated. Two days later, Madero's father and uncle, who had narrowly escaped with their lives, arrived in New York, claiming that Ambassador Wilson had assisted Huerta in the coup.[25]

Victoriano Huerta is still referred to in Mexico as *El Chacal* (the "jackal") or *El Usurpador* (the "usurper"). He was a pure-blooded Indian "with a flat nose, a bullet head, a sphinx's eyes behind incongruous spectacles, and a brandy bottle never far from hand. Wily, patient, laconic, and rarely sober."[26] Woodrow Wilson called him a butcher, but he was now the president. Unfortunately for Huerta, he did not control all of Mexico. In the state of Morelos, south of Mexico City, the land reformer Emiliano Zapata, 35, who had fought to oust Diaz and then Madero, continued the fight against Huerta. In late March, the governor of the northeastern state of Coahuila, Venustiano Carranza, became head of the "Constitutionalists," proclaiming *himself* the president of Mexico. For Carranza, it was both practical and ideological. If Huerta could oust a president, he could also oust a governor. Carranza formed a tenuous alliance in northern Mexico with Gen. Francisco ("Pancho") Villa.

Huerta craved foreign *de jure* (i.e., official) recognition of his regime, especially American recognition. For one, recognition would strengthen him against the Constitutionalists; the failure of recognition would embolden them. Secondly, Huerta's treasury was empty, but conservative foreign bankers would hesitate to lend to an unrecognized government. In the waning days of Taft's presidency, Secretary of State Knox had withheld recognition, wishing not to tie the new administration's hands. Taft had also imposed an embargo on arms shipments to Mexico. Now, in Mexico City, Ambassador Wilson was pressing for recognition. There were forty thousand Americans in Mexico, and he felt that continued disorder could threaten both their safety and American business interests, and that only Huerta could restore order.

Bryan then called upon John Bassett Moore, a Columbia University professor of international law and former assistant secretary of state who had spent a career shuttling between academia and government. Moore counseled recognition: "The Government of the United States having originally set itself up by revolution has always acted upon the *de facto* principle. We regard governments as existing or as not existing. We do not require them to be chosen by popular vote. We look simply to the fact of the existence of the government and its ability and inclination to discharge the national obligations.... The government at present existing at Mexico City is the only government professing to be able and willing to discharge the international obligations of the country. It has no competitors. There are certain States along the northern frontier that refuse to recognize its authority, but none of them claims to be the national government of Mexico. It is said that Carranza, of whom the opponents of the government we hear has the most, has in all perhaps 8,000 troops. However this may be, he is merely maintaining an opposition to the central authority, and does not profess to be maintaining a government which could in any sense be called the government of Mexico."[27]

Wilson considered Moore's advice, but did not take it. Wilson would grant recognition only if the government obeyed constitutional principles, which meant free elections in which Huerta himself was not a candidate. Soon the United States would stand alone. First the United Kingdom granted recognition (which included the presentation to Huerta of an autographed picture of the king), then France, Germany, Japan and most Latin American countries.

Wilson then decided to circumvent his own state department, which he would do repeatedly. With Bryan's acquiescence, he asked the journalist and former priest William Bayard Hale, who had authored Wilson's campaign biography in 1912, to go down to Mexico "in order that...we might find out just what is going on down there..."[28] Hale knew nothing of Mexico before his arrival, but he was nothing if not diligent. In a memo dated June 18, he gave Wilson a chilling, hour-by-hour account of the "Ten

Tragic Days," and Ambassador Wilson's active participation in it. He concluded that Huerta's coup could not have taken place without Wilson's active encouragement, that Wilson was open and proud of his participation in the coup, and that Wilson was at least indirectly responsible for Madero's murder. If there had been a chance of President Wilson recognizing Huerta's government, there was none after he read Hale's memo.

In a short memo to Wilson dated June 25, Hale reported on Constitutionalist military gains, including the fall of the northern city of Durango and government losses in southern Mexico. He also reported that "Huerta dines by invitation American Embassy next Thursday, irritating, causing comment." In forwarding the telegram to Bryan, the president noted: "I think Wilson should be recalled." Bryan returned it with the note "What do you think of Huerta dining with Wilson?" to which the president noted "Think it most seriously unwise."[29] It was the beginning of the end of Henry Lane Wilson.

On July 9, Hale composed another long memo to Bryan. He reported on Huerta's worsening military situation. The Constitutionalists held Durango and Matamoros. The army was rife with corruption, with generals engaging in fake engagements with the rebels, often selling ammunition to them. Huerta's soldiers would desert to the rebels *en* masse rather than fight them. But he opined that the rebel forces were no better, were mere armed bands with no intent of holding the territory they had won. Of Huerta himself, he painted the portrait of "an ape-like old man, of almost pure Indian blood. He may almost be said to subsist on alcohol. Drunk or only half-drunk (he is never sober) he never loses a certain shrewdness. He has been a life-long soldier, one of the best in Mexico, and he knows no methods but those of force." But he concluded that anarchy would ensue if and when Huerta were overthrown.[30]

On July 17, the president held a press conference. He was asked if he had determined not to recognize the government until after there was an election. He answered: "I can't say there is a determination about anything. I mean, we hold our minds perfectly open to do the right and necessary thing, until we find out what it is." He was asked if he felt that "Ambassador Wilson has been too friendly to the Huerta government?" He responded: "Oh, I don't permit myself to feel anything about it."[31]

The president fired Henry Lane Wilson later that day. But to name an ambassador in his place would confer recognition. Instead, Wilson appointed former Minnesota governor John Lind, a lawyer and Spanish-American War veteran with no diplomatic experience and who could not speak Spanish, as his unofficial envoy to Mexico. In the interim, American affairs in Mexico would be in the hands of the *chargé d'affaires* in Mexico City, Nelson O'Shaughnessy. In his instructions to Lind, Wilson made it clear that his policy was one of "disinterested friendship," and not a policy of protecting private interests. His goal was a cease fire of all the warring factions and free elections in which Huerta was not a candidate. He concluded his instructions to Lind by forwarding a message to all sides in the conflict: "Taking all the existing conditions into consideration, the Government of the United States can conceive of no reasons to justify those who are attempting to shape the policy or exercise the authority of Mexico in declining the offices of friendship thus offered. Can Mexico give the civilized world a satisfactory reason for rejecting our good offices? If Mexico can suggest any better way in which to show our friendship, serve the people of Mexico, and meet our international obligations, we are more than willing to consider the suggestion."[32] When Sen. Henry Cabot Lodge, the chairman of the foreign relations committee, learned of Wilson's missive, he could not contain his contempt, finding it "almost unbelievable... not merely amateurish but crude and ignorant."[33]

Worse, Wilson did not inform our embassy in Mexico City of Lind's appointment, or Huerta's government, or the Constitutionalists, all of whom learned of it in the newspapers. Huerta's reaction: "The limit of patience has been reached over the policy of non-recognition made by the United States. I intend to absolutely ignore Lind's presence unless he bears official credentials as Ambassador...I refuse to accept mediation or intervention by the United States here. The republic's dignity and decorum demand that we accept no compromise with the revolutionists."

Lind arrived in Mexico City on August 11. Two days later, he met with Huerta's minister of foreign affairs, Federico Gamboa. Lind advised Gamboa that President Wilson would never recognize Huerta as the rightful president of Mexico. Lind then offered Gamboa what was essentially a bribe: The United States was prepared to offer Mexico a large loan if Huerta would allow for a free election. Gamboa responded that "When the dignity of the nation is at stake, I believe there are not loans enough to induce those charged by the law to maintain it to be lessened."[34] Lind stayed on, but it was essentially the end of his mission.

On August 27, Wilson addressed a joint session of Congress on the situation in Mexico: "The peace, prosperity, and contentment of Mexico mean more, much more, to us than merely an enlarged field for our commerce and enterprise. They mean an enlargement of the field of self-government and the realization of the hopes and rights of a nation with whose best aspirations, so long suppressed and disappointed, we deeply sympathize. We shall yet prove to the Mexican people that we know how to serve them without first thinking how we shall serve ourselves."[35] His policy would be one of "watchful waiting." There would be no American intervention. Wilson would wait for the inevitable Constitutionalist victory, after which there would be free elections.

The Mexican Chamber of Deputies had been generally hostile to Huerta. In October, after a deputy disappeared after publicly rebuking Huerta, the Chamber passed a "resolution of warning" to Huerta. Huerta demanded they rescind the resolution, and after they refused, Huerta's troops invaded the premises and arrested 110 deputies, all of whom were opposed to him. In what was essentially a self-*coup d'etat*, Huerta dissolved the Chamber and pronounced himself Mexico's dictator. He scheduled new legislative elections for October 26. The elections were a farce, with only Huerta supporters daring to stand. The new Chamber of Deputies then proclaimed Huerta the interim president, with new presidential elections scheduled for July, 1914. Bryan cabled O'Shaughnessy advising him to inform Foreign Minister Gamboa that the United States would "view with concern and displeasure" any harm that might come to the imprisoned members of the Chamber of Deputies.[36]

On December 2, Wilson delivered his first State of the Union address as president, then known as the "Annual Address." He broke precedent in determining to deliver the address in person, becoming the first president to do so since Jefferson. He devoted more time to foreign affairs than he would have hoped or planned. After stating that "The country, I am thankful to say, is at peace with all the world", and pointing with pride to the mediation treaties Bryan had concluded, he stated that "There is but one cloud upon our horizon," and that was Mexico. "There can be no certain prospect of peace in America until General Huerta has surrendered his usurped authority in Mexico; until it is understood on all hands, indeed, that such pretended governments will not be countenanced or dealt with by the Government of the United States. We are the friends of constitutional government in America; we are more than its friends, we are its champions; because in no other way can our neighbors, to whom we would wish in every way to make proof of our friendship, work on their own development in peace and liberty." But Wilson would not abandon "watchful waiting." He believed that the end was near for Huerta: "By a little every day his power and prestige are crumbling and the collapse is not far away."[37]

He didn't say it, but Wilson's thinking was evolving. He was giving up on a cease fire leading to popular elections free of Huerta's influence. This was particularly true after he received a series of reports from Hale following a number of meetings Hale had had with Carranza. Carranza bluntly told Hale that the Constitutionalists' only goal was the violent overthrow of Huerta, that the Constitutionalists would purchase arms from outsiders but otherwise wanted no help from the United States, and, most importantly, were as opposed to American armed intervention as was Huerta. Wilson's options were now clear: It was now Huerta or Carranza; there was no middle ground. Wilson also realized that in backing Carranza he would be going it alone. Most European countries with financial interests in Mexico backed Huerta, and within Mexico, the landowners, the businessmen and the Church supported Huerta; they were terrified of life after a Constitutionalist takeover. In early February, 1914, Wilson lifted the Taft-imposed arms embargo. Huerta was receiving arms from Europe. Lifting the embargo was designed to permit arms to flow to Carranza.

On February 17, 1914, William Smith Benton, a British cattle rancher living full-time in Chihuahua, Mexico, went to see Gen. Villa at his headquarters in Ciudad Juarez. He was never seen again. According to Villa, and argument arose in which Benton allegedly drew a gun on Villa. Benton was disarmed, was "tried" and executed for attempting to kill Villa. What actually happened will never be known. Wilson was asked at his next news conference if his administration had asked for the return of Benton's body. He admitted that they had, without any response. He was also asked if he contemplated sending troops into Mexico to retrieve the body. "Oh, no," he said, "that would be an act of war."[38] Otherwise, the event went unnoticed in the United States. It caused a furor in Europe. The American ambassador, Walter Hines Page, cabled from London: "Kill an Englishman at home and there is no undue excitement. But kill one abroad, and gun-boats and armies and reparations are at once thought about..."[39]

It also drew the attention of Georges Clemenceau. Seated at the horseshoe desk in the rue Benjamin on February 24, he devoted his *L'Homme Libre* column to Mexico. He blamed the hostilities on Wilson: "[T]he whole strength of the Mexican rebellion comes exclusively from the United States. President Wilson never wanted to recognize the government of Gen. Huerta, on the pretext that he had shed blood, which we can see that Gen. Villa is not in want of. What makes it still worse is that one fine morning President Wilson, in order to get the better of Gen. Huerta, is advised to authorize the export of arms and ammunition, thus creating the latter insurrection of Gen. Villa." Clemenceau noted that "General Huerta's government can do nothing about Villa except by force of arms, and even if it could do anything, the very serious question would remain to know if it would be possible for England to push its demands, because the United States is there who watches over the entire American continent, which they claim to protect, in the name of the Monroe Doctrine, against any foreign interference.... The English newspapers are not overflowing with kind words for President Wilson and his Secretary of State, Mr. Bryan. They quite rightly observe that the pretense of guaranteeing the American continent against foreign intervention is difficult for the

American government to convince itself of, having facilitated the fomenting of the disturbances itself, the first result of which is to provoke attacks on the property of the United States and the lives of foreigners." With respect to the recovery of Benton's body, "What measures of recovery can be conducted? And who will do it? The government of the United States, whose right of intervention loses some of its authority, since it has created the disorder itself, or England or the European powers, whose colonists may be threatened, which the American government seems not to be able to admit, in any case."[40] This column was the first time the Clemenceau had taken notice of President Woodrow Wilson.

The official policy was still "watchful waiting," but Wilson was growing tired of waiting. In late December, Huerta's army recaptured Torreon from Carranza. The Constitutionalists' advance seemed to have stalled. Wilson needed to find an excuse to push Huerta out, and in early April, 1914, he found it.

The city of Tampico lies on Mexico's east coast, three hundred miles south of the U.S. border. It was Mexico's primary oil-producing area. Huerta, fearing that arms might be offloaded at Tampico destined for the rebels, ordered it blockaded. On April 8, 1914, heavy fighting broke out in the area between the Constitutionalists and the federal army, with foreigners being warned to be ready to be evacuated. The next day, an officer and six sailors in a whaleboat off the U.S.S. *Dolphin* docked at Tampico, ostensibly looking for gasoline. They were arrested on orders of one Col. Hinojosa. Within the hour, they were ordered released by Hinojosa's commanding officer, Gen. Morelos Zaragosa, who apologized for the misunderstanding, and who ordered Hinojosa's arrest. There the matter might have ended, except that Zaragosa's apology was not sufficient for the commander of the navy squadron lying off Tampico, Rear Adm. Henry T. Mayo, who demanded that Huerta raise the American flag over a Mexican fort in Tampico's harbor, and that they fire a 21-gun salute at the flag. Huerta expressed his regrets, but declined the 21-gun salute. Both Bryan and Navy Secretary Daniels were satisfied with Huerta's limited apology, no doubt sensing the absurdity of demanding a formal apology from a government they did not recognize. Bryan expressly stated that he believed Gen. Huerta's apology was sufficient "so that this government could permit this matter to pass."[41] Daniels stated: "I am inclined to believe that Admiral Mayo, who, after all, has the whole matter in his hands, will regard the apology of Huerta as sufficient."[42] But neither of them had checked in with their boss, who was vacationing in White Sulphur Springs, W. Va. The *Dolphin* affair was not over; it was just beginning.

On April 12, Huerta agreed to a flag salute. He then entered into negotiations with Chargé Nelson O'Shaughnessy as to the exact nature of the salute. The next day, Huerta changed his mind; no flag salute. Wilson interrupted his vacation for the express purpose of taking control of the matter. He demanded a flag salute. On April 14, Wilson ordered the entire North Atlantic battleship fleet—seven battleships and two cruisers—to Tampico. It would reach Tampico on April 21.

The next day, April 15, was a very busy one for Wilson. He met with the chairman and ranking members of the House and Senate foreign relations committees. As a flag salute was rather thin gruel for the possibility of a war with Mexico, Wilson felt obliged to find additional reasons for sending the fleet. He mentioned "the studied manifestation on the part of Gen. Huerta and his subordinates of ill will and contempt of the United States," and "the repeated snubbing of Chargé O'Shaughnessy," and "the snubbing of John Lind on the occasion of his first visit to Mexico City…"[43] He met with Col. House, who advised Wilson to "[S]tand firm and to blaze the way for a new and better international code of morals than the world had yet seen. If a man's house was on fire he should be glad to have his neighbors come in and help put it out, provided they did not take his property, and it should be the same with nations. If Mexico understood that our motives were unselfish, she should not object to our helping adjust her unruly household."[44] Wilson announced he would impose a "peaceful blockade" of Mexico's west coast ports, and would seize the east coast ports of Tampico and Veracruz. The customs house at Veracruz was Huerta's largest source of revenue.

Huerta continued negotiating with O'Shaughnessy over the flag salute. On April 16, Huerta changed his mind again, agreeing to a flag salute. O'Shaughnessy agreed that following the Mexican salute, the United States would return fire in salute, as a way of expressing acceptance of the apology. But Huerta insisted on a *simultaneous* salute, with Mexico firing one shot followed by the United States firing a return shot, until each nation had fired twenty-one. Wilson had Bryan rejected this. The next day, Huerta relented, agreeing to non-simultaneous salutes. O'Shaughnessy drafted a protocol to the effect that the United States agreed that it would respond with a salute after Mexico had fired its salute. To this Bryan responded that the United States would not agree to anything in writing, as this might be interpreted to confer recognition.[45]

On April 20, Wilson addressed a joint session of Congress solely for the purpose of explaining his Mexico policy. He drafted the speech himself. He recounted the events of April 9 culminating in the arrest and immediate release of the *Dolphin* crew. In his first draft of the speech, he wrote "The incident itself was of no great importance." He then changed his mind, scratched out the sentence, and in the speech he delivered said: "The incident cannot be regarded as a trivial one."[46] He then repeated the series of incidents that he deemed sufficient to warrant military intervention, concluding: "General Huerta has set up his power in the City of Mexico, such as it is, without right and by methods for which there can be no justification. Only part of the country is under his control. If armed conflict should unhappily come as a result of his attitude of personal resentment towards this government, we should be fighting only General Huerta and those who adhere to him and give him their support, and our object would be only to restore to the people of the distracted republic the opportunity to set up again their own laws and their own government."[47] The House, by a vote of 337 to 37, approved a resolution granting Wilson the authority to use armed force "in enforcing certain demands made upon Victoriano Huerta."[48]

The next day, there occurred an event that pushed the *Dolphin* into the background. The American consul in Veracruz, William W. Canada, cabled Bryan that the German-American line steamer *Ypiranga* would arrive in Veracruz to unload thirty railroad cars of ammunition for Huerta's army. Three trains, each of ten cars, were speeding towards Veracruz harbor to effect the transfer. Bryan roused Wilson from his sleep, and in a 2:30 A.M. conference call with Navy Secretary Daniels and Tumulty on the line, informed Wilson of the news of the *Ypiranga's* imminent arrival. Bryan and Daniels agreed that immediate action was necessary. Wilson ordered Daniels: "*Take Vera Cruz at once.*"[49]

On April 22, a thousand sailors and marines landed. If Wilson had hoped that they would be unopposed, his hopes were immediately dashed. Consul Canada reported heavy fighting, with at least four servicemen killed and twenty wounded. The Mexicans split into small bands, taking up positions on rooftops. They fired artillery, which was answered by the guns of the U.S.S. *Prairie*. By nightfall, American forces were in control of the entire city, with American losses now up to twelve. (Nineteen Americans would be reported killed in the hostilities). At least two hundred Mexicans—many of them naval cadets from a local academy—were dead.

Huerta broke off diplomatic relations, kicked Chargé O'Shaughnessy out of Mexico City, and proclaimed: "Mexico will fight to the extreme limit of her power against the colossus. Better to die fighting than purchase peace at the price of national dignity."[50] Worse was Carranza's reaction: He demanded that the United States get out of Veracruz. He added that Huerta, being a usurper, had no right to accept or reject any kind of flag salute. But Gen. Villa announced that he would not fight the United States, signaling the rift between himself and Carranza. Worse still was the reaction in Europe and throughout Latin America, where anti-American riots broke out. A wave of patriotism surged through Mexico, one observer noting that "three years of fratricidal war was forgotten in a day."[51] In order not to further inflame the Mexican people, and in part stung by Carranza's response, Wilson canceled plans to seize Tampico and blockade the west coast ports. It was felt that eventually Huerta would fall to the Constitutionalists.

In his April 25 column, Clemenceau reflected on the *Dolphin* affair, and it was blistering. "Supported by the guns of the fleet," he began, "an American landing party has taken over Vera Cruz, after a short exchange of gunfire less with the Mexican army than with its inhabitants." He then reviewed the arrest and immediate release of the *Dolphin* crew. "No one can take this…seriously. However, it did not take more for President Wilson to see the occasion as a *casus belli*." He then summarized the negotiations over the flag salute. "In Europe, President Wilson's policy with regard to the Mexican Republic does not have many admirers. In the name of the Monroe Doctrine, the United States has the pretension of exercising, with regard to all other peoples, a general protectorate over the whole American continent. In the state of instability created by the frequent South American revolutions, it is an appreciable guarantee for the European governments to have to deal with the Washington cabinet rather than with the adventurous dictators who settle in and disappear in the course of a day. On the other hand, the president of the United States assumes…rather heavy responsibilities. Of all this, President Wilson did not appear to be troubled. He did not recognize Huerta's government. His policy, simply, was to use it by insurrection. And as the insurrection seemed powerless to promptly secure this result, Mr. Wilson thought it expedient to provoke a new outbreak of civil war, by suddenly authorizing the export of weapons of war and ammunition into the rebel territory. The effect did not take long.…Mr. Wilson was not moved by the atrocities, the pillaging by which the generals of the insurrection dishonored their cause. But the trivial incident at Tampico, followed by the immediate apologies, seemed to him an intolerable attack on the dignity of the United States, and, without declaring war, he seized the territory of a friendly republic, stopped without any right the shipment of arms destined for the Mexican government, to give to their good neighbors a lesson in civilization.…It is the same American government, and the same Wilson, who…throws himself into bloody adventures that will lead him he knows not where."

He concluded: "The Americans are the masters of Vera Cruz. Will it be possible for them not to go further? I dare to hope. Easy beginnings of an enterprise whose end has not been sufficiently considered. If the American army crosses the Rio Grande into Mexican territory, she will be in an insurgent country…in the presence of a population and soldiers for whom, as of yesterday, they demonstrated their sympathies." [Here Clemenceau was being prescient. Later, American troops would later cross the Rio

Grande into Mexico.] "I attended the last Pan American Congress in Buenos Aires," he wrote. "The demonstrations of friendship of the South American republics with regard to the United States were, without doubt, very cordial, but I was able to note some worries about the appetites of the people that they sometimes, with a wink of the eye, called the…Great Brother, the Very Great Brother. I would not be surprised if the Latin Americans were unanimous in regretting the brutal aggression against a Latin American republic of the Great Anglo-Saxon brother."[52]

Two days later, Wilson granted an extended interview to Samuel G. Blythe of the *Saturday Evening Post*. Wilson revealed that he had concluded that Mexico's unending upheavals were rooted not in political but in economic origins, specifically in the need for land reform for the peons. "I challenge you," he told Blythe, "to cite me an instance in all the history of the world where liberty was handed down from above. Liberty is always attained by the forces working below, underneath, by the great movement of the people. That, leavened by the sense of wrong and oppression and injustice, by the ferment of human rights to be attained, brings freedom…It is a curious thing that every demand for the establishment of order in Mexico takes into consideration, not order for the benefit of the people of Mexico, the great mass of the population, but order for the benefit of the old-time regime, for the aristocrats, for the vested interests, for the men who are responsible for this very condition of disorder. No one asks for order because order will help the masses of the people to get a portion of their rights and their land; but all demand it so that the great owners of property, the overlords, the hidalgos, the men who have exploited that rich country for their own selfish purposes, shall be able to continue their processes undisturbed by the protests of the people from whom their wealth and power have been obtained….They want order—the old order; but I say to you the old order is dead. It is my part, as I see it, to aid in composing those differences so far as I may be able, that the new order, which will have its foundation on human liberty and human rights, shall prevail."

Blythe related that Wilson's passion was for the great masses of the Mexican people, and that Wilson's sole object was to secure for them the liberty that is theirs by right. "The function of being a policeman in Mexico has not appealed to me, nor does it appeal to our people….I hold this to be a wonderful opportunity to prove to the world that the United States of America is not only human but humane; that we are actuated by no other motives than the betterment of the conditions of our unfortunate neighbor, and by the sincere desire to advance the cause of human liberty." He concluded: "It will be a great thing not only to have helped humanity by restoring order, but to have gone further than that by laying the secure foundations for that liberty without which there can be no happiness."[53]

Wilson refused to evacuate Veracruz, in the hope that keeping the city occupied, and denying him the revenues of its customs house, would speed Huerta's downfall. But it was not Wilson, it was Carranza and the forces allied with him that relentlessly pushed south and which finally caused Huerta to give up. He went into exile on July 20, 1914. But Carranza took his time, and did not enter Mexico City until a month later. He would serve as Mexico's president until 1920. But Wilson's involvement with Mexico was far from over.

Hindsight now reveals that the manner in which Wilson dealt with the Mexican revolutionaries would presage his future dealings with foreign leaders, including the Allies during the First World War. For one, he preferred to rely on inexperienced but trusted friends rather than professionals. In Mexico it was Hale and Lind; in Europe it would be Col. House. In addition, Wilson's policies were, in his mind, the *moral* policies; those opposing his policies were, perforce, not only wrong, they were immoral. If he was being selfless, his opponents had to be selfish. Wilson, having convinced himself that he was unmindful of America's commercial interests in refusing to recognize Huerta's government, he concluded that any country that granted Huerta recognition could do so only out of selfish—*immoral*—motives.

The first and foremost plank in the 1912 Democratic party platform dealt with the need for tariff reform: "The federal government…has no right or power to impose or collect tariff duties, except for the purpose of revenue….The high Republican tariff is the principal cause of the unequal distribution of wealth; it is the system of taxation which makes the rich richer and the poor poorer…" This proposition was consistent with Wilson's lifelong belief that tariffs diverted resources from efficient enterprises in favor of uncompetitive ones. In the era before the federal income tax, a tariff's sole purpose, Wilson believed, was to raise the limited revenue needed to run the government, not to favor producers over consumers. A lowering of tariffs would reduce revenues, but three weeks before Wilson was inaugurated the Sixteenth Amendment, making the federal income tax legal, was ratified. The path was now open for tariff reform.

The history of tariff reform is a history of failure. A powerful senator or representative demands that his special interest must be protected. If his pet industry is protected, another senator or representative demands equal treatment. Soon wholesale logrolling breaks out, as each demands favoritism, and no reform is achieved. This was the case of the most recent attempt at tariff reform, the Payne-Aldrich Act of 1909. Even before Wilson became president, Oscar Underwood, the Alabama Democrat and chairman of the House Ways and Means Committee, began working on a tariff bill.

The committee finished its draft on March 17, two weeks after Wilson's inauguration. Wilson immediately determined to use the power of his office to prevent a repeat of the 1909 failure. On the day that Underwood reported out his tariff bill, Wilson called for a special session of Congress to consider the bill.

The biggest obstacles to tariff reform would be the powerful Congressional defenders of commodities such as sugar and wool. Wilson determined to be hands-on, and he immersed himself in the minutia of tariff schedules. On April 1 he met with Underwood. Wilson wanted wool on the "free" list, i.e. no tariffs at all. He was, however, willing to compromise on sugar. He then met on an almost daily basis with the Democratic leaders in Congress to review the bill. On April 7, barely a month after he assumed office, Wilson appeared before a joint session of Congress for the sole purpose of pushing the tariff bill. It was the first time in more than a century (since John Adams) that a president had appeared personally. The galleries were packed and overflowing, with Ellen and the three daughters in attendance. Wilson immediately disarmed his audience: "I am very glad indeed to have this opportunity to address the two Houses directly and to verify for myself the impression that the President of the United States is a person, not a mere department of the Government hailing Congress from some isolated island of jealous power...that he is a human being trying to cooperate with other human beings in a common service."[54] He spoke for only ten minutes, and got right to the point: "We must abolish everything that bears even the semblance of privilege or of any kind of artificial advantage, and put our business men and producers under the stimulation of a constant necessity to be efficient, economical and enterprising, masters of competitive supremacy, better workers and merchants than any in the world...[T]he object of the tariff duties henceforth laid must be effective competition, the whetting of American wits by contest with the wits of the rest of the world."[55]

The next day he was back in the Capitol to meet with Democratic members of the Senate Finance Committee. The road would be more difficult in the Senate, where the Democrats held a slim majority. The Capitol provides the president with an office for his use. Other than for ceremonial purposes such as the inauguration, Wilson was the first president to use the office for business since President Grant. He was breaking traditions almost every day. Throughout April he lobbied small groups of Democratic senators. To those that came around, he sent small notes of appreciation. He met with Sen. Joseph E. Ransdell, a Louisiana Democrat who was the champion of the sugar producers, who was unmovable. Wilson offered to compromise, offering the cut the sugar tariff by 50% for three years, after which it would go on the free list. But he lobbied only Democrats; Republicans played no part in the process. He attempted to go over Congress' head in an appeal to the public: "I think the public ought to know the extraordinary exertions being made by the lobby in Washington to gain certain alterations in the tariff bill. Washington has seldom seen so numerous, so industrious, or so insidious a lobby. The newspapers are being filled with paid advertisements calculated to mislead the judgment of public men not only, but the public opinion of the country itself. There is every evidence that money without limit is being spent to sustain this lobby, and to create an appearance of a pressure of public opinion antagonistic to some of the chief items of the tariff bill."[56]

What became known as the "Underwood tariff" passed the House on May 8, by a vote of 281-139. But it was almost a straight party-line vote. Only five Democrats— four of them from Louisiana—opposed the bill. The bill then went to the Senate, the usual burial ground of tariff reform where, on September 9, it passed by a vote of 44-37. Only two Democrats, Ransdell and his fellow Louisianan, opposed it. The bill then went to a conference committee to iron out the differences. The House approved it on September 30 and the Senate on October 2. The "Underwood tariff" did not eliminate tariffs, but it reduced the tariff on many items, and many others—including wool—went on the free list. It was a breakthrough achievement, and Wilson deserved the praise that followed.

There was a signing ceremony in Wilson's "executive office" (now known as the Oval Office) that evening. The cabinet was invited, as were nine Democratic members of the Ways and Means Committee and four Democratic members of the Finance Committee. No Republicans were invited, including Robert La Follette, the Wisconsin Republican who defied his party to support the bill. As the small gathering pressed in, Wilson signed the bill with two gold pens, giving one to Oscar Underwood and the other to Sen. Furnifold Simmons, the North Carolina Democrat who headed the Finance Committee. He said: "I have had the accomplishment of something like this at heart since I was a boy..."[57] But he added that their work was now only half complete; legislation reforming the nation's currency and banking was now necessary.

The United States has had a fraught relationship with banks since its beginning. The first and greatest treasury secretary, Alexander Hamilton, realized the need for a national currency as well as a source of credit to enable the funding of internal improvements. His brainchild was the First Bank of the United States. He was met with the fierce opposition of Jefferson and Madison, who questioned the constitutionality of Congress chartering a national bank short of an explicit Constitutional grant. They also objected on the ground that a central bank vested too much power in the nascent nation's commercial (i.e. *northern*) classes. Hamilton won over President Washington, and Congress agreed to charter the bank, but gave it only a twenty-year lease. When the lease ran out in 1811, Congress let it expire.

But the need for a central bank remained. In 1816 Congress chartered the Second Bank of the United States, modeled after Hamilton's original idea. The Second Bank was a private bank, twenty percent of its stock owned by the federal government, with the balance owned by four thousand private investors. Its principal *raison d'etre*, just as with the First Bank, was to create a sound national currency, and it was opposed on the same grounds as was the First Bank, with one additional argument: If Congress had the power to create a national bank, it might also deem itself empowered to free a slave. But even for opponents of slavery, there was something about paper money they simply could not abide, and their opposition was fueled by the Second Bank's mismanagement of the Panic of 1819. In November of that year, Jefferson wrote "[T]he paper bubble is then burst," no doubt feeling vindicated.[58] The Second Bank was also given only a twenty-year charter. It had no greater foe than President Jackson, who killed it off in 1836.

But without a central bank empowered to provide liquidity, the nation suffered through a series of multi-year depressions that belied their names: the "Panic" of 1837, the "Panic" of 1857, the "Panic" of 1893. After a single individual—J. Pierpont Morgan—effectively acted as the nation's central bank by providing the liquidity to end the "Panic" of 1907, a consensus was reached that reform of the nation's banking and currency system was long past due. The first attempt was made by Sen. Nelson Aldrich, the conservative Rhode Island Republican. The "Aldrich Plan" contemplated a series of regional banks owned and controlled by the banks in each region, empowered to issue currency and provide liquidity. Wilson and most other Democrats opposed the plan during the 1912 presidential election on the ground that it increased the power of the "money trust." The plan died.

After Wilson's election, but before his inauguration, Wilson met with Carter Glass, the Virginia Democrat who chaired the House Banking and Currency Committee. They agreed that, as with the Aldrich Plan, a series of regional banks was needed. Then, as if out of thin air, Wilson proposed that there be created a "capstone" in the capital, some agency to coordinate the regional banks. This "capstone" would become the Federal Reserve Board. But Glass initially assumed that the coordinating agency would itself be controlled by bankers, and that the liquidity generated by the regional banks would be the obligations of those banks. This was met with the ferocious opposition of Bryan, who had devoted his career to fighting the money power. He insisted that the Federal Reserve Board be controlled by the public, and that the new money be the obligation of federal government, not the banks. Wilson was every bit as pro-active in the fight for banking reform as he had been for tariff reform. He addressed a joint session of Congress for the second time, lobbying for passage of a compromise bill that won Bryan's support, tying banking reform to tariff reform: "It is absolutely imperative that we should give the business men of this country a banking and currency system by means of which they can make use of the freedom of enterprise and of individual initiative which we are about to bestow upon them."[59] The eventual compromise resulted in there being no bankers on the Federal Reserve Board, whose members would be appointed by the president. But the bankers appointed a majority of the boards of the regional banks. The currency they created became the obligation of the United States, not the banks themselves.

Banking reform was not the last legislative achievement of Wilson's first term. In 1914, he pushed through the Clayton Anti-Trust Act, an omnibus anti-trust bill designed to curb many anti-competitive practices that the Sherman Act didn't address, and which created the Federal Trade Commission empowered to enforce the Act. But the creation of the Federal Reserve system may well have been his greatest and most lasting domestic achievement.

On March 1, 1914, Ellen Axson Wilson suffered a fall in the White House, a fall from which she would never recover. She was only fifty-four, and she had been active, championing the fight to clean up Washington's slums. But she began to weaken, and by May was confined to her room. Wilson wrote his friend Mary Hulbert: "There is nothing at all the matter with her organically: it is altogether functional; and the doctors assure us that all with care will come out right. But a nervous break down is no light matter and my heart is very heavy."[60] Of course, she had not suffered a "nervous break down." We now know the she was suffering from a renal ailment that would later be called Bright's disease.

With Wilson heavily occupied with his domestic agenda and with the Mexican revolution and later with his wife's declining health, Wilson left the conduct of foreign policy vis-à-vis the European continent in the uncertain hands of Col. House, who was only too glad to accept the portfolio. The first thing House needed to do was to assure himself that he, and only he, was in charge, and that meant shunting aside the secretary of state, writing Ambassador Walter Hines Page that no one other than House himself "knew how thoroughly out of sympathy the president was with Mr. Bryan's excessive zeal for universal peace."[61] He solidified his position with an unending series of obsequious letters to Wilson singing Wilson's praises. For example, writing Wilson in May, 1913: "I do not think you can ever know, my great and good friend, how much I appreciate your kindness to me. All that I have tried to do seems so little when measured by the returns you have made...I believe you will be successful in all your undertakings, for surely no one is so well equipped as you to do what you have planned. My faith in you is as great as my love for you—more than that I cannot say."[62] And in September, 1913: "It is a splendid future that I see before you, and God grant you strength to carry all your noble undertakings to completion.... Your confidence in me and your affection for me is the greatest reward that has ever been given me, and I pray that I may prove worthy of it."[63] Whereas Wilson's cabinet secretaries addressed their chief as "Dear Mr. President," (McAdoo, Daniels) or "My dear Mr. President," (Bryan, Garrison), House addressed his fawning letters to "My dear friend." It worked. Wilson wrote: "Mr. House is my second personality. He is my independent self. His thoughts and mine are one."[64] With this, House was able to cultivate the not unreasonable impression in the minds of his European interlocutors that when speaking to House, they were speaking to Wilson.

Even before Wilson's inauguration, House decided that the role he wished to play would be to avert a European conflict by forging "a better understanding between England and Germany." This might be achieved "if England were less intolerant of Germany's aspirations for expansion," with the result that "good feeling could be brought about between them." House thought he could "encourage Germany to exploit South America in a legitimate way; that is, by developing its resources and by sending her surplus population there; that such a move would be good for South America and would have a beneficial result generally."[65]

After Wilson took office House continued to formulate his plan. He would attempt to mediate a reduction in the military and naval arms race between Great Britain and Germany. He posited giving Germany "a zone of influence in Asia Minor and Persia," also giving Germany "a freer hand commercially in the Central and South American republics."[66] Rather than confront each other, Great Britain and Germany, as well as the United States and France, would coordinate their energies to develop the underdeveloped countries, the "waste places" of the world. He called his scheme "The Great Adventure." He pitched his ideas to Germany's ambassador, Count Joachim von Bernstorff, and to Sir William Tyrrell, Grey's private secretary. Both cautioned him that his chances of success were slim, but neither rejected his ideas out of hand. House felt encouraged. In December, 1913, he discussed his ideas with Wilson, House.

In mid-May, 1914, House was off to Europe, writing in his diary "I am ready for Berlin and the great adventure."[67] No sooner did he arrive in Berlin than his idea for a reduction in naval armament was immediately scotched by Grand Admiral Alfred von Tirpitz, who insisted that Germany needed to develop naval supremacy in order to counter the British navy. He wrote Wilson that in Germany jingoism had "run stark mad," and that unless someone acting for the American president could intervene, there would be an "awful cataclysm."[68] He left no doubt as to who that "someone" should be. On June 1, House got what he came for: a meeting with Kaiser Wilhelm. They spoke privately for a half-hour on the terrace of the kaiser's palace at Potsdam. The kaiser denounced Great Britain's alliance with France and the "Slavs,"—Russia, urging that the West should stand together to counter the "Oriental" race. He echoed von Tirpitz in his insistence that Germany must have a strong navy, going beyond Tirpitz in his insistence that Germany needed a navy equal to the *combined* navies of France and Russia. The kaiser also advised House that he opposed arbitration treaties, in that they would impede Germany's need for rapid mobilization in the event of war. House, unfazed, offered his belief that a disinterested third party (himself) should attempt to mediate peace, and he suggested that his next stop along these lines would be London. Not hearing a definite "no" from the kaiser, House felt encouraged. Two days later, House wrote to Wilson: "I am glad to tell you that I have been successful as anticipated and have ample material to open discussions in London. I told the kaiser that you thought perhaps an American could compose the situation better than a European. He concurred in this view and seemed pleased that I had undertaken to start the work."[69] This was pure moonshine. There was nothing that House had heard in Berlin that could give him the slightest cause for optimism, and he failed to advise Wilson that official Berlin had rejected a reduction in naval armaments. But he was heartened by a response he received from Wilson: "You have, I hope and believe, begun a great thing and I rejoice with all my heart. You are doing it, too, in just the right way with your characteristic tact and quietness and I wish you Godspeed in what follows. I could not have done the thing nearly so well."[70] Six days later, Wilson again cheered him up: "I cannot tell you how constantly my thoughts follow you and how deeply interested I am and thankful besides to have a friend who so thoroughly understands me to interpret me to those whom it is most important we should inform and enlighten with regard to what we are really seeking to accomplish. It is a great source of strength and relief to me and I thank you from the bottom of my heart."[71]

From Berlin he was off to Paris, where he spent a week and accomplished nothing, the Paris newspapers not even acknowledging his presence. Yet from Paris he wrote

Wilson: "Their [France's] statesmen dream no longer of revenge and the recovery of Alsace and Lorraine. The people do, but those that govern and know, hope only that France may continue as now....It is this spirit in France which fills me with hope.... France, I am sure, will welcome our efforts for peace."[72] How House derived a consensus of the thought of French statesmen is difficult to fathom since he met neither with Poincaré nor Viviani nor any other French official.

From Paris he was off to London, where he cooled his heels for a week before he was granted a meeting with Sir Edward Grey on June 17. He reported to Wilson that "I gave it as my opinion that international matters could be worked out to advantage in much the same way as individuals would and I thought that most of the misunderstandings were brought about by false reports and mischief makers and if the principals knew of the facts, what appeared to be a difficult situation became easy of solution."[73] He also reported that he had breakfasted with Lloyd George, and "I found him particularly ill informed regarding America and its institutions."

Wilson wrote to House on June 26 that "Your letters bring me a peculiar pleasure whenever they come. They bring with them an air of sincere thought and constant endeavor for the right thing, which is just what I need to sustain the energies in me."[74]

Had House reread all of Wilson's letters, he might have noticed that nowhere did Wilson, an extraordinarily detail-oriented man, inquire as to the actual substance of House's negotiations. It is possible that Wilson held out no hope for House's "Great Adventure," and was simply jollying his friend and emissary along. It is also possible that, burdened as he was with his domestic agenda and his wife's declining health, he was simply too distracted to care.

Three days after he posted his June 26 letter to House, Wilson was compelled to draft a short letter to Francis Joseph I, the emperor of Austria-Hungary: "Deeply shocked at the atrocious murder of his Imperial and Royal Highness Archduke Francis Ferdinand and Consort at an assassin's hands. I extend to Your Majesty, to the Royal Family, and to the Government of Austria-Hungary the sincere condolences of the Government and people of the United States and an expression of my own profound sympathy."[75] The "July crisis" was on. It was the end of the "Great Adventure."

On July 4, Wilson traveled to Philadelphia to attend the Independence Day celebration at Independence Hall. He was the first president to do so. Before he addressed the large crowd, he met with the mother of a sailor who had been killed at Vera Cruz, telling her: "It must be a great comfort to you to have been the mother of such a hero."[76] He stood at the desk at which John Hancock had been seated throughout the Second

Continental Congress. His address, delivered extemporaneously, contained little of the usual Fourth of July boilerplate. In it, Wilson laid out what his foreign policy would be based upon throughout his presidency.

"[I]t is one thing to be independent and another thing to know what to do with your independence."….What are we going to do with the influence and power of this great nation?" He answered his question by announcing that the previous policy of using American diplomatic leverage in the aid of commercial interests—"dollar diplomacy"—was dead. "If American enterprise in foreign countries, particularly in those foreign countries which are not strong enough to resist us, takes the shape of imposing upon and exploiting the mass of the people of that country it ought to be checked and not encouraged. I am willing to get anything for an American that money and enterprise can obtain except the suppression of the rights of other men. I will not help any man buy a power which he ought not to exercise over his fellow-beings."[77] Making specific reference to Mexico, he noted that 85% of the people had no power over the land on which they lived; that power having been usurped by the other 15%. "A patriotic American is a man who is not niggardly and selfish in the things that he enjoys that make for human liberty and the rights of man. He wants to share them with the whole world, and he is never so proud of the great flag under which he lives as when it comes to mean to other people as well as to himself a symbol of hope and liberty. I would be ashamed of this flag if it ever did anything outside America that we would not permit it to do inside of America."[78]

Then he got to the heart of his foreign policy: "I am sometimes very much interested when I see gentlemen supposing that popularity is the way to success in America. The way to success in this great country with its fair judgments is to show that you are not afraid of anybody except God and his final verdict. If I did not believe that, I would not believe in democracy. If I did not believe that, I would not believe that people can govern themselves. If I did not believe that the moral judgment would be the last judgment, the final judgment, in the minds of men as well as at the tribunal of God, I could not believe in popular government. But I do believe these things, and, therefore, I earnestly believe in the democracy not only of America but of every awakened people that wishes and intends to govern and control its own affairs."[79]

So there it was. Wilson, who believed in his heart that God had *ordained* that he be the president of the United States, knew that it was his mission to spread democracy and self-government among the nations. Only America could undertake the task: "What other great people has devoted itself to this exalted ideal?"….America has lifted high the light which will shine unto all generations and guide the feet of mankind to the goal of justice and liberty and peace."[80]

On July 29, Col. House returned from his "Great Adventure." Upon his arrival, he learned that Austria had declared war on Serbia the previous day. He wrote to Wilson, advising that he had tried, without success, to convince Grey and the other members of the British government of the imminence of war, "but they seemed astonished at my pessimistic view and thought that conditions were better than they had been for a long time," and offered his continued services: "Both Germany and England know that I hold your confidence, and I would perhaps understand better how to proceed than one new to the situation as I am in close touch with both Governments."[81] The next day, he wrote Wilson again, explicitly urging him to keep Bryan out of it: "Please let me suggest that you do not let Mr. Bryan make any overtures to any of the powers involved. They look upon him as purely visionary and it would lessen the weight of your influence if you desired to use it yourself later."[82]

On August 3 Wilson held a regularly-scheduled news conference, which he opened with a lengthy statement. He urged calm. He pressed the reporters not to spread rumors. He stated that the United States "owes it to mankind to remain in such a condition and in such a state of mind that she can help the rest of the world," adding that "I want to have the pride of feeling that America, if nobody else, has her self-possession and stands ready with calmness of thought and steadiness of purpose to help the rest of the world. And we can do it and reap a great permanent glory out of doing it, provided that we all cooperate to see that nobody loses his head."[83] He then sent a special message to Congress, asking that $250,000 be appropriated to assist Americans trapped in Europe.

The next day, Wilson released to the press a message he had sent to Kaiser Wilhelm, King George V, Emperor Francis Joseph I and Czar Nicholas II: "As official head of one of the powers signatory to the Hague convention, I feel it to be my privilege and my duty…to say to you in a spirit of most earnest friendship that I should welcome an opportunity to act in the interest of European peace, either now or at any other time that might be thought more suitable, as an occasion to serve you and all concerned in a way that would afford me lasting cause for gratitude and happiness."[84] He sent a short telegram to Col. House: "[D]o you think I could and should act now and if so how."[85]

As he did every day lately, Wilson went to Ellen's bedside and took her hand, praying for her recovery. Thirty-six hundred miles east, David Lloyd George waited in the cabinet room for Britain's ultimatum to Germany to expire, as Georges Clemenceau sat at his horseshoe desk in Paris awaiting the onslaught that would determine if France and the Third Republic would survive, and hoping that he would die if it did not. But within hours Ellen Axson Wilson, his bride of twenty-nine years, would be taken from him.

It was August 4, 1914.

William Jennings Bryan,
the "Great Commoner," in 1896, age 36

Tenement life, by Jacob Riis

"Oom Paul" Kruger

The last moments of
"General Revanche,"
Georges Boulanger

Joseph Tumulty

George B. McClellan Harvey

Dreyfus degradation

LE COMMANDANT ESTERHAZY

Esterhazy

Emile Zola by Eduard Manet

PART TWO

THE WAR

13

THE "MIRACLE" OF
THE MARNE

*My centre is giving way, my right is in retreat, situation excellent.
I attack.*

—Gen. Ferdinand Foch

Most everyone believed it would be a short war. They had every reason to believe it. The recently-concluded First- and Second Balkan Wars in 1912 and 1913 had lasted all of eight months and five weeks, respectively. In 1904-1905, Japan had knocked out the Russian army and navy in fifteen months. An older generation could remember Prussia's 1866 defeat of Austria (seven weeks), and Prussia's 1870 humiliation of France at Sedan (six weeks). That the American Civil War had lasted four years and had cost six hundred thousand lives was too long ago and an ocean away for anyone to remember. One French soldier, ordered to report on the *tenth day* following mobilization in August, 1914, feared that he might miss the action altogether. Nor was this optimism confined to the troops. Two months into the conflict the French commanding general, Joseph Joffre, was advised that the army should replace the soldiers' traditional soft hat—the *kepi*—with a steel helmet, such as the enemy was using. He replied: We shall not have time to manufacture them for I will have wrung the Boches within two months."[1]

The German general staff had a detailed plan for war with France; it called for France's defeat in six weeks. It was a plan borne of necessity and geography. Ever since France's 1894 treaty with Russia, the general staff knew that a war against either France or Russia would be a two front war against France *and* Russia. Russia, weakened by its defeat by Japan and slow to mobilize its forces, could nonetheless bring millions of troops to bear. The German plan was to first concentrate overwhelming power in the West before Russia could fully mobilize. After France had been defeated, the German army would shift east to face Russia.

The plan was the handiwork of Field Marshal Alfred von Schlieffen (1833-1913). Appointed chief of the general staff in 1891, he devoted the remainder of his life in the single-minded effort of working out the details of his plan for the six-week defeat of France. He retired in 1906, but even in retirement he kept working on the plan. It would be no easy task, as it entailed moving *two million* men and their horses, artillery pieces and provisions over woods, canals and few and inadequate roads. Up to a point, the army could be transported by train, but for most of the army's progress through Belgium and France, the soldiers would have to walk. The Schlieffen Plan, as it has come to be known, contemplated an enormous wheel, the hub of which was centered in Luxemburg. Seven-eighths of the German Army, strung out from Luxemburg in the center to the North Sea on the far right, would swing counterclockwise, south and southwest. "Let the last man on the right," Schlieffen wrote, "brush the Channel with his sleeve." Critical to the plan was that the army on the German far right would swing to the *west* of Paris, thus enveloping the city. Paris would be the next war's Sedan.

The Schlieffen Plan entailed one great calculated risk: It meant shredding Belgium's neutrality, which Great Britain (and, ironically, Prussia) had guaranteed. Schlieffen hoped that the Belgians would allow the German Army free passage through their country en route to France, but if not, it would bring Great Britain into the war. Schlieffen calculated that whatever army Great Britain (a *naval* power) could bring to bear would be too small and would arrive too late to matter. It also had the benefit of avoiding the great French fortified cities of Verdun, Toul, Epinal and Belfort, strung out in eastern France. Finally, Schlieffen assumed that striking through Belgium is where he would find the enemy. Surely the French would not make the same mistake as in 1870, striking directly east into Alsace and Lorraine.

Schlieffen worked and re-worked the plan until his death in 1913. Legend has it that his dying words were "keep the right wing strong."[2] The military historian John Keegan reviewed Schlieffen's original plan and all its iterations. He concluded that Schlieffen had never worked out how the German right wing would be able to envelop Paris; there simply were not enough men to do it. At his death, the Schlieffen Plan was still a work-in-progress. Nonetheless, it was the plan upon which the German Army went to war. Executing the plan was left to Schlieffen's successor as head of the general staff, Helmuth von Moltke, (the "Younger") the nephew of Field Marshal Helmuth von Moltke (the "Elder"). The Elder had defeated France in 1870, in six weeks. No one compared the Younger favorably to the Elder.

The French general staff had a war plan of its own, one borne of the humiliation of Sedan. In the 1890's, young French officers sought an explanation for France's defeat. The answer was provided by a captain at the *Ecole Polytechnique*, Georges Gilbert. His message was that the principal cause of France's defeat was the army's defensive state of mind. Never mind that Prussian artillery had been superior, or that France's mobilization had been chaotic, or that von Moltke the Elder had allowed his artillery officers the discretion to change direction as the battle warranted. France had been defeated, Gilbert reasoned, because the enemy had had a more aggressive spirit. One of Capt. Gilbert's classmates at *Ecole Polytechnique* was Joseph Joffre.

The idea of the supremacy of the offensive spirit was advanced by Gen. Ferdinand Joseph Marie Foch, then a professor of strategy and tactics at the *Ecole de Guerre*, France's equivalent of the United States Army War College. Foch's message to his students was that the only time a battle is lost is when one believes it is lost. He reduced it to an equation ("Victory = Will") and a slogan: *attaque à outrance* ("attack to excess.") Foch did not believe that the advent of new weapons such as machine guns and heavy artillery tipped the balance to the defender. Rather, small arms and light artillery favored the attackers, who would "march straight on to the goal…preceded by violent fire…[who would] throw themselves into the midst of the enemy ranks and finish the contest by means of cold steel, superior courage and will."[3] One of Foch's students was Maj. Louis Loyzeau de Grandmaison. In his 1906 book "Training of the Infantry for Offensive Combat," he wrote: "For the attack, only two things are necessary; to know where the enemy is and to decide what to do. What the enemy intends to do is of no consequence."[4] He posited that Japan had defeated Russia in their recently-concluded conflict simply because the Japanese possessed a greater offensive spirit. The result of Gilbert, Foch and Grandmaison's teachings was the "cult of the offensive;" the French soldier's principal weapons were his bayonet and his own élan, his sense of drive.

The French Army purged itself of its defensive-minded commanders in 1911. Out went Chief of Staff Gen. Victor Michel, who believed that if war came, the Germans would attack through Belgium, and who wanted the French Army positioned on the

Belgian border. Michel was replaced by Gen. Joseph Jacques Césaire Joffre (1852-1931). Joffre, an engineer, had served in Indo-China and North Africa. He was corpulent, imperturbable, and absolutely devoted to his table, never missing a full noonday repast, even at the front. He slept soundly. His calm once deserted him, when, in observance of Lent, meat was omitted from his luncheon and he flew into a rage. Joffre was a devotée of *attaque à outrance*. Unlike Michel, Joffre did not believe that when war came the Germans would strike through Belgium. For one, he did not believe that Germany would risk bringing Great Britain into the war by violating Belgium's neutrality. He also did not believe the Germans had the manpower for a strike through Belgium. As war approached, he took heart when Kaiser Wilhelm announced that "no fathers of families would be in the armies of the first line," i.e. they would remain in the reserves. Armed with the cult of the offensive, Joffre's General Staff—the *Grand Quartier Général* (GQG)—adopted as its plan for a war with Germany "Plan XVII." It called for a strike at Germany due east straight through Alsace and Lorraine, where Joffre assumed he would find the bulk of the German Army. He would attack first. He issued a regulation: "The passive defense is doomed to certain defeat; it is to be absolutely precluded."[5] The author of Plan XVII was Gen. Ferdinand Foch.

The first thing France's Parliament did when war broke out on August 4, 1914 was go out of business. The Chamber of Deputies suspended itself with members shouting "Vive la France! Vive le république! Vive l'Alsace!"[6] It might have had difficulty conducting business had it not prorogued itself. Members of Parliament were not exempt from military service, and two hundred of them left for their units, fully expecting to return from a short war. But without a legislature, there could be no check on the government; no minister could be called for *interpellation*. And as the war ministry became a tool of the GQG, France quickly became a military dictatorship, governed from GQG headquarters at Chantilly, thirty miles north of Paris.

The cult of *attaque à outrance* permeated every aspect of French military operations. At the outbreak of the war, French artillery officers manning their "75's" (the main light artillery weapon) refused to use the gun's shield: "Frenchmen must look the enemy face to face."[7] (By November, 1914, they were using the shield.) The French soldier, the *poilu* ("hairy," after his bedraggled, unshaven appearance) came to battle outfitted in a blue coat (with tails to the calf) and red woolen trousers, which added to the *poilu*'s misery in August. Before the war, the British had adopted khaki and the Germans had retired their Prussian blue in favor of field gray. When it was suggested that France do the same, a former war minister summed up French military thinking: "Eliminate red trousers? Never! *Le pantalon rouge c'est la France!*"[8] By the end of 1914 the red trousers were gone. The soft *kepi* was not replaced by steel helmets until the autumn of 1915.

More important was the choice of weapons. The French relied on light artillery—the "75"—which would prove ineffective against entrenched positions, as it could not dislodge barbed wire. As for machine guns, the inspector-general of infantry opined that in combat the gun would "not make the slightest difference to anything."[9] What was most antithetical to the doctrine of the offensive was having *poilus* dig trenches. The Germans had no such disdain for the entrenching tool. They even had a slogan for it: "Sweat saves blood."

Not everyone assumed it would be a short war. One who did not was Field Marshal Herbert Horatio Kitchener–Earl Kitchener of Khartoum–who by 1914 was the most honored (Order of Merit, Most Noble Order of the Garter, etc.) and revered soldier in Great Britain. Educated in Switzerland and fluent in French, he had enlisted as a private in the Franco-Prussian War. He became a national hero when he defeated the Dervishes at Khartoum in 1898. He then defeated the Boers in the South African War, but at a horrible cost to the civilians he had herded into concentration camps. On August 3, 1914, he was about to board a boat at Dover that was to ferry him to France en route to his post in Egypt, when he received a message from Prime Minister Asquith, ordering him home. Asquith had appointed him Secretary of State for War, the *civilian* head of the War Office. Four days later, Kitchener sat at his first Cabinet meeting. To his left sat David Lloyd George, who opined to Kitchener that he thought the war might last nine months. Kitchener replied: "The Chancellor of the Exchequer will find that war is not a matter of simple gestation. It will last for three to four years."[10] (Lloyd George soon changed his mind about the duration of the war.) Kitchener advised that Great Britain, always a sea power with a miniscule army, would need to quickly build a million-man army.

Kitchener turned out to be a terrible administrator. He was incapable of delegating, and he kept everyone, including his fellow ministers and employees, completely in the dark. Lloyd George compared him to "one of those revolving lighthouses which radiate momentary gleams of revealing light far out into the surrounding gloom, but then suddenly relapse into complete darkness. There are no intermediate stages."[11] But Kitchener had one great asset that compensated for all of his weaknesses: his face. His stern, mustachioed visage was soon seen on posters plastered all over Great Britain, over the words: "Your country wants you! Join your Country's Army! God Save the King!" As Lloyd George later wrote in his *War Memoirs*: "From farm and village and city street young men thronged into the recruiting offices at the sound of Lord Kitchener's call to arms."[12] Within fifteen months he had raised an army of 2.2 million men.

One other who anticipated a long war was Georges Clemenceau. On August 4, President Raymond Poincaré offered to bring Clemenceau into the government, possibly as minister of justice. Clemenceau refused. He would be prime minister, or at least minister of war, or nothing. He stayed out, and continued as a senator and journalist for the next three years. At first he supported the strict censorship the war ministry imposed on all war information, but he soon regretted it, chafing under the censorship of any and all negative news. With little or no news from the front, he was left to bucking up the morale of his readers, and of himself. On August 6, he reported in his *L'Homme Libre* column that "Everywhere the mobilization is taking place in admirable order, on which we congratulate the Minister of War and especially General Joffre, who prepared it."[13] The next day, as the French First Army crossed into Alsace pursuant to Plan XVII, he wrote: "The strength is in the consciousness of a superior nobility; the weakness, in the unworthiness of the sentiments which have led the man into battle. That is why we are strong, we Belgians, we French, we Russians, we Britons. That is why, O Germans, we know that Destiny has already pronounced the supreme verdict against you."[14] On August 10, he cheered at the report that French forces had taken the town of Mülhousen in Alsace. But the next day the Germans counter-attacked and brought the French advance to a halt. As the bad news began to filter in, his columns became more nuanced, writing on August 13: "I feel that...the brusque attack seems to have miscarried..." adding: "Strong or weak, our soldiers await the German onrush, in the redoubtable serenity which bespeaks an invincible resolution, and behind those who fall others are already advancing, and others, and yet others; and there will come so many that these murderers of wounded and of children will be weary unto death before we shall have ceased to call to the combat their reluctant companions." *L'Homme Libre*, whose daily circulation had never been more than a few thousand, soared to over a hundred thousand. The troops loved it.

As late as the end of the second week of August, Joffre still did not believe that the main German assault would be through Belgium. Gen. Charles Lanrezac, the French general whose Fifth Army faced the German far right ("keep the right wing strong") and who would bear the brunt of the onslaught, was becoming frantic. In reply to Lanrezac's increasingly desperate pleas for help, Joffre cabled Lanrezac: "the threat is as yet only a long-term possibility and we are not absolutely certain that it exists."[15] As Joffre was drafting this cable, the German siege guns were destroying the last of the forts of the

Belgian fortress city of Liege. On August 20, the German counter-offensive began. The French abandoned Mülhousen and retreated to Nancy. The Germans had two million men rampaging into Belgium and France. On that day Clemenceau advised his readers: "A defeat of our soldiers—which our generals are very far from foreseeing—would only be one of those preliminary checks promptly reparable, while for Germany to be repulsed from our frontiers would be, for her, a wound which many would believe incurable and which would quickly spread discouragement among her people as well as in her army. Undoubtedly the war would be far from finished, for everything indicates that it will last until great resources are exhausted, but it is one thing to fight, like us, with full confidence in final success, and another to fight in the daily anguish of seeing one's hopes betrayed."[16]

Two days later, as the last Belgian fortress of Namur was overrun, the French Third and Fourth Armies were in full retreat, retiring behind the Meuse. They suffered twenty-seven thousand killed on that day alone. Not only were the French on the run, but their newly-arrived allies, the five divisions of the British Expeditionary Force (BEF), under Field Marshal Sir John French, were also repulsed. The soldiers of the BEF were not the boys who would answer the call from Kitchener's posters. They were professionals, many of them veterans of the South African War. But they too fell back under the onslaught. A fourth of them would become casualties.

On August 26, President Poincaré reorganized the government, ordering a *Union Sacrée*—a "sacred union"—essentially a coalition government. René Viviani remained as prime minister, but Clemenceau's *bete noire,* Theophile Delcassé, was back as minister of foreign affairs, and two Socialist stalwarts, Aristide Briand (who had already taken two turns as prime minister) and Alexandre Millerand were in as minister of justice and minister of war, respectively. Even the old Marxist, Jules Guesde, joined the government, explaining his decision: "When the house is on fire it is no time for controversy. The only thing to do is take a hand with the buckets."[17] Millerand replaced Adolphe Messimy because Joffre advised Poincaré that he could not work with Messimy, but that since Joffre could not resign in the face of the enemy, he would go out and kill himself, leaving a note explaining why. Millerand was so deferential to Joffre that he spent the next fourteen months as little more than Joffre's spokesman. Viviani offered Clemenceau a place in the government, who refused, again.

By the end of August the outlook for the French and their British allies was dire. Sir John French considered withdrawing the BEF altogether; Kitchener traveled to Paris and convinced him otherwise. At the British Embassy they burned confidential papers at the increasingly-likely prospect of the German occupation of Paris.[18] It appeared that the Schlieffen Plan would, after all, result in the six-week conquest of

France. If France were conquered again it would mean the end of the Third Republic and of revolutionary France. It is what Clemenceau had spent his adult life dreading, and he was becoming unhinged by the lack of news. When, on August 29, Minister of War Millerand announced that nothing had changed the previous day on the Somme, Clemenceau became enraged. "*On the Somme*?" he wrote the next day, "how did the army land on the Somme?"[19] It suggested a retreat of greater scope than he had imagined. Clemenceau stormed into Poincaré's office in the Elysée Palace like a man gone mad. Poincaré quickly showed him the door, noting in his diary that "this irritated old man relieved his anxieties and vomited over me a flood of injuries."[20] They did not meet again for three years.

Clemenceau was now thinking about the possible investment of Paris, writing on August 31: "The enormous tide has overflowed us from a direction where it was not expected and as a result has more easily ravaged the country. It has spread further and more rapidly than we should have thought possible in so short a time."[21] But he refused to give up hope: "After the surrender of Sedan and the investment of Metz, France was without an army. There is nothing comparable in her situation today. The French army keeps the field. It has suffered severely, but it has inflicted no less heavy losses on the enemy, and our own ought to be more easily reparable. It is resisting indefatigably everywhere, with varying fortune, as in the history of every war. It has had to retreat at certain points. It has advanced at others. And the battle is so closely joined that even if we give ground in certain places, the Germans do not always easily regain their freedom in the offensive." But he was hoping against hope that France had inflicted "no less heavy losses on the enemy." He could not know it, but in the first month of the war France had suffered approximately (no exact figures would ever become available) 260,000 casualties, of which 75,000 were men killed in action, 27,000 on August 22 alone. The Germans, relying more on heavy artillery, suffered only 18,000 casualties in that month.

With the siege of Paris in sight, Joffre recommended that the government evacuate. Once again, as it had in 1870, the government fled to Bordeaux. Clemenceau found himself in the exact same place (outside the Apollo theatre, where the senators met, informally) and under the same circumstances as he had found himself half a lifetime ago. He took *L'Homme Libre* with him. Mobilization had decimated the staff; the paper now consisted of himself and two others. Before he departed, in a column he titled "All our Efforts," he wrote: "France is a history, a life, an idea which has taken its place in the world, and the bit of soil whence this history, this life, this idea has radiated cannot be sacrificed without sealing the tomb over ourselves and our children and the generations that shall be born of them. And since no man of France could accept this ghastly end of so great a destiny, it remains for the men to fight to the last, and for the others to accept their trials and to offer all that they have, in order to sustain and aid and hearten each one of our soldiers facing the enemy. To what should we be first attached, of all that our ancestors have bequeathed to us, if not to the land itself which their valor and their labor made to blossom? What interest could we put above the very soil out of which what we call France has sprung? And if this is so, why encumber ourselves with concerns, from now on secondary, which, unrelated to the salvation of France, had held our interest?…Such are the thoughts that haunt me at the hour when it is announced that the German hordes may soon be approaching the entrenched camp of Paris."[22] They were, in fact, twelve miles from Paris. Their cavalry officers could spot the Eiffel Tower.

For a century historians have debated why the German advance slowed, then stalled. Some things are certain. The key to the success of the Schlieffen Plan was the German army on the far right wing, the First Army, under the command of Gen. Alexander von Kluck. The First Army was to swing west of Paris. The German Second Army, under Gen. Karl von Bülow, was to invest Paris from the east. Instead, as he approached Paris, von Kluck moved his entire army *east*, in support of von Bülow. The First and Second Armies had become dangerously separated, inviting a counterattack into the gap by the French, the BEF, or both. But in shifting to the east, von Kluck exposed the right flank of his army to attack from a newly-created Sixth Army, formed in Paris. (Many of these troops were ferried to the front in commandeered Paris taxicabs, adding to the legend of the ensuing battle). The mystery lies in the cause of the effective abandonment of the Schlieffen Plan. It may have resulted, in part, from the continued resistance of the Belgians in the German rear, or von Moltke siphoning off his forces in the west to aid in fighting the Russians. In any event, von Moltke violated Schlieffen's guiding principle, to "keep the right wing strong." By the the time that Joffre counterattacked, von Kluck and von Bülow's armies were exhausted and outnumbered.

The soldiers who fought on both sides between September 6 and 12 did not know they were engaged in what would be called the "Battle of the Marne." There was no such battle. Rather, there were a series of engagements on the Marne, the Ourcq, the Oise and elsewhere. Incredibly, the man principally responsible for calling off the entire German advance was not von Moltke (who was far from the front and out of touch with von Kluck and von Bülow) or any other general officer, but a mid-level intelligence officer, Lt. Col. Richard Hentsch, whom von Moltke had dispatched to survey the front. After conferring with von Bülow and then with von Kluck (but not with von Moltke) on September 8 and 9, Hentsch concluded that there was no chance of bringing the Schlieffen Plan to fruition. He ordered a retreat along the entire 250-mile front. In so doing, he made the most consequential decision of the war: He ordered the right wing to entrench itself behind the Aisne. The Germans chose their positions with care. For the next four years, the Germans would be defending high ground, shooting downhill. The British and the French, the reverse.

Reputations were made and unmade during that week. Gen. Joseph Gallieni, 65, called out of retirement at the start of the war, but with the energy of a man half his age, organized the defense of Paris. He was the one who commandeered the Paris taxicabs for the men he fed to the Sixth Army. He would replace Millerand as minister of war. Robert Nivelle entered the war as a fifty-eight-year-old colonel. He raced an artillery unit through retreating French infantrymen, blasting the onrushing Germans at point blank range. As Gen. Nivelle, he would replace Joffre. On September 8, commanding the newly-formed Ninth Army, Ferdinand Foch drafted (but perhaps never sent) the telegram that would make him famous: "My center is giving way, my right is in retreat, situation excellent. I attack."[23] Early in the battle, Joffre dismissed Gen. Lanrezac, the commander of the Fifth Army, perhaps for no other reason than Lanrezac had been correct and Joffre had been wrong about where von Moltke would attack. Lanrezac was replaced by the aggressive Gen. Louis Franchet d'Esperey, beloved by the BEF as "desperate Frankie." As for von Moltke himself, the strain of command proved to be too much. He suffered a breakdown and was dismissed by Kaiser Wilhelm on September 14, six weeks after the start of the war. (Six weeks into the Franco-Prussian war, his namesake uncle had defeated the French at Sedan.) He was replaced by Gen. Erich von Falkenhayn, who had his own ideas about how to defeat the French.

No one had his reputation burnished better than Joffre himself. He was the man who had saved France, the indispensable man, at least for now. With the threat to Paris alleviated, in early December he invited the government to return to Paris. Clemenceau and *L'Homme Libre* returned to the rue Franklin. But the censorship was not lifted. In late September, he penned an article critical of the medical treatment of the wounded. He had learned from his daughter, Madelaine, who was working as a volunteer nurse, that the wounded were contracting tetanus from being transported from the front in the same cars as the horses. He refused the censor's cut, and renamed the paper *L'Homme Enchaine* ("Man in Chains") to avoid the censor. The ruse failed. He mailed copies of censored passages to subscribers, politicians and friends. He became the principal target of the censor, and on occasion the paper was shut down for days at a time in punishment. For the next three years, he had to choose his words carefully, but despite his self-censorship his articles frequently appeared with whited-out gaps, courtesy of the censor.

On the day before what became known as the Battle of the Marne began, the governments of the United Kingdom, France and Russia issued a joint statement declaring that none of them would sign a separate peace with the Germans. The policy held until March 3, 1918, when Vladimir Lenin took Russia out of the war.

The end of the Battle of the Marne did not bring an end to the fighting. Joffre still believed that the key to victory lay in staying on the offensive. For Falkenhayn, the end of the Battle of the Marne meant that Germany still had to fight a two-front war, the avoidance of which was the *raison d'etre* of the Schlieffen Plan. Joffre ordered an attack across the Aisne on September 14. It stalled and he called it off four days later. Franchet d'Esperey's Fifth Army attacked and found itself blocked by entrenched soldiers whose flank could not be turned. In late October, Foch attacked; it failed. Falkenhayn counterattacked, without success. The BEF, whose numbers were growing with every day, were entrenching, as were the French. It was the beginning of what became known as the "race to the sea," which was not a race at all, but a series of engagements in which each side sought to outflank the other to the north. The First Battle of Ypres—actually a series of engagements—took place between October 19 and November 22 in western Flanders, in Belgium. There was no victor.

A week after the Battle of the Marne ended, David Lloyd George delivered a speech to an audience of fellow-Welshmen in London. Its ostensible purpose was to assist in Kitchener's call for enlistments, particularly among the Welsh residing in London, who he hoped to form into a distinct fighting unit. It was an audience of successful, comfortable men, "layers of fat," he called them. He began: "There is no man who has always regarded the prospect of engaging in a great war with greater reluctance and greater repugnance than I have done through all my political life. There is no man more convinced that we could not have avoided it without national dishonor....Why is our honour as a country involved in this war? Because we are bound by an honourable obligation to defend the independence, the liberty, the integrity of a small nation that has lived peaceably, but she could not have compelled us because she was weak. The man who declines to discharge his debt because his creditor is too poor to enforce it is a blackguard."[24] (In Lloyd George's day, there were few epithets worse than "blackguard." Referring to another member as one was sufficient to have a man expelled from the House of Commons.) He continued, referring to Belgium: "There she was—peaceable, industrious, thrifty, hardworking, giving offense to no one. And her cornfields have been trampled, her villages have been burnt, her art treasures have been destroyed, her men have been slaughtered—yea, and her women and children, too. Hundreds of thousands of her people…are wandering homeless in their own land."[25] He blamed the German military, not the German people: "[They] are under the heel of this military caste, and it will be a day of rejoicing for the German peasant, artisan and trader when the military caste is broken. You know its pretensions. They give themselves the air of demi-gods. They walk the pavements, and civilians and their wives swept into the gutter; they have no right to stand in the way of the Prussian soldier."[26] He admitted that he had changed his mind about the war's likely duration: "They think we cannot beat them. It will not be easy. It will be a long job; it will be a terrible war; but in the end we shall march through terror to triumph. We shall need all our qualities…prudence in counsel, daring in action, tenacity in purpose, courage in defeat, moderation in victory; in all things faith!"[27]

The speech was a triumph, not merely in the droves of men who enlisted in response to his call, but in the millions who read it in the newspapers. It was reproduced as a recruiting pamphlet, then translated into fourteen languages. Asquith congratulated him with tears in his eyes. Foreign Secretary Edward Grey said he wept when he read it. The *Times*, never a Liberal stalwart, opined that never since the Mansion House address had he "spoken so clearly for us all."[28] Most importantly, the speech made Lloyd George the *de facto* civilian leader of the war effort, as Kitchener was the military leader. Two days after the speech, Frances Stevenson began to keep a diary, one she would keep for the next twenty-two years. In her first entry, she wrote that Lloyd George was depressed, feeling that he had not gotten through to the "layers of fat." But the next day, as the letters of congratulations poured in, "He is quite content now, and begins to think it was a good speech after all."[29]

With the conclusion of the First Battle of Ypres, the fighting in 1914 came to an end. The toll was staggering. The Germans on the Western front alone (they were also fighting the Russians) suffered 241,000 deaths. France suffered 306,000 killed in action, Belgium lost 30,000 killed and Great Britain another 30,000, a *fourth* of the BEF at the start of the war.[30] Tens of thousands more had been wounded or taken prisoner. But the year ended with the Germans entrenched on French soil, and the territory they occupied accounted for two-thirds of France's steel production, 90% of its iron mines, 40% of its sugar production, and substantial percentages of its coal, wool and chemical production.[31] For the French, there was, and could only be, one "war aim:" to expel the invader.

One man who surveyed the results of 1914 and realized that *attaque à outrance* had failed was Ferdinand Foch. He gathered his staff before him and advised: "It remains for you to forget what you have learned, and for me to do the opposite of what I have taught you."[32]

In late August, 1914, with the German armies approaching Paris and France's prospects at their bleakest, President Poincaré thought of Clemenceau and wrote in his diary: "If ever the real moment comes, I shall call on him without hesitation. The more I think of the matter, the more I say to myself: 'So long as victory is possible, he is capable of upsetting everything.' A day will perhaps come when I shall add: 'Now that everything seems to be lost, he alone is capable of saving everything.'"[33]

14

FROM NOWHERE TO
NOWHERE AGAIN

Peace-talk ...is yet mere moonshine.

—Walter Hines Page

On the day the war erupted in Europe, President Wilson issued a proclamation. It began: "Whereas a state of war unhappily exists between Austria-Hungary and Servia and between Germany and Russia and between Germany and France..." It then imposed upon all Americans "the duty of impartial neutrality..." Every American would, "during the existence of the contest," be prohibited, upon threat of imprisonment, from enlisting in the army or navy of any of the belligerents, or recruiting any other person to enlist, or outfitting any ship destined for any of the belligerents. It also denied to any belligerent ship the use of any domestic port."[1] It was the first of ten such proclamations he would issue between August 4 and November 6. Neutrality would be the official policy of the United States throughout the war.

Also on that day, Wilson addressed a personal letter to Kaiser Wilhelm, Czar Nicholas II, Emperor Franz-Joseph, King George V and President Poincaré: "I should welcome an opportunity to act in the interest of European peace, either now or at any other time that might be thought more suitable, as an occasion to serve you and all concerned in a way that would afford me lasting cause for gratitude and happiness."[2]

None declined the invitation outright, but Franz-Joseph expressed the sentiments of all the belligerents that he would welcome mediation "at such time as the honor of the flag will permit and when the objects of the war shall be attained."[3] Soon the news would roll in of German atrocities in Belgium, including the shooting of hostages and the burning of the city of Louvain. Wilson had no comment.

Ten days after the first proclamation of neutrality, on August 14, the British cabinet met. Great Britain then had a miniscule army, but it had the world's most powerful navy. The cabinet resolved that day that "the best means of bringing economic pressure to bear upon Germany" would be by "cutting off her supplies of imported food." Not only would the navy blockade every German port, cutting her international cables, denying her access to war materials such as rubber and copper, but Great Britain hoped to starve Germany into submission. In early November, she declared the entire North Sea a war zone. Any ship, *including neutral ships*, were subject to inspection and capture. Wilson acquiesced.

Wilson soon learned that implementing neutrality was infinitely more difficult than proclaiming it. Before the war, American exports to the Allies were ten times greater than exports to the Central Powers; the outbreak of the war increased the demand for everything. The Allies were desperate for American munitions; Germany was self-sufficient in munitions. Cotton was used in the manufacture of explosives, and the majority of the South's cotton crop was destined for export. Southern senators, a powerful bloc in Congress, would not abide the interruption of cotton sales to Germany. In short, the need to maintain America's export trade often conflicted with its declared policy of neutrality. Generally, the United States—like any neutral—wanted to keep the sea lanes as free as possible, and except for the sales of munitions, Great Britain wanted those sea lanes closed.

Matters might have been easier if under international law there existed a clear set of rules setting forth the rights of neutrals in wartime, but there was not. The closest was the 1909 Declaration of London, a treaty that had not been officially adopted by any of the belligerents or by the United States. The Declaration generally favored the rights of neutrals and limited the blockading powers of belligerents. It created two classes of "contraband." "Absolute contraband," such as munitions, could be seized by a blockading power on the high seas even if destined for a neutral port. "Conditional contraband" could be seized only if destined for an enemy government or the enemy's armed forces, but never if it was destined for a neutral port. The Declaration also created a "free list," which included copper and rubber. The man in charge of implementing the policy of neutrality was the number two man in the State Department, Counselor Robert Lansing. (There were no undersecretaries then.) Lansing, 50, a New York international lawyer prior to the war, was the son-in-law of President Benjamin Harrison's secretary of state, John W. Foster. (His nephew was a future secretary of state, John Foster Dulles.) He was "poised, handsome, and formal in dress and manners."[4] He asked the belligerents to abide by the Declaration of London. Germany, self-sufficient in munitions, readily accepted. Great Britain fudged its reply, saying it would act "in accordance with the provisions of…the Declaration of London *so far as may be practicable*."[5]

The man in charge of Great Britain's foreign policy, as he had been since 1905, was Foreign Secretary Sir Edward Grey. The blockade required Great Britain to act with extreme delicacy, and no one was better suited for this than Grey. On the one hand, he needed to maximize the blockade; on the other, he dared not offend the United States, upon whom Great Britain relied for munitions. Grey's problem was that the blockade would be ineffective if neutrals could ship contraband to the ports of neutral countries such as the Netherlands and Scandinavia, only to have the contraband transshipped to Germany. So Grey adopted the policy of "continuous passage," permitting the seizure of a neutral ship sailing for a neutral port if it could be shown (and the British Navy would make the determination) that the goods were destined for Germany. Grey placed copper and rubber on the "absolute contraband" list, but refrained from listing cotton, sensitive to the southern bloc in Congress. Wisely, the British did not actually confiscate any American goods. Ships were stopped in the North Sea and escorted to Allied-controlled ports for inspection. The process was time-consuming and costly, and on occasion the British would purchase the cargo rather than see it in the hands of the enemy. As Grey wrote years later: "[B]lockade of Germany was essential to the victory of the Allies, but the ill-will of the United States meant their certain defeat…. The object of diplomacy, therefore, was to secure the maximum of blockade that could be enforced without a rupture with the United States."[6] Great Britain's chief diplomat in Paris, Ambassador Sir Francis Bertie, put it less diplomatically: "It is fear of the United States, who see fine opportunities for driving a roaring trade with Germany, that prevents us from asserting ourselves."[7] But in the end, the United States acquiesced to the British blockade policy.

Two weeks into the war, at Lansing's urging, Wilson issued "An Appeal to the American People" in which he warned against "that deepest, most subtle, most essential breach of neutrality which may spring out of partisanship, out of passionately taking sides. The United States must be neutral in fact as well as in name during these days that are to try men's souls. We must be impartial in thought as well as in action, must put a curb upon our sentiments as well as upon every transaction that might be construed as a preference of one party in the struggle before another." He continued: "My thought is of America. I am speaking, I am sure, of the earnest wish and purpose of every thoughtful American that this great country of ours, which is, of course, the first in our thoughts and in our hearts, should show herself in this time of peculiar trial a nation fit beyond others to exhibit the fine poise of undisturbed judgment, the dignity of self-control, the efficiency of dispassionate action; a nation that neither sits in judgment upon others nor is disturbed in her own counsels and which keeps herself fit and free to do what is necessary and disinterested and truly serviceable for the peace of the world."[8] Wilson intended to enforce the sentiment. When he learned that audiences were cheering (or hissing) at newsreels, he had the following notice appear on the screen:

> It would be a patriotic act in the interest of the neutrality of the nation and the peace of mankind if the audience in this theatre would refrain during the showing of pictures connected with the present war from expressing either approval or disapproval.
>
> Woodrow Wilson.[9]

Most Americans could be impartial in "action," but hardly anyone was impartial in "thought," including Wilson himself, Col. House and Counselor Lansing, all of whom, to a greater or lesser extent, expressed concern over what the German domination of Europe—still a very real possibility in August, 1914—might mean for American security. Most Americans favored the Allies, especially after the reports of German atrocities in Belgium became widespread. Nor did Chancellor Bethmann Hollweg help his cause when it became widely known that he had referred to the German guarantee of Belgian neutrality as a mere "scrap of paper." And if there was in 1914 still some lingering resentment towards Great Britain, there was none towards the land of Lafayette. But not everyone favored the Allies. The 1910 census had revealed that a third of Americans were foreign-born. There were eight million German-Americans, many of whom were swayed by the ferocious pro-German propaganda effort that sprang up immediately after the outbreak. There were also more than four million Irish Americans still resentful of the British, and four million American Jews who loathed the tsar.

Regardless of which side Americans favored, no one counseled intervention. For one, there was a strong tradition of avoiding European entanglements, and few Americans could see the point of becoming involved in a struggle that had its origins in a dispute between Austria-Hungary and Serbia. Moreover, many Progressives (Wilson among them) believed that the war had been fomented by European profiteers. As reports of the casualty rates and the atrocities poured in, the desire to stay out intensified. Even Roosevelt, who later ardently pressed for intervention, in 1914 counseled non-intervention.

The one man truly neutral in deed and in thought was the secretary of state, William Jennings Bryan. A pacifist to the bone, he had no thought of causes, or guilt, or geopolitical consequences. He was horrified by the carnage, and simply wanted it stopped. In early September, he seized upon a hint by the German ambassador, Johann von Bernstorff, that the Kaiser might accept mediation. He instructed Ambassador James W. Gerard to push the matter in Berlin. He called in the British and French ambassadors and demanded that they inquire of their governments' conditions for peace. Bryan's goal was not so much a mediation but a public airing of each side's war aims. Bryan abhorred secret negotiations, conducting his diplomacy in public. Each of the belligerents responded by claiming that they desired peace, but each shifted the blame for continuing the war to the other. When Germany's response, claiming that it was willing to talk peace if the Allies would only state their terms, appeared on the front page of the *New York Times*, it marked the end of Bryan's efforts as a peacemaker.[10] His active participation would have soon ended in any event. At a time when nothing prevented secretaries of state from engaging in party politics, Bryan set off on an extended vacation and then campaigned for Democrats in the upcoming Congressional elections, not returning until mid-November. He left the State Department to Lansing. But he continued pressing for peace. In the first of a series of plaintive letters to Wilson, he wrote (on September 19, from Asheville, North Carolina): "The European situation distresses me. The slaughter goes on, and each day makes it more apparent that it is to be a prolonged struggle....The responsibility for *continuing* the war is just as grave as the responsibility for *beginning* it, and this responsibility, if pressed upon the consideration of the belligerent nations, might lead them to consider mediation. [Italics in the original].[11] And again on December 1: "I beg to submit for your consideration the following: Our interests justify us in suggesting mediation to the belligerent nations....Mediation does not mean that any of the combatants shall accept terms that are unsatisfactory, but that they shall propose terms, and surely these Christian nations ought to be willing to state to the world the terms upon which the acceptance of which they are willing to cease hostilities, leaving responsibility for the continuance of the war to rest upon those who propose unreasonable terms or reject reasonable terms."[12]

On December 8, 1914, Wilson personally delivered his "Annual Message"to Congress, now known as the "State of the Union" address. As always, he wrote it himself, first in shorthand and then tapping it out on his typewriter. After covering a number of domestic matters, he turned his attention to the war. "We are at peace with all the world," he began, "We are, indeed, a true friend to all the nations of the world, because we threaten none, covet the possessions of none, desire the overthrow of none. Our friendship can be accepted and is accepted without reservation, because it is offered in a spirit and for a purpose which none need ever question or suspect. Therein lies our greatness. We are champions of peace and concord." Moreover, he was quick to add, our neutrality gave us the opportunity to act as peacemakers. "[I]t is our dearest present hope that this character and reputation may presently, in God's providence, bring us an opportunity which has seldom been vouchsafed any nation, the opportunity to counsel and obtain peace in the world and reconciliation and a healing settlement of many a matter that has cooled and interrupted the friendship of nations."

But he was equally opposed to any increase in military preparedness. "[W]e shall not turn America into a military camp. We will not ask our young men to spend the best years of their lives making soldiers of themselves....We must depend in every time of national peril, in the future as in the past, not upon a standing army, nor yet upon a reserve army, but upon a citizenry trained and accustomed to arms."[13] When he said: "We shall not alter our attitude toward it because some amongst us are nervous and excited" he looked directly at Massachusetts Representative Augustus P. Gardner, who was then floating a resolution (opposed by Wilson) for the creation of a commission to examine the state of military and naval preparedness.[14]

As the casualties mounted with the Germans firmly entrenched in France, statesmen on both sides of the English Channel began to consider that if the Germans could not be outflanked in France, perhaps they could be outflanked somewhere else. They fixed their gaze on southern Europe. They became known as the "Easterners," opposed to the "Westerners" who held fast to the idea that Germany could be defeated in the West only by defeating it militarily in the West. In November, 1914, Turkey joined the Central Powers. The Easterners reasoned that Austria-Hungary was the weakest of the Central Powers, and if it could be knocked out of the war it would add to the pressure on Germany and ease the pressure on Russia. Greece was neutral, but its prime minister, Eleftherios Venezelos, (the "Lion of Crete," who had wrested that island from Turkey in 1905) promised that he could deliver Greece to the Allies if they would come to the aid of Serbia. The logical lodgment for a Balkan invasion was the Aegean seaport of Salonika, in western Greece.

There was no greater proponent of the Salonika operation than David Lloyd George. In October, 1914, he went to the front, clambered through the trenches, met and was impressed by Foch and Joffre, but wrote to Margaret: "I went to the English headquarters. Had a great time. Gave me a new idea of what is happening. It is *stalemate*. [His italics]. We cannot turn them out of their trenches & they cannot turn us out."[15] In early 1915 he proposed the Salonika operation at a meeting of the War Council, the sub-cabinet body that included Asquith, Kitchener, Churchill and Grey. Asquith supported the idea, as did Kitchener, who had become perplexed by the stalemate in the trenches. ("I don't know what is to be done," he mused, "This isn't *war*").[16] Churchill had his own idea for outflanking the enemy, a *naval* invasion of the Dardanelles, with its goal of capturing Constantinople and thereby knocking Turkey out of the war. Kitchener supported the idea, provided it remained a purely naval operation. "I shall be the biggest man in Europe if this comes off," he told Lloyd George.[17] When it failed, it quickly became a military operation against heavily fortified positions in the Gallipoli peninsula. By the time the operation was finally abandoned at the end of the year, the British had suffered 115,000 casualties, and another 100,000 from illness, and Churchill, far from being the biggest man in Europe, was out of the Admiralty.

In February, 1915, Lloyd George traveled to Paris, and lobbied Poincaré, Viviani, Delcassé and Briand on the idea of a joint invasion at Salonika. Briand was as much an Easterner as Lloyd George, Generals Galleini and Franchet d'Esperey were in favor, but Joffre vehemently opposed the idea, and he controlled French military policy. He was so opposed to the idea that he threatened to resign if France opened a front in the Balkans. When Poincaré responded that he would not accept Joffre's resignation, forcing him to serve, Joffre replied that he would go out and get himself killed rather than serve.[18] Later in 1915, Serbia's position would become desperate when Bulgaria, eager to regain the territories she had lost in the Second Balkan War, joined the Central Powers. But Joffre was planning further operations in the West, and the Salonika invasion was placed on hold.

One French "Westerner" who shared Joffre's view that the war in France could be won only in France was Georges Clemenceau. Throughout his career he had opposed France's colonial adventures in North Africa and Indo-China, largely because he feared the diversion of troops away from the real threat just across the Vosges. And now, as Clemenceau kept repeating, *"Les Allemands sont a Noyon"* ("The Germans are in Noyon"), Noyon being the site of the German trench closest (fifty-five miles) to Paris.

In January, 1915, Clemenceau was appointed to the Senate Army Committee, and the next month he was appointed to its Foreign Affairs Committee. The Army Committee was the more important of the two, and both carried greater weight than their counterparts in the Chamber of Deputies. The president of both Senate committees was the elderly Charles de Freycinet, who had been Gambetta's second-in-command during the 1870 resistance and who had already taken four turns as prime minister. When de Freycinet retired later in 1915, Clemenceau became the president of both committees. He was one of thirty-six senators on the Army committee. It met in secret, had no executive authority, and could only recommend. It could not summon an army officer to appear, but could summon any minister, including Prime Minister Viviani and Minister of War Millerand, to its thrice-weekly sessions. The transcripts of its hearings were secreted in the Senate files and did not come to light until after the war. Clemenceau became privy to the true state of France's military, but could share his knowledge with no one, least of all his readers of *L'Homme Libre*.

Like most Frenchmen, Clemenceau supported Joffre after the "miracle" of the Marne, but as the skyrocketing casualties led to no end to the stalemate, by the spring of 1915 the Army Committee had become frustrated at the government's uncritical support of Joffre. During a May 29, 1915 sitting, after hearing a critical report delivered by Sen. Jules Jeanneney, Clemenceau fumed: "When I thought that the government was guilty only of negligence and *laisser-aller* ("let it go"), I did not despair of the final result. But today has been a revelation to me: there has been treason everywhere, and I will not collaborate with treason."[19]

Clemenceau in the chair of the Army Committee was not the same man who, as a young deputy in the Chamber, could bring down a ministry with his oratory and his wit. He was now an elder statesman. He often gave the gavel to another senator. He would sometimes interject no more than a sentence, leaving the interrogation to others. But that was not Clemenceau on July 31, 1915, when he exploded at Viviani, who dodged his interrogators by blandly repeating "That is a matter for command." Clemenceau: "I consider that the parliament, through the medium of the government, has an absolute right over the commander-in-chief. It is clear....You name a general-in-chief because of his abilities. It is obvious that you must give him a very great freedom of action, but not for a moment can you cease to watch over him. Take this word in the most honorable sense. You must keep an eye on him. You are the judge of his strategic operations because you are responsible to the nation....I have not said to the prime minister how he must act with regard to the commander-in-chief; that is ground upon which I will not go. But I claim that not at any time may you say: 'That is the business of command.' Everything is the prime minister's business; there is nothing that must escape him. He must proceed with particular discretion vis-à-vis the commander-in-chief, who must be made to feel at all times that he has a superior in the chain of command."[20]

He voiced a number of concerns that day, including the personal irritation that Joffre was refusing him permission to go to the front, despite the fact that a number of foreigners (Lloyd George included) had been granted permission. More important, he raised the specter of religious favoritism in the army. He told of a general who had given his officers badges of the Sacred Heart to wear on their uniforms, itself a violation of army regulations. "Do you know what happens when one returns from an attack?" he asked Viviani. "We see that the officer distributes the first rewards to those who wear the insignia….I am not putting the government on trial; I am stating a fact. But you must know it; you must know what happens at the front. You cannot say that it is a matter for the general-in-chief. You must, in a moral sense, always be at the first line in the trenches."[21] He also decried the fact that there were able-bodied young men attached to the General Staff who got there only through their connections. "[T]he General Staff is composed of an innumerable number of men—I have the figures in this regard—who have no reason to be there except that they are daddy's sons. They are—their officers say—the friends of aunt of a cousin of my good friend, and we can render service from man to man. The service that I give to the father, Mr. Very Important, he will be able to return to me."

But he was not done. Far worse than the nepotism were the "generals-in-chief who are never seen in the trenches—I will not name names, but I will name them if necessary–who settled in thirty or forty kilometres from the front. This would still not be anything, because they could have something to do, if they would prepare for operations. But the returning officers say that they were forced to drive their men to the butcher because the operations were not prepared. I could very well command an army by this method; it's very simple: 'You will bring such army in such direction and at 1:45 you will attack.' You respond that this is impossible, I would respond that it's all the same to me! And you know the result of these attacks? I speak here with complete freedom, but I believe that the moment has come where the prime minister must hear these things that are inspired by single feeling, the love of the country and the desire that the national defense be triumphant. Why are the attacks not prepared? Because there are not infantry officers in the General Staff, because those who command, excellent at giving orders, are monstrously incapable at executing them, not knowing the difficulties of terrain….[I]t would be excellent if the officers of the General Staff would spend six month in the trenches. You say that this is the business of command. I respond that this is the business of the government."[22] Neither Viviani nor Clemenceau could foresee it, but Clemenceau that day gave a preview of himself as prime minister, when the day would come.

In late August, 1915, Minister of War Millerand told the Army Committee that Joffre intended to strip the great eastern fortresses, Verdun, Belfort, Epinal and Toul, of all their men, artillery and materiel, and incorporate them into other units under Joffre's personal command. Defensive fortresses were, after all, antithetical to the offensives that Joffre was still pursuing. Clemenceau objected. "There is one element that must be taken into account, and that we have not sufficiently considered, and that is the element of time. As early as 1870, we were told that the siege would be surrendered. You could read it in all the newspapers at the time. Paris well knew that there would be an end to its ammunition and its provisions. Why did we hold out? It was to give to Gambetta, it was to give to the other rescue armies, time to arrive. The role of fortresses has not changed. A place does not surrender immediately if it has an emergency army maneuvering and who may need to rely on it....Is it then nothing for a place to hold out for a fortnight, for three weeks, when there is all of France behind, when you have on the front 1,300,000 more men than the Germans, and with the possibility of maneuver? It is more or less prolonged resistance, is that not an element that should not at least be taken into account?"[23] But Clemenceau was powerless to oppose the decision, and equally powerless to publicize it. The public learned of it later, when Falkenhayn's invading armies found the Verdun fort of Douaumont defended by little more than a platoon.

The outbreak of the war produced no change in the British government. Asquith and the Liberals continued in office; the Tories continued in opposition. Party conflict was moderated for the sake of national morale, but there was nothing like the coalition government, the *union sacrée*, that there was in France. That changed in the spring of 1915. The first cause of the government's undoing was the "shells crisis." The stalemate in the trenches, coupled with Kitchener's haphazard administration of the War Ministry resulted in a deficiency in high explosive shells, as it became apparent that artillery, not infantry, would be the principal offensive weapon in this war. On May 15, 1915, the *Times* war correspondent filed a dispatch from the front headlined "Need for Shells— British Attacks Checked—Limited Supply the Cause" claiming that the lack of shells had led to the failure of British troops to capture German trenches.[24] The writer's source was probably Sir John French himself. But the immediate cause of the end of the Liberal government was the failure of the Dardanelles operation. When the First Sea Lord, Admiral John A. "Jackie" Fisher, who had opposed the operation from the start, ("Damn the Dardanelles—they will be our grave!") resigned on the same day that the *Times* story broke, it was the end. The Tories insisted that Churchill, the turncoat former Tory they despised, be sacked, and a coalition government formed. Churchill took it very hard, even having his wife, Clementine, write a letter to Asquith imploring him to retain her husband at the Admiralty. Lloyd George tried to get Churchill a minor post in the government, such as Viceroy of India. In the end, Asquith appointed Churchill as Chancellor of the Duchy of Lancaster, a ceremonial post, and Churchill's humiliation was complete.

In the ensuing coalition government, a new Cabinet department was created: minister of munitions, with the duty of overseeing the manufacture and delivery to the armies of the weapons and ordnance they needed to fight the war. It meant removing these responsibilities from Kitchener, who originally was unaware of his loss of power. Asquith chose Lloyd George to fill the post, Kitchener cabling Lloyd George "Delighted to hear you are coming to help me."[25] The Tories got Arthur Balfour to succeed Churchill at the Admiralty. Kitchener, a nominal Tory but really of no party, remained as the somewhat truncated Secretary of State for War. Reginald McKenna replaced Lloyd George at the Treasury, but the appointment was intended to be only temporary, Asquith having assured Lloyd George that he could return as chancellor of the exchequer once the crisis passed. He remained at 11 Downing Street.

One man who exulted over Lloyd George's appointment was Clemenceau, who wrote: "They sought the man who could inspire the most confidence in the country, both by the brilliance of the services rendered and by the soundness of his views and the firmness of his character. They went to M. Lloyd George, whose name, at this particular hour, certainly enjoys the greatest authority in the whole country."[26]

Lloyd George risked his career in accepting the position. Had he failed to solve the munitions crisis, he would have suffered Churchill's fate. He was more suited to the new position than he was to the Treasury, never having been comfortable delivering the annual budget message to the House of Commons. Now, he had a job where he could *get things done*. He later recalled that he never worked harder than when setting up the ministry. At first, they gave him an office on the ground floor of a two-story town house at 6 Whitehall Gardens, one that had recently been vacated by an art dealer. The furnishings consisted of one table and one chair. He divided the ministry functionally: There was an explosives department, a shells department, a machine guns department, etc. On his first day on the job, he was visited by Col. House, then making the rounds of European capitals. By the time he left sixteen months later, the ministry would have twelve thousand employees, 40% of them women. He solved the shells shortage. Under Kitchener, the War Office delivered 871,000 shells in December, 1914. A year later, in

December, 1915, the Ministry of Munitions delivered 23.6 *million* shells, and a year after that, 128.4 million.

Scarcely a month after assuming his new office, on June 3, 1915, Lloyd George delivered a major address to a group of engineers in Manchester. Referring to the city of his birth, he began by noting that "This is by no means my first visit to Manchester—in fact, my first was timed over 52 years ago." More seriously: "Now I come as an emissary of the State to carry the most urgent errand ever told to the ears of a Manchester audience. Our country is fighting for its life; our country is fighting for the liberties of Europe, and upon what it does, upon what it is prepared to sacrifice, will depend the issue." The success of the struggle depended, more than anything else, on "the men who are occupied in running the workshops of this country....I would almost say at the present moment everything depends on the workshops of Britain....I have come here to tell you the truth. Unless you know it you cannot be expected to make sacrifices."[27] He referred to a recent German victory over the Russians in Galicia, a victory won "not by the strategy of the German generals or by the greater gallantry of their troops, but by the use they have made of their skilled industry and especially by the superior organization of the German workshop." He noted that the Germans were able to concentrate 200,000 shells *in a single hour* on "the devoted heads of the gallant Russians, 700,000 fired away in a single battle." And, to put a fine point on it, "Had we been in a position to apply the same process to the Germans on our front, broken their lines, driven them back the same number of miles as they have driven back the Russians in Galicia, what would have happened? They would have been turned out of France; they would have been driven half way across the devastated plain of Flanders..."

He was not there merely to deliver a pep talk or waive the flag. His purpose was to talk about *conscription*, not of soldiers (enough were answering Kitchener's call to make that unnecessary) but of industrial workers. So many skilled men were enlisting that there was a shortage of men where they were needed most, in industry. "Let us be frank with ourselves. Frankness is the beginning of wise action; it is the beginning of victory. We were the worst organized nation in the world for this war." He wanted to not only conscript skilled workers, he wanted to end the restrictive policies of the trade unions that he claimed hurt the war effort. A month later, he got his wish. With the enactment of the Munitions of War Act, skilled workers could be conscripted into service, restrictive trade union regulations were suspended, a cap was placed on profits, strikes and lockouts in "controlled establishments" (defined broadly enough to include not only munitions workers but docks and textile workers) were made illegal. It became a crime for a munitions worker to leave a plant without permission, and permission was rarely granted. The unions groused that the pain fell disproportionately on the workers. Not everyone was pleased with the Manchester speech or the statute that followed it.

One man who was very pleased with the Manchester speech was Clemenceau. Writing a few days later, he devoted his column to an extensive summary of the speech. He opined: "We must stop at the words that Mr. Lloyd George has just pronounced at Manchester, for they are so universal that they go beyond their audience and must hold the attention of all who think and act among the world powers....It is Lloyd George, who asks from his audience a prodigality of effort for a prodigality of munitions."[28]

Shortly after Lloyd George became Minister of Munitions, an aide asked Kitchener how many machine guns should be ordered. Kitchener, who never quite realized that he was no longer fighting spear-carrying Dervishes in the Sudan, replied: "two machine-guns per battalion as a minimum, four as a maximum and anything over four is luxury." The aide brought Kitchener's estimate to Lloyd George, who ordered: "Take Kitchener's maximum and square it, multiply it by two, and when you're in sight of it, double it again for good luck."[29]

At the outbreak of the war, Col. House determined that he would bring the warring nations together and mediate its end, confiding to his diary: "I am laying plans to make myself persona grata to all the nations involved in this European war so that my services may be utilized to advantage and without objection in the event a proper opportunity arrives...I do not believe in leaving things to chance."[30] Toward that end, he first had to sideline the secretary of state, writing Wilson: "Please let me suggest that you do not let Mr. Bryan make any overtures to any of the Powers involved. They look upon him as absolutely visionary, and it would lessen the weight of your influence if you desire to use it yourself later." After Bryan's inglorious attempt at public diplomacy, it took little to convince Wilson that Bryan was not the man to mediate an end to the war.

For House, then fifty-seven and in fragile health, brokering the end to the war would be the culmination of his life's work. Slight of stature and with no rhetorical gift, he realized early on that he could never win public office. He turned these liabilities into an asset. He made it clear to the powerful men he advised in Texas and later with Wilson that he had no ambition for office, and on occasion declined the offers. He would work behind the scenes, avoiding the spotlight. He would be remembered to posterity by his diary; it runs to three thousand pages.

On September 5, 1914, the day before the offensive on the Marne began, House wrote to the German Under Secretary for Foreign Affairs, Arthur Zimmermann: "If I could serve in any way as a medium it would be a great source of happiness to me, and I stand ready to act immediately upon any suggestion that your Excellency may convey, or have conveyed confidentially to me."[31] House had met with Zimmermann during the spring, and felt that he had established a personal relationship with him. But on the very day that House was penning this letter France, Great Britain and Russia issued their *public* declaration that none of them would make a separate peace. That meant that the war aims of each would have to be satisfied, including Russia's territorial ambitions in Turkey and the return to France not only of the territory Germany had captured in 1914 but the territory—Alsace and Lorraine—that it had captured in 1870. It is no wonder that three days later France's ambassador to the United States, Jules Jusserand, advised his foreign office that the chances of mediation were "infinitesimal."[32]

None of the belligerents had any desire for mediation at this time, but none was willing to admit it, lest it be blamed for continuing the war. German Ambassador Bernstorff wanted to "leave the odium of rejection to our enemies."[33] The British ambassador, Sir Cecil Spring Rice, wrote to Grey, warning that public opinion in the United States would swing to Germany if "we had refused a fair offer for peace which the Germans had made us, or had refused to listen to a peaceful suggestion from the United States government."[34] The American ambassador in London was Walter Hines Page, a journalist who had befriended Wilson when Wilson was a struggling lawyer in Atlanta. Page was an Anglophile to the bone, but he was a wise and capable observer of the mood in London. On September 10 he met with Grey, who advised Page that any peace would have to satisfy the demands of each of the Allies, and that Great Britain's minimum price for peace was German reparation for the ruination of Belgium and the "end of militarism forever," so that there could be no recurrence of a German invasion. He left vague what the "end of militarism" meant. Grey also warned that talk of mediation would play into the hands of the German propaganda machine. Page duly reported this meeting to his superior, Secretary of State Bryan.[35] Bryan was unaware at this time that it was House, and not he, who would act as Wilson's mediator when the time came.

House was undeterred. He tried to arrange a meeting between himself, Bernstorff and Spring Rice. Such a meeting would have been a breach of diplomatic norms, which held that when the ambassadors of warring nations accredited to a neutral nation encountered each other at diplomatic functions, they were to eye each other coldly from a distance. The last thing they could do is negotiate, especially in the light of Great Britain's commitment not to negotiate a separate peace. Nonetheless, House advised Wilson that "If we can get these two together we can, at least, make a start. For the moment, England dominates her allies. Later she may not. She would probably be content now with an agreement for general disarmament and an indemnity for Belgium.

Germany, I think, would be glad to get such terms."[36] Wilson did not question why House believed that "England dominates her allies." In any event, shortly after floating the idea of a meeting, House had to advise Wilson that Spring Rice had declined.

On two occasions in the autumn of 1914 House lamented in his diary that Wilson was not as interested in foreign affairs as he was in domestic issues. That is undoubtedly true, as Wilson was preoccupied with labor strife in the Colorado coal fields, the ongoing revolution in Mexico and his domestic agenda, not to mention his grief over the loss of his wife. But it may also be that Wilson was simply not as hopeful of House's mediation efforts as was House himself. In early November House confided in his diary that he had mentioned to Wilson that once "the Germans were driven back within their own borders" it would be a propitious time for House to travel to Germany, meet with the kaiser, and have the kaiser ask Wilson to mediate. House added: "The President did not express an opinion one way or the other as to the advisability of this, excepting he thought the Kaiser would hesitate to admit defeat, which that would practically be doing."[37]

House's (and Wilson's) hopes brightened considerably on December 15, when House received a long-delayed response from Zimmermann to his September 5 letter ("If I could serve in any way as a medium…"). The letter, written by Chancellor Bethmann Hollweg but conveyed through Zimmermann, stated: "We have greatly appreciated the President's and your own good offices…Germany has always desired to maintain peace, as she proves by a record of more than forty years. The war has been forced upon us by our enemies and they are carrying it on by summoning all the forces at their disposal, including Japanese and other colored races. This makes it impossible for us to take the first step towards making peace. The situation might be different if such overtures came from the other side. I do not know if your efforts have been extended in that direction and whether they have found a willing ear. But as long as you kindly offer your services in a most unselfish way, agreeing to act upon any suggestion that I convey to you, it seems to me worth while trying to see where the land lies in the other camp."[38] What House could not know is that shortly before sending the letter, Bethmann Hollweg confided to Zimmermann's boss, Foreign Secretary Gottlieb von Jagow, that "We have to avoid the appearance of favoring, in principle, the continuation of the war."[39]

Upon receipt of Zimmermann's letter, House instructed Page to advise Grey that the Germans would accept mediation based upon the evacuation of Belgium and a pledge of general disarmament. Grey responded openly as von Jagow had secretly, that it would be unwise for Great Britain to be in a position where it was seen as the nation seeking to continue the war. As if to underscore disdain for mediation, Grey sent Spring

Rice a long telegram, instructing Spring Rice to share its contents with House (Spring Rice *memorized* it), which Spring Rice did on December 22. In it Grey emphasized that there could be no negotiations until Germany had evacuated Belgium and paid reparations for the destruction it had caused, and no settlement unless it included a general disarmament. Grey further advised that: "[T]here are also the views of the Allies to be considered. We have not yet discussed terms of peace with them and we are bound to do so when the time comes."[40]

Prior to this, on December 20, House met with Russia's ambassador, Boris Bakhmetieff, who was even more pessimistic than Grey. Bakhmetieff advised his foreign office: "[I] reminded him (House), if Bethmann Hollweg had called treaties scraps of paper—how much trust can you put in their words, if he conveys them through a third and unofficial and personally unanswerable individual? He appeared embarrassed and assented to all we said; finally he explained it to be his mission at the desire of the President to become acquainted with 'the true feeling of Germany'....I finally declared to him that if Germany really wants peace, she knows the way by which she can attain it—through a direct approach to the allied powers, and not through private talks and empty promises."[41]

None of this deterred House. According to his diary, he went to the White House, gave Wilson the news of Zimmermann's letter, which "much elated" the President. Wilson asked House if he could go to Europe "as early as the coming Saturday."[42] They agreed that it was time to advise Bryan that House was in charge in mediating the end of the European war.

But Grey was not finished in his efforts to cool House and Wilson's ardor. In late December he in called in Chandler P. Anderson, who had served as counselor to the State Department and was on his way home after a posting as counselor to Page. Grey asked Anderson to convey a message directly to Wilson. He stressed to Anderson that he believed that the time was not ripe for peace overtures, or even a discussion of possible terms. He also wanted Wilson to know that at the end of the war, the Allies would press for reparations for Belgium, an indemnity to France, the return of Alsace-Lorraine and Russian acquisition of Constantinople and the Dardanelles."[43] In early January, 1915, Grey again wrote Spring Rice: "President's friend must not forget that France and Russia have to be consulted about European peace and that I could not open discussion with them unless very sure of the ground respecting Germany's real disposition."[44] Coincidentally, at this time Great Britain's ambassador to France, Sir Francis Bertie, dined with Clemenceau. Bertie noted afterwards that Clemenceau "pooh-poohs American intervention; peace must be the concern of the belligerents only with no outside mediation or interference."[45]

On January 12, 1915, House met with Wilson. In a meeting that, according to House, lasted all of twelve minutes, House and Wilson decided that House would travel to Europe on January 30, House admitting that "I had practically decided before I came to Washington that this was necessary. And I was certain, when I gave my thoughts to the President, he would agree with me it was the best thing to do....I thought we had done all we could with the Ambassadors at Washington, and that we were now travelling in a circle. It was time to deal directly with the principals...and that it was essential to take the matter up directly with London and afterward with Berlin."[46] France's war aims apparently did not cross his mind. Despite his feeling that he had done all he could "with the Ambassadors at Washington," he met the next day with all of them, first alone with Spring Rice, and then with Spring Rice, Jusserand and Bakhmetieff. He related in the diary that he first found Spring Rice "in a rather sulky mood," advising House that "the Allies would not receive the good offices of the President cordially," but that "I soon got him in a good humor by telling him what a wonderful thing it would be to have the United States throw its great moral strength in behalf of a permanent settlement, and it was my purpose not to discuss terms with Germany so much as to discuss a plan which would assure permanent peace." Later, when Jusserand and Bakhmetieff arrived, they were at first "violent in their denunciation of the Germans and evinced a total lack of belief in their sincerity. They thought my mission would be entirely fruitless." But again, House reports that he convinced these two career diplomats that his trip would expose the Germans' "false pretenses" to the world.[47] House's diary is replete with instances where he believed he had skillfully brought others around to his point of view.

House met again with Wilson on January 24. Wilson instructed House to inform Grey that "while you are abroad, I expect to act directly through you and to eliminate all intermediaries." Wilson gave House no instructions, believing none were necessary, telling House: "We are both of the same mind and it is not necessary to go into details with you."[48] Then it was time for House to leave. Wilson, his eyes moist, told House that "Your unselfish and intelligent friendship has meant much to me," that House was "the only one in the world to whom he could open his entire mind." House told Wilson how grateful he was: "I had tried all my life to find some one with whom I could work out the things I had so deeply at heart, and then I began to despair, believing my life would be more or less a failure, when he came into it, giving me the opportunity for which I had been longing."[49] House had fallen into a trap common to diplomats and negotiators the world over. He had allowed himself to become personally invested in the success of his mission. His failure to reach a deal would be his personal failure, and, to his mind, the failure of his life's work.

If House was "the only one in the world to whom [Wilson] could open his entire mind," he would not be for long. While House was shuttling among the capitals of Europe, Wilson met forty-two-year-old Edith Bolling Galt, an attractive, vivacious, Washington widow fifteen years his junior. She became his sounding-board, he even sharing confidential documents with her. Six weeks after meeting her he confessed his love and asked her to marry him. At first she resisted. They were married in December, 1915.

House set sail on the British liner *RMS Lusitania* on January 30, 1915. While he was at sea, Germany announced that, effective on February 18, it would begin unrestricted submarine warfare against all Allied merchant ships in the waters around Great Britain. Neutrals were warned that on occasion Allied ships flew the flags of neutral nations, and mistakes might be made. As the *Lusitania* neared port, the captain, in a *ruse de guerre*, ran up the Stars and Stripes.

The purpose of House's mission may have been secret, but the fact of it was not, the *New York Times* headlining "Col. House in London" the day after he arrived.[50] But as his mission was unofficial, House met Grey at his residence at 33 Eccleston Square, a townhouse Grey leased from Winston Churchill. During their first meeting, on February 7, Grey advised House that there was no chance of mediation at that time. He informed House that he was in talks with Italy and Romania on their entering the war on the side of the Allies, and therefore this would not be a propitious time to be seen throwing out peace feelers to the Germans. During that meeting, House suggested that, if France insisted on the return of Alsace and Lorraine, it might be possible that the two provinces be neutralized, "like Luxemburg is now."[51] They met again three days later. Grey advised House that he had informed France's foreign minister, Theophile Delcassé, of House's plans, and that Delcassé agreed with Grey that any German expression of a desire to discuss peace terms was intended solely for propaganda. House disagreed, saying that while the German military class might not be ready to talk peace, the kaiser was. But with this, House's mission subtly, imperceptibly, changed. What began as an effort at mediation became something far less ambitious, viz. an effort to express Wilson's desire to act as a mediator at some opportune time. On February 12, House received a letter from Zimmermann, inviting him to Germany, but making it clear that the payment of reparations to Belgium was out of the question. The next day, House met with Grey again. In a further attempt to deter House, Grey, with Asquith's concurrence, advised House that the Germans were launching a campaign in Poland with the goal of encircling the Russians, and that it might be best not to go to Germany until that campaign either succeeded or failed. House reported this meeting to Wilson, who, in a February 20 telegram, mildly chided House: "It will of course occur to you that you cannot go too far in allowing the English Government to determine when it is best to go to Germany because they naturally desire to await some time when they have the advantage because of events in the field or elsewhere. If the impression were to be created in Berlin that you were to come only when the British Government thought it the opportune time for you to come, you might be regarded when you reached there as their spokesman rather than as mine."[52]

But if Wilson was still not convinced of the hopelessness of mediation, House now was. In an extended reply to Wilson two days later, House gave Wilson a strong dose of reality: "Up to now, all we know is that Germany refuses to indemnify Belgium, and also refuses to make any proposition herself. She may or may not be willing to evacuate Belgium and consider proposals looking to permanent peace. But even if she considers these two critical points, it is well to remember that neither Russia nor France is willing to make peace on any such terms....Since the war has begun and since they [the British public and cabinet] consider that Germany was the aggressor and is the exponent of militarism, they are determined not to cease fighting until there is no hope of victory, or until Germany is ready to concede what they consider a fair and permanent settlement....If there was any reason to believe that Germany was ready to make terms as the Allies are ready to accept, then it would be well to go immediately, but all our information is to the contrary, and the result of my visit there now would be to lose the sympathetic interest of England, and through her, the Allies...without accomplishing any good in Germany."[53] Wilson replied: "Your cables enable me to understand the situation in all its phases, and I greatly appreciate them. I am of course content to be guided by your judgment as to each step."[54]

On February 28, House met with King George, at the king's invitation. House afterwards wrote: "He is the most bellicose Englishman that I have met so far....His idea seemed to be that the best way to obtain permanent peace was to the knock all the fight out of the Germans....He seemed more certain than anyone I have met that France and Russia would stick to the last man," concluding that "I had hoped that he might be useful to us as an instrument of peace, but we will have to change his attitude before that hope can be realized."[55] Two days later, House wrote his son-in-law, Gordon Auchincloss: "If I succeed in doing nothing more than keeping out of trouble, I shall consider I have been fortunate."[56] House had now been in London almost a month, and it appears that Grey also began to believe that House at least could do no harm. When House received another encouraging letter from Zimmermann, Grey did not attempt to dissuade him from visiting Berlin. Grey advised House that the French would insist upon the return of Alsace-Lorraine, that the French believed that the Allies would win the war and they would be able to impose peace terms.[57] Before he left (sailing to Paris en route to Berlin), he dissembled to Wilson: "Just a last word to say that I leave everything here in admirable shape. It could not be better."[58]

House arrived in Paris on March 11 and checked into the Hotel Crillon. He had a pleasant, inconclusive meeting with Delcassé, whose attitude brightened when House advised him (before Delcassé could say anything) that Wilson had no intention of pushing peace negotiations on anyone. Before heading for Berlin, House met with British Ambassador Sir Francis Bertie and the new American ambassador, William G. Sharp. Afterwards, Bertie noted in his diary that: "[House] is, I understand, looking around to see what opportunity the President may find for proposing peace, and so securing the German vote for a second Presidential Election. I had some conversation with him, but nothing worth noting."[59]

Around this time, House hit upon a new idea, one he termed "Freedom of the Seas." It was to be a guarantee the safe passage of neutral shipping in wartime, with the definition of "contraband" limited to arms and munitions. If adopted, it would eliminate Great Britain's notion of "continuous voyage;" a ship carrying war materiel such as rubber and copper could proceed unmolested to a neutral port, even if its cargo was consigned to the enemy. House intended "Freedom of the Seas" to be negotiated only after the war's end, but raising it now, he reported to Wilson, would "throw across the chasm the first thread, so that the bridge might have its beginning."[60] It would at least give House something to talk about in Berlin.

House arrived in Berlin on March 20, and was met immediately by Zimmermann. He advised Zimmermann of "the lack of bitterness in England towards Germany"(!), which surprised Zimmermann, who was equally surprised when House advised him that the real "difficulty" was with France.[61] He later met with both Zimmermann and Bethman Hollweg, which was cordial but unproductive. They wanted America to stop selling munitions to the Allies, which House advised was not going to happen. They were, however, enthusiastic about "Freedom of the Seas." House left Berlin on March 30, and after stopovers in Rome and Madrid, returned to Paris, just as the Allies' campaign in Gallipoli was getting underway. He met again with Delcassé, who was relieved to learn that House carried with him no peace proposals, and that America would continue selling arms to the Allies.

While House was still in Paris, Great Britain, France, Russia and Italy finalized the secret Treaty of London, under which Italy agreed to declare war on Austria-Hungary and Germany the following month. It did so vis-à-vis Austria-Hungary, but waited a year to declare war on Germany. The price for Italy's support was Austrian territory: parts of the Austrian Tyrol and the Austrian Adriatic including the port of Trieste.

Italy's king, Emmanuel III, favored entering the war, as did Prime Minister Salandra and Foreign Minister Sonnino and some Italian revolutionaries, including Benito Mussolini, then a Socialist. Most Italians opposed the entry into the war. The Italian army was so weak that it proved to be as much of a burden as an asset to the Allies. Worse, when the Bolsheviks took over the Russian government in 1917, they exposed the treaty. Still worse, the Italians came to the Peace Conference after the war, demanding payment.

House returned to London on April 28. He broached "Freedom of the Seas" to Grey, even suggesting negotiations start now, not at the end of the war. Grey advised House that anything and everything was contingent on the German evacuation of Belgium. In fact, Grey had no interest in the idea, as it would neuter Britain's most effective offensive weapon, its navy. House wrote in his diary: "His [Grey's] mind and mine run nearly parallel, and we seldom disagree."[62] Page summarized House's efforts in his diary: "Peace-talk…is yet mere moonshine."[63] In Sir Edward Grey's two-volume memoir of his time as Great Britain's foreign secretary, he devoted two scant pages to House's 1915 efforts at mediation.

At the outbreak of the war, Grand Admiral Alfred von Tirpitz gave an interview for the American press, in which he asked, rhetorically, "What will America say if Germany declares submarine war on all the enemy's merchant ships? Why not? England wants to starve us. We can play the same game."[64] But as he spoke, it was not England or America that prevented von Tirpitz from carrying out the threat; it was his own government. Bethmann Hollweg feared that attacking merchant ships might bring the United States into the war, for little military advantage. Germany then simply did not have enough U-boats to matter. The man who mattered, the kaiser, agreed. But in February, 1915, he relented, and on February 15 Germany announced that any ship—including passenger liners—plying "the waters around Great Britain" ran the risk of being sunk by a U-boat. But the conflict between the aggressive German admirals and Bethmann Hollweg's more cautious civilians for the mind and heart of the kaiser would continue for another two years.

On March 28, *U-24* torpedoed and sank the British passenger liner *RMS Falaba* en route from Liverpool to west Africa. One hundred twenty-eight were killed, including a thirty-one-year-old American mining engineer, Leon Thrasher. State Department counselor Robert Lansing advised sending a strong note of protest. Bryan disagreed, fearing it might lead to war. He counseled that Americans be advised not to sail on ships in the war zone. Wilson pondered for a fortnight. Fearing that it might lead to a war in which the United States was unprepared, no protest note was sent.

On May 1, Ambassador Bernstorff published a warning that was printed in the *New York Times*. He warned that anyone sailing on a British ship that ventured into the "war zone" near the British Isles would do so at his own risk.

On Friday afternoon, May 7, a torpedo fired from *U-20* sank *RMS Lusitania*, eleven miles off the coast of Ireland. Twelve hundred civilians, including 128 Americans, perished. May 7 was a busy day for Col. House. He first met with Sir Edward Grey. They fell to talking of "the probability of an ocean liner being sunk." House told Grey that "if this were done, a flame of indignation would sweep across America, which would itself probably carry us into the war." An hour later, House met with the king at Buckingham Palace, and the two also spoke of the possibility of an ocean liner being torpedoed. King George even remarked: "Suppose they sink the *Lusitania* with American passengers on board…"[65]

It was still Friday afternoon when Wilson learned of the sinking of the *Lusitania*, but it was only in the evening that he learned of the full extent of the carnage. Eluding the Secret Service, he went through the front door of the White House and walked alone, in the rain, through the streets of Washington. For the next two days, Saturday and Sunday, he met with no one, but on Saturday the White House issued a statement: "Of course the President feels the distress of the gravity of the situation to the utmost and is considering earnestly, but very calmly, the right course of action to pursue. He knows that the people of the country wish and expect him to act with deliberation as well as with firmness."[66] On Monday morning the *New York Times* headlined: "All Eyes on the President, Who Keeps His Own Counsel."[67]

Roosevelt was the first to weigh in, issuing a statement immediately after the attack: "This presents not merely piracy, but piracy on a vaster scale of murder than old-time pirates ever practiced…It is warfare against innocent men, women and children traveling on the ocean, and our fellow countrymen and countrywomen who are among the sufferers. It seems inconceivable that we can refrain from taking action in this matter, for we owe it not only to humanity, but to our national self-respect."[68] But a careful reading of TR's statement reveals that it was not an explicit call for a declaration of war.

On Sunday, Col. House cabled his advice: "I believe an immediate demand should be made upon Germany for assurance that this will not occur again. If she fails to give such assurance, I should inform her that our Government expected to take such measures as were necessary to assure the safety of American citizens….If war follows, it will not be a new war, but an endeavor to end more speedily an old one. Our intervention will save rather than increase, the loss of life….America has come to a parting of the ways, when she must determine whether she stands for civilized or uncivilized warfare. We can no longer remain neutral spectators. Our action in this crisis will determine what part we play when peace is made, and how far we may influence a settlement for the lasting good of humanity. We are being weighed in the balance, and our position amongst nations is being assessed by mankind."[69] That same day, Great Britain's ambassador to France, Lord Bertie, noted in his diary: "I do not think that war between the United States and Germany would be of advantage to us, for the Americans could not aid us in any fighting yet, and they would claim to join in settling the terms of peace."[70]

Wilson did not heed House's advice, and in so doing was more attuned to the American people than was House. Americans were outraged, but not enough to clamor for war. The mood may have been best expressed by Col. Harvey, writing in his *North American Review*: "Because Great Britain refused to permit the United States to supply the German army with foodstuffs, Germany officially assassinated a hundred American citizens. That is a naked fact from which escape is impossible. Explanations cannot explain; excuses cannot palliate; the monstrous crime was premeditated, was threatened and was perpetrated." But Harvey stopped short of calling for intervention: "This Nation is confronted by no necessity of inflicting punishment upon Germany. The reprobation of all mankind, whose effect will continue for years to come is a fully adequate penalty which, unfortunately but inevitably, the innocent German people, in common with the guilty German government, must prepare to suffer."[71]

Wilson was scheduled to address an audience of four thousand newly-naturalized citizens the evening of Monday, the tenth, in Philadelphia. He had not spoken publicly since before the *Lusitania* went down. His address was titled "American and the Foreign Born." He had delivered hundreds of such addresses, had vaulted to the governorship of New Jersey and then to the White House largely on the felicity of his speech. But on this night, when the nation hung on his every word, he heard himself utter the most unfortunate phrase of his public life. Speaking of nothing in particular, he said: "The example of America must be the example not merely of peace because it will not fight, but of peace because peace is the healing and elevating influence of the world and strife is not. *There is such a thing as a man being too proud to fight.* There is such a thing as a nation being so right that it does not need to convince others by force that it is right."[72] There was no mention of the *Lusitania* anywhere in the speech, and if Wilson was even thinking of the *Lusitania,* only he knew. But immediately he recognized the blunder. The next day he told a friend: "I have a bad habit of thinking out loud. That thought occurred to me while I was speaking, and I let it out."[73] But the damage had been done.

Down through history, "too proud to fight" has become associated with his attitude toward the 128 Americans who went down with the *Lusitania*.

At almost the same hour that Wilson was speaking in Philadelphia, Clemenceau was writing in Paris. Never having forgiven Wilson for his silence following the destruction of Belgium, Clemenceau viewed the *Lusitania* as Wilson's come-uppance. "Moved by inspirations that do more honor to his legal conceptions than to his general views of the profound causes of this war, Wilson had taken comfort in the vain hope of being able to keep, until the end, a balance between the combatants which would enable him, at the right moment, to present himself to Europe as the engine of mediation, bringing peace to the world by deploying the supreme virtue of impartiality. I have denounced this dream—for it was only a dream—from the first day, as the effect of a rare incomprehension of the political, economic and moral forces which are now in mortal combat across the vast plains of Europe and Asia. If the president of the great American republic had been able to feel (I do not even say to have understood) the irresistible power of the state of mind that has compelled Russia, France, and England to rely on the fate of arms against an enemy incredibly superior in military preparation, he would have been spared a resounding disappointment." He continued: "When the Pilgrim fathers embarked on the Mayflower to seek, in a new continent, the liberty that had been refused them in their country…they had the good fortune to find virgin lands before them. We cannot propose to Great Britain, to France, to Russia, to emigrate to make room for the Kaiser. We are condemned to fight for our land, for the defense of our homes. Mr. Wilson would not argue that our cause may be any less exalted than that of the great 'pilgrims' who…brought an extraordinary development of freedom….From the entry of its soldiers in Belgium, the most odious brutalities and savageries came to mean to the civilized world that the days of the ancient barbaric invasions had returned….If men who were in possession of speech had uttered the exalted words of reproof expected of the human conscience, perhaps Wilhelm II would have found himself capable of reflection. We can do him the honor, perhaps excessive of supposing so. In any case, a great service of humanity, of civilization, would have been accomplished, and something that was lost would have been preserved." He concluded: "President Wilson was waiting, without knowing exactly what. Now he knows, because something happened. The *Lusitania*'s torpedo may have awakened him. We will see. In any event, the American people rise up as one man to throw the curse of the human conscience to the imperial assassin of innocent passengers, whose previous warning shows that the murder was premeditated."[74]

Wilson drafted a note to Germany, and read it to his cabinet the next day. In it, Wilson demanded that Germany account for its actions against the *Falaba*, the *Lusitania*, and two other sinkings. With respect to Bernstorff's published warning, Wilson responded: "no warning that an unlawful and inhumane act will be committed can possibly be accepted as an excuse or palliation for that act or as an abatement of its responsibility for its commission." The heart of the note was that "This Government... must hold the Imperial German Government to a strict accountability for any infringement of [its] rights, intentional or incidental."[75] The note was a protest. It was a warning. It was not an ultimatum.

Following a three-hour discussion, the cabinet unanimously approved sending the note. But Bryan agreed only reluctantly, pushing for a second note, to be sent to Great Britain, protesting its violations of American neutrality. He may have agreed to the note only on the assumption that such a note would be sent to the British. Wilson considered such a note, and had Lansing draft it. But he wisely reconsidered, on the ground that sending a note to Great Britain before the Germans could reply to its note would weaken the force of the note.

The note won wide approval, the sentiment best summarized by President Taft, who called the note "Admirable in tone, moderate in the judicial spirit that runs through the entire communication...[Wilson] puts the case of the United States in such a way that it may well call for our earnest concurrence and confirmation."[76] But it caused consternation in Berlin. Von Tirpitz and his admirals wanted no interruption in unrestricted submarine warfare. Bethmann Hollweg and the civilians feared a diplomatic break leading to war with the United States, just as Italy had joined the Allies in the fight against Austria-Hungary. The German response to the note was therefore neither an outright rejection nor an acceptance of Wilson's demands; it was an evasion. In response to Wilson's demand that Germany explain the *Lusitania*, Bethmann Hollweg made justifications, viz., that the *Lusitania* had been built as an auxiliary cruiser, that it carried ammunition, and that it had ferried Canadian troops, adding "The German government believes that it acts in just self-defense when it acts to protect the lives of its soldiers by destroying ammunition destined for the enemy with the means of war at its command."[77] But in light of the policy disputes then raging in Berlin, Bethmann Hollweg's response made it clear that it was only an "interim" reply, "The Imperial Government begs to reserve a final statement of its position with regard to the demands made in connection with the sinking of the *Lusitania* until a reply is received from the American government."[78] The ball was back in Wilson's court.

Wilson had become aware of the struggle in Berlin between the civilians and the admirals, but he could not know that just at this time, the civilians had won out. By the end of the first week of June, Bethmann Hollweg first imposed a ban on submarine attacks on all neutral shipping and then a ban on attacks on all *large* passenger liners, including the enemies' liners. But the decision was kept secret. German public opinion favored the U-boats as a legitimate response to the blockade.

Wilson and his cabinet met on Tuesday, June 1, the day after receipt of the German reply to the note. According to Agriculture Secretary David Houston, Bryan "seemed to be laboring under a great strain and sat back in his chair most of the time with his eyes closed."[79] There was a discussion of sending a second note. Secretary of War Lindley Garrison urged that "Germany should be urged to say, first, whether or not she accepted the principle we stood for. If she did not, there was nothing to discuss; if she did, we could then canvass details with her." Then, again according to Houston, "Bryan got excited. He said that he had all along insisted on a note to England; that she was illegally preventing our exports going where we had a right to send them; and that the Cabinet seemed to be pro-Ally. All the rest of the Cabinet strongly protested against a note to England, and no note was sent. The President sharply rebuked Bryan, saying that his remarks were unfair and unjust. He had no right to say anyone was pro-Ally or pro-German."[80] Years later, another Cabinet participant, Attorney-General Thomas Gregory, recalled Bryan saying: "You people are not neutral. You are taking sides!" To which Wilson replied, sharply and coldly, "You have no right to make that statement. We are all honestly, trying to be neutral against heavy difficulties."[81] It was either during this cabinet meeting or shortly thereafter that Bryan decided to resign as secretary of state.

The next day, Wilson asked Bryan and counselor Lansing to compose a second note to Germany. Neither did. Lansing sent Wilson a legal memorandum countering the points the Germans had raised in their reply to the first note. Bryan sent Wilson two letters, one recommending an appeal to the "cooling off" treaties that many nations—but not Germany—had signed with the United States, and the other suggesting that Americans be warned not to sail on the ships of warring nations. Wilson drafted the second note himself. He began during the evening of the third and worked through the night. Wilson had lost none of his rhetorical flair: "Whatever may be the contentions of the Imperial German Government regarding the carrying of contraband of war on board the *Lusitania*, or regarding the explosion of that material by the torpedo, it need only be said that in the view of this Government these contentions are irrelevant to the question of the legality of the methods used by the German naval authorities in sinking the vessel....[T]he sinking of passenger ships involves principles of humanity which throw into the background any special circumstances of detail that may be thought to affect the cases; principles which lift it...out of the class of ordinary subjects of diplomatic discussion or of international controversy. Whatever the other facts regarding the *Lusitania*, the principal fact is that a great steamer, primarily and chiefly a conveyance for passengers and carrying more than a thousand souls who had no part or lot in the conduct of the war, was torpedoed and sunk without so much as a challenge or a warning and that men, women and children were sent to their death in circumstances unparalleled in modern warfare....The Government of the United States is contending for something much greater than mere rights of property or privileges of commerce. It is contending for nothing less high and sacred than the rights of humanity, which every Government honors itself in respecting, and which no Government is justified in resigning on behalf of those under its care and authority."[82] That morning, lacking sleep, Wilson reviewed this second note with Bryan and Lansing, and with the entire cabinet.

The second note was not delivered until June 9. In the interim, Bryan met with Wilson again, inveigled against sending the second note, and pressed for a warning against traveling in liners carrying contraband. When Wilson refused, Bryan announced his firm decision to resign. Highly agitated, Bryan told Wilson that "Col. House has been secretary of state, not I, and I have never had your full confidence."[83] Readers of the *New York Times* awoke on the morning of the ninth to a banner headline: "*BRYAN RESIGNS AS SECRETARY OF STATE, TELLING WILSON HE CANNOT SIGN THE NEW NOTE TO GERMANY 'IN FAIRNESS TO THE CAUSE NEAREST MY HEART, PREVENTION OF WAR.' LANSING, ACTING SECRETARY, TO SIGN AND SEND IT TODAY.*"[84] Bryan did not go quietly, issuing a series of statements. The first, delivered on June 10, stated, in part: "Among the influences which Governments employ in dealing with each other are two which are pre-eminent and antagonistic—force and persuasion...Force represents the old system—the system that must pass away.... If I correctly interpret the note to Germany, it conforms to the standards of the old system rather than to the rules of the new, and I cheerfully admit that it is abundantly supported by precedents—precedents written in blood upon almost every page of human history."[85]

Bethmann Hollweg did not respond to the second note until the second week of July, a reply made difficult by the fact that his government had already secretly determined that it would not torpedo passenger liners. An absurd offer was made to have German ships lying at anchor in American ports ferry Americans across the Atlantic. But Bethmann Hollweg refused to call a halt to all submarine warfare. Wilson responded with a *third* note at the end of July. In his strongest language yet, Wilson insisted that submarines observe the international rules of naval warfare, viz., giving warnings and providing time for civilians to disembark from threatened ships. He made it clear that he would break diplomatic relations if there was a repeat of the *Lusitania*. But by now almost three months had elapsed since the *Lusitania* went down, and the fervor had subsided. Bethmann Hollweg decided not to respond at all to the third note, and the affair seemed to peter out.

Then, on August 18, the commander of *U-24*, mistaking the British liner *Arabic* for a cargo ship, torpedoed it fifty miles southwest of Ireland. Forty-four lives were lost, including two Americans. At first, Bethmann Hollweg wondered if the secret policy against torpedoing passenger liners had been abrogated without his knowledge. Wilson, having threatened Germany with a break in diplomatic relations if there was a repeat of the *Lusitania*, saw in the sinking of the *Arabic* his challenge being answered. He turned to Col. House: "I greatly need your advice what to do in view of the sinking of the *Arabic*, if it turns out to be the simple case it seems…Two things are plain to me: 1. The people of this country count on me to keep them out of the war; 2. It would be a calamity to the world at large if we should be drawn actively into the conflict and so deprived of all disinterested influence over the settlement."[86] House responded immediately, stiffening Wilson: "Our people do not want war, but even less do they want you to recede from the position you have taken. Neither do they want to shirk the responsibility which should be ours. Your first note to Germany after the sinking of the *Lusitania* made you not only the first citizen of America, but the first citizen of the world. If by any word or act you should hurt our pride of nationality you would lose your commanding position over night."[87]

What Wilson did was issue a press release, published on the front page of the *New York World* on August 23. In it, Wilson averred that *if* an investigation revealed that the German government had acted wantonly in the sinking of the *Arabic*, it *would* result in a break in diplomatic relations. With this, Bethmann Hollweg demanded that the kaiser finally resolve the issue of submarine warfare. Wilhelm was then ensconced in his residence at Pless Castle, now located in southwestern Poland. Von Tirpitz, von Falkenhayn and other naval and military leaders attended. Bethmann Hollweg pressed his case, that it was insane to have the mistake of a submarine commander result in a war with the Americans. The admirals pushed back, claiming that requiring submarine commanders to give warning to passenger liners was impracticable and dangerous, and would effectively deprive them of the use of the submarine. The kaiser vacillated, but eventually Bethmann Hollweg won out. It was agreed that the government would make public the policy that had been decided in early June, that no passenger liner would be torpedoed unless passengers and crew had first been warned and allowed safe passage off the ship. The government failed to state if the sinking of the *Arabic* had been a mistake. To Wilson, the crisis was over. Germany would never be able to conclude its investigation. At the end of August, the British sank *U-24*, its crew and captain going down with it.

As early as January, 1915, Lloyd George had proposed to the War Council, the military sub-committee of the cabinet, that an expedition be mounted to land at Salonika. The next month (while still chancellor of the exchequer) he traveled to Paris, ostensibly to discuss war loans. While there, he lobbied Poincaré, Viviani, Briand and Delcassé for the Salonika operation, his argument being that Austria-Hungary was the weakest of the Central Powers, and that a successful operation could knock it out of the war. While in Paris, Lloyd George met with Clemenceau, whom he had not met since their brief encounter in Carlsbad in 1909, the meeting in which Clemenceau had urged Great Britain to build an army commensurate with its status as a world power. Lloyd George omitted this second encounter in his *War Memoirs*, but Clemenceau, writing on May 6, the day before the sinking of the *Lusitania*, did not, quoting Lloyd George: "Four years ago, at Carlsbad, you told me what is happening. I did not believe you. I was mistaken, and I have come to tell you." Clemenceau reminisced: "I can still see him…furiously agitated by the desire to prove that if France were truly peaceful, no war test was to be feared. That was the state of mind of English statesmen at that time—deceptions of Germanism to the point of believing that the great danger to the peace of Europe was in the bellicose soul of the French." However: "If there was one man who was not stuck in this lamentable idea that what would happen would not happen, it was Mr. Lloyd George. His superiority is that, having understood his fault, he began with a youthful ardor, despite his white hair, to prepare."[88]

Clemenceau's admiration for Lloyd George blossomed throughout 1915. He exulted when Lloyd George was appointed minister of munitions, writing: "They sought the man who could inspire the most confidence in the country, both by the brilliance of the services rendered and by the soundness of his views and the firmness of his character. They went to M. Lloyd George, whose name, at this particular hour, certainly enjoys the greatest authority in the whole country."[89] When, in July, Lloyd George settled a strike in the South Wales coalfields, Clemenceau opined: "M. Lloyd George is not a man content to speak. He was able to put an end to the Welsh miners strike, which if prolonged, could have become one of the most formidable incidents of the war.…It was here that M. Lloyd George's power of action manifests itself. The thought of civil strife that could have resulted in bloodshed, must have been hateful to him. It was necessary to persuade. The life of the leader, worthy of his high office, was focused on persuasion, where he would not accept the possibility of failure.[90] And later: "[I]n

England there is a man who is at work, and who only persists in acting on the mind of his compatriots by urging them, with irresistible force, to always act energetically. The readers already know that I am speaking of M. Lloyd George."

At the outbreak of the war, Bulgaria put itself up for auction to the Allies and the Central Powers. Bulgaria wanted what Berlin could offer but what London could not: the return to Bulgaria of the territory she had lost to Serbia in the Second Balkan War. In July, Bulgaria signed on with the Central Powers and Serbia's position became desperate. Greece's president, Eleftherios Venezelos, asked the Allies to intervene on the side of Serbia, which prompted Greece's pro-German king, Constantine, to dismiss Venezelos. But Greece was not powerful enough to resist an Allied invasion, and on October 5, French and British troops, mostly withdrawn from Gallipoli, landed at Salonika. Two days later, the Bulgarian army, 250,000 strong, invaded Serbia from the west, as a combined German-Austrian force of 200,000 invaded from the north. The rout was on, the Serbs retreating into Albania. On October 9, German and Austrian forces entered Belgrade.

At this point, the British—Lloyd George included—were having second thoughts about Salonika, and considered pulling out. Briand, however, argued that maintaining the operation would keep Greece and Romania neutral, and would ease pressure on their Russian ally. The issue became who would lead the operation, and the issue was political. One of the many generals Joffre had dismissed was Maurice Paul Sarrail, openly Socialist and very well connected with the Republican left in the Chamber. Yielding to pressure (Joffre detested Sarrail), Joffre offered him a command in the Dardanelles, but when that venture collapsed he was offered instead the command at Salonika. Sarrail, unsure if he should accept, asked Clemenceau's advice. "Tell Millerand you definitely won't go," Clemenceau advised. When Sarrail said that he believed in the success of the operation, Clemenceau replied: "But, my poor fellow, you don't understand, then, that you're being drawn into a trap? There never will be an Allied front in the East....We haven't enough troops in France. The Germans are at Noyon, and England will never follow us into such a harebrained scheme."[91] Sarrail didn't take the advice. He arrived on October 12, and with only one French and one British division at his command, he immediately set out to relieve the pressure on the Serbs by advancing north into Macedonia. The Bulgarians were too strongly entrenched in their mountain strongholds, and by the middle of December he was back in Salonika, where he began. Clemenceau lamented, in *L'Homme Libre*: "Is it so difficult to understand that with the French front in the position that it is, the conquest of France is the vital concern of the war, which can end only with a German victory in France or a French victory in Germany?"[92]

In late October, René Viviani's government collapsed, partly as a result of the failure of the Salonika operation, partly as a result of the failure of Joffre's September offensives. Viviani was replaced by Briand, for what would be his *fifth* (but not last) turn as prime minister. Joffre's spokesman, Millerand, was out as minister of war, replaced by Gen. Joseph Galleini, selected to watch over Joffre. Delcassé was out as foreign minister, Briand electing to be his own foreign minister. Briand asked Clemenceau to accept a ministry, and Clemenceau again refused. There were so many octogenarians and septuagenarians in Briand's cabinet that it was reported that Clemenceau refused Briand's offer on the ground that he was "too young."[93] But with Briand as prime minister, there was no chance that the Salonika operation would be terminated; more troops were added. In 1917, when there were still 500,000 Allied troops in Salonika with nothing to do, Clemenceau called Sarrail's troops "the gardeners of Salonika."[94]

Joffre's September offensive in northeast France kicked off on September 25. It was a combined British-French operation, including the Battle of Loos, the Third Battle of Artois and the Second Battle of Champagne. One of the corps commanders at Loos, Gen. Henry Rawlinson, opined before the battle that "it will cost us dearly, and we will not get very far."[95] That summarized Joffre's September offensive in its entirety. After some initial successes, the Germans were always able to regroup and recover whatever precious yards had been gained in the initial hours. The cost in blood was frightful. By the time Joffre called off the campaign in November, the French had suffered 143,000 casualties. Joffre claimed that the Germans had suffered more. It was a lie. The French had been fighting for fifteen months, approximately the same number of months as the Americans after they entered the war in 1917. Yet France, with a population only a third of the United States, would lose *seven times* as many men as would the Americans. By the end of 1915, France had suffered two million casualties, of whom 600,000 were dead, as many dead as the British would lose in the entire war.[96] And things were about to get worse.

Much worse.

15

....

LA VOIE SACRÉE

Today the word peace is a sacrilege.

—Aristide Briand

Woodrow Wilson entered the White House with no experience and little interest in foreign affairs. He became president decades before the creation of the National Security Council. He had no assistant to the president for national security affairs. There were not as yet any civilian intelligence agencies. At the State Department Wilson could call on the secretary—Robert Lansing—and a counselor; there were no undersecretaries. (By the time Franklin Roosevelt became president, he had a talented "brain trust" he could call upon.) But it is doubtful that Wilson would have called on any of these men had their offices then existed; Wilson preferred to work alone. He had a cabinet, but the secretaries usually learned of important policy decisions only after the fact, often from the newspapers. Only rarely did he call in men for the private chats that other presidents before and since would deem so beneficial. He dined with his family. The British ambassador, Sir Cecil Spring Rice, wrote to his Foreign Office: "The President rarely sees anybody. He practically never sees ambassadors, and when he does, exchanges no ideas with them. Mr. Lansing is treated as a clerk who receives orders which he has to obey at once and without question."[1] Walter Hines Page wrote of him: "He does his own thinking, untouched by other men's ideas. He receives nothing from the outside."[2]

The notable exception was Wilson's reliance on Col. House, who Wilson entrusted implicitly and to whom Wilson outsourced much of the conduct of foreign affairs. But House was every bit the amateur that Wilson was; he lived in New York City and refused to venture into the capital during the summer months. For much of 1916, Wilson's principal foreign policy functionaries, House and Lansing, would work at cross-purposes, confusing the Allies, as the presidential election impended, causing both the Allies and the Central Powers to suspect that Wilson's words and deeds were motivated by domestic politics. And all of this occurred as two of the greatest battles in human history, the French defense at Verdun and the Anglo-French offensive on the Somme, raged.

The sinking of the *Lusitania* did not end House's goal of mediating an end to the war; it only interrupted it. In June, 1915, after House returned from Europe, he met with Wilson. They agreed that they would leave it to House to determine when it would be "propitious" for House to return to Europe. They also agreed that Lansing would be a good man to replace the recently-departed Bryan as secretary of state. They considered Lansing an "office man" who would leave the conduct of foreign affairs to Wilson and House.

The summer and fall of 1915 was the time of Wilson's intense courtship of Edith Bolling Galt. Wilson wrote her constantly, some of his letters running to twenty pages. Tumulty warned him that he might lose the election if he married Mrs. Galt so soon after Ellen's death. Wilson ignored the advice. House wrote in his diary in November that Wilson was "so engrossed with his fiancée that he is neglecting business."[3] As Wilson's mind was occupied with his fiancée, House's was occupied with the war, and he hit upon a plan for ending it. It coincided with the failure of the Allied offensives on the Western front and the collapse of the Russian armies in the East. House's plan was to propose to the Allies a plan for an end to the war based upon the *status quo ante* and an end to militarism and navalism. The Allies would need to be convinced to accept the plan, and if they did, the plan would be presented to the Central Powers. If Germany accepted, the war would end. If it refused, the United States would break off diplomatic relations and enter the war on the side of the Allies. He broached the idea to Sir Edward Grey in a September 3 letter, asking, "Will you not advise me?"[4]

On October 8, Wilson and House met in House's apartment in New York City. The occasion was the presentation of the engagement ring to Mrs. Galt. As House and Wilson were dressing for dinner, House presented the plan to Wilson. House later recorded in his diary that Wilson was "startled" by the plan, but "He seemed to acquiesce by silence. I had no time to push it further, for our entire conversation lasted no more than twenty minutes."[5] They then left for dinner, then to the theater. They met again the next morning, as House accompanied Wilson to the train station, but did not discuss the matter further.

House received Grey's reply to his September 3 letter on October 13. It was dated September 22, indicating that Grey was in no great hurry to respond. As he had been at all times in the past and would again be in the future, Grey was courteous and friendly. He replied that "I cannot answer without consulting the Cabinet here and the Governments of the Allies," adding that "It would not be easy to do that, unless I was in a position to say that the President really was prepared to make such a proposal..."[6] Grey was thinking about American mediation *after* the war, not during it, adding: "To me the great object of securing the elimination of militarism and navalism is to get security for the future against aggressive war. How much are the United States prepared to do in this direction? Would the President propose that there should be a League of Nations binding themselves to side against warfare on sea or land...or which refused, in case of dispute to adopt some other method of settlement than that of war...?"

House advised Wilson of Grey's letter, and Wilson authorized House to respond. House then drafted what he considered one of the most important letters he had ever drafted, for Wilson's review: "It has occurred to me that the time may soon come when this Government should intervene between the belligerents and demand that peace parleys begin upon the broad basis of the elimination of militarism and navalism....In my opinion, it would be a world-wide calamity if the war should continue to a point where the Allies could not with the aid of the United States bring about a peace along the lines you and I have so often discussed. What I want you to know is that whenever you consider the time is propitious for this intervention I will propose it to the President. He may then desire me to go to Europe in order that a more intimate understanding as to procedure may be had....I would not let Berlin know of course of any understanding had with the Allies, but would rather lead them to think that our proposal would be rejected by the Allies. This might induce Berlin to accept the proposal, but if they did not do so it would nevertheless be the purpose to intervene. If the Central Powers were still obdurate, it would *probably* be necessary for us to join the Allies and force the issue."[7] Wilson inserted the "probably" himself, and approved the rest.

Grey's response was received on November 11. Courteous as ever, Grey advised House that "I wish you were here, so that we could talk things over, but the situation at the moment and the feelings here and among the Allies, and in Germany so far as I know, do not justify me in urging you to come on the ground that your presence would have any practical result at the moment."[8] House relayed Grey's response, and his own disappointment, to Wilson, lamenting that the proposal "should have met a warmer reception," and that "the British are in many ways dull."[9] Just who was being "dull" is open to debate. What House and Wilson could not then and throughout 1916 allow themselves to understand was that there was then absolutely no desire on the part of the Allies to have Wilson or anyone else mediate an end to the war. The British were raising a million-man army that they had not yet deployed; the French were still filled with hope of evicting the Germans from their territories seized in 1914 and in 1870. But the Allies, so reliant on American munitions, the raw materials used to make munitions, and, later, on American cash, could not risk alienating the Americans, even as they prevented American goods from reaching German ports. The man charged with this delicate mission was Sir Edward Grey.

In early December, House received a letter from James Bryce—Viscount Bryce— the British Liberal statesman and historian. Bryce, whose *The American Commonwealth* had inspired the young Woodrow Wilson, had served as Great Britain's ambassador to Washington. As president of Princeton, Wilson had arranged for Bryce to receive an honorary degree. Now Bryce wrote to House with a warning: "I write to say that there is not the slightest change in the British sentiment regarding the duty and necessity of prosecuting the war with the utmost vigour, and listening to no suggestions for negotiations with the German Government....We know that they would not listen to any terms we could propose, at the best, the evacuation of Belgium with ample compensation for her for all she has suffered, and also, of course, the evacuation of Northern France and Luxemburg....She on the other hand would insist on indemnities, for without them bankruptcy stares her in the face. So there is nothing for it but to fight on."[10] Bryce's advice was ignored.

According to House, Wilson saw the problem not as the belligerents' lack of desire to come to terms, but the inability of the respective ambassadors, Spring Rice for the British and Bernstorff for the Germans, to effectively communicate House's plan for mediation. Wilson had so little faith in Spring Rice that he threatened to have him recalled. House recorded in his diary in mid-December that: "I asked him [Wilson] to remember the slowness of the British mind as exhibited even in such a crisis as this war."[11] Wilson wanted House to go to Europe "immediately," and House concurred, in order "to save the British from their own obtuseness."[12] This was not the first or the last time that House would remind Wilson how superior in intellect and temperament he felt he was to his European counterparts, writing to Wilson "It is hard to estimate the effect of flattery and politeness upon Europeans, and this may be said of the British and the Germans as well as of the Latin races. They value such things far beyond our conception."[13] But Bernstorff urged Chancellor Bethmann Hollweg to invite House to Berlin, and with that, decision for House to resume his efforts in Europe became fixed.

Before House departed, he asked Wilson for instructions. Wilson, writing on Christmas Eve from his honeymoon in Hot Springs, Virginia, replied that House needed no instructions: "You know what is in my mind and how to interpret it." But Wilson did flesh out what "is in my mind." He advised House: "We are concerned only in the future peace of the world and the guarantees to be given for that. The only possible guarantees…are (a) military and naval disarmament and (b) a league of nations to secure each nation against aggression and maintain the absolute freedom of the seas. If either party to the present war will let us say to the other that they are willing to discuss peace on such terms, it will clearly be our duty to use the utmost moral force to oblige the other party to parley, and I do not see how they could stand in the opinion of the world if they refused."[14] In these instructions, Wilson had no thought of forcing mediation, or going to war with Germany if they refused. House certainly had no remit to discuss territorial readjustments. House knew what was in Wilson's mind. Once in Europe, he would go far beyond it.

House's trip to Europe was not a secret, but its purpose was, and toward that end House and Lansing devised a cover story: House was traveling to Europe to "advise" our ambassadors. "Col. House Sent to Advise Ambassadors," headlined the *New York Times*, noting House's emphatic denial that his trip was in any way a peace mission.[15] Lansing advised the British, French and German governments that House was not on a peace mission. House departed on December 28. While he was at sea the British passenger liner *Persia* exploded and sank off the coast of Crete. Hundreds of lives were lost, including some Americans. It was assumed that it had been torpedoed, and a new crisis loomed. But the issue died down when the surviving passengers testified that they had seen no submarine and no torpedo. An internal explosion may have sent the *Persia* down.

The *Persia* imbroglio masked the fact that a tug-of-war raged within the German government, one that would continue throughout 1916. It pitted the German admiralty and military, who demanded unrestricted submarine warfare, against Bethmann Hollweg and his foreign minister, Gottlieb von Jagow, who feared that a repetition of the *Lusitania* would bring that United States into the war. The man in the middle was Kaiser Wilhelm. The admirals (supported by Gen. von Falkenhayn) argued that the U-boats could break the stalemate and win the war, that restricting the use of the U-boats rendered them both ineffective and placed their crews at risk if the merchantmen and passenger liners they were stalking were armed. They deprecated the threat of American entry into the war. The American military, they argued, was too weak to help the Allies. The admirals had the support of the German public. Bethmann Hollweg would win the argument through most of 1916, but it was a near thing. And there was always the danger that a negligent or overly aggressive U-boat captain might render the kaiser's decisions moot.

House arrived in London on January 6 and immediately went into separate meetings with Grey and Arthur Balfour, the Tory head of the Admiralty in the Asquith War Cabinet. The next day House cabled Wilson that their [Grey and Balfour] "minds run parallel with ours but I doubt their colleagues."[16] He added: "it would help…if you could cable me some assurance of your willingness to cooperate in a policy seeking to bring about and maintain permanent peace among civilized nations."[17] In light of Viscount Bryce's warning that there was absolutely no desire on anyone's part for negotiations with the Germans, it is difficult to imagine how House could have concluded that Grey's and Balfour's minds ran "parallel" with his. Indeed, even to be seen engaging in talks with House was perilous. House could not set foot in the Foreign Office. Ministers who met with House in a private residence needed to arrive and leave separately. Of course, House had to be treated with delicacy. He was the emissary of the man who controlled the Allies' access to munitions and the raw materials needed to make the munitions without which Great Britain could not survive. Nonetheless, Wilson dutifully supplied House with the cable he had requested, replying on January 9: "Your cable of yesterday received. Would be glad if you would convey my assurance that I shall be willing and glad when the opportunity comes to cooperate in a policy seeking to bring about and maintain permanent peace among civilized nations."[18]

Throughout the time that House was in Europe, Secretary of State Lansing was negotiating with German Ambassador Bernstorff over the *Lusitania*. Lansing was taking a hardball approach. Bethmann Hollweg was willing to pay reparations to the families of the victims, and express "regrets." But in light of Bethmann Hollweg's own difficulties with his admirals, Bethmann Hollweg would not—could not—admit responsibility for the sinking, which was the one thing Lansing insisted upon. Lansing advised Wilson that if the Germans refused to accept responsibility, the United States should sever diplomatic relations with Germany, which might well lead to war. What made Lansing believe that the American people, who did not favor going to war with Germany in the immediate aftermath of the sinking, would agree to go to war *seven months* later, when the issue had all but been forgotten, is anyone's guess. Wilson tried to calm down his secretary of state, asking: "Do you think we could frame a handsome apology from Germany which we could accept without explicit disavowal…"[19] The fact of Lansing's negotiations over the *Lusitania* was an open secret, and became entangled in British minds with Lansing's next project, that of the arming of merchant ships.

On the day after House arrived in London, and simultaneous with his *Lusitania* negotiations, Lansing proposed a new policy regarding armed merchant ships. Under international maritime law, a merchant ship could arm itself for its *defense*. Anything more, and it could be considered a *warship*. But with the advent of the submarine, Lansing considered this to be outdated and unfair…to the submarine! He argued that if a merchant ship was heavily armed, a submarine would be defenseless if it obeyed the rules requiring the giving of notice and allowing crew to abandon before sinking the vessel. The submarine's only weapon in the face of an armed merchant ship was stealth; the ability to submerge and torpedo its quarry before the surface ship could bring its guns to bear. Lansing proposed a *modus vivendi*: All merchant ships would be prohibited from carrying any weapons at all, offensive or defensive. Once disarmed, a submarine commander would not need to torpedo a merchant ship; he would have no fear of being fired upon if he came to the surface, gave proper warning, and allowed the crew to abandon ship. Similarly, merchant ships would have no fear of being torpedoed. Lansing believed that the British would go along with the *modus vivendi*, since the British had their own submarine force in the Baltic. On January 7, the same day that House cabled Wilson for Wilson's assurances regarding his willingness to cooperate in a plan for peace, Lansing wrote Wilson asking for permission to proceed with his plan to disarm all merchant ships. Implicit in the plan was a threat: If the United States imposed the *modus vivendi* unilaterally, and treated an armed merchant ship as a warship, it could dock in an American port for no more than twenty-four hours. After that, it was subject to seizure.

It did not occur to either Lansing or Wilson that the Allies would consider Lansing's proposed *modus vivendi* as being nothing short of insane. They assumed it would result in nothing more or less than the German U-boat force having free rein to rampage against all Allied shipping. Worse, the Allies would suspect Lansing and Wilson's motives. Coming at the same time as Lansing's *Lusitania* negotiations, they assumed a *quid pro quo*: the disarming of Allied shipping in exchange for German concessions with regard to the *Lusitania*. Lansing finalized his *modus vivendi* in a memo he sent to Wilson on January 17. Wilson gave it his "entire approval" on the same day. Lansing forwarded it to Ambassador Spring Rice the following day. The day after that, it landed on Sir Edward Grey's desk.

House spent the week of January 10 to the fifteenth in meetings with members of the War Cabinet. On the tenth, he met with Grey and Balfour for lunch. He recorded in his diary that he confided in them the real purpose of his visit, which they met with "suppressed excitement," although House admitted that Balfour seemed "analytical and argumentative," wanting to know the extent of Wilson's commitment to an agreement concerning European affairs, and whether Wilson could obtain American approval for such a plan. House replied that his job would be easier than theirs, since he had only one man to convince, and "I know him sufficiently well to know what he would accept and what refuse."[20] But if Grey and Balfour now knew the real purpose of House's trip, the American ambassador, Walter Hines Page, did not. Nevertheless, the next day Page hosted a dinner in House's honor at the American Embassy. The guests included Lloyd George, Secretary of State for India Austen Chamberlain, and Reginald McKenna, the chancellor of the exchequer. According to House, Page expressed the feeling of the British politicians when he asked House: "what the United States wished Great Britain to do," to which House replied, "The United States would like Great Britain to do those things which would enable the United States to help Great Britain win the war," to which Page replied: "You have answered the question with more cleverness than I had the wit to do."[21]

On January 12 House lunched at the American Embassy with Grey and Undersecretary of State for Foreign Affairs Lord Robert Cecil. The subject of the Anglo-French blockade arose. Grey and Cecil both advised House that if they suggested any easing of the blockade, it would end their political careers. The French, they added, were even more adamant in maintaining the blockade than they were.[22]

Two nights later, House dined in a private room at the Savoy Hotel with Lloyd George, McKenna, Chamberlain and Lord Reading, the Lord Chancellor, who had arranged the meeting. Reading was the former Rufus Isaacs, the barrister who had represented Lloyd George in a number of cases, more than one of which involved Lloyd George being named the co-respondent in a divorce. House did not mention his peace plan to Lloyd George, but Lloyd George became very expansive on the issue of peace, all of which House dutifully reported to Wilson the next day. According to House, he and Lloyd George agreed that "the war could only be ended by your [Wilson's] intervention," but that "George thought intervention should not come until around the 1st of September." At that time, "public opinion in the belligerent countries would force the governments to accept your mediation. George goes even further than I had thought and says that you can dictate terms of peace, and he does not believe any agreement is possible without such dictation." He became specific, saying that Wilson could insist that France and Belgium be evacuated, Alsace-Lorraine be returned to France, Poland be created as an independent nation (with territories taken from Russia, Germany and

Austria) and that Turkey cease to be a European power. But he advised House that England would never agree to the German idea of "freedom of the seas." House then corrected him: "freedom of the seas" was not a German idea, it had been his own. Lloyd George added that "it would enormously strengthen your hand in intervening, for you to put through as large a military and naval program as possible. Not that it would be finally carried out, but because of the power it would give you. He believes that unless you do this your intervention might fail." Lloyd George believed that "[T]his peace should be a peace to make friends and not enemies, meaning that when the war is over, Germany and England should have no differences such as were left after the Franco-Prussian War." House quoted Lloyd George to Wilson as saying: "[N]o man had ever lived with such an opportunity, and that if the world went on for untold centuries, history would record this as the greatest individual act of which it had record."[23] For whatever reason, Lloyd George made no mention of this meeting in his *War Memoirs*.

House met the next afternoon—January 15—with Grey and Balfour. House asked them if they had discussed with Lloyd George his plan for the post-war division of the world and the part Wilson would play in it. They advised House that they had not, and that Lloyd George was still in the dark regarding House's peace plan. House noted in his diary that "Balfour and I did most of the talking—I proposing, he always objecting. He has an argumentative mind....He is unalterably distrustful of Germany, and was forever coming back to whether Germany could be counted upon to keep any bargain or play any game fairly. That, I told him, was beside the mark. What should be done is to get all nations together, and at least a majority of them would play fairly under the lead of Great Britain and the United States; and Germany would be the loser if she failed to keep to her agreement."[24] House wrote Wilson the next day: "I believe I have convinced those to whom I have been able to talk freely, that it is best for all concerned for us to keep out, conserving our strength so at the proper moment, we may lead them out of their troubles."[25] Not for a second did House "convince" anyone in London that the United States should "keep out." No one had even hinted that the United States should intervene. On January 19, House confided to his diary: "I wish Lloyd George was Prime Minister with Sir Edward Grey as Foreign Minister, for I believe then we could do something. The Cabinet are all too conservative, and boldness is needed at this time."[26] That same day, Grey read Lansing's memo proposing the disarmament of British merchant ships.

Grey called on Ambassador Page on the afternoon of the twenty-fifth. Later that day, Page reported to Lansing and Wilson that "I have only once before seen Sir Edward so grave and disappointed and that was when he informed me that the British had sent the

German Government an ultimatum."²⁷ Grey advised Page that he dared not mention Lansing's memorandum in the House of Commons, lest it set off a firestorm. There was nothing Page could tell Grey; Page had been completely in the dark regarding Lansing's proposal.

Still later that day, Grey responded in a telegram marked "Strictly confidential and unofficial" addressed to Ambassador Spring Rice that Spring Rice handed to Lansing on January 27. Grey regarded Lansing's proposal with "painful surprise…it had seemed to me incredible that [the] upshot of controversy about German submarine warfare would be that United States Government would propose to justify and legalise wholesale sinking of merchant vessels by German submarines and to deprive British vessels of the chance of defence which United States Government have hitherto recognised as legitimate.…Defensive armament of merchant vessels does not render them superior in force to submarines: it does not enable them to take the offensive against submarines when guns are placed in the stern: it gives no protection against torpedoes." Grey averred that Lansing's plan would destroy the Anglo-French blockade, and, in a nice touch, noted that if adopted it would prevent the Allies "from applying to present conditions the principles applied by the United States Government itself in the Civil War." He added: "I cannot adequately express the disappointment and dismay with which such an attitude on the part of the United States will be viewed here." Grey instructed Spring Rice to deliver the telegram "privately and unofficially;" he had not yet discussed it with anyone. In handing Grey's telegram to Lansing, Spring Rice opined that the proposed *modus vivendi* would result in German U-boats sinking unarmed ships, and that the United States would do nothing in response, just as the United States had done nothing after the sinking of the *Lusitania* other than to send notes which the Germans would disregard and then sink more ships.

House departed London for Berlin on January 20, making stops in Paris and Geneva. He met with no one in Paris, intending to have meetings on his return. He arrived in Berlin on the twenty-sixth. He met with Bethmann Hollweg, who insisted that Allies would have to pay an indemnity *to Germany* for the evacuation of Belgium. House advised Bethmann Hollweg that this was a complete non-starter. During this stay, House became convinced that Falkenhayn and Tirpitz would win the battle for the kaiser's mind, which would eventually draw the United States into the war. Once again trying to convince Wilson that he was the superior of every man he met, he advised Wilson that Bethmann Hollweg "is an amiable, well-meaning man with limited ability."²⁸ He added in his diary that the copious amounts of beer Bethmann Hollweg consumed didn't affect him, because "his brain was as befuddled at the beginning as it was at the end. Into such hands are the destinies of the people placed."²⁹

House returned to Paris on February 1 and on the third met with Jules Cambon, the seventy-year-old career diplomat then in effective charge of the Quai d'Orsay, Briand having named himself as foreign minister. House astounded Cambon when he advised him that the United States would enter the war *before the end of the year*, provided the Allies refrain from doing anything that would inflame American public opinion against the Allies. Not believing his ears, Cambon had House repeat it. Cambon then read it back to House—in English, to which House replied, "Exactly." With remarkable prescience, House predicted that the incident that would bring the United States into the war would be Germany's resumption of unrestricted submarine warfare.[30]

While House was in Paris, Wilson criss-crossed the Midwest by train, often speaking from the rear platform. His message was preparedness, making the case that if war became inevitable, national honor demanded America be prepared. By January 29 the news of Lansing's proposed *modus vivendi* was public knowledge. House learned of it from Lansing. House advised him to do nothing until he returned.

House met with Cambon and Briand on February 7, a meeting House referred to in his diary as "an important—perhaps the most important, conference I have had during this visit to Europe." Following the meeting, House reported to Wilson that thus far he had been frank only with the British, leaving it to them to bring their Allies along. But he was disappointed with the British "slowness and lack of initiative," and decided therefore to speak frankly with the French. He reported to Wilson that "It was finally understood that in the event the Allies had some notable victories during the spring and summer, you would intervene, and in the event that the tide of war went against them, or remained stationary you would intervene. This conversation is to go no further than between Briand, Cambon and myself and I promised that no one should know of it in America excepting yourself and Lansing." He concluded his report of the meeting: "A great opportunity is yours, my friend, the greatest perhaps that has ever come to any man. The way out seems clear to me and when I can lay the facts before you, I believe it will be clear to you also....In each government I have visited I have found stubbornness, determination, selfishness and cant. One continually hears self-glorification and the highest motives attributed to themselves because of their part in the war. But may I tell you that my observation is that incompetent statesmanship and selfishness is at the bottom of it all."[31] Cambon's report of the meeting is far more detailed than House's. With respect to House's peace plan, "I pointed out to the Colonel...that the moment for such propositions had not arrived. The situation would not allow any initiative of this sort—neither from the military point of view nor from the point of view of public opinion. I added that England and France were not alone in the cause; they had allies, and they could bring up the question of peace only in agreement with them."[32] House communicated none of this to Wilson, who was left with the impression that the Allies were receptive to his mediation. Ignoring Wilson's instructions, House engaged in detailed discussions regarding post-war territorial arrangements. He advised Cambon that he believed Germany could be convinced to return Alsace-Lorraine to France in exchange for territory in Asia Minor. Russia, he opined, could take Armenia, with Turkey disappearing in Europe. Neither Briand nor Cambon were entirely frank with House. Just as Grey had kept the territorial promises made to Italy secret, so did Briand and Cambon. They also failed to mention that as they were meeting, Great Britain and France were in negotiations for the carve-up of the entire Ottoman Empire, which when finalized would result in the Sykes-Picot Treaty. Cambon forwarded his report to his brother, Paul, France's ambassador to Great Britain, who read it to Grey.

House was back in London on February 9, meeting Page for dinner. House took this opportunity to advise Page of the peace plan, of which Page by then was not entirely unaware. The meeting was very unpleasant. Page called the plan "purely academic nonsensical stuff." When House advised Page—falsely—that the French approved of the plan, Page countered that they must have misunderstood it. He told House that the plan was a trick to get the United States into the war, was "a morally weak, indirect scheme, doomed to failure—is wrong, in fact."[33] House wrote in his diary: "The man hinders me in my work because he tries to discourage me and I would totally do so if I were of a different temperament."[34] This bit of self-appraisal was on the mark; nothing discouraged him.

It was no secret that just as House was touring Europe with his peace plan, Lansing's months-long negotiations with Ambassador Bernstorff over the *Lusitania* were being finalized, the *New York Times* headlining on February 9, somewhat prematurely "Lusitania Terms are Agreed Upon; Germany Admitting Full Liability." On the next day, no doubt taking a cue from Lansing's proposed *modus vivendi*, Germany announced that it would begin sinking any and all *armed* Allied merchantmen without warning, effective March 1. The order, Bernstorff advised Lansing, would go out to all U-boat commanders the next day. Negotiations regarding the *Lusitania* were placed on hold. It was in this atmosphere that House went into further meetings with the British.

House met with Asquith, Grey and Balfour for lunch on February 11. He reported to Wilson "They [Asquith and Balfour] were not as amenable to the plan as Grey, but adopted it tentatively and I have little doubt now that when I leave we will have an absolute understanding that you are to propose a peace conference and act as mediator when the time is propitious."[35] But Grey made it clear to House that the time was anything but "propitious," advising House that Grey, personally, believed that the time had come for Wilson to demand a peace conference, but that "this feeling is not shared by the other members of the Cabinet, or if it is, they do not want to express it. Public opinion here would condemn any Minister who would dare endorse such a proposal..."[36]

House met with Asquith, Grey, Balfour and Lloyd George for dinner at the home of Lord Reading on the fourteenth. House recorded in his diary that evening his astonishingly prescient prediction that the Germans "would probably attack the Allies in the west and perhaps at Verdun, and would attack quickly, not waiting for the spring weather to open."[37] It was a lengthy meeting, not concluding until midnight. House summarized in his diary: "While the conference was not conclusive, there was at least a common agreement reached in regard to the essential feature; that is, the President should at some time, to be later agreed upon, call a halt and demand a conference. I could not expect to go beyond that, and I was quite content."[38] House also noted that "I drew George out upon this subject and thoroughly committed him to the idea that the President should act in this capacity."[39] The following day, House wrote in his diary that Grey "congratulated me upon committing Lloyd George so thoroughly to the proposition of intervention by the President.[40]

That is not how Lloyd George recalled the meeting. In his *War Memoirs*, he wrote that he insisted that before there could be any peace conference, there would first have to be an agreement as to the minimum terms that the Allies would accept. "In my opinion," he wrote, "it was undesirable to take such a risk unless we were practically assured beforehand that if Germany proved intractable on these terms the U.S.A. would throw in her lot with us."[41] In light of an interview Lloyd George gave later in the year pouring cold water on any form of American intervention, Lloyd George's version of the meeting is the more plausible.

By February 15, both Wilson and Lansing realized that Lansing's proposed *modus vivendi* regarding armed merchant shipping had been a blunder, and needed to be rescinded. The problem was that in the interim, the Germans had announced they would sink any Allied armed merchantman, making the comedown rather delicate. On that day, Lansing called in reporters to the State Department. He announced that merchant vessels did indeed have the right, under international maritime law, to arm themselves for *defensive* purposes. However, in an attempt to avoid a total humiliation, he noted that "The Government is seriously impressed with the reasonableness of the argument that a merchant vessel should not carry armament of any sort," adding that "[T]he State Department is hoping that the Entente Allies will assent to the disarmament of the merchant craft and be willing to make such a declaration, conditioned upon their Teutonic enemies making a similar declaration....Instead of thus declaring a change in, or departure from, international law permitting merchant vessels to arm for the sole purpose of defense, the Government will rely on existing international law, and stand by the right of belligerent merchant ships to arm only for defense."[42]

Lansing's sudden comedown raises an unanswerable question. Lansing called in the reporters to announce he was abandoning a policy the British deemed to be hateful just at the hour when House was hoping to conclude an agreement to open the way for Wilson to mediate an end to the war. Were the two related? When, later that day, House learned of Lansing's reversal, he cabled Wilson: "There is great feeling against disarming merchantmen and I am glad you are holding this in abeyance."[43]

House and Grey met on February 17 and concluded what became known as the "House-Grey Memorandum." It was not a treaty; it was not even an agreement. It was initialed only by Grey, and was intended as his memorandum to the War Cabinet. It is worth reading in full:

"Confidential:

"Colonel House told me that President Wilson was ready on hearing from France and England that the moment was opportune, to propose that a Conference should be summoned to put an end to the war. Should the Allies accept this proposal, and should Germany refuse it, the United States would probably enter the war against Germany.

"Colonel House expressed the opinion that, if such a conference met, it would secure peace not unfavorable to the Allies, and if it failed to secure peace, the United States would leave the conference as a belligerent on the side of the Allies, if Germany was unreasonable. Colonel House expressed an opinion decidedly favorable to the restoration of Belgium, the transfer of Alsace and Lorraine to France, and the acquisition of Russia of an outlet to the sea, though he thought that the loss of territory incurred by Germany in one place would have to be compensated to her by concessions to her in other places outside Europe. If the Allies delayed accepting the offer of President Wilson, and if, later on, the course of the war was so unfavorable to them that the intervention of the United States would not be effective, the United States would probably disinterest themselves in Europe and look to their protection in their own way.

"I said that I felt that the statement, coming from the President of the United States to be a matter of such importance that I must inform the Prime Minister and my colleagues; but that I could say nothing until I had received their consideration. The British Government could under no circumstances, accept or make any proposal except in consultation or agreement with the Allies. I thought that the Cabinet would probably feel that the present situation would not justify them in approaching their Allies on this subject at the present moment; but as Colonel House had had an intimate conversation with M. Briand and M. Jules Cambon in Paris, I should think it right to tell M. Briand privately through the French Ambassador in London, what Colonel House has said to us; and I should, of course, whenever there was an opportunity be ready to talk the matter over with Briand if he desired it."

[Initialled]

E.G.

In his memoirs, Grey made a casual reference to Wilson's acceptance of the memorandum, noting that Wilson modified it by adding one word.[44] Grey failed to mention what that one word was. In the second paragraph, Wilson inserted the word "probably" between "would" and "leave," so that the final memorandum read that the United States "would probably leave the conference as a belligerent on the side of the Allies, if Germany was unreasonable." Lloyd George thought little of the memorandum, since the addition of "probably" made it innocuous. When Paul Cambon read it, he asked Grey if it was serious, or merely a way to influence Britain and France favorably to the president, "in order that it might have a bearing upon the presidential campaign."[45] Great Britain's ambassador to France, Lord Bertie, always cynical of Wilson's motives, believed that House was on an "electioneering mission" so that Wilson could "pose as the arbiter of the destinies of Europe and at the same time obtain great advantages for America."[46] Grey's own opinion of the memorandum was more nuanced. The fact that he failed to show it to his Allies before he initialed it underscores the fact that it bound the Allies to nothing. In a March 5 letter to Bertie, he reminded Bertie that as long as the Allies believed they could win the war without Wilson's intervention, there would be no conference for Wilson to call. Even if the war produced a stalemate, if the Allies felt they could do better without Wilson, they could still keep Wilson on the sidelines, since they controlled when it was "opportune" to "propose a conference." He advised Bertie that these were not times "in which to neglect any profitable friend."[47]

House's and Wilson's reactions to the memorandum were very different. They both believed the House-Grey Memorandum was a significant event, and were ecstatic at its achievement. They both believed that the Allies *wanted* Wilson to intervene, with only the timing to be determined. House believed the time was near, remarking to one British politician before he departed London that the United States would soon be "in the thick of it," perhaps within thirty days.[48]

The very different reactions to the House-Grey Memorandum on the opposite sides of the Atlantic highlight their very different perceptions of the war itself. Wilson could not understand that to the British and the French the war was not about territories, or colonies, or markets, all of which were amenable to negotiation. To them, the war was about finally ridding the continent of Europe of Prussian militarism, so that as the casualties and the costs skyrocketed, the Allies became more certain of the need to rid Europe of the German bacillus, not less so. Conversely, the British and the French failed to grasp that the Americans, with their isolationist traditions, could not view the war as they did. Thus, the British and the French could only assume that Wilson was motivated solely to protect American commercial interests and to foster his own re-election. Wilson and House never imagined that British and French cordiality and their seeming acceptance of his offers of mediation were motivated principally not to offend the industrial behemoth without whose continued support the war was lost.

Georges Clemenceau could not conceal his contempt for Wilson's proposals. As yet unaware that Lansing had the day before rescinded the proposed *modus vivendi,* in a February 17 editorial titled "President-Candidate," underscoring his belief that Wilson's actions were motivated by the upcoming election, he began: "The good president scratches his head. Is there no way of reconciling the conflicting interests? Once upon a time, lawyers used to make a game of it. And now, because the Germans have roughed up Belgium and northern France a bit, is there not some way to make the Belgians, the French and even the British themselves understand that with a few good words of submissiveness, all this can be arranged?" He continued: "A friend of Col. House told me that the president's desire was first to determine whether the offer of a Wilsonian mediation was likely to be accepted," and that House advised Wilson that it would not. "So how—peace through Mr. Wilson's mediation being recognized as impossible—could the eminent statesman believe that, thanks to his support in the service of Germany, a peace of violence could be imposed on us?" With respect to

Lansing's proposed *modus vivendi*, Clemenceau asked if Wilson expected Great Britain and France to "send ships, men, defenseless cargo in front of German submarines, according to the invitation of the Secretary of State? The *Lusitania* was not armed, and carried no munitions."[49]

Early in the morning of February 21, General Erich von Falkenhayn launched his artillery against the fortress city of Verdun, 150 miles east of Paris. It was the largest artillery bombardment in history. Shells fired from twelve hundred guns on an eight-mile sector rained down on the French *poilus* on the east bank of the Meuse at the rate of two hundred per minute. Some of the guns could hurl a two-thousand pound shell a distance of twenty miles. The shell bursts could be heard a hundred miles away. Then, in the afternoon, the bombardment ceased and the infantry advanced.

Verdun occupied a place in French consciousness far beyond its limited military value. As Churchill wrote: "Verdun was the historical scene of the triumph of Gaul over the Teuton. It was regarded throughout France as the corner-stone in the French rampart against Germany…Honor would compel them to defend positions which a cool view of war would have yielded at a certain price."[50] This was von Falkenhayn's strategy. His goal was not to seize ground or win a battle; it was to create casualties. "The forces of France," he said, "will bleed to death whether we reach our goal or not."[51] He would destroy the French Army, and in doing so he would destroy France. The French had already suffered *two million* casualties before the battle began; there were no reserves.

The assault should not have come as a surprise. There was intelligence from captured German soldiers and aerial reconnaissance showing the German build-up around Verdun. General Joffre maintained that everything was in a perfect state of readiness. But after the death toll spiraled upwards in the first days of the battle (the French lost twenty-three thousand killed in the first five days), on February 24 Joffre decided to abandon Verdun as being militarily unnecessary. At that moment, Briand realized that his government would collapse if Verdun were abandoned. He summoned his chauffeur and raced to Joffre's headquarters at Chantilly, thirty-five miles north. He demanded to see Joffre. He was advised that Joffre was asleep and could not be awakened. He insisted on seeing Joffre—now. Joffre was roused and Briand advised the sleepy Joffre and his fellow officers: "If you abandon Verdun I sack you all on the spot." Joffre replied: "We fight to the end."[52]

Thus was cemented in place von Falkenhayn's strategy of a battle of attrition. To give an idea of its size and scope, the most consequential battle of the American Civil War, the Battle of Gettysburg, lasted three days, and resulted in 51,000 casualties.

The Battle of Verdun resulted in approximately 976,000 casualties, and raged for ten months. This battle, and the Battle of the Somme that began in July, were background to the actions of every French and British politician in 1916.

Joffre was not slow to act. He immediately formed a new Army of Verdun, appointing Gen. Henri-Phillipe Pétain to head up the defense. Pétain had never adhered to the *attaque-a-outrance* school of offensive action, and it hindered his military career. He began the war as a fifty-eight-year-old colonel. But he was an organizational genius. The rail lines in eastern France all ran the wrong way. The only means of supplying Verdun was by a narrow road from the railhead in the town of Bar-le-Duc, southwest of Verdun. Pétain improved the road and ordered the *poilus* off the road, freeing the road for the trucks bringing supplies. The little road that became Verdun's lifeline became known as *"la voie sacrée"*—the sacred way.

Two days into the battle, Clemenceau co-chaired a meeting of French and British parliamentarians in Paris. He addressed the conferees: "We did not want war, *we want it now*, and shall want it as long as need be. That total victory will repay us for bloodshed such as no soul in history has ever seen."[53]

As early as the summer of 1915, Lloyd George had become dissatisfied with Asquith's lackadaisical conduct of the war. He told a friend: "The prime minister cannot make up his mind. Having formed the War Committee, he rendered it practically useless by bringing in the cabinet on all important decisions."[54] The result was that some ministers spent too much time in meetings and not enough running their departments. Asquith's method of conducting meetings was to solicit each man's opinion, and then defer his decision until the next meeting. Asquith would often conclude a meeting not when the time was appropriate, but by the hands of the clock.

The issue that divided Lloyd George from most Liberals and from Asquith himself was conscription. In all its wars, the British had never forced men into the ranks. It was anathema to most Liberals, and Lloyd George himself was initially opposed to it. But then the number of men answering Kitchener's call to service began to decline. A hundred thirty-five thousand enlisted in May, 1915, which declined to ninety-five thousand by September.[55] By February, 1916, the Army was seventy-five thousand men below strength.[56] Lloyd George changed his mind, and began to press for conscription, causing him to fall out with his fellow Liberals (other than Churchill), aligning him with the Tories. But Asquith was won over. In January, 1916, Asquith introduced the Military Service Bill, which made unmarried men between eighteen and forty-one (later increased to fifty-one) subject to call. Initially, the

Liberals opposed it, but in the end few voted against. By June, 1916, Lloyd George and the Tories favored extending conscription to married men, which even Asquith opposed. Lloyd George threatened to resign on the issue, and Asquith relented. The Liberal press accused Lloyd George of favoring conscription in order to advance himself to be prime minister.

In truth, he wanted to be prime minister. He told a friend: "I do not boast; I am not a braggart. But I will tell you this: if I were put in charge of this war, I would see the thing through; as I shall not be, it will end in a bad peace." He believed there was no alternative, the Tory leader, Bonar Law, being "limp and lifeless," and Balfour "can never make up his mind about anything."[57]

One thing that Lloyd George and Asquith did agree upon was Kitchener's maladministration of the War Office. As early as October, 1915, Lloyd George threatened to resign if Asquith did not rid himself of Kitchener, who was then still immensely popular. Instead, Asquith sent Kitchener on an "inspection" trip to the Middle East, advising Kitchener that he need not hurry back, and took over the War Office himself in Kitchener's absence.

The *Sussex* was a small ship that ferried passengers to and from Folkestone, England, and Dieppe, France. It was British-owned and flew the French flag. It was unarmed. On March 24, 1916, it was torpedoed by a U-boat. It did not sink, and was towed to Boulogne. Of its 325 passengers, eighty died. None were Americans, but four Americans were wounded. The next day, another unarmed steamer, the *Englishman*, was torpedoed. Two days later, two more unarmed British freighters were torpedoed, the *Manchester Engineer* and the *Eagle Point*.

Lansing's immediate reaction was to send an ultimatum to Berlin, demanding that the Germans admit guilt and pay reparations, with the threat of the rupture in relations if they refused. Wilson restrained him. House, residing in New York City and feeling unwell, rushed to the White House anyway, noting in his diary on March 27: "It looks as if we should have to act this time without further parley...I feel I ought to advise the President during these critical hours. I am afraid he will delay and write further notes, when action is what is needed."[58] His fears were justified. He met Wilson for only a few minutes the following day, confiding in his diary: "I am inclined to believe that he intends to make excuses for not acting promptly in this new submarine crisis forced upon him by the sinking of the *Sussex*...He does not seem to realize that one of the main points of criticism against him is that he talks boldly, but acts weakly."[59] House met Wilson again the next day. In the wake of the House-Grey Memorandum, Wilson was hoping to lead a peace conference as a neutral, not as a belligerent. House warned Wilson that if he did nothing, he would lose the support of the Allies, giving him little influence in any peace conference that was convened. Wilson instructed House to see Bernstorff, and to warn Bernstorff that the United States would enter the war if there was no change in German submarine policy.

On April 3, back in New York, House wrote Wilson the letter that, according to House, stirred Wilson to act. He wrote: "Unless the Germans discontinue their present policy a break seems inevitable. Before it comes do you not think it would be well to cable Grey telling him the status of affairs and asking him whether it would not be wise to intervene now rather than to permit the break to come?...Our becoming a belligerent would not be without its advantages in as much as it would strengthen your position at home and with the Allies....Your influence at the peace congress would be enormously enhanced instead of lessened, for we would be the only nation at the conference desiring nothing except the ultimate good of mankind."[60]

House met with Bernstorff, and following the meeting Bernstorff cabled Berlin for instructions. The reply was handed to Lansing on April 10. In it, the Germans denied having torpedoed the *Sussex*. This was the worst possible reply; the United States had conclusive evidence that they had, including affidavits from the survivors.

Upon receipt of House's April 3 letter, Wilson asked Lansing to draft a strong note to the Germans. The note Lansing drafted was so strong as to be a threat of war unless Germany ceased all submarine warfare. It was also insulting, accusing the Germans of a "return to barbarism." Wilson dismissed it, and began his own draft. He wrote and rewrote for a week, and finished on April 18. He began: "A careful, detailed, and scrupulously impartial investigation by naval and military officers of the United States has conclusively established the fact that the *Sussex* was torpedoed without warning or summons to surrender and that the torpedo by which she was struck was of German manufacture." Then, at great length, he reviewed the entire history of German submarine warfare to date. He concluded: "If it is still the purpose of the Imperial Government to prosecute relentless and indiscriminate warfare against vessels of commerce by the use of submarines without regard to what the Government of the United States must consider the sacred and indisputable rules of international law and the universally recognized dictates of humanity, the Government of the United States is at last forced to the conclusion that there is but one course it can pursue. Unless the Imperial Government should now immediately declare and effect an abandonment of its present methods of submarine warfare against passenger and freight-carrying vessels, the Government of the United States shall have no choice but to sever diplomatic relations with the German Empire altogether. This action the Government of the United

States contemplates with the greatest reluctance but feels constrained to take in behalf of humanity and the rights of neutral nations."[61]

It is important to note that Wilson did not demand that Germany abandon submarine warfare altogether, only its "present methods," viz., torpedo attacks without warning and without the opportunity for passengers and crew to abandon ship. There was also no mention of any distinction between armed and unarmed merchant ships.

The next day, Wilson addressed a joint session of Congress. He spoke for sixteen minutes, and was not once interrupted by applause. The speech was essentially the note he had the day before sent off to Germany, often verbatim. He concluded: "This decision I have arrived at with the keenest regret, the possibility of the action I am sure all thoughtful Americans will look forward to with unaffected reluctance. But we cannot forget that we are in some sort and by the force of circumstances the responsible spokesmen of the rights of humanity, and that we cannot remain silent while these rights are in process of being swept utterly away in the maelstrom of this terrible war. We owe it to a due regard for our own rights as a nation, to our sense of duty as a representative of the rights of neutrals the world over, and to a just conception of the rights of mankind to take this stand now with the utmost solemnity and firmness....I have taken it, and taken it with the confidence that it will meet with your approval and support. All sober-minded men must unite in hoping that the Imperial Government, which has in other circumstances stood as the champion of all that we are now contending for in the interest of humanity, may recognize the justice of our demands and meet them in the spirit in which they are made."[62]

The speech was met with widespread approval. Bryan opposed it, believing it would lead the country into war. Clemenceau loved it, believing it would lead the country into war. Whatever contempt Clemenceau had felt for Wilson's foreign policies, both in Mexico and in Europe, was suddenly forgotten. Writing on April 22 in a column he titled "America in Europe," he began with a little faint praise: "It may be Mr. Wilson's decision was a little slow." But he quickly added: "Yet he has made up his mind, and no one will dispute he has done it with impressive dignity. Without any ambiguity, he stated to Germany that, if it did not cease its work of destruction on the merchant shipping of the neutrals, contrary to the law of nations, diplomatic relations would definitely be severed. It is a straight shot that the Kaiser would try in vain to parry with feints of conversation. The president of the American Republic wanted his diplomatic demonstration to be—at the first hour—greatly assisted by the apparatus of the legislature, which did not allow the adversary—that is the word—to expect any help from hesitations or divisions of the country. He thus gives the feeling of a force that will not bend. Sent by the quickest route, the dispatch had arrived at the Wilhelmstrasse when the President had entered the room where the Congress met to receive the communication. In silence that conveyed the gravity of the hour, all the representatives of the American people rose to receive the Chief of State, and who, in a voice clear and firm, read the now-historic document....[T]he passage relating to the *Lusitania* was marked by a momentary pause, where the general emotion was barely able to contain itself. When the President was at the point of his message where he announced the irrevocable willingness to demand, on pain of rupture of relations, the cessation of the criminal German policy, the audience was struck as if by a jolt, whose impression was heightened by the bipartisan silence." He then quoted Wilson's speech at length for his Parisian readers. He concluded his article with a reminiscence: "In my youth, I almost wept in the Nantes theatre at the misfortune of Uncle Tom. The most moving scene of the drama was of the judge who, after sternly pronouncing the verdict required by the law against runaway slaves was, little by little, drawn by the respect of the rights of humanity, to take his gun and free him." In the judge who slowly but certainly came to the rescue of Uncle Tom, Clemenceau saw Wilson. "This is what makes, today, the high moral power of the great American republic, throwing down the gauntlet as champion of the neutral countries, at the savage work of German domination, which claims to put Germany alone above all considerations of humanity...Champion of neutrals! Yes, it is certainly a qualification that one can be proud of, when one has taken in hand the weapon of right, and that one feels in the heart that he will use it."[63]

Wilson's ultimatum intensified the split between Bethmann Hollweg and the military, with Wilhelm once again in the middle. The German public, largely supportive of the U-boat campaign, also needed to be considered. Bethmann Hollweg feared that a complete capitulation to the American president would bring down his government. With the Battle of Verdun raging, von Falkenhayn presented the kaiser with an astounding argument in favor of rejection of Wilson's ultimatum: The attack on Verdun, he said, had been predicated on submarine warfare weakening the Allies. If the U-boats had to surface and give warning, the assault on Verdun would have to be halted. Wilhelm turned to Bethmann Hollweg: "You have to choose between America and Verdun."[64]

In the end, Bethmann Hollweg convinced the kaiser that unrestricted submarine warfare was not worth the risk of bringing the United States into the war. In a meeting on May 1, they agreed that the German public would not accept a total capitulation. The note that Bethmann Hollweg sent in reply to Wilson's ultimatum was, therefore, harsh. Bethmann Hollweg made the fatuous claim that Germany's submarine campaign was conducted in self-defense, to counter the British blockade: "The German Government cannot but reiterate its regret that the sentiments of humanity which the Government of the United States extends with such fervor to the unhappy victims of submarine warfare are not extended with the same warmth of feeling to the many millions of men and children who, according to the avowed intentions of the British Government, shall be starved..."[65] But the ultimatum was accepted. Merchant ships would not be sunk "without warning and without saving human lives, unless these ships attempt to escape or offer resistance." But this acceptance was conditioned on the United States demanding that the British terminate their blockade, and "Should the steps taken by the Government of the United States not attain the object it desires to have the laws of humanity followed by all the belligerent nations, the German Government would then be facing a new situation in which it must reserve itself complete liberty of action."[66]

Wilson asked his advisors what they thought of the German note. Lansing thought it not sufficient and that the United States should sever relations, likely leading to war. House advised Wilson that "I do not see how we can break with Germany on this note," and counseled that Wilson need not even reply.[67] Wilson rejected Lansing's advice, but also rejected House's advice not to reply. Wilson drafted a reply himself, rejecting the notion that the rights of non-combatants were contingent on the doings of third parties.

The *Sussex* affair was an enormous political victory for Wilson. He had demonstrated steady resolve without seeming warlike. To a public that more than anything wanted to remain out of the war, he had accomplished that while achieving a diplomatic victory. In the months that followed, with the threat of Americans dying at sea at the hands of U-boat commanders abated; German-American relations improved. At the same time, Anglo-American relations worsened. American attitudes towards the British became particularly strained over an issue that refused to die: Ireland.

On Easter Monday, April 24, 1916, a group of armed men appeared in front of the Dublin general post office. In what became known as the "Easter Rising," they proclaimed the Irish republic. British forces quickly and brutally suppressed the "Rising." Sixteen of the "leaders" of the rebellion were quickly court-martialed. Then, in groups of two or three over the next few days, they were executed. Some of the men executed had little to do with the uprising; some of the leaders suffered no punishment. Irish public opinion, which initially had not supported the uprising, turned against the British. Asquith ordered the executions halted. After the man who had been the chief secretary for Ireland resigned, Asquith looked for a replacement. He turned to Lloyd George, telling him: "It is a unique opportunity and there is no one else who could do so much to bring about a permanent solution."[68] Lloyd George was then still the minister of munitions, and wished to remain as such. He effectively became the interim chief secretary for Ireland, without the title.

Lloyd George believed that the Irish uprising would hurt the war effort. He also saw that the executions were damaging Anglo-American relations, which were growing worse over the tightening blockade, just as German-American relations were improving. He resolved to settle it, quickly. He negotiated a deal with Sir Edward Carson, the Unionist leader, which was essentially the deal negotiated in 1914 which was shelved at the outbreak of the war. The six Ulster counties would remain in the United Kingdom; the rest of Ireland would gain Home Rule to last until one year following the end of the war, which could be extended if Parliament did not act during that time on Ireland's permanent status. During that time, Ireland would keep its seats in the House of Commons. He acted so quickly that he failed to get cabinet consent before announcing the deal, effectively presenting the Tories in the government, who opposed Home Rule, with a *fait accompli*. The deal died in the House of Commons, when Tories, opposed letting Ireland keep its seats during the period of Home Rule, killed it.

Lloyd George's brief service as chief secretary for Ireland may have saved his life. In early June, Asquith sent Kitchener on a military mission to Russia. Lloyd George was scheduled to accompany him, but begged off when he received the appointment for Ireland. On June 5, the *Hampshire*, the ship carrying Kitchener, hit a mine in the North Sea, and went down. Lloyd George wrote his brother: "I used to get on well with Kitchener. Great driving force but no mental powers—that is my reading of him. Hard eyes—relentless—without a glimmer of human kindness."[69] At first, Asquith appointed himself as head of the War Office. He wanted Lloyd George to assume the post. The problem was that early in 1916, in order to circumvent Kitchener's inept handling of the ministry, Asquith had issued an Order in Council to the effect that military decisions would be made by the Chief of the Imperial General Staff (C.I.G.S.), reporting directly to the Cabinet, effectively neutering the secretary of state for war. Lloyd George was reluctant to leave the ministry of munitions, where he had real power, for a ministry where he would be a figurehead. He lobbied to have the former powers of the War Office restored. The man who was the C.I.G.S., Gen. Sir William Robertson, the rare general who had risen up from the enlisted ranks, balked. Robertson was opposed to Lloyd George at the War Office in any capacity, even with reduced powers. Asquith backed Robertson. Lloyd George tried to get Bonar Law to take the post. He refused. In the end, Lloyd George relented. The War Office may have been an empty vessel, but it was the steppingstone to 10 Downing Street. Thus, on July 5 he became the secretary of state for war. It was four days after the outbreak of the Battle of the Somme.

Throughout the war, entrenched soldiers had such an enormous advantage over riflemen charging with fixed bayonets that it was said that "three men and a machine gun could defeat a battalion of heroes." In the end, those three men with a machine gun would also bring down the British government and later a government in France.

If anything can be said in defense of Gen. Sir Douglas Haig's decision to send his army over the top directly into the German machine guns it is that he ordered the attack earlier than he had planned in order to relieve the pressure on the French at Verdun. Also, the French could afford to contribute only three divisions to the operation. Nevertheless, Kitchener had opposed the operation as being futile. Lloyd George, writing years later, claimed that he was the only member of the cabinet who echoed Kitchener's pessimism.[70]

The first day, July 1, was the greatest military catastrophe in the history of Great Britain. Twenty thousand were killed that day; another sixty thousand wounded. There were between fifteen and seventeen thousand casualties during the first forty-five *minutes*. These were not the hardened *tommies* of the Marne; these were the "pals" units that had answered Kitchener's call, many of whom had never seen action. The German casualties were a tenth of the British. But by the end of July, the German casualties began to soar apace with the British: 160,000 for the Germans, 200,00 for the Allies. Haig was undaunted. When Lloyd George visited the Somme in September, he saw long rows of mounted cavalry approaching the front. Haig told him that these horsemen were going to crash through the German lines to exploit the holes the infantry would make. It was while at the front that Lloyd George learned that Asquith's son, Raymond, had been killed at Ypres.

Haig finally called it off mid-November. The Allies' farthest advance had been all of seven miles. To gain those seven miles, the Allies suffered six hundred thousand casualties; the Germans suffered an equal number defending those seven miles. The butcher's bill exceeded that of Verdun. It was the bloodiest battle of the war.

After the *Sussex* crisis was put to rest and German-American tensions eased, Anglo-American relations worsened. Wilson decided that it was time to pressure the British on the blockade, just as he had pressured the Germans after the *Sussex* went down. In mid-April, Britain's ambassador to France, Lord Bertie, met with Lloyd George. He noted that Lloyd George was pessimistic about the fighting, but "confident of the ultimate victory and is for continuing the struggle until Germany is thoroughly beaten. No lame peace for him."[71]

Military victory not what Wilson wanted. He wanted the House-Grey Memorandum implemented. On May 10, House cabled Grey, advising him that Wilson wished to "serve humanity in a large way." He added that Wilson was ready to commit the United States to a convention "looking to the maintenance of peace after the war. History would," he added, "bring a grave indictment against British leaders if they failed to act quickly."[72] Grey responded the next day, with the slow walk. He advised that implementing the House-Grey Memorandum was, he felt, "premature." However, this was only his personal opinion and that he had not consulted Asquith, who was in Ireland, "but if you desire it I will consult him upon his return."[73] Grey was well aware of how quickly Asquith made decisions. This response left House "distinctly disappointed," who perceived "a distinct feeling of cock-sureness in the Allies since Verdun."[74] Albeit at a terrible cost, the French defense at Verdun had stiffened and were counterattacking under newly-appointed Gen. Robert Nivelle. On May 16, Wilson wrote House, stating his position. The United States was, he wrote, at a crossroads with the British. There must be a move for peace now, or the United States must demand neutral shipping rights from the British, and obviously Wilson preferred the former to the latter. "Our interest is only in peace and its guarantees…a universal alliance to maintain freedom of the seas and to prevent any war begun either…contrary to treaty covenants or… without warning and full inquiry–virtual guarantee of territorial integrity and political independence." "This crisis," he added, "can not be postponed."[75] In response to Wilson's letter, House cabled Grey, warning that the United States must either "inaugurate some sort of peace discussions," or insist on neutral shipping rights." He added: "Your seeming lack of desire to cooperate with us will chill the enthusiasm here—never, I am afraid to come again, at least in our day." Grey promised to consult with Asquith at once."[76] The next day, Grey provided his answer, in the House of Commons. Speaking extemporaneously, he said: "I have no prepared statement or speech to make. If I believed that the German Government, German opinion, and the War had arrived at a stage when members of the Allied Governments could bring nearer the peace which is essential to their interests, and the interests of Europe, by making speeches about peace, I would prepare any number of them. I do not believe the time has come. I see no sign of it, adding, "The prowess of the French Army through the long battle of Verdun is saving France, and saving her Allies, too. Is this a moment for us to do anything but concentrate upon expressing our determination to give the fullest support in our power to those Allies?"[77] He added that any peace talks could come only after full consultation with all of the Allies.

If there had been any doubt about the position of the Allies, it came earlier in the week. Speaking to a group of Russian parliamentarians, Briand said: "Today the word peace is a sacrilege; if it means that the aggressor will not be punished it would be a dishonor to the Allies."[78] Briand added that peace could come only after a decisive victory which would ensure the world against a similar catastrophe in the future.

House met with Wilson as Grey was speaking in the House of Commons. He wrote in his diary that he had explained to Wilson what France's real feeling was, that "she had best stick to this war until Germany is crushed…she could never again hope to have Great Britain, Russia, Italy and Belgium fighting on her side."[79] Wilson did nothing. The Democratic convention was a month off.

Clemenceau's favorable opinion of Wilson lasted less than a month. What set him off anew was a May 15 address to the National Press Club in which Wilson said: "There are two reasons why the chief wish of Americans is for peace. One is that they love peace and have nothing to do with the present quarrel. And the other is that they believe the present quarrel has carried those engaged in it so far that they cannot be held to the ordinary standards of responsibility, and that, therefore, as some men have expressed it to me, when the rest of the world is mad, why not simply refuse to have anything to do with the rest of the world in the ordinary method of transaction?"[80] In a May 27 column he titled "Friendly People," Clemenceau began, "Now that the excellent man (I speak of the President") believed, in a speech in which he described us as 'mad,' he was serving the cause of peace. It was long ago announced that the President of the American Republic intended to present himself to us as a mediator.…If he believed he could attract the sympathies of the belligerents, perhaps he strayed. I do not know if he was aware of the famous program of annexations of the "National Liberal" party that Wilhelm II produced, unanimously. If America had neighbors to offer it negotiations of this kind, and Poincaré offered himself as mediator, I would like to see the amiable figure that Mr. Wilson would cut.…The fact that he did not protest against the violation of Belgian neutrality did not exactly serve as a qualification for Mr. Wilson to judge.…It seems that Mr. Wilson thinks that his refusal to judge gives him grounds to intervene. He is mistaken. To have tolerated the violation of Belgian neutrality does not give him the right to participate in the restoration of Belgium."

Clemenceau also made it clear who he favored in the up-coming election: Roosevelt. "We know that M. Roosevelt is in the ranks, and…we ardently wish for the election of the man who, in peace and war, has never ceased to show himself to be our friend.… The immense force of public sentiment is increasingly coming out in our favor every day, and, since the Republican Party has taken a clear stand on our side, it seems that Mr. Roosevelt has the greatest chance of success at the Republican convention.

It would undoubtedly be so, if this excellent candidate had not been wrong, in other circumstances, to openly break with the discipline of his party. This is a mistake that cannot be easily forgotten."[81]

He was not finished. The following day, in a column titled "Errors of Perspective," Clemenceau wrote: "With an ingenuity that does him honors, and in the hope, perhaps of forcing our hand, he publicly proclaimed his offer of intervention. As any man with good sense would have predicted, his proposition was met with a courteous coolness. And as he needed an explanation for his miscalculation, and that in such a case few people are resigned to take it upon themselves, he found it easier to pronounce us "mad." It may well be that there is madness in this. Events will show where it lies. Mr. President, don't rush to judge."[82]

As Clemenceau was penning "Errors of Perspective," Wilson was at the Willard Hotel to address the League to Enforce Peace. Wilson predicted that the speech "may be the most important I shall ever be called upon to make."[83] The League, founded in 1915, was not pacifist. Its goal was to foster international arbitration and collective security. Taft was its president, who sat beside Wilson on the dais. Most of Wilson's cabinet, former cabinet secretaries, Alexander Graham Bell, and the financier Jacob Schiff were among the scores of luminaries present. He was preceded to the lectern by Sen. Henry Cabot Lodge. In light of Briand's and Grey's expressed recalcitrance, Wilson and House decided to omit any reference to immediate peace moves, and to concentrate on the post-war. There was nothing in most of his speech objectionable to the Allies. "The interests of all nations," he said, "are our own also. We are partners with the rest. What affects mankind is inevitably our affair as well as the affair of the nations of Europe and of Asia." He continued: "[T]he principle of public right must henceforth take precedence over the individual interests of particular nations, and that the nations of the world must in some way band themselves together to see that the right prevails against any sort of selfish aggression; that henceforth alliance must not be set against alliance, understanding against understanding, but that there must be a common agreement for a common object and that at the heart of the common object must lie the inviolable rights of peoples and of mankind. The nations of the world have become each other's neighbors. It is to their interest that they should understand each. In order that they may understand each other, it is imperative that they should agree to cooperate in a common cause, and that they should so act that the guiding principle of that common cause shall be evenhanded and impartial justice."[84]

That is not what was heard in London or Paris. With a rhetorical blunder equal to "too proud to fight," Wilson opened his speech: "With its [the war's] causes and its objects we are not concerned."[85] To the British, who had not been invaded by the Germans but who had gone to war over the violation of Belgium's neutrality, and whose sons had died by the hundreds of thousands to maintain that principle, this statement was an affront. The *London Times* editorialized: "President Wilson must not think that his refusal to judge the case of Belgium confers upon him a title to mediate between those who treacherously assailed and those who rightfully defended her." And echoing the sentiment of many that it was all electoral politics, the *Times* added: "the Allies are not and will not be disposed to allow American internal politics to be intruded into their righteous quarrel."[86] House tried to repair the damage, writing to Grey: "If we are to take part in maintaining the peace of the world we could hardly be indifferent to the war and its causes and the President never intended to leave such an impression."[87] Grey replied: "No Englishman would at this moment say to France after Poincaré's and Briand's speeches made in [the] face of the Verdun struggles 'Hasn't the time come to make peace?'"[88]

Roosevelt may have had Clemenceau's support, but his hawkish stance on the war put Roosevelt, in his own words, "completely out of sympathy with the American people."[89] The Republicans were divided between conservatives and moderates when they convened in Chicago on June 7. Roosevelt, opting not to split the party again, rejected the nomination of the Progressive Party, which nominated him anyway. The Republicans resolved their differences and nominated the spade-bearded associate justice of the Supreme Court, Charles Evans Hughes. Hughes, 54, had been a progressive governor of New York. In 1910, Taft had elevated him to the high court. He had the advantage of not having taken a public position on any issue for the past six years. He said he would not campaign for the nomination, but would accept if it were offered. He was nominated on the third ballot. In their platform, the Republicans proclaimed their belief in "a strict and honest neutrality between the belligerents in the great war in Europe," but "We believe that peace and neutrality, as well as the dignity and influence of the United States, cannot be preserved by shifty expedients, by phrase-making, by performances in language, or by attitudes ever-changing in an effort to secure votes or voters. The present Administration has destroyed our influence abroad and humiliated us in our own eyes." They also opted for "the pacific settlement of international disputes, and favor the establishment of a world court for that purpose." They favored "the extension of the suffrage to women," but recognized "the right of each state to settle this question for itself." During the campaign, Hughes pivoted away, coming out in favor of a constitutional amendment guaranteeing women's suffrage.

There was no doubt who the Democrats would nominate when they convened the following week in the St. Louis Coliseum. Wilson honored the tradition of remaining away. Bryan, who had been defeated as a delegate from Nebraska, showed up anyway, and sat in the press gallery. His fears that Wilson would lead the nation into war thus far having been proven groundless, Bryan supported the nominee. He intended not to speak, but was inveigled to do so. "I join the people in thanking God that we have a president who does not want the nation to fight." He closed his address: "As a Democrat I want my party to have the honor of bringing peace and I want the country to give Woodrow Wilson a chance to bring it about."[90] Bryan would spend the fall campaigning for Wilson throughout the West. The platform was an almost verbatim recitation of the League to Enforce Peace speech, calling for the United States to join an international organization to promote peace. The platform also opted for women's suffrage, leaving the decision to the states. But this came only after a grueling fight, with many Southern delegates opposed to female suffrage everywhere. The platform closed: "We commend to the American people the splendid victories of our great President, who has preserved the vital interests of our Government and its citizens, and *kept us out of war.*" It was not intended as such, but the phrase caught on. "He kept us out of war," appeared on placards, banners, lapel buttons, and every place else it could be fitted for the rest of the campaign. It became the slogan that vaulted Wilson to victory.

In early June, the Russian armies, which had been suffering everywhere, launched a counterattack in Galicia against the Austro-Hungarian armies. Under the brilliant leadership of General Aleksei Brusilov, the "Brusilov Offensive" achieved a breakthrough, almost knocking Austria-Hungary out of the war and thereafter making Austria-Hungary a German dependent. It was momentarily so successful, that, in late August, it caused Romania to enter the war on the side of the Allies, a decision it would quickly regret. [Four days after it entered the war, Bulgaria declared war on Romania. By the end of the year, Romania had been totally defeated by Bulgarian and Turkish forces.] It also caused von Falkenhayn to draw troops away from Verdun in order to aid his beleaguered forces in the East, effectively ending offensive operations at Verdun, but not the battle. On August 29, von Falkenhayn was removed as chief of the general staff, replaced by Gen. Paul von Hindenburg, 68, and his alter ego, Gen. Erich Ludendorff.

Bethmann Hollweg surveyed the terrain and decided it was time to enlist Wilson's aid in ending the war. He feared that Austria-Hungary might quit the war just as

Romania was entering it, and that Hindenburg and the admirals might convince the kaiser to revert to all-out submarine warfare, bringing the United States into the war. It is also possible that he had one eye fixed on the upcoming presidential election. He feared that Wilson might lose. He was willing to evacuate Belgium, and was even willing to abandon Alsace-Lorraine. In the early fall, he tried to enlist Wilson's aid. But the election was pending; any moves for peace would have to wait.

At the same time, Lloyd George's pessimism was deepening, caused by his frustration at Asquith's handling of the war. By September, Haig's costly failure at the Somme was apparent. Allied troops were bogged down at Salonika and the Romanians were in retreat, and the government was doing nothing to aid them. The War Committee, which Asquith had formed to act as a stream-lined body, was now bloated and ineffective. Asquith's physical and mental decline many have been exacerbated by the loss of his son. But unlike Bethmann Hollweg, and unlike cabinet members like Lord Lansdowne, McKenna and even Grey, who were starting to go wobbly on the possibility of ending the war through mediation, it was the last thing that Lloyd George contemplated, and he determined to put an end to any thought of it. Seated at his desk at the War Office on September 27, he gave an interview to Roy Howard of the United Press of America. "Britain," he told Howard, "is not prepared to stop the war because of the squealing done by Germans or done for Germans. We must fight to the finish, to a *knock-out blow*. There can be no outside interference at this stage. Britain can tolerate no intervention. The enemy is whimpering and whining. With regard to the duration of the war there is neither clock nor calendar in the British army today. Time is the least vital factor. It took England twenty years to defeat Napoleon, and the first fifteen of those years were bleak with British defeats. It will not take twenty years to win this war, but whatever time is required it will be done."[91] The "knock-out blow" is the phrase that stuck. Lloyd George reviewed and edited the interview before it ran in the *London Times*, and a world-wide press, on September 29.

It is interesting to speculate to whom the interview was intended. Certainly to House, the interview being his way of advising House that his January prediction that the fall of 1916 would be the proper time for Wilson to intervene was now inoperative. Certainly to Wilson, Lloyd George advising Frances Stevenson that, but for the interview, "Wilson would most probably have made the proposal to us, and it would have been difficult for us to refuse to discuss terms."[92] It may also have been intended for his fellow cabinet members, who did not share the favorable opinion British press accorded it. McKenna called Lloyd George's "affront to America" as being "sheer lunacy."[93] McKenna's fears were not unfounded. As head of the treasury, he was borrowing £2 million *per day* from the United States, to fund a war effort costing £5 million per day. Grey was also displeased, and told Lloyd George so, advising him that until the Allies could be assured of military victory, it was best not to displease the United States. After the interview, Roy Howard wrote to his boss: "I am convinced that Lloyd George not only voiced the official but the popular British attitude. Also that peace proposals at this time would be fore-doomed to certain British rebuff."[94]

In response to Lloyd George's *Times* interview, on November 13 the Marquess of Lansdowne, the Tory leader in the House of Lords who was a member of Asquith's cabinet as Minister without Portfolio, penned a lengthy and confidential memorandum to the cabinet. "What," he asked, "does the prolongation of the war mean?" He provided the answer. "Our own casualties already amount to over 1,100,000. We have had 15,000 officers killed, not including those who are missing. There is no reason to suppose that, as the force at the front in the different theatres of war increases, the casualties will increase at a slower rate. We are slowly but surely killing off the best of the male population of these islands. The figures representing the casualties of our Allies are not before me. The total must be appalling....The financial burden which we have already accumulated is almost incalculable. We are adding to it at the rate of over £5 million per day. Generations will have to come and go before the country recovers from the loss which it has sustained in human beings, and from the financial ruin and the destruction of the means of production which are taking place....All this it is no doubt our duty to bear, but only if it can be shown that the sacrifice will have its reward. If it is to be made in vain, if the additional year, or two years, or three years, finds us still unable to dictate terms, the War with its nameless horrors will have been needlessly prolonged, and the responsibility of those who needlessly prolong such a War is not less than those who needlessly provoke it."[95] The "Lansdowne Memorandum" was discussed in the cabinet on November 22. The discussion was inconclusive, and it was agreed that it should be discussed again. Lloyd George believed that if Lansdowne was outvoted Lansdowne would have to leave the Cabinet: "You cannot have a man in a War Cabinet who thinks we ought to make peace."[96]

Things now moved very quickly, and ended with Asquith's resignation. A principal player, albeit entirely in the shadows, was Max Aitken, 37, the Canadian-born proprietor of the *Daily Express*, later to become Lord Beaverbrook. With Aitken's assistance, a cabal formed consisting of Lloyd George, Bonar Law and the head of the Irish Unionists, Sir Edward Carson. Their objective was not to depose Asquith, but to circumvent him. On November 25, three days after the Lansdowne Memorandum was discussed in the cabinet, with the Somme campaign halted and Romanian armies crumbling, the three drafted a memorandum to Asquith. They proposed that the War Committee be replaced by a three-member "War Council"—*not* to include Asquith—who would meet in continuous session and who would have no other duties but to conduct the war. That evening, Law personally delivered the memorandum to Asquith. Characteristically, Asquith neither accepted nor rejected it, but said he would consider it. He responded in a letter delivered to the three the next day. He rejected the proposal on the ground that a committee to run the war must have at least one cabinet member. As to the personnel, he rejected Carson as being too junior, since it would pass over men such as Balfour and McKenna. As for Lloyd George, "you know as well as I do both his qualities and his defects. He has many qualities that would fit him for the first place, but he lacks one thing needful—he does not inspire trust…"[97] Bonar Law presented the plan to his fellow Tories. Many of them opposed it on the ground that it would lead to Lloyd George becoming prime minister.

Lloyd George met with Asquith on December 1, and personally proposed the three-person War Council. Asquith considered it again, and rejected it again, writing: "In my opinion, whatever changes are made in the composition of the War Committee, the Prime Minister must be its chairman. He cannot be relegated to the position of arbiter in the background or a referee to the Cabinet."[98] On December 3, Law met with the Tory members of the Cabinet. They demanded that Asquith resign, and advised him they would quit the Cabinet *en masse* if he did not. Later that day, Asquith asked to see Lloyd George and Law. Asquith had changed his mind. He agreed that Lloyd George would head the War Council, of which Asquith would not be a member, but over whose decisions Asquith would retain a veto. Then he changed his mind again, insisting that the prime minister must be a member of the War Council.

Then, on December 5, Asquith changed his mind yet again. He resigned. Only he knew why. He had been prime minister for eight years, longer than any prime minister for almost a century. It is possible that he believed he would be invited back in the event Lloyd George or Law were unsuccessful in forming a government. King George asked Bonar Law to form a government, with Asquith in it. Asquith advised that he would not serve under Law. The king asked Lloyd George to form a coalition government. The key man was Arthur Balfour, who announced: "If he thinks he can win the war, I am all for him having a try…I have no prejudices in favour of Lloyd George. I have opposed every political principle that he holds…but I think he is the only man who can, at this moment, break down the barriers of red tape and see that the brains of the country are made use of."[99] With Balfour on board, the other Tories fell in line. They agreed to Lloyd George forming a government, provided that the despised turncoat Churchill not be in it and that Lloyd George not dismiss Haig. But every Liberal in

Asquith's cabinet (except Edwin Montagu, the man who had married Venetia Stanley), including McKenna and Grey, opposed Lloyd George. For Sir Edward Grey, it was the end of his career as foreign secretary, the office he had held since 1905.

At 7:30 P.M. on December 7, Lloyd George went to Buckingham Palace and "kissed hands" with the king. The "cottage-bred man" from North Wales, who had not attended high school much less university, the apprenticed solicitor who had entered the House of Commons at the age of twenty-seven and who had risked his career and on one occasion his life in his lonely opposition to the South African War, was now prime minister. When he returned from Buckingham Palace he remarked to Frances Stevenson, very uncharacteristically, "I'm not at all sure I can do it. It is a very big task."[100]

But a fissure had developed in the Liberal Party, one that would not heal. He would be the last Liberal ever to enter 10 Downing Street as prime minister.

16

FALLING APART

Peace without Victory.

—Woodrow Wilson

A s 1917 dawned, more than a million German soldiers were dead. France, with a population a third smaller than Germany's, counted almost nine hundred thousand dead. Five hundred thousand British and British Empire soldiers had perished. Italy, late to enter the war and with a smaller population, had lost four hundred thousand. The patriotic fervor that had propelled the armies at the war's beginning was long gone, replaced by a weariness on both sides of the Vosges and the feeling that no end was in sight. The Allied blockade had reduced the German civilian economy to tatters; eggs, butter, meat and sugar, despite rationing, could not be had. Turnips replaced potatoes; there were demonstrations and food riots. The German general staff was shocked at the condition of their new recruits. But the Germans, at least, could show something for the price paid: They had overrun Serbia and Romania, the Russians had been pushed east; the early conquests of Belgium and eastern France had held; their U-boats menaced Allied shipping. What gains the Allies had made on the Somme and at Verdun had been measured in kilometers at the cost of thousands of lives. And Great Britain was quickly running out of money. They assumed that by April they would be completely broke.

But 1917 would witness two cataclysmic events occurring within a fortnight of each other that would alter not only the course of the war but of the twentieth century: the Russian Revolution and the entry of the United States into the war.

David Lloyd George entered 10 Downing Street with one goal: to win the war. He was fifty-three when he became prime minister. His great friend, George Riddell, described him then: "His energy, capacity for work, and power of recuperation are remarkable. He has an extraordinary memory, imagination, and the art of getting at the root of a matter…He is not afraid of responsibility, and has no respect for tradition or convention. He is always ready to examine, scrap or revise established theories and practices. These are the qualities that give him unlimited confidence in himself…" But these qualities carried with them their own defects, chiefly his "lack of appreciation of existing institutions, organizations and stolid, dull people…fondness for a grandiose scheme in preference to an attempt to improve existing machinery…disregard of difficulties in carrying out big projects…he is not a man of detail."[1] Looking back on his youth, Lloyd George told Riddell: "I have grown more tolerant; I have come to see that there is something to be said for the other side. For instance, I have grown to realize that Dissenters are not always in the right and Anglicans always in the wrong, and that all landlords are not scoundrels of the deepest dye."[2]

He determined from the outset that his would be a small cabinet charged with no function other than running the war on a daily basis. He selected Andrew Bonar Law, 58, his chancellor of the exchequer and the Tory leader in the House of Commons. Law, like Lloyd George, had not attended university. A widower since 1909, he would lose both sons in the war in 1917. As chancellor, he resided at 11 Downing Street, and he and Lloyd George worked through the corridor separating 10 and 11. Lloyd George selected Lord Curzon, 58, the Tory leader in the House of Lords, and Lord Milner, 64, the Tory who had been Lloyd George's bitterest opponent during the Boer War. He now called Lord Curzon "the best all-round brain" in the Conservative Party, and he tapped Curzon for his brilliance as an administrator. The men Milner selected became known as "Milner Men." Rounding out the War Cabinet was the Labourite Arthur Henderson, chosen because Lloyd George needed Labour support. He selected Arthur Balfour to succeed Edward Grey as foreign secretary, Lord Derby as secretary of state for war, and Sir Edward Carson to head the Admiralty. But Balfour, Derby and Carson did not serve in the War Cabinet. They attended when a matter affecting their ministries was on the agenda; otherwise, they were left to run their departments. Lloyd George realized he could lead the war effort or lead the House of Commons but not both; he would appear only infrequently in the House of Commons.

Lloyd George met with Milner every day promptly at 11:00 A.M. The rest of the War Cabinet convened at noon. They met every weekday, meeting five hundred times before the war's end. Seated to Lloyd George's right was the indispensable cabinet secretary, Sir Maurice Hankey, who seemed to be everywhere and who knew everything. Lloyd George was the youngest member of his War Cabinet. He was also its only Liberal, as most of the Liberals remained loyal to the ousted Asquith, and refused to serve. He could not have succeeded without Bonar Law's support, who early on announced "This is essentially Lloyd George's government and my own intention…is to back him to the full extent I can."[3] But relying on the opposition party would hamper him. It meant that, at least at the beginning, Churchill was still out, and Haig was still in. The ministers met for the first time on December 9, two days after Lloyd George became prime minister. After the meeting, Sir Edward Carson told his wife that "more had been done in a few hours than used to be done in a year."[4]

Shortly after Lloyd George became prime minister, the "three men and a machine gun" claimed their biggest victim: Gen. Joseph Joffre. This hero of the "miracle" of the Marne of 1914 had produced little since, and after Prime Minister Aristide Briand won votes of confidence in late November and early December by smaller margins than in the previous June, he sensed that Joffre's continued failures could cost him his government, and so he decided to replace him. He did so in a manner so deft and subtle that Joffre himself failed to realize it until his ouster was a *fait accompli*. On December 12, Briand named Gen. Louis Lyautey as minister of war. Lyautey, 62, had helped crush the "Black Flag" rebellion in Indo-China, had served as France's administrator in Madagascar, and was serving in Morocco at the time of his appointment. Very conservative, a royalist, he was also France's only openly gay general. At the same time, Briand named Gen. Robert Nivelle as Commander in Chief of the Armies of the East and the Northeast, and appointed Joffre as "technical advisor to the government." At this point, Joffre still had no idea what was afoot. But then Nivelle changed Joffre's 1917 war plans without informing Joffre, and the acting war minister, Adm. Lucien Lacaze (Lyautey still en route from Morocco) advised Joffre that henceforth Nivelle would be receiving orders directly from Lyautey, not from Joffre. That is when Joffre realized he had been sidetracked. When Briand made it official by naming Joffre a "Marshal of France," the first so named under the Third Republic, Joffre asked to resign. Having Joffre resign, rather than dismissing him, had been Briand's goal all along. Joffre received a hero's welcome when he visited the United States later in 1917, but his career was over.

Shortly before Lloyd George became prime minister, Col. House wrote to Wilson: "If the Lloyd George-Northcliffe-Carson combination succeed in overthrowing the government and getting control, there will be no chance of peace until they run their course."[5] The day after Lloyd George succeeded in "overthrowing the government," Wilson wrote to House: "The time is near at hand for something. We cannot go back to those old plans. We must shape new ones."[6] By the "old plans" he meant the House-Grey Memorandum. He now despaired of the British ever invoking it, especially in light of Lloyd George's recent "hands off" interview. The next day—December 9—the same day Lloyd George and his Cabinet met for the first time, Wilson began drafting his "peace note," a note he addressed to all of the belligerents.

But before Wilson could finish his draft, he was chagrined to receive from Chancellor Bethmann Hollweg Germany's own peace note. The impetus for this note was no doubt Bethmann Hollweg's own concern that his worsening economy could result in the military overthrowing his government and instituting unlimited U-boat warfare. He hoped that if Germany could keep most of the gains it had achieved on the battlefield, it would be a peace the kaiser, his military and certainly the German people could live with. But this "peace note" had no chance of success. He boasted of Germany's "military and economic strength" and "our readiness to continue the war (which has been forced upon us) to the bitter end," and the "gigantic advantages over adversaries superior in number and war material. Our lines stand unshaken against ever-repeated attempts made by armies." It offered no concessions. It was an invitation to the Allies to give up.

Lloyd George's new foreign minister, Arthur Balfour, was ill when the government was formed, and his place was filled by his able undersecretary, Lord Robert Cecil, who would go on the earn a Nobel Peace Prize for his work in the creation of the League of Nations. In the week following the formation of the new government, Cecil wrote a trenchant memo to Lloyd George. Of Wilson, he wrote that the recently-reelected president "has nothing to hope for in domestic politics; he is known to be a genuine and ardent lover of peace; and the role of mediator may well be attractive to him." He warned Lloyd George that Wilson had the power to cut off the Allies' lifelines to credit and to war materiel: "[I]f he desired to put a stop to the war, and he was prepared to pay the price for doing so, such an achievement is in his power."[7] His warning was clear: just as Edward Grey had had to walk a fine line not to appear to dismiss Wilson's overtures while actually doing so, Lloyd George would have to do the same.

On December 19, twelve days after becoming prime minister, Lloyd George rose in the House of Commons to respond to the German peace note. "I should like to quote the very well known words of Abraham Lincoln under similar conditions," he began. "We accepted this war for an object, and the war will end when that object is attained. Under God I hope it will never end until that time."[8] Anticipating Wilson's own peace note, which as he spoke had been transmitted but not yet received, Lloyd George summarized, as bluntly as he could, the Allies' war aims: "Restitution, reparation, guarantee against repetition, and so there shall be no mistake, and it is important that there should be no mistake in a matter of life and death to millions[,] [l]et me repeat again—complete restitution, full reparation, effectual guarantees." Oozing sarcasm, he suggested that Germany had been "Menaced, I suppose, by the overwhelming armies of Belgium, the Germans had been intimidated into invading that country, to the burning of Belgian cities and villages, to the massacring of thousands of inhabitants, old and young, to the carrying of the survivors into bondage...I suppose these outrages are the legitimate interests of Germany?...[I]s there, I ask in all solemnity, any guarantee that similar subterfuges will not be used in the future to overthrow any treaty of peace you may enter into with Prussian militarism?"[9]

The speech infuriated Ludendorff, who telegrammed Bethmann Hollweg that the *Sussex* pledge should be abandoned in favor of all-out U-boat warfare. Hindenburg echoed it, and both of them threatened to resign if Bethmann Hollweg failed to do so.

Clemenceau was cheered not only by Lloyd George's speech, but by the aggressive spirit of his new government: "We have now in the United Kingdom a Government program the worth of which lies not in fine words...but in the fact that it gives us an irresistible sensation of a will which is going to act. That is where the strength is of Mr. Lloyd George's government....It only remains for France and also Russia to reply to the definite organization Mr. Lloyd George has announced by corresponding acts. If we decide to do it, victory is certain. If we do not, where are we going?"[10]

Wilson rushed to complete his own peace note, advising House that there was not sufficient time to have House review the final draft. Wilson may have felt that the Allies would react to the German peace note with such hostility as to kill any hope of mediation. He finished it on December 17. It took the form of a long telegram from Secretary of State Lansing to the ambassadors accredited to the belligerent nations, instructing them to transmit the note to their respective ministers of foreign affairs. Lansing transmitted the note the next day, instructing each ambassador that "He [Wilson] wishes the impression clearly conveyed that it would be very hard for the Government of the United States to understand a negative reply."[11] The note did not call for a peace conference, but instead, "The President suggests that an early occasion be sought to call out from all the nations now at war an avowal of their respective views as to the terms upon which the war might be concluded and the arrangements which would be deemed satisfactory as a guaranty against its renewal or the kindling of any similar conflict in the future..." adding, "The President...feels altogether justified in suggesting an immediate opportunity for a comparison of views as to the terms which must precede those ultimate arrangements for the peace of the world."[12] But there was a veiled threat in his call for an airing of peace terms. The belligerents needed to act, "lest the situation of the neutral nations, now exceedingly hard to endure, be rendered intolerable..." By the "neutral nations," he meant the United States.

Whatever positive reception Wilson's peace note might have achieved in Allied capitals was eliminated by one of Wilson's extraordinarily misguided sentiments: "He [i.e., the president] takes the liberty of calling attention to the fact that the objects which the statesmen of the belligerents on both sides have in mind are virtually the same, as stated in general terms to their own people and to the world." The "objects" of the belligerents "virtually the same"? Upon reading the final peace note, House wrote in his diary that "He seems obsessed with that thought, and he cannot write or talk on the subject of the war without voicing it," noting that it "will give further impetus to the belief that he does not yet understand what the Allies are fighting for," predicting that "it has done more to make him unpopular in the Allied countries than any one thing he has done, and it will probably keep him from taking the part which he ought to take in peace negotiations..."[13] House was prescient; the reaction in London was outrage. Lest this single sentence cause a rupture in Anglo-American relations, the Foreign Office censored the Associated Press report of the note. Ambassador Page reported that Lord Bryce "came to see me in a state of great depression," that Asquith's reaction was: "Don't talk to me about it. It is most disheartening," and that, according to Asquith, when the king heard of it, he *broke down*."[14] London newspapers were warned to tread lightly in reporting it. Despite this, the *London Times* opined on Wilson's comment that the belligerents' war aims were "virtually the same": "The same? We should have supposed that by this time the irreconcilable conflict between the objects of the Allies and the objects of the Central Powers was plain to all mankind. Our aims have never changed from the day Germany began hacking her way through neutral Belgium until this hour."[15] France's ambassador to London, Paul Cambon, said that Wilson, "with his dogmatism and inspired airs, is acting like a knave,"[16] which recalled Clemenceau's remark that Wilson's constant moralizing "was like a professor standing on a riverbank lecturing a drowning child on how to avoid floods."[17]

Clemenceau had on more than one occasion pointed out the absurdity of asking the "war aims" of a country that had been invaded and was still being occupied. In his

Christmas Day editorial, he asked what American reaction would be if some foreign statesman, at the time of the American revolution, had asked Washington and George III why they were fighting. "Mr. President, there is what we say and what we do. If one were to refer to words, there would be no criminals who were not motivated by pure intentions, and instead of jail we could do less than award them the Nobel Prize....Asking the *Lusitania* assassins what they intended to accomplish may seem superfluous."[18]

The next day, Lloyd George and Balfour met visiting French Prime Minister Aristide Briand. They "replied" to Bethmann Hollweg's peace note by stating that they could not reply because the note contained no specifics. They agreed that any reply to Wilson's peace note would be a joint reply.

On December 29, Lloyd George granted an interview to American Ambassador Walter Hines Page, who followed up with a long telegram to Wilson. Page reported that he and Lloyd George had agreed to speak personally, confidentially, and frankly. "The future of the whole world depends on our understanding one another," Page quoted Lloyd George. "Do I make myself quite clear? We do make mistakes. We do have irritations. They will be forgotten if we are both conciliatory. But the harm done to all mankind if we drift apart will never be forgotten nor forgiven." But Page also reported that Lloyd George felt Wilson's peace note was premature and that he wished some understanding could have been reached before it was sent, and that neither his government nor his Allies could consent to talk peace, "to say nothing of meeting the enemy in conference....They could not even talk of peace. The British were determined. If he were now to consent to a peace conference his Government would be swept out of office overnight, and the people would become ferocious....Peace talk now therefore is harmful to the Allies' cause."[19] After Page sent this telegram, he felt he had not fully imparted his impressions. The following day, he penned another one: "Lloyd George is not a spent force, but one of the most energetic projectiles that I've ever watched or come in contact with. He said more in half an hour yesterday than Asquith ever told me in his life.... He is very direct. He does not use circumlocution. He doesn't 'intimate', he says things straight out. 'Call me on the telephone any time you like' was his parting word."[20]

Lloyd George's interview with Page should be viewed in context. Lloyd George had reorganized and streamlined the British war effort. Haig was planning a spring offensive. Briand had ousted Joffre and had begun streamlining his ministry along the lines that Lloyd George had. The French had held at Verdun, and Joffre's replacement, Gen Nivelle, who had achieved some success at Verdun, recapturing the Douaumont and Vaux fortresses, was highly optimistic that he could effect a breakthrough. The Allies were still full of hope. They believed they would win the war.

On January 8, 1917, Bethmann Hollweg, Hindenburg, and Ludendorff motored to Pless Castle in Silesia to meet with Kaiser Wilhelm. They were joined by Adm. Henning von Holtzendorff, the Navy's most ardent proponent of unlimited submarine warfare. For two years, Bethmann Hollweg had been arguing that the wanton sinking of allied *and neutral* ships would bring the Americans into the war. He now lost the argument. Ludendorff argued that the Allies were planning a huge spring offensive on the western front, and that it was imperative to prevent munitions and materiel from reaching the Allies. As for the Americans entering the war, he deprecated the effect: The U-boats could knock the British out of the war within six months, long before the Americans could raise and train an army, and with the British out of the war France would sue for peace. An Imperial Order had been prepared in advance. Wilhelm signed it. Beginning on February 1, all merchant shipping destined for the Allies, whether armed or unarmed, would be sunk without warning. Neutral ships—including American ships—found in the designated area around France and Great Britain would be sunk without warning starting on February 13. The decision would be kept secret until it was implemented. Hindenburg demanded—and was refused—Bethmann Hollweg's removal as chancellor. Bethmann Hollweg promised to do his best to keep the United States out of the war.

Hindsight reveals that this decision was Germany's biggest blunder of the war, and the direct cause of its defeat. The U-boats did not knock the British out of the war, nor did they prevent American troops and materiel from reaching the continent. The British, who were at the edge of bankruptcy, would be saved by their new ally. What is worse, it was all unnecessary. Within weeks, the czar would be overthrown, and the process of disengaging Russia from the Allies would begin.

The Allies did not respond to Wilson's peace note until January 10, 1917. They rejected the notion that the Allies' and the Central Powers' war aims were "similar," noting the violation of Belgian neutrality and the U-boat atrocities. They spelled out their territorial demands: the evacuation of France, Belgium, Romania and Serbia, with indemnities. These were demands that could be met only by smashing the German military machine. That was the Allies' "war aim."

The severity of the Allies' response shocked both the kaiser and Wilson. Wilhelm issued a proclamation: "The God who planted his glorious spirit of freedom in the hearts of our brave peoples will also give us and our loyal allies, tested in battle, the full victory over all the enemy lust for power and rage for destruction."[21] House correctly guessed that Germany was planning to commence unrestricted submarine warfare, advising Wilson that "If we can tie up Germany in a conference so that she cannot resume her unbridled submarine warfare, it will be a great point gained, and if a conference is once started it can never break up without peace."[22]

Wilson received the Allies' response just as he was finalizing a speech he asked to give to the Senate for the purpose of outlining his own ideas for a post-war world. It was a long and carefully-wrought explication of his views that would presage the "Fourteen Points," but, as with "too proud to fight," the speech would be remembered for one phrase. At noon on January 22, speaking in a low voice, he addressed the assembled senators. He began by acknowledging the Allies' and Germany's responses to his peace note, concluding somewhat disingenuously that from their responses "We are that much nearer a definite discussion of the peace which shall end the present war." He then got down to substance: "In every discussion of the peace that must end this war it is taken for granted that that peace must be followed by some definite concert of power which will make it virtually impossible that any such catastrophe should ever overwhelm us again. Every lover of mankind, every sane and thoughtful man must take that for granted." He added: "It is inconceivable that the people of the United States should play no part in that great enterprise." While not using the term "league of nations," he noted that the "concert of power" must have teeth: "It will be absolutely necessary that a force be created as a guarantor of the permanency of the settlement so much greater than the force of any nation now engaged or any alliance hitherto formed or projected that no nation, no probable combination of nations could face or withstand it. If the peace presently to be made is to endure, it must be a peace made secure by the organized major force of mankind....There must be, not a balance of power, but a community of power; not organized rivalries, but an organized common peace." In other words, the politics of the "balance of power," which had resulted in a regional conflict ballooning into a world war, was finished, replaced by collective security.

He warned the belligerents against a Carthaginian peace: "The present war must first be ended....The treaties and agreements which bring it to an end must embody terms which will create a peace that will win the approval of mankind, not merely a peace that will serve the several interests and immediate aims of the nations engaged." He would go on to speak of "freedom of the seas," and the right of all people to self-determination, "unhindered, unthreatened, unafraid, the little along with the great and powerful." He touched on the need for disarmament: "There can be no sense of safety and equality among the nations if the great preponderating armaments are henceforth to continue to be built up and maintained."[23]

But one phrase would stick. For all that he proposed to eventuate, he said, there must be "a peace without victory." The following morning, the *New York Times* headlined: "Wilson's Terms for League of Peace: Freedom of Seas, Reduced Armaments and Security for Weak Nations; Peace Without Victory Now Essential to its Success." But one sub-head was more succinct: "'We Must Win' Say British."[24]

Domestic reaction to the speech was generally favorable. But Sen. Henry Cabot Lodge, then a member of the foreign relations committee and soon to be its chairman, commented, ominously: "I once regarded the idea of a league favorably, but in the last two years the more I have thought of it the more impossible it has seemed to me."[25] Oddly, William Jennings Bryan also opposed the idea of a league to enforce peace. He reasoned that it might pull the United States into a war against its will. The Allies, focusing on "peace without victory," were hostile. Lord Bryce wrote: "[C]an he really think we could make peace now on a *status quo ante* basis?"[26] Page summarized the feeling in London: "'Peace without victory' brought us to the very depths of European disfavor."[27] Lloyd George himself did not comment publicly, and there is no evidence that the War Cabinet even discussed it. But Bonar Law, in a speech the following day, said: "We have rejected the proposal to enter into peace negotiations not from any lust of conquest; not from any longing for claiming victories; or even a desire for revenge; we have rejected it because peace now would mean peace based on a German victory. It would mean a military machine still unbroken....What President Wilson is longing for we are fighting for."[28] Although silent in the immediate aftermath of the speech, Lloyd George blistered Wilson in his *War Memoirs*: "Without an Allied triumph," he wrote, "there was no faintest hope of realising any of the ideals he was advancing so eloquently. Germany was in possession of vast territories, much of which she had no intention of surrendering after the War—some of which she did not intend to restore without imposing conditions of practical vassalage. To talk of self-determination of the peoples, an independent Poland, democratic governments, universal liberty, with an undefeated Imperial Germany was a mockery. Peace without victory? The President's detachment from realities was more than ever obvious. To the Allies the phrase was an offence—to the Germans a jest."[29]

The reaction in Paris was equally hostile, the *London Times* Paris correspondent writing: "The phrase 'peace without victory' is one which stick most in French throats. The French see in all this passage the logical development of M. Wilson's inability to distinguish between the responsibility of the two opposing camps."[30]

But no one deprecated Wilson's speech at greater length and with greater vitriol than Clemenceau. In an editorial he titled "The Idealism of a President," with an argument that presaged their clash at the Peace Conference, he mocked the concept of collective security. He began: "When reading the pacifist message that President Wilson read to the American Senate, a member of that assembly wrote to himself: 'we have just experienced an historic hour.' These words are probably correct in the sense that never before has a political assembly heard such a beautiful sermon on what humans could do if they were not humans." Addressing Wilson directly, he wrote: "Our

[European] nations have a history older than yours, a history of continual struggles, providence having allotted to us very unstable borders. We can no more suppress the history of the last two years than that of the ages of which they are the consequence. You offer us, I understand, the guarantee of America for a peace without victory. Do you realize what this American guarantee will cost you? An army of ten million men, ready to face all coalitions of violence, a war navy with a fleet capable of transporting troops despite submarines to all places that might revolt, to say nothing of fortresses to ward against surprises. What would the American people think of it?" America would become a "universal police," but "If the policeman strikes, it is not always that he does not receive one in return. On which side will it intervene in the battles? It will not always be easy to decide. One thing appears certain, which is, that by your gospel of peace, you will have made war universal." He concluded: "Believe me…you do not destroy violence on earth until the earth and its creatures are changed. When a passerby is murdered the crowd on the sidewalk comes to the rescue. It is neither we, nor England, nor Belgium, who have raised the knife against Germany. We were murdered, sir. It is not time to talk."[31]

Two days after Wilson's address, the German ambassador, Johann von Bernstorff, fired off a cable to his foreign office. He pleaded that they hold off on the decision for unlimited submarine warfare. He reasoned that, in light of Wilson's speech, the immediate resumption of unrestricted U-boat warfare would be seen as a personal affront to Wilson which would surely bring the Americans into the war. He also suggested that if Germany appeared conciliatory and the Allies did not, it would make it difficult for America to declare war on Germany if it later resorted to unrestricted warfare. "Thus," he wrote, "at present all we need is a brief delay in order to improve our diplomatic position."[32] Bernstorff soon received a reply. On January 31 he handed Lansing a letter from his foreign office: "From February 1, 1917, all sea traffic will be stopped with every available weapon and without further notice," in an area around the British Isles and around Italy, including large stretches of international waters. This represented the withdrawal of the *Sussex* pledge to Wilson. It was unlimited warfare against neutral and belligerent shipping, armed and unarmed.[33] According to Lansing, Bernstorff's eyes were filled with tears as he said goodbye.

Lansing met with Wilson that evening. Wilson was still not convinced that it would be best for the United States to break diplomatic relations with Germany. He ordered Lansing to draft a note breaking relations, but not to send it. House learned of the German response as Lansing and Wilson were meeting. He boarded a midnight train and met with Wilson for breakfast. Wilson had recently told him: "There will be no war. This country does not intend to become involved in this war. We are the only one of the great white nations that is free from war today, and it would be a crime against civilization for us to go in."[34] But now they agreed not to wait for some hostile act to break diplomatic relations; it would be best to do it now. House returned home to New York.

The following day—February 2—Lansing handed Wilson the note he had prepared breaking diplomatic relations. He also advised Wilson to declare war: "The present military oligarchy must be eliminated for the sake of civilization and the future peace of the world."[35] Wilson demurred. That afternoon, Wilson met with his cabinet. He opened the meeting with a question: "Shall I break off diplomatic relations with Germany?" and according to Agriculture Secretary David Houston, Wilson answered his own question: "He would say frankly that, if he felt that, in order to keep the white race or part of it strong to meet the yellow race—Japan, for instance, in alliance with Russia, dominating China—it was wise to do nothing, he would do nothing, and would submit to anything and any imputation of weakness or cowardice."[36] Wilson asked the assembled secretaries which side they wished to see win the war. According to Interior Secretary Franklin K. Lane, Wilson opined that he did not wish to see either side win, "for both had been indifferent to the rights of neutrals—though Germany had been brutal in taking life, and England only in taking property."[37] When Lansing stated that it would be in the interest of the world for the United States to join the Allies so that the Allies could succeed in ending absolutism, Wilson replied: "I am not so sure of that," arguing that "greater justice would be done if the conflict ended in a draw."[38]

Did Wilson really believe this? At the onset of the war, Wilson had implored his fellow citizens to be neutral *in thought* as well as in deed. Most Americans were quite ready to act as neutrals, but few were neutral in thought. House was not; Lansing was not. It is interesting to compare Wilson with his wartime successor, President Franklin Roosevelt. From September 1, 1939 until the United States was invaded in December, 1941, Roosevelt maintained America's neutrality. But not for a moment did anyone believe that Roosevelt felt indifferent to the outcome, nor did Roosevelt attempt to conceal his partiality. It is likely that Wilson, unlike Roosevelt, truly felt neutral as to the belligerents. If so, it explains his persistent failure to condemn the invasion of Belgium and the consistent trope in his speeches and writings that he did not care about the origins of the war, a fact not lost on Lloyd George and Clemenceau. Wilson would soon bring into the war the political and military authority of the United States. He had long since forfeited any moral authority.

Following his meeting with his cabinet, Wilson went to the Capitol. He met with Missouri Senator William J. Stone, the chairman of the Foreign Relations Committee. It was late in the day; the Senate had adjourned. Stone rounded up as many senators as he could find—sixteen—all of them Democrats. They all assured him that the voters would back him if he broke diplomatic relations. Wilson returned to the White House and instructed Tumulty to arrange for a joint session of Congress for the following day. He then began writing his speech, working into the night.

The next morning—Saturday—he met with Lansing, informed him of his decision, and instructed Lansing to hand Bernstorff his passports as he was speaking. At 2:00 P.M. he appeared before the packed House chamber. He wore a cutaway coat. Edith and the family listened from the gallery. He first reviewed the whole history of Germany's submarine warfare, including the sinking of the *Sussex*, Germany's pledge to refrain from sinking neutral ships without warning, and Wilson's warning if they broke the pledge. Now, he said, "I have, therefore, directed the Secretary of State to announce to the German Ambassador that all diplomatic relations between the United States and the German Empire are severed and that the American Ambassador at Berlin will immediately be withdrawn..."[39] It was met with thunderous applause, led by Sen. Lodge. But what might have been lost in the cheering was that Wilson had broken off diplomatic relations only with Germany, and not with any of its allies, neither Austria-Hungary, Turkey nor Bulgaria.

Wilson then left the door ajar to reconciliation. "I refuse to believe that it is the intention of the German authorities to do in fact what they have warned us they will feel at liberty to do. I cannot bring myself to believe that they will indeed pay no regard to the ancient friendship between their people and our own or to the solemn obligations which have been exchanged between them and destroy American ships and take the lives of American citizens..." And in case anyone missed the point that he was referring only to *American lives* on *American ships*, he underscored it: "[I]f American ships and American lives should in fact be sacrificed by their naval commanders in heedless contravention of the just and reasonable understandings of international law and the obvious dictates of humanity, I shall take the liberty of coming again before the Congress, to ask that authority be given me to use any means that may be necessary for the protection of our seamen and our people in the prosecution of their peaceful and legitimate errands on the high seas."[40]

So there it was. The United States would go to war over unrestricted U-boat warfare only if American lives were lost. The Allies were on their own. It was a distinction that may have been lost on the cheering crowds that gathered in front of the American embassy in London that Saturday night. Bands played, speeches were made, and a chorus of visiting New Englanders sang "John Brown's Body."[41] The distinction may also have been lost on Clemenceau himself. In his February 5 editorial, titled "Against the Whole World," he put "peace without victory" behind him in his praise of Wilson's rupture with Germany. "On this day," he wrote, "the American people and their president are one and the same. There is an inflexible logic that now prevails between the United States and Germany. Neither side can back down…It will be Germany's war against the whole world."[42] Lloyd George was less effusive, telling George Riddell: "So he is not going to fight after all! He is waiting for another insult before he actually draws the sword."[43] Opinion was divided as to whether war could be avoided. Many believed war was inevitable, others that it could be avoided with America's honor preserved. Wilson hoped he could still avoid declaring war. After an inconclusive February 20 cabinet meeting, Interior Secretary Franklin K. Lane wrote: "We evidently are waiting for an 'overt act' which I think Germany will not commit."[44] On the same day, Page wrote in his diary: "I am now ready to record my conviction that we shall not get into the war at all."[45] This despite the fact that Lloyd George had advised Page that he had instructed his chief of the general staff, Gen. Robertson, and First Sea Lord Admiral Jellicoe to share with the Americans all information the American armed forces might find useful.

On the day following his speech severing diplomatic relations with Germany, Wilson called on the other neutral nations to do the same, stating : "it will make for the peace of the world if other neutral powers can find it possible to take similar action."[46] Commenting the following day, Clemenceau wrote: "The great neutral has come, and the other neutrals will come, in ways in which they (as well as I myself) do not know, which will impose themselves on them." He believed that there was a "logic" that was 'inexorable, in that Germany would continue to torpedo their ships."[47] He was mistaken, and Wilson was disappointed. Neither the Dutch, nor Spain, nor any of the Scandinavian neutrals severed diplomatic relations, and none ever joined the Allies.

In November, 1916, the Austro-Hungarian Emperor, Franz Joseph, finally passed away, having reigned for sixty-eight years. The throne passed to his grand-nephew, Karl, the result of Franz Joseph's son, Prince Rupert, having taken his own life in a suicide pact with his mistress, and then his nephew Franz Ferdinand having died at the hands of a Serb terrorist. The thirty-year-old Karl would be the last Hapsburg emperor. He assumed the throne at a time when the Austrian armies were reeling everywhere, and bread lines were forming in Vienna. (Ludendorff best summed up his ally: "We are shackled to a corpse.") Kaiser Karl, who had had nothing to do with getting Austria into the war, now wanted to save his empire and his throne by getting Austria out.

Three days after Wilson severed diplomatic relations with Germany, but not with Austria, Secretary of State Lansing received a telegram from the American ambassador to Vienna, Frederick Penfield, transmitting a letter from the Austrian foreign minister, Count Ottokar Czernin. It was a plea for peace: "I sincerely hope that [the president] will continue the work of peace he began in the spirit of impartiality and I sincerely hope that he will induce the powers of the Entente to accept, like us, the American point of view, that there should be neither victor nor loser and that the peace concluded should be an honorable one for both sides—a lasting one for the whole world."[48]

Austria's desire to enter into peace negotiations heartened Wilson. But there was a problem. Kaiser Karl wished to keep as much of his polyglot empire intact as he could; the Allies were intent on dismembering it following the war. Wilson had come out four-square for "self-determination" of peoples; Austria-Hungary was the living contradiction of "self-determination." What followed was the first—albeit indirect—communication between Wilson and Lloyd George. Writing to Page, Wilson instructed him to advise Lloyd George "with all earnestness and directness" that the Allies should advise Kaiser Karl that they really did not wish to sever Austria from the "older units of the Empire," such as Hungary, and that "Austria can be satisfied without depriving the several Balkan states of their political autonomy and territorial integrity."[49] Lloyd George responded in the same manner, viz., through Page. He advised Wilson that the Allies preferred to keep Austria in the war as an albatross to the Germans, and that the Allies would give Austria no assurances against dismemberment. Lloyd George then made this remarkable appeal to Wilson, urging him to enter the war: "We want him to come into the war not so much for help with the war as for help with peace... not mainly [for] the military nor naval nor economic nor financial pressure...I have a far loftier reason. American participation is necessary for the complete expression of the moral judgment of the world on the most important subject ever presented to the civilized nations...The President's presence at the peace conference is necessary for the proper organization of the world which must follow peace. I mean that he himself must be there in person. If he sits in the conference that makes peace he will exert the greatest influence that any man has ever exerted in expressing the moral value of free government. Most of the present belligerents will have suffered so heavily that their judgment also may have suffered...The United States wants nothing but justice and an ordered freedom and guarantees of these for the future. Nobody therefore can have so commanding a voice as the President...He must help make peace if the peace made at that conference is to be worth keeping. American participation in the war would enable him to be there and the moral effect of this participation would shorten the war, might even end it very quickly."[50]

Except for wishing that the United States enter the war as quickly as possible, it is unlikely that Lloyd George believed a word of this. To the contrary, he knew that Wilson's presence at a post-war peace conference, with all his palaver of "freedom of the seas" and "self-determination of peoples," would complicate matters, not simplify them. But he knew what would appeal to Wilson.

In early January, Lloyd George traveled to Rome to meet with his Entente partners. Ever the "Easterner," he wanted the Allies in 1917 to avoid another direct assault in the West; he preferred that the Allies concentrate on the Italian front, his greatest fear being casualties on the order of the Somme. Although Briand was also an "Easterner," Lloyd George's idea was rejected. Briand had just replaced Joffre with Gen. Robert Nivelle, appointing him over the more senior generals Pétain and Foch, and Nivelle had planned a spring offensive in the area of the trench line in the valley of the Aisne river known as the "Chemin des Dames," the "ladies' road" so named for the two daughters of Louis XV who traveled it by coach to and from Paris. Briand was in no position to oppose his new general-in-chief. Nivelle was not present at the Rome conference, but Lloyd George met him afterwards, and was very impressed. He was "tall, youthful-looking, of elegant bearing…proud and clean-cut."[51] Raised by an English mother, he spoke perfect, unaccented English. He told Lloyd George that his offensive would be primarily a French offensive, and that it would win the war. Having had some success at Verdun, he possessed a certain amount of credibility. He promised that if the offensive did not succeed after two days, he would call a halt. For Lloyd George, terrified of casualties on the scale of the Somme, it was the clinching argument. Lloyd George invited Nivelle to London, where on January 15 he presented his plan to the War Cabinet. Gen. Haig was not convinced, but went along. Clemenceau also liked Nivelle, but after visiting with Pétain, who advised Clemenceau that the French should stay on the defensive until the Americans entered the war, Clemenceau shared Pétain's skepticism (which was also shared by Foch) of Nivelle's offensive. History has credited Clemenceau with the maxim "War is too important to be left to the generals." There is no evidence that he was the first to utter it, but he did adopt it as his own.

Lloyd George was never one to leave war to the generals, which in part explains the mutual loathing between him and Haig. He told Frances Stevenson: "Haig does not care how many men he loses. He just squanders the lives of these boys. I mean to save some of them in the future. He seems to think they are his property. I am their trustee."[52] Haig called Lloyd George a "cur," (another slander sufficient to have one expelled from the House of Commons), but not to his face.[53] Haig had his own idea for a summer offensive, in Flanders, which Lloyd George also opposed. Lloyd George would have loved to have replaced Haig, but could not. For one, he had promised the Tories that he would not when he formed the coalition government. Even absent the promise, replacing Haig would have been difficult. He was well-placed politically, with a direct line to the king. In February, Haig gave an interview to a French journalist in which he complained of a lack of guns, an indirect swipe at Lloyd George, who had been the minister of munitions. Their relations worsened.

In November, 1916, the German secretary of state for foreign affairs, Gottlieb von Jagow, retired. He was succeeded by the undersecretary, Arthur Zimmermann, a Prussian lawyer who became the first non-aristocrat to hold the office. Scarcely two months in office, on January 19, 1917, Zimmermann wrote a coded telegram to Heinrich von Eckhardt, the German minister in Mexico City, which was transmitted to Eckhardt from the German embassy in Washington, D.C. What became infamous as the "Zimmermann Telegram" reads as follows:

> "It is our purpose on the 1ˢᵗ of February to commence the unrestricted U-boat war. The attempt will be made to keep America neutral in spite of it all. In case we should not be successful in this, we propose Mexico an alliance upon the following terms: Joint conduct of the war. Joint conclusion of peace. Ample financial support and an agreement on our part that Mexico shall gain back by conquest the territory lost by her at a prior period in Texas, New Mexico and Arizona. Arrangement as to details is entrusted to your Excellency.
>
> "Your Excellency will make the above known to the President in strict confidence at the moment that war breaks out with the United States, and you will add the suggestion that Japan will be requested to take part at once and that he simultaneously mediate between ourselves and Japan.
>
> "Please inform the President that the unrestricted use of our U-boats now offers the prospect of forcing England to sue for peace in the course of a few months.
>
> "Confirm receipt. Zimmermann."[54]

As British Naval Intelligence had broken the German diplomatic code, it is possible that British officers had read Zimmermann's missive before Eckhardt did. Their problem was how to disclose it without revealing that they were reading everything that Zimmermann wrote. So they sat on the telegram for a month, inventing a cover story about purchasing the telegram in Mexico. Then, on February 23, a Friday, they called Ambassador Page to the Foreign Office. In what Page later described as "the most dramatic moment of my life,"[55] Foreign Secretary Arthur Balfour solemnly handed Page the telegram.

Zimmermann's proposal to Mexico was the height of hypocrisy. There was no chance that Mexico could ever recover Texas, Arizona or New Mexico, but it could not hurt to tie down a few American divisions in the event America entered the war. Page transmitted the telegram to State Department Counselor Frank Polk, (Lansing was on vacation) who deciphered it and transmitted it to the White House on Sunday evening. When Lansing returned and read the telegram, he assumed that this was the "overt act" that surely would bring the United States to war with Germany. House, Page and most of Wilson's cabinet now believed that war was inevitable, and that if the Zimmermann Telegram was not the "overt act," some other event would end America's neutrality. Wilson had other ideas. He still hoped that the Germans might abandon unlimited submarine warfare, and that the United States could avoid entry into the war.

When Wilson broke diplomatic relations with Germany but did not declare war, it left up in the air what would happen to American merchant shipping. What happened was that American shippers kept their ships bottled up in port, fearing the U-boats. Wilson then determined to adopt a policy of "armed neutrality," as a middle ground between declaring war and doing nothing. He had the authority to authorize the arming of merchant ships, but wanted Congress to back him up. He drew up a proposed "Armed Ship Bill" that gave Wilson the authority to arm merchant ships. But it went further, authorizing him to "employ such other instrumentalities and methods as he may in his judgment and discretion deem necessary and adequate to protect our ships and the citizens of the United States in their legitimate pursuits on the high seas."[56] On February 26, the day after he read the Zimmermann Telegram, Wilson again appeared before a joint session of Congress, pleading for passage of the Armed Ship Bill. He did not disclose the Zimmermann Telegram, possibly in fear that it was a British ruse to bring the Americans into the war. The Democrats enthusiastically applauded Wilson, as did Clemenceau: "What other reply," he wrote from Paris, "could the chief of the great American republic make, than to ask the representatives of the people to provide him with the greatest powers of action? This is precisely what he came to the Capitol to do, in the most measured language, with such overtones of decisiveness, that there can be no doubt as to what must inevitably follow."[57] He was mistaken. The Republicans, including Sen. Lodge, were willing to arm American ships. They were not willing to give Wilson "such other instrumentalities and methods," which to them smacked of the authority to wage war without Congressional approval.

When Wilson broke diplomatic relations with Germany on February 3, he said: "I refuse to believe that it is the intention of the German authorities to do in fact what they have warned us they will feel at liberty to do." Almost as he spoke to Congress on February 26, he received his answer. A U-boat sank the armed Cunard liner *Laconia* without warning off the coast of Ireland. Two Americans from Chicago, Mrs. Mary Hoy and her daughter, who coincidentally were friends of Mrs. Wilson, perished. The next day, Mrs. Hoy's son was quoted: "What is America going to do? If this is not the overt act for which the President was waiting, then I don't know what to call it."[58] It was not until March 1 that Wilson received the confirmation of the authenticity of the Zimmermann Telegram. Wilson authorized Secretary Lansing to release it, first to Sen. Gilbert Hitchcock of the Foreign Relations Committee, and then to the Associated Press.

Since the outbreak of the war, something of a geographic divide had developed with reference to Americans' attitude toward the conflict. Along the eastern seaboard and in the larger cities, people followed the war with great interest. But in the West, the war was something "out there" that they could, and did, ignore. The Zimmermann Telegram changed that. People in the West awoke one morning to realize that the war might come home to them, and might be fought in their back yards.

German-American newspaper editors were quick to denounce the Zimmermann Telegram as a forgery. They were embarrassed when Zimmermann, in answer to a question at a press conference, freely admitted that he had indeed authored the infamous telegram. He was nonplussed by its revelation, but made no apologies for his motivation. After all, he explained, bargaining for alliances, especially in wartime, is what nations do.

The outrage over the Zimmermann Telegram resulted in the House passing the Armed Ship Bill, 403-13, most of those voting believing it was the step that would lead America into the war. It would have passed overwhelmingly in the Senate but for a filibuster led by Republican Progressives Robert La Follette and George W. Norris. The bill would die if they could maintain the filibuster until March 4, when, by statute, the Senate term would end. And so, to Wilson's fury, it did. Wilson denounced the filibusterers as: "A little group of willful men, representing no opinion but their own," who had "rendered the great Government of the United States helpless and contemptible."[59] The next day, Wilson was sworn in for his second term. In his inaugural address, he made it clear that he would adopt "armed neutrality," the Senate filibuster notwithstanding: "We stand firm in armed neutrality since it seems that in no other way can we demonstrate what it is we insist upon and cannot forgo. We may even be drawn on, by circumstances, not by our own purpose or desire, to a more active assertion of our rights as we see them and a more immediate association with the great struggle itself."[60] He spoke through a cold, raw wind, caught a cold, and closeted himself for a week.

On March 15, Tsar Nicholas II abdicated. A week later, he and his family were arrested. The House of Romanov, which had ruled Russia for more than three hundred years, was finished. The Russians had suffered an estimated *six million* casualties in the war. The British military attaché estimated that one million Russian soldiers had deserted. The new provisional government promised to be democratic, relieving the Allies of the embarrassment of being allied with a dictator. House urged Wilson to recognize the new government immediately, and Wilson acted on the advice. On March 22, the United States became the first nation to recognize the new government. Lloyd George hoped that the change in the Russian government might result in a more vigorous prosecution of the war. Clemenceau, never a supporter of the tsars, also initially favored the new government, but soon began to worry that a peace party might seize power. The House of Commons sent its "fraternal greetings" to the Russian parliament, the Duma. But within weeks it became clear that the overthrow of the tsar had plunged the country into chaos, which might result in Russia quitting the war altogether. It revealed what a colossal blunder Germany's decision to revert to unrestricted U-boat warfare had been. In his war memoirs, Grand Admiral Alfred von Tirpitz rued the decision: "Had we been able to foresee…the Russian Revolution, we should perhaps not have needed to regard the submarine of 1917 as the last resource."[61]

Two days after the tsar's abdication, Aristide Briand's government collapsed. In June of 1916 Briand had survived a no-confidence vote in the Chamber of Deputies by a huge margin, 444-80. By December, his margin was down to 344-160, Clemenceau denouncing Briand in the Senate: "After two years of war France had arrived at an alarming degree of disorder, economic, diplomatic and military."[62] Briand considered the reduced margin a defeat, and reorganized his government, ousting Joffre and bringing in Gen. Lyautey as minister of war. It proved to be his undoing. Lyautey was a respected general, but he was clueless as a politician. He refused to discuss the state of military aviation even in a *secret* session of the Chamber of Deputies. A firestorm erupted in the Chamber. He simply stalked out. When Briand could find no one to serve as his minister of war, he resigned. President Poincaré asked seventy-five-year-old Alexandre Ribot to form a government. It would be Ribot's fifth turn as prime minister. Ribot, like Clemenceau, had married an American, the former Mary Burch of Chicago.

Suddenly, American ships were being torpedoed at what seemed like one every day. On March 14, the steamer *Algonquin* was torpedoed without warning. No Americans were killed, but the U-boat commander refused to rescue the survivors in their open boats in the North Atlantic. Three American ships were torpedoed between March 16 and 18. On the *Vigilancia,* fifteen American crew members perished. The next day, President Roosevelt demanded that Wilson declare war, issuing a statement from Sagamore Hill: "Let us wage war on Germany with all our energy and courage, and regain the right to look the whole world in the eyes without flinching." Of the three torpedoed ships: "If these are not overt acts of war, then Lexington and Bunker Hill were not acts of war."[63] Lansing met with Wilson that day, urging him to declare war. He left the meeting not knowing what Wilson would decide. He wrote to House, urging House to convince Wilson to declare war. House wrote to Wilson, saying he was prepared to visit Wilson if Wilson wished him to. House was wise enough to know when not to push Wilson, and this was such a time. House would take no part in the decision to enter the war.

The following day, March 20, at 2:30 P.M., Wilson met with his cabinet. Wilson knew they were unanimous in their desire that he declare war. Wilson calmly greeted and shook hands with each of them, then took his seat at the head of the table. He asked each of them for their advice. Each of them stated that war was inevitable. Lansing spoke so forcefully that Wilson asked him to lower his voice, lest someone in the corridor listen in. After more than two hours, Wilson adjourned the meeting: "Well, gentlemen, I think that there is no doubt as to what your advice is, and I thank you,"[64] and he left, not indicating his decision. According to Attorney-General Thomas Watt Gregory, he had left them in "something akin to a panic."[65]

Wilson probably made the decision to declare war the following day. He called the Congress into special session for April 2, "to receive a communication concerning grave matters of national policy."[66] There was now little doubt as to what he would say, the *New York Times* headlining the following morning: "War Preparations Under Way," "War Policy Taking Shape," "Getting the Navy Ready for War," and "Has Plan to Call a Million Men."[67]

It is interesting to speculate as to why Wilson finally decided to declare war when he did, rather than giving "armed neutrality" a chance to succeed. In his magisterial five-volume biography of Wilson, Professor Arthur S. Link lists what were *not* the reasons he declared war: He did not believe the Allies were losing the war and needed to be rescued. He did not go in on the side of the Allies because he believed in the righteousness of their cause; he was truly agnostic about the causes of the war. He was not pushed into the war by public opinion. The most likely reason that Wilson opted for belligerency over neutrality is that he finally came to believe what House had advised him months before, that he would be able to exert his influence over a post-war settlement only if the United States participated in the war. As he told Jane Addams shortly before he made his decision, "as head of a nation participating in the war, the President of the United States would have a seat at the Peace Table, but that if he remained the representative of a neutral country he could at best only 'call through a crack in the door.'"[68]

Wilson finally invited House to the White House, and they met in the afternoon of March 27. If House can be believed, it was an extraordinary meeting. Wilson told House that he had decided to declare war. By now everyone assumed it, but House was the first to hear it. House advised Wilson that the situation Wilson now found himself in was not as difficult as others he had faced, but that it was one for which he was not "well fitted." "He admitted this and said he did not believe he was fitted for the Presidency under such conditions," to which House agreed: "I thought he was too refined, too civilized, too intellectual, too cultivated not to see the incongruity and absurdity of war. It needed a man of coarser fiber and one less of a philosopher than the President to conduct a brutal, vigorous and successful war."[69]

Anticipating that Wilson would call for a declaration of war on April 2, William Jennings Bryan made a desperate appeal, "exercising the citizen's right to petition," which he addressed to every member of Congress: "To you, and only to you, is given the constitutional authority to declare war—war which, in this case, may mean the signing of the death warrant of thousands, even millions, of your countrymen..."[70] He asked that an arbitration treaty be implemented. Unfortunately, Germany had never entered into such a treaty with the United States. But Bryan was by no means alone. The nation was divided, especially in the mid-West and West. Cities with large German populations were solidly against.

The day before Wilson went to Congress to ask for a declaration of war, Lloyd George asked his friend George Riddell: "I wonder if America will come in this week? It would be the best piece of luck we have had for some time. But I fear Wilson will only half come in."[71] But if Lloyd George, House and Wilson himself believed that

Wilson was not "well fitted" to vigorously prosecute the war once committed to it, they were all mistaken.

Wilson wrote the address himself, tapping it out on his Hammond portable typewriter. He delivered the address at 8:30 P.M. in the packed House chamber. Before he could be ushered in, police had to clear a mob of anti-war demonstrators from the Capitol steps. One struck sixty-six-year-old Sen. Lodge. Lodge returned the blow. When Wilson arrived, he was accompanied by a company of cavalry. No one was admitted without first being vetted and issued a ticket. Wilson was announced to an ovation that lasted for two minutes. Directly in front of him, in a small island of chairs, were the justices of the Supreme Court. To his side was the diplomatic corps in evening dress, seated as a group for the first time. Most senators (but not Robert La Follette) wore or carried a small flag.

He spoke for thirty minutes. He began: "I have called the Congress into extraordinary session because there are serious, very serious, choices of policy to be made, and made immediately, which it was neither right nor constitutionally permissible that I should assume the responsibility of making." He then reviewed the recent history of Germany's declaration of unrestricted U-boat warfare and the destruction that followed. He admitted: "I was for a little while unable to believe that such things would in fact be done by any government that had hitherto subscribed to the humane practices of civilized nations....I am not now thinking of the loss of property involved, immense and serious as that is, but only of the wanton and wholesale destruction of the lives of non-combatants, men, women and children, engaged in pursuits which have always, even in the darkest periods of modern history, been deemed innocent and legitimate. Property can be paid for; the lives of peaceful and innocent people cannot be. The present German submarine warfare against commerce is a warfare against mankind."

It had been less than two months since he had stood before this same body asking for "armed neutrality," and now he was at pains to explain the change of course. "[A]rmed neutrality, it now appears, is impracticable." Armed freighters were, in fact, warships, and the Germans would treat them as such. "Armed neutrality is ineffectual enough at best...It is likely to produce what it is meant to prevent; it is practically certain to draw us into the war without either the rights or the effectiveness of belligerents."

"With a profound sense of the solemn and even tragical character of the step I am taking and of the grave responsibilities which it involves, but in unhesitating obedience to what I deem my constitutional duty, I advise that the Congress declare the course of the Imperial German Government to be in fact nothing less than war against the government and people of the United States; that it formally accept the status of belligerent which has thus been thrust upon it; and that it take immediate steps not only to put the country in a more thorough state of defense but also to exert all its power and employ all its resources to bring the Government of the German Empire to terms and end the war." It was a distinction without a difference, but he was not asking Congress to declare war. He was asking Congress to recognize that the United States was already at war with Germany.

He set out what must be done. The Army must be expanded by five hundred thousand men, chosen "upon the principle of universal liability to service,"—the draft. To the Allies, he would extend "the most liberal financial credits, in order that our resources may so far as possible be added to theirs." Many details would need to be ironed out, but with these words, Great Britain, now teetering at the edge of bankruptcy, was saved.

He then arrived at the fundament of his address, and the words that would forever be his legacy. With the "Prussian autocracy…there can be no assured security for the democratic governments of the world." The German government was the "natural foe of liberty." Defeating Germany was not enough; the German government was a menace and had to be overthrown. "*The world must be made safe for democracy.*" He had gone from "peace without victory" to the overthrow of the German government in less than three months.[72]

He had asked that war be declared only against Germany. He had pointedly not declared war against Austria-Hungary. More importantly, he had not signed America on as an "ally" of Great Britain, France and Italy; the United States would be an "associated" power. It would give Wilson a freer hand in the post-war settlement. The Allies would have to trust that Wilson would not negotiate a separate peace with the Germans.

After Wilson's address, American flags began appearing all over Paris. The newly-installed prime minister, Alexandre Ribot, addressed the cheering Chamber of Deputies: "Entrance of the war with us of the most pacific democracy is a historic fact without equal…[T]he great American nation solemnly declares it cannot remain neutral to the great conflict between right and violence, between civilization and barbarism."[73] He turned to Ambassador William G. Sharp, seated in the gallery, who rose and bowed in acknowledgement of their cheers. The same scene was repeated in the Senate, where handkerchiefs and flags were waved and Ambassador Sharp again rose and acknowledged the cheers. Leading the cheers was Clemenceau.

The next day Clemenceau wrote his most hopeful column of the war. Whatever he had thought and said of Wilson following "peace without victory" was forgotten in the moment: "The adventurous spirit of our new allies will not fail to make itself felt by a series of astonishing blows…Henceforth, fate will speak. To begin with, the tragedy of this new great phase of history has found the man it needed to work out its ends….The chief of this great nation has had the immortal honor of rising up and declaring in the name of his fellow citizens: 'We will not choose the path of submission'…When has the world ever witnessed a finer spectacle of the heights a human mind can rise to in the hour of such a tragic decision? Who dared say the people of the United States were incapable of generous ideas? What more splendid refutation could be possible?"[74]

A week after declaring war, Wilson received President Roosevelt in the White House, who praised Wilson for his call for a draft. During the meeting, Roosevelt asked Wilson if Wilson would permit him to lead a division he would raise and equip himself, a revived *Rough Riders*. Wilson did not reject the suggestion outright, but he did not agree to it either. A month later, Clemenceau authored what must have been his strangest missive of the war, an "open letter" to Wilson, pleading for Wilson to allow Roosevelt to lead troops in France. Unfortunately, it was rife with put-downs and faint praise: "Perhaps it would have been possible to advance the hour of your intervention. It is no longer time to discuss the problem, since fate has decided….The slower we have been in realizing our joint action, the greater the need of hastening the final decision on the battlefield which will give us lasting peace." He added: "If I have the temerity of addressing you it is because it may be permitted to me to throw light on certain aspects of ourselves which perhaps are not sufficiently clear to you. Allow me to say, in all candor, that at the present moment, there is in France one name which sums up the beauty of American intervention. It is the name of Roosevelt…It is possible that your own mind, inclosed in its austere legal frontiers, which has been the source of so many noble actions, has failed to be impressed by the vital hold which personalities like Roosevelt have on popular imagination. But you are too much the philosopher to ignore that the influence on the people of great leaders of men often exceeded their personal merits thanks to the legendary halo surrounding them."[75]

If Clemenceau really intended his letter to have any effect, he could have delivered it privately, through Ambassador Sharp or to House. An open letter in which he compared Roosevelt's "vitality" to Wilson the "philosopher" who had unduly delayed American intervention was surely not the way to do it. What could he have been thinking? In the event, Wilson did not consent to Roosevelt forming his own division.

Since the onset of the war on the Western front, the Allies had expended tens of thousands of lives for every square kilometer they gained. Then, beginning in mid-March, Gen. Ludendorff pulled the front line of his trenches back by 140 kilometers, eliminating a dangerous salient and freeing up nine divisions. The new strengthened line became known to the Allies as the "Hindenburg" line. Clemenceau, whose watchword since the beginning of the war had been "The Germans are at Noyon," could no longer claim it; they no longer were at Noyon. As the Germans retreated, they laid waste to everything. They cut down trees, poisoned wells, destroyed buildings and smashed furnishings. "We have orders," a German soldier remarked to one local, "to leave you nothing but your eyes with which to cry."[76]

Ludendorff's withdrawal presented Gen. Nivelle with a problem. His spring offensive, which he had sold to Briand and Lloyd George with such assurances, was premised upon an attack on a salient that no longer existed. He should have altered the plan. He did not, and his failure to do so is what caused professional soldiers like Pétain and Foch to deprecate it. Before the attack, Nivelle deputized one of his colonels, Georges Renouard, to travel to Paris to explain the plan to the minister of war, Gen. Lyautey. Coincidentally, Renouard had served under Lyautey in Algeria. Renouard dutifully and without a hint of his true feelings reviewed the plan for Lyautey. When he finished Lyautey said: "Come, come, my dear Georges…tell me the truth…what do you think of [the plan]?" To which Renouard replied: "I think as you do…it is mad."[77]

On April 3, the day after Wilson declared war, Nivelle met with Prime Minister Ribot, assuring him that "under no circumstances would he repeat a battle of the Somme."[78] The British, in what was intended to be a diversion, attacked at Arras on April 9. Rain caused Nivelle to delay his attack on the Chemin des Dames, at the southern end of the Hindenburg Line, until 6:00 A.M. on April 16. The assault was effectively stopped by machine gun fire by 7:00 A.M. His promise to Lloyd George and Briand that he would terminate the assault if it failed after forty-eight hours was forgotten. By the fifth day, the French had suffered 130,000 casualties, of which 29,000 were fatalities. They had gained four miles on a sixteen-mile front. The British fared no better at Arras. After some initial success, the Germans brought up reserves and blunted the attack. Another battle of attrition set in. Nivelle continued the offensive into early May, to mounting casualties. He refused to resign. Ribot sacked him, replacing him with Pétain. The casualties were not greater than those at Verdun, but the expectations had been higher, expectations fueled by Nivelle himself.

It was, at least for now, the end of the French Army as a fighting force. For the first time in thirty-three months, the *poilus* refused to fight. What became known as the "mutinies" were not mutinies in that there was no violence directed against their officers. But in half of all the units in the army they simply refused to return to the trenches. They demanded better food, regular leave and better accommodations while on leave, and an increase in the meager pensions that forced their families into penury while they fought at the front. The man who took it upon himself to rebuild the army was Pétain. He toured the entire line, meeting with soldiers of all ranks, promising to heed their complaints, appealing to their honor. He asked a young lieutenant what was the main cause of discontent in the army. The reply: "The neglect of the men by their officers." Pétain turned and addressed the officers: "Well, gentlemen, you heard that?"[79] There would be no great assaults until the army had been rebuilt. His motto was "Lavish with steel; stingy with blood."[80] By August, Pétain had sufficiently restored the morale of the army to launch another attack at Verdun, and another in October. But this was, after all, the army. The ringleaders were rounded up; forty-nine of them met a firing squad.

It was fortunate that, due to the ferocious censorship, the Germans never learned of the "mutinies." Clemenceau knew of them. Of course, he could not even hint of them in his daily column. They could not be mentioned in the Chamber of Deputies, and only indirectly in the Senate Army Committee that Clemenceau chaired. The concern among the politicians was the extent to which the revolts had been fomented by anarchist propaganda. The generals believed they were, and no one was more eager to crack down on the "anarchists" than Clemenceau himself.

By mid-1917, after the failure of Nivelle's offensive and the collapse of the Army, it is likely that Clemenceau had come to believe that France, by herself, could never evict the Germans from his country. This must have been a crushing realization to the man who had daily championed the French soldier and the inevitability of victory. The French had but one hope—the Americans. The French, he now believed, needed to hold body and soul together for the year in which it might take the Americans to recruit, train and deliver their army of deliverance. In that year, France had to maintain its morale, and in order to do that, everything that could be done had to be done to prevent the anarchists from undermining civilian morale, which was weakening. The U-boat war resulted in rising food prices. There were strikes, some violent. And in the background of all of this was the Russian Revolution.

On June 25, Prime Minister Ribot and his minister of war, Paul Painlevé, appeared before the Senate Army Committee, chaired by Clemenceau. As always, they met in secret. He warned Ribot: "Every day we receive these documents. We have some you don't know about. I received just this morning a letter from a man whose name is very well known in the Army (Nivelle?); he warned the government a long time ago...he gave indications of the state of the troops...This is what is happening; these are the men—he names them—who are making the propaganda; this is what I am told when I speak to the soldiers." Clemenceau continued: "All the soldiers say it: 'Someone sent me a brochure.' The soldiers on leave repeat the speeches they have heard. This cannot continue."[81] Clemenceau singled out one man for blame: the minister of the interior, Louis Malvy.

In Third Republic France, the minister of the interior was a far more powerful figure than the secretary of the interior in the United States or the home secretary in Great Britain. In France, the minister of the interior was in charge of state security. The censorship that Clemenceau suffered under was directed by him. Louis Malvy was a radical Republican, a protégé of Joseph Caillaux. First elected to the Chamber of Deputies in 1909 at the age of thirty-four, he had served as the pre-war minister of the interior under Viviani, and had remained as such under Briand and now under Ribot. He maintained excellent relations with the CGT, the umbrella labor federation. As an extreme left-wing politician in Ribot's cabinet, he was the embodiment of the *Union Sacrée*. Before the war, his ministry had compiled "Carnet [list] B" a list of 2,500 suspected subversives, spies and labor leaders who might organize a general strike. Only seven hundred on the list were considered spies, but these were targeted for arrest in the event of war. When war came, Malvy came to Clemenceau and asked him if he should lock up the suspected spies on Carnet B. According to legend, Clemenceau advised: "I do not see how you can do otherwise."[82] Malvy elected not to take Clemenceau's advice.

Now, before the Senate Army Committee, Clemenceau accused Malvy of putting politics before country, specifically seeking to maintain his good relations with the labor unions and the socialists, who "thought that in order to have a few socialists, it was necessary to spare this or that anarchist."[83] He continued: "In times of peace, we can be more or less brutal, more or less soft; it's not important. We throw a man on the floor when he's wrong and its over. But it's not more of the same today. At this point, we are almost victorious. I believe that, if we stand firm, it is impossible that we should not be victorious…It will take a little more time and we will have to hold on until the end. As for America, she arrives with her men, her materiél, her ships, her cannon." [Here, a senator interrupted: "With her money!"] "The plan is to hold for a year. In a year, we will have a million Americans on the front. We must, therefore, hold, and for this we must maintain the state of morale." Referring to the anarchists: "These are men we must crack down on."[84]

On July 22 Clemenceau denounced Malvy in an open session of the Senate. He believed it was the greatest speech of his life. Years later, his secretary Jean Martet recalled: "I can still hear that speech. Whoever heard it will be hearing it for the rest of his life. What a speech! Neither was it composed, nor reasoned, nor, even, apparently, meditated, prepared: but it was played, lived, admirably. The words were thrown out in armfuls."[85] "I am not a minister," Clemenceau began, "I am nothing. I am an old man who is at the end of his political life....I knew that the war would come. I claimed it a thousand times. I warned my fellow citizens. I didn't believe I would see it...It came! Like all of you, I spent the most harrowing three years of my life....A force of idealism led me to believe that, perhaps, in a relatively short time, all of France could throw itself at Germany, and with England win an immortal victory that would have gone beyond all the splendors that history had recorded. This was not given to us. The Germans were too prepared, and we not enough. One organization of all means without honor, the other all honor without sufficient organization of means; that is the truth."[86] He was met, according to the official report, with "vigorous applause."

Then he got down to cases. Clemenceau had never seen "Carnet B," but he assumed (correctly) that one of the men listed on it was one "Miguel Almereyda," a pseudonym for Jean-Baptiste Vigo, a notorious anarchist. Almereyda's prison record, which dated back to 1901, included convictions for manufacturing explosives, incitement to murder and attempted sabotage. And yet, he was now not only walking the streets but writing a column—uncensored—for a daily anarchist rag, *Le Bonnet Rouge*. Almereyda had won this largesse through a deal he had cut with Malvy before the war; for his freedom, Almereyda agreed not to cause trouble when France mobilized. *Bonnet Rouge* was subsidized by Joseph Caillaux. When, in 1917, Caillaux's subsidy ended, support for *Bonnet Rouge* was taken up by the Germans, a fact that became known when a *Bonnet Rouge* staffer was caught at the Swiss border carrying a check for 150,000 francs, the check signed by a German.

Now Clemenceau had Malvy in his sights. Without mentioning the "mutinies," he blamed Malvy for not intercepting the pacifist propaganda that made its way to the troops. He mocked Malvy's defense of refusing to arrest anarchists because he didn't want to upset members of the working class by arresting their leaders, the same men whose support Caillaux would need should he ever return to power. Malvy's defense was that by treading lightly on the anarchists, France's mobilization had in fact gone smoothly. "You have reproached me for not bringing you enough heads; I bring you results," said Malvy, to which Clemenceau retorted: "I reproach you for having betrayed the interests of France."[87] To those old enough, it recalled Clemenceau's 1885 denunciation of Jules Ferry. ("These are no longer ministers whom I see before me. They are men charged with high treason..."[88]) The *New York Times* reported that: "Clemenceau, despite his 76 years, attacked M. Malvy for two and a half hours with a vigor and ferocity that well-justified his nickname of the Tiger."[89]

Malvy did not resign immediately; he took a holiday. But Almereyda was finally arrested. On August 20, he was found dead in his cell, strangled by his own shoelaces, an apparent suicide. Malvy resigned ten days later. Ribot tried to reshuffle his cabinet, but when the Socialists withdrew their support, his government collapsed. They were angered by his refusal to allow them to participate in an international Socialist congress to be held in Stockholm. (The Army opposed their attendance at a conference that would include German delegates). When Ribot refused to issue passports for them to attend, they walked. It was the end of the *Union Sacree*. Ribot's minister of war, Paul Painlevé, tried to form a government without the Socialists. He named himself minister of war, and installed Ribot as minister of foreign affairs. Painlevé asked Clemenceau to join the government; Clemenceau again refused. He had recently told his friend and future biographer, Georges Wormser, that Poincaré would call on him to form a government before the end of the year. Painlevé's government lasted eight weeks. During his short ministry, Lenin came to power and took Russia out of the war.

On the last day of July, Gen. Haig launched his own offensive, in Flanders. He had been warned that this season always brought the heaviest rain, with the regularity of the Indian monsoon. He ignored the warning. This, the Third Battle of Ypres, would go down in history by the name of a Belgian village—Passchendaele. Lloyd George, ever the "Easterner," opposed it, in a memo addressed to Haig and Gen. Robertson, fearing it would lead to nothing except "the driving of the enemy back a few barren miles—beyond that nothing to show except a ghastly casualty list."[90] Pétain opposed it, as did Foch, who termed Haig's plan "futile, fantastic and dangerous."[91] But Chief of the General Staff Gen. Robertson supported Haig, and Bonar Law did not wish to oppose the military. Lloyd George, a coalition prime minister dependent on the support of the Tories, had no alternative but to go along.

The assault began in some of the heaviest rain in thirty years. Haig's rolling artillery barrage filled low-lying Flanders with water-filled shell holes in which the advancing soldiers became mired and drowned. Cloud cover prevented aerial reconnaissance. By mid-August it was still raining. Guns were stuck in mud to their axles; men in mud to their knees. Haig was advised to call it off. Haig, who never wavered in his optimism, replied: "Attack!" The casualties were censored, and at its height Great Britain employed four thousand censors combing through the newspapers and the mail. It finally ended with a late-October assault by the Canadians on the village of Passchendaele. They suffered fifteen thousand casualties. After the battle, at the start of a meeting with Canadian Prime Minister Sir Robert Borden, Borden took Lloyd George by the lapels and shook him. In the end, the Allies had advanced an average of one mile *per month*. They had suffered 260,000 casualties. Haig insisted the offensive had been a triumph. In a backhanded reference, Lloyd George remarked: "We have won great victories. When I look at the appalling casualty lists I sometimes wish it had not been necessary to win so many."[92] Just as Lloyd George could not dismiss Haig before Passchendaele, he was powerless to do so afterwards. Later in the year, Lloyd George asked his secretary of state for war, Lord Derby, to fire Haig. Derby refused, and Lloyd George backed down. Haig had too many supporters, not the least of whom was the king.

On August 1, Pope Benedict XV make a public appeal to end the war. His proposal echoed much of what Wilson had propounded in his "peace without victory" speech, including disarmament and a "concert of nations" enforcing arbitration. But it was essentially a call for the *status quo ante* without indemnities. Wilson met with a group of senators to discuss the proposal, one of whom was Sen. Lodge, who noted in his diary that Wilson had opined that "there could be no peace, no real peace, until we and our Allies were able to dictate it, but the President was of the opinion that this could not be said at this time."[93]

Wilson responded to the Pope's appeal on August 27. Wilson wrote it himself; it could have been written by Clemenceau. After acknowledging the Pope's "moving appeal" and "the force of the humane and generous motives which prompted it," Wilson quickly poured cold water on the Pope's appeal: "Our response must be based upon the stern facts and upon nothing else." This is the heart of it: "The object of this war is to deliver the free peoples of the world from the menace of the actual power of a vast military establishment controlled by an irresponsible government which, having secretly planned to dominate the world, proceeded to carry out the plan without regard either to the sacred obligations of treaty or the long established practices and long cherished principles of international action and honor; which chose its own time for the war; delivered its blow fiercely and suddenly; stopped at no barrier either of law or of mercy; swept a whole continent within the tide of blood, not the blood of soldiers only, but the blood of innocent women and children also and of the helpless poor; and now stands balked but not defeated, the enemy of four-fifths of the world. This power is not the German people. It is the ruthless master of the German people....Can peace be based upon a restitution of its power or upon any word of honor it could pledge in a treaty of settlement and accommodation?"[94] So there it was: for Wilson to make peace, the German military must first be overthrown. Clemenceau, not burdened by the requirements of diplomatic politesse, was much more succinct: "[T]he proposals of

Benedict XV emanate from an inadequate sense of realities. The fact, however brutal, cannot be contested. It is an Austrian peace, that is to say, a German peace, to call it by its proper name, that is proposed to us by the Germanified Vatican. A peace against France, a peace against the people of the Entente, a peace to profit the violators of right, against those whose rights have been violated."[95]

Even before Lloyd George became prime minister, he chafed under what he saw as the lack of military coordination among the Allies. The British and French would assign responsibility for various sectors of the trench line, but beyond that, they acted completely independently. He now began to press for a combined Allied command. It would have an added benefit: If Haig could not be removed, a combined command might at least circumvent him.

On September 3, Lloyd George wrote a very long (upwards of three thousand words) letter to Wilson, which Lord Reading, then visiting Washington, personally delivered to Wilson on September 20. Headed "Private and Personal," it began by noting that: "We are approaching a very difficult period in which it will be necessary to take far reaching decisions which will be of the utmost importance in our future campaign..." Then the hard truth: "The hard fact which faces us today is that...the Germans at the end of 1917 as at the end of each of the previous years' campaign, find themselves in possession of more and not less Allied territory." Part of this he attributed to the collapse of Russia, "But I am convinced from my experience of the last three years that the comparative failure of the Allies in 1917 is also in some measure due to defects in their mutual arrangements for conducting the war....As compared with the enemy the fundamental weakness of the Allies is that the direction of their military operations lacks real unity." He noted that the Germans had effectively taken over the Austrian and Turkish militaries, so that the Central Powers were "one command and one front." The Allies, however, were four separate governments and four separate General Staffs...each of which is possessed of complete knowledge only of its front and its own national resources, and which draws up a plan of campaign which is designed to produce results mainly on its own sector of the front." There had been occasional conferences, but these were "an attempt to synchronize what are in reality four separate plans of campaign. There has never been an Allied Body which had knowledge of the resources of all the Allies and which could prepare a single co-ordinated plan..."

He then reviewed the military history of the war to date. The Allies had concentrated on knocking Germany out of the war, since it was the undoubted leader of the Central

Powers, and that if Germany could be defeated the others would follow suit. This might have been the right strategy at the outset, but each summer offensive had not yet "produced any decisive results in breaking down the enemy military organization. It still opposes a solid and hitherto impenetrable defence." He proposed an alternative strategy, to concentrate on Germany's allies. "[I]f the inability of the Prussian military machine to defend its allies were thus proved, and the dream of Eastern domination thus destroyed by the defection of one of these allies, the whole enemy military edifice might fall rapidly in ruins."

Lloyd George was writing at a time when Haig was still trumpeting the eventual success of his campaign. He alerted Wilson: "We have now reached a point when it is becoming more and more difficult to maintain, not only the national unity of each of the Allies, but unity among the Allies themselves, in the vigorous prosecution of the war. Every nation in Europe is becoming exhausted. The desire for peace in some quarters is becoming almost irresistible. The argument that any kind of peace is better than the continuation of the present suffering and carnage is daily increasing its appeal. At the same time people are beginning to ask themselves whether victory is obtainable at all and this question will be asked with all the greater insistence in a few weeks time if the end of the campaigning season shows that the whole campaign of 1917 has made no decisive impression upon the German military position…The preservation of that moral unity and greater tenacity will be our principal task during the forthcoming winter, and I believe that it depends more and more upon the British Commonwealth and the United States."[96]

Wilson would later heed Lloyd George's appeal. He would appoint Army chief of staff Gen. Tasker H. Bliss, as his permanent representative to the Allied War Council.

Lloyd George now began to press for an inter-Allied war council. What he (and Clemenceau) wanted was a combined command headed by a generalissimo, which was anathema to Haig and Robertson. What he got was a council whose members were the respective prime ministers of the Allies and senior generals they appointed, charged with advising the operational commanders. On October 30, Painlevé arrived in London and agreed to the formation of the council. Three days later, the War Cabinet signed off on its creation. That same day, Lloyd George and Painlevé set off for Rapallo, on the Italian Riviera, to confer with their Italian ally, newly-installed Prime Minister Vittorio Emanuele Orlando, accompanied by Chief of the General Staff Gen. Robertson and Field Marshal Sir Henry Wilson for the British and Gen. Foch for the French. Lloyd George stopped off in Paris, breakfasted with Gen. Pershing, followed by a "serious" talk with Gen. Haig, advising Haig that he would let the public know the truth about the casualties. While en route to Rapallo, they learned of a catastrophic defeat the Italians had suffered at Caporetto, on the Isonzo River, where thirty-three Austrian and German divisions had mauled forty-one Italian divisions, the Italians suffering 600,000 casualties. They arrived on November 6 to meet the stunned and demoralized Italians. It was here that Lloyd George determined that he had to get rid of Robertson as well as Haig. The first meeting of what was to become the Supreme Allied War Council took place in the New Casino Hotel. Lloyd George promised to send troops to shore up the Italians. The price he exacted was the dismissal of Gen. Luigi Cadorna who, like Haig, had made repeated assaults that produced little except huge casualties. Cadorna was sacked three days later. But the immovable Robertson was another matter. When it was agreed that a permanent Supreme Allied War Council would be set up in Versailles (Painlevé wanted Paris, settled for Versailles), Robertson stormed out, muttering "I wash my hands of this present business."[97]

While they were meeting, Lenin and Trotsky's Bolsheviks overthrew the provisional government of Alexander Kerensky. On December 17, in the Russian town of Brest-Litovsk, the new government, in violation of the pact that Russia had entered into with its Allies at the start of the war, signed an armistice with Germany. By the end of 1917, the eastern front had ceased to exist. Russia was out of the war.

Lloyd George returned from Rapallo by way of Paris. Speaking at a luncheon hosted by Painlevé at the banquet hall of the War Ministry on the rue St. Dominique, he explained that the need for immediate action in light of the Italian disaster had made it necessary to start the Supreme Allied War Council without first consulting the Americans or the Russians. He then made good on his promise to Haig of the previous week: "When we advance a kilometer into the enemy's lines, snatch a small shattered village out of his cruel grip, capture a few hundred of his soldiers, we shout with unfeigned joy...But what if we had advanced 50 kilometers beyond his lines and made 200,000 of his soldiers prisoners and taken 2,500 of his best guns, with enormous quantities of ammunition and stores. What print would we have for our headlines? Have you any idea how long it would take the arsenals of France and Great Britain to manufacture 2,500 guns?"[98] Lloyd George spoke in English, so that many in the room failed to grasp its meaning, but after it was translated it was hailed by the French for the tough talk that the French knew was needed. Afterwards, he told George Riddell: "It was necessary. I had to speak strongly to secure attention both here and in France and Italy."[99] The speech created a furor in the London press, a furor fomented by Gen. Robertson himself.

The day before the luncheon, Lloyd George visited Clemenceau at his office in the rue Franklin. They spoke for approximately thirty minutes. Lloyd George could not possibly know that Clemenceau's transition from journalist to prime minister was imminent. His goal was to enlist Clemenceau's approval for a Supreme War Council headed by a powerful general.

Lloyd George had been Painlevé's guest at that Paris luncheon. The next day—November 13—Painlevé was voted out of office. He was replaced by Georges Clemenceau.

France stood at a crossroads. It could follow the ready example of Russia, and conclude the best peace possible with the Germans, ending the bloodletting but permanently ceding to the Germans some or all of Alsace-Lorraine and perhaps more. The Socialists were ready to bargain, with Caillaux as prime minister. The alternative was to fight to the finish, and the only man who fitted that role was Clemenceau, who now embodied the will to win the war. When Painlevé's government collapsed after only eight weeks, having lost the support of the Socialists, the Socialists in the Chamber of Deputies shouted "Down with Clemenceau."[100]

The next day—November 14—President Poincaré telephoned Clemenceau. The call came as no surprise, and he came immediately. When Clemenceau arrived, Poincaré thought Clemenceau looked fatter, and his deafness had increased. He worried about his health, and his will-power, and noted in his diary: "I feel more and more the risk of this adventure. But this *diable d'homme* ("devil of a man") has all patriots on his side, and if I do not call him his legendary strength would make any alternative cabinet weak."[101] The meeting was friendly, and Clemenceau was conciliatory, even towards Malvy and Caillaux. Clemenceau told Poincaré that he thought Pétain was their best military leader, despite Pétain's pessimism. But Poincaré did not ask Clemenceau to form a government during that interview. He sought the advice of three former prime ministers. The Socialist Viviani advised against. Briand opined that there would be difficulties with Clemenceau. Ribot advised Poincaré to risk it. Finally, Poincaré decided: "One has to choose between Caillaux and Clemenceau. My choice is made."[102] Poincaré called Clemenceau again, who promised to form a government within twenty-four hours. The following day was his last ever as a journalist, writing: "Isn't the problem for us simply one of a concentration of usefully apportioned forces until the crushing blow of the American avalanche?"[103] On November 16 *L'Homme Enchaine* announced that he had agreed to form a government.

He was seventy-six. He had diabetes. His hands itched from eczema. He didn't sleep well. As prime minister, he would be older than all of the other politicians and soldiers leading the war. (The next oldest—Hindenburg—was six years younger.) Most all of the old antagonists—Gambetta, Ferry, Déroulède, Jaurés—were dead, as was the sainted Louise Michel. The comrades-in-arms from the Dreyfus trials–Scheurer-Kestner, Picquart, Zola—were gone. The old friends from *La Justice* and *L'Aurore*—Camille Pelletan, Cornelius Herz and Arthur Ranc—were long since in their graves. Of his fellow members of the old National Assembly who had made peace with the Germans in 1871, he was the last one left; he had survived them all. And the greatest test of all was still before him him.

17

LA GUERRE A L'OUTRANCE—
TOTAL WAR

Home policy? I wage war! Foreign policy? I wage war! All the time I
wage war!

—Georges Clemenceau

They had met before, Clemenceau and Lloyd George, in Karlsbad in the summer of 1908, and it had not gone well. Lloyd George, then the chancellor of the exchequer, was desperately trying to balance his budget. Clemenceau, ever fearful of the enemy across the blue line of the Vosges, wanted Great Britain to increase the size of her army, which he called a "play-thing" unworthy of her name. Clemenceau came away from the brief encounter believing Lloyd George to be woefully ignorant of European affairs. They had met again in 1917, shortly before Clemenceau assumed office. Lloyd George was in Paris soliciting support for a unified command structure. Clemenceau was non-committal.

But now, in 1918, that was all behind them. Lloyd George's uncompromising execution of the war effort since becoming prime minister late in 1916 had changed Clemenceau's opinion, writing that Lloyd George was the one European statesman "up to the big events," capable of speaking "of great things greatly."[1] Lloyd George's opinion of Clemenceau was more nuanced, telling George Riddell that Clemenceau "is a great man, but he is nothing more than an intellectual machine, with great courage. He has no heart,"[2] and later: "Clemenceau is a wonderful old man, but wants humouring, considering his age…He is a remarkable old man, full of vitality and energy—a real human tiger. He governs in the old fashioned way. He gives no quarter and expects none.[3] Now that Clemenceau was prime minister* and he and Lloyd George (and Italian Prime Minister Vittorio Orlando) were the *ex officio* heads of the Supreme War Council, they would meet monthly throughout 1918. After one such meeting, Clemenceau twitted Lloyd George: "You like me, you can't help yourself."[4] It was true; he did. In his *War Memoirs*, Lloyd George recalled: "I have never transacted more important business with any man than with Georges Clemenceau, and I have never met any man during the whole course of my public life with whom I more enjoyed doing business. The many opportunities I had of exchanging views with him are amongst the most delightful and treasured memories of my life."[5]

Time may have softened Lloyd George's recollection, for there were times when their differences were serious, and at least once they fought "like fishwives." What brought them to loggerheads was the fact that as 1918 dawned the Allies had simply exhausted their supply of men, and the French believed that the British were not doing enough to bring more men to the colors and to the trenches. And what exacerbated their mutual frustration was that the Americans, who had declared war on Germany in April, 1917, still had no army in the field, and would not commit their army to battle for many months. This at a time when it became increasingly apparent that, with Russia out of the war, the Germans would transfer hundreds of thousands of battle-tested troops to the West before the great American armies could make a difference.

On November 20, 1917, three days after forming his government, Clemenceau mounted the tribune of the Chamber of Deputies in the Palais Bourbon. The hall was packed; spectators sat in the aisles. Crowds outside pressed against the grilles. Clemenceau had not appeared in the Chamber in eight years. Two-thirds of the deputies knew him only by reputation; they had never seen him speak. Seated in the diplomats' gallery was the British minister of munitions, Winston S. Churchill, who later described the scene: "He ranged from one side of the tribune to the other, without a note or a book of reference or scrap of paper, barking out sharp staccato sentences as the thought broke upon his mind. He looked like a wild animal pacing to and fro behind bars, growling

---

*   In the Third Republic, the formal title of French prime ministers was "president of the council of ministers. For convenience, Clemenceau is referred to herein as the "prime minister."

and glaring; and all around him was an assembly which would have done anything to avoid having him there, but having put them there, felt they must obey."[6]

The single thought Clemenceau wished to convey that day was that of a nation united behind the *poilu*: "We present ourselves before you with the unique thought of a total war…These Frenchmen whom we were forced to throw into battle, they have rights over us. They want none of our thoughts to be diverted from them. We owe them everything, with no reservation. All for France bleeding in its glory; all for the apotheosis of law triumphant….One duty, one simple duty: to remain with the soldier, to live, to suffer, to fight with him. To abdicate all that is not of the nation. Rights of the front, duty of the rear, today let all be the same. Let every zone be a zone of the army. If there must be men who uncover in their souls old seeds of hatred, cast them aside….There have been faults. Let us only think on how to repair them. Alas! There have also been crimes, crimes against France which call for prompt chastisement… Weakness would be complicity. We will be without weakness, as without violence. All the guilty to the court martial. The soldier in the court, in solidarity with the soldier in combat. No more pacifist campaigns, no more German intrigues. Neither treason, nor demi-treason: war. Nothing but war. Our armies shall not be caught between two lines of fire. Justice comes through. The country shall know that it is defended…"[7]

These were not mere rhetorical flourishes. His ministry would be based on the goal of showing the *poilu* that the nation was behind him, and of rallying the nation behind the *poilu*. He would be unsparing in rooting out anything that smacked of collaboration or defeatism. By year's end he would have both Louis Malvy and Joseph Caillaux arrested and tried for treason. His frequent visits to the trenches, often at physical risk, were intended to show the *poilus* that France had not forgotten them. In return, the *poilus* named him *"le père la victoire"*—the father of victory—before there was any victory. The name spread through every village in France. On this day, following his speech, 418 deputies gave him a vote of confidence. Sixty-five of them, all but one a Socialist, voted against. Louis Malvy and Joseph Caillaux both abstained.

Clemenceau began each day at 5 a.m. at his home in the rue Franklin. He read and wrote until 7:30 A.M., when his physical trainer arrived for massage and some fencing exercises. Clemenceau had named himself minister of war, and so it was off to the war ministry in the rue Saint-Dominique at nine. There were two offices off of Clemenceau's second floor office. One was occupied by Clemenceau's principal military aide, Gen. Jean Jules Henri Mordacq, 50, a decorated veteran who would accompany Clemenceau on all of his trips to the front, and who would later accompany Clemenceau to the Peace

Conference. The other office was occupied by Clemenceau's principal civilian aide, Georges Mandel, 33, an Alsatian whose family had left Alsace in order to retain French citizenship. Mandel was Clemenceau's domestic eyes and ears. He knew everyone and everything and forgot nothing. Sharing Mandel's office (which was larger than Clemenceau's) were his assistants, Jean Martet (Clemenceau's post-war secretary) and Georges Wormser, 30, later to serve as the secretary to the French delegation to the Peace Conference. They comprised the inner circle; none of Clemenceau's other ministers were in it. Clemenceau rarely convened his cabinet, and since the French president—Poincaré—presided at cabinet meetings, it meant that Poincaré was completely sidelined. France, which had begun the war as a military dictatorship under Gen. Joseph Joffre, was now a civilian dictatorship under Clemenceau. The British ambassador wrote: "The Tiger did not invite the individuals to be members of his cabinet in order to hear what they might have to say but to carry out his views."[8] It was, of course, a dictatorship under the French constitution; he could have been voted out of office at any time; he had been once before. Lloyd George did not think Clemenceau would last very long.

After a morning at the war ministry he returned home for lunch, eating alone. He dined alone. He went to bed early. He hated the telephone, and no one dared call him at night. He had no social life and kept required ceremonial functions to a minimum. He did, on occasion, pass a pleasant hour with his grandchildren.

His trademark became his visits to the front, intended to symbolize the bond between the French people and the *poilus*. He also wanted to see things for himself, rather than relying solely on official reports. The *poilus* told him they were not getting enough tobacco. They began rationing tobacco in Paris so they would have enough.[9] His first trip to the front, to Champagne and Lorraine on January 19—20, was the first of sixty-four he made in 1918, visiting the front at least every week during the year. He clambered down into the trenches with his cane, his trousers tucked into hobnail boots, sporting a fedora or hunting hat. He joked with the men and sampled their food. Mordacq was always with him, respected and relied upon when he conferred with Foch, Pétain, Haig or Pershing.

Clemenceau, who had chafed under military censorship from the first days of the war, lightened it, but did not end it. He would permit political opinions, but any news of strikes, all military and diplomatic news and anything "susceptible of troubling civil order" was subject to being suppressed.[10] The nominal censor was the minister of the interior, Jules Pams. The real censor was Mandel; Pams worked for him.

Clemenceau's desire to demonstrate his support of the *poilus* is what informed his relentless pursuit of Malvy and Caillaux. "Do you believe," he told the army commission of the Chamber, "that it is a good state of mind for the *poilus* to be in, knowing these things vaguely, but feeling them all the same, to think that while they are fighting there are behind them people who betray them? Anything but that!"[11] There had been other treason investigations before him, but it was Clemenceau who went after Caillaux, who had kept a low profile during the war, maintaining his appeasement activities through the likes of Malvy and Almereyda. Poincaré wanted him arrested for treason, but Clemenceau's predecessors, Briand and Ribot, fearing the political fallout from the French left, refused. Caillaux, a member of the Chamber of Deputies, could not be arrested unless the Chamber revoked his parliamentary immunity. Upon assuming office, Clemenceau demanded it, threatening to resign if the Chamber failed to act. Caillaux and Malvy were both arrested. Malvy was charged with treason but convicted of "malfeasance in office." Caillaux spent the rest of the war in prison awaiting trial. He was eventually convicted of high treason and sentenced to three years in prison, years that he had already served. Clemenceau won the grudging respect of none other than Gen. Erich Ludendorff, who wrote in his post-war memoir: "Clemenceau knew what he wanted. His policy was a war policy; he suppressed every sign of peace agitation and strengthened the spirit of his country. His proceedings against Caillaux showed clearly what we were to expect of him."[12]

On November 7, 1917, while Lloyd George was in Rapallo convening the Supreme War Council, Col. House and Gen. Tasker Bliss arrived in London, just at the time when the Allies' fortunes were at a low ebb. Haig's offensive at Passchendaele had just ended in failure and the Italians had been routed at Caporetto. House met with Foreign Minister Arthur Balfour, after which House cabled Wilson that the Italian situation was "desperate," advising that the United States should appoint a representative (Gen. Bliss) to sit in on the military (but not the political) deliberations of the Supreme War Council. Wilson replied that he not only acceded to the plan for a single war council, but "insisted" on it, agreeing to the appointment of Gen. Bliss.[13] House and Bliss issued a statement announcing that President Wilson "considers that unity of plan and control between all Allies and the United States is essential in order to achieve a just and lasting peace."[14]

The day after House arrived in London, the Bolsheviks stormed the Winter Palace in St. Petersburg. The following day, Lenin seized power. One of his first acts was to issue a "Decree of Peace," calling for an end to the war "without annexations or indemnities." Three weeks later, during armistice negotiations with Germany, Lenin's commissar for foreign affairs, Leon Trotsky, called on the Allies to "declare clearly and definitely before all mankind the aims for which the peoples of Europe may be called to shed their blood during the fourth year of war."[15] If Russia could negotiate peace with Germany "without annexations or indemnities," people in the West might begin to wonder why the Allies could not do so as well. The need arose, once again, for the Allies to state their war aims.

On November 20, the same day that Clemenceau addressed the Chamber of Deputies, House and Gen. Bliss met with Lloyd George and the War Cabinet. Lloyd George urged them to send troops into battle as soon as they could be trained and equipped.[16] They would hear the same urgent request in Paris. Many months would pass before the request would be honored.

On November 23, six days after Clemenceau formed his government and three days after he addressed the Chamber of Deputies, House arrived in Paris. Two days later he met with Clemenceau and Pétain, cabling Wilson afterwards that the meeting had resulted in "a clear understanding as to the military situation. They gave us information about the number of fighting men left in France and what would be necessary from us....If we send over a million men by autumn 1918 they will continue to use their own actual fighting men for offensive operations & use ours for defensive purposes until then."[17] After a number of meetings with House, Clemenceau told the Senate Army Commission that House was "a highly civilized gentleman from the wilds of Texas,"[18] and that he and House "are now a good pair of friends."[19] The feeling was mutual, House noting in his diary that "Clemenceau is one of the ablest men I have met in Europe…There can be no doubt of his great courage and his unusual ability."[20] But neither Clemenceau nor the British attempted to conceal from House their anxiety over the slowness of the American mobilization. The United States had been at war for seven months, but had yet to fight in it. They also complained about Pershing's refusal to integrate American units into Allied units, insisting that Americans fight separately, under American commanders.

On November 29, House attended a largely ceremonial (the meeting lasted for all of eight minutes) inter-Allied conference in the ornate Salle de l'Horlage ("Clock Room") in the Quai d'Orsay, the same room in which the opening sessions of the Peace Conference would take place. Lloyd George and Balfour attended for the British, Prime Minister Orlando for Italy. Clemenceau chaired the meeting and opened the proceedings: "The high passions which animate us must translate into acts. Our order of the day is to work. Let us work."[21] The conference then broke into various committees, for munitions, armaments, finance and the like.

On the same day that Clemenceau and Lloyd George were meeting in Paris, there appeared in the London *Daily Telegraph* yet another letter from Lord Lansdowne advocating a compromise peace. "We are not going to lose this war," he wrote, "but its prolongation will spell ruin for the civilized world and an infinite addition to the load of human suffering which already weighs upon it."[22] He called for the creation of a league of nations and adoption of freedom of the seas. Lansdowne had not advised the government in advance of its publication; Lloyd George dismissed it out of hand, telling George Riddell: "Lord Lansdowne advocates making a treaty with a nation whom we are fighting because they have broken a treaty. He advocates that the treaty should be enforced by a League of Nations consisting of the nations who are now engaged in attempting to enforce the treaty already in existence."[23] The government issued a statement: "The views expressed in the letter do not in any way represent the views of his Majesty's Government, nor do they indicate in the slightest degree that there is any change or modification in the war policy of this country....This war policy has been spoken of in different words, but perhaps is summed up in the recent utterance of M. Clemenceau, 'the war aims for which we are fighting are victory.'"[24]

Lloyd George was unaware of the "Lansdowne Letter" before its publication, but it is likely that House was aware of it (as Lloyd George believed) and approved of it, at least to the extent that it called for the Allies to state their war aims. House had met with Lansdowne on November 14, finding Lansdowne in a "peculiarly pacific turn of mind," noting that Lansdowne believed that in a peace settlement Great Britain should not expect to get "twenty shillings to the pound."[25]

On December 1, House, Clemenceau, Lloyd George, and Orlando, accompanied by the generals Bliss, Foch, Robertson and Wilson, and others, met in the ornate Hotel Trianon in Versailles, for the first of series of monthly meetings of the Supreme War Council. Lloyd George had favored Versailles as an alternative to Paris, as a way to get out from under the influence of the entire French bureaucracy. Clemenceau opposed Versailles as the former home of French kings. He grumbled at the cost of needlessly moving archives and staff to Versailles, but relented. This was the organizational meeting of the Council. The Allies had not yet worked out the politico-military lines of authority, and months would pass before they did. From the start, Clemenceau pressed for a unified command under a French generalissimo, with that man being Foch. This would place Haig under Foch, to which Haig (at least for now) was adamantly opposed. When Clemenceau first broached the possibility to Haig: "[B]oth hands shot up to heaven...*Monsieur* Clemenceau, I have only one chief and I can have no other. My King." Ruefully, Clemenceau called this "A bad beginning." Lloyd George also wanted a unified command, but in light of Haig's and Robertson's opposition, he could not press it. He also realized that the British people were cool to it. They remembered

Haig's brief subordination to another French general—Nivelle—and they were not eager to have it repeated.

Lloyd George wrote in his *War Memoirs* that Clemenceau "throughout the whole of his contentious career…never went out of his way either to seek accord or to shun disagreement,"[26] and he did not do so at this first meeting of the Supreme War Council. The issue was the extent of the trench line for which Haig was responsible. At the start of the war, when the BEF consisted of only six divisions, of necessity it occupied only a small part of the front in France. But now that the BEF had hundreds of thousands of men in arms, Pétain pressed for Haig to occupy a larger sector, extending himself south. Clemenceau backed Pétain, demanding that Haig extend his line as far south as the town of Berry-au-bac. Clemenceau threatened to block Lloyd George's train if he tried to leave the meeting without agreeing to the extension. Lloyd George agreed, verbally. Clemenceau demanded it in writing. Lloyd George refused. In the end, Pétain and Haig agreed that the British would extent their line south to the town of Barisis, thirty-seven miles *northwest* of Berry-au-bac. Clemenceau would raise it at a later meeting of the Council, where it was agreed that *Italian* troops would fill the gap.

It was agreed that Allies would mount no big offensives in 1918, much to Haig's disappointment, who was planning on another Passchendaele offensive in the spring. In his *War Memoirs*, Lloyd George noted that the steady stream of German divisions diverted from the East to the French front did "not seem to have made any impression on the stubborn and sticky mind of the British commander."[27]

After the meeting, Clemenceau reported to the Army Commission of the Chamber of Deputies that "at present, unity of command is unattainable. The question of national sensibilities increases the complexity of the problem. So it is necessary at present to rest content with a unity of direction which, I recognize, is a most complicated arrangement."[28] Lloyd George wanted the Council to be under political control, headed by the three Allied heads of government. He did not want the Council's military operations to be headed by the Allied field commanders. House perceptibly saw (and so advised Wilson) that if Lloyd George could not rid himself of Haig (and Robertson), he might use the Supreme War Council to circumvent them. Lloyd George appointed Gen. Sir Henry Wilson as Great Britain's military representative on the Supreme War Council.

But the issue of "war aims" would not go away. House came to the meeting armed with a proposed resolution: "The Allies and the United States declare that they are not waging war for the purpose of aggression or indemnity. The sacrifices they are making are in order that militarism shall not continue to cast its shadow over the world and that nations shall have the right to lead their lives in the way that seems to them best for their general welfare."[29] House cabled the proposed resolution to Wilson, who immediately cabled back his approval: "Our people and Congress will not fight for any selfish aim on the part of any belligerent, with the possible exception of Alsace-Lorraine, least of all for divisions of territory such as have been contemplated in Asia Minor."[30] House pressed for the adoption of his resolution as a response to the Lansdowne Letter. Both Lloyd George and Clemenceau were opposed, and the matter was dropped.

One of Lloyd George's considerable talents was his sense of the public mood. With the war now in its fourth year, war-weariness had set in. Worse, the pending Russia-Germany peace negotiations had led to a spike in pacifist sentiment. The *Manchester Guardian* on December 12 published the secret treaties that the Bolsheviks had released. Lloyd George was not alone in fearing that the bacillus of revolution might spread west. It was a threat that had to be dealt with. It was now, indeed, time to speak publicly of "war aims."

With the House of Commons in recess, Lloyd George chose to address a group of trade unionists crowding into Caxton Hall (a short walk from Buckingham Palace) on Saturday, January 5. He emphasized that what he was about to say had been approved by Asquith, Lord Grey, the leaders of the Labour Party and the heads of the Dominions. His speech, therefore, represented not only his opinions, but that of a united Empire. "When men by the million are being called upon to suffer and die," he began, "and vast populations are being subjected to sufferings and privations of war on a scale unprecedented in the history of the world, they are entitled to know for what cause or causes they are making the sacrifice."[31] He then summarized the causes for which Great Britain was *not* fighting: "We are not fighting a war of aggression against the German people...Nor are we fighting to destroy Austria-Hungary or to deprive Turkey of its capital, or of the rich and renowned lands of Asia Minor..." Turning to Great Britain's war aims, he said that post-war Europe must be "based on such grounds of reason and justice as will give some promise of stability." To achieve that, "government with the consent of the governed must be the basis of any territorial settlement in this war." The first requirement, therefore, must be "the complete restoration, political, territorial and economic, of Belgium and such reparation as can be made for the devastation of its towns and provinces." But he emphasized that by "reparation" he was excluding the types of indemnities Germany had imposed upon France in 1871. "Serbia, Montenegro and the occupied parts of France, Italy and Romania" would have to be restored. He made specific reference to Alsace-Lorraine, "two French provinces" that had been seized "without any regard to the wishes of the population." They too must be restored to France. He supported an independent Poland, recently severed from Russia by

Germany, and self-government for the various nationalities within Austria-Hungary. He spoke of the "crushing weight of modern armaments…the vast waste of wealth and effort involved in warlike preparation…blots on our civilization of which every thinking individual must be ashamed." He concluded thus: "For these and other similar reasons we are confident that a great attempt must be made to establish by some international organization an alternative to war as a means of settling international disputes."[32] He made no mention of "freedom of the seas."

At a luncheon following the speech attended by Winston Churchill and Albert Thomas, the former French Socialist minister of munitions, Lloyd George told George Riddell: "I went as near peace as I could. It was the right moment. The time had come to speak definitely."[33] He told those gathered that he had spoken directly to the German people, over the head of their government, in the hope of detaching Austria-Hungary from Germany.

The following day, Lloyd George received a telegram, immediately made public, from Clemenceau: "I hasten to send to you my heartiest congratulations and those of all Frenchmen at the front and behind the front on the admirable speech in which you have so happily summarized the actual truths we must never grow weary in affirming against German falsehoods."[34] That telegram was important to Lloyd George. He said it would serve to blunt any Tory criticism of the speech.

The one man who felt somewhat depressed by Lloyd George's speech was Woodrow Wilson. He was about to deliver his own address on American war aims, and felt that Lloyd George had stolen his thunder. He considering abandoning the speech. House advised him against it, counseling that once he delivered his war aims, Lloyd George's speech would be forgotten and Wilson's would go down in history. House had never—and would never—give Wilson more prescient advice. Wilson's address—the "Fourteen Points"—would be Wilson's enduring legacy, far more than "too proud to fight" and "peace without victory." More importantly, when the Germans and the Austrians sought to sue for peace months later, they would do so based upon the principles of the Fourteen Points, which in turn became the agenda for the Peace Conference. The Fourteen Points came to stand for mankind's hope for a stable, peaceful world after the war.

Back in September, 1917, House had formed a study group of academics tasked with formulating ideas for the Peace Conference. Known as the "Inquiry," it grew to approximately 150 men who met regularly in the New York Public Library. It was headed by Sidney Edward Mezes, related by marriage to House, a philosopher who was president of the City College of New York. Its director of research—and its guiding light—was the twenty-eight-year-old journalist Walter Lippmann, then at the start of a career that would make him one of the most influential journalists of the twentieth century. Twenty-one of its members would accompany Wilson to the Peace Conference, among them David Hunter Miller, the lawyer who would serve as Wilson's the legal advisor.

But for now, the work of the Inquiry would serve a more immediate purpose: to formulate the ideas for Wilson's address on war aims. On January 4—the day before Lloyd George's address—House, recently returned from Paris, presented Wilson with the Inquiry's report, as drafted by Lippmann. The following day, Wilson met with House again and, according to House, within two hours they had "finished remaking the map of the world."[35] The cabinet had been left completely in the dark, and Secretary of State Lansing was given the finished text of Wilson's address only for purpose of making stylistic revisions. His "lucky number" was thirteen, and he hoped that the "points" would amount to that number, but it was not to be. As finalized, there were six aspirational principles and eight articles dealing with territorial adjustments.

On January 8 Wilson stood before a joint session of Congress. He introduced the Fourteen Points: "We entered this war because violations of right had occurred which touched us to the quick, and made the life of our own people impossible unless they were corrected and the world secured once for all against their recurrence. What we demand in this war, therefore, is nothing peculiar to ourselves. It is that the world be made fit and safe to live its own life, determine its own institutions, be assured of justice and fair dealing by the other peoples of the world as against force and selfish aggression. All the peoples of the world are in effect partners in this interest and for our own part we see very clearly that unless justice be done to others it will not be done to us. The program of the world's peace, therefore, is our program and that program, the only possible program, as we see it, is thus:"[36] He then enunciated the Fourteen Points:

> "I—*Open covenants of peace, openly arrived at, after which there shall be no private international understandings of any kind but diplomacy shall proceed always frankly and in the public view.*"

"Open covenants of peace," caused no difficulty, but "openly arrived at," the manifest absurdity of requiring diplomats to negotiate treaties in the open, caused considerable anxiety. Ten months later, when House was back in London representing Wilson in the armistice negotiations to end the war, he had Lippmann and and the journalist Frank Cobb prepare a memo explaining "openly arrived at." They defined the infelicitous phrase to meaninglessness, stating that the phrase did not preclude "confidential diplomatic negotiations involving delicate matters," but rather that anything negotiated in secret would not be binding unless included in a treaty made public. In other words, in "open covenants."[37]

> "II—*Absolute freedom of navigation upon the seas, outside territorial waters, alike in peace and in war, except as the seas may be closed in whole or in part by international action for the enforcement of international covenants.*"

The "except as the seas may be closed" clause was added by House, in the hope that it would assuage the expected hostility of the British. It did not. Lloyd George never agreed to it, and even such liberal journals as the *Manchester Guardian* deprecated it. In the Lippmann-Cobb memo, they attempted to soften it by noting that it was intended to ensure the navigation rights of neutrals in a war in which the League of Nations took no part. The British knew that without the blockade, they might well have lost the war. Their opposition to this provision was unceasing.

> "III—*The removal, as far as possible, of all economic barriers and the establishment of an equality of trade conditions among the nations consenting to the peace and associating themselves for its maintenance.*"

At first blush, this provision seemed to call for the removal, or at least the lowering, of tariff barriers. But in a letter to North Carolina Democrat Sen. Furnifold Simmons, Wilson underscored that he meant no such thing. In fact, nations would be free to maintain tariffs and other import restrictions as high as they pleased, provided they did so on a non-discriminatory basis against other members of the League of Nations, and with respect to those nations who were not in the League, a nation could impose whatever discriminatory tariffs it pleased.[38]

> "IV—*Adequate guarantees given and taken that national armaments will be reduced to the lowest point consistent with domestic safety.*"

In the Lippmann-Cobb memo to House, the authors made it clear that "consistent with domestic safety" meant not only the means to maintain internal order, but also sufficient armaments to deter foreign invasion. The stockpiling of arms not necessary to repel a foreign invader would be a violation of the principle. Clearly, this provision envisioned future negotiations as to what did and did not constitute arms "consistent with domestic safety."

> "V—*A free, open-minded, and absolutely impartial adjustment of all colonial claims, based upon a strict observance of the principle that in determining all such questions of sovereignty the interests of the populations concerned must have equal weight with the equitable government whose title is to be determined.*"

No provision of the Fourteen Points has been misinterpreted more than this. The Fourteen Points has become synonymous with national "self-determination," which caused the French to be concerned that it applied to their colonial empire. But nowhere does this phrase appear in the Fourteen Points, and Wilson did not intend it as such. As Lippmann and Cobb made clear in their memo to House, this provision applied only to "those colonial claims which have been created by the war. That means the German colonies and any other colonies which may come under international consideration as a result of the war."[39] In other words, it applied to the Bantus of German East Africa and the Papuans of German New Guinea, but to little else, and certainly not to the three hundred million inhabitants of the Indian subcontinent.

The next eight Points dealt with territorial adjustments, which Wilson did not deem to be as important as the general, aspirational, Points. The Inquiry (and Wilson and House) had difficulty with Russia (Point VI) calling for the "*evacuation of all Russian territory and a settlement of all questions affecting Russia...*" They realized that the Poles, Finns, Estonians, Lithuanians and the host of other nationalities had conflicting claims to the former Russian Empire. Wilson asserted that Belgium *must* be "evacuated and restored," (Point VII), but that Romania, Serbia and Montenegro *should* be evacuated (Point XI); that the people of Austria- Hungary...*should* be accorded "*the freest opportunity to autonomous development,*" (Point VIII), that Italy's borders *should* be readjusted "*along clearly recognizable lines of nationality*" (Point IX), that "the the *Turkish portion of the present Ottoman Empire should be assured a secure sovereignty* (Point XII), and that an independent Polish state *should* be erected (Point XIII).

Wilson and House had the most difficulty with Alsace-Lorraine. Lloyd George had simply called for its restoration to France, but Wilson and House were not willing to go that far. They did not wish to place Alsace-Lorraine, which had been part of Germany in 1914, on a par with the rest of France, or with Belgium, which had been invaded in violation of a treaty. They worked and re-worked the language of Point VIII up the last moment before Wilson delivered the address, and settled as follows:

"VIII—*All French territory* should *be freed and the invaded portions restored,*
and the wrong done to France by Prussia in 1871 in the manner of Alsace-
Lorraine, *which has unsettled the peace of the world for nearly fifty years,*
should *be righted, in order that peace may once more be made secure in the*
interest of all."

Wilson intentionally moved the final aspirational point to the end, saving the
best for last:

"XIV—*A general association of nations* must *be formed under specific covenants*
for the purpose of affording mutual guarantees of political independence and
territorial integrity to great and small states alike."[40]

"For such arrangements and covenants," he said, "we are willing to fight and to
continue to fight until they are achieved."[41] As for Germany, "We do not wish to injure
her or to block in any way her legitimate influence or power...We wish her only to
accept a place of equality among the peoples of the world—the new world in which we
now live—instead of a place of mastery." But Wilson warned that this could be achieved
only if the world dealt with "the Reichstag majority," and not with "the military party
and the men whose creed is imperial domination." Wilson would treat with a German
democracy, not with the kaiser.

When Clemenceau heard of the Fourteen Points, he is said to have remarked "The
Lord Almighty limited Himself to ten,[42] and if Clemenceau recognized Wilson's less
than whole-hearted treatment of Alsace-Lorraine in Point VIII, ("All French territory
should be freed...") he let it pass, ordering that the Fourteen Points be presented to
the Chamber of Deputies, which approved it by a vote of 377-113. But in an interview
with the daily *Le Matin*, he said: "The League of Nations? Do you believe it? In a world
built upon violence?"[43]

Wilson did not use the phrase "self-determination" in the Fourteen Points address, but
he did use it the next month, when he yet again addressed a joint session of Congress
to report of German Chancellor von Hertling's evasive, lukewarm response to the
Fourteen Points. (Hertling could not do otherwise; Germany then was a military
dictatorship controlled by Hindenburg and Ludendorff.) In reply, Wilson said that
"'Self-determination' is not a mere phrase. It is an imperative principle of action, which

statesmen will henceforth ignore at their peril. It then outlined the four "principles" upon which the territorial settlements at the Peace Conference must be applied:

"First, that each part of the final settlement must be based upon the essential justice of that particular case and upon such adjustments as are most likely to bring a peace that will be permanent;

"Second, that peoples and provinces are not to be bartered about from sovereignty to sovereignty as if they were mere chattels and pawns in a game, even the great games, now forever discredited, of the balance of power; but that

"Third, every territorial settlement involved in this war must be made in the interest and for the benefit of the populations concerned, and not as part of any mere adjustment or compromise of claims against rival states; and

"Fourth, that all well-defined national aspirations shall be accorded the utmost satisfaction that can be accorded them without introducing new or perpetuating old elements of discord and antagonism that would be likely in time to break the peace of Europe and consequently of the world."[44]

These principles would form the basis for most of Wilson's struggles with Clemenceau, Lloyd George and Italian Prime Minister Orlando at the Peace Conference. Lloyd George and Clemenceau would be happy to tear up the Treaty of London, freeing them from their territorial concessions to Italy. They had no intention of tearing up the Sykes-Picot Treaty, carving up between themselves the Ottoman Empire. And as far as Germany's colonies were concerned, Lloyd George had already advised House that Great Britain wished to control them following the war.

By the time the Supreme War Council re-convened in the Trianon Hotel in Versailles on January 30, 1918, it was clear to all that, with fifty additional divisions of battle-hardened troops pouring into the Western Front from the East, and the Americans nowhere close to being able to render support, a great German onslaught would soon befall the Allies. (Ludendorff later wrote: "All the world, including the Entente, knew we were going to attack in the West."[45]) The issue before those gathered was how to deal with it. Haig wished to launch a Third Ypres campaign in the spring. Lloyd George now so feared another Passchendaele that he actually withheld available troops from Haig. Even Haig's consistent backer, Gen. Robertson, was cool to the idea.

The annual struggle between Clemenceau, the "Westerner," and Lloyd George, the "Easterner," re-emerged at this meeting. Clemenceau wanted the Allies to hold on the Western Front until the Americans arrived. He deprecated Lloyd George's plan to press on to Jerusalem, thus knocking Turkey out of the war. To Clemenceau, these troops (and the ones idling in Salonika) were needed on the Western Front. In this, Robertson supported Clemenceau over his own boss. More than ever, Lloyd George wanted to rid himself of Robertson.

The Allies did not know when they would be attacked, or *where*. The respective military representatives of the Council—generals Foch, Bliss, Wilson and Cadorna—pressed for the establishment of a thirty-division general reserve comprised of British, French and Italian units. In the event of a German breakthrough, the reserve would be sent to whatever sector was in distress. This general reserve would be in addition to the reserve units under each of the field commanders. Clemenceau opened the discussion, posing four questions: "Shall we constitute a general reserve?" "Will it be a reserve on the whole front, from the North Sea to the Adriatic?" "How shall it be composed?" and "Who shall command it?"

In answer to the fourth question, for Clemenceau that man was Foch, the man whom Clemenceau had appointed to head the *ecole de guerre* in 1909. Clemenceau was turned off by Foch's clericalism, (his brother was a Jesuit) but there was no doubting Foch's talents. After the Italians were routed at Caporetto, Foch—then Pétain's chief of staff—commanded the eleven-division Anglo-French force rushed to shore them up. Foch bucked up Gen. Cadorno, convincing him to make a stand on the Piave River and not retreat from it. "I care a lot about Foch," Clemenceau told the Senate Army Commission back in December, 1917, "[H]e has a supreme quality in my eyes. He is a man who is never discouraged. He is stopped by nothing. When he finds himself in difficulty, he calls himself to resolve it, and it is resolved."[46] But it was Lloyd George who nominated Foch to the post of president of the "executive committee" of the Council (Bliss and Gen. Henry Wilson, a French-speaking devotee of Foch, would be the other members) in charge of the reserve, noting that Foch was a man loyal not only to France, but to all of the Allies, having assisted the Italians in their hour of need, and who had selflessly assisted the British in Flanders. Lloyd George knew that with Foch heading the reserve, it would be a way of circumventing Haig.

Haig knew it too. Haig would later tell Clemenceau that he would turn over no troops to the reserve, and would resign if forced to do so. For now, it was agreed *in principle* that the reserve would be established, with the details to be worked out at the next meeting. Gen. Bliss had no authority to approve of Foch's appointment, but agreed on the assumption that the president would consent.

This meeting spelled the end of Gen. Robertson as chief-of-staff ("C.I.G.S."). When Lloyd George appointed Gen. Wilson as his military representative on the Council, it meant that Wilson would report directly to Lloyd George, one of the three political heads of the Council. Lloyd George offered to appoint Robertson instead of Wilson, but Robertson refused. He then offered to keep Robertson as C.I.G.S., under a new arrangement, which Robertson also refused, and resigned. As Robertson's replacement as C.I.G.S., Lloyd George appointed Gen. Wilson!

In his *War Memoirs*, Lloyd George said of both Haig and Robertson: "Their abilities were average; their obstinacy was abnormal."[47]

On March 3, in the town of Brest-Litovsk (in present-day Belarus), the new Bolshevik government finalized its peace treaty with the Central Powers. The terms that Ludendorff imposed on the Bolsheviks were so harsh that they surprised even his own negotiators. All of Ukraine, Lithuania, Estonia, Finland and Russian Poland were detached from Russia. The Bolsheviks in return obtained peace, a respite they needed to wage their own civil war. After March 3, everyone in the West recognized what would befall any nation defeated by the German militarists. The incipient peace movement in the West was dead. A month later, speaking at a Liberty Loan celebration in Baltimore, Wilson reacted: "Germany has once more said that force, and force alone, shall decide whether Justice and Peace shall reign in the affairs of men....There is, therefore, but one response possible from us: Force, Force to the utmost, Force without stint or limit..."[48] The following year, when the German negotiators at the Peace Conference learned of the conditions to be imposed upon them, they were hard pressed to complain. It was pointed out to them that the conditions were far less harsh than those they had imposed on the Russians.

The Supreme War Council next convened in London on March 14. The predominant issue once again was the general reserve. Both Haig and Pétain refused to contribute to it, each of them arguing that he was facing too many German divisions to afford the loss of a single man. Both Lloyd George and Clemenceau acquiesced. Foch remonstrated heatedly, demanding that the general reserve be formed immediately. After a heated argument between Clemenceau and Foch, Clemenceau ended it with a wave of his hand at Foch: "Be quiet," he said, "it is I who represent France here."[49] France had come a long way from Millerand's toadying to Joffre. Before the meeting broke up, Foch warned that disaster would befall them if they persisted in divided command and scattered reserves. Afterwards, Clemenceau admitted to Gen. Henry Wilson that Foch had been right on the issue of the general reserve.

There were only three hundred thousand American troops in Europe in March of 1918, but soon they would be arriving at the rate of two hundred fifty thousand *per month*. Since the start of the war, the Allies had enjoyed a manpower advantage over the Germans. That advantage was now gone, but would revive with a vengeance once the Americans began arriving. To Ludendorff, all this meant that if he could win the war in the West, he had to attack *right now*. He was confident he would succeed. Hindenburg said to one of his generals: "The drama is nearing its close; now comes the last act."[50]

At dawn on March 21, 190 German divisions—three million men—hurled themselves at the British lines on a forty-mile front between Arras in the north to San Quentin to the south. Employing new tactics that emphasized speed rather than sheer strength (which in the next war would be termed "*blitzkrieg*") the objective of what Ludendorff called "Operation Michael" was to drive the British as far back as possible, ideally to the Channel ports. With the British defeated, the Germans would then direct all of their forces on the French. Haig, focused exclusively on his own attack plans, had devoted very little attention to defense. The British Fifth Army, situated directly in front of the assault, disintegrated. Of course, there was no general reserve. Pétain rushed two hundred thousand troops to assist Haig, not nearly enough.

By March 23, the Germans were in sight of Amiens, the rail, road and communications hub at the intersection of the British and French armies. If it fell, the Germans would separate the British and French armies. It might spell the end of the war. On that day Clemenceau, in order to avert a panic, strolled the halls of the Chamber of Deputies with a smile on his face, exuding calm.[51] But also on that day, the first of the German artillery shells fired from "Big Bertha" flew into Paris. On March 29 a shell fell directly on the Church of Saint-Gervais in the heart of the city, killing seventy-five. But the shells caused more panic than actual destruction. A half million Parisians fled the city the following week, clogging roads.

On March 24, Clemenceau visited Pétain and Foch at headquarters in Compiègne. Pétain prophesized defeat, lamenting that "if we are beaten, we shall owe it to the English."[52] On their return, Clemenceau told Mordacq: "After an interview like that, you need an iron-bound spirit to retain your confidence."[53] But at the same moment, Lloyd George expressed his own pessimism to George Riddell: "Things look very bad. I fear it means disaster. They have broken through, and the question is what there is behind to stop them." He also expressed his bitterness: "Unless President Wilson hurries up, he may be too late. He has wasted too much time; he has been nine months in the war and has done very little which is of real service at the front."[54]

It is probable that on this day Gen. Haig changed his mind about serving under a French generalissimo. He cabled Minister of War Alfred Milner and Gen. Henry Wilson, urging them to hurry over to France. He likely realized he would get no more support from Pétain; he might get it from Foch.

On March 26, Clemenceau and President Poincaré motored to the town of Doullens, 122 miles due north of Paris, to meet the British for the purpose of determining what could be done to prevent an irreparable breach in the line. Before the meeting, Foch's chief of staff, Gen. Maxime Weygand, received a note from Haig informing him that Haig might have to abandon Amiens and retreat to the Channel ports, a move that would have imperiled Paris itself. Also before the meeting, Clemenceau confided to Poincaré what Pétain had confided to him: "The Germans will beat the English in open country; after that, they will beat us also." Clemenceau asked Poincaré: "Should a general speak or even think in that fashion?"[55]

The meeting was scheduled for 11:00 a.m. in the Doullens city hall. Outside, the tramp of retreating British troops could be heard. They were sixteen miles from Amiens; the German guns could be heard in the distance. The British—Milner, Wilson and Haig—arrived shortly after noon. Before they arrived, Milner and Wilson had agreed that Foch should "coordinate" all of the Allied armies. Foch then arrived with a flourish, surrounded by his entourage of officers. Asked his opinion of the military situation, he immediately took charge: "My plan is not complicated. I want to fight. I would fight without a break. I would fight in front of Amiens. I would fight in Amiens. I would fight behind Amiens. I would fight all the time…we must dig in and die where we stand if need be; to withdraw a foot will be an act of treason."[56] Years later, Clemenceau recalled that when he heard these words, "I could hardly refrain from throwing myself into the arms of the admirable chief in the name of France in deadly peril."[57] But he did restrain himself, saying of Foch: "He is a chap!"[58] Milner then pulled Clemenceau aside. They agreed that, if there were no objections, the British would nominate Foch as "coordinator" of the Allied armies on the Western front. Haig readily agreed, his prior stance that he could serve under no one but his king now forgotten. Later, President Wilson agreed to the arrangement.

There is today a stained glass window in the Doullens city hall that depicts the scene in which all of the participants are bent over a table, constituting Foch as the generalissimo of the Allied armies. But far less actually happened at Doullens. As "coordinator," he could give orders to no one; he could direct no troops. As Foch soon related to Clemenceau: "I came up against some unfortunate events because I have to persuade, which is not always easy, instead of directing. I encounter too often difficulties in obtaining execution of measures that I judge necessary, even urgent. That is why a power of direction superior to that which I am provided seems to me indispensable for the achievement of success."[59] According to Clemenceau, Lloyd George had told him to summon him any time he thought his presence necessary, and so Clemenceau asked Lloyd George to come to sort out Foch's authority. They, together with Pétain, Foch, Haig, Wilson, Pershing and Bliss, met in the town of Beauvais on April 3. After Foch threatened to resign due to his lack of real authority, Clemenceau proposed, and the Allies accepted, that Foch be provided "all the powers necessary" for the strategic direction of military operations. According to Gen. Bliss, the agreement, formalized in writing, "resulted in the nearest approximation to giving General Foch supreme command that was ever attained." Haig at last expressed his acquiescence: "There should be only one head in France."[60] But as a sop to Haig, the agreement provided that "Each Commander-in-Chief will have the right to appeal to his government if in his opinion the safety of his Army is compromised by any order received from General Foch."[61] On April 14, Foch was given the title "General in Chief of the Allied Armies," to make it clear to all that Foch was Haig's (and Pétain's) superior. But whether Haig intended to take orders from the Frenchman was still in doubt.

The meeting ended late in the day, too late for the British delegation to obtain a meal anywhere on the road to the Channel. As Lloyd George remembered it, Clemenceau's staff had prepared a luncheon basket for the French delegation. But as Clemenceau had already lunched with President Poincaré, Clemenceau "dispensed with his rations and passed them on to us." The British delegation picnicked by the roadside, feasting "sumptuously on the *charcuterie* (sausages) which had been provided for the Tiger."[62]

By the time of the Beauvais conference, Operation Michael had failed. The troops that Pétain had rushed north to assist Haig spelled the difference. Ludendorff's troops outran their artillery and their supplies. They became exhausted; their discipline broke down; they began looting. The British were not thrown back to the Channel; the French and British forces were not separated. Amiens had held. The British had suffered a hundred sixty thousand casualties, but they had inflicted a similar number on the Germans.

Operation Michael was finished, but Ludendorff was not. Having promised his kaiser victory, he was now faced with the inexorable numbers of the arriving Americans.

Eighty thousand had arrived in March, an additional 118,000 would arrive in April, and 245,000 more in May. On April 9 he launched "Operation Georgette," ("Fourth Ypres") directly against the British in Flanders. As with "Operation Michael," the first day's assault appeared promising, the British losing in a single day all of the ground that Haig had spent months and a quarter of a million casualties to gain. But like "Operation Michael," it stalled.

Ludendorff's offensives made the Allies' manpower shortage, always acute, now desperate, particularly in infantry and machine-gun units. What added to Clemenceau and Lloyd George's frustration was that, with every month, Pershing had more and more of these vitally needed men, but refused to commit them to battle, insisting that no American troops would be committed to battle unless and until they were fully trained in France and committed as complete divisions, including artillery, staff officers, medics, telephone operators and clerks. "But this took time," Clemenceau noted ruefully. "And it was heart-rending to see our men being mown down unceasingly while, under the command of their good leaders, large bodies of American troops remained idle, within earshot of the guns....And the more I insisted the more the American general resisted."[63] In private, his bitterness spilled over, telling the Senate Army Commission that "General Pershing is dominated by the idea that a large American army should be formed as soon as possible to unfurl its flag and that, under the command of an American general, will win an American victory, which I have no doubt will be worth to the American commander-in-chief an equestrian statue next to the one of Washington!"[64] Lloyd George expressed the same sentiment at the same time: "It is maddening," he wrote to Lord Reading, "to think that though the men are there the issue of the War may be endangered because of the short-sightedness of one General and the failure of his Government to order him to carry out their undertakings."[65] By this time, both Great Britain and France had been at war for almost four years, and each had suffered casualties in the hundreds of thousands. The United States had been at war, at least technically, for a year, and its casualties were in the hundreds.

These and other manpower issues erupted at the May 1-2 meeting of the Supreme War Council in the town of Abbeville, France, a short drive from the English Channel. The immediate issue was the deployment of the arriving American troops. Prior to the meeting, Pershing and Lloyd George's Secretary of State for War, Alfred Milner, had agreed between themselves that all of the American troops arriving in May and June would be deployed in the British sector. Foch and Clemenceau came to the meeting wishing to force the issue. Lloyd George and Milner wished to avoid a confrontation. Lloyd George and Clemenceau forged a compromise over Foch's objection: The first six American infantry divisions arriving in each of the months of May and June would be divided between the British and the French; above that, Pershing would determine how they would be deployed. But when Pershing said that he would rather see the Allies driven back to the Loire rather than commit American troops before they were ready, Lloyd George threatened to report Pershing's obstinacy to President Wilson, to which Pershing retorted: "Refer it to the President and be damned."[66]

Col. House sided with Lloyd George and Clemenceau. On April 9, the same day that Ludendorff launched "Georgette," he wrote to Wilson that he was anxious "because of the effect which a grave disaster in France would have upon your administration…. Pershing's feeling that an American army under his command should be established and made as formidable as possible is understandable. Nevertheless, the thing to be done now is to stop the Germans, and to stop them it is evident that we must put in every man that is available."[67]

The manpower crisis brought to the fore an issue that separated Lloyd George and Clemenceau, who believed that the British were simply not bringing enough men to the front. It was the British practice to keep their reserves at home, rather than in France, which meant that there were thousands of men in khaki roaming the streets of London. When Ludendorff launched "Operation Michael," it took the British two weeks to send more than a quarter-million men to the front. France was sending men to the front who previously had been classified as fit only for auxiliary work. Clemenceau told Lloyd George that there were more than a million men in Great Britain so situated, who could be sent to fight. Clemenceau also could not understand why there was no conscription in Ireland, not realizing that it might require more men to force the Irish to the front than the conscription would yield.

On May 27, Ludendorff struck again, this time against the French, in what became known as the Second Battle of Chemin des Dames. His strategy was to draw off the French troops in Flanders that Pétain had sent to aid Haig, his main goal still being to drive the British to the Channel. This had been a quiet sector; some British veterans of the recent fighting in Flanders had been sent there for a rest. The attack came as a complete surprise, the French having ignored American intelligence predicting the attack. In retreat, the French had failed to destroy the bridges over the Aisne. By May 30 the Germans had advanced thirty miles, had taken fifty thousand prisoners, had reached the Marne, and were forty miles from Paris. It was 1914 all over again. There was panic in the Chamber of Deputies. But unlike 1914, the Americans were now in the fight, getting their first taste of battle at Chateau-Thierry.

Clemenceau was at the front or at military headquarters every day between May 28 and May 31. On May 29 he visited the headquarters of Gen. Jean Degoutte, later recalling "A tragic sight to see the General silently weeping over a tattered remnant of a map....I left him with no hope of ever seeing him again. For me this is one of the most poignant memories of the War.[68] On the return drive to Paris, Clemenceau lamented to Mordacq: "Yes, the Germans might take Paris, but that will not prevent me from waging war. We will fight them on the Loire, then on the Garonne...even in the Pyrenees. If...we are driven from the Pyrenees, we will continue the war at sea. But make peace, never!"[69]

Winston Churchill was then in Paris. In his office in the War Ministry, Clemenceau told him: "I will fight in front of Paris. I will fight in Paris. I will fight behind Paris."[70] The words, and the cadence, obviously stayed with Churchill, for use in 1940.

With Paris imperiled, the Supreme War Council—Lloyd George, Clemenceau and Orlando—reconvened in Versailles on June 1. Clemenceau now voiced his belief that the British were not recruiting enough men and not sending enough of the men they recruited to the front. "The British Empire has mobilized six million men," he challenged Lloyd George, "they must be somewhere or other and they ought to be forthcoming."[71] Lloyd George then rather cavalierly replied that if the French thought they could do better, they could send a man to London to look into British recruitment practices. Clemenceau replied that he had just such a man. He insisted that Lloyd George commit the promise to writing. The man was a certain Col. Rouve, a recruitment specialist. He was dispatched to London, poked around, and three weeks later issued his report, concluding that of the men the British recruited, too few were in the trenches, that the British could comb more men out of the transport services, and that too many were engaged in home defense. The British rejected Col. Rouve's statistical assumptions, and hence his conclusions.

During the meeting, Foch asked the British to reduce the number of their battalions on the Italian front. Lord Milner replied that he didn't want Italy to "fall down," to which Clemenceau replied that he didn't want Paris to fall down either.[72] The meeting concluded with the drafting of a telegram to Wilson signed by Lloyd George, Clemenceau and Orlando, pleading for more men. It was sent to France's ambassador, Jules Jusserand, who handed the telegram to Wilson on June 6. It began by thanking Wilson for the aid he had sent. "The crisis," they wrote, "however, still continues," and in light of the inability of the British and the French of increasing their numbers, "there is a great danger of the war being lost unless the numerical inferiority of the Allies can be remedied as rapidly as possible by the advent of American troops." They specified that Foch "urges with the utmost insistence that the maximum possible number of infantry and machine gunners" be shipped during the months of June and July "to avert the immediate danger of an Allied defeat in the present campaign, owing to the Allied reserves being exhausted before those of the enemy." A sentence was included at the behest of Clemenceau: "We are satisfied that General Foch, who is conducting the present campaign with consummate ability, and on whose military judgment we continue to place the most absolute reliance, [who] is not overestimating the needs of the case..."[73] A separate telegram broke down the immediate manpower needs, totaling 250,000 in each of June and July. When Jusserand handed the telegram to Wilson, Wilson responded by saying he would try to send the troops requested, and might even exceed it.[74] When Jusserand met with Wilson again on June 12, he reported that Clemenceau agreed with the importance of an independent American army *at the proper time*, and that "every facility" would be provided toward that end.[75]

The Chemin des Dames debacle constrained Clemenceau to rally to Foch's defense. On June 3 he appeared before the Army Commission of Chamber of Deputies, admitting that mistakes had been made, promising an investigation. "We must have confidence in Foch and Pétain, those two great chiefs who are happily complementary of each other."[76] With all of Paris in an uproar, he mounted the tribune of the Chamber of Deputies the following day. The Socialists were in full throat, screaming for a secret session. He brushed it aside, asserting that it would become public, fostering rumors and political intrigue. "If, in order to obtain approval from certain people who make hasty judgments one is obliged to abandon the commanders who well merit their country, this is an act of cowardice of which I am incapable. Don't expect me to do it."[77] He was shouted down. He left the tribune. When quiet resumed, he returned and pressed on. "These soldiers, these great soldiers have commanders, good commanders, great commanders, commanders worthy of them from every point of view...."[78] "General Foch possesses the confidence of the Allies and the Inter-Allied Council in Versailles has decided to thank him publicly. The Germans have flung themselves headlong into this adventure. Withdraw though we may, we shall never capitulate. If you are resolved to persevere to the end, victory is ours....The Americans are coming. The French and British effectives have become exhausted, like those of the Germans. The result of the struggle depends on the help of America. Our Allies are determined to pursue the war to the end. We shall have victory if the public authorities rise to the height of the situation[79]...It remains for the living to complete the magnificent work of the dead."[80]

But afterwards Clemenceau ruefully opined: "I had to hold both of them (Foch and Pétain) by the scruff of their necks...I've saved them, but they don't deserve it."[81] He would later remind Foch how he had covered for him. And he exacted his price: He drove to Foch's headquarters and handed him a list of generals that Clemenceau wanted removed, some of them Foch's old friends. Foch acquiesced.

As in 1914, the Germans stalled at the Marne. The French linked up with two American divisions (American divisions were twice the size of British or French divisions) and at Chateau-Thierry and halted the advance. Ludendorff tried again on June 9, and failed. Two days later, American Marines counterattacked, and in fighting so desperate that today Belleau Wood occupies a place in Marine lore. The Americans were now arriving at the rate of two hundred fifty thousand per month. At the July 2-4 meeting of the Supreme War Council, Gen. Bliss announced that there were twenty-two complete American divisions in France, and he expected there would be thirty by the end of August. On July 15, Ludendorff launched his final offensive, east and west of Rheims, the last of his offensives. It failed, and Foch counterattacked three days later. On July 24 Pershing, Foch, Pétain and Haig met and coordinated their offensives. On August 8 Haig launched an offensive near Amiens. Ludendorff's army was demoralized, weary and hungry, but the Allies could not know just how deteriorated his army had become. They still believed the war would not be won until 1919. At the same time, Ludendorff advised the kaiser that a German military victory was now impossible, and the only hope of retaining the territories they had conquered would be through diplomacy.

On September 15, Gen. Louis Franchet d'Esperey ("desperate Frankie"), recently appointed by Clemenceau to head the army in Salonika, attacked the Bulgarian forces. With the help of 250,000 Greek troops, he rolled north. On September 29, Bulgaria sued for peace. It became the first of the Central Powers to be knocked out of the war. When Clemenceau heard the news, he said: "I almost went mad...mad with joy!"[82]

As Foch's armies moved east, Clemenceau increased his visits to the front, now traveling the areas the Germans had left behind in their retreat. He saw entire villages reduced to rubble. What buildings remained had been completely sacked, denuded of everything. They had even cut down all of the trees.

On July 4, Paris celebrated American Independence day. There was a parade down the Avenue Trocadéro, which that day was renamed the Avenue du Président Wilson, the name it bears to this day. Seated in the reviewing stand at the Place d'Iéna were

Clemenceau and Lloyd George. Before leaving Lloyd George was overheard saying to Clemenceau: "Did you realize, old friend, you have just forced me to attend the celebration of Britain's greatest defeat?" Clemenceau, who had spent five of his formative years in the United States, replied: "After all, do you really regret American independence? What harm has it done you? Anyway, Britain and France have had a brush or two and yet, just now, you saw with what a heart and with what respect the British saluted the French flag, and the French saluted the British flag."[83]

On July 31, Lloyd George delivered a tough speech to two hundred members of the National Union of Manufacturers. "There is a good deal of discussion about a league of nations," he said. "I am certainly one of those who believe in it. But there are two leagues of nations already in existence—the British Empire and the great alliance against the Central Powers. And whatever decision we come to must be one in which we can march hand in hand and side by side with these two great leagues of nations of which we are members....The longer the war lasts the sterner must be the economic terms we impose on the foe. I think the sooner he realizes that the better. He is fighting in order to impose his own economic terms on the Allies. He will never succeed in doing so....If he goes on fighting, imposing greater burdens on us, destroying our young manhood and guilty also of outrages which shock humanity and which make it difficult to shake hands with him when the war is over, the sterner will be the terms imposed upon him.[84] Chancellor of the Exchequer Bonar Law followed Lloyd George. He stressed that the trade policy of the British Empire was founded upon imperial preferences, and would remain so after the war: "We are one empire, and there shall be preference within that empire."[85] Not mentioned was Point III of the Fourteen Points ("*equality of trade conditions among the nations.*")

Lloyd George's speech distressed Wilson, who met with Sir William Wiseman, Great Britain's liaison to Col. House. Wiseman wrote that Wilson "is convinced... that it is a great mistake to threaten Germany now with any kind of punitive post-war measures against her trade....The President thinks that we ought to adopt the line that we have no desire to deny Germany her fair share of the world's commerce, and that it is her own militarists who are ruining her trade by prolonging the war and obliging us to maintain a blockade."[86]

On August 1, Walter Hines Page submitted his resignation as America's ambassador to the Court of St. James's, due to failing health. He had been unfailing and outspoken in his support of the British cause, which placed him completely out of step with Wilson's policy of neutrality "in thought and in deed." His letters and diaries are literature, eloquently evoking the quiet stoicism of the Londoners who gently pressed him— usually in vain—for news of a missing son or husband. He related that one woman told him she had lost one son to a U-boat and another son at the front. "How brave they were," he commiserated. She gave him a quizzical look. "No," she said, "they were just doing their duty." Wilson called him the "damnedest fool we ever appointed."[87] Arthur Balfour said: "I loved that man. I almost wept when he left England."[88] Page returned to his home in North Carolina, and died on December 21, 1918.

Some time in June of 1918, Col. House began thinking about the structure of the League of Nations, writing Wilson: "Now if war can be made impossible, what a glorious culmination of your other accomplishments."[89] On July 16 House delivered to Wilson a draft of what would become the "covenant" (Wilson's word) of the League. House's draft provided for economic sanctions and the possibility of a blockade against any nation found by the League to be in breach of the peace. It provided for mandatory arbitration of disputes and for an international court, but did not provide for the use of force against a nation violating the peace. Wilson reworked House's draft, inserting a provision for the use of force against miscreant nations.

House and Wilson met on August 15. House's draft did not put smaller nations on the same footing in the League as the great powers. According to House, Wilson disagreed "warmly." House suggested that Wilson press the Allies to immediately sign the Covenant of the League, his rationale being that if Wilson waited until the Peace Conference, he would be nearing the end of his second term, with his leverage diminished. Wilson disagreed. For now, he wanted to keep the League of Nations quiet, telling House that revealing it would create too much criticism, "particularly by senators of the Lodge type."[90] The conversation then drifted to a discussion of the possible makeup of the American delegation to the Peace Conference. House suggested that the delegation include one or more Republicans, suggesting Roosevelt, Taft or former Secretary of State Elihu Root. Wilson dismissed Roosevelt and Taft as "impossible," and argued against Root.[91]

Allied forces were making steady progress (combined British-French forces would breach the Hindenburg Line on September 22), but the Allies still believed the war would not end until 1919. Foch told Clemenceau that it would be foolish for the Allies to drive all the way to Berlin, which would cost another hundred thousand French lives. Foch told House: "One makes war only for the results; when these results are achieved, no one has the right to shed another drop of blood." Clemenceau told Foch: "Marshal, I am entirely of the same opinion."[92] They were unaware of how desperate were the German and Austro-Hungarian economies, and were surprised when the peace offers began coming their way.

On September 16, Wilson received a note from the Austrian foreign minister, Count Burian, in which Burian requested a peace conference of all of the belligerents. The note was received at 6:20 p.m. Wilson rejected at 6:45 p.m. The rejection, drafted by Lansing stated: "The Government of the United States feels that there is only one reply which it can make…It has repeatedly and with entire candor stated the terms upon which the United States would consider peace and can and will entertain no proposal for a conference upon a matter concerning which it has made its position and and purpose so plain."[93] Although Wilson had declared war against Germany on April 2, 1917, he had waited until December 7 to declare war against Austria-Hungary. Yet Austria directed its peace feeler only to Wilson, and not to the Allies against whom she had been waging war since 1914. Foreign Secretary Balfour rejected Austria's note for the British, calling it a cynical attempt to divide the Allies. Clemenceau rejected it as well, saying that the Allies would fight until the enemy recognized that "right cannot negotiate with crime."[94]

On September 27, Wilson gave what would be his last major address of the war to a group of five thousand sellers of "Liberty Bonds" at the Metropolitan Opera House in New York City. The purpose of this speech, he said, was "to try to make it clear once more what the war really means." The purposes of the war "were perhaps not clear at the outset, but they are clear now…The common will of mankind has been substituted for the particular purposes of individual states. Individual statesmen may have started the conflict, but neither they nor their opponents can stop it as they please. It has become a peoples' war, and peoples of all sorts and races…are involved in its sweeping processes of change and settlement." He said "we can accept no outcome which does not squarely meet and settle" the issues of the war…" Those issues are these:" He then enumerated them:

> "Shall the military power of any nation or group of nations be suffered to determine the fortunes of peoples over whom they have no right to rule except the right of force?

"Shall strong nations be free to wrong weak nations and make them subject to their purpose and interest?

"Shall peoples be ruled and dominated even in their own internal affairs, by arbitrary and irresponsible force or by their own will and choice?

"Shall there be a common standard of right and privilege for all peoples and nations or shall the strong do as they will and the weak suffer without redress?

"Shall the assertion of right be haphazard and by casual alliance or shall there be a common concert to oblige the observance of common right?"

The agency to "oblige the observance of common right" would be "a League of Nations formed under covenants that will be efficacious. Without such an instrumentality, by which the peace of the world can be guaranteed, peace will rest in part upon the word of outlaws and only upon that word." And, he added, "the constitution of the League of Nations and the clear definition of its objects must be a part, is in a sense the most essential part, of the peace settlement itself."

But in order that these principles sound "less like a thesis and more like a practical programme" he specified what the peace settlement must contain:

"First, the impartial justice meted out must involve no discrimination between those to whom we wish to be just and those to whom we do not wish to be just.

"Second, no special or separate interest of any single nation or any group of nations can be made the basis of any settlement which is not consistent with the common interest of all.

"Third, there can be no leagues or alliances or special covenants or understandings within the general and common family of the League of Nations.

"Fourth, and more specifically, there can be no special, selfish economic combinations within the League.

"Fifth, all international agreements and treaties of every kind must be made known in their entirety to the rest of the world."[95]

The reaction to Wilson's speech in official London or Paris was…silence. Neither Lloyd George nor Clemenceau nor any of their ministers would comment publicly.

The Allies could not know it, but Ludendorff was becoming desperate for an armistice. On September 29—two days after Wilson's speech and the same day that Bulgaria sued for peace—Chancellor Georg von Hertling submitted his resignation to the kaiser. On October 3, Prince Max of Baden, 51, was appointed as his successor. Prince Max was a cousin of the kaiser, but he spoke perfect English and had a reputation as being something of a liberal. Dr. Wilhelm Solf, a career diplomat who had opposed unrestricted submarine warfare, was appointed foreign secretary. There was no doubt what Max's mission was: It was to obtain an armistice. Initially, Max thought he had been summoned to office at "five minutes before twelve." He later rued that "actually I was summoned five minutes after twelve."[96] On the very day that he assumed office, at the insistence of Ludendorff, Max drafted the following cable, which was dispatched to Wilson the following day: "The German Government requests the President of the United States of America to take in hand the restoration of Peace, acquaint all belligerent States with this request, and invite them to send plenipotentiaries for the purpose of opening negotiations. The German government accepts the programme set forth by the President of the United States in his message to Congress of January 8, 1918 [the Fourteen Points address], and in his later pronouncements, especially his speech of September 27, as the basis for the peace negotiations."[97] On the same day, Austria sent a similar cable to Wilson. Once again, as with Austria's September 6 note, these notes were addressed only to Wilson and not to the Allies against whom the Central Powers had been warring since 1914. Gen. Sir Henry Wilson called the sending of the notes directly to Wilson a "pretty piece of impertinence."[98]

In his inaugural address to the Reichstag, Prince Max made public the terms upon which Germany would be willing to halt the fighting, which included the full restoration of Belgium to its pre-war status and the renunciation of Brest-Litovsk. They would also be willing to make Alsace-Lorraine an independent state *within the German confederation.*

Wilson did not receive Max's note (delivered through the Swiss) until October 7. French intelligence, having intercepted and decoded it on October 5, read it before Wilson did. Neither the British nor the French realized how desperate the Germans were, and assumed that the note was a trap, designed to lead to "peace without victory." But they could not reject it out of hand, fearing it would stiffen the resolve of the

German people. When Wilson read the note he telephoned House, ordering him to Washington. House arrived that evening.

Wilson's October 8 reply to the German note, as Secretary Lansing told the press that afternoon, was "not a reply but an inquiry."[99] It began: "Before making reply to the request of the Imperial German Government and in order that that reply shall be as candid and straightforward as the momentous interests involved require, the President of the United States deems it necessary to assure himself of the exact meaning of the note of the Imperial Chancellor." It concluded: "The President feels bound to say with regard to the suggestion of an armistice that he would not feel at liberty to propose a cessation of arms to the Governments with which the Government of the United States is associated against the Central Powers so long as the armies of these powers are upon their soil. The good faith of any discussion would manifestly depend upon the consent of the Central Powers immediately to withdraw their forces everywhere from the invaded territories....The President also feels that he is justified in asking whether the Imperial Chancellor is speaking merely for the constituted authorities of the Empire who have so far conducted the war. He deems the answers to these questions vital from every point of view."[100]

As Wilson was drafting his reply, the Supreme War Council—Clemenceau, Lloyd George, and Orlando—were meeting in Versailles. On October 7, they drafted their own armistice terms, which they submitted to the Council's military advisors (but not to Foch.) As an armistice is considered to be a military, and not a political, matter, they deemed it appropriate that armistice demands should be presented by military men to military men. Their terms called for the "total evacuation by the enemy of France, Belgium, Luxemburg and Italy....Alsace-Lorraine to be evacuated by German troops without occupation by the Allies....Servia and Montenegro to be evacuated by the enemy....Evacuation of the Caucasus....Immediate steps to be taken for the evacuation of all territory belonging to Russia and Roumania before the war....Immediate cessation of submarine warfare."[101] It did not, however, provide a timetable for the German withdrawal of France, Belgium, Alsace-Lorraine and the other territories.

The next day, Foch submitted his own armistice proposals to the Council. Foch maintained that he did it on his own initiative; Mordacq claims he did it at Clemenceau's urging. In any event, they were much tougher than the armistice proposals the Council had submitted to their military men the previous day. Foch called for the evacuation of all of the occupied territories "within a fortnight," and their populations "immediately" repatriated. Far more significant was Foch's demand for Allied occupation of three bridgeheads on the *right* bank of the Rhine, in Germany proper, each comprising a thirty-kilometer semi-circle. Lloyd George thought Foch's terms amounted to unconditional surrender, which is exactly what many politicians, including Sen. Lodge, were calling for.

At the same time, Wilson's reply to Prince Max's note was delivered to the Council. It presented the three prime ministers with a serious problem. Wilson, who had not deigned to consult them, was basing the armistice on Germany's acceptance of the Fourteen Points in full, *to which the Allies had not agreed*, and to which they could never agree. Lloyd George could never accept "Freedom of the Seas," Point VIII regarding the future of Alsace-Lorraine was hopelessly vague, and Orlando would resist (to the point of stalking out of the Peace Conference) Point IX and its call for Italy's borders readjusted "along clearly recognizable lines of nationality."

Even though Wilson had ignored the Allies, they could not ignore him. The meeting of the Supreme War Council having concluded, they met in the French Foreign Ministry on the Quai d'Orsay the following day, October 9. According to Gen. Wilson, Clemenceau wanted to ignore Wilson's reply because they had not been consulted. Lloyd George convinced him a response was necessary. That evening, the three prime ministers sent a joint note directly to Wilson, implicitly backing Foch's tough armistice conditions: "The Allied Governments…recognize the elevated sentiments which have inspired the reply. Limiting themselves to the most urgent question, that of the armistice, they agree with the President of the United States that the preliminary condition of all discussion of this question is the evacuation of all invaded territory. But they think for the conclusion of an armistice itself this condition, while necessary, would not be sufficient. It would not prevent the enemy from profiting by a suspension of hostilities to install himself, after the expiration of an armistice not followed by peace, in a better military position than at the moment of the expiration of hostilities…. The conditions of an armistice cannot be fixed until after consultation with military experts and in accordance with the military situation at the moment of engaging in negotiations. These conditions have been forcibly exposed by the military experts of the Allied Powers and especially by Marshal Foch….To these considerations the Allied Governments draw the entire attention of President Wilson."[102]

Still later that evening, again at Lloyd George's urging, they dispatched a second cable to Wilson: "[T]he time has come when decisions of supreme importance in regard to the war may have to be taken at very short notice." Therefore, the Allied Governments "think it would be of very great assistance if an American representative possessing the full confidence of the United States Government could be sent to Europe to confer when occasion arose with the other Associated Governments so as to keep them accurately and fully informed of the point of view of the United States Government."[103] No one was under any allusions as to who the "American representative possessing full confidence" might be. It was House; they trusted him. House departed on October 17 accompanied by a corps of secretaries and assistants, and arrived on the twenty-fifth. Before he left, Wilson told him: "I have not given you any instructions because I feel you will know what to do."[104] House would not return for another year.

On Friday, October 11, a U-boat torpedoed and sank the Irish mail boat *Leinster*. Of approximately six hundred on board, four hundred perished.

Saturday evening, October 12, as Wilson dined with Mrs. Wilson and House at the Waldorf Hotel in New York, Joseph Tumulty handed Wilson a note. It was Germany's acceptance of his October 8 reply. Immediately made public, it sought to answer all of Wilson's "questions": "The German government," it began, "has accepted the terms laid down by President Wilson in his address of January the eighth and in his subsequent addresses as the foundations of a permanent peace of justice. Consequently its object in entering into discussions would be only to agree upon practical details of the application of these terms....The German government in accordance with the Austro-Hungarian government for the purpose of bringing about an armistice declares itself ready to comply with the propositions of the President in regard to evacuation." And in direct reply to Wilson's final question, whether the Chancellor was merely the mouthpiece of the kaiser who had brought about the war, the note concluded: "The present German government which has undertaken the responsibility for this step towards peace has been formed by conference and in agreement with the great majority of the Reichstag. The chancellor supported in all of his actions by the will of this majority speaks in the name of the German government and of the German people."[105]

The next morning, October 13, Lloyd George met with his War Cabinet. According to Gen. Henry Wilson, "Everyone [was] angry and contemptuous of Wilson." The result was a cable Secretary Balfour drafted to the British *chargé* in Washington, who handed it to Secretary Lansing, who the following day handed it to Wilson: "President Wilson's fourteen points as supplemented by his later utterances have apparently been accepted by the Germans....His Majesty's Government fully agree with the general tenour of the President's policy but they wish to make the following observations: (a) That there has been no discussion by the Associated Powers of the points at issue. (b) That various interpretations can be put upon certain of these points, to some of which His Majesty's Government would object most strongly. (c) That there are probably in existence other terms to which the President has not referred, such for instance as terms with regard to outrages on shipping, on which, if full justice is to be done, we shall have to insist.... His Majesty's Government are of opinion that in framing the conditions of armistice care must be taken to prevent the Allies from being deprived of the necessary freedom of action in the settlement of the final terms in the Peace Conference and that steps should immediately be taken by the chief belligerent Powers to discuss the doubtful points and come to some agreement amongst themselves with regard to them."

Item "c" in Balfour's telegram is telling. Nowhere in the Fourteen Points did Wilson mention the possibility of *reparations* for sunken shipping, the despoliation of Belgium and occupied France, or anything else. The "principles" upon which Wilson believed the peace must be based in fact precluded reparations. If the armistice was to be based on Germany's acceptance of the Fourteen Points, reparations might be precluded at the Peace Conference. Lloyd George's government was not prepared to concede the point.

Upon receipt of the German note, Wilson and House rushed back to Washington. They met after breakfast on the fourteenth, a date House described as "one of the stirring days of my life."[106] Wilson's mood had changed. He now found himself in a back-and-forth of notes similar to the exchanges over the *Sussex*, from which he could not extricate himself. He decided to put an end to it, reasoning that if Germany was beaten they would have to agree to anything, and if they weren't beaten he did not want to deal with them at all. But neither he nor House wished to sign on to a "vengeful" peace, House noting that "It is difficult to do the right thing in the right way with people clamoring for the undesirable and impossible."[107]

Wilson's reply to the Germans went out that afternoon, and it was very tough. He advised them that "the process of evacuation and the conditions of an armistice must be left to the military advisors" [read: "Foch"] of the Allies and the Unites States. However, "no arrangement can be accepted...which does not provide absolutely satisfactory safeguards and guarantees of the maintenance of the present military supremacy of the armies of the United States and of the Allies in the field." He pointed out that neither he nor the Allies would even *consider* an armistice as long as U-boats were still sinking passenger ships and retreating German armies were plundering French and Belgian villages. And he saved the best for last: as a "condition precedent to peace" the German people must either overthrow or neuter the militarists [read: the kaiser]: "It is indispensable that the governments associated against Germany should know beyond a peradventure with whom they are dealing."[108] The note was received in Berlin at 5:20 p.m. of the sixteenth. Kaiser Wilhelm read it and knew exactly what it meant: "It aims directly at the overthrow of my house, at the complete overthrow of monarchy."[109] But the Allies were also dissatisfied with Wilson's note. It was the second one Wilson had dispatched to the Germans, and he had consulted with them with respect to neither.

It was evident now that victory was only a matter of how much time and the amount of suffering that would have to be endured before it ended. On Friday, October 18, huge crowds gathered in Paris, awaiting the opening of the Chamber of Deputies. Every seat was filled, except those seats draped in a *tricolor*, indicating a deputy who had died in battle. The president of the Chamber, Paul Deschanel, announced that the Belgian port cities—Lille, Douai, Ostend and Bruges—had been liberated. Then Clemenceau mounted the tribune. He first announced that two additional Belgian cities—Roubaix and Tourcoing—had also been liberated. Then: "Our victory does not spell revenge. Our victory and the victory of our allies means the liberation of civilization and liberation of human conscience."[110] He added: "I have but one sentiment in my heart—immense joy over the recovered *patrie*, gratitude to our great soldiers, our great chiefs, our noble allies. With victory, hope spread its wings, and it is our duty to see that this hope, for which the purest French blood has been shed, shall become a reality. We have fought for our right. We will have our whole right, with the necessary guarantees against the offensive return of barbarism."[111] These words were met with thunderous cheers.

Wilson's tough note put Prince Max, his government and the German military in a quandary. Prince Max wished to keep dealing with Wilson, on the assumption that any armistice he could finalize with Wilson would be better than anything his military people could negotiate with Foch. The admirals had no intention of giving up the U-boat; to do so, they argued, really was unconditional surrender. Even Ludendorff, who had been pleading for any form of armistice, now stiffened. An armistice that locked in the Allies' military supremacy in the field—as Wilson now demanded—was exactly what he had been fighting to prevent.

Prince Max's reply was dispatched on October 20. It began by accepting the demand for the evacuation of "occupied territories." It protested against accusations of predations on the part of retreating German troops. It denied that U-boat commanders were firing on survivors in lifeboats. It tried to assure Wilson that only the Reichstag, and not the kaiser, had the power over war and peace. It was a total non-starter.

The German reply was received in London the following day, during a day-long meeting of the cabinet convened to discuss armistice terms. All present were alarmed that Wilson might accept the German reply, which they believed was a trap to permit the Germans to retreat unmolested behind the Rhine and regroup. The reference to the acceptance of the proposal to evacuate the "occupied territories" would likely not include Alsace-Lorraine. Under Balfour's signature, a "Very Urgent" telegram was dispatched to the British *chargé* and delivered to Wilson on the twenty-second. "The German reply," it began, "is plainly designed to obtain a conditional armistice, which would be most disastrous to the cause of the Associated Powers....About military terms they assume that an undisturbed retreat for the German army to their own frontier has been already accepted in principle....It seems to us clear that any armistice must contain securities both against the resumption of hostilities by the enemy if peace negotiations unhappily break down; and probably also against any violations of the final Treaty of Peace when that is concluded." To avoid this, Balfour urged that some enemy territory, "including at least Alsace and Lorraine be at once occupied by Allied troops," and that adequate precaution be taken against the resumption of naval warfare." The cable concluded: "We greatly hope that the President will not commit himself on these vital questions without previous consultations with the Allies."[112]

If Balfour was hoping that Wilson would consult with the Allies before sending off his next missive, he was hoping against hope. But with House still somewhere in the Atlantic, Wilson himself drafted his third note to the Germans. In it, he transferred all further talk of armistice terms to the military, i.e. Foch. With respect to his insistence that the Allies could treat only with a democratically elected German government not beholden to the German military, he was blunt. He did not believe that Prince Max's government, no matter how it was constituted, met his standard, and if "[the United States] must deal with the military masters and the monarchical autocrats of Germany now, or if it is likely to have to deal with them later in regard to the international obligations of the German Empire, it must demand, not peace negotiations, but surrender."[113] Wilson's critics, such as Roosevelt and Sen. Lodge, opposed the note, wanting no more negotiations. They wanted unconditional surrender.

The mid-term elections neared, wherein a third of the Senate and all 435 House seats would be contested. Wilson decided to nationalize the elections, making them a test of his leadership and his policies. House and Tumulty had both opposed the idea. On October 19, he drafted a direct appeal to the American people. It began: "*My fellow countrymen*: The Congressional elections are at hand. They occur in the most critical period our country has ever faced or is likely to face in our time. If you have approved of my leadership and wish me to continue to be your unembarrassed spokesman in affairs at home and abroad, I earnestly beg that you will express yourselves unmistakably to that effect by returning a Democratic majority to both the Senate and the House of Representatives." The pith of it was "The return of a Republican majority to either House of the Congress would, moreover, certainly be interpreted on the other side of the water as a repudiation of my leadership."[114] Before issuing it, he showed it to Edith. "I would not send it out," she counseled, "it is not a dignified thing to do."[115] He ignored her advice, telling Vice President Marshall, "I have no doubt they will give it [a Democratic Congress] to me. They have refused me nothing so far.[116]

House arrived in Paris on October 26 and took up residence at 78 rue de l'Université, a short walk from the Quai d'Orsay. He first met Secretary of State for War Alfred Milner and Gen. Haig. He found that Haig believed that the German army facing him still had plenty of fight in it, and hence was willing to give them moderate armistice terms. That evening, House met with Clemenceau, who revealed to House the armistice terms that Foch had finalized: the "immediate evacuation [of] France, Belgium, Alsace-Lorraine [and] Luxemburg," under a strict timetable, measured in days, "in order to prevent [the] enemy from withdrawing great part of war material and provisions of every character." The Germans would have to abandon 2,500 heavy guns, 2,500 field artillery, 30,000 machine guns, 3,000 mine throwers, 5,000 locomotives and 150,000 railway cars "in good running order." The naval terms included the delivery of 150 submarines and the entire surface fleet gathered in Baltic ports. But this was not the worst. There would be no lifting of the Allied blockade. The Germans would also be required to evacuate the left bank of the Rhine. The Rhine cities of Mainz, Coblenz, Cologne and Strassburg would be occupied, and a "neutral zone to be established on [the] *right bank* of [the] Rhine forty kilometers wide from Swiss to Dutch frontiers."[117] Clemenceau told House that Germany was so beaten that she would accept any armistice terms.

House cabled Foch's armistice terms to Wilson the following morning, Sunday the twenty-seventh. Wilson cabled his response the following day: "My deliberate judgment is that our whole weight should be thrown for an armistice which will prevent the renewal of hostilities by Germany but which will be as moderate and reasonable as possible within those limits, because it is certain that too much success or security on the part of the Allies will make a genuine peace settlement exceedingly difficult if not impossible."[118]

Since the creation on the Supreme War Council in November, 1917, Wilson had authorized the presence of an American military (Gen. Bliss) but not an American political representative at its deliberations. Wilson now changed that, explicitly appointing House as his political representative. With his *carte blanche* authority, he was now Wilson's power-of-attorney in France. The Supreme War Council was set to meet in Paris on October 29. At a luncheon preceding the meeting, Lloyd George told House that he could not accept Point II of the Fourteen Points, ("Freedom of the Seas") "without qualification," unless it was incorporated into a League of Nations charter generally acceptable to the British. Lloyd George advised House that Germany was being asked to accept an armistice based on the Fourteen Points, and if the Allies signed such an armistice, the Germans might correctly assume that the Allies also accepted all of the Fourteen Points, which was simply not the case.

Following the luncheon, House, Lloyd George, Balfour, Clemenceau, Foreign Minister Stephen Pichon and Italy's Foreign Minister Sonnino (Prime Minister Orlando not yet having arrived) repaired to the Quai d'Orsay for the opening meeting of the Supreme War Council, and all hell broke loose. Lloyd George reiterated that if the Allies accepted an armistice based upon the Fourteen Points, the Allies would be committed to it, which none of them were willing to do. "I ask Colonel House," said Lloyd George, "whether the German Government is accepting terms of an armistice on the President's conditions of peace? The question is, do we or do we not accept the whole of President Wilson's Fourteen Points? I am going to put quite clearly the points which I do not accept. Should we make it clear to the German Government that we are not going in on the Fourteen Points of Peace?" Clemenceau stated that he was not willing to commit himself or France blindly. He turned to Lloyd George and asked: "Have you ever been asked by President Wilson whether you accept the Fourteen Points? I have never been asked." To which Lloyd George replied "I have never been asked either." Lloyd George then turned to House: "What is your view? Do you think that if we agree to an armistice we accept the President's peace terms?" To which House replied: "That is my view." Foreign Secretary Balfour responded: "For the moment, unquestionably, we are not bound by President Wilson's terms; but if we assent to an armistice without making our position clear, we shall certainly be so bound." "Then," said Clemenceau, "I want to hear the Fourteen Points." "Yes," said Sonnino, "and the five more and the others."

Point I ("*Open covenants of peace, openly arrived at…*") was read aloud. "I cannot agree," said Clemenceau, "never to make a private or secret diplomatic agreement of any kind." Lloyd George agreed: "I do not think it possible so to limit myself."

The now-infamous Point II was read. "This point," said Lloyd George, "we cannot accept under any conditions; it means that the power of blockade goes; Germany has been broken almost as much by the blockade as by military methods; if this power is to be handed over to the League of Nations and Great Britain were fighting for her life, no league of nations would prevent her from defending herself. This power has prevented Germany from getting rubber, cotton and food through Holland and the Scandinavian countries. Therefore my view is that I should like to see this League of Nations established first before I let this power go. If the League of Nations is a reality, I am willing to discuss the matter."[119]

Foreign Minister Sonnino interjected that it was absurd to base an armistice on permanent peace terms, and that President Wilson should be so advised. This was exactly what House wished to avoid. Once the Germans were defeated, Wilson's leverage to force a peace based on the Fourteen Points would decrease. House now unsheathed his ultimate weapon. He advised Clemenceau, Lloyd George and Sonnino that, in light of the Central Powers having requested an armistice based on the Fourteen Points, Wilson would have to inform them that the Allies refused to accept an armistice on this basis, and that henceforth they would have to treat with the United States as a separate belligerent, and not as one of the "Associated Powers." "That amounts to a separate peace between the United States and the Central Powers," said Clemenceau. "It might," replied House. Lloyd George and Clemenceau were unmoved. "If the United States made a separate peace," said Lloyd George, "we would be sorry, but we could not give up the blockade, the power which enabled us to live; as far as the British public is concerned, we will fight on."[120] After the meeting concluded, Lloyd George told George Riddell: "We had a lot of trouble with the Americans regarding the freedom of the seas. The Americans threatened to make a separate peace. I said 'We shall fight on, even if we have to go on alone.' Clemenceau said, slapping his chest, 'Yes, and we shall fight with you.'"[121]

House cabled the results of the meeting to Wilson, who was unyielding, cabling back: "I feel it my solemn duty to authorize you to say that I cannot consent to take part in the negotiation of a peace which does not include freedom of the seas because we are pledged to fight not only to do away with Prussian militarism but with militarism everywhere. Neither could I participate in a settlement which did not include [the] league of nations because peace would be without any guarantee except universal armament which would be intolerable. I hope I shall not be obliged to make this decision public."[122]

In the end, a compromise of sorts was reached. House asked Lloyd George if the British would be willing to discuss the "principle" of freedom of the seas at the Peace Conference, even if they could not accept it now. Lloyd George said he would. House asked if he could put this in writing, and Lloyd George agreed to do so.

On November 3, as they were meeting to discuss the conditions to be imposed upon Germany, came word that an armistice had been reached with Austria. According to Lloyd George, Prime Minister Orlando was in tears, the otherwise stern Sonnino was "radiant," and even the "iron-hearted Frenchman," Clemenceau, was "overcome with emotion."[123] The second of the Central Powers was out of the war.

The following day, the Supreme War Council voted on and approved the final wording of the armistice with Germany. Their approval included two "reservations."

While agreeing to an armistice based upon the Fourteen Points, the first "reservation" noted that "clause two, relating to what is usually described as freedom of the seas, is open to various interpretations, some of which they do not accept." The second "reservation" dealt with reparations, of which the Fourteen Points were silent. The Allies insisted that "compensation will be made by Germany for all damage done to the civilian population of the Allies and their property by the aggression of Germany by land, by sea, and from the air."[124]

The following day, November 5, House cabled Wilson that a "great diplomatic victory" had been won in getting the Allies to accept an armistice based upon the Fourteen Points. But he warned Wilson that both Clemenceau and Lloyd George had indicated that they wanted the League of Nations to be considered only *after* the Peace Conference had concluded.[125]

November 5 was the first Tuesday after the first Monday, and America voted. Just as Wilson had sought to nationalize the election, so had the Republicans. They ran against the League of Nations. They picked up twenty-five seats in the House and five in the Senate, enough to give them control of both houses of Congress for the first time since 1908. They would not give up control until 1930. For the first time in his political career either as governor or as president, Wilson did not have a legislative majority. The new chairman of the Foreign Relations Committee would be Henry Cabot Lodge. When Lloyd George heard the news he could not contain his *schadenfreude*: "The elections show that America is not behind Wilson. He does not properly appreciate our share in the war."[126]

Wilson had warned that a GOP victory would be interpreted abroad as a "repudiation" of his leadership. Now, he was defiant: "You may be sure that the stubborn Scotch-Irish in me will be rendered no less stubborn and aggressive by the results of the election."[127]

One of Wilson's biographers, Arthur Walworth, best summed up Wilson's stance: "The last act of the tragedy of Woodrow Wilson had begun."[128]

With the Allies now having accepted, albeit grudgingly, all of the armistice terms, Wilson, by means of a rearranged signal, notified the Germans to proceed to meet Foch to finalize the armistice. Prince Max appointed new Secretary of State without Portfolio Matthias Erzberger, 43, the leader of the Catholic Center Party, to head the negotiating team, which included Maj. Gen. Detlof von Winterfeldt, representing the

Army, Count Alfred von Oberndorff, representing the Foreign Office, and Capt. Ernst Vanselow, representing the Navy. Accompanying Foch was his chief of staff, Gen. Maxime Weygand. First Sea Lord Adm. Rosslyn Wemyss and Rear Adm. George Hope, the Deputy First Sea Lord, represented the Allied Navies.

Erzberger and his *parlementaires* departed Berlin on November 6 and arrived within the French lines the next day. The following day, Friday the eighth, they were escorted to a train in the Compiègne forest, near the town of Rethondes. The dining car of the train had been converted into a conference room. Foch and his delegation were seated along one side of the conference table when Erzberger and his party entered and took their places opposite them.

Foch opened: "What brings these gentlemen here? What do you wish of me?" Erzberger replied that he awaited proposals relative to the conclusion of an armistice on land, on sea and in the air, and on all fronts. "I have no proposals to make," said Foch. Erzberger tried again, asking for the conditions of the armistice. "I have no conditions to offer." Erzberger then read President Wilson's last note, saying that Marshal Foch is authorized to make known the conditions of the armistice. Foch then ordered Weygand to read the armistice conditions, clause by clause, so that they could be translated from the French. No one spoke as Weygand read. Foch sat as immovable as a statue. When Weygand read the condition related to the occupation of the Rhineland, tears flowed down Capt. Vanselow's cheeks.

When Weygand finally finished reading the armistice conditions, Erzberger asked that there be an immediate end to the fighting. Revolution had erupted throughout Germany, and Erzberger feared that armed Bolsheviks could seize the government. Weygand was in constant telegraph communication with Mordacq. Mordacq relayed the request to Clemenceau, who declined. Foch told Erzberger that the fighting would not cease until the armistice had been signed.[129] Foch made it clear to Erzberger that there would be no negotiations of the armistice terms. He could accept or reject them; there was no alternative, and Foch gave Erzberger until 11 A.M. on Monday morning—the eleventh—to give his answer. Erzberger dispatched a courier with the armistice terms back through the French lines to his government, advising them that Foch had given them until Monday at 11:00 A.M. to finally decide.

All of Paris was now on tenterhooks awaiting news. At 3:00 P.M. Mordacq rushed to Clemenceau's second floor office in the War Ministry, delivering the message from Foch that the Germans had accepted the armistice proposals "in principle." Mordacq remembered that when Clemenceau finished reading the message his eyes moistened. Then he put his head in his hands and began to weep. After a moment Clemenceau pulled himself together. "It's absurd," he said, "I am no longer master of my nerves…

all of a sudden, I saw 1870 again, the defeat, the shame, the loss of Alsace-Lorraine, and now all that is wiped out. Is it a dream?"[130]

The following day, November 9, as Erzberger awaited final confirmation from his government, Kaiser Wilhelm abdicated his throne and fled to Holland. His son, the crown prince, renounced the throne. The House of Hohenzollern, which had ruled all or parts of Prussia, Romania and Germany through countless dukes, kings, emperors, margraves and electors since the *eleventh century*, was finished. Germany was a republic. Friedrich Ebert, the head of the Social Democrats, became chancellor. Clemenceau became concerned that there might be no government to deal with.

At noon on the tenth Ebert met with his cabinet in the chancellery. The armistice terms were read. He read a note from the Army high command that the terms be accepted "without delay and without change." A telegraph was sent to Erzberger, authorizing him to sign.

At 2:05 A.M. on Monday the eleventh, Erzberger advised Foch that he was ready to conclude the armistice. The final session began at 2:15 A. M. All of the articles were read and discussed. Erzberger protested the continuation of the blockade, but did obtain from Foch an informal promise that food would be provided during the period of the armistice. The armistice would go into effect at 11:00 A.M. They began signing at 5:20 A.M. Tears flowed from the faces of Winterfeldt and Vanselow as they signed. Within ten minutes, all had signed. "Tres bien!" said Foch. There was no shaking of hands.

When Mordacq told House that the armistice had been signed, House said "at last our dead on the *Lusitania* are avenged."[131] House sent Wilson a telegram advising that the armistice had been concluded. In a separate telegram to Wilson, House expressed his feelings: "Autocracy is dead. Long live democracy and its immortal leader. In this great hour my heart goes out to you in pride, admiration and love."[132] Wilson had been asleep when the telegrams arrived. He learned at breakfast that the war was over. He telephoned Lansing, instructing him not to announce the terms, which he would announce to a joint session of Congress later in the day.

At 6:00 A.M., Mordacq rushed to the rue Franklin to give Clemenceau the news. He told Clemenceau: "The task is accomplished at last. It is a great one, and France will know what it owes to you." "To me and others," Clemenceau replied. He then penned a note to House: "My very dear Friend," he wrote, "in this solemn moment of great events in which your noble country and its worthy chief have played so fine a role, I cannot restrain the desire to open my arms to you and press you against my heart. Your sincere Georges Clemenceau."[133]

He then paid a courtesy call at the Élysée Palace to formally advise President Poincaré of the armistice. He then headed to his office in the War Ministry, to the deafening cheers of the crowds that lined the boulevard St. Germain. His car reached the courtyard of the edifice, blocked by hundreds of children waving the *tricolor*. By 9:30 A.M. he was in his office. His children were there. At 10:00 A.M., Foch arrived, carrying the signed armistice in his brief case. Handing the document to Clemenceau, Foch said: "My work is finished; your work begins.[134]

At 4:00 P.M, Lloyd George entered the House of Commons to announce the terms of the armistice, by prearrangement at the same time Clemenceau entered the Chamber of Deputies. Breaking protocol, the members cheered him as he entered the chamber. He read the terms of the armistice. There were no emotional outbursts, but they cheered when he read the part about "Reparation for Damage Done." He concluded "This is no time for words. Our hearts are too full of gratitude to which no tongue can give adequate expression."[135] The body rose as one and, with Lloyd George and Asquith—side by side—leading the procession, they made the short walk to St. Margaret's, the parish church of Parliament.

At almost the same hour, President Wilson read the armistice terms in the House chamber, and was cheered as he did so. But he concluded: "To conquer with arms is to make only a temporary conquest; to conquer the world by earning its esteem is to make permanent conquest. I am confident that the nations that have learned the discipline of freedom and that have settled with self-possession to its ordered practice are now about to make conquest of the world by the sheer power of example and of friendly helpfulness.[136] No one cheered.

Clemenceau read the terms of the armistice to the Chamber of Deputies in a voice trembling with emotion. "In the name of the French people and the French Republic, greetings to France, one and indivisible, to France liberated by the power of arms, to Alsace-Lorraine and their honor to our great dead. France has been liberated by the power of arms. Let us salute our heroes of yesterday, soldiers of God, and our heroes of today, soldiers of humanity. Our soldiers will always be soldiers of the ideal."[137] When he finished, cannons boomed on the Esplanade des Invalides. Then the entire chamber rose and thundered out the *Marseillaise*.

He then drove to the Palais du Luxemburg to address the Senate. In 1871, as a very young member of the National Assembly huddled in Bordeaux to accept the peace that Bismarck had imposed on France, Clemenceau had been one of 107 who signed the document under which they refused to accept the annexation of Alsace-Lorraine into Germany. One of the senators now read that document. Of the 107 *protestataires*, Clemenceau was the only one still living. Of all of them who had seen the Germans march into Alsace-Lorraine, he was the only one who would see them march out. He had waited forty-seven years.

That evening, back in the rue Franklin, he took a long walk with Mordacq. "Yes," he told the general, "we have won the war, and not without difficulty. But now we must win the peace, and perhaps that will be harder."[138]

PART THREE

PARIS

THE DEFEATED

In Defeat: Defiance! In Victory: Magnanimity!

—Winston Churchill

The First World War was fought in places far afield from France and Flanders: in Russia, in the Balkans, in Jerusalem, in Mesopotamia. British Empire troops fought in East and West Africa, in New Guinea and in Samoa. But after the first thirty days, *the war was not fought in Germany.* The great Rhineland cities of Cologne and Mainz, not to mention Berlin and Munich, lay untouched by war. Germany's industries were intact, the coalfields of the Ruhr operating. But it was very different west of the Vosges, where the devastation was total. Four thousand French villages had been utterly destroyed; twenty thousand factories were in ruins. What the Germans could not carry off they wrecked. As they retreated, the Germans wrecked the coal mines. Millions of acres were so ruined that a plow could not cut a furrow. There were shell holes in the Tuileries Gardens from the "Big Berthas" that had terrorized Paris. All this meant that following the war, German industry was up and running and ready to compete in world markets; France was not.

France's post-war debt to its principal creditors, the United States and Great Britain, was 147 billion francs. Germany's post-war debt amounted to 160 billion marks, but with a population a third larger than France's. It is no wonder that shortly after the end of the war Clemenceau told the press: "In industry and commerce, between France and Prussia, victory for the moment rests with the latter."[1]

When the final butcher's bill was finally tallied, 1.4 million Frenchmen lay dead or were missing and presumed dead. The tally was somewhat higher for the Germans (1.7 million), but Germany emerged from the war with a population of sixty-eight million; France's population was only forty million.[2] There were an estimated six hundred thousand French widows and seven hundred thousand children without fathers.

What was worse from the French standpoint was that Germany emerged from the war strategically *stronger* than at the start. In 1914, Germany's neighbor to the east had been Russia. There now emerged a new buffer state—Poland—astride between it and Russia. To Germany's south and east, Austria-Hungary, a rather ramshackle empire but an empire nonetheless, had ceased to exist on November 11, replaced by a collection of new, small, weak states. And Germany would grow larger still if the German-speakers of Austria would be allowed to effect an *Anschluss* with Germany.

In November, 1911, Clemenceau had addressed the French Senate, speaking, as he often did, of Germany. For centuries there had been an ebb and flow of conflicts on the banks of the Rhine. "It is in the highest interests of civilization" he said, "that these conflicts cease, that a wise settlement, which should be hailed with joy by all civilized nations, should put an end to these alterations of peace and massacre, resulting from the victory of the one side or the other." But this would not be possible, he added, "until there shall be a conqueror superior to his conquest, a victor who shall be [a] hero in his moderation."[3] But a "conqueror" could be "superior to his conquest" only if he considered himself the victor; not if he deemed that he had emerged from the conflict as the defeated, more in fear of the conquered than the conquered feared the victor. This was Clemenceau and France in November, 1918.

For the nations of continental Europe, for centuries national security had been largely a function of *frontiers*. If the frontiers were secure, so was the nation. It was a concept lost on the British, whose security as an island nation was guaranteed by its navy, or on Americans, sheltered until the nuclear age by two oceans. For the French, the frontier that would provide that security was the Rhine. As Clemenceau's friend Gen. Mordacq wrote, Clemenceau was "hypnotized, like all men who had seen the defeat of 1870, by...the question of the Rhine. There, for the men of his generation, was the real danger, the weak point *par excellence*; there we must concentrate all our resources, all our efforts, all our thoughts."[4] Mordacq might have added that one man equally "hypnotized" by the Rhine was Marshal Ferdinand Foch. But the war had taught

Clemenceau one thing that was lost on Foch: In the next war, aircraft would breach whatever infantry and artillery guarded the frontier. Clemenceau emerged from the war with the realization that bridgeheads on the Rhine were not sufficient security. To ensure that a revivified Germany would not one day seek to overturn its defeat, Clemenceau knew that the one thing that France needed was the guarantee that Great Britain and the United States would come to France's aid in her hour of need. He knew that rescue in the next war was not a sure thing. No one had come to France's aid in 1870. The British had entered the war in 1914 only as a result of the kaiser having shredded the "scrap of paper," the violation of Belgium's neutrality. The sinking of the *Lusitania* had not brought the Americans into the war. Only after its merchantmen had been torpedoed on a daily basis was Wilson forced to abandon "peace without victory." Clemenceau's Peace Conference goal, therefore, was an alliance with the British, and particularly with the Americans. Foch's goal was very different.

The Peace Conference would convene in the midst of a continent wrecked and in upheaval. A civil war raged in Russia, with the Bolsheviks fighting to consolidate their grip on the nation. The westward spread of Bolshevism loomed: A short-lived "Bavarian Soviet Republic" was proclaimed; there would be a brief Soviet republic in Hungary. With the sudden disappearance of Austria-Hungary, new nations sprang up in Czecho-Slovakia and Jugo-Slavia, all with ill-defined, and in many cases contested, borders. In the case of the new Czecho-Slovak state, hundreds of thousands of ethnic Germans found themselves in a new nation in which they were strangers. The crack-up of the Ottoman Empire produced a jumble of unsettled territorial claims. And all of this as hunger and an influenza pandemic wracked the continent. The Peace Conference, therefore, would be more than an assembly to make permanent the armistice that had been signed in the railway car in Compiègne. It would be the *ad hoc* temporary government of a continent.

There was never a doubt that Lloyd George and Clemenceau would attend the Peace Conference. There was some doubt about Wilson. Three days after the war's end, House cabled Wilson, advising him that his supporters did not wish him to attend, fearing that it would result in the loss of his dignity and moral authority. Implicit in House's cable was House's concurrence that Wilson should stay home. House confided in his diary that he wished to head the delegation himself, with Treasury Secretary McAdoo and the Republican Herbert Hoover as fellow commissioners ("If I could have had these two men as associates and only these, I would have been able to guarantee results.")[5] But House also advised Wilson that Lloyd George, Clemenceau and Italian

Prime Minister Vittorio Orlando would be heading their delegations. Wilson fired back that House's telegram "upsets every plan we have made," that "I infer that French and English leaders desire to exclude me from the Conference for fear I might there lead the weaker nations against them....The program there proposed for me by Clemenceau, George, Reading and the rest seems to me a way of pocketing me."[6] On November 18, Wilson told Lansing that he had decided to attend the Peace Conference. Lansing then confided in a memo that "[H]e will undoubtedly lose the unique position which he now holds in world affairs. He will have to sit there on an equality with the Premiers of the Allies."[7] The Allies came to accept Wilson' attendance: "If he chose to step down from his pedestal," wrote Winston Churchill, "why were they [the Allies] the losers?"[8] Others may have doubted whether Wilson should not only show up but actively participate; Wilson did not.

Wilson not only intended to participate, he intended to preside. Unlike Clemenceau, Lloyd George and Orlando, who were their respective heads of government but not their heads of *state*, Wilson was both the head of the American government and its head of state, placing him in a position above that of the others. Clemenceau had anticipated the problem, and it concerned him. If Wilson participated as the American head of state, the French head of state, Clemenceau's *bete noire,* Raymond Poincaré, might wish to chair the French delegation, a prospect that horrified Clemenceau, Poincaré being as unbending on the issue of the Rhineland as Foch. Even before the war's end, Clemenceau said "I represent France, and I will not yield the presidency [of the Peace Conference] to anyone."[9]

It is traditional that the presiding officer of any international gathering is the representative of the host country. If the Peace Conference were to be held in France, Clemenceau would be its presiding officer. Initially, Wilson (and the British) favored a neutral site, such as Geneva or Lausanne, Switzerland. Needless to say, Clemenceau lobbied hard for Paris or Versailles. Shortly before the war's end, an editorial appeared in the semi-official *Temps,* (which may have been induced by Clemenceau) opining that the Conference should be held in Versailles, since it had been "the cradle of the German Empire, and ought to be its grave."[10] In any event, Wilson changed his mind about Switzerland, calling it "saturated with every poisonous element," referring to the increased Bolshevik influence there. Wilson now favored Versailles, because of the "friendly influences and authorities there."[11] To the French, conducting the Conference at a neutral site was pointless. Most of the Peace Conference would be the "preliminary" conference, in which the victors would determine among themselves the peace terms they would present to the Germans and their Central Powers allies. (The Peace Conference was officially designated the "Preliminary Peace Conference.") As the Germans would not be invited to the Peace Conference until the end, there was no need to conduct the Conference at a "neutral" site.

House initially was opposed to conducting the Conference in Paris, writing in his diary that "It will be difficult enough at best to make a just peace, and it will be almost impossible to do so while sitting in the atmosphere of a belligerent capital."[12] But when Wilson changed his mind about Paris, so did House, who now needed to convince the British. He "induced" Lord Northcliffe, the proprietor of the *Times,* to insert an editorial in the November 11 edition—the date of the Armistice—strongly favoring Paris as the site of the Conference. It turned the trick. But it was a mistake. Paris still seethed with anger. Captured German cannons lined the quays along the Seine; shell holes from the German "Berthas" were still evident; the women everywhere dressed in black were a constant reminder of the death toll. Paris was the worst place to conduct the Peace Conference.

But it ensured that Clemenceau would preside. When House advised Wilson that precedent and courtesy required Clemenceau to preside, Wilson advised House that he would attend the Conference not as a head of state but as a head of government, and graciously offered that "If the French Prime Minister is uneasy about the presidency of the Conference, I will be glad to propose that he preside."[13] And so he did.

Having decided to head the American delegation, Wilson needed to decide upon the other "commissioners" who would round out the delegation. Wilson was duty-bound to select Lansing, but was not duty-bound—and would not—use him in any meaningful way. Of course, he selected House, he only man he trusted. In a November 14 telegram to Wilson, House suggested a seven-man delegation, (the Allies had agreed upon delegations of five "plenipotentiaries") including two prominent Republicans. He repeated his suggestion of former Secretary of State Elihu Root. Attorney-General Thomas Gregory visited Wilson, urging him to choose a Republican senator for the delegation. Wilson rejected the idea, countering that it would require a senator to vote on a treaty that he had negotiated. Gregory pushed for Root and President Taft, noting that both were supporters of the League of Nations, and that they could push it through the Senate. Joseph Tumulty also pushed for Root. Wilson seemed to agree, but Tumulty later learned that Wilson thought Root to be too conservative. Richard Hooker, the editor of the Springfield *Republican,* wrote Wilson, urging Taft. Wilson replied, rejecting Taft: "I have lost all confidence in his character."[14] When the Czech patriot Tomas Masaryk visited Wilson, urging him to include Republicans in the delegation, Wilson rejected the idea, telling Masaryk that he didn't want to have to settle differences within the delegation. Finally, he told Masaryk: "I tell you frankly, I am descended from Scottish Presbyterians and am therefore somewhat stubborn."[15]

Wilson's refusal to name a prominent Republican is rooted less by his Scottish ancestry than in his philosophy of government. From his days as a graduate student, Wilson believed in party government, that the party in power should shoulder all of the responsibility, taking all of the credit and all of the blame, for its policies. It is what attracted him to Britain's parliamentary system. In the end, Wilson did select one Republican, semi-retired diplomat Henry White, 68, but only after Wilson assured himself that White was on board with the Fourteen Points. White's appointment sent Republicans scrambling to determine if he still was a Republican, and his appointment did not please them. What was known of him was that one of his daughters was married to a Prussian count who had been a member of the kaiser's personal guard. White was well-regarded by everyone he encountered in Paris, but, like Lansing, was not used by Wilson in the slightest. Wilson rounded out the delegation by selecting Gen. Tasker Bliss, the Army chief-of-staff, already in Paris. In mid-December, House wrote in his diary: "The President and I are doing everything."[16]

Four days after the Armistice, Clemenceau wrote to Lloyd George that they should not hurry into concluding a final peace: "I think it is not a bad idea to let the German Revolution settle down for a while in order that we may know, before proceeding, what we have before us."[17] A delay would also permit the nations that had sprung up following the Armistice—Poland, Jugo-Slavia and Czecho-Slovakia—to get their footing. But the Allied armies were quickly demobilizing, which with every day would make it more difficult to renew the conflict if no agreement could be reached with the Germans.

Once Wilson decided to head the American delegation, delay became inevitable. He needed to deliver his "Annual Message on the State of the Union" on December 2; he could not arrive in Paris until mid-December. And another, more serious delay eventuated: Lloyd George decided to hold elections for the House of Commons.

In his State of the Union address, Wilson noted (not entirely accurately) that the Central Powers and the Allies had accepted the Fourteen Points as the basis for the Armistice, and that they "very reasonably desire my personal counsel in their interpretation and application." Wilson now appealed for the bipartisan support that had been denied him in the Congressional elections: "The gallant men of our armed forces on land and sea have consciously fought for the ideals which they knew to be the ideals of their country....It is now my duty to play my full part in making good what they offered their life's blood to obtain. I can think of no call to service which could transcend this....May I not hope, Gentlemen of the Congress, that in the delicate tasks I shall have to perform on the other side of the sea, in my efforts truly and faithfully to interpret the principles and purposes of the country we love, I may have the encouragement and the added strength of your united support?"[18]

Roosevelt's reaction was immediate. He ridiculed the notion that American soldiers had fought for the ideals of the Fourteen Points. America fought "to smash Germany," and that "not one soldier in a 1000 ever heard of the Fourteen Points." Moreover, the American people had rejected the Fourteen Points on Election Day, concluding, "[I]t is earnestly to be hoped that it is his business not to try to be an umpire between our allies and our enemies, but to act loyally as one of the Allies."[19]

Two days later, Wilson boarded the liner *George Washington* (so named by its prior German owners to attract American tourists) at Pier 2 in Hoboken. He would be the first American president to set foot in Europe while in office. Before he set sail, he told his secretary: "Well, Tumulty, this trip will either be the greatest success or the supremest tragedy in all history; but I believe in Divine Providence."[20] Mrs. Wilson accompanied him, as did Secretary Lansing and the newly-appointed delegate Henry White, and a select group from the Inquiry, the historians, economists and geographers that would act as Wilson's technical advisors.

For the first six days at sea, Wilson kept his own counsel, strolling the deck alone, dining only with Mrs. Wilson, as the *George Washington*, escorted by the battleship *Pennsylvania* and three destroyers, steamed toward the Azores. But on December 10 Wilson called in the members of the Inquiry, and unburdened himself. Dr. Isaiah Bowman, the Inquiry's executive director, took copious notes. Wilson began by remarking that he was glad to meet the members of the Inquiry and to give his views of the impending Peace Conference. "The Americans" he said, "would be the only disinterested people at the Peace Conference," and that the men they were about to deal with "did not represent their own people." With respect to the matter of German indemnities, they should be determined by a commission "to determine the just claims of the Allies against Germany" and that after that determination had been made, "Germany should be made to pay." He stated that the Peace Conference would be "the first conference in which decisions depended upon the opinion of mankind, not upon the previous determinations and diplomatic schemes of the assembled representatives, and that "unless the Conference was prepared to follow the opinions of mankind and to express the will of the people rather than of their leaders at the Conference, we should soon be involved in another breakup of the world, and when such a breakup would come it would not be a war but a cataclysm." With respect to the League of Nations, it implied "political independence and territorial integrity plus later alteration of terms and alteration of boundaries if it could be shown that an injustice had been done or

that conditions had changed." The key was the establishment of the League. Once
established, territorial claims could be revised and adjusted. Only under the League
could "elasticity and security be obtained." The opposite was the idea of the Great
Powers and the balance of power, and these ideas had produced only "aggression and
selfishness and war," and "the people are heartily sick of such a course and want the
Peace Conference and the Powers to take an entirely new course of action."

According to Dr. Bowman's notes, the League would have a "Council," whose
members would be "the best men that could be found." Whenever trouble arose in the
world, it would be called to the attention of these men, who would give it the widest
publicity. A miscreant nation would be disciplined by cutting off its trade, postal
and cable access to all other League members. "No nation would be permitted to be
an outlaw, free to work out its evil designs against a neighbor or the world." More
specifically, Germany's former colonies would be "declared the common property of
the League of Nations and administered by small nations," the "resources of each colony
should be available to all members of the League." Wilson realized he was calling for a
new world order: "If it won't work, it must be made to work." The American delegation
would fight for the new order, "agreeably if we can, disagreeably if necessary.... [W]e
should only go so far in backing the claims of a given Power as justice required, and
not an inch farther."

He concluded the conference by stating that he hoped to see the members of the
Inquiry frequently, working through the commissioners, but that if any of them felt
that there was an emergency, he should bring the matter to him directly. He concluded
with the words that every man present would remember forever: "Tell me what's right
and I'll fight for it; give me a guaranteed position."[21]

There had not been an election in Great Britain in eight years. In the interim,
women over thirty and men over twenty-one had gained the franchise, tripling the
electorate and making the House of Commons unrepresentative of the people. Lloyd
George had assumed that the next one would be a war-time election, with his and
his coalition's stewardship of the war being the issue. But the war had ended sooner
than expected. What better time, he reasoned, to hold an election than now, in the
full glow of victory?

Lloyd George's coalition had been dominated by Tories; he was the only Liberal
in his own cabinet. Asquith and his followers sat in sullen silence, not in formal
opposition (only Labour formally opposed the coalition) but in grudging support.
Lloyd George wanted to continue the coalition into peacetime. So did Andrew Bonar
Law, the Tory leader.

On November 12, the day following the Armistice, Lloyd George invited two hundred Liberal supporters to 10 Downing Street. He shared with them his policies for the post-war world. He outlined a domestic program that included more housing ("We must have habitations fit for the heroes who have won the war"), increased minimum wages, and shorter working hours. But his principal focus was on the post-war world. "No settlement that contravenes the principles of eternal justice will be a permanent one." He noted that the 1871 treaty that Germany had imposed on France "outraged all the principles of justice and fair play," and must not be repeated. Therefore, "The mandate of this Government at the forthcoming election will mean that the British Delegation to the Peace Congress will be in favor of a just peace....We must not allow any sense of revenge, any spirit of greed, any grasping desire to overrule the fundamental principles of righteousness." To achieve that end, the establishment of an effective League of Nations, "more necessary now than ever," would be one of his prime objectives. "A large number of small nations have been reborn in Europe, and these will require a League of Nations to protect them against the covetousness and ambitions of grasping neighbours...The League of Nations is an absolute essential to permanent peace." To these gathered Liberals he concluded: "I was reared in Liberalism. From the old leaders of Liberalism I learned my faith. Even if I had the desire, I am too old now to change. I cannot leave Liberalism. I would quit this place tomorrow if I could not obtain the support of Liberals. I must have Liberal support."[22]

Wilson took note of the speech, and sent Lloyd George a short note, expressing his "sincere admiration of the admirable temper and purpose of your address....It is delightful to be made aware of such a community of thought and counsel in approaching the high and difficult task now awaiting us."[23]

Lloyd George had said that he "must have Liberal support," but in fact the reverse was true; each of them needed him. Only those Liberals who had sufficiently supported the coalition received Lloyd George's support, in the form of a letter of recommendation; those who had remained loyal to Asquith did not get one. A Liberal receiving such a letter had the assurance that the Tories would not contest his election. Seven hundred and even seats were up for election; only 150 Liberals received letters, which Asquith derisively called "coupons," referring to the wartime ration coupons. It became the "coupon election." More Tories received "coupons" than Liberals. Asquith himself did not receive one.

The most powerful of the Fleet Street press barons was Dublin-born Alfred Harmsworth—Lord Northcliffe—the proprietor of the *Daily Mail,* the *Daily Mirror* and the *Times.* As the campaign got under way, Northcliffe launched the twin campaigns to bring the kaiser to justice and to "make Germany pay." According to Lloyd George,

Northcliffe wanted to be named as one of Britain's five plenipotentiaries to the Peace Conference, and when Lloyd George refused, it set Northcliffe off. He became an implacable foe of Lloyd George during and after the Peace Conference. Northcliffe's campaigns resonated with the voters in the immediate aftermath of the Armistice. Bringing the kaiser to justice became "Hang the Kaiser." "Making Germany Pay" received its most famous utterance from Eric Geddes, Lloyd George's own Tory head of the Admiralty, who opined that the German "lemon" should be squeezed "until the pips squeak."

Lloyd George knew what Eric Geddes probably and the average voter certainly did not know, which was that "making Germany pay" was a far more complicated matter than it might appear. "They must pay," he explained to his friend George Riddell, but there were only two ways in which they could pay, either in gold or in goods. The Germans did not have nearly enough gold to pay what they owed, and "we do not mean to take their goods, because that would prejudice our trade." He gave Riddell an example: If Britain insisted that the Germans pay in aniline dyes every year, it would ruin the British dyes industry. He related to Riddell that "I said to [Australian Prime Minister William] Hughes the other day 'Shall you take their goods? We shant!' He did not know what to reply."[24] He also knew what it might cost to keep British troops stationed in Germany to assure payment. And so throughout the election campaign Lloyd George had to tread a fine line, as only a master politician could. He would promise the British people that he would require the Germans to pay "to the utmost of their ability," knowing that this was far less than what they expected.

Lloyd George made only six speeches during the campaign. He made two in Newcastle-upon-Tyne, in northeast England on November 29. To the readers of Northcliffe's *Daily Mirror* and *Daily Mail*, he wanted to show that he was just as eager as Northcliffe to prosecute the kaiser. He asked, rhetorically, if there should be one law for the common criminal and another for kings and emperors. He listed the kaiser's crimes, the chief of which was invading a country without its consent: "burning their cities, killing their old men and children and devastating the land in defiance of the law." But a careful listener might have noticed that Lloyd George made no mention of the punishment to be meted out to the prosecuted kaiser, certainly not hanging the kaiser. With respect to reparations, he explained: "When Germany defeated France, she made France pay. That is the principle which she herself has established. There is absolutely no doubt about the principle and that is the principle we should proceed upon—that Germany must pay the cost of the war up to the limit of her capacity to do so." They cheered lustily. But he added: "We are not going to allow her to pay in such a way as will wreck our industries."[25]

On December 7, while preparing to deliver a speech in the north-central city of Leeds, he was handed a telegram from Lord Northcliffe. The public, declared Northcliffe, was dissatisfied with "limit of her capacity," and wanted a definite figure, just as the French had done. There is a rule known to most American politicians: "Never argue with someone who buys ink by the barrel." Lloyd George now disobeyed the rule. He fired back his own telegram: "You are quite wrong about France. No Ally has named figure. Allies in complete agreement as to demand for indemnity. Inter-Allied commission will investigate on behalf of all on identical principles. Don't be always making mischief."[26] But two days later, in a speech in the southern city of Bristol, he caved in to Northcliffe's demand. He had been advised, he said, that the cost of the damages the Germans had inflicted was £24 billion. However, he hastened to add, the pre-war value of all of Germany had been only £20 billion, so Germany obviously could not pay the full amount. "Why have I always said 'up to the limit of her capacity'? he asked. "Well, I will tell you at once. It is not right for the Government to raise any false hopes in the community, and least of all is it right to do so on the eve of an election. You have no right to mislead your public at any time." After the speech, he announced that Germany would have to pay to "the utmost farthing," adding "we will search their pockets for it."[27] But what people remembered was the number–£24 billion.

The people voted on December 14, but the results were not announced for two weeks, in order to give the *tommies* still in France time to vote and have their ballots counted. The result was an astounding victory for Lloyd George and his coalition, far more than he had expected or had hoped for. Of the 707 seats contested, the Coalition had won 525. But of the 525 members of the new House of Commons, 379 were Tories and only 127 were Liberals whom Lloyd George had supported. The Asquith Liberals were almost eliminated, winning thirty-six seats; Asquith himself was defeated. The only formal opposition—Labour—won fifty-seven seats. Sinn Fein won seventy-three seats, one of whom, Constance Markievicz, became the first woman ever elected to Parliament. But she, like all of her Sinn Fein colleagues, refused to swear the Oath of Allegiance, thus failing to take their seats, effectively increasing Lloyd George's majority even more. Writing years after the war, Lloyd George compared his election victory to Wilson's recent defeat: "President Wilson was considerably weakened by an electoral disaster which indicated that his countrymen had lost faith in him. We were strengthened by the knowledge that the country trusted us."[28]

But it was not an unalloyed triumph. The Liberal Party, the party of Gladstone, of Richard Cobden and James Bryce, the party of free trade and social justice that had nurtured Lloyd George and that young "Tommy" Wilson had revered, was effectively dead. It exists as a fringe to this day, but Lloyd George would be its last prime minister.

He would enter the Peace Conference with a jingoist House of Commons and a powerful press lord in implacable opposition.

On November 15, Clemenceau wired Lloyd George, suggesting that each of the Allies submit a plan for the organization of the Peace Conference. Lloyd George, House and Orlando agreed. Two weeks later, Ambassador Jules Jusserand presented to Lansing the French plan, which Lansing sent to Wilson before he boarded the *George Washington*. It was the work of André Tardieu, 42, a wounded veteran and member of the Chamber of Deputies who Clemenceau would select as one of his commissioners at the Peace Conference and who would, years later, serve three terms as prime minister. Tardieu's plan was very detailed. It assumed that the Allies would determine all of the issues among themselves and then impose the terms on the Germans and the other defeated powers; there would be no negotiations. It is what made the Peace Conference officially the "Preliminary Peace Conference." It is surprising that Wilson would accept this arrangement. In his "peace without victory" address, he anticipated that an imposed peace would mean peace forced on the defeated: "It would be accepted in humiliation, under duress, at an intolerable sacrifice, and it would leave a sting, a resentment, a bitter memory upon which peace terms would rest, not permanently, but only as upon quicksand." Tardieu assumed that only the Allies would attend all of the discussions. The smaller nations, the neutrals during the war and the new nations forming out of the wreckage of the dissolved empires would be heard only as their specific issues were being discussed.

Tardieu's plan assumed that all of many items dealing directly with the peace (Alsace-Lorraine, Belgium, Germany's colonies, reparations and indemnities, etc.) would be discussed first, followed by the organization of the League of Nations. The treaties that had not been entered into by all of the Allies, including the Treaty of London which had brought Italy into the war, would be abrogated, as would Brest-Litovsk, by which Russia had exited the war. The plan called for discussion of all of the aspirational items in the Fourteen Points, such as freedom of the seas, limitation of armaments, and international trade. But it also called for the "Recognition by Germany of the responsibility and premeditation of her rulers justifying the measures of penalization and precaution taken against her. Solemn disavowal of the breaches of international law and of the crimes against humanity."[29] Germany would have to accept her "war guilt."

Wilson rejected Tardieu's plan with silence; there was no response. He wanted the League of Nations to be discussed first. Lloyd George wanted the kaiser's guilt to be discussed first.

Shortly before Tardieu delivered his plan for the Peace Conference to the Allies, Marshal Foch delivered to Clemenceau his plan for France's permanent security. In a five-page memo, Foch called for the effective annexation of the entire left bank of the Rhine (and its more than five million inhabitants) by means of the creation of a new Rhineland state wholly controlled by France. The right bank of the Rhine would thereafter be Germany's western frontier, subject to the right bank bridgeheads that Germany had ceded in the Armistice, which would be made permanent. "Without this fundamental precaution" Foch maintained, "Western Europe would still be deprived of all natural frontiers, and would lie open to the dangers of an invasion which remained as easy as in the past."[30] Foch would beat the drum for this new state, despite the opposition of the Allies and his own prime minister, right up until the signing of the treaty and beyond. André Tardieu called this "an extreme proposal amounting to annexation in disguise which had never been endorsed by the French government."[31] Clemenceau wrote that Foch "did not trouble his head to think what would happen to five and a half millions of inhabitants who, as a result of the principles of the French Revolution, would perhaps feel a certain dissatisfaction at being disposed of without a previous consultation, the result of which could be in very little doubt."[32] Clemenceau's opposition to Foch's scheme was also practical: It had no chance of winning the support of Wilson or Lloyd George, and it was to the United States and Great Britain that Clemenceau would look to guarantee against the next invasion from the East.

Foch was not alone in France in his desire to sever the Rhineland from Germany. In early December, the Foreign Affairs Committee of the Chamber of Deputies came up with its own plan, which called for the internationalization and demilitarization of the Rhineland (including a thirty-kilometer strip on the right bank) under French control. The plan also called for the return to France of the entire Saar basin, the coal-rich enclave through which, in 1870, French forces, led by Napoleon III, had marched, and held by Germany ever since.

The Allies had decided to meet informally in London in early December to iron out pre-Conference matters. Unfortunately, House fell ill and could not travel from Paris. It is a measure of Wilson's trust in House—and only in House—that Wilson left the United States unrepresented at this meeting rather than appoint anyone to fill House's shoes. And with the United States absent, it meant that nothing of substance could be finalized. Clemenceau assured House of this before he embarked for London.

Before the meeting convened, Foch met with Lloyd George, Balfour, Bonar Law and Gen. Henry Wilson at 10 Downing Street. Amazingly, Clemenceau begged off attending, citing a "previous social engagement." There is no record of what that "social engagement" was; it is likely Clemenceau simply did not wish to be in the room when

Foch presented his ideas for the annexation of the left bank of the Rhine. After patiently listening to Foch's exposition, they pressed him for details. He was asked how he could reconcile the scheme with the Fourteen Points. He replied that Germany was an aggressor that had disregarded its treaty obligations and whose signature could not be trusted in the future. Asked how the inhabitants of the Rhineland might to be induced to accept this arrangement, he replied that they might find compelling economic advantages in siding with the winner, such as being exempt from the payment of indemnities. When pointedly asked if this would not create an Alsace-Lorraine in reverse, with Germany bent on revenge, he contended that precautions could be taken "to conciliate the feelings and interests of these people," to which Bonar Law pointed out that Germany had said the same thing of the inhabitants of Alsace-Lorraine, adding that "We ourselves had tried for years to conciliate the Irish."[33] Foch promised to rework his plan into a written memorandum. Lloyd George's pithy comment upon reading it: "On my last trip to Paris my strongest impression was the statue of Strasbourg in its veil of mourning. Do not allow Germany to erect such a statue."[34]

When they got down to business, they agreed that each of the Allies would have five delegates to the Peace Conference. There were a host of smaller nations such as Cuba and Nicaragua that had declared war on the Central Powers but had not participated in the war. They would be represented only as the need arose. A resolution was adopted creating an Inter-Allied Commission (which would include Belgium) to determine and report on "the amount enemy countries are able to pay for reparation and indemnity." House later advised them that the United States would agree to the resolution only if the words "and indemnity" were deleted. A resolution was proposed to bring the kaiser to trial. Clemenceau said he mildly favored it. Italian Foreign Minister Sonnino opposed it on the grounds that the Dutch would never give him up and that it was not worth trying. A resolution favoring a trial of the kaiser by an international court was adopted, but delayed pending Wilson's approval. From the *George Washington*, Wilson cabled House that all resolutions should be held in abeyance until he arrived. House cabled back that "I have not committed you to any of the resolutions."[35] It was agreed that after Wilson's arrival in Paris and the prior to the opening of the Peace Conference, the Supreme War Council would meet to finalize the pre-Conference procedural matters.

While Lloyd George was campaigning and with Wilson still at sea, Clemenceau (and President Poincaré) made a ceremonial, emotional tour of Alsace and Lorraine. Poincaré did most of the honors, but on December 9, Clemenceau addressed the crowd in the city of Metz. It had been the site of Gen. François Bazaine's ignominious surrender of his entire army in 1870, in which almost 200,000 officers and men were marched into captivity. Now, Clemenceau turned to Metz's mayor: "[W]hen the Germans entered Metz as a result of an act of treason [Bazaine's surrender] and violated the city, General Lepasset was fortunate to be able to put the keys of the city into safety. They were carefully preserved by his family, who gave them to me, and today I entrust them to your use. Guard them well." The mayor replied: "We shall know how to guard them forever."[36]

On Friday, December 13 (Wilson's lucky number) the *George Washington* docked at Brest. The quay was festooned with American flags. The crowd cheered and a band played *The Star-Spangled* Banner as Wilson and Edith debarked. France's foreign minister, Stephen Pichon, Ambassador William Sharp and Generals Bliss and Pershing, among other lesser dignitaries, greeted him. After a few words of greeting to the crowd, they boarded the train for Paris.

After an overnight stay at a siding aboard the train, the presidential party arrived at the Bois de Boulogne station at 10:00 A.M. On the platform, dressed in a morning coat, stood the president of the republic, Raymond Poincaré. Behind him stood Clemenceau, in a high hat and dress coat. He was heard to say "Now I am going to see him. This is where we take each other's measure."[37] But there is no record of what words, if any, were actually exchanged when the two first met.

The four-mile carriage parade from the Bois de Boulogne to the Murat Palace, the opulent residence built by one of Napoleon's nephews which would be Wilson's home for the first part of the Peace Conference, was unlike anything Paris had ever witnessed. Half of Paris' population of four million lined the streets, surging forward, restrained by *poilus,* screaming "Vive Wilson," "Vive l'Amerique," "Vive la liberté." Wilson rode in the first open carriage with Madame Poincaré, followed by Edith and President Poincaré, whose carriage was quickly showered with flowers. No man could have resisted the overwhelming and unrestrained display of reverence that these people exhibited that morning for Wilson, and it would be the same when the crowds greeted Wilson in London and in Rome. But what, exactly, were they cheering for? The man who had sent the troops that had delivered the continent or the man of the Fourteen Points and the League of Nations? Might they have cheered just as lustily to "hang the kaiser?" There is no doubt that the conviction Wilson drew from these crowds was that he was the man who embodied their hope for permanent peace in the world. Half of the voters in America might have rejected him, but not these people.

After a brief stopover at the Murat Palace, the Wilsons were back in their carriages for a luncheon at the Élysée Palace hosted by President Poincaré. Following the sumptuous meal, Poincaré rose and, speaking without notes, toasted the president. He was very tough. "Eager as they were to meet the enemy," he began, referring to France's advancing armies, "they did not know when they arrived the enormity of his crimes. That they might know how the German armies make war, it has been necessary that they see towns systematically burned down, mines flooded, factories reduced to ashes, orchards devastated, cathedrals shelled and fired—all that deliberate savagery, aimed to destroy national wealth, nature and beauty, which the imagination could not conceive at a distance from the men and things that have endured it and today bear witness to it....In your turn, Mr. President, you will be able to measure with your own eyes the extent of these disasters, and the French government will make known to you the authentic documents in which the German General Staff developed with astounding cynicism its programme of pillage and industrial annihilation. Your noble conscience will pronounce a verdict on these facts."[38] But Poincaré was mistaken in his assumption that Wilson would ever "measure with your own eyes" the devastation. In the six months that Wilson was in Europe, he never once visited most of the devastated areas. It did not go unnoticed.

In his toast, Wilson answered Poincaré's challenge. "From the first" he said, "the thought of the people of the United States turned to something more than the mere winning of this war. It realized that...it must be won in such a way as to ensure the future peace of the world..."[39]

Later that day (as the British went to the polls) Wilson met with House for the first time since October. He told House that he intended to make the League of Nations part and parcel of the peace treaty. "Once that is a *fait accompli*" he said, "nearly all the very serious difficulties will disappear."[40] So there it was. If the articles that comprised the organization of the League of Nations were part of the peace treaty itself, the Senate could not possibly reject it. They would not reject the peace that tens of thousands of American *doughboys* had given their lives to achieve. They wouldn't dare.

The following day, Wilson's first full day in Paris, he met with Clemenceau for the first time other than their brief encounter the previous day at the Bois de Boulogne train station. In late November, House had taken pains to assure Clemenceau that the rumors of Wilson being "dictatorial, arbitrary or hard to get along with," were untrue. "I assured him" he confided in his diary, that "I had always found him more amenable to advice than any public man with whom I had been thrown in close contact."[41] Clemenceau came to the Murat Palace, and he Wilson and House met for an hour. Following the meeting, House wrote: "I have never seen an initial meeting a greater success. The President was perfect in the matter and manner of his conversation, and Clemenceau was not far behind." (Clemenceau, remember, was fluent in English.) "Neither said anything that was particularly misleading. They simply did not touch upon topics which would breed discussion....I took Clemenceau downstairs afterwards and he expressed keen delight over the interview and the President personally. The President was equally happy when I returned upstairs and discussed the matter with him. It was a pleasant augury for success."[42]

Three days later, on December 18, Wilson telephoned House, who was now residing with the American delegation in the Hotel Crillon, suggesting that he and Clemenceau have another, more serious meeting, focused on the League of Nations. They met the following day at the Murat Palace. House made a point of arriving fifteen minutes before Clemenceau. He suggested to Wilson that the best way to bring the conversation around to the League of Nations was to first discuss freedom of the seas. The three met for ninety minutes, with Wilson doing most of the talking. According to House, Clemenceau agreed "in a mild way" to freedom of the seas. With respect to the League of Nations, Clemenceau thought that the League should be attempted, but was skeptical of it being formed or being workable if it could be formed.[43] Had House or Wilson done their homework, they would have known that Clemenceau had spent the better part of the war deprecating the idea of a League of Nations in his *L'Homme Enchaine* editorials. After the meeting, Clemenceau told Great Britain's ambassador to France, Lord Derby, that Wilson was an "amiable" fellow but "shockingly ignorant of the European situation."[44] House concluded that Clemenceau had little faith in the League. "[H]e believes in war. He has something of the Roosevelt idea that war ennobles," he wrote.[45]

The Peace Conference could not begin until the results of the British election became known, so Wilson occupied himself with ceremonies and social events at the Murat Palace. He visited Lafayette's tomb, he was acclaimed a citizen of Paris at the Hotel de Ville, and received an honorary doctorate from the University of Paris (the "Sorbonne.") at which he called the League of Nations "the moral force of mankind throughout the world."[46]

Wilson spent the next two days with Italian Prime Minister Vittorio Orlando and his foreign minister, Baron Sonnino. It did not go well. The Italians would not be moved off of the Treaty of London. They claimed they would be at the mercy of whomever controlled the Dalmatian Coast (the eastern shore of the Adriatic), and the Treaty had promised it to them, not to mention the city of Fiume, the Trentino region, the Brenner

Pass and parts of the southern Tyrol, on the Austrian border, which they deemed essential to their security. Wilson was equally unmoved. The eastern Adriatic was filled with ethnic Slavs, the southern Tyrol with Germans, and nothing would violate the principle of self-determination more than to hand these people over to Italy simply because they had been on the winning side. Wilson had a technical argument in his favor. The Treaty of London purported to award the spoils of a defeated belligerent—Austria-Hungary—which now no longer existed. The Treaty, he reasoned, should not apply to Jugo-Slavia. The Italians were unmoved. Wilson suggested a compromise. If the Italians' security was at issue, would they not accept a provision in the peace treaty under which any nation that occupied the Dalmatian Coast would be prohibited from having a navy? Orlando and Sonnino would have none of it. It was a stalemate. Worse was to come.

As Wilson was meeting with Orlando and Sonnino, there appeared in the *Times* of London an interview that Wilson had ostensibly given to the *Times'* Paris correspondent. In fact, there had been no interview. What appeared in the *Times* was a script drafted by House and Sir William Wiseman, House's liaison to the British delegation. In the "interview," Wilson was asked what he believed "was the great purpose of the Conference and the great goal towards which the delegates should strive." His "response" was: "I think the plain man in the street could answer that question as well as I can. The plain people of all nations are now looking with anxious expectation towards Versailles, and I am sure they are asking themselves this one question, 'Will there be found enough wisdom and purpose among the statesmen there assembled to create a safeguard against future wars?' The difficulties and responsibilities, some of them very urgent and pressing, which are presented by the successful termination of the great war must of course be shared by the great nations of the world as comrades of the less powerful....I am confident that by common counsel the statesmen of the world will be able to reach a just and reasonable solution to the problems which will be presented to them, and thus earn the gratitude of the world for the most critical and necessary service which has even been rendered it."[47]

On the same day that Wilson's "interview" appeared in the *Times,* Sen. Henry Cabot Lodge took the floor of the Senate. He wished to speak, among other things, of the League of Nations. Lodge, 68, was tall, slender and elegant with an Edwardian moustache and spade beard. He could trace his lineage to *before* the *Mayflower,* to Francis Higginson, the first Puritan minister of the Massachusetts Bay Colony. His grandfather had been George Cabot, who on March 4, 1791 became the state's first full-time senator. It was in Sen. Cabot's home in Boston that Lodge was born in 1850. Graduated from Harvard College in 1871 (his mentor had been Henry Adams) and Harvard Law School in 1875, he first won election to the House of Representatives in 1886. In 1890 he co-sponsored the Federal Elections Bill, a failed effort to shore up the voting rights of southern blacks, who then voted overwhelmingly Republican, the party of Lincoln. He was elected to the Senate in 1892. Now, following the Republican takeover of the Senate following the mid-term elections, he was both the chairman of the Foreign Relations Committee and the majority leader. He believed that Wilson had left the nation insufficiently prepared for war. He derided Wilson's lack of bipartisanship. He believed that Wilson "does not want the truth told to him. It wearies him and makes him nervous to see people."[48] But the divide was more than about policy; it was personal. As he confided to his friend Teddy Roosevelt, "I never expected to hate anyone in politics with the hatred I feel toward Wilson."[49]

Lodge began his address by recommending that all of the aspirational points of the Fourteen Points ("freedom of the seas," "open covenants" etc.) should be laid aside as likely to cause division among the Allies and delay in concluding a peace treaty. In recommending this, he said that he was not reflecting on Wilson's "failure to give the Senate representation among the delegates charged with the work of formulating the peace." He came out in favor of Germany being forced to pay huge indemnities, including indemnities for the sinking of the *Lusitania* and for the expenses Germany had forced on the Allies in defending themselves. Then he came to the heart of it, Point XIV, the League of Nations. "Are we prepared to allow any association of nations" he asked, "by a majority vote to order the troops and the ships of the United States to go to war? Unless we are prepared to do so we are not prepared to join a league of nations which is going to enforce peace, and we should never put our name as a nation to any treaty or agreement which we are not ready to carry out both in letter and in spirit. To sign a treaty and then evade or disregard its provisions is not only bad faith and dishonor, it is the surest breeder of wars....Let us be honest with ourselves. It is easy to talk about a league of nations and the beauty and necessity of peace, but the hard, practical demand is, Are you ready to put your soldiers and your sailors at the disposition of other nations? If you are not, there will be no power of enforcing the decrees of the international court or the international legislature or the international executive, or whatever may be established."[50]

Wilson and House agreed that before the Peace Conference Wilson should visit London. The goal was that the people there would greet Wilson as tumultuously as in Paris, so that, according to House, "Lloyd George and his colleagues would not dare oppose his policies at the Peace Conference."[51] For some reason known only to House, he chose not to accompany Wilson, sending instead his son-in-law, Gordon Auchincloss, who House had attached to the American delegation and whose officiousness rankled Wilson.

The Wilson party crossed the Channel on December 26, "Boxing Day," which Lloyd George had designated as a bank holiday. They arrived at Dover shortly before noon, in perfect weather. Wilson and Edith boarded a train for the short trip to London's Charing Cross station. When the train arrived and Wilson emerged, the king stepped forward and greeted Wilson with outstretched hand. He introduced Wilson and Edith (carrying a bouquet of white flowers) to Queen Mary and Princess Mary. The king and Wilson then proceeded along the platform to review an honor guard of Scots Guardsmen, as the band played the *Star-Spangled Banner*. The king then presented Wilson to all of the members of the cabinet, and it was at that moment that Wilson and Lloyd George first met. Lloyd George recalled that "the frankness of his countenance and the affability and almost warmth of his greeting won my goodwill, and, as far as I was concerned, he never lost it….The favorable personal impression made on my mind by our first handshake was deepened by my subsequent meetings. He was even-tempered and agreeable. He had the charm which emanates from a fine intelligence, integrity of purpose and a complete absence of querulity or cantankerousness. He was stiff, unbending, uncommunicative but he was pleasant almost to the confines of geniality."[52]

When Wilson emerged from the station, he was met by a wall of two million cheering Londoners. Wilson, with the king seated to his left in an open, gilded carriage drawn by six horses, received the cheers of the crowd as they proceeded down the Strand to Trafalgar Square, through the Mall, around Piccadilly to and through the gates of Buckingham Palace. He emerged from the balcony and received more cheers from the surging throngs. Spotting wounded soldiers below, he said: "I honor you men who have been wounded in this fight for freedom, and I want to thank you for the welcome you have given me so generously."[53]

The following day, Wilson had his first substantive meeting with Lloyd George and Foreign Minister Arthur Balfour, the essence of which Lloyd George later relayed to the Imperial War Cabinet. He reported that Wilson had been an "attentive and receptive listener," with none of the professorial condescension that he had come to expect.[54] Wilson had opened immediately on the issue of the League of Nations, leaving the impression that it was the only thing that he cared about. He wanted the League of Nations to be the first thing discussed at the Peace Conference, since he might have to return to Washington for the conclusion of the Sixty-Fifth Congress on March 4, and wished to have the League of Nations in hand before then. Lloyd George had received a draft plan for a League of Nations that had been drawn up by South African Gen. Jan Christiaan Smuts. Lloyd George asked Wilson if he had drafted his own plan. Wilson replied that he had none, which was curious, since he had the written plan that House had drawn up, which he and House had discussed and reworked months before. With respect to Germany's colonies, Wilson agreed that they should not be returned to Germany, but that (as he had explained to the Inquiry aboard the *George Washington*) they should be given to a small, neutral nation acting as a League of Nations "mandatory." Lloyd George responded that this would be impossible with respect to South-West Africa (present-day Namibia), which the Afrikaaners of the South African Union considered part of their country. In 1914, a rebellion of Boer never-enders had broken out in that territory, which Gen. Smuts and Prime Minister Louis Botha, leading South African troops, had suppressed. There was no chance they would give it up now. If there was to be a "mandatory" for South West Africa, it would be the South African Union, and no one else.

Wilson, Lloyd George reported, was very vague on just what was meant by "freedom of the seas," and was willing to put off discussion of it until after the League of Nations had been established. Wilson had lost interest in Point III of the Fourteen Points, the one dealing with the reduction of tariff barriers. Lloyd George had found Wilson "stiffer" on the issue of indemnities than on any other issue. Wilson said he was willing to discuss claims for "pure" reparations; other claims might be discussed afterwards. Lloyd George expressed to Wilson that limiting the discussion to "pure" reparations would result in France and Belgium receiving everything, Great Britain receiving almost nothing and the Dominions—Canada, Australia and New Zealand— receiving nothing. The fact that Great Britain had expended £6 billion to prosecute the war did not make an impression on Wilson."[55] As a result of Wilson's recent meeting with Orlando and Sonnino, Lloyd George found Wilson very hostile to the Italians, and would oppose their territorial claims. But Wilson was prepared to accept French control of the West Bank of the Rhine.

Gen. Smuts spoke up. "We must from the very start of the conference cooperate with America, and encourage and support President Wilson as far as is consistent with our interests."[56] Smuts recommended that the British support Wilson in his effort to establish the League of Nations as quickly as possible. Having succeeded in that, "I believe he will…be prepared to drop some of the other contentious points he has unfortunately raised."[57]

Australian Prime Minister William Hughes spoke next. "Billy" Hughes, 57, was born in London of Welsh parents. After his mother died when he was six, he returned to Wales with his father. (He and Lloyd George would banter in Welsh.) He emigrated to Australia when he was twenty-two. He was short, wiry, and very deaf, and would signal his boredom with a speaker by placing his electric ear trumpet on the table. What he wanted from the Peace Conference was the former German colony of New Guinea. During the Conference, he would point out to Wilson on a map that the islands of New Guinea ringed Australia like a fortress, and possession of them was essential to Australia's security. When Wilson suggested to Hughes that he spoke for only a few million Aussies, Hughes shot back: "I speak for sixty thousand dead! How many do you speak for?" Behind his back, Wilson referred to Hughes as a "pestiferous varmint."[58] Now Hughes reminded the Imperial War Cabinet that "unless we were not very careful, we should find ourselves dragged quite unnecessarily behind the wheels of President Wilson's chariot,"[59] observing that the United States had made less of a contribution to the war than had Australia, that Lloyd George had just won a huge electoral victory while Wilson "did not speak for half of the Americans." He said that the League of Nations was to Wilson "what a toy [is] to a child—he would not be happy until he got it."[60] He suggested that the British not agree to the League of Nations until all of the other work was done—including New Guinea for Australia.

The evening of the twenty-seventh, the day following Wilson's arrival in London, was the occasion of a state dinner in Wilson's honor at Buckingham Palace. Lloyd George recalled it as one of "unsurpassed splendor," the most dazzling scene that he had witnessed in his lifetime. Wilson, accompanying Queen Mary, led the procession into the great hall, followed by Edith and the king, followed by the other members of the royal family in order of precedence.

The king gave a short, gracious speech, in which he thanked "with all our hearts your valiant soldiers and sailors for their splendid part in [the] victory, and we thank the American people for their noble response to the call of civilization and humanity."[61] The band then struck up the *Star-Spangled Banner*, and Wilson rose and responded. His tone was very different. "There is a great tide running in the hearts of men" he said. "The hearts of men have never beaten so singularly in unison before….I believe, sir, not only to apply the moral judgments of the world to the particular settlements which we shall attempt, but also to organize the moral force of the world to preserve those settlements, to steady the forces of mankind, and to make the right and the justice to which great nations like our own have devoted themselves the predominant and controlling force of the world….There is something inspiring in knowing that this is the errand that we have come on. Nothing less than this would have justified me in leaving the important tasks which fall upon me upon the other side of the sea, nothing but the consciousness that nothing else compares with this in dignity and importance."[62] Not a word of appreciation to the British Empire soldiers and sailors that had fought and died. As Lloyd George remembered it, when Wilson sat down there was a "perceptible chill of disappointment."[63]

Lloyd George feared that Wilson's oversight might damage Anglo-American relations, just at a time when his and Wilson's attitudes with respect to most of the issues to confront the Peace Conference would more likely converge than would Wilson's and Clemenceau's. So Lloyd George asked Lord Reading to reach out to Wilson, in the hope that Wilson would correct the error in a speech the following day at a banquet in his honor at the Guildhall, in which Wilson would be formally welcomed by the City of London. Lord Reading was assured that it was indeed an oversight, but when Wilson addressed the gathering, he made scant mention of Britain's soldiers and none of their sacrifices. Instead: "As I have conversed with the soldiers I have been more and more aware that they fought for something which not all of them had defined, but which all of them recognized the moment you stated it to them. They fought to do away with the old order and establish a new one. And the center and characteristic of the old order was that unstable thing which we used to call the balance of power; a thing in which the balance was determined by the sword which was thrown in on the one side or the other; a balance which was determined by the unstable equilibrium of competitive interests; a balance which was maintained by jealous watchfulness and antagonism of interests…The men who have fought in this war have been the men of free nations who were determined that that sort of thing should end now and forever."[64]

He was then off to northern England for a sentimental visit to Carlisle, the birthplace of his mother.

It was nearing midnight of the next day when Clemenceau mounted the tribune of the Chamber of Deputies. "People say," he began, "'Premier Lloyd George has spoken. President Wilson has spoken, but you have said nothing.' I have given explanations whenever you have asked me. But it isn't because Mr. Lloyd George has spoken, or because Mr. Wilson has arrived from America with elevated thoughts that I am obliged to explain myself and keep running to the Speaker's rostrum….France was in an especially difficult situation. It was the country nearest Germany. America was far away and took her time coming into the war. England came at once at the call of Mr. Asquith. We suffered and fought; our men were mowed down and our towns and villages were destroyed….This must not occur again, but how? There is an old system of alliances called the 'balance of power.' It seems to be condemned nowadays, but if such a balance had preceded the war, if England and the United States, France and Italy had agreed, say, that whoever attacked one of them attacked the whole world, the war would not have occurred. This system of alliances, which I do not renounce, will be my guiding thought at the Peace Conference if your confidence sends me there." Then he challenged them: "Whether this Chamber gives me a vote of confidence or not, I am ready to resign office. If you have a minute's hesitation, now is the time to change your pilot. You cannot do it when we are under way."[65] The vote of confidence passed, 386-89, with only the Socialists in opposition. Clemenceau's four-to-one majority caused House to write in his diary that it was "about as bad an augury for the success of progressive principles at the Peace Conference as we could have."[66] Following the speech, Clemenceau headed for his boyhood home in the Vendee for a few days rest.

The previous day, Lloyd George's overwhelming electoral victory had been announced. Both he and Clemenceau now headed into the Peace Conference with the wind at their backs. Wilson was undeterred. In a meeting with C.P. Scott, the editor of Manchester's *Guardian*, Scott told Wilson not to regard the results of the election as a demonstration against the League of Nations. Wilson agreed: "[T]his was strictly analogous to what had happened in the recent congressional elections in America." He did not think it would be the British so much as the French and the Italians who would give him trouble at the Peace Conference, adding that he "could always summon the public opinion of the world to his side."[67]

Following Clemenceau's speech in the Chamber, Wilson addressed a crowd in Manchester. Prior to Wilson's speech, House, in Paris, mused if Wilson would respond to Clemenceau. He did: "You know that the United States has always felt from the very beginning of her story that she must keep herself separate from any kind of connection with European politics. I want to say very frankly to you that she is not now interested in European politics, but she is interested in the partnership of right between America and Europe. If the future had nothing for us but a new attempt to keep the world at a right poise by a balance of power the United States would take no interest, because she will join no combination of power which is not a combination of all of us. She is not interested merely in the peace of Europe, but in the peace of the world."[68]

On the first day of the new year Wilson was off to Italy. It was the same as Paris and London; he was greeted by tumultuous crowds screaming "Vive Wilson" as he rode through the streets of Rome in an open carriage accompanied by King Victor Emanuel. Urged on by Joseph Tumulty, he paid a courtesy call on Pope Benedict, becoming the first American president to meet a pope. At yet another state dinner in his honor, he touched on his now-familiar theme: "[T]here must be something substituted for the balance of power, and I am happy to find everywhere in the air of these great nations that the thing must be a thoroughly united League of Nations."[69] It was the same when he toured Turin and Milan.

On January 6, Wilson's train stopped in Modena on the return to Paris. During the stopover, Wilson was handed a telegram. President Roosevelt had suddenly died at his home in Oyster Bay, New York, at the age of sixty. Wilson composed a note of condolence to Roosevelt's widow, in which he wrote that he was "grieved" at the news of the president's death. When he finished the note, he scratched out "grieved," and wrote in "shocked" before sending it off. Shortly thereafter, Lloyd George met with Wilson at the Murat Palace, and as Lloyd George entered the room he expressed his sorrow at Roosevelt's passing. "I was aghast," Lloyd George wrote, "at the outburst of acrid detestation which flowed from Wilson's lips. He was a man of burning animosities—against persons as well as principles, and he took no trouble to conceal either."[70]

Wilson returned to Paris on January 7, and met again with Clemenceau at the Murat Palace. Before the two met, House took Clemenceau aside. He tried to make Clemenceau see that, with Germany and Russia "gone under," France was now the biggest military power in Europe. The military guarantee that Clemenceau wanted would be provided by the League of Nations. Under it, the United States and Great Britain would be compelled to come to France's aid if she were attacked again. As for the Senate's "brag and bluster" about rejecting the League (they both must by now have read Lodge's Senate speech), House assured Clemenceau that the Senate would not dare reject a treaty made with its Allies, thereby forcing the United States to either continue the war alone or sign a separate peace. Then, according to House, "The old Tiger seemed to see it all and became enthusiastic. He placed both hands on my shoulders and said, "'You are right. I am for the League of Nations as you have it in mind and you may count upon me to work with you. '"[71] There are two possible explanations for this scene. The first is that it never happened. What is more likely is that it represents another example of House's belief that he could convince anyone—especially the emotional Latins—of almost anything. In Clemenceau's midnight address to the Chamber, he let slip what his strategy at the impending Peace Conference would be. His "directing thought" would be that "nothing must happen which might separate after the war the four Powers that were united during it. To this unity I will make every sacrifice."[72]

During his meeting with Wilson, Clemenceau brought up the matter of the huge debt that France had incurred to the United States during the war. If the debt burden could not be reduced, it would result in irresistible demands to have it paid by the

Germans in the form of indemnities. Wilson was noncommittal. Clemenceau also pressed Wilson about when Wilson might visit the devastated regions east of Paris. Wilson put him off. But they agreed to try to get Lloyd George to the peace table as quickly as possible. Wilson did not want the ardor of the crowds that he had seen and heard in Paris, London and Rome to cool.

The next day, House fell ill again, with either kidney or gall stones. He would be indisposed for the next two critical weeks.

Lloyd George and the rest of the 207 members of the British delegation arrived on January 11. They took over the Hotel Majestic. In order to assure that no latter-day Mata Hari might masquerade as a *femme de menage* (a cleaning lady), they turned out the entire French hotel staff and replaced them with British cooks(!), waiters and servants. Lloyd George occupied a flat on the rue Nitot, with Arthur Balfour occupying the flat above him. The Americans had taken over the entire Hotel Crillon, with Secretary Lansing on the ground floor. It meant that on those occasions when Wilson traveled from the Murat Palace to visit House, ensconced on the third floor, he had to walk past the office of his little-used secretary of state. In all, a thousand delegates from twenty-seven countries, plus their secretarial staffs and teams of experts and advisors, poured into Paris. Delegations from smaller nations such as Cuba and Nicaragua, that had declared war on Germany but had not participated in the fight, were accorded official status; neutral nations were not. Of course, none of the defeated powers were invited; for now, this was to be the *Preliminary* Peace Conference. Five hundred journalists were accredited to the Peace Conference. Every one of them was aware of Point I of the Fourteen Points ("Open covenants *openly arrived at*"); they assumed that the delegates' deliberations would be open. They would all be disappointed.

If Wilson's overarching goal at the Peace Conference was the League of Nations, and Clemenceau's was the security of France in the form of an alliance with the United States and Great Britain, Lloyd George arrived with goals more modest, but no less important. With the surrender and internment of the German High Seas Fleet, the Royal Navy was now more dominant than ever, and Lloyd George was committed to keeping it that way. "Freedom of the seas" would be opposed at all costs. A million Dominion soldiers—all volunteers—had aided the cause of the Allies, and their causes became his at the Peace Conference. He would fight for Australian control over German New Guinea and South Africa's claim for German South-West Africa and German East Africa. Lloyd George had little interest in these former German colonies; his goal was Imperial unity. More important were Britain's rights under the Sykes-Picot Agreement with France, viz., its control over what is present-day Iraq and, most important, its protectorate over Egypt, the guardian of the Suez Canal. But more than anything was the maintenance of good relations with the United States. Like France, Britain had incurred huge war debts to the United States, and like France, the possible cancelation of these debts was tied to the issue of German indemnities. But unlike France, which had a huge claim for *reparations*, Great Britain had a scant claim for reparations, and the Dominions, physically unscathed by the war, had none.

Wilson, Clemenceau and Lloyd George met for the first time in the same room on Sunday, January 12, 1919. The place was the ground-floor office of Foreign Minister Stephen Pichon in the Palais Bourbon on the Quai d'Orsay. The occasion was a meeting of the Supreme War Council, the inter-Allied body that Lloyd George had forged at Rapallo in 1917. Their purpose was to make preparations for the "Plenary" (i.e. public) sessions of the Peace Conference, at which all of the twenty-seven nations accredited to the Peace Conference would be present. Wilson, in diplomatic cutaway coat, arrived with Admiral Grayson, accompanied by Secretary Lansing and General Bliss. Clemenceau was accompanied by Pichon, Louis Loucheur (his point man on the League of Nations), Marshal Foch and Gen. Weygand. With Lloyd George that day were Foreign Minister Balfour, Gen. Henry Wilson and Lloyd George's ever-present eyes and ears, Sir Maurice Hankey. Prime Minister Orlando and Baron Sonnino headed the Italian delegation. Pichon's high-ceiling, large office was made small by the thirty to thirty-five men who crowded inside. Pichon's large desk had been placed by the west wall, and behind it, under tapestries depicting the life of Henry IV, sat Clemenceau, who had arrogated to himself (without opposition) the role of chairman. To Clemenceau's right, at the south wall, before the glass doors which led to a small courtyard, were the desks reserved for the British, American, Italian and (later) Japanese heads of government. A table was placed at the north wall for those who might be called upon to render advice or plead their cases. Wilson, the only head of state, was given a high-backed gold-leaf chair. Behind them sat their foreign ministers. Also seated behind Clemenceau was professor Paul Mantoux, the interpreter who would record for posterity their secret deliberations.

The meeting began promptly at 3:00 P.M., and they got right down to business. A pressing issue was the renewal of the Armistice, set to expire in five days. Foch reported that the Germans had not complied with all of its requirements. Only 1,956 of the required five thousand locomotives had been turned over. Four hundred fifty-eight thousand French prisoners had been returned; but twenty-eight thousand were still interned. The Germans still held over *one million* Russian prisoners, and as they were being released, the Bolsheviks were giving these newly-freed men the choice of joining the Red armies in the civil war, or starving. Foch now wished to use force to check the westward advance of the Bolsheviks. Wilson objected, noting that it was doubtful whether their advance could be stopped by intervention. Lloyd George and Clemenceau agreed, and they agreed to postpone the issue of stopping the Bolsheviks. Foch was authorized to extend the Armistice for another thirty days.

After an hour of discussion, Clemenceau dismissed the military men; the heads of government and their foreign ministers remained. After the Japanese joined them the following day, these men became the Council of Ten, and would remain as such until late March. Clemenceau arrogated to himself the chairmanship of this body as well. Clemenceau circulated the (somewhat revised) memorandum of procedure that André Tardieu had prepared in late November and which Wilson had ignored. In their London meeting on December 2-3, at which no American was present, it was agreed that each of the five Allies would have five delegates at the Peace Conference, but nothing was decided regarding the representation of the Dominions—Canada, Australia, New Zealand, South Africa and India. A dispute now arose between Wilson and Lloyd George regarding the number of delegates each of the Dominions would have at the Plenary sessions. The issue was entirely symbolic—there would be no "voting" at the Plenary sessions—but significant nonetheless. Wilson objected to the Dominions being separately represented, arguing that their interests would be championed by Great Britain. He argued that if the British Empire were given too many delegates, the smaller nations might perceive that big powers were running the Peace Conference, to which Lloyd George retorted "After all, they ran the war. Those who fought the hardest should talk the loudest."[73] They had originally hoped that the first Plenary session—the formal Preliminary Peace Conference—would convene the following day. They now postponed it. The Council of Ten would meet for most of the following week.

The next day (with Japan now joining the other four) the issue arose whether any substantive matters would be discussed at the Plenary sessions at which all of the nations would be present. Clemenceau put his opposition bluntly: "I have hitherto always been of the opinion that it was agreed that the five great Powers should reach their decisions upon important questions before entering the halls of the Congress to negotiate peace. If a new war should take place, Germany would not throw all of her forces upon Cuba or upon Honduras, but upon France; it would always be upon France. I request that...meetings be held in which the representatives of the five countries mentioned shall participate, to reach decisions upon the important questions, and that the study of secondary questions be turned over to the commissions and the committees before the reunion of the conference."[74] Lloyd George agreed. The smaller nations would be represented on the commissions and committees, and would be heard as their direct interests warranted, but all the final decisions would be made behind closed doors by the five powers. So much for "open covenants openly arrived at." Wilson also conceded on the issue of the Dominions' representation. It was agreed that Canada, Australia and South Africa would each have two delegates, New Zealand would have one, "British" India would have one and "native" India would have one. Also, each of the Dominions would have a delegate in Great Britain's delegation, on a rotating basis. Curiously, Wilson raised the issue of Brazil's representation. He noted that Brazil had contributed to the war effort, that it was a nation of over thirty million and, more importantly, that it was heavily influenced by Germany. In order to wean Brazil away from Germany, he suggested that it be given three delegates, and this resolution was carried. Wilson then presented his own agenda for the Peace Conference, much shorter than Tardieu's detailed memorandum. It contained only five items: the League of Nations, reparations, new states, frontiers and territorial changes, and colonies. The League of Nations was listed first. They then fixed January 18 as the first Plenary session of the Peace Conference which, coincidentally, would be the forty-eighth anniversary of Bismarck's proclamation of the German Empire in the Hall of Mirrors in Versailles. Following this day's meeting, Wilson rushed to House's bedside in the Hotel Crillon, as he did following every meeting.

The Council of Ten did not meet the following day, the fourteenth, but Wilson met with Lloyd George, who was accompanied by Balfour and Bonar Law. They discussed Italy. Balfour advised Wilson that Great Britain felt honor-bound to observe the Treaty of London, which had promised to Italy the Dalmatian Coast and parts of the Tyrol, with its 250,000 ethnic Germans. To Lloyd George, it was "a bond which had to be honoured...for by that time Italy had paid the price in full in blood and treasure."[75] To Wilson, it was everything he opposed.

The Council of Ten met on the fifteenth, the sixteenth and the seventeenth. They finalized the number of delegates to be awarded Serbia (two), Montenegro (one) and the new state of Jugo-Slavia (none). They agreed that no sensitive matters, such as the representation of Russia or Poland, would be discussed at the Plenary sessions, but would be ironed out by the big five in closed session. A mild dispute arose over the official language of the Peace Conference. Historically, French had been the official language of diplomacy, and Foreign Minister Stephen Pichon pressed for it. Wilson countered that that was then and this was now, and that more English-speaking than French-speaking nations had contributed to the war effort. (Wilson spoke no French; Lloyd George hardly any.) Clemenceau, who was fluent in English, backed Pichon, on the ground that French was the more "precise" language. (Clemenceau had once mused that English was nothing but French with bad pronunciation.) In the end, they compromised; French and English were both made the official languages.

There was a serious discussion of whether the Plenary sessions should be open to the public. Clemenceau, who had spent the war railing against censorship, recommended that even these largely ceremonial sessions be closed to the press, on the ground that otherwise delegates would be required to take positions for home consumption that they had already conceded in private. Wilson wanted the Plenary sessions to be open to the public. He carried the day on this issue, but it was an empty victory: There would be only six Plenary sessions of the Peace Conference.

The Salle d'Horloge ("Clock Room") is a very large and very ornate assembly hall in the Ministry of Foreign Affairs in the Quai d'Orsay. On this day—January 18—a long table was placed in its center to accommodate the seventy plenipotentiaries from twenty-five countries in attendance. Four large chandeliers grace its high ceiling. At one end is a large fireplace. Above it is a clock, whence the room derives its name, and above the clock is a statue representing France.

The meeting was scheduled to begin at 3:00 P.M. As Wilson and the rest of the American delegation (minus House, still ill) approached the front door, one of the American soldiers guarding the hall suddenly left his post, approached Wilson and introduced himself. He was Hardin Craig. He had been one of the fifty "preceptors" who Wilson had hired while president of Princeton. Wilson, somewhat startled, looked at Craig. Yes, he said, he remembered Craig from Princeton, and wished him well. He then strode into the hall.

And with that, the Peace Conference was under way.

Lord Kitchener, and the poster that brought a million men to the colors

Foch, Clemenceau, Lloyd George, Orlando and Sonnino

Wilson and Colonel House

Arthur Balfour and
Robert Lansing

Gen. Jan Christian Smuts

Australia's William
("Billy") Hughes

China's Wellington Koo

Sen. Henry Cabot Lodge

Clemenceau, Wilson and Lloyd George
minutes after signing the treaty

THE PEACE CONFERENCE BEGINS

President Wilson, the inspired prophet of a noble ideological venture,
to which he was unfortunately destined to become a slave.

—Georges Clemenceau

Woodrow Wilson entered the Peace Conference with certain strengths, but with a number of weaknesses. His greatest strength was that the British emerged from the war owing the United States $4.2 billion, and the French owing the United States $2.7 billion. Wilson had the power to cancel these debts, or modify them, or insist upon full and prompt payment. Worse for the British and the French, they would require still more financial assistance from the United States, which Wilson had the power to grant or deny. He also had the power to grant or deny the one thing Clemenceau wanted and needed more than anything: America's guarantee that it would come to France's aid if Germany attacked again. This is why Clemenceau told his Chamber of Deputies that he would sacrifice anything to assure that France's wartime alliance with Great Britain and the United States would survive the Peace Conference.

But Wilson came with a number of weaknesses, most of his own making. For one, he entered the Peace Conference with no moral authority whatever. Neither Lloyd George nor Clemenceau nor any of the gentlemen seated at the tables in the

Quai d'Orsay had forgotten that Wilson had failed to denounce Germany's violation of Belgium's neutrality, or that he had equated Germany's war aims with the Allies' war aims, or that his policy was "peace without victory" before the kaiser had forced him into the war, a policy Lloyd George termed a "jest" to the Germans and an "insult" to the Allies. As Clemenceau wrote after the war: "You had put your trust in a policy of procrastination that cost us dear....It was not enthusiasm that flung you into our firing lines; it was the alarming persistence of German aggression."[1] The United States had entered the war very late and had suffered relatively little. Fifteen French *poilus* had died for every American *doughboy*.

Wilson was politically weak relative to Lloyd George and Clemenceau, both of whom had just won resounding votes of confidence. Wilson had lost both houses of Congress, and a number of observers wondered if he could carry the Senate at the conclusion of the conference. Wilson had foolishly let slip to the British that he wanted the League of Nations more than anything; they would use this against him. They also knew that time was not on Wilson's side; he would need to leave the Peace Conference in mid-February in order to be home for the March 4 end of the sixty-fifth Congress. He needed to have at least a draft of the League of Nations treaty in hand before he left.

These weaknesses are certain. There is another that is conjectural: Wilson, relative to Lloyd George and Clemenceau, may simply not have been up to the task. Lloyd George alluded to this in his memoirs, noting that both he and Clemenceau had spent their adult lives in the rough and tumble of their legislatures, honing their adversarial skills. "But the moment he appeared at our Councils, he was there on equal terms with the rest of us. His training had never qualified him for such a position. Whether as principal of a college, as Governor of New Jersey, or President of the United States, he was always...amongst subordinates. He was not accustomed to confer with equals. He found it exceedingly difficult to adapt himself to that position. In the capacities he had filled he might have debated but he also decided. But when he came to the Peace Congress his decisions counted to no more than those of the Prime Ministers with whom he conferred."[2] Harold Nicolson, a young member of the British delegation who on occasion sat in on the Council of Ten, was more blunt: "It was the actual slowness of the President's own mental processes which placed him at such a disadvantage in his conversations with such men as Clemenceau and Lloyd George."[3]

André Tardieu had presented Wilson with a highly-detailed plan for the organization of the Peace Conference. Wilson ignored it, which Tardieu attributed to "the instinctive repugnance of the Anglo-Saxons to the systemized constructions of the Latin mind."[4]

It was defective in one important particular: It assumed that the Allies would settle upon the terms of peace before they tackled the charter of the League of Nations. As a result, the Peace Conference began and would proceed on an *ad hoc* basis, it being unclear to everyone whether their goal was a "preliminary" treaty to be negotiated with the Germans, or a completed treaty to be presented as a *fait accompli*. The Five Great Powers determined at the start that all of the substantive decisions would be made by them, sitting as the "Council of Ten." The "smaller" nations would have no voice, the "Plenary" sessions which they were permitted to attend would be largely ceremonial. But the five delegation heads and their five foreign ministers soon realized they could not possibly carry out all of the work they had arrogated to themselves, House noting in his diary "They are not getting anywhere, largely because of the lack of organization."[5] So they delegated the work to a proliferating array of "commissions" and "committees." There were territorial commissions studying Czecho-Slovakia, Romania/Yugo-Slavia, Poland and Greece/Albania. There were commissions on reparations, finance, international waterways, labor and general economic issues. By the end, fifty-eight commissions had been created, holding 1,646 meetings, each acting completely independently of all the others. In an attempt to coordinate them, at the end of February a Central Commission on Territorial Commissions was created. All of the commissions were ordered to complete their work and report to the Council of Ten by March 8.

But the real locus of decision-making was neither the Plenary sessions, nor the Council of Ten (which was later divided into a Council of Five and a Council of Four), nor the commissions. More often than not, decisions were made informally, in private meetings between House, Wilson, Lloyd George, Arthur Balfour, Clemenceau and a few others. After the first Plenary session, the veteran diplomat Jules Cambon, a member of Clemenceau's delegation, remarked to Balfour's private secretary: "You know what is going to be the result of this conference? An improvisation."[6]

The Peace Conference formally began in the mid-afternoon of January 18. Seventy-two plenipotentiaries representing twenty-four nations crowded around the horseshoe-shaped table in the Salle d'Horloge. They were welcomed by President Poincaré, who was gracious towards Wilson: "[T]he lofty moral and political truths of which President Wilson has nobly made himself the interpreter, and in the light of these truths, you intend to accomplish your mission....You will, therefore, seek nothing but justice." He then quoted Wilson: "Justice that has no favorites, justice in territorial problems, justice in financial problems."[7] But Poincaré left no doubt about where he stood on indemnities, encouraging the delegates "to render to each his due and not to encourage crime through leaving it unpunished." He also encouraged them the establish a "general

League of Nations which will be a supreme guarantee against any fresh assaults upon the rights of peoples." He concluded: "This very day forty-eight years ago, on the 18th of January, 1871, the German Empire was proclaimed by an army of invasion at the Chateau at Versailles. It was consecrated by the theft of two French provinces....Born in injustice, it has ended in opprobrium. You are assembled in order to repay the evil that it has been done and to prevent the recurrence of it. You hold in your hands the future of the world. I leave you Gentlemen to your grave deliberations and I declare the Conference of Paris open."[8] As Paul Mantoux read the translation, he went around the table shaking every hand, and left.

Wilson rose and, as pre-arranged, nominated Clemenceau as president of the Conference. "We have learned to admire him and those of us who have been associated with him have acquired a genuine affection for him."[9] Through a mix-up, Lloyd George had arrived mid-way through Poincaré's address. The always-prepared Col. Hankey passed Lloyd George a note, advising him that he had to second Clemenceau's nomination, which Lloyd George then proceeded to do, extemporaneously. He noted that Clemenceau had already been a "compelling and conspicuous" figure in French politics when he was still a schoolboy. "Were it not for that undoubted fact, Mr. President, I should have treated as a legend the common report of your age," noting that in any meeting that he attended with Clemenceau, it was always Clemenceau who was the most vigorous. "He is indeed the 'Grand Young Man of France.'"[10]

After nominations for Conference vice-presidents and secretary were received and approved, Clemenceau rose and spoke, in English, without notes. "Here we have met, as friends, from here we must go as brothers. That is the thought that is uppermost in my heart today...all else must be subordinated to the necessity of a union growing ever closer between the peoples who have taken part in the Great War. The League of Nations is here. It is in you, but you must inspire it with the breath of life, and this cannot do unless that purpose and determination is in your hearts. Gentlemen, let us try to act quickly and well."[11] He then instructed the delegates to lodge any of their special claims (there would be many of these) with the Secretariat, noting that memoranda for the guilt and punishment of the kaiser had already been received. Finally, accepting Wilson's bare-bones agenda, he announced that the first topic of discussion at the next Plenary session would be the League of Nations. He adjourned the session at 4:35 P.M. It had lasted all of ninety minutes. On the way out, Arthur Balfour, who had worn a top hat to the meeting, caught up with Clemenceau, who had worn a bowler. Balfour apologized, saying that he had been told he had to wear a top hat. "So was I," replied Clemenceau.

The improvisational nature of the Peace Conference represented Lloyd George with an opportunity. Big issues loomed, such as the boundaries of the new states of Poland and Czecho-Slovakia (who had competing claims), reparations and the Rhineland. But at the January 23 meeting of Council of Ten, Lloyd George suggested that they begin with consideration of the disposition of the German colonies, since the interested parties were present and ready to make their cases, and the European claimants were not. His proposal was accepted. It permitted Lloyd George to show his support for the Dominions—South Africa, Australia and New Zealand—whose support he might need when they proceeded to issues dearer to him. Clemenceau was in full agreement. He too wanted to get an item he cared little about out of the way, hoping it would give him more leverage when it came to dealing with a weightier matter—the Rhineland.

In the years after Bismarck created the German nation in 1871, it had conquered an overseas colonial empire of more than a million square miles, five times larger than Germany itself. There was now no question but that Germany would be stripped of all of these colonies, the issue now being what to do with them. The Allies and the Germans had signed an Armistice based on the Fourteen Points, Point V of which was "A free, open-minded and absolutely impartial adjustment of all colonial claims." Shortly after the end of the war, Gen. Smuts circulated an outline for a League of Nations, which provided for the the states succeeding to the collapsed Austro-Hungarian and Turkish Empires to be administered as League of Nations "mandates," with the "mandatory" acted as a trustee for the League. But Smuts' plan did not call for mandates over the former German colonies. Before the war ended, Lloyd George advised House that German South-West Africa (present-day Namibia) must go to the Union of South Africa, and shortly after the war's end South African Prime Minister Louis Botha told George Riddell that South Africa also had to have German East Africa (present-day Rwanda, Burundi and mainland Tanzania): "The Americans do not understand that. The situation must be explained to Wilson."[12] On the *George Washington*, Wilson had told the members of the Inquiry that he favored the smaller, neutral nations as the mandatories.

On Friday, January 24, the Council of Ten began dealing with the former German colonies. All agreed that Germany would be stripped of all of them. Lloyd George announced that he opposed a League of Nations mandate over German South-West Africa, because it had been conquered by the Union of South Africa, which was already in possession, and therefore should be directly annexed by South Africa. Similarly, New Guinea should be annexed by Australia and Samoa annexed by New Zealand. With respect to New Guinea, Lloyd George referred to the inhabitants as "cannibal colonies, where people are eating each other." When Australian Prime Minister William

Hughes entered the room, Clemenceau put both arms on Hughes' shoulders: "I hear, Mr. Hughes, that you are a cannibal," to which Hughes replied: "I can assure you that the report is grossly exaggerated."[13]

"Billy" Hughes then made the case for Australia's annexation of German New Guinea. Australia was already in possession of Australian New Guinea, and wished to administer the remainder of the island as a single unit. Using a map, Hughes demonstrated that the islands ringing New Guinea were like fortresses. "Any strong power controlling New Guinea controlled Australia."[14] He felt that Australia was owed as much, pointing out that Australia had lost sixty thousand men (all of them volunteers) and had incurred a £300 million ($7.2 billion) debt fighting the war.

Next came Gen. Smuts, in the uniform of a lieutenant general of the British Army. The earliest proponent of the mandate system, he now opposed it for South-West Africa. He noted that there was no defined border between it and the South African Union, that South African troops had conquered it and were in possession, and that anything less than annexation would be taken as justification for the 1914 Boer rebellion that he and Louis Botha had crushed. He was followed by New Zealand Prime Minister William Massey, who argued for direct annexation of German Samoa, calling it the strategic key to the Pacific. As with South-West Africa, New Zealand had conquered Samoa and was in possession. He noted that New Zealand treated its native population with care and respect, and could be counted on to do so with the natives of Samoa. Like Australia, it had sacrificed in the war, losing sixteen thousand men. It was owed. Clemenceau thanked the presenters, and adjourned the meeting. Wilson had not uttered a word.

They resumed the discussion of the German colonies on Monday, the twenty-seventh. Lloyd George spoke in favor of the Australian, South African and New Zealand claims for direct annexation, as did the Japanese and Italians. Canada's Prime Minister Sir Robert Borden supported his fellow Dominions, despite Canada having no colonial claims. Only Wilson opposed. The idea of smaller, neutral countries acting as mandatories, which he had mooted on the *George Washington*, was long gone; he accepted South Africa as the logical mandatory over South-West Africa, but he opposed annexation: "If any nation could annex territory which was previously a German Colony, it would be challenging the whole idea of the League of Nations."[15] If any nation threatened a nation under a mandate, it would bring the whole world against it. Looking at Billy Hughes, he said Hughes' position represented a "fundamental lack of faith in the League of Nations….If the League of Nations did not prove adequate to its task, general chaos and confusion would arise in all parts of the world. Therefore, the League of Nations must succeed, and if all the delegates in this room decided that it must succeed, it would succeed."[16]

But Lloyd George saw problems. Under its system of "Imperial Preference," Great Britain gave South Africa a three percent tariff concession. He asked Wilson whether, if South-West Africa were not an integral part of South Africa, but only a South African mandate, could the preference be extended to it? Wilson replied it could not, which meant that two sets of customs rules would be imposed on a country with no defined borders. Then there was the issue of the expenses of the administration of the mandate. If the mandatory ran a deficit, how would the League of Nations raise the money to fund the shortfall? Would countries, he asked, "be able to raise money by taxation in order to enable…France to develop the Cameroons?"[17] Wilson had no answer; there was none. "That essential detail," Lloyd George later wrote, "had somehow escaped his consideration."[18] Wilson's principal argument against annexation was that it would look to all the world as if, immediately after the war, the victors were divvying up the spoils. But Smuts, Hughes and Massey, supported by Lloyd George, argued that there were no "spoils," that the cost of maintaining an undeveloped nation exceeded any economic gain, and that a mandate over the subject nation would be worse for the natives than annexation. The difference between annexation and a mandate, Massey argued, was the difference between ownership and a leasehold. "No individual would put the same energy into a leasehold as into a freehold. It would be the same with governments."[19]

The Japanese plenipotentiaries usually remained mute throughout the proceedings. But Baron Nobuaki Makino now made the claim for the annexation of the Chinese territory of Kiaochow, in the south coast province of Shantung, and the Marianas, Carolines and Marshall Islands in the northern Pacific. Japan had entered the war against Germany right at the start. It had presented the Germans with an ultimatum to deliver "on a date not later than September 15, 1914 to the Imperial Japanese authorities, without condition or compensation, the entire leased territory of Kiaochow, *with a view to eventual restoration of the same to China.*[20] The ultimatum went unanswered, and the Japanese overran the entire province. The Japanese were in possession, and now wished to annex what they had conquered. They had a clinching argument for the Pacific Islands: Under a secret treaty they had entered into with the British in 1917, they had been promised these islands. (It is questionable whether Balfour advised Wilson of this treaty when he advised him of the other secret treaties.).

The debate continued the following day, with only Wilson opposing annexation. France's Minister of Colonies, Louis H. Simon, led off, presenting France's case for the annexation of Germany's former west African colonies of Togoland and Cameroons. (Under a war-time agreement with the British, they had agreed to carve up the territories.) Simon averred that the natives had been well-treated by the French prior to the German takeover, and that they now wished to be reunited with France. Clemenceau supported Simon, the entire proceeding tinged with irony; Clemenceau had long opposed France's acquisition of colonies in the first place.

Arthur Balfour now took up the Dominions' argument for annexation. He again raised the question of how the League of Nations would pay for the costs of the mandates, a question Wilson had clearly never considered. He also raised the knotty question of whether a mandate, once granted, was to be permanent or temporary. If only temporary, there was little incentive for the mandatory to invest in its development, and nothing to prevent the Germans from continuing to stir up trouble among the natives. Wilson had no answer. Balfour also raised a fundamental question regarding the nature of the League of Nations itself. Was it merely a defensive alliance, or would it have executive powers, to grant, administer, and if necessary cancel a mandate? Both Lloyd George and Clemenceau opposed a League of Nations with executory powers.

Wilson responded, forcefully. He appreciated the difficulties mentioned by Balfour, but he believed they were soluble, but "they could not be solved by discussion until they arose in concrete form." He again asked his fellow delegates to "consider how the Treaty would look to the world....The world would say that the Great Powers first portioned out the helpless parts of the world, and then formed a League of Nations. The crude fact would be that these parts of the world had been assigned to one of the Great Powers....[T]he world would not accept such action; it would make the League of Nations impossible, and they would have to return to the system of competitive armaments with the accumulating debts and the burden of great armies. There must be a League of Nations, and they could not return to the *status quo ante*. The League of Nations would be a laughingstock if it were not invested with this quality of trusteeship....[T]he people of the world would not permit the parceling out among the Great Powers of the helpless countries conquered from Germany." Wilson urged his fellow delegates to consider that if they failed in this, it would give the world "its initial cold bath of disappointment."[21]

Clemenceau then called upon the plenipotentiary from China, Dr. V.K. Wellington Koo. Koo had been born in Shanghai in 1888, the son of a wealthy merchant. He had earned BA, MA and PhD degrees from Columbia University, and as an undergraduate was Columbia's star debater and orator of the class of 1909. He would go on to be China's ambassador to France, the United Kingdom and the United States, and would briefly serve as China's prime minister. He would sign the United Nations Charter. He died in his home in Manhattan in 1985, at the age of ninety-seven. But on this day Koo, 31, asked to be heard in opposition to Baron Makino's claim for the annexation of Shantung province. He noted that he stood there representing four hundred million people, a fourth of the human race, and that China was not New Guinea, Samoa or South-West

Africa. Japan, he explained, had taken Shantung province from Germany by force, but Germany had acquired it only by force. There were thirty-eight million inhabitants of Shantung province, all of them ethnic Chinese; there were only thirteen million natives on all of Germany's former African colonies combined. China had a right to Shantung province on the principles of nationality and territorial integrity. Moreover, the province was a "Holy Land" to the Chinese; it was the birthplace of Confucius.[22] Secretary Lansing, who sat facing Koo throughout, noted afterwards that Koo "simply overwhelmed the Japanese with his argument."[23] Baron Makino must have felt the same. Afterwards, he sought out Lansing. He advised Lansing of the "intense feeling" in Japan over Shantung, and that Japan would hold the United States responsible if the province were returned to China.

The mandates/annexation dispute threatened to collapse the Peace Conference as it began. The men who rescued it were Lloyd George and Gen. Smuts. On the morning of the twenty-ninth (there being no meeting of the Council of Ten that day) Smuts devised a compromise: a three-tiered set of League of Nations mandates for the former Ottoman states and German colonies. "Class A" mandates would be those former states in Mesopotamia, Syria, Armenia and Palestine that had reached an advanced stage of development requiring minimal stewardship. The "Class B" mandates were for Germany's former colonies in central Africa, viz., Togoland and Cameroon, requiring greater supervision, where the mandatory would be required to guarantee the civil rights of the natives, and would be prohibited from engaging in the slave trade, arms and liquor traffic, from fortifying the subject country with naval or military bases, or providing military training to the natives other than for police purposes. The Class C mandates were specifically reserved for Germany's former colonies in southern Africa and in the Pacific, which, "owing to their small size, or their remoteness from the centres of civilization, or their geographical contiguity to the territory of the Mandatory" permitted the mandatory to administer the subject nation as an "integral portion of his territory," subject to the same prohibitions as the Class B mandates. All of the mandates would be subject to League of Nations oversight. The Class C mandates were substantively indistinguishable from annexation, without calling it that.

At 10:30 A.M., Smuts met with House. He advised House that Lloyd George had approved the compromise, but had not mentioned it to either Hughes or Massey, wishing first to know if Wilson would approve. Lloyd George was scheduled to meet with all of the Dominion heads later that day. House accepted without consulting Wilson. (Later that evening, Wilson advised House that he might not be ready to accept Japanese control of the northern Pacific Islands as a strategic threat to the United States.)

When Lloyd George met with the Imperial War Cabinet later in the day, he convinced Hughes and Massey to accept the compromise. He asked Hughes if he was willing to accept a prohibition on the slave trade and liquor trafficking in New Guinea. Hughes replied that he was. He asked Hughes if he was willing to accept missionaries in the colony. "Of course," replied Hughes, "The natives are very short of food and for some time they have not had enough missionaries."[24] That being the case, argued Lloyd George, there was no effective difference between annexation and a Class C mandate. And besides, argued Lloyd George, the British Empire really did not need the enmity of Woodrow Wilson. The deal was done, and Smuts' compromise would become Article 22 of the League of Nations charter.

But that did not prevent the next day's meeting of the Council of Ten from turning ugly, which Lloyd George later described as the only unpleasant episode of the Peace Conference. The previous day, Billy Hughes had given an interview to an Australian reporter in which he had said that Lloyd George had "kowtowed" to Wilson in giving away the Dominions' case for the colonies. The interview was cabled around the world, and in the morning all of the plenipotentiaries, and their governments, had read it. Wilson was furious. He demanded to know from Hughes if the acceptance of the Class C mandates represented an ultimatum to the Peace Conference, and if refused whether "Australia is prepared still to defy the appeal of the whole civilized world?" To which Hughes replied "That's about the size of it, President Wilson."[25] At which point South Africa's Louis Botha asked to be heard. According to Col. Hankey, who was seated behind Lloyd George, Botha spoke "with great deliberation, but obviously under great emotion, in rather broken English that, if anything, added force to his remarks."[26] Botha pleaded for compromise. He recalled that the Union of South Africa was itself the result of a compromise between Englishmen and Afrikaaners, and that they all had to submerge their differences in order to achieve the high ideal, the South African nation. He praised Lloyd George and Wilson for their idealism, and pleaded that they too reach a high ideal. His speech rescued the day. When the session ended, Hankey heard Wilson say that Botha's was one of the most moving speeches he had ever heard.

But one last issue remained. Stephen Pichon questioned the provision prohibiting the military training of the natives. France had recruited and trained hundreds of thousands of Senegalese and other African troops, many of whom had served on the Western front. Pichon was not about to cede that right. Clemenceau, who had sat silent throughout the entire debate, now spoke up, revealing what was uppermost in his mind, and it was not Togo or the Cameroons. "The French," he said, "were the nearest neighbors of Germany, and could be at all times, and had been in the past, suddenly attacked." The British had responsibilities all over the world, and the

Americans could not come at once to the assistance of France. "If the League of Nations and the peace of the world were to be established, it must not begin by putting France in a position of peril which would be much more dangerous for them than for any other Power. America was protected by the whole breadth of the ocean, and Great Britain by her fleet. If the French could not find any territories for which they would have to take the responsibility…if they could not raise volunteers without compulsion…the people of France would resent this very much, and would have a grievance against the government."[27] Only after Lloyd George and Wilson assured Clemenceau that the prohibition on compulsory military training did not prevent France from training volunteers for defensive purposes was the issue laid to rest.

The second Plenary session of the Peace Conference was held on January 25 in the Salle d'Horloge, attended by plenipotentiaries of twenty-six nations, Clemenceau presiding. He announced that it had been decided that commissions would be appointed to consider the League of Nations, the responsibility for the war and the punishment of the criminals, reparations, international labor legislation and international control of waterways and railways. It had also been decided that each commission would have fifteen members, two from each of the Five Great Powers, and five from the other nations, who would (somehow) select the delegates to represent them. The first matter to be discussed would be the adoption of a resolution, previously adopted by the Council of Ten, making the charter of the League of Nations an integral part of the peace treaty. That resolution provided, in part: "It is essential to the maintenance of the world settlement…that a League of Nations be created to promote international cooperation to ensure the fulfillment of accepted international obligations, and to provide safeguards against war….The League should be created as an integral part of the general treaty of peace, and should be open to every civilized nation which can be relied on to promote its objects."[28] Clemenceau then introduced Wilson.

"I consider it a distinguished privilege to open the discussion in this Conference on the League of Nations," he began. "We have assembled for two purposes—to make the present settlements which have been rendered necessary by this war, and also to secure the peace of the world not only by the present settlements but by the arrangements we shall make in this Conference for its maintenance." He rehearsed many of the arguments he had pressed for the past months throughout England, France and Italy: "The United States in entering the war never for a moment thought it was intervening in the policies of Europe, Asia, or any part of the world. Its thought was that all the world had now become conscious that there was a single cause which turned upon the issues of this war. That was the cause of justice and all liberty for men of every kind and place. Therefore the United States would feel that its part had been played in vain if there ensued upon it merely a body of European settlements…I would feel I could not take part in guaranteeing this European settlement unless that guarantee involved the continuous superintendence of the peace of the world by the Associated Nations of the world."[29] Clemenceau sat passively, believing not a word of this. Wilson was followed by Lloyd George, Orlando and Léon Bourgeois (Clemenceau's man on the League of Nations), all of whom seconded Wilson's call for a League of Nations as part of the peace treaty.

The Five Great Powers intended the Plenary sessions to be ceremonial rubber stamps for the work of the Council of Ten. They were therefore surprised when a small revolt broke out. Brazil's João Pandiá Calógeras spoke first: "It is with some surprise that I constantly hear it said 'This has been decided, that has been decided.' Who has taken a decision? We are a sovereign assembly, a sovereign court. It seems to me that a proper body to take a decision is the Conference itself."[30] Others joined in. The Belgian delegate wanted assurance that Belgium would sit on the League of Nations commission. The delegate from China wanted representation on the commission on international labor, in light of the 150,000 Chinese laborers who had served on the Western front. The Polish delegate wanted representation on every commission.

After all the pleadings had been heard Clemenceau, who had sat impassively, now sprang to his feet: "I will remind you that it was we who decided that there should be a conference at Paris, and that the representatives of the countries interested should be summoned to it. I make no mystery of it—there is a conference of the Great Powers going on in the next room….The Five Great Powers whose action has to be justified before you today are in a position to justify it. The British Prime Minister just now reminded me that, on the day the war ceased, the Allies had twelve million men fighting on various fronts. This entitles them to consideration. We have had dead, we have had wounded in millions, and if we had not kept before us the great question of the League of Nations we might have been selfish enough to consult only each other. It was our right. We did not wish to do this, and we summoned all the nations interested. We summoned them, not to impose our will upon them, not to make them do what we wish, but to ask them for their help. That is why we invited them to come here…. A few days ago Mr. Lloyd George was cruel enough to remind me that I was no longer very young. I entered Parliament for the first time in 1871…and I have noticed—as most of you perhaps have also noticed—that the larger the Committees are the less chance they have of doing any work….We have, therefore, decided to appoint two delegates each, and then—may I be pardoned for it—we have decided to ask you to appoint five delegates in common."[31]

But the little revolt did have some effect. The League of Nations commission was increased from fifteen to nineteen members, with the smaller nations given the additional four seats. Of course, Wilson became its chairman. Resolutions making the League of Nations charter a part of the peace treaty, and for the appointment of a commission to examine the kaiser's war guilt, were adopted in Clemenceau's dismissive fashion: *"Sans objection"? "Adopté!"*

The plenipotentiaries who met in Stephen Pichon's office during the final days of January had much more on their plate than Germany's former colonies. Newly-revived Poland was at war with the Bolsheviks to the east, Germany to the west and newly-created Czecho-Slovakia to the south. On January 22, Marshal Foch appeared before the Council of Ten. He proposed to assist the Poles in their struggle against the Bolsheviks by supplying them through the German port of Danzig (present-day Polish Gdansk.) They all knew that Germany would oppose it. They agreed to send a combined military-civilian commission to Poland to investigate the situation on the ground.

Then there was the matter of Russia. The Bolshevik takeover of Russia was far from complete as the Peace Conference opened, with "White" armies under Admiral Aleksandr Kolchak in Siberia and General Anton Denikin in the Ukraine fighting (with some success) the "Reds." Partly as a result of the uncertain outcome of the revolution, and partly from the almost-universal revulsion against the Bolsheviks, none of the Allies had recognized any Russian government, and no Russians were invited to the Peace Conference. But in early January, Lloyd George suggested to the French Foreign Office that all of the warring factions and the Russian exiles be invited to Paris to work out a truce. Clemenceau vetoed the idea of any Bolsheviks in Paris. So on January 22 the Council of Ten, per a resolution drafted by Wilson, "every organized group that is now exercising or attempting to exercise political authority or military control,"[32] was invited to attend a February 15 conference with Allied representatives on the resort island of Prinkipo, twelve miles from Constantinople. None of the exile governments accepted, and the Bolshevik reply was so contingent as to constitute a rejection. Nothing came of it.

On the following day, they agreed to appoint a commission "to examine and report on the question of the amount of the sum of reparation which the enemy countries should pay, and are capable of payment, as well as the form in which the payment should be made."[33] When the resolution for the commission was first proposed, it was styled as "reparations and indemnities." Wilson asked that "indemnities" be deleted.

The commission consisted of the Five Great Powers, together with Belgium, Greece, Romania and Serbia. A commission was also appointed to inquire and report on "The responsibility of the authors of the war"…and "The Constitution and procedure of a tribunal appropriate to the trial of these offenses."[34] This pleased Lloyd George; it fulfilled a campaign promise.

On the twenty-third and the twenty-fourth, they took up the matters of German disarmament and demobilization. Prior to the the Armistice, Gen. Bliss had pressed for the complete disarmament of Germany as a condition to the Allies' agreeing to the Armistice. Foch opposed it, on the ground that it would require the occupation of all of Germany to enforce it. The Armistice had required the Germans to turn over specific amounts of guns, aircraft and locomotives, but did not require them to completely disarm or to demobilize. Moreover, there was nothing in the Armistice that prevented the Germans from continuing to manufacture arms, which they were doing. Lloyd George now pressed for Germany's demobilization as a condition to the renewal of the Armistice, set to expire on February 16. Germany still had thirty-seven divisions on the Western front and fifteen to eighteen in the East, a total of 600,000 to 700,000 men under arms. This, according to Foch, required the Allies to keep eighty to ninety divisions—1.8 million men—on the Western front. Lloyd George advised his fellow delegates that, as far as Great Britain was concerned, this was politically untenable. Clemenceau was also feeling pressure from the Chamber of Deputies to speed up French demobilization. But the last thing that Clemenceau was willing to do was allow France to become militarily weaker than Germany. As he kept reminding his interlocutors, the Armistice had not ended the war, and it might have to be resumed if the Allies and the Germans could not agree to an extension.

Clemenceau pressed for requiring further German disarmament and demobilization as a condition for the extension of the Armistice. The Allies were willing to allow the Germans thirty divisions, deemed sufficient to maintain internal order. Beyond that, Clemenceau wanted to reduce German manpower, require the surrender of more war materiel, and control its principal arms factories. As security for German compliance, he pressed for the occupation of Essen (site of the principal Krupp works) if the Germans cheated. Foch did not oppose tougher Armistice terms, but in a remarkably prescient look into the future, he warned: "In a country like Germany it would be very easy for the people to take up arms again. Should a real leader arise, it would not be difficult for him to reconstruct the armies—trained men, officers and staffs and a skeleton organization existed. In a short time it would be possible to have a good army, in splendid fighting trim."[35] They could insist on further disarmament as a condition to the continuation of the Armistice, "but it would be ineffective."

Gen. Bliss, who had initially pressed for the total disarmament of Germany, now opposed it, on the ground that if the Allies had not initially required it, they could not require it now. Wilson suggested that the best solution was the early conclusion of a peace treaty, which would eliminate the necessity of the Allies having to keep troops in Europe indefinitely. Lloyd George agreed. Wilson also said that the real danger was Bolshevism, and that the only real protection against it was providing food and reviving German industry, that it was in the Allies' interest to give Germany the means to restore her economic life, not only to reduce unemployment (and the risk of revolution), but to "enable her to pay the reparations which the Allies had a right to expect."[36]

The debate continued throughout the first week of February. Wilson, siding with Gen. Bliss, opposed the idea of increasing the quantum of arms that the Germans would be required to turn over. He explained that when the initial Armistice terms were announced in America, the people regarded them as the terms of a final surrender. If the Germans were now required to turn over (as the French suggested) 82,000 additional machine guns, 12,000 field guns and 3,000 heavy guns, if this request were received in America, "the people would say that the original figures of the Armistice must have shown astonishing ignorance of the situation in Germany, if the demand then made was so insufficient that an almost equivalent demand must be made now, three months later."[37] He added that "It is very important that the Allies should make a good impression on the world. These continual aggravations of the armistice put the Allies at a moral disadvantage."[38] Clemenceau disagreed. "France would be placed in a situation of great danger if a firm attitude were not adopted." The Americans and the Australian troops, he noted, were leaving, and it was essential to act quickly. "The forces at the call of the Allies had not yet diminished appreciably," he said, adding that he "knew the German people well. They become ferocious when any one retires before them. Was it forgotten that they were still at war? The Germans had not forgotten it….A state of war existed, and any appearance of yielding would be construed as an evidence of weakness."[39]

On February 10 they heard reports of the Germans' widespread evasion of the Armistice terms. They were cheating not only with respect to the military terms, but they had not turned over the merchant ships required of them, and they had not complied with the financial terms, not having turned over the French securities they had removed from the occupied areas. With the Armistice scheduled to expire in just four days, they debated extending the Armistice for two weeks, demanding that the Germans comply with the Armistice in the interim. Time was running out in another respect: Wilson was scheduled to depart on the fourteenth. They rejected the two-week extension as being pointless. On February 12 Wilson again objected to increasing the Armistice demands, for which, he said, the Allies were not prepared to go to war. The Allies, he maintained, should set the final military and naval terms as quickly as possible, being prepared to resume the war if these terms were breached.

Clemenceau strongly disagreed, and in so doing highlighted the split between himself and Wilson. The final military and naval peace terms could not be severed from the political (i.e. territorial), and financial terms. Clemenceau feared what would happen after the Allied forces left. France had fifty-one divisions in the field, but "The final military conditions to be imposed might be extremely difficult, and it might be that the enemies, having been left free to act on the other side of the frontier, a great deal of blood would have to be shed to conquer them a second time."[40] He reminded the delegates that during four years of war the French countryside had been devastated "and subjected to the worst kind of savagery." The Germans had then been forced to surrender, but, "left to themselves, the Germans had created order, just as the Russians had created disorder. The Germans had succeeded in forming a government, and the first words spoken in the National Assembly had been 'Deutschland Über Alles.'" The German nation, he said, "had not suffered from invasion, its aggressive morale had been preserved intact...probably the Germans had come to think that the Allies were quarreling and they were incapable of action...The Germans must not be allowed to think that they would be able to face successfully France's fifty-one divisions after the Allied troops had dispersed."[41] As for providing Germany with the means to restore its economic life in order to prevent revolution and pay the reparations, as Wilson suggested, he observed that as a result of the occupation French industries that had been "scientifically destroyed, not for military reasons, but in order to prevent France from recovering in peace time;"[42] France would be unable to compete with Germany for two years. What he left unsaid, but clearly implied, was that he had no faith in a League of Nations to provide France with the security it needed. Whatever aid the League could provide would come too late, if at all. The security that France required needed to come now, before the Allies went home.

In the end, they agreed to extend the Armistice indefinitely, with no additional terms, and to advise the Germans that the Allies were speeding to prepare final military and naval peace terms. But severing those terms from the other terms—including the disposition of the Rhineland—was something to which Clemenceau would never agree.

During the latter part of January and the first week of February, the Council of Ten entertained a steady stream of claimants to the pieces of the fractured Austro-Hungarian and Ottoman Empires, who brought with them maps, charts, photograph albums and centuries-old histories. Clemenceau, Wilson and Lloyd George had to keep straight in their minds Silesia, in Poland, from Cilicia, in Turkey, and to remember that Lower Silesia is *north* of Upper Silesia. In whatever language the claimant spoke, it then all had to be translated in English or French, and if the claimant spoke neither, into English and French. It was interminable. Lansing kept himself awake by doodling expert caricatures of the speakers. One of the technical advisors seated next to Lansing asked if he could have one. Lloyd George leaned over and asked if he could have one, too.

Point XIII of the Fourteen Points called for an independent Poland composed of "indisputably Polish populations," with "free and secure access to the sea." Poland had had a truly tortured history. After the fall of Napoleon, it had ceased to exist, partitioned between Russia, Germany and Austria. On the day of the Armistice, it was reborn. Prior to the war's end, the Inquiry had recommended to Wilson that the East Prussian port of Danzig be awarded to Poland, in order to provide it with access to the sea, with a "corridor" connecting Danzig to the rest of Poland. But Danzig was indisputably German, and the "corridor" would separate East Prussia from the rest of Germany. Fighting had broken out between Poland and Czecho-Slovakia over the coal-rich district of Teschen. (Lloyd George later admitted in the House of Commons that he had never heard of Teschen.)[43] In late January, the Council of Ten sent a committee to Poland to investigate and to arrange a cease-fire between the Poles and the Czechs. On January 29, the Council of Ten heard from the Polish delegate, Roman Dwomski. He spoke for five solid hours, in French and English. He pressed for Poland's ancient frontiers, which included parts of East Prussia, claims that Lloyd George asserted were "extravagant and inadmissible."[44] Clemenceau supported the Poles, for reasons having nothing to do with the Fourteen Points. The stronger was Poland, the more secure was France vis-à-vis Germany. Clemenceau not only supported the Poles' territorial claims, he pressed for military assistance to them. On February 12, the Council of Ten created a Commission on Polish Affairs, headed by Jules Cambon. In mid-March, Cambon presented the Commission's findings, ceding large chunks of coal-rich Upper Silesia, parts of Western Prussia and Danzig to Poland, severing East Prussia from the rest of Germany.

On February 1 the Council of Ten welcomed Romania's prime minister, Ion Bratianu, who presented Romania's claim for the provinces of Transylvania, (also claimed by Hungary) Bukovina and Bessarabia (present-day Moldova). He also claimed part of the Banat district, which lies at the intersection of eastern Hungary, western Romania and northern Serbia, and claimed by all three. Romania's claim was based on the unassailable fact that it had entered the war in August, 1916 on the side of the

Allies, the result of a secret treaty with Great Britain, France and Italy. But when Russia, its principal military ally, exited the war in October, 1917, Romania found itself almost completely surrounded by Germany, Austro-Hungary and Bulgaria, and by May, 1918, was almost completely overrun, and with the signing of the Treaty of Bucharest was out of the war. (It re-entered the war on November 10, 1918, the day before the Armistice.) Of course, the United States had not signed (or even been aware of) the treaty, and was not bound by it. Clemenceau made the point that the Treaty of Bucharest should have nullified the secret treaty. Lloyd George pointed out that Bratianu was now claiming more than even the secret treaty awarded him. Wilson was willing to have a committee of experts examine Bratianu's claims based on the facts on the ground, and this was agreed to. Orlando was willing to go along, but made it clear that letting the ethnic make-up of a region vitiate a treaty must not be considered a precedent. He had his own secret treaty with Great Britain and France to protect.

And so it went. On the third and fourth they heard from Greece's prime minister, Eleftherios Venizelos, one of most charismatic figures of the Peace Conference. Venizelos had supported the Allies throughout the war, despite the opposition of his German-leaning king, Constantine I. He now presented Greece's claims for the former Ottoman territories of Thrace, the Dodeconese Islands, and the island of Rhodes. The following day, they heard from Edvard Benes, Czecho-Slovakia's foreign minister, who presented his newly-created country's claims for highly-industrialized Bohemia, which contained as much as two million ethnic Germans. As with the other claimants, it was referred to a committee. And on the following day they heard from the Emir Faisal, a son of King Hussein, representing the kingdom of Hejaz, modern-day western Saudi Arabia. He appeared in flowing Arab dress. He pleaded only for self-government. He spoke no English or French. His interpreter, also appearing in Arab dress, was Col. T.E. Lawrence—"Lawrence of Arabia."

Lloyd George had promised to make Great Britain "a land fit for heroes." With the war now ended, there was mounting pressure on him to redeem the pledge. Returning soldiers wanted jobs. Workers demanded a shorter working day, in order to alleviate the threat of rising unemployment. Many workers in essential industries had become accustomed to decent wages. Their employers, seeing their markets shrinking due to a world-wide recession, needed to reduce wages, just as the cost of living was rising. The result was labor unrest and a wave of strikes throughout Great Britain. The London tube workers struck, demanding a *paid* thirty-minute lunch. In Glasgow, the Clyde shipyard workers struck. The lights went out in Belfast as the electrical workers struck. The miners, railwaymen and transport workers, united as The Triple Industrial Alliance, all threatened to strike at once. Even the waiters and cooks in London restaurants walked out. With the existence of his government imperiled, on February 8 Lloyd George left for home, leaving the Peace Conference in the capable hands of Arthur Balfour. He would not return until March 5.

February 3 was a very busy day for Wilson. In the morning he sat through Venizelos' pleas for parts of the former Ottoman Empire. In the evening, he addressed the Chamber of Deputies. President Poincaré, Clemenceau and Antonin Dubost, the president of the French Senate, called on him at the Murat Palace. They proceeded to the steps of the Palais Bourbon, where the president of the Chamber, Paul Deschanel, waited to greet him. A band played the *Star-Spangled Banner* and the *Marseillaise* as he entered the Chamber, festooned with the *tricolor* and the Stars and Stripes. Lloyd George, Balfour, Secretary Lansing and a host of lesser dignitaries filled the galleries.

Deschanel introduced Wilson. Deschanel had devoted his legislative career to offending no one by avoiding controversy. His efforts were rewarded with the largely ceremonial presidency of the Chamber of Deputies. Not today: "As this war was unlike any preceding war, so must this peace be unlike any preceding peace. Guarantees must be taken against the recurrence of the horrible things which have been an opprobrium to the world and which no one has stigmatized with more force than you; territorial, military, economic and financial guarantees to protect the victims of German ambition against perpetual alarms, guarantees for free peoples, with efficacious sanctions to punish the crimes against the peace of the world first; then, to prevent them."[45]

Wilson began by graciously paying homage to "the soldiers of France [who] came to the help of the struggling little Republic of America to get on its feet and proclaim one of the first victories of freedom....America was fighting Great Britain. And now she is linked as closely to Great Britain as she is to France." Then he got to the heart of his message: "The rulers of the world have been thinking of the relations of Governments and forgetting the relations of peoples," he began, with two of the "rulers of the world," Lloyd George and Clemenceau, in the galleries. "They have been thinking of the maneuvers of international dealings, when what they ought to have been thinking of was the fortunes of men and women and the safety of home, and the care that they should take that their people should be happy because they were safe.... They know that the only way to do this is to make it certain that the same thing will not always happen that has happened this time, that there never shall be any doubt or waiting or surmise, but that whenever France or any free people is threatened, the whole world will be ready to vindicate its liberty....It is for that reason, I take it, that I find a warm and intelligent enthusiasm in France for the Society of Nations—France with her keen vision, France with her prophetic vision....The nations of the world are about to consummate a brotherhood which will make it unnecessary in the future to maintain those crushing armaments which make the peoples suffer almost as much in peace as they suffered in war."

His words drew appreciative applause. The words that drew the most enthusiastic applause were these: "[T]he people of France may rest assured that their prosperity is secure, and men everywhere not only wish her safety and prosperity, but are ready to assure her that with all the force and wealth at their command they will guarantee her security and safety."[46]

Wilson's address was followed by an editorial in the semi-official Le Temps, one that might have been induced by Clemenceau. It was not kind. Titled "Guarantees of France," it began by asking "Why did the rulers of Germany make war? Because they hoped to crush France in a few weeks. To avoid a new war, what is necessary above all? No German can make this villainous calculation again. Without guarantees for France, there are no guarantees for peace....It is a universal truth. Let us first make the peaceful people strong; on this condition, but only on this condition, will they be able to guarantee each other and ensure peace in the world." To Wilson's assertion that the world would assure France's safety, Le Temps called it a "wise recommendation," that failed to touch on the "crucial problem," the wait France might have to endure before the aid might come. Referring to the war just ended, "If there had been a general impulse to defend freedom, how can we explain that the American people waited almost three years to take part in it?...Victory came nevertheless, but at a price of what sacrifices did we have to hold out until then? If the future League of Nations were to promise its adherents only triumphs so dearly paid, it would find few supporters. Should we therefore renounce international guarantees of peace? No, but they have to be made effective."[47]

Between his morning meeting at the Council of Ten and his evening address to the Chamber of Deputies, Wilson chaired the first meeting of the commission charged with drafting the Covenant of the League of Nations.

Lloyd George supported the creation of a League of Nations, as did the other Dominion prime ministers except, of course, Australia's Billy Hughes. In late December, House wrote to Wilson that the British cabinet was ready to support him on the League of Nations "almost to the extent of letting you write the covenants of it yourself."[48] Clemenceau was always dismissive, calling it a "super-Parliament, whose sole occupation when action was needed would be super-talking."[49] But Clemenceau never publicly opposed it, or publicly attacked Wilson. What Clemenceau wanted and France needed was an Anglo-American guarantee, and for that he needed Wilson. He knew that Wilson would be president for two more years; he couldn't trust Wilson's successor. So he gave the impression of supporting the League, appointing its most ardent advocate, Léon Bourgeois, to the League of Nations Commission. But as with all of his ministers, Clemenceau tightly controlled Bourgeois.

Lloyd George and the rest of the British delegation knew before the Peace Conference began that Wilson cared more about the League of Nations than anything else. They knew it because Wilson advised them of it when they first met in Buckingham Palace. They also knew that he wished the League of Nations to be the first thing discussed at the Peace Conference, and that the charter (the "covenant") of the League to be an integral part of the Peace Treaty itself, to which Lloyd George and Clemenceau were indifferent.

Starting on February 3, the League of Nations Commission held ten meetings in eleven days. But in fact, most of the work of drafting the covenant had already been done. In the summer of 1918, Col. House had prepared and sent to Wilson a draft treaty, one that had relied on a draft prepared by a British Parliamentary Commission headed by Sir Walter Phillimore. The "Phillimore Plan" contemplated a league comprised only of the large states that met only occasionally, as the need arose. But the Phillimore Plan contained a feature central to all of the plans that followed it and the final Covenant itself: Every signatory nation committed that it would not go to war with another nation without first submitting its dispute or grievance to some form of binding arbitration, and that if it went to war in violation of this provision, it would—*ipso facto*—be deemed to be at war with all of the other nations, subject to whatever economic and/or military sanctions the other nations might impose. In the summer of 1918, Léon Bourgeois also prepared a draft treaty for a "Society of Nations," one that had Clemenceau's support. Unlike all the other plans, it contemplated an international army to enforce peace, directed by a permanent general staff, with the power to inspect international forces and armaments. His plan gained no traction outside of France. Shortly after the war, Gen. Smuts drafted a "Practical Suggestion" for a League of Nations. It dealt only with Europe, but was the first draft to introduce the system of "mandates."

Wilson and House had together refined House's draft, which Wilson then proceeded to rewrite completely. He completed what became known as his "First Paris Draft" on January 10, and it was close to the final product. It established a "Body of Delegates" consisting of every democratic, self-governing nation, and an

"Executive Council" of the Great Powers and some of the lesser powers, selected annually and serving on a rotating basis. A decision on any matter would be made first by the Executive Council, and if approved by the Body of Delegates would become the decision of the League. The heart of the treaty was Article V, in which each of the "Contracting Parties" agreed that "they will in no case resort to armed force without previously submitting the questions and matters involved either to arbitration or to inquiry by the Executive Council...until there has been an award by the arbitrators or a decision by the Executive Council; and that they will not even then resort to armed force against a member of the League of Nations who complies with the award of the arbitrators or the decision of the Executive Council."[50] If any nation violated this provision, "it shall *ipso facto* become at war with all the members of the League," immediately subjecting that nation to economic boycott, a cutoff of trade and travel, and "whatever effective military or naval force" the Executive Council should advise. But Wilson's legal advisor, David Hunter Miller, advised Wilson that declaring a miscreant nation to be "ipso facto" at war usurped Congress' war-making power, and the language was modified in the subsequent draft.

The provision of the draft closest to Wilson's heart (and deprecated by the French as being meaningless) was Article III, in which "The Contracting Powers unite in guaranteeing to each other political independence and territorial integrity" of each nation. The First Paris Draft also included a flat prohibition on conscription "and all other forms of compulsory military service," a reduction in armaments and a prohibition on the private manufacture of arms. David Hunter Miller objected to this last provision, on the curious ground that Congress could not prohibit a *state* from permitting private manufacture. The draft also automatically abrogated all treaties inconsistent with it, notably (without mentioning them) the wartime secret treaties. Finally, Wilson tacked on a "Supplementary Agreement" that the League of Nations "shall require all new States to bind themselves as a condition precedent to their recognition as independent or autonomous States, to accord all racial or national minorities within their several jurisdictions exactly the same treatment and security, both in law and in fact, that is accorded the racial or national majority of the people."[51] This provision bound only "new States," not the original members of the League. He would come to grief over this.

As Wilson was finalizing the First Paris Draft, Lloyd George's principal advocate for the League of Nations, Lord Robert Cecil, was preparing his own draft, also modeled on the Phillimore Plan. The two drafts were substantively very similar, but there were differences. Cecil's plan called for an Executive Council comprised only of the Great Powers. He provided for separate admission to the League of all of the British Dominions, including India, which then was not self-governing. Like Wilson's, his draft also provided that a nation violating its commitment to bring any dispute to binding arbitration before going to war was "ipso facto" at war with all the other nations.

On the evening of January 30, following Wilson's row with Hughes over the mandate for New Guinea, Wilson and House met with Orlando, who had his own ideas for a League of Nations. Wilson apparently won Orlando over. House convinced Orlando to sit on the League of Nations Commission, as a way of getting closer to Wilson. But Wilson paid a price for bringing Orlando on board; he made a territorial concession—the Brenner Pass—to Orlando in the course of the meeting.[52]

The following evening, Wilson, House, Smuts, Lord Cecil and David Hunter Miller met in House's rooms in the Crillon to iron out the differences between the Wilson and Cecil drafts. In deference to Congress' exclusive war-making powers, the provision making a miscreant nation "ipso facto" at war with all other League members was softened; it would "*ipso facto* be deemed to have committed an act of war" against all other members of the League.[53] The five members of the Executive Council were named—the United States, France, the British Empire, Italy and Japan—each with two delegates, and each of the Dominions was given separate representation. A provision in Wilson's First Paris Draft relating to "Freedom of the Seas" was dropped, never again to appear. David Hunter Miller and Sir Cecil Hurst were appointed to finalize a joint draft.

With the first meeting of the League of Nations Commission scheduled for February 3, Miller and Hurst worked into the night to revise and print the final draft. On the second, Wilson read it, and decided he didn't like it, saying "it has neither warmth nor color." But he accepted it at House's urging, having convinced Wilson that he need not risk alienating Lord Cecil, the man in the British delegation who most favored the League of Nations.

Each of the five Great Powers was permitted two delegates to the League of Nations Commission. Wilson selected House—not Lansing—as his second. Lord Robert Cecil and Gen. Smuts represented the British Empire. Léon Bourgeois and Prof. F. Larnaude, the dean of the Sorbonne law faculty, represented France, both totally controlled by Clemenceau. Orlando and Vittorio Scialoja, an Italian senator (*not* Sonnino) represented Italy, and Baron Makino and Viscount Chinda represented Japan. Belgium, Brazil, China (Dr. Koo), Portugal and Serbia each had one. Portugal's delegate, J.B. Reis, was noteworthy in that every day he insisted that the League of Nations could not possibly succeed unless the Deity, (specifically, the Holy Trinity) were prominently mentioned in the covenant. Following strenuous objections from the smaller nations, membership after February 6 was expanded by four nations, to include Greece, Poland, Romania and Czecho-Slovakia. Neither Clemenceau nor Lloyd George (who after February 8 was in London) ever appeared.

The delegates sat around House's dining room table in the Hotel Crillon. In order to give the proceedings a more official appearance, the tablecloth was removed and replaced by a green baize cloth. They met in the afternoons and evenings, Wilson having to attend Council of Ten meetings in the mornings and afternoons. Wilson, who attended every meeting except the last, sat at the head of the table. To his right sat Orlando, in deference to his being the Commission's only other head of government. House sat at Wilson's left. At the far end of the table sat Makino and Chinda, "silent, unemotional but watchful," according to House.[54] But House also kept silent, and according to him, "Cecil and I do nearly all the difficult work between meetings."[55]

Wilson convened the first meeting on the evening of the third, stating (according to the notes that translator Stephen Bonsal retained) that "never again should civilization be confronted with a situation as they had faced in 1914," and it was their task to see that it never happened again."[56] He told them that the League of Nations was no longer optional; it was compulsory, and it was their task to write its constitution.[57] The issue arose as to whether they should keep minutes of their deliberations. Wilson opposed it, on the ground that he wanted to express himself freely, so that he could change his mind without being bound by what he had said.[58] "We must get under way, the record will take care of itself."[59] Bourgeois objected, and prevailed; a secretary was appointed. But Wilson was successful in suppressing the transcript until late March. Wilson then presented the delegates with the Miller-Hurst draft. Unfortunately, in their haste to complete it, no French draft had been prepared. A day was wasted.

The convened again at 8:30 P.M. the following evening. Wilson suggested that the Miller-Hurst draft be their discussion draft, which they would review line by line. They first had to decide what the world would call this thing they were creating around this table. Sen. Pessoa, the delegate from Brazil, suggested "Union of States," but it was finally determined that it would be the "League of Nations" in English and "Societé des Nations" in French. The Belgian delegate asked that the membership of the Commission be expanded by four states, enlarging the Commission to nineteen delegates. Wilson opposed it, as did Lord Cecil. Bourgeois voted in favor, and the motion carried. They debated one important matter that evening. In the Miller-Hurst draft (and in Lord Cecil's draft), only the five Great Powers were to sit on the Executive Council. The delegates from the smaller powers objected vehemently, and Wilson and Lord Cecil himself yielded. They amended the draft to provide them with two additional seats. By the ninth meeting, they had upped it to four. The meeting adjourned close to midnight. Exiting the room, a reporter asked House how it had gone. "Talk, talk, talk," he replied.[60]

And so it went, for the next nine days. The Miller-Hurst draft provided for compulsory arbitration of any dispute before a nation could resort to war, a provision to which all the other nations concurred. On February 6, Lord Cecil announced his opposition: "I hate to be the stumbling block to the realization of a dream, a world without war, which I confess has a strong appeal to me....[I]n the end, we must have the right to seek the arbitrament of arms."[61] Since compulsory arbitration had been a part of Lord Cecil's own draft, the word must have come down from either Balfour or Lloyd George that compulsory arbitration was out. The Miller-Hurst draft called for the abolition of conscription, to which both Bourgeois (at Clemenceau's direction) and Orlando objected. The provision was deleted. The Miller-Hurst draft called for the reduction of arms to the lowest possible level consistent with national safety. After Bourgeois objected on the ground that if war came France would be the first to bear the brunt of it, the provision was softened to require the reduction of national armaments *"having special regard for the geographical situation and circumstances of each State."*[62] Later that evening, Lord Cecil confided to his diary: "Now that I have sat for two or three days with the President I am coming to the conclusion that I do not personally like him. I do not quite know what it is that repels me: a certain hardness, coupled with vanity and an eye for effect. He supports idealistic causes without being in the least an idealist himself...in 99 out of 100 cases we are agreed, but all the same I do not like him."[63]

Article III of the Hurst-Miller draft was reworded and became Article X of the final draft: "The High Contracting Parties undertake to respect and preserve as against external aggression the territorial integrity and existing political independence of all States members of the League. In case of any such aggression or in case of any threat or danger of such aggression the Executive Council shall advise upon the means by which this obligation shall be fulfilled." Wilson considered it the "king pin of the whole structure....Without it, the Covenant would mean nothing."[64] His opponents shared that view. Article X would become the centerpiece over the fight for the League.

But nothing bedeviled the delegates more than the dispute between Bourgeois and Wilson on the issue of what armed force the League would have, and it highlighted the fundamental divide between Wilson and Clemenceau on how France could be made secure. Bourgeois' own League of Nations draft had provided for an international army, and now he wouldn't let go of it. Wilson tried to explain to Bourgeois that the United States Constitution simply forbad the sending of armed forces to foreign soil absent Congressional approval. "I know how France has suffered," he said, "and I know that she wishes to obtain the best guarantees possible before she enters the League, and everything that we can do in this direction we shall do, but we cannot accept proposals which are in direct contradiction to our Constitution."[65] It is certain that Clemenceau, having lived in the United States for five years, knew all this. His insistence on an international armed force, something he knew he could never get, was a bargaining ploy for what he hoped to get, the security offered by the Left Bank of the Rhine and a written Anglo-American guarantee. He later told Lord Cecil that Bourgeois' constant plea for an international army was at his direction, that he wanted to be able to later say that he had tried every other means to obtain security for his country.[66]

So Bourgeois kept at it, at one point causing Lord Cecil to throw up his hands: "Oh, M. Bourgeois, do not begin that all over again. We have heard you so often and so patiently. Your plan will lead you nowhere..."[67] On February 9, Bourgeois brought with him a sheaf of Wilson's wartime speeches. He quoted to Wilson his own words when Wilson called upon America to enter the war: "The new world order must make provision for common action against aggressors. If the moral force will not suffice, the physical force of the world shall." Bourgeois continued: "And now today you are asking my countrymen and all of the devastated lands of our Allies to be content with the shield of a Covenant without striking arms but merely illuminated with the noble words and the note which you hurled against the invaders—but to stop them you needed force, and it was, at last forthcoming. I beseech you to look at the situation once again. Without military backing in some force and ready to act, the League and our Covenant will be filed away, not as a solemn treaty, but simply as a rather ornate piece of furniture."[68] Bourgeois' words were translated, and after a short, whispered aside with House, Wilson responded: "I am grateful to the French delegate for his gracious comment on words which came from my heart....Need I assure him that my attitude has not changed, but the situation has."[69] And with that, Wilson moved on to other matters. With a despairing gesture, Bourgeois slumped back into his chair. House wrote in his diary: "The President excels in such work. He seems to like it and his short talks in explanation of his views are admirable."[70]

Not everyone shared that view. The Miller-Hurst draft provided that all treaties inconsistent with the covenant to be deemed abrogated. On February 10, Prof. Larnaude, the Sorbonne law faculty dean, asked Wilson who would decide whether a treaty was "inconsistent." Would the Executive Council decide, or would a special tribunal? To which Wilson replied: "The decision will lie with the court of public opinion." To which Larnaude turned to Bourgeois and asked, *sotto voce* (but loud enough for the translator to hear) "Tell me, mon ami, am I at the Peace Conference or in a madhouse?"[71]

On February 11, Lloyd George reported to the House of Commons on the Peace Conference. With respect to the League, he said its progress was "exceedingly satisfactory," that "There was a general feeling in favor of it, especially among the smaller nations, who felt very helpless without the protection which a body of that kind can afford them in the future."[72] He termed the League "an experiment full of hope for the future."

Two meetings of the Commission were held on February 13. Wilson chaired the morning meeting. The French continued to press for an international army, or at least for a permanent general staff having the power of "surveillance," i.e. the ability to monitor whether a nation was complying with the disarmament terms. This too was rejected.

In the afternoon, Wilson had to attend a Council of Ten meeting, and he deputized Lord Cecil—who he could trust with a quick gavel—to chair the meeting. This was to be the final meeting, as Wilson was to leave for home the following day. The Japanese delegates, who had sat mute at the end of the table for more than a week, now raised the issue of racial equality. The Miller-Hurst draft contained a "Supplementary Agreement" prohibiting discrimination on religious grounds; it made no mention of racial discrimination. Baron Makino had previously told House that his government had instructed him to raise the issue of racial equality. They specifically wanted a provision calling for nondiscrimination in immigration, and were making their joining the League contingent upon it. Neither the United States nor the British could agree to this, but House hoped he could forge a compromise. He met with Balfour, who was sympathetic. The problem, said Balfour, was Hughes, and Australia's "whites only" immigration policy. "Hughes will not admit them to Australia," he told House, "and if I am not mistaken your people in California are opposed to even limited immigration."[73] At the February 13 afternoon meeting, Makino proposed his amendment, a prohibition on discrimination of minority races. Lord Cecil said that this raised "extremely serious questions within the British Empire."[74] China's Dr. Koo said he was without instructions from his government. House said the issue should be postponed. The result was that the final Commission draft deleted any mention of either religious or racial discrimination. They had not heard the last of this. Lord Cecil called for a vote, and the draft Covenant was adopted, unanimously.

Wilson called for an immediate Plenary session, to present the draft Covenant to all of the delegates. They convened in the Salle d'Horloge at 3:30 P.M. of the following day. Lloyd George, still in London, was absent, but all of the plenipotentiaries from twenty-eight nations attended. That morning, Wilson gave the draft Covenant to his fellow commissioners—House, Secretary Lansing, Gen. Bliss and Henry White—who, with the exception of House, had had nothing to do with its drafting. He instructed them that, in his absence, not a single word could be changed.[75]

The minutes of the first and second Plenary sessions were approved. Then Wilson rose and addressed his fellow delegates. "I have the honor, and, as I esteem it, the very great privilege of reporting, in the name of the Commission constituted by this conference, on the formulation of a plan for the League of Nations."[76] He reported that it was the unanimous report of the representatives of fourteen nations. He read the entire draft treaty. He then expounded on it, notably: "[T]hroughout this instrument we are depending primarily and chiefly upon one great force, and that is the moral force of the public opinion of the world, the cleansing and clarifying and compelling influences of publicity; so that intrigues can no longer have their coverts, so that designs that are sinister can at any time be drawn into the open, so that those things that are destroyed by the light may be promptly destroyed by the overwhelming light of the universal expression of the condemnation of the world....Armed force is in the background of this programme, but it is the background, and if the moral force of the world will not suffice, the physical force of the world shall. But that is the last resort, because this is intended as a constitution of peace, not as a League of War....[W]hile it is elastic, while it is general in its terms, it is definite in the one thing that we are called upon to make definite. It is a definite guarantee of peace. It is a definite guarantee by word against aggression. It is a definite guarantee against the things which have just come near to bring the whole structure of civilization into ruin. Its purposes do not for a moment lie vague. Its purposes are declared and its powers are unmistakable."[77]

The Commission had not touched the issue of mandates. That had been decided by the Council of Ten, and the Commission incorporated the three-class compromise it had reached on January 30 into the treaty without discussion. Wilson mentioned it now: "We are done with annexations of helpless people, meant in some instances by some Powers to be used merely for exploitation." He concluded: "So I think I can say of this document that it is at one and the same time, a practical document and a humane document. There is a pulse of sympathy in it. There is a compulsion of conscience throughout it. It is practical, and yet it is intended to purify, to rectify, to elevate."[78]

Wilson was followed by Lord Cecil, who praised it. He was followed by Orlando, who praised it as well. Wilson had hoped that the encomiums would be unanimous, but then Bourgeois rose to speak. While he praised the covenant, he noted that "Special dangers exist for certain countries, for France, for Belgium, for Serbia and for the States which have just been created or reconstituted in Central Europe. These States will need to prepare and elaborate effective guarantees." He noted that the treaty provision calling for the reduction in armaments carved out a special provision for "the geographical situation and the circumstances of each country." "Finally," he said, "we shall be obliged to find a way of fortifying the guarantees of which we stand in need....That is the reason for which…we have asked for the creation of a permanent organism which shall endow the League of Nations with necessary guarantees….We firmly believe that the Plan now laid before you comprises, in the general aspect of the clauses, the measures which are necessary for the attainment of our purposes; in our opinion, however, and we have expressed it in all sincerity, the Plan is yet only the foundation on which we shall have to work."[79]

Contrary to popular opinion, the Plenary session did not "accept" the draft covenant that day. There was no vote. Clemenceau noted that President Wilson's report had been deposited with the secretary of the Conference, for examination by all interested parties, and adjourned the meeting.

No issue divided the American, French and British delegations more than the amounts and nature of the reparations the defeated powers would be required to pay to the Allies. On November 5, 1918, the Germans had accepted Wilson's final note, which obligated them for "all damage done to the civilian populations of the Allies and their property by the aggression of Germany by land, sea, and from the air." The British, French and Italians had agreed. This "Pre-Armistice Agreement" had incorporated the Fourteen Points, which required the "restoration" of France, Belgium, Romania, Serbia and Montenegro, and Wilson's Fourteen Points address, which proclaimed "no annexations, no contributions, no punitive damages." To the Americans, Germany had contracted to repay only for the cost of what they had actually destroyed or had physically carried off; the actual "damage done to the civilian populations." And it was a contract; it was binding.

But between November 5 and November 11, Clemenceau had slipped a provision into the Armistice agreement that the German representatives signed in the railway carriage at Compiègne. It was a "reservation that any future claims and demands of the Allies and the United States of America remain unaffected, and the following financial conditions are required: Reparation for damage done." The French conveniently interpreted this as abrogating the Pre-Armistice Agreement, permitting them to demand their full "war costs," an open-ended term that could include the billions they had expended in training, clothing and feeding an army, the cost of millions of shells and rifles, and pensions for hundreds of thousands of disabled men and war widows. To Billy Hughes, if an Australian farmer had had to mortgage his home to pay the increased taxes needed to fund the war, that too was a "war cost" recoverable from the Germans.

Every Frenchman, remembering the huge indemnity the Germans had extracted in 1871 (despite having suffered no physical damage itself), supported this view. Now bankrupt, if France were to revive itself it would need to squeeze still higher taxes from its citizens (which the Chamber of Deputies had no intention of doing) or squeeze it from the Germans. A headline in the Paris daily *Matin* summed it up: "Who Ought to be Ruined? France or Germany?"[80] When Clemenceau's minister of finance, Louis-Lucien Klotz, told the Chamber of Deputies *"L'Allemagne paiera!"* ("Germany will pay") it drew huge applause. On Paris walls appeared placards: *"Que L'Allemagne paye d'abord"*–Let Germany pay first."[81] It became unofficial French policy. Before the Peace Conference opened Klotz' Finance Ministry produced two memoranda defining "reparations" in the extreme, including disability payments and widows' pensions, and the return of the 1871 indemnities, *with interest.* Harold Nicolson termed these memoranda "fantastic."[82] But a young (36) British economist attached to the British delegation, John Maynard Keynes, saw through it. He wrote David Hunter Miller that the "fantastic" French reparations demands would form the basis for the continued occupation "and ultimate acquisition" of the Rhine provinces."[83] Clemenceau himself let this fire rage. But huge reparations were not his principal objective, which was security for France, and he would be willing to trade the one for the other.

The man in the middle was Lloyd George. He had just won an election on a platform demanding war costs "shilling for shilling, ton for ton,"[84] and he now had a Tory-dominated House of Commons determined to collect. He had couched his speeches on the stump by promising to extract from the Germans everything "up to their ability to pay," but he knew (as Wilson and Clemenceau also knew) that what Germany could reasonably pay could not possibly cover the Allies' "war costs," and would not even cover the Americans' more conservative interpretation of reparations. A Board of Trade study prepared shortly before the war ended had told him that.[85] When the Peace Conference opened, Sir William Wiseman asked David Hunter Miller: "How are we going to get out of the statements made by Lloyd George during the campaign?"[86] How, indeed.

The Allies were also divided over something more basic than philosophy. The French owed the Americans $2.7 billion, and the British owed $4.2 billion. If the Americans would cancel or stretch out these debts, it would palliate the Allies' need for reparations. Before Wilson arrived in Paris, House wrote in his diary that "We have to meet the growing demand of the Allies that the United States not only cancel the sums that they owe us, but help them pay their own debts....I want to treat the matter sympathetically and generously, but I do not want to see the United States forced into an impossible and unsatisfactory position."[87] If House wanted to deal with it "sympathetically and generously," Wilson did not. On January 21, Wilson met at the Murat Palace with Vance McCormick, one of his representatives on the Reparations Committee, who reported that Wilson had heard that the Allies wanted to "pool the total expense of the war and have us pay our proportionate share of the whole," that Wilson was "considerably exercised over this proposal," and ordered his commissioners not to discuss it, and to keep clear of any discussions "which have nothing to do with Germany."[88] This became Wilson's fixed policy. When his principal financial advisor, Norman H. Davis, told Wilson of a "concerted movement…to obtain an interlocking of the United States with the continental governments on the whole financial situation," Wilson assured him that he was aware of it "and on my guard against it."[89] Later in March a Treasury Department official wrote that the Treasury "will not assent to any discussion at the peace conference, or elsewhere, of any plan or arrangement for the release, consolidation or reapportionment of the obligations of foreign governments held by the United States."[90] To underline how serious Wilson was, Davis warned Klotz that even mentioning reducing Allied debt would result in the cutoff of further American assistance. The threat worked; Klotz advised that he would not raise the matter again.[91] But Wilson's posture on Allied indebtedness explains why Wilson's assertions that the United States would itself eschew any claims for reparations fell on Allied deaf ears. Their need for reparations was based in large part on their indebtedness to the Americans, and the Americans would not budge.

With the Americans fixated on the "damage done to the civilian populations," they set out to determine what that was. In December, Gen. Pershing, at House's request, appointed Brigadier Gen. C.H. McKinstry, who set up a team of experts to comb through France and Belgium to determine, as best they could, the extent of the damage. At the same time, Paul D. Cravath, a Wall Street lawyer attached to the American delegation, drafted a detailed memo which spelled out the American negotiating position. His starting point was that the uppermost that the Allies could claim was what the Germans had agreed to in the Pre-Armistice Agreement, which excluded all "war costs." He then assumed what everyone, including Lloyd George, already knew, which was that whatever the quantum of "damage done to the civilian population" turned out to be, Germany did not now have the means to pay it. Cravath proposed Germany pay a modest ($3 billion) amount in the first year, followed by $15 billion over twenty-eight years, bearing five percent interest, which resulted in a $1 billion annual payment. Cravath reasoned that a fixed sum would enable Germany to enter the credit markets in order to retire the debt. (It had worked for France in 1871.) No one would lend to Germany if her debt burden was open-ended. He also advised that, whatever the final number might be, it should err on the side of leniency. A debt burden that reduced every German worker to serfdom would be counter-productive. It would require an expensive Allied occupation, and would prove to be uncollectable.[92]

Cravath also pointed out what Wilson, Lloyd George and Clemenceau also knew, but which was hidden from the man-in-the-street in London and Paris, which was that the economies of Germany and her former enemies were so intertwined that Germany would be able to pay reparations only out of the profits of her revived export trade. If France and Great Britain wished their domestic tax burdens to be alleviated by German reparations, they needed to help Germany rebuild. Keynes knew this as well as anyone. When, in the end, the Peace Conference did everything Cravath suggested it not do—impose an indeterminate indemnity that Germany could not possibly pay—Keynes' jeremiad against the treaty, *The Economic Consequences of the Peace*, became the lens through which generations of scholars viewed the treaty.

But fixing a definite, payable sum was anathema to Lloyd George and Clemenceau. Both knew that any fixed sum would fall short of political expectations; their constituents wanted every cent owed to be paid. They both told Wilson that a fixed sum would result in the Peace Conference having to start all over, because they would both be turned out of office. In early March, Lloyd George told House that he (Lloyd George) knew that the Germans could never pay what the British and French were demanding, but he needed the sum to be large, even if it was later reduced and even if the Germans never paid it. He didn't want the Tories to "throw him" over a matter dear to their hearts.[93] Clemenceau had his own reason for an indeterminate sum: The longer it remained unpaid, the longer France would occupy the Left Bank of the Rhine. He remembered, as perhaps the others did not, that the Germans did not evacuate France until the last of the 1871 indemnities was paid.

In the January 22 meeting of the Council of Ten, Lloyd George proposed that a commission be set up to study and report on "reparation and indemnity." Wilson insisted that "indemnity" be deleted. Lloyd George yielded, provided that "reparations" be taken "in its widest terms,"[94] and so the "Commission on Reparation of Damage" was created, with the Five Great Powers, Belgium, Greece, Poland, Romania and Serbia as its members. The only delegation that would consistently hold to the position that the Pre-Armistice Agreement bound the Allies to "damage done to the civilian populations" was the United States.

Wilson appointed Vance McCormick, the head of the War Trade Board, Norman H. Davis, the commissioner of finance, and the Wall Street financier Bernard M. Baruch to the reparations commission. Their legal advisor was another Wall Street lawyer, John Foster Dulles, Lansing's nephew. Clemenceau appointed Klotz (who would act as the commission's chairman), Minister of Reconstruction Louis Loucheur, and Minister of Liberated Areas Albert Lebrun. If Lloyd George believed that the Germans should be made to pay only up to the limit of their ability, as he had maintained on the stump, he chose three men who believed anything but. He selected Australia's Billy Hughes, whose expansive views of indemnities were well known, Lord Walter Cunliffe, a former governor of the Bank of England, and Lord Sumner, a respected judge. In December, 1918, a "Cabinet Committee on Indemnity" had reported that Germany would be able to pay all of the Allies' "war costs," up to the truly astronomical sum of £24 billion ($480 billion!) The report was signed by Hughes and Cunliffe. Lloyd George termed the report "a wild and fantastic chimera,"[95] but he appointed them anyway. In his *War Memoirs*, Lloyd George maintained that he appointed Sumner to bring a "judicially moderate view" on the issue of reparations, and to exert a moderating influence on Cunliffe, but that Sumner "caught the infection," and sided with Hughes and Cunliffe.[96] It is more likely that Lloyd George got from these men what he wanted, a high enough reparations bill that would please the Tories and protect his government. As their economic advisor, Lloyd George selected John Maynard Keynes. According the McCormick, "all of the other nations on the committee were playing politics for home consumption and claiming the earth."[97]

The commission held its first meeting around a U-shaped table on February 3 in (according to McCormick) a "magnificent salon" in the Ministry of Finance. On February 5 they agreed to constitute three subcommittees. The first, headed by Lord Sumner, was charged with determining the "scope" of reparations, where the United States stood alone. The second, headed by Lord Cunliffe, was to determine Germany's ability to pay. Since, under any definition of the "scope" of reparations Germany would be unable to pay, this became the most important subcommittee. The third subcommittee was charged with determining "guarantees" for payment, but it never submitted a report.

The commission next met on February 10, and it was here that Billy Hughes made his pitch for the broadest possible indemnities, to include the increased tax burden that Australian farmers would suffer to pay for Australia's part in the war. He realized that if the American position prevailed, Australia would receive nothing, since no Australian property had been damaged. Hughes was not a man who minced words. Pointing his finger at the American delegates, he shouted: "Some people in this war have not been so near the fire as we British have, and, therefore, being unburned, they have a cold, detached view of the situation."[98]

It fell to John Foster Dulles to give the other delegates, particularly the French, a dose of reality, which he did on February 13. Since the Germans could not possibly pay the Allies' "war costs," or even the less grandiose "damage done to the civilian populations" the real issue was how the sums that the Germans would pay would be apportioned among the Allies. He pointed out that since France (and to a lesser extent Belgium) had suffered the most actual damage, under the American interpretation France and Belgium would receive more in reparations than under the expansive "war costs" interpretation. Specifically, the American experts had calculated that under the American view, France would receive 43% of the reparations, Belgium would receive 24%, and all of the British Empire nations combined, which had suffered shipping losses but no physical damage, would receive 19%. The United States itself, which had suffered no "damage to the civilian populations" would receive nothing. But if all of the Allied nations' "war costs" had to be apportioned, France's share would *decrease* to 25%, the British Empire share would increase to 40%, and the Americans' share would rise from zero to 25%.[99]

But Lord Sumner and Billy Hughes would not be moved. The following day— the day that Wilson left for home—they both stuck to their positions that the Pre- Armistice Agreement did not bind the Allies to any reparations formula. The reparations commission was deadlocked, and the issue would be resolved only by Wilson, Lloyd George and Clemenceau among themselves.

Wilson met with House on the evening before his departure, in the presence of Wilson's interpreter, Stephen Bonsal. What instructions Wilson did or did not give House would later become critical. Bonsal quoted Wilson in his diary: "During my unavoidable absence, I do not wish the questions of territorial adjustments or those of reparations to be held up." Bonsal interpreted this to mean that Wilson had left House in charge, but House did not interpret it this way, later explaining to Bonsal: "The president does not mean that I am authorized to definitely settle anything, but he does hope that I will get the problems, one and all, in such shape that on his return they can be submitted to him for final judgment. I am glad of these limitations on my powers. The President has been so absorbed by his struggle for the Covenant that he does not fully appreciate the obstacles that still beset his path. Let me give you but one illustration. The President is unalterably opposed to the creation of the Rhenish republic, and justly so, because if we acquiesced it would torpedo our doctrine of self-determination upon which the future of our better world order depends. And yet, if we close an eye for a moment there it is—rearing its ugly head."[100] Bonsal noted in his diary, with remarkable prescience, "I think the Colonel is taking quite a risk in accepting merely verbal instructions from his Chief."[101]

The following morning—the fourteenth—Wilson and House met alone for three hours. According to House, they "settled all the important questions that were on my mind to take up with him before he left for America. I outlined my plan of procedure during his absence: we could button up everything during the next four weeks. He seemed startled and even alarmed at this statement. I therefore explained that the plan was not to actually bring these matters to a final conclusion but to have them ready for him to do so when he returned."[102] The matters that he wished to bring "to a final conclusion" were the reduction in the German army and navy, the delineation of Germany's boundaries and the cession of her colonies, the amount of reparations and the time the Germans would have to pay them, and "an agreement as to the economic treatment of Germany." House then asked Wilson "if he had anything else in addition… He thought they were sufficient." Then, also according to House, "I asked him to bear in mind while he was gone that it was sometimes necessary to compromise in order to get things through; not a compromise of principle but a compromise of detail; he had made many since he had been there. I did not wish him to leave expecting the impossible in all things."[103]

The railway station was bedecked with flowers and palms, which helped to offset the drizzling rain. A red carpet had been laid out. President Poincaré and Mme. Poincaré were there to see him off, as were Clemenceau and his entire cabinet. Just before Wilson entered the railway car, he placed his hand on House's shoulder, and said: "Heavy work before you, House."[104]

INTERREGNUM

Entangling alliances or entangling leagues are nothing to the entanglements of cash owing.

—John Maynard Keynes

Wilson departed and House and Stephen Bonsal walked from the station, engaged in conversation. House began: "He goes to meet the Senate..." and Bonsal interrupted: "You do not seem hopeful of the encounter." "Hopeful, yes," replied House, "but not confident. In the Washington battle the President will need diplomacy, patience." In fact, House hoped that Wilson would conduct the rest of the Peace Conference from Washington, but he dared not raise the point.

House continued: "It is clear to me that not nearly as many senators, as the President thinks, are sold on the Treaty and the Covenant, but if he plays his cards well he will win. So today in our talk I told him I was already counting noses, and as that made him laugh I went into details. I urged the President to extend some courtesies, to even extend an olive branch to Hoke Smith, the senator from Georgia with whom, as I knew, he had been feuding for some years....'If you whistle Hoke will not come to heel...but if you ask him to come to the White House and assist you he will come and stay with you.'" "'I will do nothing of the sort,' "and for a moment his eyes blazed with anger. 'That man is an ambulance chaser. I scorn to have any relations with him whatsoever. I don't think his role will be important, and I'm sure it will not be decisive. I shall receive him…but…no olive branches in that direction.'"

Hoke Smith's successful career was to Wilson an accusation. Decades before, at the same time that Wilson tried and failed to establish a law practice in Atlanta, Smith also set up his law practice, also in Atlanta. Smith was willing to provide the small courtesies to prospective clients that every young lawyer—but not Wilson—was willing to give to build his practice.

House continued to relate his talk with Wilson:

> "Governor, I hope you haven't lost your admiration for Burke…"
> "Of course not, but why your question?"
> "Because I recall your Burke said: 'To govern is to compromise…'"

"He laughed and shook his fingers at me and then he grew serious. 'I know the situation you have in mind, but for once I do not agree with you or Burke, if you have quoted him correctly. I have found that you get nothing in this world that is worthwhile without fighting for it.'" "And so you see why I am hopeful, but not confident of the outcome of the battle that awaits the President in Washington," concluded House.[1]

The Armistice had been signed more than three months past, with the warring nations still technically at war. The Peace Conference had dragged on for more than a month, having finalized nothing except a draft of the covenant of the League of Nations, when Wilson sailed for home with only one objective, to secure consent for the covenant. But that was not the objective uppermost in the minds of the sixty-nine other delegates to the Peace Conference. Clemenceau and the French wanted security more than a League of Nations. The British wanted naval supremacy, the Italians wanted the eastern Adriatic, the Japanese wanted Shantung and the Poles wanted Danzig and the Silesian coalfields and Billy Hughes wanted a fair share of reparations for Australia more than they wanted a League of Nations, if they wished for one at all. After Wilson had left for home Lloyd George mused to his friend George Riddell that he (Lloyd George) had left the Peace Conference with "a pocket full of sovereigns (gold coins) in the shape of German colonies, Mesopotamia, etc." while Wilson had left with a "bundle of *assignats* [i.e., worthless currency]; Everyone to his taste."[2]

And now the pressure to just get the Peace Conference done was becoming intense. Lloyd George, Wilson and even Clemenceau were feeling increasing pressure to bring their occupying troops home. The blockade, which had not been lifted since the Allies were still at war, now resulted in American troops seeing German children starve, all of which terrified Western politicians that the war that had been won against the Germans might be lost to the Bolsheviks. The one man who, more than anyone else, now set himself up to get the Peace Conference done was Edward M. House.

On February 23, the *George Washington* docked at Boston, the home of Henry Cabot Lodge. The day before, during a shipboard luncheon in honor of Washington's birthday (at which Franklin and Eleanor Roosevelt were present), Wilson advised his guests that the failure of the United States to back the League of Nations "would break the heart of the world, for the world considers the United States as the only nation represented in this great conference whose motives are entirely unselfish."[3] Wilson had entreated the members of the Senate who would be entrusted with considering the covenant not to discuss it publicly until he had had the opportunity to discuss it with them over dinner. Many senators ignored Wilson's plea; Lodge felt honor-bound to accept, "as he is the president of the United States."[4]

The following day, at Boston's Mechanic's Hall, Wilson addressed an adoring crowd. He first noted that the cheering that he had received in Europe was not personal; it was not directed at him so much as toward the people he represented, and that the competing nations at the Peace Conference did not look to each other to resolve their differences, but "resort to that nation which has won the enviable distinction as being regarded as the friend of mankind." He went on to say that America had been created "to make men free, and we did not confine our conception and purpose to America, and now we will make men free." He did not mention the League of Nations by name, but there was no mistaking his meaning when he said that if all the nations did at the Peace Conference was to sign a peace treaty, "with no nations united to defend it, no great forces combined to make it good," it would be "nothing but a modern scrap of paper." He continued: "Any man who thinks that America will take part in giving the world any such rebuff and disappointment as that does not know America. I invite him to test the sentiments of the nation....I should welcome no sweeter challenge than that. I have fighting blood in me, and it is sometimes a delight to let it have scope, but if it is a challenge on this occasion it will be an indulgence."[5] Lodge was offended by Wilson's fighting speech on his home turf, viewing it as a breach of their implied agreement not to publicly mention the League of Nations until they met. "The President," Lodge wrote to Henry White, "does not seem to look at it the same way[6]...while I am reduced to silence because I wish to observe what I think is required of an honorable man."

"Very characteristic," was Lodge's reaction.[7] Henry Cabot Lodge was not a man one offended lightly.

The dinner was held on the evening of the twenty-sixth, in the State Dining Room. All of the members of the Senate Foreign Relations Committee and the House Foreign Affairs Committee had been invited. Senator William Borah, the Idaho Republican who was a leader of the "irreconcilables," declined, as did New Mexico's Albert Fall, on the ground that there was nothing Wilson could possibly say to change their minds. During dinner, Edith Wilson, seated beside Lodge, could not help but mention how enthusiastic had been her husband's reception in his home city. Lodge was offended, again.

Following dinner, Lodge escorted Edith into the East Room, where chairs had been arranged in an oval, the chair reserved for Wilson at its center. Wilson opened with a brief statement, saying that there was a consensus in Paris that a League of Nations was necessary to prevent future wars. He implored them to be completely frank with him, and for the next two hours they peppered him with questions. He spoke without notes, and did not have a copy of the covenant before him. He was asked whether joining the League would involve relinquishing American sovereignty. He responded that it would, but that every treaty entailed a certain relinquishment of sovereignty. He was correct in this, and Lodge knew it. Any treaty results in a nation agreeing to do or refrain from doing something it is otherwise free to do. He added that every other nation would be making a similar sacrifice, for the good of the world, with each nation yielding something of its sovereignty to protect the weak nations from the strong. But in response to a pointed question as to whether the covenant impinged upon Congress' exclusive power to declare war, Wilson claimed it would not, since only Congress could do so. But Lodge no doubt noticed that if the Executive Council of the League voted to declare that a nation had committed an act of war upon all of the other members, a nation's failure to declare war was a violation of the treaty.

He was asked whether the provision in the covenant regarding disarmament would entail the surrender by Congress of its right to fix the level of arms, and he replied—again correctly—that it would not. But here Wilson had to admit to a failure in the covenant draft: Nowhere did it specify what vote of the Executive Council was required to take any action. Wilson averred that the draft implied the unanimous consent of the Executive Council to fix any level of arms, and that even following such unanimous consent, each nation would have to approve its respective arms appropriations.

In response to a statement from Connecticut Republican Frank Brandegee, that "the League of Nations will not prevent war," Wilson stated: "Nothing will prevent war, but it will bring about a discussion before the beginning of a war. If there had been one week's discussion before the beginning of the European war it would not have occurred."

Wilson was on the weakest ground in response to the assertion that joining the League meant the abrogation of the Monroe Doctrine, the nineteenth-century doctrine that declared the Western Hemisphere off limits to European colonization, a doctrine that then still resonated. Wilson's weak response was that the League did not abrogate the Monroe Doctrine, but extended it to the entire world.[8]

The meeting broke up after midnight. No minds had been changed. Worse, Wilson's responses were freely misquoted in the press. Lodge had sat through it all, uttering hardly a word. But following the meeting he issued a statement: "The President…told us nothing.…He did not seem to know it [i.e. the covenant] very thoroughly and was not able to answer questions. For example, he did not know that it was not stated by whom mandatories were to be appointed until I pointed it out to him. He was civil and showed no temper. We went away as wise as we came…[T]he President's performance under [Sen.] Brandegee's very keen and able cross-examination was anything but good."[9]

The public had to wait only two days for Lodge to respond. He rose in the Senate on the morning of the twenty-eighth. The galleries were filled, people having waited up to two hours to enter. Almost every senator was present, and House members filled the lounges. Lodge had devoted his career to foreign policy, and during the war had favored some form of league of nations, but by war's end had changed his mind. He knew that there were a handful of Senate Republicans who favored the League, and more who could be brought over. He had to be careful. He spoke for two-and-a-half hours.

He began: "We ought to lay aside once and for all the unfounded and really evil suggestion because men differ as to the best method of assuring the world's peace in the future," anyone against the League of Nations is opposed to permanent peace.[10] His first objection was that the covenant "seems to have been hastily drafted, and the result is crudeness and looseness of expression, unintentional, I hope." He claimed that there were already disagreements in the interpretation of many of its provisions, which, he claimed, would not reduce the chances of conflicts between nations but exacerbate them. The burden of proof lay with the proponents, not the opponents, of the treaty. "Glittering and enticing generalities will not serve. We must have facts, details, and sharp, clear-cut definitions."[11]

He then moved on to the substance of the treaty, line by line. If Article 10,* with its guarantee of every nation's "territorial integrity" and "existing political

---

*   "The High Contracting Parties undertake to respect and preserve as against external aggression the territorial integrity and existing political independence of all States members of the League."

independence" was to Wilson the linchpin of the entire covenant, to Lodge it was the principal objection, and removing it was his principal aim. He felt that nations would not always honor it, but that any nation that failed to would dishonor itself. Lodge pointed out that the result might be the United States being drawn into a war or participate in economic sanctions in order to protect some border in the Balkans. Wilson's co-author of the covenant, Lord Robert Cecil, was willing to delete "and preserve against external aggression." Canada's Sir Robert Borden, a League supporter, recommended deleting Article 10 in its entirety, on the ground that a guarantee of the "territorial integrity" of every nation implied that all existing territorial arrangements were just, and would continue as such in the future.[12] With respect to Article 12, and its three-month waiting period following arbitration before a nation could resort to war,* Lodge's criticism was extremely deft. With Pancho Villa's 1916 raid into New Mexico still fresh in everyone's mind, he pointed out that once Mexico became a member of the League, Article 12 might require the United States to wait three months before retaliating. In fact, since a nation had to wait three months until *after* an arbitrator's award, which might be delayed indefinitely, retaliation might also be delayed indefinitely. "That," he said, "would be a little hard on the people who live on the border."[13] He suggested that the covenant be amended to make provision for sudden inroads or invasions. But what was worse, he suggested, was that requiring every nation to submit every international dispute to arbitration might subject a nation's immigration policies to outside interference, "a very lively question," which might result in a "flood of Japanese, Chinese or Hindu labor." And any nation that became subject to an arbitration would not, presumably, have the right to vote on that dispute in the Executive Council. "We are asked, therefore, in a large and important degree to substitute internationalism for nationalism and an international state for pure Americanism. Certainly such things as these deserve reflection, discussion and earnest thought."[14]

He then focused on Article 16, the provision under which a nation breaking the covenant would thereby "*ipso facto* be deemed to have committed an act of war against all other members of the League," subjecting that nation to the "severance of all trade or financial relations" and, significantly, to the possibility of war against the

---

* "[The High Contracting Parties] agree that should disputes arise…they will in no case resort to war without previously submitting the questions and matter involved either to arbitration or to inquiry by the Executive Council and until three months after the award by the arbitrators or a recommendation by the Executive Council…"

other members of the League.* Here Lodge was on shakier ground. At David Hunter Miller's urging, Wilson had watered down the "*ipso facto*" clause so that a miscreant nation was only *deemed* to have committed an act of war, and not *be* at war, so as not to infringe upon Congress' sole authority to declare war. But Lodge maintained that this was not sufficient. By signing the covenant, the United States would be "morally bound to contribute what the Executive Council recommends to the armed forces called forth to protect the covenants of the League." This, Lodge claimed, was "a direct interference with the power of Congress to raise armies and maintain navies."[15]

Lodge also focused on what was not in the Covenant, viz., any provision permitting a nation to withdraw from the League. Lodge correctly pointed out that every treaty contained such a provision. What he probably did not know, but which Wilson admitted, was that the omission was not an oversight. Most of Wilson's fellow commissioners assumed that a nation joining the League could freely withdraw. Wilson, as he confided to some of his fellow passengers on the *George Washington,* believed that once in, a nation could not withdraw. Lodge now claimed that the possibility that the United States could not withdraw from the League violated the fundament of Washington's *Farewell Address,* the warning against "permanent alliances." It also violated its corollary, the Monroe Doctrine, since not only would it bind the United States to purely European affairs, it would involve European nations in matters touching solely on the Western Hemisphere. Wilson had sent troops into Haiti in 1915 and into the Dominican Republic the following year. No one imagined that any European nation would, or could, become involved. Lodge had held a long-standing and publicly stated belief that any treaty the United States entered into should explicitly exclude both the Monroe Doctrine and immigration.[16] Lodge suggested a three-line amendment explicitly preserving the Monroe Doctrine, an amendment explicitly excluding all immigration matters, and a provision permitting a nation to withdraw from the League.

In his lengthy address, he touched on other matters before the Peace Conference. He wanted the United States to claim reparations for the sinking of the *Lusitania* and other ships, but nothing further, but wholeheartedly supported France's reparations claims and its security demands. "The debt of the free and civilized world to France is inestimable....She has bared her breast to the storm and stood between us and the advancing hordes of Germany in the darkest days....France should be made as strong as possible. Alsace and Lorraine she must have without question and without reduction,

---

*   "It shall be the duty of the Executive Council in such case to recommend what effective military or naval force the members of the League shall severally contribute to the armed forces to be used to protect the covenants of the League."

and other barriers if necessary to make her impregnable to German assault, for on the strength of France more than anything else, because she is the neighbor of Germany, rests the future peace of the world."[17]

Nowhere in his address did he suggest that he was opposed to any League of Nations; just the draft Wilson had presented. "Is it not possible to draft a better, more explicit, less dangerous scheme than the one here and now presented?"[18] Which brought Lodge to his concluding point. "What I ask, and all I ask, is consideration, time, and thought." He asked only that the covenant be separated from the peace treaty, and that the peace treaty be concluded as quickly as possible.

Wilson wasted no time in responding, later that day, in a White House address to members of the Democratic National committee. Lodge had not mentioned Mrs. Wilson's *faux pas* at the White House dinner, but Wilson did: "Innocently she dwelt upon the magnificent reception we had gotten in Boston....And I understand that if not that, at any rate something, had an interesting effect upon the speech that was delivered today by the senior senator from Massachusetts."[19] Wilson had long held the belief that the party in power should govern; should take the credit for success and suffer the consequences for failure. It is what endeared him to the British parliamentary system. Now he reiterated his belief: "I am in one sense an uncompromising partisan. Either a man must stand by his party or not. Either he has to play the game or get out of the game, and I have no more sufferance for such a man than the country has, not a bit."[20] However, he added, the League of Nations should be a non-partisan issue, "Because, believe me, gentlemen, the civilized world cannot afford to have us lose this fight. I tried to state in Boston what it would mean to the people of the world if the United States did not support this great ideal with cordiality, but I was not able to speak when I tried to express my thoughts. I tell you frankly, I choked up. I could not do it. The thing reaches the depths of tragedy."[21]

On Sunday morning, March 2, Sen. Frank Brandegee came to Lodge's home with an idea. It was for a "sense of the Senate" resolution opposing the covenant in its present form and asking that the covenant be stripped from the peace treaty so that that Peace Conference could expeditiously conclude the peace with Germany. Lodge immediately agreed. They both then went to the home of Pennsylvania Senator (and former Taft secretary of state) Philander Knox, who drafted the resolution. On Monday morning they took the resolution to Iowa Senator Albert Cummins, who made a few changes. The three then signed it, and circulated it all of the incumbent Republican senators (but no Democrats) and those who would be entering the sixty-sixth Congress. What became known as the "Round Robin" resolution gained thirty-nine signatures by March 5. As a two-thirds majority is required to enact any treaty, the Round Robin Resolution meant that, at least in its current form, and as part of the peace treaty, Lodge had enough adherents to kill American participation in the League of Nations and, in Wilson's words, to "break the heart of the world."

A few minutes before midnight on the third, Lodge rose in the Senate and asked for unanimous consent for the Round Robin resolution. Kentucky Democrat George B. Martin, in his last day as a senator, objected on the ground that Lodge's motion was out of order, of which Lodge was well aware. But it permitted Lodge to read the motion— and the list of signers—into the record, which was Lodge's sole intent. Days later, as Republican senators returned to the Capitol, the roster of senators supporting Lodge's resolution grew. Many supported it not because they opposed the League of Nations, but because they wanted the covenant divorced from the peace treaty. One Democrat lamented that the covenant had to be amended, or it would fail in the Senate. Shortly after reading the resolution, Nebraska Democratic Senator Gilbert Hitchcock wrote to Wilson, advising him that he believed that a number of Republicans would vote for the covenant if it was part of the peace treaty, and even more would vote for it if it were amended. He suggested some amendments that would bring them around, including a reservation that each nation have exclusive rights over its domestic affairs, a specific exclusion for the Monroe Doctrine, and a provision that a nation could withdraw upon proper notice.[22] The following week, North Dakota Senator Porter McCumber, a Republican who supported the League, also advised Wilson that there were a number of Republicans who had signed the Round Robin but who would support the covenant if it were amended to make it "clear that our sovereignty over domestic affairs and our Monroe Doctrine are not jeopardized."[23]

News of the Round Robin set off alarm bells in Paris. The French, who in the person of Léon Bourgeois had fought to toughen the covenant, now feared that the covenant might fail entirely, leaving them with nothing. The British had the same fear. Since the covenant was an integral part of the peace treaty, its failure might imperil the entire Peace Conference. But others calculated that with the covenant as part of the peace treaty, the Senate would not dare reject it and leave the United States as the only nation still at war with the Germans. For now, the Round Robin resolution meant that Wilson had been weakened even further, and would have to return with hat in hand, seeking amendments. Other nations might offer amendments of their own.

A nation-wide outbreak of strikes had threatened Lloyd George's government, causing him to return home. He now set out to put out the fires. On February 14, the day that Wilson left for home, he rose in the House of Commons and presented his program. He would welcome an inquiry into the causes of the industrial unrest, but he would resist "Prussianism" at home, just as he had in Europe. But he would be almost alone in the effort, as a prime minister essentially without a party. He quipped afterwards that when he looked straight ahead of him at the opposition (Labour) benches, he felt he was addressing the Trades Union Congress, and when he turned and looked behind him, at the Tories who backed him, he felt he was addressing the Chamber of Commerce. Walking the middle ground would not be easy.

What followed over the next two weeks was vintage Lloyd George, as he employed the same skills he had brought to bear when he headed the Board of Trade. He invited the executives of the Miners' Federation to 10 Downing Street. Union locals were holding strike votes, and a national strike of coal miners loomed. The issue was mostly wages (they demanded a 30% increase) but they also pressed for nationalization of the mines. He asked them to delay a strike pending the issuance of a government commission report. But he warned them that their demands, if fully met, would result in an increase in the cost of coal to all industries, crippling those industries at a time when the country was crippled by the cost of the war. He made a thinly-disguised threat. This time, he said, it was different. A nation-wide strike would be more than a conflict between labor and employer; it would be between labor and the government. "The threat of force on either side is not a rational means of settling, whether it is on the side of the Government or on the side of the miners, and I am making no threat. I am only pointing out to you…what the effect is going to be, and I am also pointing out to you that it would be impossible, once it began, in a conflict between the State and one section of industry, for any Government to give in without surrendering the functions of all government."[24] The following month, the commission issued its report, recommending a seven-hour day for the miners, and a wage increase of two shillings *per day*. The government accepted. The threat of a miner's strike was diffused.

Another issue in an era of high unemployment was the amount and duration of unemployment insurance. He arranged for a National Industrial Conference, which convened on February 27. Lloyd George was the last of the many government and labor representatives to speak. "It is always assumed that it [i.e. money] is inexhaustible," he said, and borrowing from *The Merchant of Venice*, "and dropping like gentle rain from heaven, blesses him who gives and him who takes…And when you have not gotten taxes like manna every morning…You have to get it out of somebody."[25] It won appreciative laughter. They agreed to the creation of a Joint Industrial Conference to examine all labor issues.

The Conference met on March 5, with Lloyd George pleading for moderation. "I am off this afternoon to take part in the Peace Congress, which I hope will settle, and settle satisfactorily, the peace of the world....You are really a peace congress; you are settling the future of this country, but you may be doing more than that. You may be settling the future of civilization, you may be making a model for civilization which all lands will turn to and say 'Let us follow Britain.'" He appealed to the patriotism of both labor and employers: "Don't try to get an advantage over the other....I want you to feel that you are the trustees for the whole country. Employers might get temporary advantages which will in the end ruin them....On the other hand, let me say a word to the workers. What is happening in Russia, and what may happen in Germany, shows that while anarchist sections may appear for the moment to be triumphant, inconceivable horrors are being suffered in those countries. A small section may be doing well, but the vast multitude of the working classes there are suffering unimaginable distress. Therefore what is needed is a prosperous community with a prosperity insured for all."[26]

The Conference issued a report recommending a forty-eight-hour week and the establishment of minimum wage rates in all industries. By the time Lloyd George set off for Paris, Frances Stevenson noted in her diary that "Everyone congratulates him most heartily in the way in which he seems to have brought comparative peace to the industrial world."[27]

Arthur Balfour wanted to speed up the Peace Conference as much as House. Before Wilson had left for home, it was agreed that the Council of Ten could proceed to finalize the military and naval terms that the Allies would present to the Germans, but that all other matters could be negotiated, but not concluded, until Wilson returned. To date, Clemenceau had opposed finalizing the military terms separate from the issues of reparations and Germany's borders on the ground that these issues were integrated, and that if the military terms were settled first, the French would lose any leverage they had. Shortly after Wilson left, Balfour and House had a lengthy meeting to discuss how they might speed up the Peace Conference. They agreed Balfour would work on the Japanese, House would work on the Italians, and both would see Clemenceau, "to get him in line with us."[28]

On morning of the nineteenth, House and Balfour planned to meet with Clemenceau at the Crillon to discuss speeding up the Peace Conference. House and Balfour met, but the meeting never happened. Shortly after entering his car at the rue

Franklin to attend the meeting, a man emerged from the crowd, dressed in worker's clothes. He fired between six to nine shots at Clemenceau. Clemenceau saw the man, and had enough time to think "he's going to miss me," later quipping that "contrary to my prognosis, I was hit."[29] One bullet lodged between his ribs, missing vital organs. The assailant was one Louis Emile Cottin, 22, who, before shooting, may have shouted "I am a Frenchman and an anarchist."[30] He was almost lynched by the crowd that had formed to see Clemenceau off. Clemenceau never lost consciousness, and he was returned to his home. "Fortunately," mused Clemenceau, "the rascal was a bad shot." The following week Clemenceau was visited by the public prosecutor, who asked Clemenceau what he thought Cottin's punishment should be. "We have just won the most terrible war in history, yet here is a Frenchman who at point-blank range misses his target six times out of seven. Of course the man must be punished for the careless use of a dangerous weapon, and for poor marksmanship. I suggest he be locked up for about eight years, with intensive training in a shooting gallery."[31] Cottin was initially sentenced to death, which was later commuted to ten years. He joined the anti-Franco forces, and was killed in the Spanish Civil War. Clemenceau, against doctors' orders, returned to the Council of Ten nine days later. But he was seventy-eight, and now tired easily. The bullet lodged between his ribs was never removed.

Before he learned of the shooting, House fired off a coded cable to Wilson on the *George Washington*. Wilson had instructed House that all of their communications be encoded and shared with no one, thus keeping House's fellow commissioners— including Lansing—completely in the dark. In this cable, House relayed a memo from Marshal Foch to the effect that the Germans (in Foch's opinion) were now desperate to conclude any peace terms the Allies might offer, "but he says there is no time to lose....Delay is dangerous." Foch said that the Germans would agree to any proposal for the strength of her armed forces, and would accept the Rhine as their Western border, and that they could quickly agree to resolve their border with Poland. Foch recommended setting a fixed sum as reparations. All this, Foch believed, could be accomplished in a few days.[32] That evening, House again cabled Wilson, advising him that their planned meeting "to discuss plans of speeding up work of [the] Conference... had to be abandoned" due to the shooting. He reported that the French appeared to have changed their position, and now also wished to speed up the Conference, which House ascribed to the "demoralization" of France's army.[33]

Wilson's response to Foch's proposals was sharp and immediate. "It seems to me," he cabled House, "like an attempt to use the good offices of the French to hurry us into an acquiescence in their plans with regard to the western bank of the Rhine, a plan to which I could, as I now see the matter, in no case accede….I know I can trust you and your colleagues to withstand such a programme immovably, except of course I am willing to have the strictly military and naval terms promptly decided and presented to the Germans. I am not willing to have anything beyond the military and naval terms settled and believe that the Council of Ten would be going very much beyond its powers to attempt anything of this sort….I beg that you hold things steady with regard to everything but the strictly military and naval terms until I return."[34]

These cables from House to Wilson, and the ones that followed in the ensuing weeks, are an important record in light of the eventual cooling of their relationship. The charge that House kept Wilson in the dark for the purpose of undermining Wilson cannot be sustained in light of the cable record.

On Saturday, the twenty-second, House met with Clemenceau at his home in the rue Franklin who, according to House, "opened his heart to me."[35] Clemenceau, seating in an armchair, was in good spirits, except for being harassed by his nurse, Sister Theoneste, to take his medicine. Clemenceau rightfully prided himself on his facility in American slang, and now announced to House: "The slogan is now full-speed ahead." More specifically: "As I cannot lie down since that madman shot me…I just naturally will not let anybody else lie down. I shall insist on a little speed being turned on. I am confident that if we 'Americans' and the British and the French would only get together we could push through the peace treaty with Germany in a few days…"[36] Balfour also met with Clemenceau that morning, who reported that Clemenceau's desire to speed up the Peace Conference did not mean he agreed to separating the military and naval terms from the other terms; he still wished all the terms to be treated as a whole. Clemenceau's *volte-face* is difficult to fathom. He may have signed on to Foch's belief that the timing was right for forcing a peace on the Germans, or (as House believed) Clemenceau was feeling pressure to speed French demobilization. The American delegates believed that the French had slow-walked the Peace Conference waiting for Wilson to leave, in order to obtain a better deal in his absence. At any rate, House, Balfour and Clemenceau were now all fully on board in an attempt to conclude the Peace Conference as quickly as possible.

The plan was put forward later that day. At the Council of Ten, Balfour introduced a resolution to the effect that, without prejudicing "Naval, Military and Air Conditions of Peace… the Conference agrees that is desirable to proceed without delay to the consideration of other preliminary Peace Terms with Germany and to press the necessary investigations with all possible speed….The Preliminary Peace Terms, other than the Naval, Military and Air Conditions, shall cover the following points," which were: "The approximate future frontiers of Germany; The financial arrangements to be imposed on Germany; Our economic relations with Germany after the war;" and "Responsibility for breaches of the Laws of War."[37] At Balfour's suggestion, House added two words to the resolution, so that the final resolution provided that the Peace Terms "shall cover, *inter alia*, the following points..." House's purpose in adding *"inter alia"* was to assure that the Peace Terms included the covenant of the League of Nations, without mentioning it as such, so as to obviate an "interminable" discussion with the French.[38] The resolution called for the "consideration" of all of these items, not their conclusion, which would have to await the return of the respective heads of government. And in order to hasten the conclusion of the Peace Conference, all of the various commissions and committees were ordered to submit their reports by March 8. One final matter needed to be ironed out. The Italians feared that if a peace treaty were quickly concluded with the Germans, they might be left as the only belligerent, fighting the Austrians. So four identical "fill-in-the-blanks" resolutions were adopted, one for each of the defeated powers. All four resolutions were cabled to Wilson. When the meeting broke up, House told waiting reporters that he expected peace to now come sooner than he had expected.

House cabled Wilson the results of his meeting with Clemenceau the following day, reporting that Clemenceau "is anxious now to speed up and make an early peace with Germany. He at last realizes the danger of delay." But House reported that Clemenceau was still adhering to Foch's demand for the creation of a Rhineland republic, with its four million Germans. Repeating the line that Foch had espoused to the British the prior December, Clemenceau maintained that the Rhinelanders would be exempt from reparations, and every attempt would be made to make the Rhinelanders prosperous so that they would not later desire to rejoin Germany, which they would not be permitted to do. Clemenceau could not possibly have believed that Wilson would consent to this. Once again, he was bargaining. House also reported that Clemenceau believed that the Poles should receive Danzig and that the Austrians had to be prevented from federating with Germany. House also reported that the Council of Ten had agreed that all of the peace terms—including the naval and military terms—be quickly concluded and presented to the Germans as a package.[39] Wilson did not respond to this cable.

In early February, House had met with André Tardieu's associate, Louis Aubert. He advised Aubert of his objection to the French plan for a Rhineland republic, that it would be bad for France as well as the United States, prompting the same reaction among the Germans that the 1871 annexation of Alsace-Lorraine had had upon the French. House added that "Our only chance for peace…was to create a League of Nations, treat Germany fairly, and see that she did not have an opportunity to again equip and maintain an army that would be formidable."[40] On the morning of the nineteenth, prior to the attempted assassination, House and Balfour discussed possible ways of circumventing French desires in the Rhineland. House mooted a plan to prohibit German conscription, limiting the size of German forces to 150,000, and limiting French occupation to the Rhine bridgeheads.

On the twenty-fourth, House met with André Tardieu in Vance McCormick's suite at the Ritz, to discuss the Rhineland. What he heard from Tardieu was very different from what he had heard from Clemenceau the previous day. According to Tardieu, the Rhineland republic would not be forever barred from reuniting with Germany, but that in "five, ten or some other number of years, when the League of Nations was working as a protection against war" they would have no objection to the Rhinelanders rejoining Germany, if they so wished. According to House, "This of course relieves that question of one of its most objectionable features, since otherwise it would be quite contrary to the policy of self-determination."[41] Arthur Balfour went along with this proposal. Whether Wilson (or Lloyd George) would agree was another matter. House duly cabled Wilson a report of the meeting: "Our territorial experts are in substantial agreement with the British and the French respecting the boundaries of Germany. Tardieu, who since the attack on Clemenceau has become more or less prominent said to me yesterday that France would be willing to have the Rhenish republic set up for only a limited period of years, at the end of which the population would be permitted to decide for themselves what the future should be….The principle of self-determination would be in this way safe-guarded."[42] He also laid out for Wilson the plan to hasten the work of the committees so that the work would be concluded by the time of his return, "so that you can consider them without delay."[43] Wilson did not respond to this dramatic turn of events. It is possible that, what with the imperfect ship-to-shore communications of the day that often rendered entire coded messages unintelligible, Wilson never received House's cable.

Two days later, House was presented with a twenty-page litigation-style brief, drafted by Tardieu but no doubt inspired by Clemenceau. The bottom line of Tardieu's brief was that France required for its security a state on the Rhineland separated from Germany. It included quotes from Wilson himself, that the Rhine should become a "frontier of freedom" and Admiral von Tirpitz, that "without the possession of the left bank, Germany would have been unable to pass her armies through a neutral Belgium."[44] The argument was based upon France's dual difficulties of distance and timing. France had almost been overrun in five weeks because Germany had had possession of the left bank and the Rhine bridges; France needed both to assure her security. Tardieu rejected a limitation in German arms, and the guarantee of the League of Nations, as sufficient. Germany could always rebuild her armed forces, and the guarantee of the other, far-away nations in the League could not solve France's inherent time and distance problem. What France needed was the complete demilitarization of the left bank and its occupation (along with the Rhine bridges) by an inter-Allied force. Tardieu claimed that this did not amount to the annexation of the Rhine. But it would result in a self-governing Rhineland state divorced from Germany. The result would be the same. House received this brief just after he had advised Wilson that the French position was softening.

At roughly the same hour of Cottin's attempt to take Clemenceau's life, Vance McCormick was discussing with Lansing the contents of a cable they intended to send to Wilson aboard the *George Washington* on the status of reparations negotiations. In the cable, sent under the signatures of Lansing, House, McCormick, Bernard Baruch and Norman H. Davis, they reviewed the American position, viz., that the terms under which the Germans agreed to the Armistice excluded the broader definition of "war costs." However, "We fear that Lloyd George, Clemenceau and Orlando will oppose the view which we have been defending." They were cognizant of the political difficulties of the Allies: "[O]ur opponents make a strong popular argument difficult to answer without appearing to be bound to legal technicalities….[T]he political situation in almost all countries will make it most difficult for their delegates to take any attitude other than insistence upon the complete reparation which they have promised their people and which all our inquiries show the people of the Allied countries feel to be just and due them." They asked if Wilson could provide them with a statement they could use in support of the American position.[45] McCormick showed a draft of the cable to House, who approved it, McCormick noting that House rather resented that McCormick had shown it first to Lansing.[46] Wilson cabled his response from the *George Washington*: "I feel that we are bound in honor to decline to agree to the inclusion of war costs in the reparation demanded. The time to think of this was before the conditions of peace were communicated to the enemy originally. We should dissent and dissent publicly if necessary now on the ground that it is clearly inconsistent with what we deliberately led the enemy to expect and can not now honorably alter simply because we have the power."[47]

Shortly after McCormick met with Lansing to draft the cable, he attended a meeting of the Reparations Committee. Completely deadlocked, they voted to refer the issue to the Council of Ten, adopting a resolution, drafted by the French, as to whether "The rights to reparations of the Allied and Associated Powers is entire," [i.e. includes war costs], or whether this is contrary to the Pre-Armistice Agreement." But on March 1, with three of the Big Four absent (Lloyd George in London, Wilson in Washington, Orlando in Rome tending to domestic matters) they agreed to hold the matter in abeyance. At Lansing's suggestion, the Reparations Committee was ordered to draft alternate reports, one allowing for war costs, the other limited to actual damages.

On February 21, McCormick and Thomas Lamont reported to House on the status of the bidding. They noted that Britain's man on the Reparations Committee, Lord Cunliffe, had put in for $120 billion in reparations, with the French asking for $200 billion, to run for fifty-five years. The American experts had concluded that the Germans could not pay more than $22 billion, and probably less. McCormick opined that the only possible solution was to not require any specific amount, since the Allies had "fooled their people with exaggerated promises of high indemnity and no taxes" with governments falling if the promises were not met.[48] Two days later, McCormick met with Tardieu, who explained to McCormick the difficulty his government faced in explaining to their people what the Germans really could be expected to pay. Tardieu felt that the British were in the same position, and both were hunting about for a compromise that would accept the American position without making it appear as such.[49]

The following day—the twenty-fourth—in the same cable in which House had advised Wilson that he had reached an agreement with the British and the French over the Rhineland (and which Wilson may not have received) House advised Wilson that "It now seems possible that we shall arrive at a solution of the reparation matter which we can accept without abandoning the principle accepted by Germany and the allies at the time of the armistice."[50] Unfortunately, House did not share with Wilson what this "solution of the reparation matter" was, other than to suggest that the United States inform its Allies that the United States would not assist in attempting to collect any reparations other than what the United States was owed. If Wilson received this cable, he did not respond to it. Three days later, House ordered McCormick and Lamont to put in a $40 billion bid in the Reparations Committee, a sum that House himself thought "absurd," noting later that "Whatever we agree will be largely a figure of speech," since the Germans would be unable to pay it.[51] But, as he had advised Wilson, he wished to underline that the United States did not consider itself legally or morally obligated to assist in the collection of such a sum.[52]

On February 27, House cabled Wilson that he had met with Balfour and Lord Robert Cecil, and had suggested that they try to start the League of Nations functioning at once, to which they agreed. The League of Nations committee, headed by Wilson, would become the *de facto* Executive Committee of the League. The Council of Ten or the full Plenary conference would refer matters to the committee, which would report back to the Council of Ten or the Plenary conference, acting as a *de facto* Body of Delegates. The neutral nations would be invited to join the League. All of this, House advised, would be contingent on the French and the Japanese not offering any amendments to the draft Covenant.[53] But in a second cable to Wilson later that day, House advised Wilson that the idea was dead: "We have not found a way to make the League of Nations function as suggested."[54] It is possible that Wilson may have interpreted House's suggestion as a means of doing the one thing of which Wilson was adamantly opposed, viz., separating the covenant from the peace treaty. In any event, House's stillborn idea shows that he was keeping Wilson fully abreast of all of his activities.

Before Wilson left for home, the Council of Ten agreed to extend the Armistice indefinitely, with the Allies formulating the "final" military and naval terms for presentation to the Germans as quickly as possible. Marshal Foch presented the final military terms on March 2, and it sparked yet another dispute among the Allies. Foch posited a German army consisting of no more than 200,000 enlisted men, and 9,000 officers. The officers would all be volunteers, serving terms of *not less than* twenty-five years. Non-commissioned officers would serve terms of not less than fifteen years. Conversely, new recruits would all be conscripts, who would serve for not more than one year. All this to assure that the Germans would be able to draw as few men to the colors as possible, and the training of those who were conscripted would be of little benefit in the one year they could serve before being mustered out. The permitted level of German armament would be limited to serving this small army. In presenting the plan, Foch begged that it be accepted quickly. With the Allied occupation forces quickly dissipating, he warned that if the Germans failed to accept permanent military terms by April 1, it would be difficult to enforce any military terms after that date.

Lloyd George returned to Paris on March 5, and at the Council of Ten meeting on March 7 refused to go along with any plan that included conscripts, no doubt on the ground that if the Germans were able to conscript an army, it would make it that much more difficult for Great Britain to abolish conscription. A compromise was reached: The Germans would be limited to a volunteer army of 200,000, each enlistee serving for twelve years. At the March 10 meeting, this number was finalized at 100,000, a number so small that Balfour, tongue firmly in cheek, inquired what would happen if Germany were attacked by Switzerland, Belgium, or some such small power.[55] But Lloyd George was pleased with the result, telling Frances Stevenson that "What I proposed practically amounts to the abolition of conscription in Europe."[56] When Wilson returned, he inquired whether an army this small would be sufficient to guard against Bolshevism in Germany. He was assured by Foch that it was.

There was an unintended consequence of the forced demobilization of the German army that no one could then foresee. Limiting Germany to 100,000 men meant that there were tens of thousands of unemployed and embittered former officers and enlisted men with nothing to do. They became the nuclei of the *Freikorps*, the S.A. and other paramilitary groups that helped to undermine the Weimer Republic.

After the attempt on Clemenceau's life, House deputized Stephen Bonsal to sit with Clemenceau. With a bullet lodged between his ribs, it was too painful for Clemenceau to lie down, so he sat in an armchair. As Clemenceau was fluent in English and Bonsal in French, there was no need for an interpreter; it was just the two of them. Fortunately for history, Bonsal kept copious notes.

"I must make peace based upon my belief and upon my own experience in the world in which we live," he advised Bonsal. "My responsibility is personal and nontransferable…Mr. Wilson has lived in a world that has been fairly safe for Democracy, I have lived in a world where it was good form to shoot a Democrat. After a few weeks of sparring I became convinced that your President wanted the same things that I did, although we were very far apart as to the ways and the means by which we could reach the desired end.…When he first developed his program, it seemed to be perfectly Utopian. I said to him: 'Mr. President, if I accept what you propose as ample for the security of France, after the millions who have died and the millions who have suffered, I believe and I would hope, that my successor in office would take me by the nape of the neck and have me shot at daylight before the donjon at Vincennes.' After that we began to get together."[57]

And later: "Now who can deny that in peacemaking France is meeting with great opposition from all her Allies who were so noble and considerate while the battle was on. During the long war years we sustained the heaviest losses, we suffered the most, and now what is our fate at the Conference? We are blocked in our plea for security, only our undoubted claim to Alsace goes uncontested. For the little else that we may obtain we shall have to fight and fight hard. I mean to do that very thing and Wilson knows it."

And still later: "I told your President that, in my judgment, the grave fault of his attitude is that he eliminated sentiment and endeavored to efface all memory of the past. A grave, a very grave fault, it seems to me. It was then I would say: 'I am the last, the only survivor of the Protest of Bordeaux—against the infamy of the treaty that the Prussians imposed at the point of the bayonet. M. le President, I speak for our glorious dead who fell in the two wars. For myself, I can hold my tongue, but not for them.'"[58]

Henry Cabot Lodge introduced the "Round Robin" resolution at 12:02 A.M. on March 4. Before the day was out, Wilson issued a public statement: "A group of men in the Senate have deliberately chosen to embarrass the administration of the Government, to imperil the financial interests of the railway system [by failing to return the railroads to private hands] and to make arbitrary use of powers intended to be employed in the interest of the people."[59] At the same time, he cabled House that he was "satisfied that the sentiment of the American people" was behind the League."[60] That evening, he was off to New York to make his last appeal before returning to Paris, a Metropolitan Opera House rally in support of the League.

Wilson was preceded to the stage by President Taft, one of the pro-League Republicans Wilson had rejected as one of his peace commissioners, who had been crisscrossing the country drumming up support for the League. Taft was no rabble-rouser. His tack was to refute Lodge's point-by-point shredding of the draft covenant. To counter Lodge's argument that the covenant's arbitration provision might require the United States to admit Japanese and Chinese immigrants, Taft argued that the United States could simply refuse arbitration. With regard to Lodge's clever argument that the covenant might prevent or delay American response to a raid from Mexico, Taft simply denied it: The inherent right of self-defense would permit immediate retaliation. He countered Lodge's argument that the covenant's disarmament provision impinged on Congress' exclusive right to raise an army: "Can we not trust our Congress to fix a limitation safe for the country and stick to it?"[61] The decision as to whether the United States goes to war, and with what forces, remains with the Congress. "This is as it should be." The covenant "fixes the obligation of action in such a way that American nations will attend to America, and European nations will attend to Europe, and Asiatic nations to Asia, unless all deem the situation so threatening to the world and their own interests as that they should take a more active part."[62] But Taft's defense of the covenant was not unqualified. He suggested amendments, such as a provision that purely American disputes should be addressed solely by American nations, obviating what was becoming one of the biggest threats to the covenant, the concern over the Monroe Doctrine. And he conceded that the covenant did not provide a mechanism for a nation to withdraw. He suggested an amendment permitting a nation to withdraw on one or two years' notice. Finally, Taft addressed the Round Robin resolution that Lodge had introduced earlier that day: "If the president insists, as I hope he will, that the League be incorporated in the peace treaty and brings it back, then the responsibility for postponing peace is with the body that refuses to ratify it."[63] At this, Wilson was seen smiling broadly.

Wilson was introduced by Governor Alfred E. Smith. In his fight for the League, Wilson was unlike modern presidents. He had no domestic policy staff and no office of Congressional liaison charged with counting votes and twisting arms. His public communications team consisted of his secretary, Joseph Tumulty. Believing as he did in party government, he was incapable of doing what House had implored him to do, to reach across the aisle, making the small obsequies that lubricate the wheels of the democratic state. Except for Taft and a few outspoken supporters such as Nebraska Senator Gilbert Hitchcock, he was all alone. His greatest gift, as it had always been, was his gift of oratory.

It was a fighting speech. He began by asserting that "an overwhelming majority of the American people is in favor of the League of Nations. I know that to be true. I have had unmistakable intimations of it from all parts of the country, and the voice rings true in every case." He said he would not defend each provision of the covenant, as Taft had already done so. "Europe is a bit sick at heart at this very moment, because it sees that statesmen have had no vision, and that the only vision has been the vision of the people. Those who suffer see. Those against whom wrong is wrought know how desirable is the right of the righteous….And I am amazed—not alarmed, but amazed—that there should be in some quarters such a comprehensive ignorance of the state of the world. These gentlemen do not know what the mind of men is just now. Everybody else does. I do not know where they have been closeted. I do not know by what influences they have been blinded; but I do know they have been separated from the general currents of the thought of mankind….Now the heart of the world is awake, and the heart of the world must be satisfied."[64]

Answering Lodge's demand that the covenant be separated from the peace treaty, he threw it back at him. Not only would the covenant be part of the peace treaty, but "gentlemen on this side will find the covenant not only in it, but so many threads of the treaty tied to the covenant that you cannot dissect the covenant from the treaty without destroying the whole vital structure."[65] If Lodge wished to destroy the covenant, he had to vote down peace itself. That was the challenge. The Senate Republicans viewed it as a threat.

Wilson concluded: "When I was in Italy, a little limping group of wounded Italian soldiers sought an interview with me. I could not conjecture what it was they were going to say to me, and, with the greatest simplicity, with a touching simplicity, they presented me with a petition in favor of the League of Nations....Their wounded limbs, their impaired vitality, were the only argument they brought with them. It was a simple request that I lend all the influence that I might happen to have to relieve future generations of the sacrifices that they had been obliged to make. That appeal has remained in my mind as I have ridden along the streets in European capitals and heard cries of the crowd, cries for the League of Nations from lips of people who, I venture to say, had no particular notion of how it was to be done, who were not ready to propose a plan for a League of Nations, but whose hearts said that something by way of a combination of all men must come out of this....It is inconceivable that we should disappoint them, and we shall not."[66]

And with that he was off to the Hoboken pier and the *George Washington*, to return to Paris.

House and Balfour had been trying to speed the Peace Conference along in Wilson and Lloyd George's absences, but the lack of progress on the biggest issues—reparations and Germany's borders—now left House in a momentary depression. On March 3, he summarized the Peace Conference to date in his diary. "It is now evident," he wrote, "that the peace will not be such a peace as I had hoped, or one which this terrible upheaval should have brought about. There are many reasons why it will not be one....The American Delegation are not in a position to act freely. The elections of last November in the United States have been a deterrent to free action by our delegates. The British elections and the vote of confidence Clemenceau received in the French Chamber of Deputies, put the finishing touches on a situation already bad."[67] House predicted that if Wilson put too much pressure on the British, French and Italians, all of their respective governments might fall, "but if he did, he would still have to reckon with our own people, and he might bring the whole world into chaos." Feeling somewhat sorry for himself, he added "I dislike to sit and have forced upon us such a peace as we are facing. We will get something out of it in the way of a League of Nations, but even that is an imperfect instrument." He enumerated the issues he faced every day, all at an impasse: "the left bank of the Rhine, Asia Minor, the African Colonies, the Chinese-Japanese differences, the economic situation over raw materials, the food situation as it affects the various countries in Europe...and the financial situation as it relates to the United States, and the Allies."[68]

House had reason to brighten three days later, shortly after Lloyd George returned. On March 6, House met with Lloyd George for lunch in the latter's flat in the rue

Nitot. Lloyd George seemed to House especially eager to discuss reparations, House noting that Lloyd George would be "extremely grateful" if House could help him out on this issue. Lloyd George wanted the amount of reparations demanded to be large, even if the Germans would never pay it, and even if it were later reduced. According to House, Lloyd George did not want to let the Tories "throw" him on a question near and dear to their hearts.[69]

House and Lloyd George met with Clemenceau the morning of the following day. They worked out a tentative solution. The Allies would accept the American definition of reparations, i.e. to exclude war costs. Whatever amount agreed upon (if any) would, however, be allocated 60% towards direct physical damages (thus going mainly to France and Belgium), with the other 40% allocated among all of the Allies based upon their war costs. It was a classic Lloyd George compromise, one that House thought fair, as not violating the Pre-Armistice Agreement or the Fourteen Points. House duly reported the compromise to Wilson (now returning to Paris aboard the *George Washington*) in a cable later that day, noting that Clemenceau thought the proposal acceptable, but wishing to reserve judgment until he could consult with his financial experts.[70] In the same cable, House reported to Wilson that they had discussed the Rhine, with Clemenceau holding out for the Rhinelanders being permanently separated from Germany. "Tardieu tells me," House advised, that "he will urge him to modify this view." Wilson received this cable, as he responded to it the following day: "Am made a little uneasy by what you say of the left bank of the Rhine. I hope you will not even provisionally consent to the separation of the Rhenish provinces from Germany under any arrangement but will reserve the whole matter until my arrival."[71] This exchange indicates, if nothing else, that House attempted to and succeeded in advising Wilson of his progress.

An exchange between Lloyd George and Clemenceau in the Council of Ten on March 8 revealed their fundamentally different fears for Europe's future. The issue was Germany's need for food. With the blockade never lifted, reports filtered in about starving German children. The Allies had reached an understanding—but not a formal agreement—with the Germans that food would be allowed through once the Germans turned over their merchant fleet, as required by the Armistice. The Germans were reneging on turning over the ships, in fear that the Allies would renege on the food. Lloyd George wanted to let the food through; Clemenceau did not. "The Allies were now on top," argued Lloyd George, "but the memories of starvation might one day turn against them....The Allies were sowing hatred for the future; they were piling up agonies, not for the Germans, but for themselves….As long as the people were starving they would listen to the argument of the Spartacists [i.e. the German Communists], and the Allies by their action were simply encouraging elements of disruption and anarchy. It was like stirring up an influenza puddle, just next door to oneself."[72]

But Clemenceau would have none of it. The Germans had promised to surrender the ships, and had not done so. The Germans, in his opinion, were simply seeing how far they could go in blackmailing the Allies, and "to yield today would simply mean constant yielding in the future….It was essential that no signs of weakness should be displayed on the eve of the settlement of other large territorial, military and economic questions. The Germans must not be given any advantage today that might give them the impression that the Allied Powers could be intimidated and made to yield."[73]

On March 9, with Wilson now at sea returning to Paris, Henry Cabot Lodge received a cable from Henry White, Wilson's sole Republican at the Peace Conference. It had been encoded and transmitted through State Department channels. In it, White requested that Lodge cable to him the "exact phraseology" of any amendments to the covenant that Lodge's Republican-controlled Senate might desire. He suggested that Lodge's return cable also be in cipher.[74] Lodge referred White's cable to Senators Frank Brandegee and Philander Knox, and to former Secretary of State Elihu Root. Root was of the opinion that the real author of the cable was not White, but Wilson, who was employing this ruse to solicit Republican amendments to the covenant. Root advised Lodge not to respond to an "unauthorized" agent, that the proper way to interpose amendments was by means of a special session of Congress, which Wilson had refused to call. Lodge did not respond to White's plea for amendments.

If Root and Lodge really believed Wilson was the motivating force, or was even aware of White's cable, they were sadly mistaken. For one, such a move would have been totally uncharacteristic of Wilson. Moreover, White's missive to Lodge was hardly a bolt out of the blue, for White had been in frequent, recent communication with Lodge, a fact that Lodge may not have shared with Root, Brandegee and Knox. In a February 10 letter to Lodge, White dispelled many of the arguments Lodge would make in his Senate address. He advised Lodge that no one on Wilson's League of Nations commission had the slightest intention of allowing an American army or navy to be under the orders of an international body, or of abandoning the Monroe Doctrine. Of Wilson, White opined that "[H]e has always been ready to listen, and in several cases to accept suggestions, particularly in the phraseology of the draft constitution of the League of Nations."[75] In a letter to Lodge the following week, White advised Lodge that, contrary to Lodge's assertion on the Senate floor, the drafting of the covenant was not holding up progress on the peace treaty.[76] The mystery of White's coded cable was solved two weeks after it was received, when Lodge received from White a twenty-page letter, dispatched via the regular mails, outlining White's views and asking for suggestions for amendments. White had sent his cable because he aware of the slowness of the mails, and deemed the need for amendments to be urgent.

On March 10, House met with Lloyd George and Clemenceau. In their discussion of reparations, both Lloyd George and Clemenceau pressed for a large sum, due to Lloyd George's problem in the House of Commons and Clemenceau's in the Chamber of Deputies. Whatever the agreed-upon sum, both were willing to call the sum "reparations." They agreed to add pensions and separation allowances to the definition of "reparations," a compromise to which Wilson later agreed. They agreed to appoint a secret committee to study reparations, comprised of Louis Loucheur, Edwin Montagu and Norman H. Davis, all known as moderates on the issue. They also agreed to set up a committee to the consider the German boundaries, consisting of Philip Kerr, Tardieu and Sidney Mezes. They discussed Italy's borders with Austria and Jugo-Slavia, concluding that Italy should not be rewarded the Tyrol or Fiume, House noting that Clemenceau and Lloyd George were even more opposed to Italy's territorial demands than was Wilson. And it was at this meeting that House suggested that when Wilson returned they should wind down the meetings of the Council of Ten in favor of the four of them—Wilson, Lloyd George, Clemenceau and Orlando—meeting in executive session.

In the early evening of March 14, the *George Washington* pulled into the harbor at Brest. The French Ambassador, M. Jusserand and Madame Jusserand, and a few other dignitaries, boarded a launch to officially greet the president. But otherwise, there were no ceremonies. A tug plied out to the ship, and returned with Wilson, Mrs. Wilson, and other members of his party. Standing on the dock, waiting to greet him, was Edward M. House.

COLLAPSE

War plays havoc with the refinements of conscience.

—David Lloyd George

Colonel House boarded the president's train for Paris late in the evening of March 13, but it was not until the following morning, as it neared the Gare des Invalides station, that House got to brief Wilson on all that had transpired in his absence. Then, according to legend, after they met, Wilson returned to his cabin and, with jaw clenched and straining to control himself, he advised Edith: "House has given away everything I had won before we left Paris. He has compromised on every side, and so I have to start all over again and this time it will be harder, as he has given the impression that my delegates are not in sympathy with me."[1]

The sole source of this legend, repeated more or less uncritically by commentators and biographers through the years, was Edith Wilson herself, in the memoir she penned twenty years after the alleged event. It did not happen. Wilson did not utter the words she ascribed to him, for he could not have. House, as Wilson well knew, had "given away" nothing in his absence. The cable traffic between House and Wilson during the preceding month reveals that House sought Wilson's counsel and dutifully advised him of all of his efforts to speed along the peace treaty. The gravest charge leveled against House is that he acceded to pressure to decouple the League covenant from the peace treaty. There is no evidence of this. When the Council of Ten drew up its resolution on all of the matters that needed to be included in the peace treaty, it was House who inserted the "inter alia" clause to include the covenant as an integral part of the treaty. If Wilson had felt that House had indeed "given away" everything in his absence, it should have produced an immediate break in their partnership. Yet House remained Wilson's principal advisor and confidante, and it was House—not Lansing—who Wilson chose to substitute for him on the Council of Four during Wilson's brief illness.

With the peace conference now headed into its third month, it was Wilson, not House, who had bargained away many of his principles. "Open covenants…openly arrived at" disappeared in the impenetrable secrecy Wilson imposed on the League of Nations Commission. "Freedom of the Seas" became a distant memory in the face of Great Britain's implacable hostility. "Impartial adjustment of colonial claims" vanished when Germany was stripped of all of her colonies and Wilson forgot about giving colonial mandates to smaller, neutral nations, and it was Wilson, not House, who had ceded the South Tyrol, and its two hundred thousand German-speakers, to Italy. And more compromises of principle were to come.

Wilson's train arrived in Paris shortly after noon. Unlike his arrival in January, there were no cheering crowds, but he was again met by Clemenceau. Wilson graciously asked if Clemenceau was still feeling the after-effects of the assassination attempt, to which Clemenceau replied "On the contrary, I think it did me good."[2] The French, having lost the lease to the Murat Palace, found a new residence for Wilson at 11 place des Etats-Unis, and Wilson went straight to it from the train station. When he arrived he found Lloyd George (whose flat on the rue Nitot was across the street) waiting for him.

Wilson arrived in Paris in a fighting mood, and the one thing he planned to fight for was the League. Wilson and Lloyd George met for an hour, Lloyd George afterwards confiding to Frances Stevenson that Wilson wanted to talk about nothing other than the League.[3] Wilson then motored to House's suite at the Crillon, where he met with Clemenceau, Lloyd George, House, Andre Tardieu and Clemenceau's reparations advisor, Louis Loucheur. For the next three hours, they discussed reparations and the Rhineland, but according to Lloyd George, "Wilson talked for an hour about the League of Nations and his ideals, but we did nothing practical."[4] But in fact they did accomplish something "practical." Wilson and Lloyd George made it clear to Clemenceau that annexation of the Left Bank of the Rhine was out of the question, of which Clemenceau was probably aware, but that they could agree to a short occupation to assure the payment of reparations. According to Lloyd George, it was here that he, on behalf of Great Britain and the United States, offered Clemenceau a joint Anglo-American guarantee against German aggression, to which Wilson agreed. Clemenceau would accept the guarantee, but wanted more, in the form of a more permanent occupation. And it is likely that it was at this meeting that Clemenceau, now convinced that France could not annex the Rhineland, began to think about annexing the tiny but coal-rich basin of the Saar.

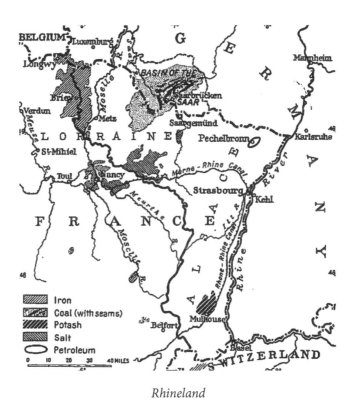

Rhineland

Following the meeting, Wilson cabled Tumulty: "The Plenary Council has positively decided that the League of Nations is to be part of the Peace Treaty. There is absolutely no truth in any reports to the contrary."[5] He also telephoned Ray Stannard Baker, ordering Baker to deny reports that the peace treaty would not include the League of Nations covenant. It appears that Foreign Minister Stephen Pichon, who was not in the meeting, didn't get the word, for on March 16 he issued a statement to the effect that the League covenant would not be included in the peace treaty. Tardieu, who was in the meeting, then tried to walk it back, advising reporters that Pichon had been "misunderstood."

That evening, Wilson met with House and Lord Robert Cecil in Wilson's new home on the place des Etats-Unis. According to both House and Cecil, Wilson was inclined to leave the covenant as it was, refusing any amendments. House noted that "The President, with his usual stubbornness in such matters, desires to leave it as it is, saying that any change will be hailed in the United States as yielding to the Senate, and he believes it will lessen rather than increase the chances of ratification."[6] Cecil reported that Wilson was in a "very truculent" mood, "fiercely refusing to make any concessions to Republican senators," but that after the meeting House advised Cecil that in the end, Wilson would agree to amend the covenant.[7] As Wilson was having dinner with House and Cecil, Lloyd George was dining with friend George Riddell, musing over Wilson and Clemenceau: "Each lacks and fails to understand the other's best qualities. When Wilson talks idealism, Clemenceau wonders what he means, and, metaphorically speaking, touches his forehead, as much as to say, 'A good man, but not quite all there.'"[8]

House's prediction that Wilson would accept amendments to the covenant proved to be prescient. As Wilson was meeting with House and Cecil, President Taft was cabling Wilson, asking if he might suggest changes to the covenant. Two days later, Wilson replied that he would welcome any suggestions. What might have helped change Wilson's mind was a report in that morning's *New York Times*, quoting Republican Senator Miles Poindexter to the effect that if the unaltered League covenant was included in the peace treaty, there would be no peace treaty, for the Senate would reject it. Taft immediately cabled back his suggested changes, including an explicit reservation for the Monroe Doctrine, a provision permitting a nation to leave the League, a requirement that the Executive Council and the Body of Delegates act unanimously, and a provision exempting purely "domestic" issues from the League's purview, thus prohibiting the League from discussing immigration or tariff issues.[9] That evening, Wilson dined with House, Cecil and legal advisor David Hunter Miller, and agreed to the changes. That afternoon, Baron Makino and Viscount Chinda visited House, advising him that they planned to re-introduce their amendment for racial equality. When Wilson, House, Cecil and Miller met, they agreed that even a provision for religious equality could never be included, Miller pointing out that in Great Britain, a Catholic was barred from acceding to the Crown. Their concern was for the proposed Monroe Doctrine amendment, the fear being that it would spark a similar insistence on the part of the Japanese to include a reference to their sphere of influence in Asia. In the end, the Japanese acceded without comment to all of Taft's proposed changes. They were waiting.

The Armistice had been signed on November 11 of the previous year, but the war was not over. Allied troops still occupied the Rhineland, the blockade had not been lifted, European industry was disabled, and famine gripped the continent. There was a general strike in Berlin in the first week of March, with labor unrest marked by rioting and violence throughout Germany. But it was in Hungary, not Germany, where the second domino fell: On March 21, Hungary succumbed to Bolshevism in the form of the "Hungarian Soviet Republic." Bela Kun, recently returned from Soviet Russia, was named "People's Commissar for Foreign Affairs," but he was the real leader of the revolution. The real fear among the Allies was that social democrats in other European countries would align themselves with the Bolsheviks, as they had done in Hungary to bring Bela Kun to power. With the prospect of Bolshevism spreading throughout Europe, everyone in Paris now felt pressure to get the peace treaties signed, lest the war that had been won at such enormous cost be lost to the Bolsheviks. The first two months had seemingly been lost in endless commissions, committees, the ineffectual Council of Ten, Wilson's and Lloyd George's absences and the attempt on Clemenceau's life. House now confided in his diary: "[S]ince the world is crumbling about us it is necessary to act with celerity commensurate with the dangers that confront us."[10] But there were so many unresolved issues: reparations, the Rhineland, Germany's eastern borders, Italy's borders, the German "war guilt," among the seemingly most pressing, all of which had to be addressed and resolved before the Germans (and then the Austrians, Bulgarians and Turks) could be called in and presented with the peace treaties.

It was just at this moment that David Lloyd George decided that he needed to go off to think.

On Friday, March 21—the day that Hungary succumbed to the Bolsheviks—Lloyd George told George Riddell that he was going off to Fontainebleau for the weekend, "and I mean to put in the hardest forty-eight hours' thinking I have ever done. The Conference is not going well, and I must try to pull things together."[11] He took with him his faithful aide, Sir Maurice Hankey, his secretary, Philip Kerr, and Gen. Henry Wilson. They arrived on Saturday afternoon, and, to disguise their conference as a pleasure trip, they first visited the Fontainebleau Palace and other tourist sights.[12] Then they got down to business, spreading maps over their sitting room. Lloyd George then assigned them roles they were to play, Hankey as the "average Englishman," Wilson as a German officer and then as a French woman. Lloyd George gave them thirty minutes to gather their thoughts before they presented their views. Gen. Wilson, according to Hankey, filled his assigned roles with great gusto, wearing his hat back to front to appear as a German officer, skillfully blending pathos and humor as the average French woman.[13] In that role, as the real source of French public opinion, pleading for all of the widows, he argued for full payment of all of France's war costs and punishment of the guilty. Lloyd George then offered his views, and Philip Kerr then spent most of Sunday writing what was modestly titled "Some Considerations for the Peace Conference Before They Finally Draft Their Terms," but which became known as the "Fontainebleau Memorandum." Considering the speed in which it was conceived and drafted, it is an extraordinary document. It could have been written by Woodrow Wilson himself, for it assured that on most, but not all, of the issues they would soon confront, the British delegation would align itself with the Americans, and not with the French, in opposing a "Carthaginian" peace.

The Memorandum began: "When nations are exhausted by wars in which they have put forth their strength and which leave them tired, bleeding and broken, it is not difficult to patch up a peace that may last until the generation which experienced the horrors of the war has passed away....What is difficult, however, is to draw up a peace which will not provoke a fresh struggle when those who have had practical experience of what that war means have passed away....The peace of 1871 was believed by Germany to ensure not only her security but her permanent supremacy. The facts have shown exactly the contrary. France itself has demonstrated that those who say you can make Germany so feeble that she will never be able to hit back are utterly wrong. Year by year France became numerically weaker in comparison with her victorious neighbor, but in reality she became ever more powerful."[14] Then, presciently predicting Europe's future: "You may strip Germany of her colonies, reduce her armaments to a mere police force and her navy to that of a fifth-rate power, all the same in the end if she feels that if she has been unjustly treated in the peace of 1919 she will find means of exacting retribution from her conquerors."[15] In his Senate speech in 1911, Clemenceau had predicted that the age-old conflict between France and Germany would end only when there was a victor greater than his conquest, a conqueror who treated the defeated with magnanimity. Lloyd George now echoed those words: "The maintenance of peace will then depend on there being no causes of exasperation constantly stirring up the spirit of patriotism, of justice or of fair play."[16]

He then got down to specifics. "I am, therefore, strongly averse to transferring more Germans from German rule to the rule of some other nation than can possibly be helped."[17] With respect to reparations, "the duration for the payments...ought to disappear if possible with the generation which made the war."[18] The Allies should "open to her the raw materials and markets of the world on equal terms with ourselves...to enable the German people to get upon their legs again. We cannot both cripple her and expect her to pay."[19] He proposed that disarmament be mutual: "To my mind it is idle to endeavor to impose a permanent limitation on armaments upon Germany unless we are prepared similarly to impose a limitation upon ourselves."[20] He wanted the Rhineland to be demilitarized, its citizens prohibited from bearing arms or receiving military training, but he opposed a Rhenish state or permanent occupation. He pressed for Germany's admission to the League of Nations as soon as she had a stable government, as an inducement to resist Bolshevism: "Might it not be safer that she should be inside the League than she should be outside it?"[21] He warned against a naval arms race among the leading naval powers, and that "not only Germany, but all the smaller states of Europe undertake to limit their armaments and abolish conscription...."[22] "Finally, I believe that until the authority and effectiveness of the League of Nations has been demonstrated, the British Empire and the United States ought to give France a guarantee against the possibility of a new German aggression."[23] He summarized the positions he would take: "From every point of view, therefore, it seems to me that we ought to endeavor to draw up a peace settlement as if we were impartial arbiters, forgetful of the passions of the war. First of all it must do justice to the Allies by taking into account Germany's responsibility for the origins of the war and for the way in which it was fought. Secondly, it must be a settlement which a responsible German government can sign in the belief that it can fulfill the obligations it incurs. Thirdly, it must be a settlement which will contain in itself no provocations for future wars, and which will constitute an alternative to Bolshevism, because it will commend itself to all reasonable opinion as a fair settlement of the European problem."[24]

According to Frances Stevenson, Lloyd George "arrived back from Fontainebleau with his plans all made. He means business this week and will sweep all before him."[25] He sent the Memorandum to its intended audience, Wilson, Orlando and, principally, Clemenceau. He did not send it to the press. Clemenceau responded immediately, and, as expected, he was indignant. His riposte was clever. He noted that all of the exactions that had been imposed upon the Germans, stripping her of her colonies and seizing her naval and commercial fleets, had redounded to the benefit of the British Empire, but none had benefitted France, and if Lloyd George wished to appease the Germans, he should do so with some of the benefits he and his Dominions had obtained. "[I]t would be an injustice," Clemenceau noted ruefully, "to impose the burden of these compensations upon those of the Allies who have felt the weight of the war the most heavily."[26]

Point XIII of the Fourteen Points provided: "An independent Polish state should be erected which should include the territories inhabited by indisputably Polish populations, which should be assured a free and secure access to the sea..." As with

all of the Fourteen Points, Germany had acquiesced to this provision in order to
gain the Armistice. It is unclear if Wilson realized that creating a state "inhabited by
indisputably Polish populations" while assuring "free and secure access to the sea"
might be contradictory, but the contradiction soon manifested itself. On March 19,
Jules Cambon, 74, the French career diplomat who headed the Polish Commission,
reported to the Allies, then still meeting as the Council of Ten, that Poland's outlet
to the sea should be the Baltic port of Danzig, which prior to the end of the war had
been a part of East Prussia. In order to connect Danzig to Warsaw and the rest of
Poland, Cambon's commission proposed a "corridor" that ran along the Vistula that
included two railways. The justification for the corridor was that this outlet to the sea
was essential for the new nation's economic survival.

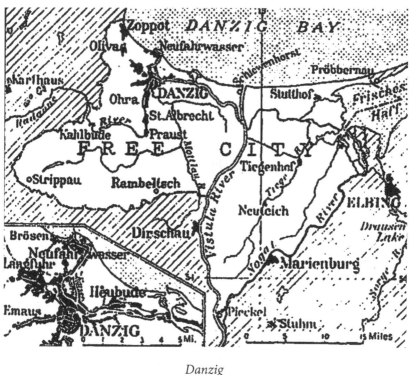

Danzig

Lloyd George immediately objected. He pointed out that Poland with the corridor
would contain two million Germans, that there were 412,000 Germans in Danzig alone,
that Danzig was, in fact, a German city, and that handing over these Germans "to a
distasteful allegiance merely because of a railway" was a mistake, creating a "Germania

irredenta" and the seed for a future war."[27] He conceded that Poland should have an outlet to the sea, but one that would include fewer Germans, arguing that the "human," i.e. ethnic, considerations should outweigh the economic or the strategic. Wilson conceded that two million Germans within Poland would violate the self-determination principle, and that the desire to rescue their fellow Germans from Polish rule might be hard to resist, but he noted that Poland having an access to the sea was one of the Fourteen Points to which the Germans had readily agreed. Clemenceau remained silent throughout. What strengthened Poland weakened Germany; his sentiments were entirely with the Poles. At Wilson's suggestion, the Council of Ten did what it always did: it referred the matter back to the Commission for further study. Jules Cambon reported back three days later, but with the same plan.

Germany's western and eastern borders and reparations were pressing issues that needed to be addressed before the treaty with the Germans could be finalized, and Italy's borders before the Austrian treaty could be signed. But first Wilson, who had instructed his fellow commissioners that not a single word of the League covenant could be changed in his absence, now needed to reconvene the League of Nations Commission to do just that, lest the League and the peace treaty fail in the Senate. The Commission met again in the afternoon of March 22, and fulfilled one of the Republican senators' demands, enacting a provision that the Executive Council and the Body of Delegates of the League had to act unanimously, if at all. But translator Stephen Bonsal detected a changed attitude on the part of the other delegates, who now realized that Wilson had been weakened during his absence. Bonsal predicted that the British would press harder for naval concessions, the French would dig in their heels on the Rhine and the Italians for the territories promised to them by the Treaty of London.

When House met with Wilson on March 24, he advised Wilson that the issues of reparations, France's security and Italy's borders needed to be addressed quickly, adding that Wilson should finally announce that the League of Nations would be part of the peace treaty, and without it the Americans would go home. He also advised Wilson to scrap the Council of Ten. Instead, he urged, Clemenceau, Lloyd George, Orlando and he should, if need be, meet in continuous session, with their fifth ally, the Japanese, being called in only when matters concerned them directly. According to House, Wilson readily agreed.[28] It was the beginning of the Council of Four. Later, Wilson met with legal advisor David Hunter Miller. Wilson handed him drafts of three proposed amendments to the League covenant that Wilson had typed on his Hammond typewriter. All three were amendments proposed by Taft, one dealing with the Monroe Doctrine, another exempting purely domestic issues from the purview of the League and a third giving any member of the League the right to quit the League upon one year's notice, but only after ten years after the formation of the League. Miller considered them poorly drafted, and reworded them.

The League Commission met on March 24, 25 and 26, hammering out the amendments that Taft had suggested and that the Senate Republicans demanded. Léon Bourgeois renewed his appeal for an international general staff, which was once again rejected. An amendment allowing a nation to withdraw from the League upon two years' notice was adopted, Wilson advising his fellow commissioners that without it Senate ratification was doubtful. An amendment to exclude strictly "domestic" matters was adopted, to mollify Senate Republicans who feared that the League might involve itself in immigration and tariff matters. The covenant was further amended to permit the covenant itself to be amended by a majority vote. The "Executive Council" became simply the "Council," and the "Body of Delegates" was changed to the "Assembly." With these amendments put to bed, only an amendment specifically excluding the Monroe Doctrine remained on Wilson's checklist. Joseph Tumulty, Wilson's faithful secretary and ear to the ground, cabled Wilson that the failure to include a Monroe Doctrine amendment in the covenant would kill the League.[29]

Sir William Wiseman, House's liaison to the British delegation, drafted a Monroe Doctrine amendment. Arthur Balfour approved it. He showed it to David Hunter Miller, who tweaked it slightly into its final form: "Nothing in this Covenant shall be deemed to affect any international engagement or understanding for securing the peace of the world such as the Monroe Doctrine."[30] But it suddenly appeared that there was one man in the British delegation opposed to any Monroe Doctrine amendment—David Lloyd George. According to Miller, there were only two matters that Cecil needed to refer to Lloyd George, being Japan's push for racial equality and the Monroe Doctrine. In all other matters, Cecil was on his own.[31] When Cecil met with Balfour, he advised Cecil that the matter was out of his hands, and that he should speak to Lloyd George directly. Lloyd George informed Cecil that he could not agree to the inclusion of a Monroe Doctrine amendment for two reasons, the first being that it would appear as a further concession to the Americans and difficult to sell to the British public, and the second that a provision dealing with only one part of the world was antithetical to the covenant, which, ironically, was the same objection Wilson himself had voiced. But on April 7, Lloyd George informed House that he could not agree to a Monroe Doctrine amendment unless the United States and Great Britain first came to an agreement on *naval armaments*!

So there it was. Lloyd George, knowing full well that Wilson needed the Monroe Doctrine amendment to get the covenant through the Senate, and pleased that he had already collected a pocketful of "sovereigns," decided to try to squeeze another out of Wilson's difficulty. The following day, in a letter to Lloyd George approved in advance by Wilson, House confirmed that Lloyd George would not consent to a Monroe Doctrine amendment "without first coming to an agreement with the United States regarding our naval building program," adding the obvious: "I cannot see what connection the two matters have." He warned that the failure to include the amendment might result in the Senate rejecting the covenant.[32] As ever, House sought to forge a compromise. In a letter Cecil sent to House—at House's suggestion—Cecil asked: "Would it be possible, for instance, for you to say that once the Treaty of Peace containing the League of Nations has been signed you would abandon or modify your naval programme. I am sure the British Government would be only too ready to give corresponding assurances."[33]

In the end, Lloyd George did not collect his "sovereign." House advised him that American naval construction was a matter for Congress, and that funds for naval construction had already been appropriated. He called what had always been a bluff, advising Lloyd George that Wilson would proceed to push a Monroe Doctrine amendment through the League Commission, and that Lloyd George could kill the League if he wished. In the end, Lloyd George consented to the Monroe Doctrine amendment.

But getting the amendment through caused Wilson some acute embarrassment. The French, like Lloyd George, cared little about the Monroe Doctrine, and, like Lloyd George, were prepared to bargain for what they did care about, an international general staff. At the April 10 meeting of the League commission, Prof. Larnaude, the dean of the Sorbonne law faculty, led off: "Before accepting this amendment, I should like very much to have clear definition of what the Monroe Doctrine is." Mr. Reis, Portugal's delegate, then chimed in: "My difficulty in approving this amendment is that I find no text of the Doctrine which is referred to. I, therefore, cannot commit my home government to an approval of something which is vague and unspecified."[34] There is, of course, no "text" of the Monroe Doctrine. "All of us are glad that America decided to come to Europe and participate in this war," he added, "nevertheless, that action of hers would seem to be rather contradictory to the Monroe Doctrine." To which Wilson confessed: "When I was in America my colleagues asked whether the acceptance of the Covenant by America would destroy the principles of the Monroe Doctrine. I replied that it was nothing but a confirmation and extension of the Monroe Doctrine, and explained to them why this is so. They then asked me if this were so, whether there would be any objection to making a specific statement to that effect in the text. It is by way of concession to this reasonable request that I am asking the Commission to state definitely something which is implicitly taken care of."[35] To which Prof. Larnaude replied: "It seems unnecessary to make a specific mention of the Monroe Doctrine. And it seems very much out of harmony with the rest of the document, since it is the only reference in the document to a particular country....Article 20 provides that all of the States which enter the League are bound to make their international engagements conform to the spirit of the League. If they are not inconsistent, they can stand. If, therefore, there is nothing in the Monroe Doctrine inconsistent with the covenant, it will not be affected."[36] Afterwards, House wrote in his diary: "It seems the irony of fate that France, who has more at stake in the League of Nations than any other country, should have tried to keep us from putting in a clause which will practically make certain the acceptance of the League by the American people and the Senate. Of all the stupid performances I have ever witnessed, this was the worst."[37]

The following day—April 15—the Commission finally approved the Monroe Doctrine amendment. But Wilson was not quite done. Toward the end of the meeting, Japan's Baron Makino and Viscount Chinda proposed to amend the *preamble* of the covenant, to the effect that the purpose of the League was to promote "international co-operation…by the prescription of open, just and honorable relations between nations *by the endorsement of the principle of equality of nations and the just treatment of their nationals…*"[38] This was their "racial equality" amendment, in much watered-down form. They insisted that this rather anodyne change to the preamble was in no way intended to affect any nation's immigration policy. Lord Robert Cecil, who personally had no objection, was forced to admit that he was under instructions from his government to oppose the change. House, seated to Wilson's left, passed Wilson a note: "The trouble is that if this Commission should pass it, it would surely raise the race issue throughout the world." Wilson then spoke at length against the Japanese amendment: "Gentlemen, it seems to me that it is wisest that we should be perfectly candid with one another.... The trouble is that not one of us wishes to deny the equality of nations or wishes to deny the principle of just treatment of nationals of any nation. The trouble is not with our decision here, but with the discussions which would certainly be raised in the Plenary Council if the words suggested were introduced into this Covenant."[39] He was making a backhanded reference to Australia's Billy Hughes, who had threatened to oppose any racial equality amendment. Wilson added: "How can you treat on its merits in this quiet room a question which will not be treated on its merits when it gets out of this room?" He was again referring to Hughes, who had threatened to campaign against such an amendment in the western United States.

In the end, Japan's amendment was defeated. More delegates supported the amendment than opposed it, but Wilson ruled that unanimity was required. The League of Nations covenant could now go to the Plenary Session for approval. But the Japanese knew they had been defeated by Great Britain's support for Australia's policy of racial exclusion. They would be heard from again.

The Council of Four met for the first time on March 25, the day that Lloyd George finalized the Fontainebleau Memorandum. They would meet almost continuously until June 28, usually in the morning and again in the afternoon, seated in a semi-circle around the hearth in Wilson's study in the place des Etats-Unis. Although termed the "Council of Four," they did not meet alone. Claimants, experts and their ministers were called in as needed. As Orlando spoke no English, but was fluent in French, Prof. Paul Mantoux volunteered himself to translate. He did not keep a shorthand record, but instead kept detailed notes, afterwards dictating his record of that day's proceedings to a Foreign Ministry secretary. His notes and extraordinary memory resulted in an almost-verbatim transcript, which survived the Second World War in the basement of the Sorbonne faculty of law, hidden by him as he fled Paris for the south of France. Later in the conference, Sir Maurice Hankey was brought in, who kept a more official but less detailed account of their deliberations.

In their first meeting, Clemenceau raised an interesting point, one occasioned by Wilson's insistence that the League covenant be included in the peace treaty. Since there could obviously be no peace treaty unless the Germans signed it, and since no one contemplated the Germans being offered initial membership in the League, could the treaty provisions related to the League be included in the treaty? Wilson assured Clemenceau that they could. Lloyd George added that he hoped to see the Germans in the League as quickly as possible: "That would give us a stronger hold over them."[40]

That day, they received the report of the reparations committee they had appointed, consisting of Edwin Montagu, Norman H. Davis and Louis Loucheur. They did not recommend any fixed sum, opting instead for a permanent commission to oversee reparations payments, one that had the authority to modify the required annual payments. In early March, Lloyd George had met with Montagu, who advised Lloyd George to accept the opinion of the American experts, that the Germans be required to pay $30 billion, half of which would be payable in German currency, effectively cutting the debt in half. Lloyd George tentatively agreed. His concurrence lasted all of two days, buckling under to his reparations hawks, Lords Cunliffe and Sumner, who pressed for double the Americans' recommendations. This highlighted the split not only within the British delegation and the split between the Americans at one extreme and the French on the other, but the split within Lloyd George himself. He realized that both "squeezing the German lemon" and hoping to recover reparations from a prostrate Germany was impossible, a truism he dared not express to his own Tory backbenchers and an aroused electorate. At the same time, House advised Balfour that it would be best for Lloyd George to admit to the British public that Germany was bankrupt, and to accept the lower amount, and if the Allies insisted on a higher amount, they would have to build up Germany's economy sufficient to make Germany a serious—if not dominant—trading competitor.[41] But Sir William Wiseman advised House that Lloyd George was worried both as to the amount and as how to satisfy the British public. House also suggested setting $30 billion as the maximum bill, with a permanent commission authorized to determine Germany's annual payment. But the French adamantly opposed naming any fixed sum, and Lloyd George supported the French.

That is where matters stood when they addressed the matter on March 26, five days after the Bolsheviks seized power in Hungary. On that day, they received a very pointed letter from Gen. Smuts: "I am seriously afraid that the peace to which we are working is an impossible peace, conceived on the wrong basis....We cannot destroy Germany without destroying Europe...My fear is that the Paris Conference may prove to be one the historic failures of the world; that the statesmen connected with it will return to their countries broken, discredited men, and the Bolsheviks will reap where they have sown."[42] His letter formed the basis of the extended debate that ensued. Lloyd George began: "If the German leaders conclude that it is best for them to imitate Hungary and ally themselves with the Bolsheviks, if they prefer to risk several years of anarchy to thirty-five years of servitude, what will we do? Areas such as Danzig and Silesia can be occupied militarily, but as for money, how will we make them pay?"[43] Wilson echoed him: "We can say: we will occupy Danzig, but we can't militarily occupy fifty billion dollars. Besides, Germany could pay very large sums only by taking an even larger share of world markets than before the war."[44] Lloyd George neatly summarized his own predicament: "Four hundred members of the British Parliament have sworn to extract from Germany the very last penny to which we are entitled; I will have to face them. But our duty is to serve our country in the best possible way. If I am defeated because I did not do the impossible, my successor, whoever that might be, won't be able to do better....I am convinced the Germans won't sign the proposals we envisage. In their place, I wouldn't sign them. Germany will go over to Bolshevism. Europe will remain mobilized, our industries will be halted, our states will go bankrupt; it will be said rightly that we are to blame because we were unable to make peace. We must decide to act wisely..."[45]

They debated reparations intermittently for the next two weeks. Referring to the Fontainebleau Memorandum, Wilson, addressing Clemenceau, said he hoped Clemenceau would agree with the moderation principle Lloyd George had espoused in it: "We don't wish to destroy Germany, nor could we do so; our greatest error would be to give her powerful reasons for wishing one day to take revenge. Excessive demands must certainly sow the seed of war."[46] Clemenceau responded that he agreed, in principle: "We must not abuse our victory; we must treat peoples with consideration and fear provoking a surge of national consciousness."[47] But he doubted that the Germans would refuse to sign the treaty. "We must be aware of possible dangers, but, after having obtained victory at the price of so many sacrifices, we must also assure ourselves of the fruits."[48] He reminded Wilson of his first meeting with Lloyd George, in Karlsbad in 1908: "I conveyed to him my uneasiness over the future of Europe, and I mentioned the German threat. Mr. Lloyd George hoped that Germany would be wise; unfortunately, he has had his eyes opened....The Germans are a servile people who need force to support an argument...We must do everything we can to be just towards the Germans, but as far as persuading them that we are just towards them, that is another matter."[49] Addressing himself directly to Wilson: "My principles are your own; I am only arguing about their application...don't believe that the principles of justice which satisfy us will also satisfy the Germans. I know them; I have forced myself to go to Germany nearly every year since 1871. I wanted to know the Germans, and, at certain times, I hoped that mutual understanding could be reached between our two peoples. I can tell you that their idea of justice is not our own....I implore you to understand my state of mind about this, just as I am making an effort to understand yours. America is far away, protected by the ocean. Not even Napoleon could touch England. You are both sheltered; we are not."[50]

They also had to deal with another reparations issue, one that did not touch the Germans directly but which had to be dealt with: how to divide the reparations payments among the Allies. It having been settled that "war costs" were off the table and that reparations would be limited to actual damages, the lion's share of reparations would go to France, the nation that had been damaged the most. Lloyd George suggested that reparations be divided 50% to France, 30% to Great Britain and 20% to all others. Louis Loucheur protested, demanding 58%, averring that "no French government could go further than that without being repudiated,"[51] but in the same meeting saying he would settle for 55%. Another issue was the extent to which Germany should be held responsible for Italy's losses, which had been caused principally by Austria-Hungary, a debtor that no longer existed. Yet another issue was whether a nation's actual damages would include pensions and separation allowances. Lloyd George was insistent that they be included, for without them Great Britain would receive little and Australia and the other Dominions nothing. Still another issue was whether Belgium should receive a preference with respect to reparations payments, in light of it having been invaded in breach of its pledge of neutrality. Wilson favored it; Lloyd George was opposed.

Two days later, on March 28, Clemenceau's finance minister, Louis-Lucien Klotz, proposed a plan that called for an initial down payment, with the final sum to be determined by a permanent commission. Lloyd George heartily concurred, noting that any fixed sum would result in both the British and French electorates screaming that the sum was too small. "If our parliaments should disapprove because we haven't asked enough, what will happen to the governments which succeed us in attempting the impossible?"[52] Only Wilson opposed not naming a fixed sum.

Wilson met with his principal reparations advisors, Vance McCormick, Bernard Baruch, Thomas Lamont, Norman H. Davis and John Foster Dulles prior to the April 1 meeting of the Council of Four. They agreed that a permanent commission would be established to determine –- not later than December 31, 1921—the amount of Germany's liability, the categories of liability, and Germany's ability to pay, the payments to run for not more than thirty years, with the commission empowered to modify the annual payments, McCormick noting in his diary that this would "relieve Great Britain and France from their troubles of making public the small amount they are to get from reparations because both Prime Ministers believe their government will be overthrown if the facts are known," adding "I am afraid this camouflage will not work but it may, as the people forget so easily."[53] They then had to confront Lloyd George's insistence that pensions and separation allowances be included in the definition of "damage to the civilian population," which was the basis on which Germany had surrendered. John Foster Dulles pointed out that including these payments was "illogical," but Wilson countered by saying he did not feel bound by considerations of logic.[54] Pensions and separation allowances would be included as a category of reparations. When the Council of Four met later that afternoon, Louis Loucheur advised them that whereas the British and the Americans might be in agreement on the reparations formula, the French were not, but he hoped to bring their conclusions to the table the following day. He did not.

The following day, a revolt of Tory MP's broke out in the House of Commons. One backbencher expressed the hope that on the matter of reparations, Britain was not "truckling to America," noting that President Wilson "was able to bear the financial embarrassments of every country but his own." Another said that he had been elected in order to support Lloyd George's demand that Germany "pay the bill," and that he would have to resign if the promise were not kept. Yet another asked if the government was sticking to its election pledge, "or is Paris today dealing with a new idea of being kind and moderate in the demand to be made upon the enemy countries?" And still another posed the question of what Germany would have done to Great Britain had Germany won the war? Answering his own question: "She would have left us without a shirt to our back."[55]

The next round of debate on reparations came on April 5, again in Wilson's study but without Wilson, who had caught the flu, which delighted Clemenceau. "He is *worse* today," Clemenceau told Lloyd George, gleefully. "Do you know his doctor? Couldn't you get round and bribe him?"[56] House filled in, shuttling in and out of Wilson's bedroom. The French were unwilling to fix any time limit for the payment of reparations, even over thirty years. Lloyd George, who in the Fontainebleau Memorandum had posited that reparations should not extent beyond the generation that had fought the war, now bowed to public pressure and sided with the French, against any time limit on reparations, and against naming a fixed sum in the treaty. Clemenceau also insisted that Germany's obligations should be based on what the permanent reparations committee determined what was owed, not on Germany's capacity to pay. In the end, it was determined that no fixed amount would be named in the treaty, but would be fixed by the permanent commission by 1921, an amount the commission could not later reduce. No time limit would be placed on reparations. After the meeting, McCormick confided in his diary: "I am thoroughly disgusted with the Allies' selfishness…afraid to tell their people they cannot get from them what they promised them at election time. I feel more discouraged today than at any time since I came over."[57] But Lloyd George was not discouraged; he was very pleased. "We are making headway," he told Frances Stevenson, "which means I am getting my own way."[58]

If Lloyd George was pleased, Lord Robert Cecil was not. In a memo to House, Cecil suggested that Wilson cut the Gordian knot by presenting the Council of Four with a draft treaty based on the Fourteen Points, telling them to take it or leave it, and that Wilson should leave if they rejected the offer. But Cecil's proposal was based on the United States canceling the Allies' debts, something Wilson was dead set against.[59] House acted on Cecil's suggestion. He recommended to Wilson that if no agreement was reached by the end of the following week on all matters, Wilson should make a statement as to what he wanted in a peace treaty, and unless the Allies agreed he would go home and let them make whatever peace they could.[60]

Wilson concurred, and on the following day, April 6—a Sunday—he summoned his commissioners. He told them that if sufficient progress was not made within the next few days, which he defined as a peace based on the Fourteen Points, he would either go home or insist that further deliberations be conducted in the open, i.e. before the Plenary

Session.[61] But Wilson did finally agree to the substance of the reparations provisions they had hammered out the previous day, all of the concessions notwithstanding.

The next day, Wilson secretly ordered the *George Washington* to sail for Brest. The order leaked so quickly that it was reported on the front page of the *New York Times* the following morning, even before the Navy had officially received the order. Sending for his ship was widely seen as a warning that Wilson meant business.

The issue closest to Clemenceau's heart, that of France's boundary with Germany, proved to be one of the easiest to solve. On March 20, House drafted and presented to Clemenceau a proposed compromise. In exchange for a joint Anglo-American guarantee against German aggression, Clemenceau would drop the idea of a separate Rhenish state. Instead, the entire Left Bank of the Rhine and a fifty-mile zone on the right bank would be demilitarized, i.e. the Germans could not bear arms or receive military training in the demilitarized zone, with the Allies occupying the Left Bank. On March 27, Clemenceau, Wilson and Lloyd George forged the agreement. Clemenceau insisted that the joint guarantee against German aggression be defined to include as any German incursion into the fifty-mile zone. Clemenceau pressed for the joint guarantee being written into the peace treaty, but Wilson objected, on the ground that the peace treaty should not mention the security needs of any particular nation. Wilson wrote, signed and handed to Clemenceau the following note: "In addition to the securities offered in the Treaty of Peace, the President of the United States has pledged himself to propose to the Senate of the United States and the Prime Minister of Great Britain has pledged himself to propose to the Parliament of Great Britain an engagement, subject to the approval of the Council of the League of Nations, to come immediately to the assistance of France in case of unprovoked attack by Germany."[62] Clemenceau wanted the United States and Great Britain to jointly occupy the Left Bank along with France. Lloyd George said that that would be impossible if it meant conscription. Clemenceau said he would settle for a British battalion, as long as the British planted their flag on the Left Bank.

In giving up on a separate Rhenish state, Clemenceau gave up on something he had long known he could never have. He knew it, but Ferdinand Foch did not, who kept pressing for it, and Clemenceau allowed him to keep pressing. Years later, Clemenceau confided to his secretary, Jean Martet, that the push for a separate Rhenish state was "a little fiction to keep Foch happy."[63]

The Anglo-American guarantee was an extraordinary act both for the United States and for Great Britain. For the British, it spelled the end of their age-old policy of "splendid isolation" vis-à-vis the continent of Europe. It also represented the one thing President Washington warned against in his Farewell Address—*permanent* alliances. Indeed, members of the American delegation were concerned that the Senate would never agree to it. Their concerns proved well-founded.

There was a small corner of the Rhineland that proved infinitely more difficult to resolve—the Saar basin–and before it was resolved it almost caused the peace conference to collapse.

Following Napoleon's defeat, the Council of Vienna first awarded the Saar to France in 1814, then reversed itself and in 1815 awarded part to Prussia and part to Bavaria. Napoleon III invaded it in 1870, and quickly lost it. By 1914, it was thoroughly German, but its coal was essential for the Lorraine steel mills. In order to compensate France for the wanton destruction of France's northern coal mines by the retreating Germans, the Allies agreed that part of the Saar's coal should go to France as reparations. The issue thus became how—or whether—to separate the coal from the people. Wilsons's own experts—the Inquiry—had concluded that the Saar should be made some sort of autonomous state administered by the French. Wilson rejected their advice, on the ground that turning the people of the Saar over to the French was a violation of the self-determination principle.

When the question of the Saar first came up in the Council of Four, Clemenceau announced that France had to annex the Saar outright, and would not sign the treaty without it. Wilson responded that annexation had nothing to do with France's security. Clemenceau angrily accused Wilson of being "pro-German," to which Wilson asked: "Then if France does not get what she wishes, she will refuse to act with us. In that event do you wish me to return home?" To which Clemenceau replied: "I do not wish you to go home, but I intend to do so myself." At which point he rose and left.[64]

Following Clemenceau's walkout, Wilson met with a group of his advisors. "Gentlemen, he said, "I am in trouble and I have sent for you to help me out...I do not know if I shall see M. Clemenceau again. I do not know whether he will return to the meeting this afternoon. In fact, I do not know whether the Peace Conference will continue. M. Clemenceau called me pro-German and abruptly left the room."[65]

But Clemenceau did return for the afternoon session. Wilson began by stating that he liked Germany less than anyone, and, addressing Clemenceau directly, said: "And yet you this morning told me that I should be wearing the kaiser's helmet. And why? Because I have protested against laying a taxation upon Germany that will make life so unattractive to the little children and the children yet unborn that existence would be a running sore and dreams of vengeance an obsession…One reason why France has held the sympathy of most of the world in this terrible war is because individuals and nations have remembered with indignation the terms which Germany imposed upon France after the Franco-Prussian war…I want to save France from being put in the place of Germany in the future.[66] Clemenceau then made a motion to rise from his chair. "You sit down," said Wilson, "I did nothing to interrupt you when you were speaking this morning," and Clemenceau sank back into his chair. When Wilson had finished, Clemenceau replied: "Mr. President, I want to say that you are not only a great man but that you are a good one, and I am with you."[67]

Andre Tardieu proceeded to make France's historical case for the annexation of the Saar, which would have resulted in 300,000 Germans residing within France. It was a weak case. Per usual, Lloyd George offered a compromise, one that had been mooted by the British and American experts, calling for an autonomous, self-governing Saar state, subject to ultimate French sovereignty. Wilson said he was ready to accept a compromise that did not amount to annexation and which indemnified the French for the destruction of their mines but which sent the Saar's output north—to Germany—as well as south to France. "Both can be done," Wilson said, "without annexation and without violation of our principles. We mustn't forget that these principles obligate us to Germany, towards which we took definite commitments at the time of the Armistice… let us avoid acting in a manner that would risk creating sympathies for Germany; neither let us seek to interpret our promises with a lawyer's cunning."[68] To which Lloyd George interjected, "Please allow me to protest on behalf of the lawyers," perhaps forgetting that Wilson was one himself.[69]

Clemenceau responded at length. "I will keep in mind the words and excellent intentions of President Wilson. He eliminates sentiment and memory; it is here that I have a reservation about what has just been said. The President of the United States fails to recognize the basis of human nature. The fact of war cannot be forgotten. America did not see this war at a close distance for its first three years; during this time we lost a million and a half men. We have no more manpower.…Our trials have created a profound feeling in this country about the reparation which is due us; and it isn't only a matter of material repairs; the need for moral redress is no less great.… You seek to do justice to the Germans. Don't believe they will ever forgive us; they will only seek the opportunity for revenge. Nothing will extinguish the rage of those who wanted to establish their domination over the world and who believed themselves so close to succeeding.…I am old. In a few months, I will leave political life forever. My disinterestedness is absolute. As Mr. Lloyd George said the other day, there is no finer role than to succumb in defending a just cause…I will support before Parliament whatever agreements we arrive at amongst ourselves. But here, amongst us, allow me to tell you that you will miss an opportunity to forge one more link in the chain of affection which binds France to America."[70] He went on to deprecate Wilson's self-determination principle as a chimera. "You don't want to make an exception to the principle? You will certainly be forced to do so by the facts…People who fought against each other for centuries have remained mingled as in battle. In the Balkans, you won't be able to create a Greece which contains no Bulgarians, a Serbia which contains no Albanians."

They did not resolve the issue that day—nothing was ever settled on the first attempt. They took up the issue again on April 8, after Wilson's implicit threat to go home by ordering the *George Washington* to port. Wilson refused to accede to an independent Saar state, but would agree to an autonomous state under German sovereignty, governed by a League of Nations commission, empowered to arbitrate all disputes regarding exploitation of the mines. The inhabitants would be granted a plebiscite after fifteen years to determine their fate. Wilson turned to Clemenceau: "I ask you now not to let world peace be hung up on this question of the Saar," to which Clemenceau responded, "No, but world peace requires that we first establish justice among ourselves."[71]

Two days later. they finalized the Saar agreement. Clemenceau agreed to the plebiscite after fifteen years, with the League commission overseeing the Saar during that period. The commission would have full executive and legislative power over the region, effectively suspending German sovereignty during the period, in fact if not in name. It is interesting that under the agreement, anyone in the Saar over the age of twenty was given the right to vote in local elections. This at a time when women in Great Britain could vote only at age thirty, and when millions of women in the United States could not vote at any age. Andre Tardieu later said that the man principally responsible for forging the agreement was Lloyd George.

One of Lloyd George's campaign promises was to bring the kaiser (now safely ensconced in the Netherlands) to justice, and now he sought to redeem the pledge. On April 8, the Council of Four considered the issue. Clemenceau joined Lloyd George in wanting the kaiser tried. Wilson was opposed. Orlando, disagreeing with his own commissioners, was also opposed. The first issue was whether the victorious Allies had any right to try the kaiser. "Suppose," said Lloyd George, "the kaiser alone, in peacetime, had crossed the frontier of Belgium with gun in hand and had fired on the inhabitants: the first Belgian policeman on the spot would have had the right to arrest him and to have him hanged; and because instead of doing it himself, he sent a million men into Belgium, he should go unscathed?"[72] "That's what our peoples would never understand," Clemenceau added.[73] "Perhaps it would not be understood in the United States either," Wilson said, "but I can only do what I believe is right, regardless of whether public feeling is for or against the judgment of my conscience." Wilson was opposed on the ground that there was no specific law that the kaiser had violated, and to set up a commission now would be to convict him based on an *ex post facto* law. "What I seek," he added, "is the severest lesson. I say, this is an unspeakable crime; but we didn't want to lower ourselves to the level of the criminal by abandoning principles of law, and we have treated him so as to spare him nothing of the universal contempt which should overwhelm him. We may have the right to take precautions against a political danger; but we mustn't exalt the culprit by summoning him before the highest tribunal we can conceive. The worst punishment will be that of public opinion." "Don't count on it," replied Clemenceau.[74]

Vittorio Orlando had been a law professor before entering politics. He opposed trying the kaiser on purely legal grounds: there was simply no legal basis, and no precedent, for the victors trying a defeated head of state. "[I]n my opinion, crime is essentially a violation of the domestic law of each national entity, a violation of a subject's obligation towards his sovereign. To create a different precedent is a serious thing."[75] "There is no precedent?" retorted Clemenceau, "There never is a precedent. What is a precedent? I'll tell you. A man comes: he acts—for good or evil. Out of the good he does, we create a precedent. Out of the evil he does, criminals—individuals or heads of state—create the precedent for their crimes....Our judges, who will meet in the tribunal we propose to establish, will be accustomed to applying different laws. We will ask them to unite their consciences in a concept of equity…We shall tell them: 'Seek amongst yourselves the principles upon which you must rely in order to judge the greatest crime in history.'"[76]

They had a secondary issue to consider. If they constituted a tribunal composed of judges from the five Allied powers, should their verdict be unanimous or by a majority? In the United States, unanimity was required in criminal courts; in France, a majority. Lloyd George raised the possibility of the effect on public opinion if unanimity were required and Japan, whose sovereign was considered a god, voted to acquit.

In the end, the peace treaty did include a provision calling upon the Dutch to hand over the kaiser. He was to be tried not for the violation of any criminal law, but for "a supreme offense against international morality and sanctity of treaties."[77] The Dutch refused, as the Council of Four well knew that they would. Wilhelm II was widowed and then remarried in Holland, living out his life in comfortable exile. He died in 1941.

On the following day, April 9, the Council of four effectively finalized the issue of Danzig. It was to be an autonomous state under the League of Nations. The Poles would control the port, its foreign affairs, and the railway connecting Danzig to Warsaw. Germany would have the right to use the railroad, in order to connect West to East Prussia. As with the Saar, the inhabitants would have the right to determine their fate in a plebiscite, one where the voting rights of women would be guaranteed. Arguing against the plebiscite that day was Poland's prime minister, the internationally-acclaimed pianist and composer, Ignacy Jan Paderewski, who had interrupted his concert career for the Polish cause. Paderewski made the standard argument that the population was predominantly Polish, especially if one counted the children. "Isn't that an argument in favor of a plebiscite?" asked Lloyd George.[78] Paderewski weakly replied that the people might be afraid to vote against the Germans. "Guarantees of a free vote would be assured," counseled Lloyd George, adding "What we don't want is to create an Alsace-Lorraine question in Danzig, so that Germany could assume the posture of a victim."[79]

On the evening of the eleventh, Lloyd George attended a dinner party at which Lady Nancy Astor, the American-born and soon-to-be member of Parliament, was present. He opened up on the subject of his fellow conferees. He opined that Wilson was "more sincere" than he had first thought. "He talks a lot of sentimental platitudes, but believes them. He is not a hypocrite nor a humbug. The difference between his point of view and that of old Clemenceau is marked. The old boy believes in none of Wilson's gods and does not understand them." He added that he thought that the assassination attempt had slowed Clemenceau. "Now he so often asks for twenty-four hours in which to make up his mind. Before, he made it up in twenty-four seconds. A truly wonderful person."[80]

The following morning, with the treaty provisions dealing with Germany's western and eastern boundaries, as well as the articles dealing with reparations, having been hammered into shape, and Wilson having obtained the amendments he needed to the League covenant on the previous day, the Council of Four began discussion of when to call in the Germans to present the treaty. At that point, Orlando called a halt. The treaty cannot be finalized, and the Germans cannot be called in, unless and until they dealt with the territorial rights granted to Italy under the 1915 Treaty of London that had brought Italy into the war. He announced that he would need to leave the conference by April 23 for the opening of his Parliament, and wished that the issue be resolved by then, in order to quell the pressure he was feeling on the issue. [The legislative session would be postponed; Orlando would leave for other reasons.] Just then, Lloyd George announced that he too would have to leave the conference, probably on the fourteenth or fifteenth, in order to deal with the revolt in his own coalition.

They did discuss when and to whom to publish the preliminary treaty. They agreed that the greatest secrecy was necessary, lest the Germans learn of the proposed treaty before the more than twenty other nations represented at the Peace Conference that were technically their Allies. But if the roughly fifty other plenipotentiaries were given an advanced look at the treaty—which was now expected to run to more than a hundred thousand words—it would surely leak to the Germans. They would eventually decide to provide the other delegates with a "summary" of what they had decided.

The following day, Orlando delivered a letter to Wilson. "A rapid solution of the Italian question is essential to a rapid conclusion of peace," he averred, for the Italian people were becoming anxious, having formed the impression that while "the peace conditions for France are now settled," the "Italian questions" had been intentionally neglected.[81] Wilson had promised Orlando that he would deliver to Orlando a memo setting forth his positions on the "Italian questions." Orlando now asked for it, and for a Council of Four meeting as quickly as possible to resolve the issues. That the Italian questions were being discussed last was partly his own fault; he had accepted House's advice that if he acceded to Wilson's desires with respect to the amendments to the League covenant, Wilson would be conciliatory when it came to Orlando's issues.

But the Italian questions would have to wait. On April 14 Lloyd George returned to Westminster, in order to quell the Tory uprising in the House of Commons that had been fomented, in large part, by the Northcliffe press. Two hundred thirty-three backbenchers had signed a manifesto addressed to him. "The greatest anxiety exists throughout the country at the persistent reports from Paris that the British delegates instead of formulating the complete financial claim of the Empire are merely considering what amount can be extracted from the enemy....Our constituents have always expected—and still expect—that the first action of the Peace Delegates would be, as you repeatedly stated in your election speeches, to present the bill in full, to make Germany acknowledge the debt and then to discus ways and means of obtaining payment.[82]

Lloyd George faced them on the floor of the House of Commons on the sixteenth. It was yet another brilliant Lloyd George performance. He painted for them a picture of the conditions in which he and his fellow conferees were working, the "crowded hours, long and late, because, whilst we were trying to build, we saw in many lands the foundations of society crumbling into dust, and we had to make haste." He doubted whether "any body of men with a difficult task have worked under greater difficulties—stones clattering on the roof, and crashing through the windows, and sometimes wild men screaming through the keyholes."[83] But he reserved his best for Lord Northcliffe, a man loved by few of the men who had signed the manifesto. Without mentioning Northcliffe by name, he referred to Northcliffe's "keen sense of disappointment" at not having been named as a commissioner to the Peace Conference, "however unjustified and however ridiculous the expectations may have been." The result was that Northcliffe would conclude that the world, without him, was badly run. "When a man has deluded himself, and all the people whom he ever permits to go near to him help him in the belief that he is the only man who can win the war, and he is waiting for the clamor of the multitude that is going to demand his presence there to direct the destinies of the world, and there is not a whisper, not a sound, it is rather disappointing; it is unnerving; it is upsetting."[84] When he had finished, few noticed that he had not mentioned the issue of reparations, the issue upon which their manifesto had been based. Lloyd George was back in Paris the following day.

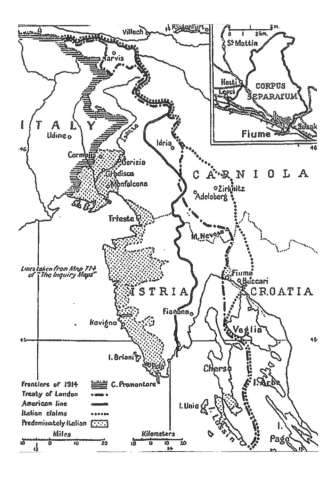

Istria

The port city of Rijeka (population 128,000) is today the third largest in Croatia. But in 1915 it was known as Fiume, a part of the Austro-Hungarian Empire. The Allies—then Great Britain, France and Russia—and desperate for help, sought to wean Italy away from its erstwhile allies, Germany and Austria-Hungary. The result was the April 26, 1915 Treaty of London. In exchange for the Italians declaring war on the Central Powers, Italy was to be awarded substantial chunks of Austria-Hungary, principally in the southern Tyrol, the Istrian peninsula and, most importantly for the Italians, the eastern shore of the Adriatic. There was no ambiguity in the Treaty; it was accompanied by a colored map. Those areas to be awarded to Italy were shaded in blue; those that were to remain in Austria-Hungary were shaded in yellow. At the insistence of the Russians, the city of Fiume was specifically excluded from the areas along the Adriatic to be awarded to Italy. Although the 25,000 Italians residing in the inner harbor constituted a majority, when one considered the entire city and its suburbs, Fiume was predominantly Slav. Hence the Russians' insistence that it not go to the Italians. To everyone's surprise, the war ended with the total collapse of Austria-Hungary. Fiume was now not within that Empire, but within the new kingdom of Serbs, Slovenes and Croats—Jugo-Slavia. The Serbs had fought heroically against the Austrians. But many Croats and Slovenes had fought against the Italians, who now viewed Croatia much as the French viewed the Germans, to be despised and feared. As part of that treaty, the Italians adopted the 1914 treaty wherein the Allies pledged not to enter into any separate peace with any of the Central Powers. The man principally responsible for the Treaty of London for the Italians was its foreign minister, Baron Sidney Sonnino. Of course, the United States was not a party to either treaty.

Shortly after the war ended, Sonnino precipitated a cabinet crisis by insisting that Italy demand Fiume and the parts of the Dalmatian coast that it had not been awarded in the Treaty of London. He was warned that the Allies would resist the claims. The shortest of Wilson's Fourteen Points was Point IX: "A readjustment of the frontiers of Italy should be effected along clearly recognizable lines of nationality." But Sonnino (and Orlando) now had cause for hope. Wilson had yielded to the French with respect to the Rhineland and to the British with respect to Germany's former colonies. He had given up on "Freedom of the Seas." It was now their turn. What they did not realize was that, having yielded so much, Wilson now chose to make a stand: at Fiume.

Wilson met with Orlando for two hours on April 14. During the meeting, Wilson read to him the memo he had promised. In it, Wilson began by saying that he felt bound by the "principles of peace" contained in he Fourteen Points and in his subsequent addresses. While the Germans had explicitly agreed to their Armistice based on the Fourteen Points, the Austrians had not. Nevertheless, averred Wilson, "I do not feel at liberty to suggest one basis for peace with Germany and another for peace with Austria."[85] He was uncompromising: "I am quite willing that Italy should be accorded along the whole length of her Northern frontier and wherever she comes into contact with Austrian territory all that was accorded her in the so-called Pact of London, but I am of the clear opinion that the Pact of London can no longer apply to the settlement of her Eastern boundaries. The line drawn in the Pact of London was conceived for the purpose of establishing an absolutely adequate frontier of safety for Italy against any possible hostility or aggression on the part of Austro-Hungary. But Austro-Hungary no longer exists."[86]

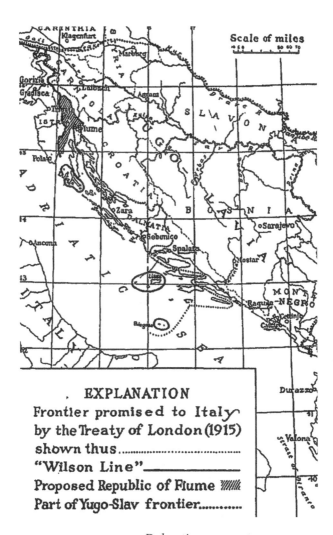

Dalmatia

So there it was. Wilson would consider Italy's security needs, but he would not recognize the Treaty of London. In doing so, Wilson placed himself at odds not only with Italy but with his own Allies, who felt honor-bound to uphold the treaty they had signed which had brought Italy into the war and which had cost it a half million lives. Indeed, the British had entered the war because Germany had violated a treaty; there was no chance they would turn their backs on one now. But on the issue of Fiume, which had not been awarded to Italy, the Allies were united. Wilson's memo continued: "There would be no justification, in my judgment, in including Fiume within the boundaries of the Italian kingdom. Fiume is by situation and by all the circumstances of its development an international port, serving the countries to the East and North of the Gulf of Fiume."[87] While he insisted that Fiume be included within the customs system of Jugo-Slavia, he was willing to make Fiume a free port. His memo concluded that in refusing Italy's claims, the Allies "will have avoided the fatal error of making Italy's nearest neighbors on the East her enemies and nursing just such a sense of injustice as has disturbed the peace of Europe for generations together and played no small part in bringing on the terrible conflict through which we have just played."[88] Wilson told Orlando that he could publish the memo, if he wished. Orlando told Wilson that the Italian troops already occupying Fiume would mutiny rather than leave, and that there would be bloodshed if the Croats tried to evict them.

Following the meeting, Wilson told Arthur Balfour that he feared that Sonnino would leave the Peace Conference, and that if Sonnino did so he felt that Orlando might feel constrained to leave as well. That might result in the Italians refusing to sign the peace treaty with Austria. It did not necessarily mean they would refuse to sign with the Germans. Wilson later confided to House that he had only once before had such an unpleasant meeting, when he was the president of Princeton and about to expel a student. The student's mother visited Wilson, pleading for Wilson to relent. She told him that she was in poor health, and that if Wilson expelled her son she would die. Wilson did, and she didn't.[89]

The following day, the Council of Four decided that on April 24, the day before they planned to present the treaty to the Germans, they would reveal the terms of the treaty to the other nations that had declared war on the Central Powers. They would do so in secret sessions to groups of three nations each. Also on that day Balfour reminded the Council of Four that there was an additional issue that still needed to be addressed, that being the Chinese province of Shantung, which the Japanese claimed by virtue of the treaty that had brought the Japanese into the war on the side of the Allies.

At the Council of Four's morning meeting of the nineteenth, Orlando got the hearing on his claims for Fiume and the Dalmatian coast for which he had been pressing. By this time, not only Wilson, but Lloyd George and Clemenceau also feared that the Italians might quit the Peace Conference if they did not get what they wanted. Orlando argued forcefully, but he did not base his claims on the Treaty of London, since under that treaty he had no claim to Fiume. His claim for the eastern Adriatic was that it was essential for Italy's defense. During the war, the Austrians had raided Italy from the Adriatic islands, and the Allies, although superior, could do little to protect the Italian coast. He argued just as forcefully for Fiume, asserting that even though the Italian enclave was small, "small people, as well as great ones, if they form a historical unit, have the same right to decide their own fate."[90] He rejected Wilson's proposal to internationalize the port, arguing that Fiume was not like Danzig, Poland's only outlet to the sea. The Jugo-Slavs, he asserted, had other ports on the southern Adriatic available to them.

Wilson countered Orlando's arguments with equal force. He had come to this meeting prepared, thoroughly briefed on the history and geography of the region. He said that Fiume was not part of the natural geography of Italy, as was the port of Trieste. The Italian population of Fiume constituted only a small island, separated from Italy. However, it was an essential port not only to Croatia but to the other nations north and east of it, who relied upon it for their trade. To unite Fiume to Italy "would be an arbitrary act so contrary to our principles that, as for myself, I could not associate myself with it."[91] With respect to Italy's security claims, he said he was "against everything that will give any great European power whatsoever a foothold in the Balkans...Intervention in Balkan domestic politics would repeat itself as in the past. That is why one of my great concerns is to keep all the great powers out of the Balkan peninsula....I believe it would be a danger to the peace of Europe if Italy insisted on establishing herself on the eastern coast of the Adriatic."[92] Italy should look to the League of Nations to preserve its security. Sonnino replied with the same argument that Clemenceau had asserted with respect to the Rhine. If Italy were attacked, the League of Nations was simply too far away to protect it.

The dispute was almost entirely between Wilson and the Italians. Lloyd George stated that the Treaty of London bound Great Britain to honor Italy's claims, pleading with Orlando not to break up the Peace Conference over 25,000 Italians in Fiume. "Great Britain stands by the treaty, but by the treaty such as it is. According to this document, Fiume must become part of Croatia. I don't see how we can consent to violate one part of the treaty whilst fully keeping the other."[93] Clemenceau echoed Lloyd George: "Italy has our word; we don't dispute it. But she also gave her word in May [sic] 1915 to leave

Fiume to the Croats. If we are upholding the treaty, let us uphold it."[94] The meeting ended with Wilson's plea: "I beg my Italian friends not to take a hasty decision, to consider everything, not to alienate their country from us and the rest of the world. In my opinion, that would be the most tragic event since the end of hostilities."[95]

The same five men met the following day—Easter Sunday. Orlando opened by reading a prepared statement that was very conciliatory. He would not leave the Peace Conference, and would abide by the Treaty of London, if Italy received what it had been granted under that treaty. This represented Lloyd George's and Clemenceau's worst nightmare; it would align them with the Italians against Wilson. There was a prolonged silence. Then Wilson spoke. "It seems unbelievable to me," Wilson began, "that the representatives of Italy should take this position." He reminded them that without the United States—which had not signed the Treaty of London—the Allies probably could not have won the war, and that when United States entered the war, "we announced the principles that would control our action." Those principles were embodied in the Fourteen Points, which provided that "Serbia was to have free and secure access to the sea and that relations amongst the Balkan states were to be established on the basis of the free will of the peoples and of historical traditions, with boundaries drawn along clearly recognizable ethnographic lines. Concerning Italy, she was to obtain boundaries which would unite her peoples of the same language and tradition."[96] He added: "If Italy declares that she insists upon the terms of the Treaty of London, she is barring the road to peace. The United States cannot associate herself with such a policy."[97] If Italy would give up on Dalmatia and Fiume, she would still have the Brenner Pass and Trieste, "she completes her unity…Five years ago, it would have been a dream whose realization would have been believed hardly possible. This dream has been realized by the valor of the Italian army and by the combined efforts of the world." Referring to Orlando's threat to leave, he added: "It would be incredible to see all that disappear in an instant. This, I declare, would be the supreme tragedy of this war. You would turn your back on your best friends, and I would deplore it profoundly. My heart would be broken; but, as the representative of the United States, having the right to speak only in its name, I have no choice in what I do. I cannot violate the principles whose establishment constitutes the very mandate which was given to me when I came to participate in these negotiations."[98] Orlando responded: "President Wilson has said with obvious sincerity that his heart is broken at the thought that we would withdraw. I thank him for that. My heart is even more broken than his."[99] Lloyd George said that "we are facing the gravest situation which has arisen since the beginning of the conference…Personally, I am not free, since I have the duty to respect the commitment taken by my country."[100] At this point, Orlando broke down. He rose, faced the window, and began to weep. Frances

Stevenson, waiting outside for Lloyd George, saw him at the window, sobbing openly, wiping his eyes an cheeks.[101] Wilson was so touched that he went to the window and shook Orlando's hand. Orlando's stress was understandable. Two days prior, he had received a telegram from the Italian Officers' and Soldiers' Union, to the effect that if he yielded, his government would be overthrown.[102] An officer attached to the Italian delegation told a reporter that this was an ultimatum, indicating that the Army was with the nation in permitting no compromise on Fiume.[103] The meeting ended with an agreement that the Council of Four would meet the following day without Wilson, to discuss Wilson's rejection of the Treaty of London.

That same day, the Japanese warned Wilson that, with the Germans soon to arrive, their dispute with China over Shantung needed to be resolved before the treaty could be signed.[104]

Some time before the Easter Sunday meeting, Wilson decided that he would go over the heads of Orlando and Sonnino and make a public plea to the Italian people, the people who had cheered him by the millions when he had toured Italy in January. On the morning of April 21 Wilson met with his fellow commissioners at the Crillon. He read them the statement, in which he rehearsed the reasons why he could not agree to the terms of the Treaty of London, and why Italy could not have Fiume. He pleaded for their understanding: "America is Italy's friend. Her people are drawn, millions strong, from Italy's own fair countrysides. She is linked in blood as well as in affection with the Italian people. Such ties can never be broken." "America," he added, "trusts Italy, and in her trust believes that Italy will ask nothing of her that cannot be made unmistakably consistent with [the] sacred obligations" upon which America entered the war.[105] Wilson was unsure if he should release the statement now or wait until there was a definite break. House advised him to consult with Clemenceau and Lloyd George.

Later that morning, Clemenceau, Lloyd George and Orlando, along with their foreign ministers, Sonnino, Balfour and Pichon, met in an attempt to extricate themselves from the box in which Wilson had placed them. Clemenceau and Lloyd George were bound by the terms of the Treaty of London if the Italians insisted on it; only if they agreed to modify its terms was there a way out. Lloyd George warned that America was essential to the recovery of Europe; they all required American credits. "All things considered," he noted, "President Wilson has in the course of these negotiations gone much further in our direction than we at first had thought possible. He has come over to our views on the question of indemnities, on the question of the Saar Basin, on many others besides."[106] To which Sonnino retorted: "America said nothing to us for five months. Now, after having made concessions right and left to legitimate interests, she wants to recover her virginity at our expense by invoking the purity of principles."[107] Orlando added: "If President Wilson's opinion prevails, there will be a revolution in Italy, don't you doubt it."[108] He said that as far back as their first meeting in January he warned Wilson that he would have to leave the conference if Wilson insisted on his own boundary line, rather than the one outlined in the Treaty of London. Balfour warned him that Italy would be bankrupted without American financial support. Orlando replied: "I acknowledge the truth of what Mr. Balfour says…We are a sober people, and we know the art of dying of hunger. The danger being equal, I prefer to stay on the side of justice and honor."[109] Nothing was solved.

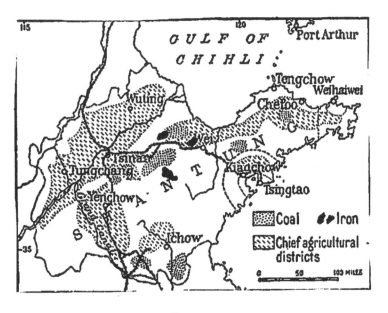

Shantung

Per usual, it fell to Lloyd George to try to forge a compromise. Later that day, he met with Wilson and Clemenceau. He suggested giving to certain islands in the Adriatic to Italy that had been earmarked for Croatia by the Treaty of London, making Fiume an international city. Wilson remarked that he had "a particular horror of paying them compensation for something which should never have belonged to them." Lloyd George replied that if Sonnino returned to Rome without having received what was promised by the Treaty of London, "he would be hanged from a lamp post."[110] Sir Maurice Hankey was dispatched to the Edouard VII Hotel, the Italians' headquarters, with the compromise. They were still meeting when Hankey returned, the Italians having rejected it. Wilson had brought his statement to the Italian people with him to the meeting, and he now proposed to publish it. They pleaded with him not to, Clemenceau arguing "If you publish it, there will be nothing doing any longer after that. When the business is dead and buried, say why, but not before."[111] Lloyd George said "It will unleash a tempest in Italy. Everything will be topsy-turvy...It would make all compromise impossible for us. It is better to say these things only when all the doors have been closed."[112] Wilson agreed to wait one more day. They agreed to advise the Italians that they would be discussing the Japanese claims the following day. The issue could wait no longer.

In 1898, Germany invaded China, the ostensible *casus belli* being the murder of two German missionaries. The result was a ninety-nine year "lease" the helpless Chinese government was forced to grant the Germans to the Shantung province port of Tsingtao, on Kiao-Chow Bay, and to the territory circumscribed by a fifty-mile radius beyond the bay. The Germans proceeded to build a railroad to the city of Tsinan, 250 miles to the west, well beyond the perimeter of their lease. They installed a civilian administration and occupied the entire province, owning it in everything but name.

When war broke out in Europe, Japan immediately declared war on Germany, and quickly expelled the Germans from China, conquering all of Shantung Province to the railhead at Tsinan. The Japanese victory in Asia was helpful to the British, for it cleared the Germans out of the Pacific, enabling the unimpeded transport of Aussie and kiwi troops to the Western front. But for the Chinese, it meant exchanging one master for another. In May, 1915, the Japanese presented the Chinese with their "Twenty-One Demands," the first of which was the transfer of all of Germany's leasehold rights in Shantung to the Japanese. Under this agreement, the Japanese did agree to ultimately restore the province to the Chinese, but it was left unclear when, and what rights Japan might retain once they had. Another of the "Demands" was a Japanese "protectorate" over all of China, this being Japan's "Asian Monroe Doctrine." With a gun to their heads (the Chinese were given forty-eight hours to decide), the Chinese agreed to the Twenty-One Demands.

In August, 1917, China declared war on Germany. In doing so, they declared all prior treaties with Germany, including the 1898 lease, to be invalid. They were now a belligerent, which in 1919 afforded China a place at the Peace Conference. Also in 1917, in an exchange of diplomatic notes, both Great Britain and France, in appreciation for Japan's prior and hoped-for continuing services, agreed to uphold Japan's accession to the German leasehold "on the occasion of the Peace Conference." Sadly for the Chinese, and again with a gun at their heads, in September 1918 they entered into a series of notes with Japan in which they ceded to Japan continuing economic rights in the province, including the right to station troops all along the Tsingtao-Tsinan railway, rights the Chinese correctly claimed were far greater than those the Germans had had under their lease. For the British and the French, they were in a similar, but not identical, box to the one they had created for themselves with respect to the Treaty of London. Their obligation to the Italians was unambiguous; not so to the Japanese. When the Council of Ten determined Japan's rights to certain islands in the northern Pacific, it ignored the question of Shantung, despite both being governed by the same 1917 series of notes between Great Britain, France and Japan. Japan's delegates, Baron Makino and Viscount Chinda, had sat almost mute throughout the Council of Ten and the League of Nations Commission. Despite being one of five Allied powers, they acceded to their exclusion from the Council of Four. They now demanded to be heard.

On April 21, the same day Wilson, Clemenceau and Lloyd George were seeking and failing to forge a compromise with the Italians, Arthur Balfour met with Viscount Chinda. Afterwards, Chinda delivered a note to Balfour. In the most emollient diplomatic language, he averred that Japan would adhere to the 1915 and 1918 agreements it had entered into with the Chinese. As to when and under what conditions Japan might return control of the province back to the Chinese, Chinda wrote: "As to how soon Kiaochow will be handed back to China, I may say that it ought not to take very much time for Japan and China to make actual arrangements for carrying out the conditions already agreed upon, and I need hardly assure you that my Government will be disposed to reach an agreement as to such actual arrangements with utmost speed upon conclusion of the Peace Treaty with Germany."[113]

The following morning, Wilson, Clemenceau and Lloyd George met with the Japanese. With the British and French bound by their commitments (at least as to whatever rights Japan had obtained from the Germans) Wilson was once again the man in the middle. He hoped that the Japanese would accept a League of Nations trusteeship over Shantung. They refused. Wilson mooted the abandonment of all foreign concessions in China (including American rights in Shanghai), but both the French and the British were opposed. Chinda was blunt. He announced that unless the peace treaty explicitly grants to Japan the rights it had acquired from the Germans, they would not sign the treaty. Wilson warned: "There are, you know, many inflammable elements in China, and we must guard against starting a fire there one day which no one could extinguish...no power in the world could restore order in a country where 400 million souls live. You know, on the other hand, what the feeling of the Chinese is regarding Shantung, to which they are attached by so many of their most ancient and sacred traditions." However, he added, "I respect all international agreements, even when I should prefer that they not be signed, and that I am not at all proposing to hold them null and void."[114]

This last sentence is nothing short of stunning. Wilson's "respect" of "all international agreements" did not extend to Italy's rights under the Treaty of London, in pursuance of which Italy had sacrificed a half million men. At least Italy could claim the presence of a few thousand Italian nationals in Fiume. Thirty-five million Chinese—and no Japanese other than as occupiers—resided in Shantung. Indeed, there was no place, not Danzig, not the Saar, not Upper Silesia, that so violated Wilson's principle of self-determination as Japan's presence in China. Yet Wilson was willing to uphold Great Britain's and France's concessions to the Japanese, despite the United States not having been a party to them, and, as with the Treaty of London, not even having been aware of them. The following day, with only Clemenceau and Lloyd George present, Wilson explained: "I realize the apparent contradiction between my stand on this question. But the difference is that Austria-Hungary has disappeared. If she still existed, I would not oppose the execution of the Treaty of London."[115] A more likely explanation is that with the Italians threatening to quit the Peace Conference, if the Japanese did so as well it might well spell the end of the League of Nations. In his post-war *Memoirs*, Lloyd George offered another explanation: "Wilson, with a nature rich and varied in animosities, cordially disliked the Italians. It was not a personal dislike of the genial Orlando or the courtly Sonnino, but he disliked them as an embodiment of the Italian policy of making war an instrument of violent appropriation of other peoples' towns and villages."[116]

The crises over Fiume and Shantung now came to a head simultaneously. Between the morning and afternoon sessions of the Council of Four, Lloyd George met with Orlando, who advised Lloyd George that he could no longer attend their meetings and, unless their demands were met, would not meet with the soon-to-be-arriving Germans. While Italy's boundaries would likely be determined in the treaty with Austria, Lloyd George deftly pointing out to him that if Italy were not present when the Germans arrived, there would be no one to present Italy's claims for German reparations.

At the afternoon session, China's foreign minister, Lou Tseng-tsiang and commissioner Wellington Koo presented China's case. Koo stressed the obvious, that China had signed the treaties with Japan under duress. "[I]f we fail to obtain justice at the conference, that can throw us into the arms of Japan....It is a question of whether we can guarantee a peace of half a century to the Far East, or if a situation will be created which can lead to war within ten years."[117] "There are serious considerations,"

Wilson countered, "But the respect for treaties by the powers which signed them is not a denial of justice…it is necessary not to confuse justice and the repudiation of treaties, even unfortunate ones."[118] Lloyd George lamented to Koo that Great Britain had to adhere to its treaty commitment: "It is impossible for us to say to the Japanese: 'We were happy to find you in time of war; but now, good-by.'"[119] As he had with the Italians, Wilson sought to convince them that China should seek its protection from the League of Nations. He also offered the Chinese a compromise: If China would accept Japan's right under the German lease, the Allies would object to Japan's greater rights under the 1918 agreement. Within a day, both the Chinese and the Japanese rejected it. After the Chinese departed, Wilson stressed to Lloyd George and Clemenceau that they must do everything possible in order to have Japan join the League.

But the Italian walkout was more pressing. The three now discussed another compromise floated by Lloyd George, to give the Italians certain islands in the Adriatic subject to plebiscites after fifteen years, with Fiume being a free city. But Wilson doubted the wisdom of floating new proposals. "Let me publish my document," he said, "that can only clear the air." "Yes, but as a storm would," replied Lloyd George.[120] They agree to let Lloyd George float his latest compromise.

They reconvened the next morning. Wilson now sought to convince Lloyd George and Clemenceau to repudiate the Treaty of London. "The Slavs have behind them the immense reservoir of the populations of Asia," he said, "whose position and destiny will be the great problem of the future. There are 800 million men there, against whom our 200 million would seem a small thing. Must we alienate half of Europe from ourselves for a strategic boundary which, in the opinion of the American experts, is of no importance?"

Lloyd George: "What matters is not one boundary or another, but the sanctity of treaties. Say, if you wish, that the Treaty of London should never have been signed… But, after all, our signature is at the bottom of that treaty."

Wilson: "I wouldn't be scandalized if I saw France and England repudiate a treaty concluded in a world situation completely changed today."

Clemenceau: "I am not inclined to do anything like that. But what I ask myself is whether the Italians, by withdrawing from the conference, are not withdrawing from the treaty."

Lloyd George: "We can tell them, 'We decided with you that Fiume should go to the Croats; if you don't accept that, the treaty no longer exists, and if you keep Fiume, you are violating the treaty.'"

Wilson: "And what will you do if they answer you: "We abandon Fiume""?

Lloyd George: "In that case, we are caught; we will have to carry out the treaty."

Wilson: "And you will be compelled to break with us."[121]

That afternoon, Wilson published his appeal to the Italian people. It appeared in the afternoon editions of the Paris newspapers, and was printed in full on the front page of the next morning's *New York Times*. Lloyd George told George Riddell: "Well, the fat is in the fire at last. It is a pity that Wilson sent out the statement so hurriedly."[122]

On the morning of the twenty-fourth, Lloyd George met with Orlando, pleading with him not to quit the Peace Conference. He acknowledged that if Orlando returned to Rome, he would be met by a surge in public opinion, but that would result in Orlando being unable to make any concessions. He warned Orlando that he could never get Fiume, and that if Italy took Fiume, it would abrogate the Treaty of London. "That," Lloyd George later told Wilson and Clemenceau, "made a great impression on him."[123] He also advised Orlando that if and when he made a public statement, he should avoid mentioning Fiume. Orlando did issue a statement, later that afternoon. He began by noting that Wilson's appeal directly to the people, over the heads of their government, was "an innovation in international discourse…which is today for the first time being used against a government which has been…a loyal friend of the Great American Republic." He rejected Wilson's argument that the collapse of the Austro-Hungarian Empire "implies a reduction of the Italian aspirations," but contrary to Lloyd George's advice, he did mention Fiume, calling it an "admirable example of a national consciousness perpetuated throughout the centuries. To deny it this right for the sole reason that it only has to do with a small community, would be to admit that the criterion of justice to world nations varies according to their territorial expansion."[124] When Lloyd George, Clemenceau and Wilson met later that morning, Wilson defended his statement: "My argument is that the circumstances which justified the treaty have completely changed since then." Clemenceau disagreed: "Unfortunately, it is impossible for me to take this point of view," as did Lloyd George: "That would mean that Italy has succeeded so well that she must not profit from her victory."[125] Wilson replied that "All I wanted to do was to inform the Italian people of my true position, in view of all that has been said by a venal press."[126] Toward the end of the meeting, they received word that Orlando and Sonnino would be returning for the afternoon meeting.

At Orlando's request, he and Sonnino came not to Wilson's residence on the place des Etats-Unis but to Lloyd George's residence, to inform Wilson, Clemenceau and Lloyd George that they were leaving Paris and the Peace Conference. They were leaving not because of their inability to agree on the territorial issues, but because of Wilson's statement. The consequence of that document, said Orlando, "is to cast doubt upon my authority as the representative of the Italian people. Such is the impression produced in Rome, and that creates a very delicate situation for me. I find it necessary to return to the sources of my authority."[127] Incredibly, Wilson responded by saying that "It was never in my mind to appeal to the Italian people over his head; if I appeared to do that, I regret it."[128]

Lloyd George was becoming desperate to achieve a compromise, again floating the idea of revising the Treaty of London by making Fiume a free city, a revision only the Italians could agree to. The Germans were scheduled to arrive the following week. Clemenceau asked: "Will Italy be represented when we meet with the Germans, or not?" "The first question the Germans will ask us," added Lloyd George, "is 'Whom do you represent?' We won't know what to reply, unless M. Orlando declares to us in writing that we can act in his name."[129] Orlando replied that it depended on what happened in Rome.[130] Wilson suggested that since the Italian territorial issues concerned only the Austrian treaty, Orlando could still sign the treaty with the Germans. Orlando replied by throwing Wilson's cherished Article X* in his face: "Italy would be obligated to guarantee the territorial integrity of other states, whilst her own boundaries would still be undetermined, and she would not be assured of what she regards as her territorial integrity."[131] And since Wilson had insisted on the League covenant being included in the peace treaty, not signing the peace treaty meant Italy not joining the League.

That evening, Orlando, Sonnino and most of the Italian delegation arrived at the Gare de Lyons. The station was filled with Italians waving the Italian tri-color. Amid cheers of "Vive Orlando" and "Vive Fiume," Orlando raised his hat, gave a faint smile, and boarded the train for home. The Council of Four was now the Council of Three. Just at that moment, Wilson received a letter from the Japanese, demanding a "definite settlement" of their claims to Shantung, "with the least possible delay."

Years later, Lloyd George wrote in his *Memoirs* about Wilson's open appeal to the Italian people. Orlando and Sonnino, he opined, regarded it as "an insult to their dignity and an offense against comradeship. They were outraged. It was not playing cricket..."[132] It begs the question why Wilson chose to do so, something so risky and ultimately foolish, in the face of Clemenceau's and Lloyd George's pleas not to do so. The answer lies in Wilson's past. Throughout his life, first as an undergraduate, then as a teacher, then as governor and finally as president, Wilson had been able to sway hundreds, then thousands, then millions by the force of his rhetoric. A man in his sixties does not suddenly unlearn the lessons of a lifetime.

---

* "The Members of the League undertake to respect and preserve as against external aggression the territorial integrity and existing political independence of all Members of the League."

The damage was immediate. There were anti-American demonstrations throughout Italy. The throngs that had welcomed Wilson only three months before now carried placards of "Down with the Americans" and "Vive Fiume." The American embassy in Rome was placed under guard. The crowds stopped and cheered before the Japanese embassy. Orlando informed the American ambassador, Thomas Nelson Page, that considering the state of popular feeling, he would not be able to sign the peace treaty. Harold Nicolson summed it up best: "The President had appealed to both his principles and to the people. And the latter gnashed their teeth at him in rage."[133]

The morning following the Italians' departure, Wilson met with Ray Stannard Baker. "They [the Japanese] are not bluffers," Wilson told him, "and they will go home unless we give them what they should not have." "The opinion of the world," replied Baker, "supports the Japanese claims." "I know that," said Wilson, adding "But if Italy remains away and Japan goes home, what becomes of the League of Nations?"[134]

Later that morning, Wilson met with Lloyd George and Clemenceau to discuss the now-urgent issue of the Japanese claims. Wilson had in hand a letter from Edward Thomas Williams, who headed the State Department's Division of Far Eastern Affairs. It was blistering. As to Japan's rights under the German lease, Williams wrote: "To claim that because Japan took Kiaochow from Germany she has any right to it is as though we were to claim from France St. Mihiel because we took it from Germany. Japan in Shantung is far more dangerous to China and to the peace of the Far East than Germany ever was." With respect to the 1915 treaty, Williams wrote that it should not be recognized at all, as it was "extorted from a peaceful and defenseless people" and was even worse than the German lease, as it would make the Japanese presence permanent. "She [Japan] does not offer to return the railway or the mines...she proposes to control the policing of the railway which Germany never attempted and she will station troops in the capital of the province, a thing Germany never did. Her offer to return Kiaochow therefore is merely an offer of the shell. She would keep the kernel."[135]

On Saturday morning, April 26, Wilson motored to the Crillon to meet with his delegation. With the Germans scheduled to arrive on Wednesday, he asked Lansing to meet with the Japanese, to offer them a League of Nations trusteeship over Shantung. They refused. Arthur Balfour also met with them that day. They advised Balfour that, for reasons of "national dignity," they would not revise the terms of any of their treaties with the Chinese. They assured him that their intention to maintain troops in the province was merely "transitory," but they refused to provide a definite timetable for their withdrawal. They further assured him that they did not intend to exclude any other nation from the port of Tsingtao.[136] The sole rights they sought to retain, they said, were *economic*, i.e. the exploitation of the Kiaochow coal mines and the ownership of the railroad.

On Monday morning, during a meeting in which the Council of Three debated how long they would give the Germans to reply to the treaty, Arthur Balfour was introduced. He announced that Baron Makino had visited him the prior evening, to advise him that the Japanese had decided that they would not join the League of Nations. Their reasons, they claimed, were twofold: "the refusal to adopt the principle of the equality of the races" and "the rejection of our claims to Kiaochow." On the latter question, the Japanese expected to be heard by that afternoon, the scheduled meeting of the Plenary Session.[137] "If not, what will they do?" asked Lloyd George. "I think they will make a protest against the refusal to accept the principle of racial equality. But if they aren't satisfied on Shantung, they could go much further," Balfour replied. Wilson asked: "Would they go so far as to withdraw from the League of Nations?" To which Balfour answered: "Not if they expect a solution acceptable to them on the Kiaochow problem."[138]

"I cannot return to America saying that I abandoned China," replied Wilson. "If the Japanese give up Kiaochow and content themselves with economic rights without any military advantage, we then would have the feeling that they are giving China better terms than the Germans did." "That is what the Japanese promise," said Balfour. "That is not quite the opinion of our experts," replied Wilson, referring to Edward Thomas Williams' memo.

It is at this exact moment that Wilson abandoned the Chinese. "What I will ask them is to be content with economic rights. Later we can propose a general renunciation of special rights for foreigners in China." Balfour agreed: "I think we can obtain assurances from the Japanese that they are content with purely economic advantages. They are prepared to give you the most explicit assurances."[139] He suggested that Wilson meet with the Japanese before the Plenary Session, scheduled for three o'clock.

Secretary Lansing never learned what Wilson said to the Japanese or they to him, but he assumed they had struck a deal. At the Plenary Session in the Foreign Ministry's ornate Salle d'Horloge, Baron Makino offered and then immediately withdrew his amendment for racial equality. It then fell to Wilson to explain to the plenipotentiaries all of the many changes that had been made to the covenant of the League of Nations. When he came to Article XXI, dealing with the Monroe Doctrine,* he could not bring himself to offer any explanation. He merely said that Article XXI was "new." There was no vote, Clemenceau simply declaring, in French, not waiting for a translation,

---

* "Nothing in this Covenant shall be deemed to affect the validity of international engagements, such as treaties or arbitration or regional understandings like the Monroe Doctrine, for securing the maintenance of peace."

that "the resolution of President Wilson with the Covenant of the League of Nations is unanimously adopted." Afterwards House commented that it had "moved with the sureness of a Texas political convention."[140]

The next day, three of Wilson's commissioners, Secretary Lansing, Henry White and Gen. Bliss, considered resigning over Wilson's cave-in. They decided against it, instead writing him a stinging letter of protest: "What moral right has Japan acquired by her conquest of Shantung assisted by the British? If Great Britain and Japan secured no moral right to sovereignty over various savages inhabiting islands in the Pacific Ocean, but, on the other hand, we held that these peoples shall be governed by mandates under the League of Nations, what moral right has Japan acquired to the suzerainty (which she would undoubtedly have) over 30,000,000 Chinese in the sacred province of Shantung?"[141] Later, Lansing told Ray Stannard Baker that Wilson should do the right thing, regardless of the consequences. "And break up the Peace Conference?" asked Baker. "Even that, if necessary," replied Lansing.[142]

The Council of Three met with Makino and Chinda the following morning. Wilson hoped to get the Japanese to renounce their 1918 treaty, but the Japanese refused, knowing they held all the cards. It now came for Wilson to try to make the best of it. The next day he issued to the press a "Statement as to the Facts as to Kiao-Chow and Shantung": "All rights in Kiao-Chow and Shantung province formerly belonging to Germany are to be transferred without reservation to Japan. Japan voluntarily engages to hand back the Shantung peninsula in full sovereignty to China, retaining only the economic privileges granted to Germany and the right to establish a settlement at Tsing-Tao. Owners of the railroads will use special police only to insure security for traffic… The Japanese military forces are to be withdrawn at the earliest possible moment.[143]

People in the West may have been fooled by this, but no one was in China. The effect was immediate. On May 4, thousands of students protested in Beijing. Milling before the Gate of Heavenly Peace, they demonstrated against foreign influence and foreign concessions. They demanded that China refuse to sign the treaty. They burned the home of an official they believed to be a Japanese collaborator. The protest spread to Shanghai, supported by local merchants. It was the beginning of the May Fourth Movement, which years later Mao Zedong credited with being an element in the radicalization of China.

On the afternoon of the twenty-ninth, just as the Germans were set to arrive, Belgium's foreign minister, Paul Hymans, appeared before the Council of Three, demanding that Belgium receive its full "war costs" as reparations. He did not threaten not to sign the peace treaty in so many words, but he did say that he would need to consult with his Parliament before he did. The Allies had agreed that Belgium was entitled to a preference in the collection of reparations as a result of its having been invaded in violation of its treaty, but the award of full "war costs" to any nation was off the table. There it stood.

As they were meeting, Orlando spoke before Italy's Chamber of Deputies. He reviewed the negotiations in the Council of Four, noting that Lloyd George and Clemenceau were willing to stand by their commitments under the Treaty of London. Wilson's memorandum of April 14, which Wilson had invited him to make public, Orlando now did for the first time. He told his audience that it was only on that date that he realized that his and Wilson's positions were irreconcilable. But he was unclear as to what he planned to do. He asked for a vote of confidence, and received it by a vote of 382-40. He then received a unanimous vote of confidence from the Italian Senate. Having achieved his mandate, Orlando declared: "Now the Italian delegation can return to Paris with increased authority to continue peace negotiations."[144]

The next day, the Germans arrived at Versailles. Jules Cambon, the elderly French diplomat, was appointed to head the delegation for the exchange of credentials the following day. "What shall we do about Italy?" Lloyd George asked, "the question is pressing." "Must the Italians be notified that we are making contact with the Germans tomorrow?" asked Clemenceau. "I would tell them nothing," replied Lloyd George. "They made no reply to the compromise proposal I made to them, but I am convinced they will end by accepting it."[145]

That afternoon, they reviewed Articles 429 and 430 of the draft treaty, the provisions the closest to Clemenceau's heart, which he had worked to achieve since the beginning of the peace conference. Article 429 provided for the occupation of the Rhine bridgeheads, with the phased withdrawal of the occupiers over fifteen years. The final paragraph of Article 429 provided that, if after fifteen years "the guarantees against unprovoked aggression by Germany are not considered sufficient by the Allied and Associated Governments, the evacuation of the occupying troops may be delayed to the extent regarded necessary for the purpose of obtaining the required guarantees."[146] Article 430 provided that if the Reparations Commission were to determine, at any time during the fifteen-year period, that Germany had refused "to observe the whole or in part, of her obligations under the present Treaty with regard to reparation," then the areas subject to occupation could be immediately occupied."[147] They also reviewed the proposed articles of the treaty dealing with China. Germany was required to return everything in China to the Chinese: buildings, barracks, forts, arms, wireless installations, etc., everything and everywhere, "*except in the leased territory of Kiaochow*."[148] That was all.

Whatever promises the Japanese had made to return Shantung to the Chinese were just verbal; they would appear nowhere in the treaty.

May 1—May Day—saw Paris completely paralyzed by a general strike. The Champs Elysees was cordoned off. Troops were stationed in the Tuileries Gardens. The strike turned violent, with bloody clashes between police and strikers in front of the Hotel Crillon. In this setting, the Council of Three met for their morning session. They were now concerned with whether the Belgians would sign the treaty, and what Jules Cambon should say to the Germans later that day if the Germans inquired about the Italians. Lloyd George predicted they wouldn't ask.

Jules Cambon and his delegation met the Germans in the Hotel Trianon in Versailles at 3:00 P.M., in the same room in which the Supreme War Council had met during the war. The German delegation was headed by Count Ulrich Karl Christian von Brockdorff-Rantzau, 53, an apolitical career diplomat, an aristocrat by birth but thoroughly democratic in belief. Fluent in French, he had recently been appointed as the Weimar Republic's first foreign minister. The 250-person delegation he headed was ensconced in the Hotel des Reservoirs, where, in 1870, Adolphe Thiers had stayed when he met with Bismarck. History had come full circle. It was reported that Brockdorff-Rantzau was "pale and almost fainting from emotion" when he entered the room and approached Cambon. Cambon announced that he was the chairman of the commission appointed to present and exchange credentials. "Here are ours," said Brockdorff-Rantzau. The meeting lasted all of five minutes.[149] True to Lloyd George's prediction, he did not ask about Italy's absence. It was later reported that Brockdorff-Rantzau had been "satisfied" with the meeting, believing there would be "negotiation and exchange" on the basis of "mutual equality," and that no "dictated peace" was planned. He later went riding through Versailles in a car provided by the French.[150]

Later that day, Wilson, Clemenceau and Lloyd George agreed to inform the Italians of when the meetings with the Germans would begin, lest the Italians claim they had never been informed. They agreed to invite the Austrians in on May 12.

They spent the following day tying up open issues. They discussed Belgium's reparations demands, which included Belgium being appointed mandatory for African colonies. Lloyd George was opposed to granting Belgium any preference. They discussed the possibility of preventing the union of Germany and Austria, which the agreed would be practically impossible and would violate the self-determination principle in any event. They agreed to include a provision in the treaty that "Germany acknowledges and will fully respect the independence of Austria within the frontiers established by the present treaty as inalienable, except by consent of the powers of the Council of the League of Nations."[151] The reparations commission appointed by the Council of Ten agreed, in Italy's absence, to cut Italy out of a substantial share of German reparations, since most of Italy's damages had been caused by the Austrians, not the Germans. They agreed to communicate this fact to the Italians, and further agreed not to ask the Italians to return. They also learned that the Italians had sent a battleship, two cruisers and a destroyer to Smyrna, bound for Fiume.

They spent the morning of the next day discussing Italy. Balfour appeared with a draft of a short message he prepared to send to Orlando: "We are not sure if you realize the serious effects on the unity of the Allies and the settlement of Europe which must be produced by your absence from Versailles while peace with Germany is being arranged…[I]f Italy refuses her concurrence and cooperation she will not only be in our opinion violating the Pact of London, but she will be taking a step which will render future unity of action a matter of the extremest difficulty. To us such a result seems little short of disaster to civilization."[152] Clemenceau had brought with him a much longer draft letter to the Italians, in which he reminded them that they had agreed not to enter into separate negotiations. He underlined that France and Great Britain still stood by the provisions of the Treaty of London, which awarded Fiume to the Croats, but that if Italy refused to return to the Peace Conference, both agreements would lapse.[153] Wilson took serious issue with this draft, saying it isolated the United States. If the Italians agreed to the Treaty of London, he would have to repudiate it.

They were suddenly faced with the prospect of what would happen if the Italians returned to the Peace Conference ready to accept the Treaty of London. Lloyd George: "We are risking a dispute either with Italy or with the United States. We know well enough which of the two would be more serious for the peace of the world. We know the importance that the Germans attach to the action of the United States in comparison to that of Italy. This is why I am more alarmed at the idea of seeing M. Orlando return than I am of seeing him remain in Rome."[154] He raised a related issue, which was the growing feeling that Europe was submitting to the "bullying" of the United States. "If Europe and America should fall apart on this Italian question, nothing could be more deplorable."

Wilson: "If you give the impression in Italy that we are divided, nothing would do more harm. On the contrary, we must show that we are united."

Lloyd George: "Unfortunately, it must be acknowledged, we are not. We are united on the question of Fiume; but the great difficulty comes from the fact that we are not in your situation; we are bound by the Treaty of London."

Wilson: "We are united not by our situation, but by our judgment."

Lloyd George: "That is not sufficient when we are compelled to take a decision."[155]

Wilson tried to convince Lloyd George that he was not bound by the Treaty of London, that by quitting the conference the Italians had abrogated the treaty. Lloyd George would have none of it. "We don't have the right to denounce a treaty which has been carried out by Italy; she lost 500,000 men in the course of its execution. I think unceasingly of the danger which could result from such a situation, and I have a downright terror of seeing the Italians come back.[156]

But now Wilson was hardening. With the Japanese safely on board, there was no chance that both the Japanese and the Italians would refuse to join the League. After the morning session, Lloyd George met with Marquis Guglielmo Imperiali, the member of the Italian delegation Orlando had left behind. He told Imperiali that the Italians should accept his compromise to make Fiume a free city in exchange for a few islands in the Adriatic. But at the afternoon session, Wilson pressed for a tough letter to the Italians, to the effect that if the Italians did not return by May 6, "Your absence will constitute a rupture of the pact."[157]

Two days later, Clemenceau reported that the Italians were returning to Paris. They would demand what they had been promised in the Treaty of London. They would deal directly with the Croats over Fiume, exchanging the Dalmatian coast for Fiume. The Germans, idling in Versailles, were complaining about the delays in getting the negotiations started, and were threatening to go home. The Belgians announced that they would sign the treaty after all. They would receive five billion in reparations, representing their full "war costs." Wilson announced that they were a special case, having been invaded in violation of a treaty. They agreed to inform all of the other belligerents of the terms of the treaty at a meeting of the Plenary Session the following afternoon. Andre Tardieu would read a summary of the treaty, which was now the size of a book: seventy-two thousand words. They then all decamped to the Trianon Palace, to personally review the arrangements for the first meeting with the Germans, set for May 7, two days hence.

Baron Makino called in the press. He wished to make it clear that Japan's policy would be to hand back the Shantung Peninsula to the Chinese, retaining only the economic privileges that had been granted to Germany. He did not specify when. The police would be used only to provide security for the railroad. The Chinese issued a statement deploring the Peace Conference's decisions regarding Shantung, saying that the Japanese had been given more than what they had granted the Germans.[158] In the end, the Japanese signed the treaty. The Chinese did not.

On the morning of the Plenary Session, Wilson, Lloyd George and Clemenceau agreed that Tardieu, in addition to reading a summary of the treaty, would announce the mutual guarantees that the United States and Great Britain had agreed to provide to France.

The Plenary Session began at 3:00 P.M. in the Salle d'Horloge. The prime ministers, foreign ministers and assorted plenipotentiaries of thirty-one nations assembled, with the notable absence of the yet-to-arrive Orlando and Sonnino. It fell to Tardieu to read his "summary," one that consumed forty-seven pages of the official State Department translation. To the many present who understood no French, including Wilson and Lloyd George, it must have been excruciating. (They did not bother to offer a translation.) But one can only imagine what went through Clemenceau's mind as he heard Tardieu intone the language of Section V of the treaty, which dealt with Alsace-Lorraine: "The High Contracting Parties recognize the moral obligation to redress the wrong done by Germany in 1871, both to the rights of France and to the wishes of the population of Alsace and Lorraine, which were separated from their country in spite of the solemn protest of their representatives at the Assembly of Bordeaux."[159] He had been one of the signers of that protest, and was the last survivor.

When Tardieu was finally finished, China's foreign minister, Lou Tseng-Tsiang, rose and registered his formal protest to the section of the treaty dealing with the Chinese settlement. And then, to everyone's surprise, Marshal Ferdinand Foch rose and asked to be heard. He admitted that he had not had the opportunity to read the treaty, but he was aware of its contents. With respect to France's right to occupy the Rhineland for five, ten and fifteen year periods, with the right to re-occupy as a guarantee for the payment of reparations, Foch called this guarantee "worthless." Moreover, after fifteen years, the barrier of the Rhine would have to be abandoned, and France would find itself back again on her 1870 frontiers, "that is to say, without any military guarantee."[160] He droned on and on. When Clemenceau finally gaveled the session to a close, he approached Foch: "And why, M. de Marechal, why did you choose to make such a scene in public?" Foch replied: "It was to ease my conscience."[161] As they were leaving, Andrew Bonar Law told Clemenceau that a British general wouldn't last five minutes following such a display of insubordination. Clemenceau replied: "You know my position. No matter how much I regret the attitude of the Marshal, we cannot forget that he led our soldiers to victory."[162]

The next day, they would meet the Germans.

22

....

ENDGAME

Nothing permanent is founded upon force.

—Napoleon

Five months after the Armistice, the preliminary treaty was finally in a shape for presentation to the Germans. It was a coincidence that Wilson, Clemenceau and Lloyd George met the Germans at 3:00 P.M. on May 7, 1919, four years to the day following the sinking of the *Lusitania*, in the conference room of the Trianon Palace in Versailles. The Allied delegations arrived to the ruffle of drums and the blare of trumpets. Sixty-two delegates from twenty-eight countries were seated in a semicircle, with Clemenceau at the center, Wilson to his right and Lloyd George to his left. Orlando and Sonnino, recently arrived, were present. There was some doubt whether Foch would appear, considering his performance of the previous day, but there he was. Behind the Germans were seats reserved for the forty-five selected journalists. In all there were 205 crowded in, all but one—a foreign office interpreter—were men. Ignacy Paderewski, accustomed to entering packed rooms, arrived last.

A French functionary intoned: "*Monsieurs les plenipotentiares Allemandes.*" As Brockdorff-Rantzau, trailed by his five delegates, all dressed in morning coats, entered the hall, they all rose. The Germans took their seats at the table directly facing Clemenceau. As the Germans sat, Clemenceau, still standing and with complete calm, opened the proceedings: "This can be neither the time nor the place for superfluous words. You see before you the accredited representatives of the Allied and Associated Powers, both small and great, which have waged without intermission for more than four years of pitiless war which was imposed on them. The hour has struck for the weighty settlements of our accounts. You asked us for peace. We are disposed to grant it to you. This volume, which the Secretary-General of the Conference will shortly hand to you, will tell you the conditions which we have fixed....I am compelled to add that this Second Peace of Versailles, which is about to become the subject of our discussion, has been too dearly bought by the peoples represented here for us not to be unanimously resolved to secure by every means in our power all the legitimate satisfactions which are our due."[1] He advised the Germans that there would be no direct discussions. They would have fifteen days to present their written "observations," in English and in French. Paul Mantoux then translated Clemenceau's remarks into English, which were then translated for the Germans.

Brockdorff-Rantzau, facing Clemenceau, began to speak. *He did not stand.* His auditors would not remember what he said, but they would never forget the effrontery, the abject breach of diplomatic courtesy, as he sat as he spoke. "We cherish no illusions as to the extent of our defeat—the degree of our impotence. We know that the might of German arms is broken. We know the force of hatred which confronts us here, and we have heard the passionate demand that the victors should both make us pay as vanquished and punish us as guilty."[2] His first sentences were interpreted into French and English. He spoke a few more sentences, and was again interrupted for the interpreters. As Brockdorff-Rantzau spoke, Australia's Billy Hughes whispered to Lloyd George: "Is Clemenceau going to allow this fellow to go on like this?"[3] He did. "We are required to admit that we are war-guilty; such an admission on my lips would be a lie. We are far from seeking to exonerate Germany from all responsibility for the fact that this world war broke out and was waged as it was...but we emphatically combat the idea that Germany, whose people were convinced they were waging a defensive war, should alone be laden with the guilt....The hundreds of thousands of non-combatants who have perished since the 11th November through the blockade were killed with cold deliberation, after victory had been won and assured by our adversaries. Think of that, when you speak of guilt and atonement." He emphasized that the Armistice had been based on Wilson's "principles," which "therefore became binding upon both belligerent parties—upon you as well as upon us..." He admitted the "wrong done to Belgium" and pledged that his foremost aim was the restoration of Belgium and Northern France, but "We cannot complete this task without the technical and financial participation of the victors; you can only carry it through with our aid." He asked that "the portals of the League of Nations must be thrown open to all peoples of good will." He concluded: "A

Peace which cannot be defended in the name of justice before the whole world would continually call forth fresh resistance. No one could sign it with a clear conscience, for it would be impossible of fulfillment."[4]

When he finished Clemenceau announced the meeting adjourned. The Germans filed out. Lloyd George said to André Tardieu: "It is hard to have won the war and to have to listen to that."[5] Wilson said: "What abominable manners…The Germans are really a stupid people. They always do the wrong thing."[6] As they were leaving, Lloyd George noted to Clemenceau that Brockdorff-Rantzau's rudeness seemed to offend the British and the Americans more than it did the French or the Italians. "Because," Clemenceau answered, "we are accustomed to their insolence. We have had to bear it for fifty years. It is new to you and therefore it makes you angry."[7] Afterwards, Lloyd George told Frances Stevenson that he felt like getting up and smacking Brockdorff-Rantzau as he spoke, adding that the incident made him angrier than any incident during the war, and that for the first time he felt the same hatred for the Germans that the French felt for them.[8]

But years later Lloyd George wrote that Brockdorff-Rantzau's insolence may not have been contrived. It was related to him that Brockdorff-Rantzau's knees trembled so badly that he simply could not stand.

The Council of Four spent the next week and beyond receiving and responding to the Germans' objections to the treaty. But on the day following their meeting with the Germans, Sir Maurice Hankey raised the issue of Europe's lack of raw materials, which if not resolved, he said, "there will be no real hope for peace for Europe."[9] Lloyd George picked up the thread, noting that "if Europe doesn't obtain these raw materials, she will find herself in a position worse, in certain respects, than that of wartime."[10] The only source of funding for raw materials was the American treasury. Great Britain owed the United States $4.2 billion, and France owed $2.7 billion. Worse, Britain had loaned $2.8 billion to the Russians, a debt that was now worthless. France owed Britain $2.5 billion and Belgium owed it almost another $500 million, sums that could be paid only through reparations payments. Lloyd George was pleading, yet again, for the cancelation of inter-Allied debts and the guarantee of Germany's debt, and again Wilson would have none of it: "The difficulty is that we will only be able to do so through taxation, which would fall in great part on persons who derived no profit from the war." Lloyd George replied: "If we could renounce all debts owed us by our allies, provided you cancel our own, I assure you we would accept, although the balance would be unfavorable to us. It is absolutely necessary for us to deal with this question without delay."[11] They did not deal with it at all.

They received their first communication from Brockdorff-Rantzau on May 9. He raised a delicate point that Clemenceau had himself raised, which Wilson had dismissed. Germany was being asked to sign the treaty, of which the League covenant was an integral part, yet Germany was not being invited to join the League. "The German Peace Delegation begs to inquire whether, and if so under what circumstances, such invitation is intended."[12] This pointed up a split within the Council of Four. In his Fontainebleau Memorandum, Lloyd George had pressed for Germany's admission to the League ("Might it not be safer that she should be inside the League…"). Wilson and Clemenceau were opposed, Wilson opining that Article I of the covenant offered membership to "all nations that govern themselves under a democratic form of government."[13] Wilson was mistaken. Article I required only that a nation be self-governing; there was no requirement that it have a "democratic form of government."

More generally, Brockdorff-Rantzau, objected to the draft treaty as a whole, as being an abandonment of the Wilsonian principles upon which the Armistice had been signed. "The draft treaty contains demands which no nation could endure, moreover, our experts hold that many of them could not possibly be carried out."[14] This was the first intimation that the Germans might not sign the treaty, and that the war might resume. They agreed to send Foch on a "secret" mission to the front, to prepare for an invasion if the Germans refused to sign. Lloyd George instructed his press representative, George Riddell, to leak Foch's mission to the press, so that the Germans would learn of it.[15] Their response to the Germans' first communication, drafted by Wilson and signed by Clemenceau, was curt: "The…Allied and Associated Powers…wish to remind the German Delegation that they have formed the Terms of the Treaty with constant thought of the principles upon which the Armistice and the negotiations for peace were proposed. They can admit no discussion of their right to insist upon the Terms of the Peace substantially as drafted. They can consider only such practical suggestions as the German plenipotentiaries have to submit."[16]

Three notes from the Germans came in on May 13 and 14. In the first, the Germans complained that the reparations provisions of the treaty would so deprive the Germans of raw materials that Germany would not be able to provide itself with food or work. The treaty, they complained, would deprive Germany of three quarters of its minerals, a fifth of its corn and potatoes, and a third of its coal, yet required huge deliveries of coal to the Allies. Germany would be required to import food and raw materials, but would be unable to do so as a result of the loss of its merchant fleet and colonies. "Those who sign this treaty," the note concluded, "will sign the death warrant of millions of

German men, women and children."[17] A second note objected to Article 231 of the treaty,* the introduction to the reparations section, which held Germany was responsible for the war. This section, which began as a rhetorical flourish to justify the demand for reparations, would be for the Germans the most hateful provision of the treaty. They accepted that they were responsible to pay reparations. They refused to admit that this responsibility resulted from the German people having willed a war of aggression. In their third note, they complained of the territorial concessions, particularly of the Saar, cleverly using Wilson's own words, objecting to "territories...made the subject of bargains between one sovereignty and another, as though they were mere chattels or pawns in a game, in order to endure the satisfaction of the financial and economic claims of the adversaries of Germany."[18] On May 22, the Council of Four rejected all of these claims but in so doing the Germans won the first of what would be very few Allied concessions. They agreed to allow the Germans to repurchase the Saar coal mines if and when they won the Saar plebiscite.

On May 12, the German Chancellor, Philipp Scheidemann, a Social Democrat, delivered a fiery speech that brought the cheering galleries to their feet. He called the treaty "unacceptable, so unacceptable that I am unable to believe that this earth could bear such a document without a cry issuing from millions and millions of throats in all lands...Away with this murderous scheme!" He called the treaty "This dreadful and murderous volume by which confession of our own unworthiness, our consent to pitiless disruption, our agreement to helotry [serfdom] and slavery, are to be extorted— this book must not become the future code of law."[19] More specifically: "At the same time as we shall have to bestir ourselves to perform forced labor for the benefit of the entire world, our foreign trade, the sole source of our welfare, is destroyed and our home trade is rendered impossible. Lorraine iron ore, Upper Silesian coal, Alsatian potash, the Saar Valley mines, and the cheap foodstuffs from Posen and West Prussia are to lie outside our frontiers."[20] Lloyd George's comment was that the German opposition to the treaty focused primarily on their losses to the East: "With the French, at least they feel that they are amongst equals, but they don't hide their contempt for the Poles."[21] The next day the Allies intercepted a message from Brockdorff-Rantzau to Scheidemann, in which the former approved the latter's speech. "Go on and play your part," the message said, "and I will play mine." To Wilson, this meant the Germans were bluffing.[22]

---

* The Allied and Associated Governments affirm and Germany accepts the responsibility of Germany and her Allies for causing all the loss and damage to which the Allied and Associated Governments and their nationals have been subjected as a consequence of the war imposed upon them by the aggression of Germany and her Allies."

As they met almost every day, war raged around them throughout most of Central Europe. The Poles, having just freed themselves from the Hapsburgs, were at war with the Germans, the Czechs, the Ukrainians and the Bolsheviks. Using arms the Allies had provided them to fight the Bolsheviks, they fought the Ukrainians, who had none. The Council proposed an armistice, which the Ukrainians accepted and which the Poles rejected. "How will we impose our terms upon Germany," Lloyd George mused, "if Poland, which wouldn't exist without our support, defies us?"[23] But they feared that if they cut off aid, Paderewksi's moderate government would fall, and the replacement would be worse. The Czechs fought the Hungarians, as well as the Poles. Hungary was at war with all of its neighbors, Romanians, Slovenes, and Czechs. Jugo-Slavs fought Austrians. "They are all little brigand peoples," said Lloyd George, "who only want to steal territories."[24] But the British and the French, supported by an American battleship (the *USS Arizona*) evicted the Turks from the city of Smyrna, installing the Greeks. It was the beginning of the dismemberment of the Ottoman Empire. It was assumed that the United States would have the mandate for Constantinople and Armenia. But Lloyd George wondered what the effect would be on the Muslim world. There were millions of Muslims in India.

They had to consider when to lift the blockade. Wilson wanted it lifted when the Germans signed the treaty. "The German people mustn't be reduced to despair by famine," he said. "We must keep in mind that economic sanctions constitute a much more terrible punishment than a simple military occupation and could not be used in all their rigor without offending the moral sentiment of humanity."[25] Clemenceau disagreed, insisting that the blockade not be lifted until all nations ratified the treaty. Lloyd George sided with Clemenceau: "If this terrible threat of the blockade were made against the German nation, she would crowd around Scheidemann and tell him with one voice: 'Sign! Sign! Sign'"[26]

They also needed to finalize the Austrian treaty. As a defeated power, it followed that Austria would have to pay reparations, but little Austria was now not the Austro-Hungarian Empire that had set off the war. They agreed that all of the constituent states of the former Empire—except Poland—should pay reparations. The Austrians arrived at the appointed place—St. Germain-en-Laye—on May 14, much too early, for the draft treaty was not near completion, Austria's border with Italy not having been finalized. On May 25 they sent a letter to the Council of Four, protesting the delay.

The issue of Fiume and the Adriatic would not go away. On May 13, Wilson proposed a plebiscite for all of Dalmatia. Italy would compensate the Jugo-Slavs for the loss of Fiume by building a new port for them, after which there would be a plebiscite for Fiume. Clemenceau and Lloyd George were both skeptical. On the same day,

Orlando met with House. House mooted a League trusteeship over the entire area. It got nowhere. The next day, Wilson gave House the green light to try to mediate the dispute. Two days later, House conducted the mediation, with Orlando in one room and Jugo-Slav Foreign Minister Ante Trumbic in the other, House shuttling between rooms. They came to no agreement, but House, with characteristic optimism, reported to Wilson that they had come close, with Orlando agreeing to make Fiume a free city, with all of Dalmatia going to the Jugo-Slavs if the Dalmatian cities of Zara and Sebenico were to remain under Italian sovereignty. Trumbic balked. Two Adriatic ports stood between them.

The following week, Lloyd George presented a comprehensive plan for the settlement of Italy's and Jugo-Slavia's territorial claims and much of Asia Minor. It would require Italy to modify the Treaty of London, since without its consent France and Great Britain were bound by it and Wilson was dead set against it. He proposed that Fiume be placed in League of Nations trusteeship until such time as the Italians, at their expense, construct a substitute port with adequate rail connections for the Jugo-Slavs. When that port was completed to the satisfaction of the League, Fiume would revert to Italy. Italy would renounce its claims to all of Dalmatia except for a few small islands. In Asia Minor, the United States would be the mandatory for Armenia, Constantinople and Azerbaijan, with the Sultan remaining in Constantinople. The Anglo-French dispute over the Middle East would be settled by France obtaining a League trusteeship over Syria and and Great Britain obtaining a League mandate over Palestine and present-day Iraq. It was a far-sighted effort at compromise designed not to inflame the Muslim world against the West. But it would have the effect of ousting the French from Asia Minor. Clemenceau balked: "[I]f our people get the idea that the English placed the Americans in Asia in order to chase out the French, that will create a frame of mind which…I would dread….I am the least colonialist of all the French; I can't be accused of having excessive ambitions in this respect. If this decision was taken, I wouldn't do what our Italian colleagues did, I would not leave the conference, but I would leave the government."[27] Lloyd George would shop this compromise to all who would listen until the end of the Peace Conference, to no avail.

There were rumblings within the Allied delegations. William C. Bullitt, 29, a member of the State Department staff who had made an unsuccessful attempt to negotiate with Lenin, resigned from the peace delegation, writing Wilson: "I was one of the millions who trusted confidently and implicitly in your leadership and believed that you would take nothing less than a 'permanent peace' based upon 'unselfish and unbiased justice.'

But our government has consented now to deliver the suffering peoples of the world to new oppressions, subjections and dismemberments—a new century of war."[28] General Smuts wrote Lloyd George, urging him to "use your unrivalled power and influence to make the final treaty a more moderate and reasonable document."[29] Smuts told House that he and South Africa's President Louis Botha had almost agreed not to sign the treaty unless changes were made, that it would cause a "world-wide revolution" if it was seen that the Allies were using the blockade to starve the Germans into signing the treaty. Lord Robert Cecil wrote Lloyd George that many people in Britain believed the treaty to be "out of harmony with the spirit, if not the letter, of the professed war aims" of the Allies.[30] John Maynard Keynes told Harold Nicolson that he considered the treaty not only immoral but incompetent, saying the Germans could gain nothing by signing the treaty and lose nothing more by refusing to sign.[31] In early June, Keynes resigned from the British delegation. Nicolson himself wrote in his diary that the "great crime" of the treaty were the reparations clauses "which were drawn up to please the House of Commons and which [are] impossible to execute." He placed the blame on "an old man called Lord Sumner and an old man called Lord Cunliffe."[32] Lloyd George himself told Wilson and Clemenceau that if he were in Brockdorff-Rantzau's place, he would not sign "a treaty which will deliver to foreigners all the colonies, the entire merchant fleet of my country."[33]

On May 20, the Germans asked for more time to respond in full to the treaty. They were given until May 29. In the interim, the Council of Four continued to wrestle with Fiume and Dalmatia. On May 25, Orlando wrote a "personal" and "unofficial" letter to Lloyd George, one that he said did not call for an answer. His theme was that the needs of the French and the British had been addressed at the Peace Conference, but that the Italians had been left out. "Public opinion in Italy, already irritated by the unusual statement which President Wilson saw fit to make, has been more and more exasperated by the neglect in which it feels it is left by the failure to come to any decision on the most important problems which concern it." Orlando predicted dire consequences if Italy were "force[d] into the ranks of the malcontents of Europe. Do you not think that a dreadful period of absolute international anarchy will dawn for continental Europe?"[34] The letter requested no response, but Lloyd George did anyway. He made it clear that Orlando and Italy wanted territory that was indisputably and overwhelmingly Slavic. Although Lloyd George and Clemenceau were bound by the Treaty of London if pressed by Orlando to do so, they were both now aligned in spirit with Wilson.

On Thursday, May 29, the Council of Four received the Germans' full response to the treaty. Lloyd George and George Riddell sat down and counted the words on a few pages, then estimated that the response covered 67,000 words, almost as long as the treaty itself. It was accompanied by a six-page cover letter addressed to Clemenceau and signed by Brockdorff-Rantzau. "The more deeply we penetrated into the spirit of the Treaty," he began, "the more convinced we became of the impossibility of carrying it out. The exactions of this Treaty are more than the German people can bear."[35] He claimed that Upper Silesia had been German for 750 years. With respect to the Saar, he said that Germany owed France "coal only, not men." Regarding reparations, "No limit is fixed save the capacity of the German people for payment, determined not by their standard of life but solely by their capacity to meet the demands of their enemies by their labour. The German people would thus be condemned to perpetual slave labour."[36] He complained that "The German people is excluded from the League of Nations to which is entrusted all work of common interest to the world."[37] He agreed that certain predominantly Polish areas should be ceded to Poland, to disarm Germany to the extent of 100,000 volunteers, and offered counter-proposals: a plebiscite for Alsace-Lorraine, Germany given a League mandate over her former colonies, Danzig as a free port but under German sovereignty, and an impartial commission to determine the causes of the war. He agreed to supply France with twenty million tons of coal annually for five years, and eight million tons annually for the next five years. With respect to reparations, he offered a fixed sum of 100 billion marks, or roughly $25 billion. Brockdorff-Rantzau concluded the letter: "We are under no delusions regarding the strength of the hatred and bitterness which this war has engendered: and yet the forces which are at work for a union of mankind are stronger now than ever they were before. The historic task of the Peace Conference of Versailles is to bring about this union."[38]

The next day, Lloyd George announced that he was calling his entire Cabinet to Paris for a Sunday, June 1, meeting with all of the British Empire delegations. The following day, Bonar Law wrote Lloyd George that the German reply "is a very able one and in many particulars is very difficult to answer." He urged concessions, particularly with respect to Upper Silesia and reparations.[39] Wilson announced he would meet with the entire American delegation on Monday.

Clemenceau's reaction to the Germans' reply was very different. The day after it was received, he told House that he intended to stand firm against any substantial changes to the treaty, regardless of the consequences. House himself felt that the treaty was "too severe." However, he confided in his diary, "the time to have the treaty right was when it was being formed, and not now." He felt that once the treaty began to unravel, there would be no stopping it, and wondered what effect amending it might have on the Germans. "We desired from the beginning a fair peace, and one well within the Fourteen Points, and one which could stand the scrutiny of the neutral world of all time." Then, in an astounding admission, he wrote: "It is not such a peace, but since the treaty has been written, I question whether it would be well to seriously modify it."[40] It would eventuate that House's opinion of the treaty, as written, was shared by Wilson.

Lloyd George met with his entire Cabinet and the British Empire delegations in his flat on the rue Nitot all of Sunday and Monday morning. Secretary of State for War Lord Milner found himself seated beside Gen. Louis Botha, his bitter enemy during the South African War. Botha turned to Milner: "This is the seventeenth anniversary of the Treaty of Vereeniging, as my friend, Milner, will remember."[41] His message was clear: rivals can emerge as friends; nothing is forever. Lloyd George began by asking each of the gathered ministers if they wanted to stand on the treaty as written or to make concessions, and if concessions were to be made, whether they should continue by means of written communications, giving the Germans a time limit to reply, or to encourage direct negotiations with the Germans. According to Lloyd George, they were all in favor of granting some concessions, apparently including Australia's hard-line Billy Hughes. The strongest in favor of concessions was Gen. Smuts. He argued that the fifteen-year occupation of the Rhineland was "indefensible from every point of view." Lloyd George agreed, saying that he had accepted it only as a compromise arranged by Wilson and Clemenceau. Smuts pushed for the revision of Poland's eastern boundary, for Germany being immediately admitted to the League of Nations in order to obviate it aligning itself with Russia, and that the reparations burden should be revised. Balfour then spoke, agreeing with Smuts. He pointed out that the treaty provision that allowed the Germans to reduce from the overall reparations bill the amount they were required to pay to support the occupation, would result in the British taxpayer supporting the French army. He wanted the size of the occupation forces reduced. They all agreed that there should be a fixed sum of reparations, Lloyd George agreeing that the Germans should be given time to come up with a reasonable sum to repair the damage they inflicted on Belgium and northern France. Lloyd George and the rest did not agree with Smuts that the Germans should be immediately welcomed into the League, a change from his stance in the Fontainebleau Memorandum, in which Lloyd George had called for its immediate admission. He now favored waiting a year or two, until the Allies could sort out their own differences.

The experts recommended, and they all agreed upon, a plebiscite for Upper Silesia. As it stood, Upper Silesia would become "a new Alsace-Lorraine grievance in the middle of Europe."[42] Lloyd George called the Poles Wilson's "protegés": "He liked them as much as he detested the Italians."[43]

Underlying all their discussions was the fear that the Germans would not sign. They agreed that if the Germans refused, the British Empire would not assist in the occupation of Germany or in the continuation of the blockade in order to enforce an unjust peace. On Monday morning, near the end of the second day of their meeting, Lord Milner reminded them all that it was moderation that had saved South Africa for the British Empire. But Lloyd George knew what he was up against: "The hatred of the French for the Germans was something inconceivable—it was savage."[44]

In the end, the British Empire delegations agreed to give Lloyd George wide discretion in his dealings with Wilson and Clemenceau in favor of the direct transfer of some territories to Poland and plebiscites in others, a reduced army of occupation in the Rhineland, a promise that Germany would soon be admitted to the League of Nations, and a fixed sum for reparations. The British Empire would not allow "the peace of the world to be tied to the chariot of French fury."[45] Before they parted Lloyd George praised them all, saying that it was "an extraordinary tribute to the temper of the British Empire that in such circumstances there could be a discussion in such a spirit." He was sure that the Germans could not believe it possible.[46]

On Monday morning, June 2, as Lloyd George was meeting with the British Empire delegations, Clemenceau was engaged in the ceremony in which he presented the peace treaty to the Austrians. This meeting was very different from the one the prior month with the Germans. For one, Clemenceau had to apologize that the treaty was very incomplete. The sections dealing with Austria's borders with Italy and Jugo-Slavia and its reparations burden, among others, had not yet been finalized. The meeting differed in another respect: the head of the Austrian delegation, Dr. Karl Renner (a future chancellor), made a very conciliatory address. The Austrian treaty would not be signed until September 10.

Lloyd George, Wilson and Clemenceau met in Lloyd George's flat at 4:00 P.M. that afternoon. After a few desultory comments, Lloyd George sprang the news. It was a long speech: "I feel it is my duty to indicate to you the position of the British delegation with respect to the peace treaty. It is difficult. Our public opinion desires peace above all else and doesn't attach excessive importance to the terms of that peace. It wouldn't support a government that would resume the war without the most compelling reasons. That is why I thought I had to invite all my colleagues in the English government who could leave London to come to confer with me....They are obviously not disposed, in the event the Germans refuse to sign, to continue the war or to resume the hostilities or the blockade unless certain amendments are made to the treaty."[47] He told them that one member of his delegation, George Barnes, "the only member of the labor world in the present government," would not sign the treaty as it stood; neither would the South African delegation. "All the others think that, if certain provisions of the treaty are not changed, they could agree neither to having the British army advance into Germany nor to having our fleet secure the blockade." Then he got down to specifics. Germany's boundary with Poland could not be justified as drawn, and that the fate of Upper Silesia could not be determined without a plebiscite. "Concerning reparation, everyone agrees that we are asking of Germany more than she can ever pay. But what they criticize most is the indefinite and unlimited character of the debt imposed on Germany." With respect to the occupation, "Since Germany has an army of 100,000 men, is it necessary…to have 200,000 men on the left bank of the Rhine to prevent the Germans from invading France?"[48] He added: "One can understand—whilst rejecting them—Marshal Foch's ideas about the permanent occupation of the bridges of the Rhine…Our military advisors say that it cannot be defended and that it will cost Germany—that is to say, in the end, the Allies—100,000,000 pounds sterling a year, unless France herself assumes the costs. In the first years, this sum is nearly all the Germany will be able to pay."[49] Regarding Germany's entry into the League, he said that if Germany showed good faith in the execution of the treaty, it should be admitted "as soon as possible," and that the issue should be addressed "as early as next year."

Wilson was equivocal. "I will have to convene my delegation tomorrow morning to discuss [the objections] with it." Clemenceau was not. "In France…we know the Germans better than anyone; we think that the more we conceded to them. the more they will ask.…I am convinced that what we have done was reasonable; but if I move one step back, I know that I will have a general uprising against me.…I have to fight every day against generals who go beyond their authority and commit errors that I regret. In this question of the occupation, many people…believe I have made excessive concessions." Clemenceau then tipped his hand: "Germany will not attack France, that is not what we fear. But she will sign the treaty with the intention of not carrying it out, she will raise difficulties on one point, then on another, and if we don't have the means to impose our will, everything will go bit by bit."[50] He took his stand: "I agree to discuss the costs of the occupation, but nothing else.…I am ready to offer my resignation and ask the President of the Republic to negotiate with you on that basis. I won't seek to recriminate."[51] Lloyd George replied: "Nor do I recriminate; I reproach you for nothing. I reproach myself for not having stood out more in our previous discussions."[52]

Following the meeting, an "excited and angry" Clemenceau went to see House. He told House that he would not yield an inch, and would not agree to reduce the fifteen-year occupation by a single day. Clemenceau admitted that he was not opposed to the

Germans in the League, but not right now. House disagreed, telling Clemenceau that "the sooner the League of Nations gets its grip on Germany, the better it would be for France." "I concede that," replied Clemenceau, "but not for the moment."[53]

Wilson met with his delegation and his experts the following day. Before the meeting, Wilson's economic advisors, Lamont, Baruch and McCormick, met with André Tardieu. They advised Tardieu that the Allies should agree to fix a sum for reparations, now that the British had come out for it. But Tardieu stood firm. He took up the line that Clemenceau had taken in the Council of Four, that all the concessions the British were willing to make were at the expense of the French. The British were not willing to give up on the German colonies or the German fleet, the parts of the treaty that benefitted them. He advised the Americans to stand with the French, that if they did Lloyd George would give in.[54] On the whole, he would prove to be correct.

Wilson and his four other commissioners—House, White, Lansing and Gen. Bliss—met with the experts in Lansing's office at the Crillon. The five sat in armchairs, the experts arrayed around them in a semi-circle. Wilson began by going around the room, shaking everyone's hand. Then Wilson led off, advising them that Lloyd George's main objections to the treaty were Upper Silesia, the Rhineland occupation, reparations and Germany's entry into the League. He asked his economic advisors: "If you gentlemen of the reparation group had a free hand…what would you propose?"[55] Thomas Lamont answered for all of them: "Mr. President, I believe our difficulties with Germany would fade away if you and Mr. Clemenceau and Mr. Lloyd George would instruct your technical committees to arrive at a definite sum within twenty-four hours instead of two years, and at the same time to reach an agreement as to how much working capital should be left in Germany's hands."[56] Lamont and McCormick favored a fixed sum at $25 billion, which was essentially the same sum the Germans had proposed. Charles Seymour, a future Yale president, noted that the Germans had a right to fear a Reparations Commission that later could do almost anything.

A lengthy discussion regarding Upper Silesia ensued. The advisors agreed that the area was very rich in iron, coal, zinc and other minerals, which is why ceding the area to the Poles would impede Germany's ability to recover. But if the area went to Germany, Poland would lose three-fourths of its coal. Upper Silesia was ethnically Polish, but the experts questioned whether a plebiscite could be conducted fairly, in light of the influence the German clergy and landlords exerted. The principal Poland expert, Dr. Robert H. Lord, favored no change in the Polish boundary at all. No consensus was reached.

Wilson advised them all that a serious split had developed between Clemenceau and Lloyd George on the length of the occupation. He also advised that the Germans wanted a speedy admission into the League on the ground that no nation in the League could be subject to occupation by other members. Gen. Bliss opined that the Germans would not accept the disarmament provisions (i.e. a 100,000 troop ceiling) unless they were admitted to the League.

Also present in the room was a future president: Herbert Hoover. Near the end, he asked Wilson "Apart from all questions of justice, how far does the question of expediency come in?" Wilson: "In order to get them to sign, do you mean?" Hoover: "In order to get them to sign. It strikes me that that is a more important thing than the question of justice or injustice, because the weighing of justice and injustice in these times is pretty difficult."[57] It was near the end of the meeting, and Wilson summarized his thinking: "Well, I don't want to seem unreasonable, but my feeling is this: that we ought not, with the object of getting it signed, make changes in the treaty, if we think it embodies what we were contending for; that the time to consider all these questions was when we were writing the treaty, that it makes me a little tired for people to come and say now that they are afraid that the Germans won't sign, and their fear is based upon things that they had insisted upon at the time of the writing of the treaty; that makes me very sick....Here is a British group made up of every kind of British opinion... they are all unanimous, if you please, in their funk. Now that makes me very tired. They ought to have been rational to begin with and then they would not have needed to have funked at the end. They ought to have done the rational things, I admit, and it is not very gracious for me to remind—though I have done so with as much grace as I could command."[58]

Lansing had suggested that each of the expert groups prepare a memo specifying what concessions might me made. Wilson quashed the proposal. "Where have they [the Germans] shown that the arrangements of the treaty are essentially unjust...they are hard—but the Germans earned that. And I think it is profitable that a nation should learn once and for all what an unjust war means in itself."[59]

So there it was. In his "Four Principles" address in February, 1918, Wilson's first principle was that "Each part of the final settlement must be based upon the essential justice of that particular case..." One of the "Five Particulars" of his September 1918 address was that "Impartial justice...must involve no discrimination between those to whom we wish to be just and those to whom we do not wish to be just." The Germans had accepted the Armistice on the assumption that these "Principles" and "Particulars," as well as the Fourteen Points, would form the basis of the treaty. Young men such as William Bullitt and Walter Lippmann for the Americans and John Maynard Keynes and Harold Nicolson for the British had eagerly enlisted on the assumption that these principles would be the foundations of the peace. But, as Lloyd George ruefully noted, the the French "hatred…for the Germans was something inconceivable," and Wilson, as he admitted, was "tired." Wilson would side with Clemenceau; there would be no softening of the treaty. Keynes summed it up best: "To his horror, Mr. Lloyd George, desiring at the last moment all the moderation he dared, discovered that he could not in five days persuade the President of error in what had taken five months to prove to him to be just and right.…Thus in the last act the President stood for stubbornness and a refusal of conciliations."[60]

It is very possible that Wilson was more than "tired." The viral infection he suffered in early April may have been followed by a small stroke later that month.[61] His health declined rapidly after the Peace Conference ended, culminating in a small stroke on July 19 and the massive stroke on October 2 that left him partially paralyzed. We cannot know with certainty the extent, if at all, to which Wilson was impaired during the important, final days of the Peace Conference, but his actions militate toward the conclusion that he was.

After Wilson's meeting with his commissioners, but before the afternoon meeting of the Council of Four, House handed Clemenceau a memorandum he had prepared giving Clemenceau his thinking regarding the German counter-proposals. House wrote that a plebiscite for Upper Silesia would not work, since the large landowners would control it. The Germans should not be admitted to the League until they exhibited their sincerity as a liberal government, and there should be no discussion of shortening the Rhineland occupation until the Germans were in the League. The treaty provisions regarding the Saar should not be changed, but House advised that the reparations burden could be reduced if it helped the Germans pay. Clemenceau promised to keep the memo secret.

Wilson picked up the thread when the Council of Four met in the late afternoon, with Wilson opposed to a plebiscite for Upper Silesia on the ground it would be controlled by the German landowners. "I know what intimidation by great landowners is like," countered Lloyd George, "I had some examples of it in Wales, where, moreover, we were able to shake off this yoke without any outside support." Their roles were now reversed. Turning to Wilson, Lloyd George said: "No one has proclaimed more forcefully than you the principle of self-determination. It means that the fate of people must be determined by the people themselves…I am doing nothing but adhering to the Fourteen Points; why, after deciding that there would be plebiscites in Danzig, in Klagenfurt, in Fiume, in the Saar Basin, must we rule out that solution in Silesia?" Wilson was now in the defensive: "I cannot allow you to say that I am not for the right of self-determination. That is absurd. What I want is the true expression of popular sentiment." But Lloyd George said that Silesia was the thing that concerned the Germans the most, and he feared the Germans might refuse to sign because of it. "It is better," he said, "to send an American or English division to Upper Silesia than an army to Berlin." "It is a little late to say that," countered Wilson. "I admit that the Germans may have something to say on the question of Silesia, and I am ready to study the question, *but nothing more.*"[62]

Lloyd George won this round, but little else. They agreed to modify the treaty to permit a plebiscite for Upper Silesia. It would be supervised by an international commission, with American troops at the ready in case the Germans attempted to coerce the residents. They also agreed that the Germans would be allowed to purchase Silesian coal on the same terms as the Poles. But contrary to the pleas of Wilson's advisors, there would be no fixed sum for reparations. Lloyd George admitted that his delegation was divided, Keynes being "moderate" and the Lords Cunliffe and Sumner "very intransigent." And in the face of Clemenceau's implacable opposition, Germany would not be admitted to the League any time soon. But they agreed that the German counter-proposals had made an impression, and that they needed to respond in kind, as so to put the onus on the Germans if they refused to sign. Later, Wilson suggested sending an emissary to tell the Germans that they were misinterpreting the treaty, that it was not intended to be as harsh as they were reading it. Clemenceau opposed even that, on the ground that it would serve only to divide the Allies.

The issue of Fiume and Dalmatia still defied resolution, Wilson predicting to Ray Stannard Baker that the Italians and the Serbs would go to war over it. On June 7, they considered Tardieu's proposal that Fiume be made a "free state," that the Adriatic city of Sebenico go to the Jugo-Slavs and the city of Zara, on the northern Adriatic, be administered by the League. Orlando said he would consider it. The day before, out of Orlando's hearing, Lloyd George lamented Orlando's position. "[He] stirred up forces he can no longer control....I am sorry to see him in this position; he is a lost man if he is compelled to capitulate."[63] On June 10, they received Orlando's answer, rejecting the compromise.

On June 9, the Council of Four received the report of the reparations commission charged with drafting a reply to the German counter-proposals. The commission was split. The Americans wanted to fix the sum at 100 billion gold marks, approximately $25 billion. All the others, including the British, the French, the Italians, even the

Japanese, were opposed on the ground that was impossible to now fix the amount of Germany's indebtedness. Lloyd George gave in, commenting that if the fixed sum was too high the Germans would not sign, and if too low French and British public opinion would not stand for it. He agreed that Germany must be left with sufficient working capital to restart its industry. His proposal, that within three to four months Allied and German experts should meet to fix the amount sufficient for the Germans to rebuild the devastated areas, became a concession that was made a part of the treaty. Clemenceau opposed discussing Germany's needs with them, or making any concessions, but he went along. "As for myself—I state it clearly—I am not for a policy which aims at making the Germans forgive us for our victory; I have known them too well; too long."[64]

House still enjoyed Wilson's confidence enough that Wilson entrusted him to arrange for the organization of the League, and on June 10, with little left to do in Paris, as he prepared to leave for London, he wrote his valedictory in his diary. "He [Wilson] is one of the most difficult and complex characters I have ever known. He is so contradictory that it is hard to pass judgment upon him...When one gets access to him, there is no more charming man in all the world than Woodrow Wilson. I have never seen any one who did not leave his presence impressed....There is little left for me to do in Paris. The answer to the Germans is practically ready, and it is not intended that I should remain in Paris with Lansing, White, and Bliss to button up the matters that will be left over after Germany signs. I have been away from home for eight strenuous months, and while I do not feel at all tired, yet I would like to shift the scene. In a way I realize that in breaking up here it means the end of an epoch in my life, for after the Peace Conference is wound up I feel that I shall do other things than those I have been doing for so many years."[65]

House and Wilson met the next day, which, House wrote "was in the nature of a farewell." Wilson apparently still valued House's counsel, for they discussed "the Adriatic question, Germany's entrance into the League of Nations, Reparations and a number of other matters." House was "disappointed" that Wilson had agreed to the Upper Silesia plebiscite. "I am afraid it cannot be honestly carried out."[66]

The next day, the Council of Four considered the draft reply to the Germans on the reparations issue, penned by Lloyd George's secretary, Philip Kerr, which, with slight modifications, they approved. The tone of the reply was correct; the substance was unyielding. It asserted that the Germans had misinterpreted the role of the Reparations Commission. Its role would be to assist in the reconstruction of Germany, not to hinder it. Contrary to the Germans' allegations, it would not interfere in Germany's domestic legislation or in its budget, and could not levy any taxes. To the extent that the Reparations Commission could later modify reparations payments, it was only to assist Germany. Adopting Lloyd George's suggestion, the Germans would be given four months to make a reasonable fixed offer (the offer of 100 billion gold marks was rejected) or to make an offer to repair the damage. The Allies would have two months to either accept or reject the Germans' offer. They promised to provide the Germans with the raw materials they needed to recover. "Meanwhile, the draft treaty must be accepted as definitive and must be signed."[67]

On the morning of the next day—June 12—Clemenceau advised the Council of Four that they had intercepted a telegram Brockdorff-Rantzau had sent to his government, advising that the Allies would make only minor changes to the treaty, and that a decision needed to be made on the treaty as a whole. They then discussed all of Germany's major objections to the treaty. They agreed to reply to the Germans that their admission to the League would depend on their performance under the treaty. Clemenceau said he could not offer the Germans hope of early admission to the League. "I will do all I can towards that end; but what I cannot do is say it today to the French people."[68] Lloyd George told Clemenceau that he might have trouble in the House of Commons unless he could say that Clemenceau would be willing to later shorten the duration of the Rhineland occupation. "Don't ask me to shorten the occupation," retorted Clemenceau.[69] He allowed that he might be willing to consider it later, depending on the Germans' performance under the treaty. But Lloyd George would not give up. He told Clemenceau that the occupation made no military sense, since it would exist when Germany was weakest, and would go away in fifteen years when, presumably, Germany would be stronger. The occupation existed only for political purposes, to protect Clemenceau's government. Clemenceau corrected Lloyd George, and in doing so revealed to him the real rationale for the occupation: "We need a guarantee for the execution of the financial clauses. Please believe that military considerations have nothing to do with this question. In 1871, the German army occupied French territory until payment of that indemnity, and it did not leave before the last sou had been paid. The situation is the same, on a larger scale. It is a matter of reminding Germany that she owes us money and must pay it."[70] But even with this admission, Clemenceau was being somewhat disingenuous, not revealing his assumption (hope?) that Germany would default, so that the occupation could continue beyond the fifteenth year. Wilson agreed with Clemenceau that the occupation provisions of the treaty should not be changed, and they were not.

On the afternoon of the twelfth, the Council of Four rejected out of hand all of the Germans' objections regarding Alsace-Lorraine, and the Germans' counterproposals regarding the cession of their colonies. But an interesting discussion ensued regarding the treaty requirement that *private* property in the former German colonies must also be turned over. It turned out that the Vatican also objected to this provision, on the ground that it owned the church property in the colonies. "In England," said Lloyd George, "even before the Reformation, the Crown always rejected this pretension of the Holy See to be the owner of property of the Church on our territory."[71] Clemenceau, that lifelong anti-clerical, heartily agreed: "[T]hat is a pretension our kings never accepted." They agreed that church property would be turned over to local missionaries of the same faith. When the meeting ended, Orlando left on a planned visit to the Italian border areas. They could not know it, but it was the last they would ever see of Vittorio Orlando.

The following day, with Sonnino sitting in for Orlando, they returned to the issue of the occupation, and Clemenceau was as unyielding as ever. "You will ask me 'Why this obstinacy?' I cannot act otherwise. Our birth rate is low. We lost 1,500,000 men. France's first need is security. Our people need to know that there is somewhere a barrier behind which they can begin to work and rebuild their ruins. I am not free as I would be in ordinary circumstances. I ask Mr. Lloyd George not to compel me to take commitments towards Germany. Between us, I state that, if proofs of good will and the guarantees furnished by Germany satisfy us, I will be ready to resume this conversation with you. I have to reckon with national feeling. That doesn't mean I fear being overthrown; that doesn't matter to me at all. I don't want to do something that would break down the vital resilience of the people."[72]

They discussed whether to continue the blockade if the Germans refused to sign and the war resumed. Wilson claimed that "you will only produce Bolshevism with the blockade," but here Lloyd George sided with Clemenceau. "Germany was defeated," Lloyd George replied, "because the morale of her people, undermined by the blockade, collapsed at the time of her military reverses. In times almost as critical, our peoples held on because they were not suffering from hunger....The blockade is the only weapon that reaches all Germans, whilst there are many whom an occupation frightens not at all. The owning classes, in particular, prefer occupation to a social revolution."[73] They agreed with Clemenceau that they would permit the newspapers to say that they were making preparations to resume the blockade if the Germans refused to sign.

The next day—the fourteenth—they informed Paderewski that they had decided upon a plebiscite for Upper Silesia, which he opposed despite the Polish majority in the region. "If the results of the plebiscite go against us," said Paderewski, "it will be a veritable calamity for our people." He hoped that the plebiscite would take place in as short a time as possible. "In the meantime," he said, "the struggle will be terrible."[74]

Lloyd George opined that the Poles would win in the eastern, industrial areas, but he wasn't as sure of the outcome in the western, rural parts of Upper Silesia. Based on Paderewski's pleas, they agreed to revise the treaty so that the plebiscite would be held within six to eighteen months.

When they reconvened two days later, Foreign Minister Sonnino read them a letter from Orlando, in which Orlando once again threatened not to sign the treaty, on the ground that Article X of the League covenant provided for a mutual guarantee of all existing boundaries, and Italy's boundary with Jugo-Slavia had not yet been determined. Wilson correctly pointed out that Italy's boundary with Jugo-Slavia had nothing to do with the *German* treaty, which impacted only Italy's treaty with Austria.

Later that day, the Council of Four called in Foch to hear his plans for the renewed invasion of Germany in the event the Germans refused to sign, and what they heard stunned them. This great exponent of bold military action now averred that he might not be able to successfully mount an advance on Berlin, despite the Germans being disarmed, demoralized and hungry. What he feared was rearguard actions from the civilian populations as he advanced. The remedy, he proposed, was separate armistices with the various German states as he advanced. What he was proposing was the political dissolution of Germany, a reversion to its pre-1870 status. After he left, Wilson said: "I don't know what to think about what Marshal Foch just told us. I can't imagine what happened since we last heard him." "Nothing at all happened," replied Clemenceau. "If he has it in his head not to go to Berlin, he won't go," advised Clemenceau. "It is dangerous to allow him to return to the field if it is to carry out a policy in Germany which is not our own." He advised that he would speak to Gen. Pétain, and perhaps to Foch again. "This crisis is serious from a general point of view; but beyond that, it greatly saddens me personally."[75]

On June 16, the Council of Four delivered the revised treaty to the Germans, accompanied by a long cover letter addressed to Brockdorff-Rantzau and signed by Clemenceau. It placed sole responsibility for the war on the Germans, and rehearsed all of the violations and crimes they committed in its execution. "Justice, therefore, is the only possible basis for the settlement of the accounts of this terrible war. Justice is what the German Delegation asks for and says that Germany had been promised. Justice is what Germany shall have. But it must be justice for all." As a result, "Germany must undertake to make reparation to the very uttermost of her power; for reparation for wrongs inflicted is of the essence of justice. That is why [the Allies] insist that those individuals who are most clearly responsible for German aggression and for those acts of barbarism and inhumanity which have disgraced the German conduct of the war must be handed over to a justice which has not been meted out to them at home."[76] With respect to those reparations, "It is not possible to fix this sum today, for the extent of damage and the cost of repair has not yet been ascertained."[77] The Allies would give the Germans four months to survey the damaged areas and make proposals for a settlement of the Allies' claims. If a settlement could not be reached within two months thereafter, the treaty terms would go into effect. The Allies rejected the German proposal that they be admitted to the League: "In the present temper of international feeling, it is impossible to expect the free nations of the world to sit down immediately in equal association with those by whom they have been so grievously wronged."[78]

The letter concluded that this was the Allies' "last word." "As such, the Treaty in its present form must be accepted or rejected." The Germans had "five days from the date of this communication" to declare that they were prepared to sign the treaty as it stood. Failing that, the "Armistice will then terminate, and the Allied and Associated Powers will take such steps as they think needful to enforce their Terms."[79]

There had not been time to reprint the treaty. Changes were made by interdelineations in red ink. When the Peace Conference secretary, Paul Dutasta, delivered the one copy of the treaty the Germans were to receive, his German counterpart, Herr Simon, asked for two more days to respond. Dutasta raced back to Paris at breakneck speed. Clemenceau telephoned Lloyd George and Wilson, who both agreed to the two extra days. Dutasta then raced back to Versailles, who advised the Germans of the extension, just as they were leaving for Weimar. They now had until exactly 6:45 P.M. on June 23 to agree to terms, or the war would be renewed. As they left, a crowd gathered around them, hurling stones. One of the German delegates, Dr. Theodor Melchior, was struck in the head by stones. Clemenceau dispatched a message: "I hasten to express my deepest regrets for such condemnable and unfortunate acts contrary to the laws of hospitality."[80] The local police commissioner was dismissed.

The Allies' reply reached Berlin by 11:00 P.M. that evening. The German press had it by the next morning. Many in Paris were certain that the Germans would sign. Others were just as certain that they would not. There were reports that the Allies had ordered an advance on Berlin beginning on the twenty-fourth if the Germans had not agreed to sign before then.

On the eighteenth, Chancellor Scheidemann and his cabinet debated the peace terms at Weimar, beginning at noon and ending late in the day. It was officially announced that no decision had been reached due to the slow translation of the official text. But this official statement was contradicted by Scheidemann himself, who stated:

"'There is nothing new in the general accusations made against the German people, but we must note with regret that the Allies have rejected the proposal for the establishment of a neutral tribunal which alone would impartially examine these accusations. It is also lamentable that the whole nation should be charged with the offenses and crimes alleged....This charge is to constitute justification for the heavy conditions which... are to be imposed on the German people."[81]

Lloyd George returned to London for a few days, and Wilson made a long-delayed trip to Belgium as the guest of King Albert and Queen Elizabeth. He toured the Ypres and Louvain battlefields, and on the nineteenth he told Belgium's parliament that "The League of Nations is the child of this great war for right...it is the expression of those permanent resolutions which grew out of the temporary necessities of this great struggle, and any nations which decline to adhere to this covenant turns away from the most telling appeal that has ever been made to its conscience and its manhood."[82] As Wilson was speaking, Brockdorff-Rantzau was in Weimar, advising the cabinet to reject the treaty, informing them that he would resign if they did not. But the left-wing democrats favored signing.

As Wilson spoke, the government of Vittorio Orlando collapsed. He had lost a vote of confidence in the Chamber of Deputies. Orlando complained that his position had been "considerably aggravated by international events during the second fortnight of April," referring to Wilson's open letter to the Italian people.[83] But his downfall may have resulted as much from such domestic travails as high unemployment and inflation as his conduct at the Peace Conference. Francesco Nitti would succeed Orlando, with Tomaso Tittoni as foreign minister. Sonnino would stay on to represent his country as a plenipotentiary, not as foreign minister.

At 2:00 A.M. Berlin time of the next day—the twentieth—the government of Chancellor Philipp Scheidemann resigned. Brockdorff-Rantzau and five other cabinet members had voted to reject the treaty. It was reported that Matthias Erzberger, the head of the Catholic Center Party who had signed the Armistice, was the new "Minister of Reconstruction and Fulfillment of the Treaty." The following day the formation of a coalition government of Social Democrat and Catholic Center parties was announced. Gustav Bauer, 49, the Minister of Labor, was the new "President of the Imperial Ministry." Dr. Herman Müller, the leader of the Social Democrats, was appointed foreign minister. It was a cabinet formed for the express purpose of getting the National Assembly to approve the treaty. There was a feeling in Berlin that the people were sick of war and wanted peace on any terms.[84] Clemenceau had predicted that the Germans would sign, if not by Brockdorff-Rantzau then by someone else.

The Armistice required the Germans to hand over their navy. The entire fleet—battleships, heavy cruisers and light cruisers—was interred by the British at Scapa Flow in the Orkney Islands north of Scotland, awaiting the Allies' decision (which might prove contentious) as to how to divvy up the ships. They were unguarded and lightly-manned by their German crews. At precisely noon on the twenty-first a red flag was hoisted on one of the ships. That was the signal. As there were no explosives on any of the ships, the crews opened the seacocks and the waters of the Atlantic flooded in. The sailors took to the lifeboats, paddled ashore, and held up their hands in surrender. All but one of ten battleships went to the bottom with their flags aloft, as did five battle cruisers. It was considered a breach of the Armistice, and would result in the cost of the ships being added to the reparations bill that everyone knew was already more than the Germans would ever pay. A group of school children from the local Stromness Higher Grade Public School, out for a pleasant summer holiday, had witnessed it all.

On June 19, former Secretary of State Elihu Root wrote a letter to Sen. Lodge, which Lodge released on the twenty-first. In it, Root averred that the covenant of the League of Nations embraces "a great deal of very high value which the world ought not lose." But Root also wrote that the changes to the covenant that Wilson had effected in March with respect to the Monroe Doctrine, the ability of a nation to quit the League and the prohibition on the League from considering purely domestic matters, were simply insufficient. "I do not think," he wrote, "that in these respects the United States is sufficiently protected against more injurious results, which are wholly unnecessary for the establishment and maintenance of the League of Nations."[85] But his most serious objection was to Article X, the mutual guarantee of every nation's territorial integrity, which Wilson believed was the heart and soul of the League. Root believed that Article X might result in the United States being dragged into a European war in which it had no interest.

What Root proposed were "qualifying" resolutions appended to the resolution to adopt the treaty, i.e. reservations which expressed the Senate's dissent to certain treaty provisions, and which would result in the United States not being bound by those provisions should a dispute later arise over the interpretation of the treaty. There was nothing new or novel in this; nations had appended reservations to treaties in the past. Of the forty-nine Senate Republicans, Lodge could count on forty-seven of them for a reservation to Article X, and on all of them for the other reservations. They were more than enough to defeat the two-thirds majority required to enact the treaty.

Wilson, Lloyd George and Clemenceau met on the evening of the twenty-second, to consider three notes received from the Germans. The first officially announced the formation of the new government. The second announced that Edgar Karl Alfons Haniel von Haimhausen, 49, had replaced Brockdorff-Rantzau as the head of the German delegation. The third was the most important. Arriving a full day before the deadline, it purported to be the Germans' acceptance of the treaty. It contained an ominous warning. The government had received "passionate expressions of opinion" from the people "in the districts to be cut off in the East." The German government, therefore, "finds itself compelled to decline all responsibility for any difficulties which may arise from the resistance of the inhabitants against their separation from Germany."

But the acceptance was not complete; it contained a qualification: "Germany… cannot accept article 231 of the Treaty of Peace which requires Germany to admit herself to be the sole and only author of the war, and does not cover this article by her signature."[86] It followed that they would also not agree to turn over anyone to the Allies. In their acceptance, the Germans had agreed to the full panoply of reparations, the relinquishment of all of her colonies, her navy and her merchant marine, the loss of Alsace-Lorraine, the Saar, Danzig and the Polish corridor and Upper Silesia, the occupation of the Rhine, her unilateral disarmament and much more, but admitting that she was solely responsible for the war was simply too much. On this, they deferred.

Matthias Erzberger, who had contacts with Americans and French representatives in Germany, believed that the Allies would accept this reservation.[87] He was mistaken. The Council of Four's curt reply was drafted by Wilson himself: "[T]he time for discussion has passed." The Allies would accept no "qualification or reservation and must require of the German representatives an unequivocal decision as to their purpose to sign and accept as a whole or not to sign and accept, the Treaty as finally formulated."[88]

At 9:00 A.M. of the twenty-third—deadline day—the Council of Four received a request from the Germans for an additional forty-eight hours. They refused. At 4:00 P.M. they intercepted a telegram from the Weimar government to their delegation informing them they would have to sign, but to await confirmation of the telegram before communicating their consent to the Allies. At 5:40 P.M., Dutasta brought to the Council of Four the message of concession, signed by Haniel von Halmhausen: "No act of violence can touch the honor of the German people. The German people, after frightful suffering in these last years, have no means of defending themselves by external action.…Yielding to superior force, and without renouncing in the meantime its own view of the unheard of injustice of the peace conditions, the Government of the German Republic declares that it is ready to accept and sign the peace conditions imposed."[89]

It was done. There would be no renewed war, no advance on Berlin. Clemenceau returned to the War Ministry, where he was met by House, returned from London for the signing ceremony. Clemenceau blessed all Americans, and the two friends embraced. Clemenceau said he intended to resign within six weeks. He did not.

The Council of Four reconvened as usual the following morning, with Clemenceau in a fighting mood. Under the treaty, the Germans were required to return the French flags that they had seized in 1870. Instead, they burned them. "I have the honor of formally demanding reparation for the burned French flags,"[90] he announced to Wilson, Lloyd George and Sonnino. He also mentioned the ships sunk in Scapa Flow. His proposed remedy? "We must take possession of Essen....Essen is still today the great manufacturing center of German artillery," which, Clemenceau maintained, was continuing.[91] His announced purpose was, "above all, to affirm the sovereign will of the Allies...Seeing how we act, the Germans will have only one idea—to give in." They continued the discussion into the next day, and Lloyd George quashed the idea. He allowed that British sailors might have done exactly what the German sailors had done at Scapa Flow, and while the destruction of the French flags was "a gratuitous and intolerable insult," but they could not have the Germans sign a treaty that defined a definite boundary, with the mental reservation to breach that boundary after the treaty was signed. "If you want to occupy Essen, that is well and good; but the Germans must be told about it today....But I hope, in any case, that France will not act alone." Clemenceau backed off: "Never fear; you know well that I am not the man to break our alliance."[92]

It was a coincidence that the date of the signing of the treaty—June 28—was exactly five years from the date that the Archduke Franz Ferdinand had been shot by the Bosnian terrorist that had ignited the conflagration; the place of the signing was not. It was in this place, the Galerie des Glaces—the Hall of Mirrors—in the Palace of Versailles, where in January 1871 Otto von Bismarck had proclaimed the formation of the German Empire.

The Hall of Mirrors is a cavernous room atop a broad staircase. It faces onto the fountains and lawns of the palace. On this day, dragoons in white trousers, black boots and dark blue coats lined the staircase past which the delegates, functionaries, newspaper reporters and guests paraded as they entered the hall. A long table extended the length of the room, with seats reserved for the Allied delegates, Clemenceau's seat at the center. Directly in front of Clemenceau was a gold table on which sat the treaty in a brown leather case. Beside the treaty were seats reserved for the various secretaries who would handle the signing. Benches behind Clemenceau had been placed for the spectators and guests lucky enough to have obtained a ticket. A side wing table was reserved for the Germans, Herman Müller and a Center Party politician, Johannes Bell.

The ceremony was scheduled to begin at 3:00 P.M. When Clemenceau arrived at approximately 2:00 P.M., he was surrounded by well-wishers, shaking hands. He spotted Robert Lansing. "This is a great day for France," he said.[93] Then Wilson arrived, deluged by people wanting his autograph, which he gave, first willingly, later grudgingly. He sat to Clemenceau's right. Lloyd George sat to Clemenceau's left. Clemenceau had arranged for a group of grizzled veterans of the 1870 war to attend, and they took their seats. Then the Germans arrived, their expressions tense. No one rose. Secretary Dutasta directed them to their seats.

Clemenceau then rose and said: "The session is open. You have before you, gentlemen, the peace treaty which I have duly authenticated as identical to the document delivered to the German delegation. The signatures will be given now and they amount to a solemn undertaking faithfully and loyally to execute the conditions embodied by this treaty of peace. I now invite the delegates of the German Reich to sign the treaty."[94] Clemenceau was interpreted into English and then into German. Müller and Bell were escorted to the table. In total silence, their hands trembling, they signed. Then Wilson rose and walked around the long table to sign. He was followed by his fellow delegates, Lansing, White, Bliss and House. After he signed, Wilson told Lansing "I did not know I was excited until I found my hand trembling when I wrote my name."[95] Then came the French, followed by the British Empire delegates. The Italians, who had threatened not to sign, did. The Japanese signed. Then, arranged in alphabetical order, the delegates of all the other nations signed. Everyone noticed the absence of the Chinese. In all it took an hour.

When it ended, Clemenceau, Wilson and Lloyd George walked onto the terrace, where they were mobbed by the cheering throngs. The fountains around them began to play, for the first time since the war began. That night, Paris erupted in joy. They danced in the streets, waved American flags, and dragged captured German cannons through the streets.

That evening, Wilson and Edith headed for the Gare des Invalides station for the trip home. Clemenceau was at the station to see them off, as was Lansing. "This is your day, Mr. President," Lansing said to Clemenceau. "And yours, yes, and yours too," replied

Clemenceau.[96] In his last conversation with Wilson, House urged him to be conciliatory with the Senate. Wilson replied: "House, I have found one can never get anything in this life that is worthwhile without fighting for it."[97] They would never see each other again. As Wilson boarded the train, Clemenceau clutched his hand: "I feel as though I were losing one of the best friends I ever had."[98] Wilson and Clemenceau were both pleased with the outcome, for each had achieved his principal objective. Wilson had in hand the covenant of the League of Nations. Clemenceau had preserved in peacetime the French-Anglo-American alliance that had won the war, and the fifteen-year occupation of the Rhineland that he believed in his heart would be permanent. Both would soon.

In his 1911 speech in the French Senate, Clemenceau had predicted that the unending conflict between France and Germany would continue "until there shall be a conqueror superior to his conquest, a victor who shall be [a] hero in his moderation." He admitted that Napoleon had not been that man, nor was Bismarck. He could not have imagined that, at the age of seventy and already a former prime minister, he might one day be the man called upon to be a "conqueror superior to this conquest," a "hero in his moderation" following the greatest of all conquests in the greatest of all wars. But he was not that man. Instead, he became the principal architect of a vengeful and bitter peace that, while it did not necessarily directly cause the next conflagration twenty years hence, certainly did nothing to prevent it. Why?

Clemenceau had devoted his life to the ideals of the French Revolution. Those were ideals not only for France, but for the world, and France's destiny was to carry those ideals to the world. But the war had seared him. He had witnessed too much German pillage, too many French villages wantonly demolished, too many civilians forced into slavery, too much rape and rapine, too many (1,500,000) French dead. And at the end, he knew, Germany was still *unconquered*. He came to the Peace Conference terrified that, unless he alone prevented it, it could happen...again. And he remembered, not only that the Germans had not departed France after 1871 until every last *sou* had been paid, but that when that war erupted no nation had come to France's aid, and they had been crushed fighting the Germans alone. That too could happen...again.

The man who wished to be "a conqueror superior to his conquest," a victor who was a "hero in his moderation," and who easily could have been that man, was Wilson, and his is by far the greater tragedy. He came to Paris with the power to enforce the peace to his liking, for he held all the cards. Not only were his British, French and Italian allies indebted to the United States, but they would require further American assistance if they wished to avoid bankruptcy. But at some point his idea for a League of Nations became an obsession, and the obsession blinded him to everything else. The others could not fathom his obsession. "We *are* the League of Nations, right here," one of them pointed out to him, as wars raged all around them. How did he suppose that this new thing would magically prevent wars from breaking out or spreading? There was no answer. He just believed it would. And so by degrees he bargained away the Fourteen Points and the ideals of justice and magnanimity behind them. He gave Orlando territory filled with Germans just to get him to sit in on the League Commission. He gave Shantung to Japan to get them to sign. Clemenceau made believe he supported the League to get his mutual guarantee. When the Germans read the treaty, believing it would embody Wilson's principles, they were shocked. No wonder.

There were no heroes at the Peace Conference, but the man who came to Paris the most clear-eyed was Lloyd George. At every turn, he sought to forge compromise from irreconcilable contenders. He realized that the one thing that had to be avoided was an "Alsace-Lorraine" on the Rhine or in Poland. The last thing he wished to do was instill a spirit of *revanche* in the Germans. He did support the creation of the League of Nations and hoped for its success. He remembered Edward Grey's frantic, failed efforts to convene a conference in late July, 1914, in the hope of heading off the conflict. He believed that had a League of Nations then been in existence, he might have succeeded. But he was under no illusions. For the Empire's safety and security, a League of Nations was no substitute for the iron bottoms of the British Navy. For a successful peace, the model was the Fontainebleau Memorandum. But in the face of Clemenceau's implacable opposition and Wilson's visions of a world remade by the League of Nations, it never stood a chance.

Lloyd George was greeted by cheering crowds at Victoria Station the day following the signing of the treaty. The king wished to welcome him personally. He was advised that there was no precedent for a king to greet a returning prime minister. "Very well, I will make a precedent," and off to the station he went. They rode together in an open carriage. Someone threw a laurel wreath into the carriage, intended for Lloyd George. It landed on the king's lap. He handed it to Lloyd George. "This," he said, "is for you."

EPILOGUE

T he Peace Conference did not end with the departure of Wilson and Lloyd George. The peace treaties with Austria, Hungary, Bulgaria and Turkey still needed to be hammered out, but they would be finalized by others. Clemenceau continued to attend what was re-styled as the "Heads of Delegations," but he stopped attending by December, 1919.

The House of Commons ratified the treaty—and the Anglo-American guarantee treaty—unanimously. Clemenceau had a more difficult time. By late September, when the Chamber of Deputies took up the treaty, it had become apparent that the United States might not ratify the treaty or the Anglo-American guarantee. Clemenceau sat on the front government bench while his ministers defended various treaty clauses, but the opponents demanded that he personally defend the treaty. By trading a permanent occupation of the Rhine for the Anglo-French guarantee, he was now accused of reducing France to a state of permanent vigilance. He rose and gave what would be his final exegesis on the treaty: "The treaty, with all its complex clauses, will only be worth what you are worth; it will be what you make it...The ideas it contains will grow and bear fruit. You have won the power to impose them on a defeated Germany. We are told that she will revive. All the more reason not to show that we fear her....[D]o you think that one could make a treaty which would do away with the need for vigilance among the nations of Europe who only yesterday were pouring out their blood in battle? Life is a perpetual struggle in war, as in peace....That struggle cannot be avoided. Yes, we must have vigilance, we must have a great deal of vigilance. I cannot say for how many years, perhaps I should say for how many centuries, the crisis which has begun will continue. Yes, this treaty will bring us burdens, troubles, miseries, difficulties, and that will continue for long years."[1] The Chamber of Deputies ratified the treaty by a vote of 372-53. Most of the votes in opposition came from the Socialists. It passed unanimously in the Senate.

The Allies never did resolve the conflict over Fiume and the Dalmatian coast. The Italians and the Jugo-Slavs tried to resolve it themselves. In 1920 they signed the Treaty of Rapallo, which created the "Free State of Fiume." A neighboring port went to Croatia. In 1924, they agreed that Fiume be ceded outright to Italy. Most of the rest of Dalmatia went to Croatia. After Italy's defeat in the Second World War, Fiume reverted to Yugoslavia (as the Croatian city of Rijeka) along with the rest of the Istrian Peninsula and Dalmatia.

The League of Nations came into existence in June, 1920, and Wilson, Léon Bourgeois and Lord Robert Cecil were all awarded the Nobel Peace Prize for the creation and operation of the League. Gen. Smuts' prediction that if the Allies refused Germany's admission into the League it would throw the Germans into the arms of the Russians proved prescient. The two nations signed a treaty of friendship in April, 1922 wherein they agreed to normalize diplomatic relations, each agreeing to renounce all territorial and financial (i.e. reparations) claims on the other. Secretly, they began military consultations. Germany was admitted in 1926; Hitler removed it upon assuming office in 1933. Russia (as the U.S.S.R.) was admitted in 1934. It was expelled in 1939 following its invasion of Finland.

The League could boast some modest successes in its early years. It resolved a few minor territorial disputes. It governed the Free City of Danzig until that was terminated by the invasion of Poland in September, 1939. The plebiscite promised for Upper Silesia went ahead under Allied supervision on March 20, 1921. Paderewski's fear that the run-up to the plebiscite would be bloody proved prescient, with Polish and German paramilitary forces fighting for control. His prediction that the Germans, an ethnic minority in the enclave, would dominate the voting also proved prescient. Sixty percent of the voters opted to remain with Germany. But just as Lloyd George had predicted, the Poles dominated the eastern, industrial regions. The result was a stalemate. In the end, Upper Silesia was partitioned by the League. The western, agricultural areas remained with Germany and the rest became part of Poland. But both Warsaw and Berlin gave considerable autonomy to their respective Silesians.

The League governed the Saar until 1935, and in that year it conducted the plebiscite that had been promised to its inhabitants. With the considerable assistance of Nazi propaganda, and a certain amount of intimidation, 91% of them voted to have the Saar—and all of its coal—revert to Germany.

The Japanese bowed to world-wide pressure and, in 1922, agreed to grant *de jure* control over Shantung Province to China. But they retained their armed forces in province, and were not evicted from Shantung until the end of the Second World War.

But the League's failures far outweighed its limited successes. In September, 1931, Japan invaded Manchuria and set up a puppet government under Pu Yi, the last emperor of China. The League "investigated," and in 1933 voted 42-1 (with only Japan voting against) to demand that Japan quit Manchuria. Instead of complying, Japan quit the League. The League did nothing. The irony was complete: Wilson had sold out the Chinese in order to placate the Japanese so that they would join the League.

On October 3, 1935, Italy invaded Ethiopia. The League condemned Italy, imposed some ineffective sanctions, but otherwise did nothing. Italy quit the League, and with Italy out, all of the Axis powers—Germany, Japan and Germany—were now out of the League. But the League's nadir came on June 30, 1936, when Ethiopia's bearded, magisterial emperor, Haile Selassie, personally appeared before the Assembly in Geneva to plead Ethiopia's case. As he began to speak, Italian journalists began blowing whistles supplied by Mussolini, in an attempt to drown out the emperor. When order was restored and he finally could speak, he referred to Ethiopia as a "small people of twelve million inhabitants, without arms, without resources." He said that the problem was not just the immediate matter of the Italian aggressor, "It is collective security; it is the very existence of the League of Nations….On behalf of the Ethiopian people, a member of the League of Nations, I request the Assembly to take all measures proper to ensure respect for the Covenant."* They did nothing. It was the effective end of the League of Nations. It went dormant during the Second World War. Some of its agencies were folded into the United Nations in 1946.

We cannot know if Clemenceau was serious in his desire to invade the city of Essen, but in January, 1923, the wish he expressed in the waning days of the Council of Four came true. In April, 1921, the Reparations Commission promulgated the final reparations bill: 132 billion gold marks ($33 billion), 58% of which was earmarked for France, 22% for the British Empire, 10% for Italy and 8% for Belgium. Almost immediately, the Germans began defaulting on the required deliveries of coal. In December, 1922, when the Germans defaulted on a required delivery of timber, the government of Prime Minister Raymond Poincaré decided that it had better do something lest the

---

*   A film of Haile Selassie's address can be viewed at *www.youtube.com*.

entire treaty collapse. France and Belgium invaded the Ruhr in January, 1923. The British refused to participate. The invasion produced little coal for France but a passive resistance and an armed occupation that lasted until August, 1925.

What ended the occupation was the Dawes Plan, the creation of the American banker Charles G. Dawes. Germany's reparations payments were reduced to one billion marks for the first year (3% of the total obligation), increasing annually to 2.5 billion marks in the fifth year. Throughout the Peace Conference, Wilson had resisted having the United States assist in Germany's recovery. Under the Dawes Plan, the United States did just that, providing it with loans funded by bonds floated on Wall Street. For his efforts, Dawes received a Nobel Peace Prize and the vice presidency under President Calvin Coolidge.

But the tortuous path of reparations did not end with the Dawes Plan. The reparations burden was reduced further in 1930 by the Young Plan under the authorship of the industrialist Owen D. Young. It called for the issuance of more U.S.-backed bonds. But thew Wall Street crash and the Great Depression put an end to American financing, and the National Socialists ended the reparations payments permanently. That, however, did not end the debt obligations under the American-backed bonds, which were finally paid in full in October, 2010, ninety-two years after the end of the war.

Twelve days after the treaty was signed, Wilson personally presented the treaty to the Senate. It was the first time that a president had ever personally delivered a treaty. All of the Republican senators rose as he entered, but only a few of them joined in the applause. In his thirty-seven-minute address, Wilson advised the gathered Senators that "Convenient, indeed indispensable, as statesmen found the newly-planned League of Nations to be for the execution of present plans of peace and reparation, they saw in it a new aspect before their work was finished. They saw it as the main object of the peace, as the only thing that could complete it or make it worth while. They saw it as the hope of the world, and that hope they did not dare to disappoint....Shall we or any other free people hesitate to accept this great duty? Dare we reject it and break the heart of the world?"[2] When he finished, only one Republican senator, North Dakota's Porter J. McCumber, joined in the applause. After his speech, Wilson repaired to an adjoining reception room, where he was greeted by approximately thirty senators, only one of whom was a Republican. Talk of reservations to the treaty was in the air. Wilson opined that since it required a two-thirds majority to ratify a treaty, a two-thirds majority would be required to pass a reservation. His dismissed as unnecessary the key reservation, the one that provided that Article X of the covenant could not require the United States to enter a war without Congressional approval. Sen. Lodge quickly demurred. He cited Senate Rule 37: "…all other motions and questions upon a treaty shall be decided by a majority vote."

The Republicans enjoyed a slim, two-vote majority in the Senate, some of whom were "irreconcilables," led by Idaho's William Borah, opposed to the League under any circumstances. By there were not enough of them to defeat the treaty on an up-or-down vote. But there were nineteen or twenty "mild reservationist" Republicans who would vote to ratify, but only if the ratification resolution contained a series of reservations, including the reservation to Article X. These senators held the key to ratification.

On July 19, Wilson may have suffered a small stroke. Adm. Grayson hid his condition, calling it "dysentery." On August 15, Sen. Key Pittman, the Nevada Democrat who was a member of the Foreign Relations Committee, warned Wilson that there were a number of Senate Democrats who also favored placing reservations in the ratification resolution. He asked Wilson to support a Senate resolution incorporating the reservations, one that would not be part of the ratification resolution. Four days later, Wilson met with Lodge and the full Foreign Relations Committee at the White House. During the three-hour meeting, he was asked why, if the League existed to prevent war, the Anglo-American guarantee to France was necessary. He responded that it was simply an extra safeguard for France. His presentation was filled with misstatements of fact and contradictions.[3] More importantly, he stated that while he would support any "interpretive resolutions," he opposed any reservations to the ratification resolution, which, he averred, would require the consent of all of the other powers signatory to the treaty.[4] No one except Wilson believed this. Thus, the dispute now reduced itself not to the fundamental question of whether the United States should or should not become a founding member of the League of Nations, but whether the Lodge reservations would be included in the ratification resolution or, as Wilson insisted, in separate "interpretive reservations." The man spearheading the effort for ratification was Minority Leader Sen. Gilbert Hitchcock, who pleaded with Wilson to "extend to Lodge and his followers the olive branch." Wilson's response was to "let Lodge extend the olive branch."

Less than a week later, Wilson decided to make a cross-country trip to sell the League. According to Arthur S. Link, a Wilson biographer and editor of the Wilson papers, his decision "was obviously made without much thought, in anger, and on the spur of the moment."[5] But it is not surprising. Wilson's entire professional life, both as an academic and as a politician, had been propelled by his ability to sway people from the podium. He had once admitted to Ellen that to him, it was like a drug. Admiral Grayson and Edith warned him against it, fearing it might kill him. It was also irrational. It had no chance of swaying any of the senators. On September 26, on board the presidential train outside Pueblo, Colorado, Wilson collapsed, and may have suffered a small stroke. The trip was canceled and he was rushed back to Washington. On October 2 he suffered the massive stroke that left him paralyzed on the left side. The effect on the rest of Wilson's presidency is now well-documented. For months, Wilson was shielded from the outside world, his condition known only to Admiral Grayson, Joseph Tumulty and Edith Wilson. They determined what mail Wilson would and would not see; correspondence was returned by Mrs. Wilson, in her own hand.

On the same day that Wilson suffered the stroke that paralyzed him, former Foreign Secretary Sir Edward Grey, called out of retirement by Lloyd George, arrived in Washington for the purpose of convincing Wilson to accept the Lodge reservations. What happened was both tragedy and farce. A member of Sir Edward's entourage had previously made a derogatory remark about Edith, and it had made the rounds. When this aide again accompanied Grey to Washington, Edith demanded that the aide be sent home before he would be granted an audience with Wilson. Grey refused, on the ground that it would ruin the young man's career. Grey spent a month cooling his heels before he returned home, never having seen Wilson. It is doubtful that Wilson ever learned of the incident.

There matters stood as Wilson, shielded from the world by Edith, Tumulty and Grayson, slowly recovered. In February, 1920, President Taft, still an ardent supporter of the League, drafted a compromise reservation to Article X.* Wilson refused it, the refusal letter penned by Edith. The Senate voted twice on ratification, and twice it failed. In its final defeat on March 19, 1920, the treaty resolution, which included the Lodge Reservations, forty-nine senators voted in favor, thirty-five opposed, thus failing to achieve the required two-thirds majority. Twenty-three democrats, *at Wilson's urging*, voted no. A few democrats voted in favor, despite Wilson's opposition. In the end, neither Henry Cabot Lodge nor the "irreconcilable" Republicans "broke the heart of the world." It was Wilson himself.

In his *Memoirs of the Peace Conference*, Lloyd George summed up America's failure to enter the League: "Had [Wilson] conquered his stubborn pride, had be subordinated his personal antipathies for the sake of a great cause of which he was an

---

* "The United States assumes no obligations under the provisions of Article X to preserve the territorial integrity or political independence of any other country or to interfere in controversies between other nations whether members of the League or not or to employ the military and naval forces of the United States under any article of the treaty for any purpose unless in any particular case the Congress, which under the Constitution has the sole power to declare war or authorize the employment of the military or naval forces of the United States, shall by act or joint resolution so declare."

outstanding champion, America would have been in the League of Nations and the whole history of the world would have been changed. Has there ever been a greater tragedy in human history?"[6]

Was it "stubborn pride" that prevented Wilson from coming to terms with Lodge and the "mild reservationists?" He had a long-standing aversion to compromise, and his Covenanter heritage made him see opponents not only as wrong-headed but as evil. But he had come to Paris with one objective, the League of Nations. It was the one thing he believed in his heart would remake the world and prevent another world war. In his obsessive drive to achieve it, he had been willing sacrifice anything and everything. Yet when he had it within his grasp, he squandered it all rather than accept the inconsequential "Lodge Reservations." This cannot be explained by "stubborn pride." The ineluctable conclusion is that it was the work of one having lost his bearings, a man mentally impaired.

Wilson's impairment was the probable cause for the exile of Edward M. House. One thing is certain: There was no "break" between the two. There was never a heated moment; there were no recriminations. The record proves it. On the day before he signed the peace treaty, Wilson wrote "My dear House," asking House's opinion of the drafts of the League of Nations mandates. "[L]et me know your opinion at the earliest possible hour," he wrote, signing it "Affectionately yours."[7] On August 15, Wilson penned a letter to House, beginning "I am glad that your letters have begun to come, though the movement of mail between us is sure to be very slow." After again commenting on the League mandates, Wilson concluded "I hope that you and the family keep well. We are going through a tremendous storm of all sorts of difficulties here…We unite in the warmest messages." Again he signed it "Affectionately yours." Later that month, after rumors surfaced that there had been a "falling out" between the two, House wrote Wilson from London: "Our annual falling out seems to have occurred. The Foreign Office received a cable the other day saying that we were no longer on speaking terms and asking that the Prime Minister and Balfour be informed."[8] Wilson responded with a short cable: "Am deeply distressed by malicious story about break between us and thank you for your message about it. The best way to treat it is with silent contempt."[9] That same day, Lansing wrote in his desk diary: "Prest much incensed at press report he had broken with House."[10]

House returned to the United States at the same time of Wilson's stroke, unfortunately also ill with kidney stones. That is when communication between House and Wilson ceased. Only when House read an October 17 letter Edith had written to House's wife, in response to a letter she had written to express her concern for the president, did House learn that Wilson did not even know he had returned from Paris. "When he is better," Edith wrote, "I will tell him of your letter and the Col.s messages, but as we keep everything from him (which is not important to have his advise about, & which would annoy or distress him, I have not told him of the Col's illness or that he has left Paris—for I know how anxious he was that he remain there for the time."[11]

Edith Wilson had despised House from the beginning. Wilson knew of it, and had tried to soften her loathing for him. He was now helpless to do so. She was assisted in House's exclusion by Admiral Grayson and the man she later chose to be Wilson's biographer, Ray Stannard Baker. In early November, Baker wrote in his diary: "The Colonel's stock has fallen to zero. He is no longer a factor."[12]

After Wilson first met House in 1911, he commented that his and House's minds worked in perfect harmony. Wilson sent House on annual diplomatic missions to Europe with no instructions. None were needed; House knew what Wilson wanted. But if in Paris their ultimate goals were the same, a peaceful world founded on the League of Nations, their means of achieving those goals diverged. House feared the onrush of Bolshevism in Europe and wanted the Peace Conference to conclude the treaty as quickly as possible. He was willing to compromise on places like the Left Bank of the Rhine and Fiume if it would speed up the process; Wilson was not. But these differences do not explain why Wilson refused to see House for remainder of his life, and House himself was baffled and saddened by it. Like so much else, the result would probably have been different had Wilson not been disabled.

The end of the Peace Conference did not end Lloyd George's interactions with Clemenceau, as they both remained the heads of their respective governments, and needed to finalize the treaties with the other defeated powers. They met in December, 1919, when Clemenceau traveled to London to discuss a wide range of issues necessitated, in large part, by the American refusal to ratify the peace treaty and the Anglo-American guarantee. Lloyd George met Clemenceau at Victoria Station. "I am very glad to see you," Clemenceau said upon greeting Lloyd George, but he could not help but comment on the inclement London weather.[13] The two, who had met for the first time in Carlsbad in 1909, met for the last time in June, 1921, when they were both in retirement. Clemenceau had been awarded an honorary degree from Oxford.

Clemenceau and Lloyd George had both come to the Peace Conference constricted by their respective publics, a common fate of politicians in democratic states. In France, the cry was "Make the Germans pay." In London, they wanted to "squeeze the German lemon until the pips squeaked." Each knew better, but each knew that if he showed too much moderation he would be replaced by someone worse. It is therefore somewhat ironic that Clemenceau and Lloyd George—and Wilson as well—did not survive in office long after the Peace Conference ended.

Clemenceau was the first to go. He had once mused that there were two things in the world utterly useless, one being the human appendix and the other being the president of France. He never officially announced that he was a candidate for the office, but let it be known that he would serve if elected. Nor was he ever officially defeated for the office. On January 16, 1920, in an unofficial caucus of his fellow Republicans in the Chamber of Deputies, he was beaten by the lackluster Paul Deschanel. Clemenceau retired. Deschanel's presidency was marked by his flying out of a moving train, occasioned by his trying to pry open a window. His fall from the train either sparked or accelerated his descent into madness. His presidency lasted seven months.

Wilson's term ended on March 4, 1921. He rode to the Capitol in an open car with President-elect Harding, but was too disabled to attend the swearing-in ceremony.

Lloyd George had been a man without a party since he assisted in the ouster of Herbert Henry Asquith in December, 1916. He had governed heading a coalition of loyal Liberals and Tories. On October 19, 1922, the Tories caucused and decided to end the coalition. Lloyd George presented his resignation as prime minister to the king that afternoon. He would be the last Liberal ever to hold that office.

Clemenceau met with Wilson for the last time during Clemenceau's triumphal visit to America in November, 1922. After a nostalgic drive through the Greenwich Village streets of his youth (failing to find the house where he had boarded, it having been razed) he went down to Washington, D.C. Of his visit with Wilson, he later told the journalist Wythe Williams: "It was pathetic, I was with him only fifteen minutes. Mentally he was as alert as ever, but could not raise himself from his chair. We didn't discuss the future—only the occasional good moments of the old days. Wilson was a man of great vigor. He fought hard for his great dream of a better world. I felt that he deeply appreciated my call. In any case we fully forgave each other for our bitter quarrels at Versailles. That was all in the past, and both of us had lost. He is preparing for his earthly departure and I suppose I shall be doing the same before long. I am a much older man. In retrospect I am sorry that he could not have fought longer, as I have great respect for his sincerity and honesty. And now, at the last, we are friends."[14]

Lloyd George last saw Wilson when Lloyd George paid a courtesy call on him in October, 1923. His impressions were similar to Clemenceau's. "His health was so precarious that his doctor warned me that the interview must be a short one," he wrote in his post-war *Memoirs*. "He was pleased to see me and his reception was cordial. He alluded with pleasure to his experiences at the Conference. Of Clemenceau he spoke in kindly terms. But when the name of Poincaré was mentioned, all the bitterness of his nature burst into a sentence of concentrated hatred. 'He is a cheat and a liar,' he exclaimed...The name of Coolidge provoked another outburst. 'Coolidge is no one in particular'....We shunned all reference to the League of Nations. The doctor signaled to me that the interview should be terminated. That is the last I saw of this extraordinary mixture of real greatness thwarted by much littleness."[15]

Woodrow Wilson was fifteen years younger than Georges Clemenceau, yet he predeceased Clemenceau by five years, dying on February 3, 1924, not three years after the end of his presidency. Edith survived him by thirty-seven years, devoting her time to the curation of his legacy, which included the publication of her own memoir and the restoration of Wilson's birthplace in Staunton, Virginia. She died in 1961, having attended the inauguration of John F. Kennedy.

Clemenceau spent his retirement writing a two-volume collection of philosophical essays, a biography of Demosthenes, and a biography of his great friend Claude Monet, whose company he enjoyed until Monet's death in 1926. He traveled far and wide, to the United States, Egypt, Japan and elsewhere. He died in his home in the rue Franklin on November 24, 1929. His remains were interred in Vendee hamlet of Le Colombier, beside those of his father.

Lloyd George's wife of fifty-three years, Margaret, died in 1941. In 1943, he married Frances Stevenson, his mistress of thirty-three years. Late in 1944, the poor Welsh boy who had been apprenticed to a solicitor, who had never attended a university or a high school, learned he was to be ennobled as the Earl Lloyd-George of Dwyfor. But this man who had broken the iron grip that the House of Lords had on British life never got to sit in it. He died on March 26, 1945. His remains are interred in the Welsh town of Llanystumdwy, the hamlet of his youth.

BIBLIOGRAPHY

PRINTED MANUSCRIPT SOURCES

Baker, Ray Stannard. *Woodrow Wilson and the World Settlement*. 3 vols. Garden City, N.Y.: Doubleday, Page. 1922.

Baker, Ray Stannard, and William E. Dodd, eds. *The Public Papers of Woodrow Wilson*, 6 vols. Vols. 1-2: ("College and State") New York: Harper & Brothers, 1925; Vols. 3-4 ("The New Democracy") New York: Harper & Brothers, 1926; Vols. 5-6 ("War and Peace") New York: Harper & Brothers, 1927.

Baldensperger, Fernand, ed. *American Reconstruction 1865-1870*. New York: Lincoln MacVeagh, Dial Press, 1928.

Clemenceau, Georges. *France Facing Germany*. New York: E.P. Dutton, 1919.

Cronon, E. David, ed. *The Political Thought of Woodrow Wilson*. Indianapolis, IN.: Bobbs-Merrill, 1965.

Hendrick, Burton J., ed. *The Life and Letters of Walter H. Page*. 2 vols. New York: Doubleday, Page, 1924.

Link, Arthur S., ed. *The Deliberations of the Council of Four (March 24—June 28, 1919)*, 2 vols. Princeton: Princeton University Press, 1992.

Link, Arthur S., ed. *The Papers of Woodrow Wilson*. 69 vols. Princeton: Princeton University Press, 1966-1993.

McEwen, John M., ed. *The Riddell Diaries*. London: Athlone Press, 1986.

Morgan, Kenneth O., ed. *Lloyd George Family Letters, 1885-1936*. Cardiff, U.K.: University of Wales Press, 1973.

Paget, Alain, ed. *Emile Zola, The Dreyfus Affair, J'Accuse & Other Writings*. New Haven, CT.: Yale University Press, 1996.

Seymour, Charles. *The Intimate Papers of Colonel House*. 4 vols. Boston: Houghton Mifflin, 1927-1928.

Temperley, H.W.V., ed. *A History of the Peace Conference of Paris*. 6 vols. London: Oxford University Press, 1920.

DIGITAL MANUSCRIPT SOURCES

Link, Arthur S, ed. *The Papers of Woodrow Wilson Digital Edition*. Charlottesville: University of Virginia Press, Rotunda, 2017. Originally published in the Papers of Woodrow Wilson © 1966—1994, Princeton University Press.

Papers Relating to the Foreign Relations of the United States, 1914, Supplement, The World War. Washington, D.C.: Government Printing Office, 1914, http://digital.library.wisc.edu.

Papers Relating to the Foreign Relations of the United States, 1916, Supplement, The World War. Washington, D.C.: Government Printing Office, 1916, http://digital.library.wisc.edu.

Papers Relating to the Foreign Relations of the United States, 1919, The Paris Peace Conference. 12 vols. Washington, D.C.: Government Printing Office, 1919. http://digital.library.wisc.edu.

BOOKS

Anderson, R.D. *France, 1870-1914*. London: Routledge & Kegan Paul, 1977.

Axson, Stockton. *Brother Woodrow, A Memoir of Woodrow Wilson*. Princeton: Princeton University Press, 1993.

Axtell, James. *The Making of Princeton University*. Princeton: Princeton University Press, 2006.

Baker, Ray Stannard. *Woodrow Wilson, Life and Letters*. 7 vols. V. 1: ("Youth") London: William Heinemann, 1928; V. 2: ("Princeton 1890-1910") Garden City: Doubleday, Page. 1927; V. 3 ("Governor") Garden City: Doubleday, Doran, 1931; V. 4: ("President, 1913-1914") Doubleday, Doran, 1931; V. 5: ("Neutrality, 1914-1915") Doubleday, Doran, 1935; V. 6: ("Facing War, 1915-1917") Doubleday, Doran, 1937; V. 7: ("War Leader, 1917-1918") Doubleday, Doran, 1939.

——. *Woodrow Wilson and the World Settlement*, 3 vols. Garden City, NY: Doubleday, Page, 1922.

Baruch, Bernard. *The Making of the Reparation and Economic Sections of the Treaty*. New York: Howard Fertig, 1970.

Begley, Louis. *Why the Dreyfus Affair Matters*. New Haven: Yale University Press, 1999.

Berg, A. Scott. *Wilson*. New York: G.P. Putnam's Sons, 2013.

Birdsall, Paul. *Versailles Twenty Years After*. New York: Reynal & Hitchcock, 1941.

Blalock, Stephanie M. *"Go to Pfaff's!" The History of a Restaurant and Lager Beer Saloon*. Bethlehem, PA.: Lehigh University Press, 2014.

Blum, John M. *Joe Tumulty and the Wilson Era*. Boston: Houghton Mifflin, 1951.

Bonsal, Stephen. *Unfinished Business*. Garden City, NY: Doubleday, Doran, 1944.

Bragdon, Henry. *Woodrow Wilson, The Academic Years*. Cambridge, MA: Harvard University Press, 1967.

Brogan, D.W. *The Development of Modern France (1870-1939)*. London: Hamish Hamilton, 1940.

Brown, Frederick. *For the Soul of France*. New York: Alfred A. Knopf, 2010.

Bruun, Geoffrey. *Clemenceau*. Cambridge, MA: Harvard University Press; 1943.

Burnett, Robert A. "Georges Clemenceau in the Paris Peace Conference 1919" (PhD diss. University of North Carolina at Chapel Hill, 1967)

Bury, J.P.T., *Napoleon III and the Second Empire*. London: English Universities Press, 1964.

Cameron, Rondo E. *France and the Economic Development of Europe 1800-1914*. Princeton: Princeton University Press, 1961.

Carroll, E. Malcolm. *French Public Opinion and Foreign Affairs, 1870-1914*. New York: The Century Company, 1931.

Chace, James. *1912*. New York: Simon & Shuster, 2004.

Chapman, Guy. *The Dreyfus Trials*. London: Granada Publishing, 1974.

Churchill, Winston S. *The Aftermath*. London: Macmillan & Co. 1941.

Clemenceau, Georges. *Grandeur and Misery of Victory*. New York: Harcourt, Brace, 1930.

———. *South America Today*. New York: Putnam, 1911.

Craig, Hardin. *Woodrow Wilson at Princeton*. Norman, OK: University of Oklahoma Press, 1960.

Cregier, Don. *Bounder from Wales*. Columbia, MO: University of Missouri Press, 1976.

Crowe, S.E. *The Berlin West African Conference, 1884-1885*. London: Longmans, Green, 1942.

Czernin, Ferdinand. *Versailles 1919*. New York: G.P. Putnam's Sons, 1964.

Dallas, Gregor. *At the Heart of a Tiger*. New York: Carroll & Graf Publishers, 1993.

Devlin, Patrick. *Too Proud to Fight -Woodrow Wilson's Neutrality*. New York: Oxford University Press, 1975.

Edwards, J. Hugh. *David Lloyd George*. 2 vols. London: The Waverly Book Co., 1930.

Elcock, Howard. *Portrait of a Decision*. London: Eyre Metheun,1972.

Ellis, Jack D. *The Early Life of Georges Clemenceau, 1841-1893*. Lawrence, KS: The Regents Press of Kansas, 1980.

Floto, Inga. *Colonel House in Paris*. Princeton: Princeton University Press, 1973.

George, Alexander. *Woodrow Wilson and Colonel House*. New York: John Day,1956.

George, Lord Riddell. *Lord Riddell's Intimate Diary of the Peace Conference and After*. London: Victor Gallancz, 1933.

George, Lord Riddell. *Lord Riddell's War Diary, 1914-1918*. London: Ivor Nicholson & Watson, 1933.

George, R.L. *David & Winston*. New York: Overlook Press, 2008.

George, William. *My Brother and I*. London: Eyre & Spottiswoode, 1958.

George, W.R.P. *Lloyd George Backbencher*. Llandysul, U.K.: Gomer Press, 1983.

Giesberg, Robert. *The Treaty of Frankfort*. Philadelphia: University of Pennsylvania Press, 1966.

Gilbert, Bentley, *David Lloyd George, a Political Life*, (2 vols.) *The Architect of Change, 1863-1912*. Columbus, OH: Ohio State University Press, 1987; *Organizer of Victory 1912-1916*. Columbus, OH: Ohio State University Press, 1992.

Gildea, Robert. *Children of the Revolution, The French, 1799—1914*. Cambridge, MA.: Harvard University Press, 2008.

Gooch, G.P. *Franco-German Relations 1871-1914*. London: Longmans, Green, 1923.

———. *Before the War—Studies in Diplomacy* London: Longmans, Green, 1936.

Goodwin, Doris Kearns. *The Bully Pulpit*. New York: Simon & Schuster, 2013.

Gould, Lewis L., ed. *The Progressive Era*. Syracuse, N.Y.: Syracuse University Press, 1974.

Grayson, Cary. *Woodrow Wilson, An Intimate Memoir*. Washington, D.C.: Potomac Books, 1960.

Grey of Fallodon. *Twenty-Five Years, 1892-1916*. 2 vols. New York: Frederick A. Stokes, 1925.

Grigg, John. *The Young Lloyd George*. Berkeley, CA: University of California Press, 1973.

———. *Lloyd George, The People's Champion*. London: Eyre Metheun, 1978.

———. *Lloyd George, War Leader*. London: Penguin Books, 2002.

Halasz, Nicholas. *Captain Dreyfus: The Story of a Mass Hysteria*. New York: Simon & Schuster, 1955.

Hankey, Maurice. *The Supreme Control at the Paris Peace Conference, 1919*. London: George Allen and Unwin, 1963.

Hardinge, Charles. *Old Diplomacy*. Frome, U.K.: Butler & Tanner, 1947.

Hattersley, Roy. *David Lloyd George, The Great Outsider.* London: Little, Brown, 2010.

Hochschild, Adam. *To End All Wars.* New York: Houghton Mifflin, 2011.

Hofstadter, Richard. *The Age of Reform.* New York: Alfred A. Knopf, 1959.

Hofstadter, Richard, ed., *The Progressive Movement*, Englewood Cliffs, N.J.: Prentice Hall, 1963.

Holt, Edgar. *The Boer War.* New York: G.P. Putnam's Sons, 1958.

———. *The Tiger.* London: Hamish Hamilton, 1976.

Horne, Alistair. *The Fall of Paris.* London: Penguin Books, 1990.

House, Edward M. and Seymour, Charles, eds. *What Really Happened at Paris.* London: Hodder & Stoughton, 1921.

Houston, David. *Eight Years With Wilson's Cabinet, 1913-1920.* vol 1. New York: Doubleday, Page, 1926.

Howard, Michael. *The Franco-Prussian War.* London: Granada Publishing, 1979.

Hunt, George L. and McNeill, John T., eds. *Calvinism and the Political Order.* London: Westminster Press, 1965.

Hyndman, H.M. *Clemenceau: The Man and His Time.* New York: Frederick A. Stokes, 1919.

Inglis, Carol Anne. *Clemenceau and French Labor: The National Assembly Debates, 1906-1909.* Privately published by Concordia University. Montreal, 1977 http//spectrum.library.concordia.ca/2719/1/MK33131.pdf.

Jackson, J. Hampden. *Clemenceau and the Third Republic.* London: Hodder & Stoughton, 1946.

Johnson, Martin P. *The Dreyfus Affair.* New York: St. Martin's Press, 1999.

Johnson, Willis Fletcher. *George Harvey, Passionate Patriot.* London: George Allen & Unwin, 1929.

Judd, Denis, and Surridge, Keith. *The Boer War, A History.* London: I.B. Tauris, 1913.

Keegan, John. *The First World War.* New York: Alfred A. Knopf, 1999.

Kennan, George F. *The Fateful Alliance,* New York: Pantheon, 1984.

Kennedy, Paul. *The Rise and Fall of the Great Powers.* New York: Random House, 1987.

Kerney, James. *The Political Education of Woodrow Wilson.* New York: The Century Company, 1926.

Keynes, John Maynard. *The Economic Consequences of the Peace.* Cambridge, U.K. Kings College, 1919.

King, Jere Clemens. *Foch versus Clemenceau.* Cambridge, MA.: Harvard University Press, 1960.

———. *Generals and Politicians.* Berkeley, CA.: University of California Press, 1951.

Lamont, Thomas M. "Reparations," in Edward M. House and Charles Seymour, eds. *What Really Happened at Paris.* London: Hodder & Stoughton, 1921.

Lansing, Robert. *The Big Four and Others of the Peace Conference.* London: Hutchinson, 1922. 1922].

———. *The Peace Negotiations, a Personal Narrative.* Boston: Houghton Mifflin, 1931.

Lennox, Lady Algernon Gordon, ed., *The Diary of Lord Bertie of Thame, 1914-1918*, Vol. 1, New York: George H. Doran, 1924.

Levin, Phyllis Lee, *Edith and Woodrow.* New York: Scribner, 2001.

Lewis, McMillan. *Woodrow Wilson of Princeton.* Livingston, AL: Livingston Publishing, 1952.

Link, Arthur S. *Wilson, Campaigns for Progressivism and Peace, 1916-1917.* Princeton: Princeton University Press, 1965.

———. *Wilson, Confusions and Crises, 1915-1916.* Princeton: Princeton University Press, 1964.

———. *Wilson the Diplomatist.* Baltimore: Johns Hopkins Press, 1957.

———. *Wilson, The Road to the White House.* Princeton: Princeton University Press, 1947.

———. *Wilson, The Struggle for Neutrality.* Princeton: Princeton University Press, 1960.

———. *Woodrow Wilson, Revolution, War and Peace.* Wheeling, IL.: Harlan, Davidson, 1979.

Lloyd George, David. *Memoirs of the Peace Conference.* New Haven: Yale University Press, 1939.

——. *The Truth About the Peace Treaties*. 2 vols. London: Victor Gollancz, 1938.

——. *War Memoirs*. 2 vols. London: Ivor Nicholson & Watson, 1933.

Lodge, Henry Cabot. *The Senate and the League of Nations*. New York: Chas. Scribner's Sons, 1925.

Longford, Elizabeth. *Jameson's Raid*. London: Weidenfeld & Nicolson, 1960.

Lowe, John. *The Great Powers, Imperialism and the German Problem*. London: Routledge Press, 1994.

MacMillan, Margaret. *The War that Ended Peace*. New York: Random House, 2013.

Mann, Arthur, ed. *The Progressive Era*. New York: Holt, Rinehart & Winston, 1963.

Martet, Jean. *Georges Clemenceau*. London: Longmans, Green, 1930.

Massie, Robert. *Dreadnaught*. New York: Random House, 1991.

Mayer, Arno. *Politics and Diplomacy of Peacemaking*. New York: Vintage Books, 1969.

Mayeur, Jean Marie and Reberioux, Madeleine. *The Third Republic From its Origins to the Great War, 1871—1914*. London: Cambridge University Press, 1973.

Maynard, W. Barksdale. *Woodrow Wilson, Princeton to the Presidency*. New Haven: Yale University Press, 2008.

McAuliffe, Mary. *Dawn of the Belle Epoque*. Lanham, MD.: Rowman & Littlefield, 2011.

McCombs, William F. *Making Woodrow Wilson President*. New York: Fairview Publishing,1921.

McCormick, Donald. *The Mask of Merlin*. New York: Holt, Rinehart & Winston, 1963.

McCormick, Vance. *Diaries of Vance McCormick*. Undated, privately published.

McCullough, David. *The Path Between the Seas*. New York: Simon & Schuster, 1977.

Meyer, G.J. *A World Undone*. New York: Delacorte Press, 2006.

Miller, David Hunter. *The Drafting of the Covenant*. 2 vols. New York: G.P. Putnam's Sons, 1928.

Mitchell, Allan. *Bismarck and the French Nation*. Indianapolis, IN.: Bobbs-Merrrill, 1971.

Myers, William Starr, ed. *Woodrow Wilson, Some Princeton Memories*. Princeton: Princeton University Press, 1946.

Nevins, Allan. *Henry White: Thirty Years of American Diplomacy*. New York: Harper & Bros., 1930.

Neu, Charles E. *Colonel House*. New York: Oxford University Press, 2015.

Newhall, David S. *Clemenceau, a Life at War*. Lewiston, N.Y.: Edward Mellen Press, 1991.

Nicolson, Harold. *Peacemaking 1919*. Gloucester, MA: Peter Smith, 1984.

Noble, George Bernard. *Policies and Opinions at Paris, 1919*. New York: Macmillan Co., 1935.

Nowak, Karl Friedrich. *Versailles*. New York: Payson and Clarke, 1929.

Osborn, George. *Woodrow Wilson, The Early Years*. Baton Rouge, LA.: Louisiana State University Press, 1968.

O'Toole, Patricia, *The Moralist*. New York: Simon & Schuster, 2018.

Owen, Frank. *Tempestuous Journey*. London: Hutchinson, 1954.

Porch, Douglas. *The March to the Marne, 1871-1914*. London: Cambridge University Press, 1981.

Porter, Charles W. *The Career of Théophile Delcassé*. Westport, CT.: Greenwood Press, 1975.

Pugh, Martin. *Lloyd George*. London: Longman Group, 1988.

Paleologue, Maurice. *An Intimate Journal of the Dreyfus Case*. Westport, CT.: Greenwood Press, 1957

Price, Roger. *The French Second Empire*. London: Cambridge University Press, 2001.

Ralston, David B. *The Army of the Republic*. Cambridge, MA.: M.I.T. Press, 1967.

Recouly, Raymond. *The Third Republic*. London: William Heinemann, 1928.

Rowland, Peter. *David Lloyd George*. New York: Macmillan Publishing, 1975.

——. *The Last Liberal Governments*. New York: Macmillan Publishing, 1968.

Rudin, Harry R. *Armistice 1918*. New Haven, CT.: Yale University Press, 1944

Schechter, Betty. *The Dreyfus Affair*. New York: Houghton Mifflin, 1965.

Schivelbusch, Wolfgang. *The Culture of Defeat*. New York: Henry Holt, 2001.

Seager, Frederic H. *The Boulanger Affair*. Ithaca, NY.: Cornell University Press, 1969.

Scott, John A. *Republican Ideas in the Liberal Tradition in France, 1870–1914*. New York: Columbia University Press, 1951.

Shotwell, James T. *At the Paris Peace Conference*. New York, Macmillan, 1937.

Smith, Daniel M. *Robert Lansing and American Neutrality, 1914-1917*. Berkeley, CA.: University of California Press, 1958.

Steed, Henry Wickham. *Through Thirty Years*, vol. 2. London: William Heinemann, 1924.

Steefel, Lawrence D. *Bismarck, the Hohenzollern Candidacy, and the Origins of the Franco-Prussian War of 1870*. Cambridge, MA.: Harvard University Press, 1962.

Steffens, Lincoln. *The Shame of the City*. Charleston, S.C.: BiblioBazaar, 2009.

Stevenson, D. *French War Aims Against Germany 1914-1919*. Oxford, U.K.: Clarendon Press, 1982.

Stevenson, Frances. *Lloyd George*. New York: Harper & Row, 1971.

Stowell, Ellery C. and Munro, Henry F. *International Cases*. Boston: Houghton Mifflin, 1916.

Striner, Richard. *Woodrow Wilson and World War I*. Lanham, MD.: Rowman & Littlefield, 2014.

Stuart, Graham H. *French Foreign Policy from Fashoda to Serajevo*. New York: The Century Co., 1921.

Szeps, Berta. *My Life and History*. New York: Alfred A. Knopf, 1939.

Tardieu, Andre. *The Truth About the Treaty*. London: Hodder & Stoughton, 1921.

Thompson, Charles T. *The Peace Conference Day by Day*. New York: Brentano's, 1920.

Tillman, Seth. *Anglo-American Relations at the Peace Conference of 1919*, Princeton, N.J.: Princeton University Press, 1961.

Tink, Andrew. *Australia, 1901-200*. Sydney: New South Publishing, 2014.

Tuchman, Barbara. *The Zimmermann Telegram*. New York: Dell, 1965.

Tumulty, Joseph. *Woodrow Wilson as I Know Him*. New York: Doubleday, Page, 1921.

Walworth, Arthur. *Wilson and his Peacemakers*. New York: W.W. Norton, 1986.

——. *Woodrow Wilson*. 2 vols. Baltimore, MD.: Penguin Books, 1969.

Warner, H. Landon, ed. *Reforming American Life in the Progressive Era*. New York: Major Issues in American History, 1971.

Watson, D.R. *Georges Clemenceau, a Political Biography*. London: Eyre Methuen, 1974.

Wawro, Geoffrey. *The Franco-Prussian War*. London: Cambridge University Press, 2003.

Wetzel, David. *A Duel of Giants*. Madison, WI.: University of Wisconsin Press, 2001.

Wilentz, Sean. *The Rise of American Democracy*. New York: W.W. Norton, 2005.

Williams, Joyce Grigsby. *Colonel House and Edward Grey*. Lanham, MD.: University Press of America, 1984.

Williams, Wythe. *The Tiger of France*. New York: Duell, Sloan and Pearce, 1949.

Wilson, Joseph R. *Mutual Relation of the Masters and Slaves as Taught in the Bible*. Augusta, GA.: Steam Press of Chronicle & Sentinel, 1861.

Wilson, Woodrow. *Congressional Government*. New York: Meridian Books, 1959.

——. *The State*. Lexington, MA.: D.C. Heath, 1898.

——. *A History of the American People*. 5 vols. New York: Harper & Brothers, 1902.

Weinstein, Edwin A. *Woodrow Wilson: A Medical and Psychological Biography*. Princeton: Princeton University Press, 1981.

Wright, Peter E. *At the Supreme War Council*. New York: G.P. Putnam's Sons, 1921.

ARTICLES

Andrieux, Louis. "Georges Clemenceau," *The North American Review* 184, no. 609, (February, 1907).

Bauer, Deborah S. "Georges Boulanger: The Third Republic's Spy Master?" *Proceedings of the Western Society for French History* 39, 2011, at http://handle.net/2027/spo.0642292.0039.018

Bigelow, John. "Did Grant, Sherman and Sheridan Teach Militarism to Germany?" *The William and Mary Quarterly* 24, no. 1 (July 1915).

Bliss, Tasker. "The Evolution of the United Command." *Foreign Affairs*, (December, 1922).

Curry, George. "Woodrow Wilson, Jan Smuts and the Versailles Settlement." *The American Historical Review*, 66, no. 4 (July, 1961).

Dockrill, M.L. "David Lloyd George and Foreign Policy Before 1914" in Taylor, A.J.P. *Lloyd George: Twelve Essays* (Atheneum, 1971).

Edwards, E.W. "The Franco-German Agreement on Morocco, 1909." *The English Historical Review* 78, no. 308 (July, 1963).

Fuller, Joseph V. "The War-Scare of 1875," *The American Historical Review* 24, no. 2 (January, 1919).

Gilderhus, Mark T. "Carranza and the Decision to Revolt, 1913; A Problem in Historical Interpretation." *The Americas* 33 no. 2 (October. 1976).

Grafton, Henry. "Precepting: Myth and Reality of a Princeton Institution." *Princeton Alumni Weekly,* 103 (March, 2003).

Greenhalgh, Elizabeth. "David Lloyd George, Georges Clemenceau and the 1918 Manpower Crisis." *The Historical Journal* 50, no. 2 (June 2007).

Henderson, Peter. "Woodrow Wilson, Victoriano Huerta and the Recognition Issue in Mexico." *The Americas* 41, no. 2 (Oct 1984).

Hewes, James E. "Henry Cabot Lodge and the League of Nations." *Proceedings of the American Philosophical Society* 114.4 (1970).

Inglis, William. "Helping to Make a President." *Colliers Weekly* LVIII, October 7, 1916.

Jones, Heather. "Algeciras Revisited, European Crisis and Conference Diplomacy, 16 January–April, 1906." *European University Institute*, EUI Working Paper MWP 2009/01 (2009).

Lamont, Thomas J. "Reparations," in *What Really Happened at Paris,* (Edward Mandell House and Charles Seymour, eds., New York: Charles Scribner's Sons, 1921).

Lévy, Claude. "Un Journal de Clemenceau: Le Bloc," *Revue d'Histoire Moderne et Contemporaine*, (April—June 1963).

Kernek, Sterling. "The British Government's Reactions to President Wilson's 'Peace' Note of December, 1916." *The Historical Journal* 13, no. 4 (December, 1970).

King, C. Richard. "Woodrow Wilson's Visit to Texas in 1911." *The Southwestern Historical Quarterly* 65, no. 2 (Oct., 1961).

Lynn, Kenneth S. "The Hidden Agony of Woodrow Wilson." *The Wilson Quarterly*, Winter, 2004.

Milwaukee Journal. "Mary Clemenceau—Discarded Wife." Nov 27, 1969.

Morton, Richard A. "It Was Bryan and Sullivan Who Did the Trick." *Journal of the Illinois State Historical Society* 108, no. 2 (Summer, 2015).

Mulder, John M. "Joseph R. Wilson: Southern Presbyterian Patriarch." *Journal of Presbyterian History* (1974).

Murray, Bruce. "The People's Budget a Century On." *The Journal of Liberal History* (Autumn, 2009).

Orthon, Guerlac. "The Separation of Church and State in France." *Political Science Quarterly 23,* (June, 1908).

Park, Bert E. M.D., "Wilson's Neurologic Illness during the Summer of 1919." In Link, Arthur S. ed. *The Papers of Woodrow Wilson*, vol. 62.

Poritt, Edward. "The British National Insurance Act." *Political Science Quarterly* 27, no. 2, (June 1912).

Rintala, Marvin. "Made in Birmingham: Lloyd George, Chamberlain and the Boer War." *University of Hawaii Press* 11, no. 2 (Spring 1988).

Rintala, Marvin. "Renamed Roses: Lloyd George, Churchill and the House of Lords." *University of Hawaii Press* 8, no 3 (Summer, 1985).

Sanders, Charles W., Jr. "No Other Law: The French Army and the Doctrine of the Offensive." *RAND* Paper P-7331 (Santa Monica, March 1987).

Subrtova, Marcela. "Great Britain and France on the Way to the Entente Cordiale." *Prague Papers on the History of International Relations* (2014).

Watson, D.R. "The Making of French Foreign Policy during the First Clemenceau Ministry, 1906—1909." *The English Historical Review* 86 no. 341 (Oct. 1971).

Trachtenberg, Marc. "Reparations at the Paris Peace Conference." *Journal of Modern History* 51 (March 1979)

Weinstein, Edwin A. "Woodrow Wilson's Political Personality: A Reappraisal." *Political Science Quarterly* 93 (Winter, 1978).

Wilson, Woodrow. "Mr. Cleveland's Cabinet." *The Review of Reviews"* April 1893 VII, quoted in 186-297, Link, Arthur, ed. *The Papers of Woodrow Wilson*, vol. I.

———.Our Course in History." *The Princetonian* 3, no. 4 (June, 1878).

———. "The Study of Administration." *Political Science Quarterly* 2, no. 2 (June 1887).

———. "The Study of Politics." *The New Princeton Review* (March 1887).

Zebel, Sydney H. "Joseph Chamberlain and the Genesis of Tariff Reform." *Journal of British Studies* 7 no. 1 (November, 1967).

NEWSPAPERS AND PERIODICALS

The Asbury Park (N.J.) *Press*

The Atlanta Constitution

L'Aurore

The Carnarvon Herald

The Commoner

La Follette's Weekly Magazine

Harper's Weekly

L'Homme Enchaine

L'Homme Libre

La Justice

London *Evening Express*

London *Times*

The Los Angeles Times

The Manchester *Guardian*

The Minneapolis Morning Tribune

The Nashville Tennessean

The New York Evening World
The New York Herald
The New York Times
The New York Tribune
The North American Review
The North Wales Express
The Oregon Daily Journal
The Princetonian
Princeton Alumni Weekly
The San Francisco Chronicle
Saturday Review
Le (Paris) *Temps*

GOVERNMENT DOCUMENT ARCHIVES

Hansard Parliamentary Debates, 3d series.
Journal Officiel, Annales de la Chambre des Députés.
Journal Officiel du Senat.
Archives of the Senate, Commission de l'Armee, Auditions des Ministres.

NOTES

The following abbreviations have been used in these Notes:

COF Link, Arthur S., ed. *The Deliberations of the Council of Four (March 24 – June 28, 1919)*, 2 vols. Princeton: Princeton University Press, 1992. Professor Link et al. translated Paul Mantoux's transcript of the deliberations of the Council of Four.

DLG The memoirs of David Lloyd George.

FRUS *Papers Relating to the Foreign Relations of the United States, 1914, Supplement, The World War*. Washington, D.C.: Government Printing Office, 1914, http://digital.library.wisc.edu, and *Papers Relating to the Foreign Relations of the United States, 1916, Supplement, The World War*. Washington, D.C.: Government Printing Office, 1916, http://digital.library. wisc.edu. The Department of State's official collection of documents related to the foreign relations of the United States during the First World War.

FRUS-PPC *Papers Relating to the Foreign Relations of the United States, 1919, The Paris Peace Conference*. 12 vols. Washington, D.C.: Government Printing Office, 1919. http://digital.library.wisc. edu. The Department of State's official collection of documents related to the Paris Peace Conference, in twelve volumes.

PWW Link, Arthur S., ed. *The Papers of Woodrow Wilson*. 69 vols. Princeton: Princeton University Press, 1966-1993.

PWW-DE Link, Arthur S, ed. *The Papers of Woodrow Wilson Digital Edition*. Charlottesville: University of Virginia Press, Rotunda, 2017. Originally published in the Papers of Woodrow Wilson © 1966 – 1994, Princeton University Press.

WW The books, articles and essays authored by Woodrow Wilson.

CHAPTER ONE

1 Wolfgang Schivelbusch, *The Culture of Defeat* (New York: Henry Holt, 2001), 107.

2 Michael Howard, *The Franco-Prussian War* (London: Granada Publishing, 1979), 221.

3 Robert T. Geisberg, *The Treaty of Frankfort* (Philadelphia: University of Pennsylvania Press, 1966), 25.

4 Geoffrey Wawro, *The Franco-Prussian War* (London: Cambridge University Press, 2003), 239.

5 Geisberg, *The Treaty of Frankfort*, 33.

6   Schivelbusch, *The Culture of Defeat,* 113.

7   Schivelbusch, 114.

8   Edgar Holt, *The Tiger* (London: Hamish Hamilton, 1976), 1.

9   D.R. Watson, *Georges Clemenceau, a Political Biography* (London: Eyre Metheun, 1974), 19.

10   Jack D. Ellis, *The Early Life of Georges Clemenceau, 1841-1893* (Lawrence, KS: The Regents Press of Kansas, 1980), 14.

11   Ellis, 15.

12   Holt, 8.

13   Ellios, 27.

14   Stephanie M. Blalock, *"Go to Pfaff's!" The History of a Restaurant and Lager Beer Saloon* (Bethlehem, PA.: Lehigh University Press, 2014), 24.

15   Blalock, 5.

16   Most, but not all of the letters were compiled, edited and translated under the direction of Fernand Baldensperger, a friend of Clemenceau's, into a 1928 book under the title "American Reconstruction 1865-1870" as if the volume had been authored by Clemenceau himself. The references to the letters herein are under the heading "Baldensperger."

17   Fernanrd Baldensperger, ed. *American Reconstruction 1865-1870,* (New York: Lincoln Mac Veagh, Dial Press, 1928), 38.

18   Baldensperger, 39.

19   Baldensperger, 41.

20   Baldensperger, 62.

21   Baldensperger, 115.

22   Baldensperger, 76.

23   Baldensperger, 132.

24   Baldensperger, 99.

25   Baldensperger, 36.

26   Baldensperger, 116.

27   Baldensperger, 118-119.

28   Baldensperger, 158.

29   Baldensperger, 163-164.

30   Baldensperger, 165.

31   Baldensperger, 167.

32   "Mary Clemenceau—Discarded Wife," *Milwaukee Journal,* Nov 27, 1969.

33   Baldensperger, 211.

34   Baldensperger, 211.

35   Baldensperger, 222.

36   Baldensperger, 226.

37   Baldensperger, 241-242.

38   Baldensperger, 241-242.

39   Baldensperger, 251.

40   Baldensperger, 260.

41   Baldensperger, 262.

42   Baldensperger, 299-300.

43   Watson, *Georges Clemenceau, a Political Biography* 37-38.

44   Ellis, *Early Life of Georges Clemenceau,* 45.

45   Jean Martet, *Georges Clemenceau* (London: Longmans, Green, 1930), 285.

46 Martet, 216, n. 6

47 Alistair Horne, *The Fall of* Paris (London: Penguin Books, 1990), 107.

48 Watson, *Georges Clemenceau, a Political Biography,* 41.

49 Holt, *The Tiger,* 24.

50 Ellis, *Early Life of Georges Clemenceau* 47.

51 Holt, 25.

52 Martet, *Georges Clemenceau,* 288.

53 Horne, *The Fall of* Paris, 269.

54 Ellis, 54.

55 Ellis, 55.

56 Ellis, 50.

57 Holt, *The Tiger,* 33.

58 Horne, *The Fall of* Paris,272-73.

59 Holt, 30.

60 Joseph V. Fuller, "The War-Scare of 1875," *The American Historical Review* 24, no. 2 (January, 1919).

61 Fuller, 201.

62 Fuller, 203.

63 Fuller, 203.

64 Fuller, 205.

65 Fuller, 206.

66 Fuller, 208

67 The *London Times,* May 6, 1875, p. 7.

68 *London Times,* p. 7.

69 Fuller, 213.

70 Fuller, 216.

71 Fuller, 216.

72 Fuller, 217.

73 Georges Clemenceau, *France Facing Germany* (New York: E.P. Dutton, 1919), 20.

74 Clemenceau, 21.

75 Ellis, *Early Life of Georges Clemenceau,* 62.

76 Ellis, 64.

77 Ellis., 93.

78 Ellis, 93.

79 The foregoing is derived principally from Watson, *Georges Clemenceau, a Political Biography,* 422.

80 Pratt, Julius, "Clemenceau and Gambetta—A Study in Political Philosophy," The South Atlantic Quarterly, Vol. XX, No. 2 (April, 1921).

CHAPTER TWO

1 Ellis, *The Early Life of Georges Clemenceau,* 64.

2 Ellis, 64.

3 Holt, *The Tiger,* 35.

4 Gregor Dallas, *At the Heart of a Tiger* (New York, Carroll & Graf Publishers, 1993), 228.

5 Louis Andrieux, "Georges Clemenceau," *The North American Review* 184, no. 609, (February, 1907).

6 Holt, 37.

7   *Journal Officiel, Annales de la Chambre des Députés*, 16 May 1876, 35-53.

8   *Journal Officiel, Annales de la Chambre des Députés*, 21 February, 180.

9   Holt, 47.

10   Dallas, 219,

11   *La Justice*, January 16, 1880, 1.

12   *La Justice*, quoted in Dallas, 222.

13   Dallas, 222.

14   *La Justice*, January 16, 1880, 3.

15   G.P. Gooch, *Anglo-German Relations, 1871-1914* (London, Longmans, Green, 1936), 21.

16   Holt, 49.

17   J. Hampden Jackson, *Clemenceau and the Third Republic* (London: Hodder & Stoughton, 1946), 63.

18   Gooch, 21.

19   D.W. Brogan, *The Development of Modern France (1870-1939)* (London: Hamish Hamilton, 1940), 148.

20   Dallas, 228.

21   Dallas, 149.

22   Ellis, 91.

23   Berta Szeps, *My Life and History* (New York: Alfred A. Knopf, 1939), 12.

24   Szeps, 13.

25   Szeps, 14.

26   Szeps, 14-15.

27   Dallas, 248.

28   Dallas, 249.

29   Brogan, 225.

30   Gooch, 22.

31   Gooch, 17.

32   *Journal Officiel, Annales de la Chambre des Députés*, Nov. 10, 1881,1967-75.

33   Ellis, 110.

34   Ellis, 110.

35   Szeps, 28.

36   Rondo E. Cameron, *France and the Economic Development of Europe, 1800-1914* (Princeton: Princeton University Press, 1961), 514.

37   Frederik Brown, *For the Soul of France* (New York: Alfred A. Knopf, 2010), 65.

38   Mary McAuliffe, *Dawn of the Belle Epoque* (Lanham, MD.: Rowman & Littlefield, 2011), 116.

39   Brown, 65.

40   Brown, 117.

41   Brogan, 232-235.

42   Ellis, 115.

43   Gooch, 22.

44   *Journal Officiel, Annales de la Chambre des Députés*, Nov. 22, 1884, 2405.

45   *Journal Officiel*, 2405.

46   *Journal Officiel*, 2497.

47   *London Times*, November 27, 1884, 5.

48   Dallas, 249.

49   Dallas, 250.

50   *La Justice*, March 30, 1885,1.

51 Dallas, 250-251.

52 *London Times*, March 31, 1885, 5.

53 *London Times*, March 31, 1885, 5.

54 Ellis, 118.

55 Dallas, 253.

56 *London Times*, March 31, 1885, 5.

57 D.R. Watson, *Georges Clemenceau, a Political Biography* (London: Eyre Methuen, 1974), 94.

58 Martet, *George Clemenceau*, 274.

59 Martet, 275.

60 *La Justice*, July 21, 1885, p. 2,

61 Frederic H. Seager, *The Boulanger Affair* (Ithaca, NY: Cornell University Press, 1969), 19.

62 Dallas, 269.

63 Szeps, 119.

64 Schivelbusch, *The Culture of Defeat*, 153.

65 Schivelbusch, 153.

66 Watson, 104.

67 *London Times*, July 15, 1886, 5.

68 Schivelbusch, 153-154.

69 Schivelbusch, 137.

70 Seager, 53.

71 Brogan, 189.

72 Seager, 66.

73 Seager, 68.

74 John A. Scott, *Republican Ideas in the Liberal Tradition in France, 1870-194* (New York: Columbia University Press, 1951), 134.

75 Seager, 113.

76 Seager. 151-152.

77 Seager, 171.

78 Brogan, 207.

79 Raymond Recouly, *The Third Republic* (London, William Heinemann, 1928), 185.

80 Allan Mitchell, *Bismarck and the French Nation* (Indianapolis, IN.: Bobbs-Merrill, 1971,) 105.

81 The following account is based largely on this work.

82 David McCullough, *The Path Between the Seas* (New York: Simon & Schuster, 1977) 198.

83 Dallas, 311. McCullough's version is slightly different. He has de Reinach visiting his nephew, Joseph Reinach, and two lady-friends following the meeting at Herz' home.

84 *London Times*, Nov, 22, 1892, 5.

85 *London Times,* Nov, 22, 1892, 5.

86 *London Times,* Nov, 22, 1892, 5.

87 Ellis, 175.

88 Ellis, 176.

89 *Journal Officiel, Annales de la Chambre des Députés*, Dec. 20, 1892, 1887.

90 *Journal Officiel, Annales de la Chambre des Députés*, Dec. 20, 1892, 1887.

91 Ellis. 177.

92 *Journal Officiel, Annales de la Chambre des Députés*, Dec. 20, 1892, 189-1890.

93 *London Times*, December 23, 1892, 3.

CHAPTER THREE

....

1   Ray Stannard Baker, *Woodrow Wilson Life and Letters*, vol. 1 ("Youth"), (London: William Heinemann, 1928), 6.

2   Arthur S. Link, *Woodrow Wilson, Presbyterian in Government*, in George L. Hunt and John T. McNeill, eds., *Calvinism and the Political Order*, (London: Westminster Press, 1965), 164.

3   Baker, *Youth*, 22.

4   Baker, *Youth*, 8.

5   Baker, *Youth*, 51.

6   John M. Mulder, "Joseph R. Wilson: South Presbyterian Patriarch," *Journal of Presbyterian History*, (1974).

7   Joseph R. Wilson, *Mutual Relation of the Masters and Slaves as Taught in the Bible* (Augusta, GA.: Steam Press of Chronicle & Sentinel, 1861), 7.

8   Kenneth S. Lynn, "The Hidden Agony of Woodrow Wilson," *The Wilson Quarterly* (Winter, 2004).

9   Edwin A. Weinstein, "Woodrow Wilson's Political Personality: A Reappraisal," *Political Science Quarterly* 93 (Winter, 1978).

10 Baker, *Youth*, 30.

11 Baker, *Youth*, 38.

12 George Osborn, *Woodrow Wilson, The Early Years* (Baton Rouge, LA.: Louisiana State University Press, 1981), 522.

13 Baker, *Youth*, 46.

14 Baker, *Princeton, 1890-1910*, 292.

15 Baker, *Youth*, 57.

16 Baker, *Youth*, 76.

17 Edwin A. Weinstein, *Woodrow Wilson: A Medical and Psychological Biography* (Princeton: Princeton University Press, 1981), 21.

18 Henry Bragdon, *Woodrow Wilson, The Academic Years* (Cambridge, MA.: Harvard University Press, 1967), 30.

19 Bragdon, 30.

20 Bragdon, 34.

21 Bragdon, 49.

22 Arthur Walworth, *Woodrow Wilson* vol. 1 (Baltimore, MD.: Penguin Books, 1969), 55.

23 PWW, vol. 1, 307.

24 PWW, vol. 1, 311.

25 PWW, vol. 1, 312-313.

26 Ray Stannard Baker and William E. Dodd, eds. *The Public Papers of Woodrow Wilson*, 6 vols. vol. 1 ("College and State") (New York: Harper & Brothers, 1925), 14.

27 Baker and Dodd, vol. 1, 11.

28 WW, *The Princetonian* 3, no. 4 (June 3, 1978).

29 Baker and Dodd, vol. 1, 23.

30 Baker and Dodd, vol. 1, 19.

31 Baker and Dodd, vol. 1, 21.

32 Baker and Dodd, vol. 1, 28.

33 Baker and Dodd, vol. 1, 33.

34 PWW, vol. 1, 515.

35 PWW, vol. 1, 519.

36 PWW, vol. 1, 518.

37 PWW, vol. 1, 526.

38 Baker, *Youth*, 104.

39 E. David Cronon, ed. *The Political Thought of Woodrow Wilson* (Indianapolis, IN.: Bobbs-Merrill, 1965), 4.

40 Bragdon, 70.

41 Bragdon, 82.

42 Bragdon, 56.

43 Bragdon, 57.

44 Bragdon, 49.

45 Bragdon, 91.

46 PWW, vol. 8, 368-380.

47 PWW, vol. 2, 51.

48 Baker, *Youth,* 155.

49 PWW, vol. 2, 148.

50 PWW, vol. 3, 135-137.

51 Baker, *Youth*, 199.

52 Bragdon, 110.

53 Walworth, *Woodrow Wilson* v. 1, 55.

54 WW, *Congressional Government* (New York: Meridian Books, 1959), 39.

55 WW, *Congressional Government*, 54.

56 Bragdon, 125.

57 WW, *Congressional Government*, 73.

58 Bragdon, 112.

59 *New York Tribune*, March 20, 1885.

60 Cronon, 10.

61 Bragdon, 151.

62 Bragdon, 149.

63 Weinstein, 91.

64 Baker, *Youth*, 266.

65 PWW, vol. 4, 625-627.

66 WW, *The State* (Lexington, MA.: D.C. Heath, 1898), 230.

67 WW, *The State*, 232.

68 WW, *The State*, 232.

69 WW, "Of the Study of Politics," *New Princeton Review* V, no. 3 (March 1887), 188-199.

70 WW, "Of the Study of Politics," 192.

71 WW, "Of the Study of Politics," 192.

72 WW, "Of the Study of Politics," 199.

73 WW, "Of The Study of Administration," *Political Science Quarterly* 2, no. 2 (June, 1887), 197.

74 WW, "Of The Study of Administration, 201.

75 WW, "Of The Study of Administration, 200.

76 WW, "Of The Study of Administration, 205-206.

77 WW, "Of The Study of Administration, 209.

78 Bragdon, 168.

79 Bragdon, 166.

80 Bragdon, 166, 169.

81   Bragdon, 170.

82   WW, "Bryce's 'American Commonwealth'" in Ray Stannard Baker and William E. Dodd, eds. *College and State* v. 1 (New York, Harper & Brothers, 1925), 159.

83   WW, "Bryce's 'American Commonwealth,'" 160.

84   WW, "Bryce's 'American Commonwealth,'" 163.

85   WW, "Bryce's 'American Commonwealth,'" 162-163.

86   WW, "Bryce's 'American Commonwealth,'" 172.

87   WW, "Bryce's 'American Commonwealth,'" 191.

88   Baker, *Princeton, 1890-1910*, 5.

89   PWW, vol. 7, 360.

90   McMillan Lewis, *Woodrow Wilson at Princeton* (Livingston, AL.: Livingston Publishing, 1952), 24.

91   Baker, *Princeton, 1890-1910*, 12.

92   Baker, *Princeton, 1890-1910*, 10.

93   Bragdon, 213.

94   PWW, vol. 7, 594.

95   PWW, vol. 9, 309.

96   PWW, vol. 9, 362.

97   The quoted address is from an 1890 version, reported at www.teachingamericanhistory.org.

98   PWW, vol. 9, 264.

99   PWW, vol. 9, 335.

100   *New York Times*, June 29, 1894, 1.

101   PWW, vol. 8, 636.

102   Baker and Dodd, vol. 1, 275.

103   Baker and Dodd, vol. 1, 276.

104   Baker and Dodd, vol. 1, 281.

105   Bragdon, 217.

CHAPTER FOUR

1   G.P. Gooch. *Franco-German Relations, 1871-1914* (London: Longmans, Green, 1923), 33.

2   *Chicago Tribune*, February 28, 1891.

3   *Chicago Tribune*, February 27, 1891.

4   David B. Ralston, *The Army of the Republic* (Cambridge, MA.: M.I.T. Press, 1967), 133-134.

5   Ralston, 143.

6   J.F.V. Keiger, *France and the World Since 1870* (London: Arnold, 2001), 82.

7   Guy Chapman, *The Dreyfus Trials* (London: Granada Publishing, 1974), 17.

8   George F. Kennan, *The Fateful Alliance* (New York: Pantheon, 1984), 12.

9   Ralston, 210.

10   Louis Begley, *Why the Dreyfus Affair Matters*, (New Haven, CT.: Yale University Press, 1999), 13.

11   Martin P. Johnson, *The Dreyfus Affair* (New York: St. Martin's Press, 1999), 23.

12   Brogan, *Development of Modern France*, 305.

13   Johnson, 27.

14   Maurice Paleologue, *An Intimate Journal of the Dreyfus Case* (Westport, CT.: Greenwood Press, 1957), 36.

15   Paleologue, 42-43.

16   Chapman, 56.

17   Brogan, 310.

18   *La Justice*, December 22, 1894, 1.

19   *New York Times*, January 6, 1895, 5.

20   Chapman, 33.

21   Betty Schechter, *The Dreyfus Affair* (New York: Houghton Mifflin, 1965), 64.

22   Johnson, 50.

23   Brogan, 331.

24   Johnson, 69.

25   Johnson, 73.

26   Dallas, *At the Heart of a Tiger,* 339-340.

27   *L'Aurore*, November 1, 1897, 1.

28   *L'Aurore*, November 2, 1897, 1.

29   Dallas, 359.

30   Paleologue, 80.

31   Nicholas Halasz, *Captain Dreyfus: The Story of a Mass Hysteria* (New York: Simon & Schuster, 1955), 113.

32   Halasz, 114.

33   *L'Aurore*, November 20, 1897, 1.

34   *L'Aurore*, November 21, 1897, 1.

35   *L'Aurore*, November 21, 1897, 1.

36   Johnson, 82.

37   Johnson, 83.

38   *L'Aurore,* December 5, 1897, 1.

39   *L'Aurore,* December 5, 1897, 1.

40   *L'Aurore,* December 5, 1897, 1.

41   Halasz, 117.

42   Schechter, 116.

43   *Le Figaro,* December 1, 1897, 1.

44   Edgar Holt, *The Boer War*, 108.

45   Begley, 75.

46   Ralston, 220.

47   Schechter, 131.

48   *L'Aurore*, January 17, 1898, 1.

49   Paleologue, 133.

50   Paleologue, 133.

51   Halasz, 135.

52   H.M. Hyndman, *Clemenceau, The Man and His Time* (New York: Frederick A. Stokes, 1919), 176.

53   Chapman, 146.

54   Halasz, 158.

55   *L'Aurore*, February 25, 1898, 1.

56   *L'Aurore*, February 25, 1898, 1.

57   Paleologue, 150.

58   *New York Times*, September 1, 1898, 1.

59   *London Times*, July 11, 1898, 7.

60   Johnson, 105.

61   Johnson, 106.

62   Halasz, 176.

63   *L'Aurore*, September 1, 1898, 1.

64   Johnson, 121.

65   Halasz, 207.

66   Schechter, 199.

67   Johnson, 137.

68   *L'Aurore*, September 10, 1899, 1.

69   *L'Aurore*, September 11, 1899, 1.

70   *L'Aurore*, September 13, 1899, 1.

71   *L'Aurore*, September 18, 1899, 1.

72   Chapman, 175.

73   Johnson, 150.

74   This description of *Le Bloc* is drawn largely from an extended essay by Claude Lévy in "Un Journal de Clemenceau: Le Bloc," in *Revue d'Histoire Moderne et Contemporaine,* (April—June 1963) at pp. 105-120 (hereinafter "Levy".) The full text of every issue of *Le Bloc* can be found at *http:gallica.bnf. fr/ark:12148.*

75   Levy, 118.

76   Levy, 117.

77   Levy, 119.

78   Levy, 119.

CHAPTER FIVE

1   Hugh J. Edwards, *David Lloyd* George v. 1 (London: The Waverly Book Co., 1930), 18.

2   Bentley Gilbert, *David Lloyd George, A Political Life, The Architect of Change, 1863-1912* (Columbus OH.: Ohio State University Press, 1987), 14.

3   John Grigg, *The Young Lloyd George* (Berkeley, CA.: University of California Press, 1973), 28.

4   Edwards, 37.

5   Edwards, 45.

6   Grigg, 37.

7   Gilbert, 34.

8   Gilbert, 37

9   Peter Rowland, *David Lloyd George* (New York: Macmillan Publishing, 1975), 86.

10 *The North Wales Express*, Nov. 5, 1880, 4.

11 Gilbert, 44.

12 Edwards, 73.

13 Grigg, 50.

14 Gilbert, 57.

15 Donald McCormick, *The Mask of Merlin* (New York: Holt, Rinehart & Winston, 1963), 36.

16 Edwards, 107.

17 Gilbert, 66.

18 Grigg, 49.

19 Gilbert, 74.

20 Edwards, 115.

21 McCormick, 18.

22 Edwards, 126.

23 Rowland, 79.

24 *The North Wales Express*, June 6, 1890, 5.

25 Rowland, 77.

26 Gilbert, 80.

27 *The Carnarvon Herald*, June 13, 1890, 8.

28 *The Carnarvon Herald*, June 13, 1890, 8.

29 Rowland, 77.

30 Rowland, 77.

31 *Hansard Parliamentary Debates*, 3d series, August 13, 1890, v. 348. cc 901-14.

32 *Hansard Parliamentary Debates*, 3d series, August 13, 1890, v. 348. cc 901-14.

33 Gilbert, 87.

34 Gilbert, 94.

35 Rowland, 36.

36 Gilbert, 102.

37 *The North Wales Express*, July 29, 1892, 5.

38 Gilbert, 103.

39 See www.measuringworth.com.

40 *London Times*, April 13, 1894.

41 Grigg, 170.

42 Rowland, 133.

43 Edgar Holt, *The Boer War* (New York: G.P. Putnam's Sons, 1958), 39.

44 Holt, 36.

45 Holt, 44.

46 Grigg, 256.

47 *The London Times*, November 12, 1895, 6.

48 *The Saturday Review*, May 4, 1895.

49 Denis Judd and Keith Surridge, *The Boer War, A History* (London: I.B. Tauris, 1913), 40.

50 Grigg, 258.

51 Grigg, 258.

52 Elizabeth Longford, *The Jameson's Raid* (London: Weidenfeld & Nicolson, 1960), 79.

53 Judd and Surridge, 46.

54 Judd and Surridge, 47.

55 William George, *My Brother and I* (London: Eyre & Spottiswoode, 1958), 177.

56 Edwards, 202.

57 Edwards, 200.

58 *Hansard Parliamentary Debates*, 3d series, March 20, 1902, v. 105, cols. 638-655.

59 *The (London) Evening Express*, November 28, 1899, 3.

60 *The (London) Evening Express*, November 28, 1899, 3.

61 Judd and Surridge, 58.

62 *Hansard Parliamentary Debates*, 3d series February 6, 1900, v. 78, cols 731-828.

63 *Hansard Parliamentary Debates*, 3d series February 6, 1900, v. 78, cols 731-828.

64 George, 178.

65 *The North Wales Express*, April 13, 1900.

66   Marvin Rintala, "Made in Birmingham: Lloyd George, Chamberlain and the Boer War," *University of Hawaii Press* 11, no. 2, (Spring 1988).

67   Rowland, 145.

68   Grigg, 270.

69   Judd and Surridge, 194.

70   *The Carnarvon Herald*, December 7, 1900, 6.

71   Grigg, 285.

72   Rintala, 128.

73   Grigg, 288.

74   Gilbert, 181.

CHAPTER SIX

1   W. Barksdale Maynard, *Woodrow Wilson, Princeton to the Presidency* (New Haven CT.: Yale University Press, 2008), 56.

2   Bragdon, *Woodrow Wilson, the Academic Years,* 272.

3   James Axtell, *The Making of Princeton University* (Princeton: Princeton University Press, 2006), 43.

4   *The New York Times,* June 11, 1902, 8.

5   Axtell, 112.

6   PWW, vol. 1, 450.

7   PWW, vol. 1, 457.

8   Bragdon, 284.

9   PWW, vol 14, 156-157.

10   Anthony Grafton, "Precepting, Myth and Reality of a Princeton Institution," Princeton Alumni *Weekly* 103, (March 12, 2003).

11   PWW, vol. 1, 470.

12   PWW, vol. 1, 469.

13   PWW, vol. 1, 488.

14   PWW, vol. 1, 468.

15   Maynard, 169.

16   Maynard, 471.

17   William Starr Myers, *Woodrow Wilson, Some Princeton Memories* (Princeton, Princeton University Press, 1946), 15.

18   Myers, 20.

19   Grafton, 18.

20   *Princeton Alumni Weekly,* April 18, 1917, 645.

21   *Princeton Alumni Weekly,* April 18, 1917, 647.

22   Edward H. Hilliard, "Woodrow Wilson & the Fence," *Princeton Alumni Weekly* 56, no. 17 (February 17, 1956), 3—6.

23   PWW, vol. 16, 300.

24   PWW, vol. 16, 301.

25   *Literary Digest,* XXXII, no. 15, (April 14, 1906), 557.

26   PWW, vol. 16, 365.

27   PWW, vol. 16, 365.

28   PWW, vol. 16, 367.

29   PWW, vol. 16, 372.

30   Edwin A. Weinstein, "Wilson's Neurological Illness," *The Journal of American History* 57, no. 2 (Sept. 1970), 324-351.

31   Maynard, 170.

32   PWW, vol. 16, 519-525.

33   PWW, vol. 16, 499-511.

34   PWW, vol. 16, 509.

35   PWW, vol. 16, 510-511.

36   PWW, vol. 16, 511.

37   PWW, vol. 16, 511.

38   PWW, vol. 17, 389-391.

39   PWW, vol. 17, 396.

40   PWW, vol. 17, 428-430.

41   Arthur S. Link, *The Road to the White* House (Princeton: Princeton University Press, 1947), 51.

42   Maynard, 168.

43   Bragdon, 322.

44   Stockton Axson, *Brother Woodrow: A Memoir of Woodrow Wilson* (Princeton: Princeton University Press, 2006), 130.

45   Baker, *Princeton 1890-1910,* 238.

46   Baker, *Princeton 1890-1910,* 254.

47   Bragdon, 325.

48   Bragdon, 324.

49   PWW, vol. 17, 271.

50   PWW, vol. 17, 335-338.

51   PWW, vol. 17, 337.

52   *The New York Times,* November 24, 1907, 35.

53   *Nashville Tennessean,* Nov. 12, 1907, 2.

54   *Indianapolis Star,* December 1, 1910, 6.

55   *The Davenport Daily Times,* Dec. 3, 1910, 3.

56   Maynard, 54.

57   Baker, *Princeton 1890-1910,* 292.

58   Axtell, 388, n. 30. The term "graduate college" should not be confused with the "graduate school." The graduate school, with its students, faculty members and administration, had been in existence since 1900. The term "graduate college" was then used to refer to the facility in which students would board, i.e. the dormitory.

59   Link, 62.

60   Bragdon, 315.

61   Baker, *Princeton 1890-1910,* 294.

62   Baker, *Princeton 1890-1910,* 294.

63   PWW, vol. 19, 162.

64   *Princeton Alumni Weekly,* (April 6, 1910), 428.

65   *Princeton Alumni Weekly,* (March 23, 1910), 391.

66   Link, 67.

67   Baker, *Princeton 1890-1910,* 317.

68   Link, 70.

69   Link, 70.

70 Link, 70.

71 *Princeton Alumni Weekly*, (March 23, 1910), 389.

72 Bragdon, 379.

73 *Princeton Alumni Weekly*, (April 20, 1910), 471.

74 Link, 85.

75 *Princeton Alumni Weekly*, (May 4, 1910), 498.

76 Bragdon, 378.

77 Bragdon, 388.

78 James Kerney, *The Political Education of Woodrow Wilson* (New York: The Century Company, 1926), 53.

79 William Inglis, "Helping to Make a President," *Colliers Weekly* LVIII, (October 7, 1916), 14.

80 Inglis, 37.

81 Inglis, 37.

82 PWW, vol. 2, 32-53.

83 Baker, *Governor*, 53.

84 Baker, *Governor*, 53.

85 Baker, *Princeton 1890-1910*, 353.

86 *Trenton Evening News*, July 16, 1910, 3.

87 PWW, vol. 21, 14.

88 PWW, vol. 21, 41, n.1.

89 *Trenton Evening Times*, Aug. 17, 1910, 1.

90 Link, 166.

91 Baker, *Governor*, 79.

92 Baker, *Governor*, 80.

93 PWW, vol. 21, 205.

94 PWW, vol. 21, 231.

95 PWW, vol. 21, 333.

96 Baker, *Princeton 1890-1910*, 104.

CHAPTER SEVEN

1 Holt, *The Tiger*, 124.

2 Guerlac Orthon, "The Separation of Church and State in France," *Political Science Quarterly* 23, (June, 1908), 272.

3 Jackson, 127.

4 Jackson, 125.

5 Holt, 124-125.

6 Holt, 124.

7 Douglas Porch, *The March to the Marne, 1871*-1914 (London: Cambridge University Press, 1981), 92.

8 *L'Aurore*, Jan 9, 1905, 1.

9 Marcela Subrtova, *Great Britain and France on the Way to the Entente Cordiale* (Prague: Prague Papers on the History of International Relations, 2014), 84.

10 Robert K. Massie, *Dreadnought* (New York, Random House, 1991), 342.

11 G.P. Gooch, *Before the War—Studies in Diplomacy* (London: Longmans Green, 1936), 96, 102.

12 Jackson, 129.

13 Holt, 126.

14 John Lowe, *The Great Powers, Imperialism and the German Problem* (London: Routledge Press 1994), 166.

15 Gooch, 42-43.

16 *London Times,* April 3, 1905, 3.

17 Gooch, 44.

18 Holt, 127.

19 Charles W. Porter, *The Career of Theophile Delcassé* (Westport, CT.: Greenwood Press, 1975), 238.

20 Porter, 242.

21 Porter, 252.

22 *L'Aurore*, June 7, 1905, 1.

23 Holt, 122.

24 *London Times*, March 15, 1906, 3.

25 Grey (Edward) of Fallodon, *Twenty-Five Years, 1892-1916*, vol. 1 (New York: Frederick A. Stokes, 1925), 101.

26 *L'Aurore*, April 15, 1906, 1.

27 *L'Aurore*, February 26, 1906, 1.

28 *London Times,* March 19, 1906, 3.

29 *L'Aurore*, March 18, 1906, 1.

30 *L'Aurore*, March 19, 1906, 1.

31 David S. Newhall, *Clemenceau, a Life at War* (Lewiston, NY: Edward Mellen Press, 1991), 257.

32 *London Times*, March 20, 1906, 5.

33 Newhall, 257.

34 *New York Times*, June 3, 1906, 29.

35 *London Times,* May 4, 1906, 4.

36 Hyndman, *Clemenceau, a Man and His Time*, 206.

37 *Journal Officiel, Annales de la Chambre de Députés*, 18 June, 1906, 1994-95,

38 *Journal Officiel, Annales de la Chambre de Députés*, 14 June, 1906, 1960.

39 *Journal Officiel, Annales de la Chambre de Députés*, 19 June, 1906, 2015.

40 Jackson, 139.

41 *London Times,* June 20, 1906, 7.

42 *Journal Officiel, Annales de la Chambre de Députés*, 19 June, 1906, 2016.

43 *Journal Officiel, Annales de la Chambre de Députés*, 18 June, 1906, 2006.

44 Watson, *George Clemenceau*, 173.

45 Hyndman, 209.

46 Newhall, 247.

47 Watson, 203.

48 Watson, 194.

49 *London Times*, June 6, 1908, 9.

50 *London Times*, June 12, 1908, 9.

51 Newhall, 280, n. 5.

52 Holt, 147.

53 Charles Hardinge, *Old Diplomacy* (Frome, U.K., Butler & Tanner, 1947), 140.

54 Newhall, 277.

55 Watson, 225.

56 Jackson, 147.

57 Don Cregier, *Bounder from Wales*, (Columbia, MO.: University of Missouri Press, 1976), 116.

58   DLG, *War Memoirs*, vol. 2 (London, Ivor Nicholson & Watson, 1933), 1605.

59   Watson, 226 n.126.

60   Newhall, 233.

61   D.R. Watson, "The Making of French Foreign Policy during the First Clemenceau Ministry, 1906-1909," *The English Historical Review* 86, n. 341 (October, 1971), 777.

62   Newhall, 293.

63   *London Times*, July 21, 1998, 5.

64   Newhall, 293.

CHAPTER EIGHT

1   John Grigg, *Lloyd George, The People's Champion,* (London: Eyre Metheun, 1978), 22.

2   Kenneth O. Morgan, ed., *Lloyd George Family Letters, 1885-1936,* (Cardiff, U.K.: University of Wales Press, 1973), 131-132.

3   Gilbert, *Lloyd George, a Political Life*, 225.

4   W.R.P. George, *Lloyd George Backbencher* (Llandysul, U.K.: Gomer Press, 1983), 354.

5   George, 359.

6   *Manchester Guardian* Oct. 19, 1905, 3.

7   George, 366.

8   Grigg, *People's Champion*,40.

9   George, 384.

10   Sydney H. Zebel, "Joseph Chamberlain and the Genesis of Tariff Reform," *Journal of British Studies* 7, no. 1 (November, 1967), 148.

11   *London Times*, May 25, 1903, 9.

12   *Hansard Parliamentary Debates*, 3d series, vol. 123, col. 185.

13   R.L. George, *David and Winston* (New York: Overlook Press, 2008), 29.

14   Rowland, *David Lloyd George*, 34.

15   Massie, *Dreadnought*, 330.

16   Grigg, *People's Champion,* 100.

17   Cregier, *Bounder from Wales*, 91.

18   Martin Pugh, *Lloyd George* (London: Longman Group, 1988), 31.

19   McCormick, *Mask of Merlin*, 57.

20   Gilbert, 317.

21   *Manchester Guardian*, Nov. 7, 1907, 7.

22   *London Times,* Nov. 7, 1907, 7.

23   McCormick, 61.

24   Cregier, 141; 143.

25   Massie, 401.

26   Gilbert, 341.

27   *Manchester Guardian*, July 28, 1908, 7.

28   *Manchester Guardian*, Aug. 24, 1908, 5.

29   Gilbert, 350.

30   DLG, *War Memoirs* vol. 1 (London: Ivor Nicholson & Watson, 1933), 30.

31   Cregier, 116.

32   Roy Hattersley, *David Lloyd George, The Great Outsider* (London: Little, Brown, 2010), 249.

33 Rowland, 48.

34 Bruce Murray, "The People's Budget a Century On" *The Journal of Liberal History* (Autumn, 2009), 5.

35 Hattersley, 250.

36 Hattersley, 251.

37 The entire text of the Limehouse speech can be found at www.beersandpolitics.com/discursos/ david-lloyd-george/limehouse-speech/1365.

38 Grigg, *People's Champion*, 208.

39 George, *My Brother and I*, 229.

40 Rowland, 238.

41 Pugh, 50.

42 Marvin Rintala, "Renamed Roses: Lloyd George, Churchill and the House of Lords," *University of Hawaii Press* 8, no. 3 (Summer, 1985), 250.

43 Rowland, 234.

44 *London Times*, Aug. 11, 1911, 4.

CHAPTER NINE

1   Paul Kennedy, *The Rise and Fall of the Great Powers* (New York: Random House, 1987), 242.

2   www.measuringworth.org.

3   James Chace, *1912* (New York: Simon & Schuster, 2004), 83.

4   Doris Kearns Goodwin, *The Bully Pulpit* (New York: Simon & Schuster, 2013), 204.

5   H. Landon Warner, ed., *Reforming American Life in the Progressive Era* (New York: Major Issues in American History, 1971), 3.

6   Link, *Campaigns for Progressivism and Peace*, 203.

7   *http//historymatters.gmu/d/5354*. Although there are no sound recordings of the actual speech, Bryan re-enacted the speech numerous times during his career. A 1921 recording of Bryan reciting excerpts of the speech are included in this site.

8   Goodwin, 263.

9   Goodwin, 292.

10 Richard Hofstadter, ed. *The Progressive Movement* (Englewood Cliffs, N.J.: Prentice-Hall, 1963), 143.

11 Lincoln Steffens, *The Shame of the* Cities (Charleston, S.C.: BiblioBazaar, 2009), 3.

12 Ray Stannard Baker, *Governor* (Garden City, N.Y.: Doubleday, Doran, 1931), 179.

13 *The New York Times*, November 9, 1910, 1.

14 WW, *History of the American People* vol. 5 (New York: Harper & Brothers, 1902), 58.

15 WW, *History of the American People* vol. 5, 62.

16 PWW, vol. 17, 337.

17 Baker and Dodd, *College and State*, vol. 2, 32-53.

18 Kerney, *Political Education of Woodrow Wilson*, 27.

19 Kerney, *Political Education of Woodrow Wilson*, 78.

20 John M. Blum, *Joe Tumulty and the Wilson Era*, (Boston: Houghton Mifflin, 1951), 22.

21 Joseph Tumulty, *Woodrow Wilson as I Know Him* (New York: Doubleday, Page, 1921), 53-54.

22 PWW, vol. 22, 43.

23 PWW, vol. 22, 47-48.

24 Tumulty, 59.

25 PWW, vol. 22, 153.

26   Link, *Campaigns for Progressivism and Peace*, 223.

27   PWW, vol. 22, 236.

28   PWW, vol. 22, 236, n. 2.

29   PWW, vol. 22, 249-250.

30   Link, *Campaigns for Progressivism and Peace*, 225.

31   PWW, vol. 22, 303.

32   PWW, vol. 22, 304.

33   *The Commoner*, February 3, 1911, 1.

34   Link, *Campaigns for Progressivism and Peace*, 252.

35   Link, *Campaigns for Progressivism and Peace*, 280.

36   PWW, vol. 22, 581.

37   PWW, vol. 22, 598.

38   PWW, vol. 22, 598.

39   *Atlanta Constitution*, March 11, 1911, 1.

40   *Asbury Park Press*, April 6, 1911, 8.

41   PWW, vol. 22, 538.

42   PWW, vol. 22, 592.

43   PWW, vol. 23, 11.

44   PWW, vol. 23, 49-50.

45   *Los Angeles Times*, May 14, 1911, 7.

46   *Los Angeles Times*, May 14, 1911, 160.

47   *Oregon Daily Journal*, May 19, 1911, 1.

48   *Oregon Daily Journal*, May 19, 1911, 1.

49   *Oregon Daily Journal*, May 19, 1911, 13.

50   *Minneapolis Morning Tribune*, May 25, 1911, 1.

51   PWW, vol. 23, 157.

52   PWW, vol. 23, 516-517.

53   PWW, vol. 23, 542.

54   PWW, vol. 22, 466.

55   Alexander George, *Woodrow Wilson and Colonel House*, (New York: John Day, 1956), 85.

56   George, *Woodrow Wilson and Colonel House*, 85.

57   PWW, vol. 23, 458.

58   C. Richard King, "Woodrow Wilson's Visit to Texas in 1911," *The Southwestern Historical Quarterly* no. 2 (October, 1961), 185.

59   Chace, *1912*, 140.

60   Chace, *1912*, 140.

61   BAKER, Governor, 249.

62   Tumulty, 84.

63   Baker, *Governor*, 250.

64   PWW, vol. 24, 45.

65   PWW, vol. 24, 45.

66   *San Francisco Chronicle*, January 17, 1912, at p. 1.

67   *New York Times*, January 9, 1912 at p. 1.

68   PWW, vol. 24, 123.

69   PWW, vol. 24, 128.

70   Link, *Campaigns for Progressivism and Peace*, 395, n.15.

71 Link, *Campaigns for Progressivism and Peace,* 382.

72 *Atlanta Constitution,* May 1, 1912, 1.

73 *Atlanta Constitution,* May 1, 1912, 1.

74 Link, *Campaigns for Progressivism and Peace,* 447.

75 Tumulty, 119.

76 Tumulty, 120-121.

77 Richard Allen Morton, "It was Bryan and Sullivan Who Did the Trick," *Journal of the Illinois State Historical Society* 108, no. 2 (Summer, 2015).

78 Link, *Campaigns for Progressivism and Peace,* 462.

79 *The New York Times,* August 8, 1912, 6.

80 Chace, *1912,* 199.

81 A sound recording of Wilson's address is available at www.youtube.com.

CHAPTER TEN

1   Newhall, *Clemenceau, A Life at War,* 293.

2   Geoffrey Bruun, *Clemenceau* (Cambridge, MA.: Harvard University Press, 1943), 104.

3   Berta Szeps, *My Life and History* (New York, Alfred A. Knopf, 1939), 204.

4   Szeps, 207.

5   Holt, *The Tiger,* 118.

6   Gooch, *Before the War,* 54.

7   Massie, *Dreadnaught,* 726.

8   Massie, 727.

9   DLG, *War Memoirs,* vol. 1, 43.

10 DLG, War Memoirs, vol. 1, 44.

11 Grey of Fallodon, *Twenty-Five Years,* vol. 1, 217.

12 Grey of Fallodon, *Twenty-Five Years,* vol. 1, 232.

13 Massie, 742.

14 Watson, 241.

15 *Annales du Senat,* 10 Feb 1912, 272-81.

16 *Annales du Senat,* 10 Feb 1912, 272-81.

17 Clemenceau, *France Facing Germany,* 24.

18 Clemenceau, *France Facing Germany,* 25.

19 Clemenceau, *France Facing Germany,* 25-26.

20 Clemenceau, *France Facing Germany,* 25-26.

21 Clemenceau, *France Facing Germany,* 11.

22 Clemenceau, *France Facing Germany,* 12.

23 Clemenceau, *France Facing Germany,* 11.

24 Clemenceau, *France Facing Germany,* 12.

25 Clemenceau, *France Facing Germany,* 10.

26 Clemenceau, *France Facing Germany,* 14.

27 Clemenceau, *France Facing Germany,* 15.

28 Clemenceau, *France Facing Germany,* 15.

29 Clemenceau, *France Facing Germany,* 16.

30 Clemenceau, *France Facing Germany,* 17.

31 Clemenceau, *France Facing Germany*, 20.

32 Clemenceau, *France Facing Germany*, 20.

33 Clemenceau, *France Facing Germany*, 19-20.

34 *New York Times,* Oct. 18, 1912, 1.

35 Brogan, *Development of Modern France*, 417.

36 Clemenceau, *France Facing Germany*, 31-32.

37 *L'Homme Libre,* May 8, 1913, 1.

38 *L'Homme Libre,* May 9, 1913, 1.

39 Clemenceau, *France Facing Germany,* 33-34.

40 Clemenceau, *France Facing Germany*, 42-43.

41 Clemenceau, *France Facing Germany,* 44.

42 *New York Times*, Nov. 23, 1913, 28.

43 *New York Times*, Nov. 22, 1913, 3.

44 *New York Times*, Nov. 30, 1913, 1.

45 *New York Times,* Dec. 6, 1913, 3.

46 Clemenceau, *France Facing Germany,* 49.

47 *London Times,* May 7, 1914, 31.

48 Gooch, 60.

49 Clemenceau, *France Facing Germany*, 65.

50 Clemenceau, *France Facing Germany,* 55.

51 *L'Homme Libre,* July 1, 1914, 1.

52 *L'Homme Libre,* July 1, 1914, 1.

53 *London Times,* July 14, 1914, 8.

54 *London Times,* July 15, 1914, 8.

55 Clemenceau, *France Facing Germany,* 99.

56 Clemenceau, *France Facing Germany*, 100.

57 *L'Homme Libre,* July 25, 1914, 1.

58 *L'Homme Libre,* July 26, 1914, 1.

59 *L'Homme Libre,* July 31, 1914, 1.

60 *L'Homme Libre,* July 31, 1914, 1.

61 *L'Homme Libre,* Aug. 2, 1914, 1.

62 *L'Homme Libre,* Aug. 2, 1914, 1.

63 *L'Homme Libre,* Aug. 5, 1914, 1

CHAPTER ELEVEN

1 Hattersley, *David Lloyd George*, 295.

2 Hattersley, 299.

3 Cregier, *Bounder from Wales*, 175.

4 Cregier, *Bounder from Wales*, 175.

5 Rowland, *David Lloyd George*, 252.

6 Hattersley, 319.

7 Cregier, 209.

8 John Grigg, *Lloyd George, War Leader* (London: Penguin Books, 2002), 51-52.

9 *London Times*, March 29, 1913, 4.

10 Cregier, 206.

11 *The Manchester Guardian*, June 19, 1913, 11.

12 Hattersley, 327.

13 Grigg, *War Leader*, 55.

14 Bentley Gilbert, *David Lloyd George, a Political Life, Organizer of Victory, 1912-1916* (Columbus, OH.: Ohio State University Press, 1992), 57.

15 Rowland, 262.

16 Grigg, *War Leader*, 91-92.

17 Gilbert, *Organizer of Victory*, 62.

18 *The Manchester Guardian*, October 12, 1913, 9.

19 Grigg, *War Leader*, 131.

20 *London Times*, January 2, 1914, 6.

21 Grigg, *War Leader*, 134-135.

22 *L'Homme Libre*, January 4, 1914, 1.

23 George, *David and Winston*, 101.

24 *The Manchester Guardian*, September 30, 1912, 7.

25 *The Manchester Guardian*, July 24, 1914, 5.

26 *The Manchester Guardian*, July 23, 1914, 8.

27 Rowland, 177.

28 DLG, *War Memoirs*, vol. 1, 54.

29 *Hansard Parliamentary Debates*, 3d series, July 27, 1914, vol. 65, cc. 947.

30 Morgan, ed., *Family Letters*, 166.

31 Gilbert, *Organizer of Victory*, 108.

32 Gilbert, *Organizer of Victory*, 167.

33 Gilbert, *Organizer of Victory*, 108.

34 Frank Owen, *Tempestuous Journey* (London: Hutchinson, 1954), 263.

35 Owen, 264-265.

36 Owen, 265.

37 Owen, 268.

38 Rowland, 283.

39 Owen, 269.

40 Rowland, 283-284.

41 Gilbert, *Organizer of Victory*, 112.

42 *Hansard Parliamentary Debates*, 3d series, August 3, 1914, vol. 65, cc. 1814-1827.

43 Rowland, 284.

CHAPTER TWELVE

1 William F. McCombs, *Making Woodrow Wilson President* (New York: Fairview Publishing, 1921), 208.

2 Charles Seymour, *The Intimate Papers of Colonel House*, 4 vols. (Boston: Houghton Mifflin, 1927-1928), vol. 1, 116.

3 Arthur S. Link, *Wilson, The New Freedom* (Princeton: Princeton University Press, 1956), 7.

4 Seymour, vol. 1, 88.

5 Kerney, *Political Education of Woodrow Wilson*, 288.

6 Link, *New Freedom*, 180.

7   Kerney, 286-287.

8   Tumulty, *Woodrow Wilson as I Know Him*, 138.

9   Link, *New Freedom*, 138.

10   PWW, vol. 27, 148-152.

11   PWW, vol. 28, 280.

12   *New York Times*, May 9, 1913, 1-2.

13   Link, *New Freedom*, 279.

14   PWW, vol. 27, at 310.

15   Peter Henderson, "Woodrow Wilson, Victoriano Huerta and the Recognition Issue in Mexico," *The Americas* 41, no. 2 (October, 1964), 164.

16   Link, *New Freedom*, 462.

17   *Washington Post,* February 3, 2007, 1.

18   PWW, vol. 27, 175.

19   PWW, vol. 27, 192-194.

20   PWW, vol. 27, 237.

21   Link, *New Freedom*, 285-286.

22   PWW, vol. 27, 172.

23   Link, *New Freedom*, 348.

24   Mark T. Gilderhus, "Carranza and the Decision to Revolt, 1913, A Problem in Historical Interpretation" *The Americas* 33, no. 2, (October, 1976).

25   *New York World*, March 7, 1913, 1.

26   Barbara Tuchman, *The Zimmermann Telegram* (New York: Dell, 1965), 40.

27   PWW, vol. 27, 437-438.

28   PWW, vol. 27, 335.

29   PWW, vol. 28, 7.

30   PWW, vol. 28, 27-34.

31   PWW, vol. 28, 39.

32   PWW, vol. 28, 111.

33   Patricia O'Toole, *The Moralist* (New York: Simon & Schuster, 2013), 93.

34   Link, *New Freedom*, 360.

35   PWW, vol. 28, 228.

36   *New York Times*, October 14, 1913, 7.

37   PPW, vol. 29, 4-5.

38   PPW, vol. 29, 294.

39   PPW, vol. 29, 300.

40   *L'Homme Libre*, February 25, 1914, 1.

41   *New York Times*, April 12, 1914, 3.

42   *New York Times*, April 12, 1914, 3.

43   PWW, vol. 29, 441.

44   PWW, vol. 29, 48.

45   PWW, vol. 29, 465.

46   PWW, vol. 29, 472.

47   PWW, vol. 29, 473.

48   *New York Times*, April 21, 1914, 1.

49   Tumulty, 152.

50   *New York Times*, April 23, 1914, 1.

51   Link, *New Freedom*, 400.

52   *L'Homme Libre*, April 25, 1914, 1.

53   Ray Stannard Baker and William E Dodd, eds. *The Public Papers of Woodrow* Wilson, vol. II ("*The New Democracy*"), 118; 122.

54   PWW, vol. 27, 269-270.

55   PWW, vol. 27, 271.

56   PWW, vol. 27, 473.

57   *New York Times,* October 4, 1913, 2.

58   Sean Wilentz, *The Rise of American Democracy* (New York: W.W. Norton, 2005), 216.

59   PWW, vol. 27, 571.

60   PWW, vol. 30, 158.

61   Charles E. Neu, *Colonel House* (New York: Oxford University Press, 2015), 98.

62   PWW vol. 27, 462-63.

63   PWW vol. 28, 270.

64   Neu, 107.

65   Seymour, vol. 1, 239.

66   Seymour, vol. 1, 246.

67   Neu, 123.

68   PWW, vol. 30, 108.

69   PWW, vol. 30, 139-140.

70   PWW, vol. 30, 187.

71   PWW, vol. 30, 201.

72   Neu, 544, n. 18.

73   PWW, vol. 30, 214.

74   PWW, vol. 30, 214.

75   PWW, vol. 30, 222.

76   *New York Times,* July 5, 1914, 3.

77   Baker and Dodd, eds. *The New Democracy*, 143.

78   Baker and Dodd, eds. *The New Democracy*, 144.

79   Baker and Dodd, eds. *The New Democracy*, 146.

80   Baker and Dodd, eds. *The New Democracy*, 147-148.

81   PWW, vol. 30, 323-324.

82   PWW, vol. 30, 327.

83   PWW, vol. 30, 332.

84   PWW, vol. 30, 342.

85   PWW, vol. 30, 342.

CHAPTER THIRTEEN

1   Dallas, *Heart of a Tiger*, 431.

2   John Keegan, *The First World War* (New York: Alfred A. Knopf, 1999), 98.

3   Charles S. Sanders, Jr., "No Other Law: The French Army and the Doctrine of the Offensive," *RAND* Paper-7331 (Santa Monica, March 1987), 9

4   Sanders, Jr., 9.

5   Sanders, Jr., 12.

6   Jere Clemens King, *Generals and Politicians* (Berkeley, CA.: University of California Press, 1951), 19.

7   Lennox, Lady Algernon Gordon, ed. *The Diary of Lord Bertie of Thame, 1914-1918*, vol. 1 (New York: George H. Doran, 1924), 64.

8   Sanders, Jr., 6.

9   Sanders, Jr. 15.

10   McCormick, *Mask of Merlin*, 88.

11   George, *David & Winston*, 117.

12   Lloyd George, *War Memoirs*, vol. 1, 125.

13   Clemenceau, *France Facing Germany*, 125.

14   Clemenceau, *France Facing Germany*, 131.

15   G.J. Meyer, *A World Undone* (New York: Delacorte Press, 2006), 115.

16   Clemenceau, *France Facing Germany*, 154.

17   Brogan, *Development of Modern France*, 483.

18   Lennox, 24.

19   *L'Homme Libre*, August 30, 1914, 1.

20   Dallas, 438-9.

21   Clemenceau, *France Facing Germany*, 168.

22   Clemenceau, *France Facing Germany*, 172.

23   Keegan, 119.

24   Gilbert, *Organizer of Victory*, 118.

25   Grigg, *War Leader*, 163.

26   Grigg, *War Leader*, 165.

27   Grigg, *War Leader*, 165.

28   *London Times*, Sept. 21, 1914, 9.

29   Frances Stevenson, *Lloyd George* (New York: Harper & Row, 1971), 2.

30   Stevenson, 135-136.

31   Meyer, 210.

32   Sanders, Jr. 29.

33   Jackson, *Clemenceau and the Third Republic*, 165.

CHAPTER FOURTEEN

1   FRUS, 1914, Supp. 547.

2   PWW, vol. 30, 342.

3   Arthur S. Link, *Wilson, The Struggle for Neutrality, 1914-1915* (Princeton: Princeton University Press, 1960), 192.

4   Link, *Struggle for Neutrality*, 45.

5   Grey of Fallodon, *Twenty-Five Years*, vol. 2, 101, n.1.

6   Grey of Fallodon, *Twenty-Five Years*, vol. 2, 103.

7   Lennox, Lady Algernon Gordon, ed. *The Diary of Lord Bertie of Thame, 1914-18* vol. 1 (New York: George H. Doran, 1924), 55.

8   PWW, vol. 30, 394.

9   Link, *Struggle for Neutrality*, 67.

10   *New York Times*, Sept, 18, 1914, 1.

11   PWW, vol. 31, 56.

12 PWW, vol. 31, 378-279.

13 PWW, vol. 31, 421-422.

14 PWW, vol. 31, 423, n. 6.

15 Morgan, ed., *Family Letters*, 173.

16 Grey of Fallodon, *Twenty-Five Years*, vol. 2, 69.

17 George, *David & Winston*, 120.

18 King, *Generals and Politicians*, 41-42.

19 Watson, *Georges Clemenceau*, 254.

20 Archives of the Senate, *Commission de l'Armee, Auditions des Ministres,* 1 July 1915, 2098-2100.

21 Archives of the Senate, 2101.

22 Archives of the Senate, 2102-2104.

23 Archives of the Senate, 2460.

24 *London Times*, May 14, 1915, 8.

25 Hattersley, *David Lloyd George*, 378.

26 *L'Homme Libre*, May 28, 1915, 1.

27 *London Times,* June 4, 1915, 9.

28 *L'Homme Libre*, June 7, 1915, 1.

29 Owen, *Tempestuous Journey*, 294-295.

30 Joyce Grigsby Williams, *Colonel House and Edward Grey* (Lanham, MD.: University Press of America, 1984), 56.

31 PWW, vol. 30, 489.

32 PWW, vol. 31, 16.

33 Link, *Struggle for Neutrality,* 198.

34 Link, *Struggle for Neutrality,* 198.

35 PWW, vol. 31, 21-22.

36 PWW, vol. 31, 45.

37 PWW, vol. 31, 282.

38 Link, *Struggle for Neutrality,* 210.

39 Link, *Struggle for Neutrality,* 209.

40 PWW, vol. 31, 520.

41 Williams, 57.

42 PWW, vol. 31, 501.

43 Link, *Struggle for Neutrality,* 213.

44 Link, *Struggle for Neutrality,* 213.

45 Lennox, Lady Algernon Gordon, ed., 82.

46 PWW, vol. 32, 61.

47 Seymour, *Intimate Papers of Colonel House,* vol. 1, 351-352.

48 Seymour, 356.

49 Seymour, 358.

50 *New York Times,* Feb. 7, 1915, 3.

51 Seymour, 363.

52 PWW, vol. 32, 265.

53 PWW, vol. 32, 276-277.

54 PWW, vol. 32, 287.

55 PWW, vol. 32, 303-304.

56 Seymour, 386.

57 PWW, vol. 32, 392.
58 PWW, vol. 32, 350.
59 Lennox, Lady Algernon Gordon, ed., 131.
60 Seymour, 410.
61 Seymour, 400.
62 Seymour, 428.
63 Williams, 67.
64 Patrick Devlin, *Too Proud to Fight—Woodrow Wilson's Neutrality* (New York: Oxford University Press, 1975), 199.
65 Seymour, 432.
66 *New York Times*, May 8, 1915, 1.
67 *New York Times*, May 10, 1915, 1.
68 *New York Times*, May 8, 1915, 2.
69 Seymour, 434.
70 Lennox, Lady Algernon Gordon, ed., 163.
71 *North American Review*, vol. CCI, June 1915, 801.
72 Link, *Struggle for Neutrality*, 382.
73 Link, *Struggle for Neutrality*, 382.
74 *L'Homme Libre*, May 11, 1915, 1.
75 *New York Times*, May 14, 1915, 1.
76 *New York Times*, May 15, 1915, 1.
77 Link, *Struggle for Neutrality*, 403.
78 Link, *Struggle for Neutrality*, 403-404.
79 David Houston, *Eight Years with Wilson's Cabinet, 1913-1920* vol. 1 (New York: Doubleday, Page, 1926), 132-133.
80 Houston, 137.
81 Link, *Struggle for Neutrality*, 411.
82 *New York Times*, June 11, 1915, 1.
83 Link, *Struggle for Neutrality*, 422.
84 *New York Times*, June 9, 1915, 1.
85 *New York Times*, June 11, 1915, 1.
86 Link, *Struggle for Neutrality*, 567.
87 Link, *Struggle for Neutrality*, 568.
88 *L'Homme Libre*, May 7, 1915, 1.
89 *L'Homme Libre*, May 28, 1915, 1.
90 *L'Homme Libre*, July 24, 1915, 1.
91 King, 81-82.
92 *L'Homme Libre*, December 26, 1915, 1.
93 Stevenson, *Lloyd George*, 81.
94 Meyer, *A World Undone*, 199.
95 Meyer, 301.
96 Brogan, *Development of Modern France*, 481-482, n.1

CHAPTER FIFTEEN

1 Devlin, *Too Proud to Fight*, 469.

2 Devlin, 469.

3 Neu, *Colonel House*, 220.

4 Arthur S. Link, *Wilson, Confusions and Crises, 1915-1916* (Princeton: Princeton University Press, 1964), 102.

5 Neu, 213.

6 Williams, *Colonel House and Edward Grey*, 75.

7 PWW, vol. 35, 81.

8 Link, *Confusions and Crises*, 106.

9 Williams, 77.

10 PWW, vol. 35, 347-348.

11 PWW, vol. 35, 357.

12 Williams, 78.

13 Seymour, *Intimate Papers of Colonel House*, vol. 2, 108.

14 Williams, 80.

15 *New York Times*, December 22, 1915, 1.

16 PWW, vol. 35, 453.

17 PWW, vol. 35, 453.

18 PWW, vol. 35, 457.

19 PWW, vol. 36, 129.

20 Link, *Confusions and Crises*, 115.

21 Seymour, vol. 2, 124.

22 Link, *Confusions and Crises*, 117.

23 PWW, vol. 35, 484-485.

24 Seymour, vol. 2, 130.

25 PWW, vol. 35, 488.

26 Seymour, vol. 2, 131.

27 PWW, vol. 35, 534.

28 PWW, vol. 36, 123.

29 Seymour, vol. 2, 142-143.

30 PWW, vol. 36, 126, n.1.

31 PWW, vol. 36, 148.

32 PWW, vol. 36, 149, n. 1.

33 Link, *Confusions and Crises*, 129.

34 Link, *Confusions and Crises*, 129

35 PWW, vol. 36, 170.

36 Grey of Fallodon, *Twenty-Five Years*, vol. 2, 176-177.

37 Seymour, vol. 2, 179.

38 Seymour, vol. 2, 182.

39 Seymour, vol. 2, 181.

40 Seymour, vol. 2, 182.

41 DLG, *War Memoirs*, vol. 1, 411.

42 *New York Times*, February 16, 1916, 1.

43 PWW, vol. 36, 180.

44 Grey of Fallodon, vol. 2, 122.

45 Seymour, vol. 2, 195.

46 Williams, 88.

47 Williams, 88.

48 Link, *Confusions and Crises,* 137.

49 *L'Homme Libre,* February 17, 1916, 1.

50 King, *Generals and Politicians,* 97.

51 Dallas, *Heart of a Tiger,* 453.

52 King, 99-100.

53 *Manchester Guardian,* February 23, 1916, 6.

54 Rowland, *David Lloyd George,* 331.

55 Grigg, *War Leader,* 329.

56 Hattersley, *David Lloyd George,* 384.

57 Stevenson, *Lloyd George,* 102.

58 Seymour, vol. 2, 226.

59 Seymour, vol. 2, 226

60 PWW, vol. 36, 405.

61 FRUS, 1916, Supp. 232-237, April 18, 1916.

62 PWW, vol. 36, 510.

63 *L'Homme Libre,* April 22, 1916.

64 Link, *Confusions and Crises,* 267.

65 PWW, vol. 36, 623.

66 PWW, vol. 36, 625.

67 Seymour, vol. 2, 243.

68 Hattersley, 395.

69 Rowland, 340.

70 DLG, *War Memoirs,* vol. 1, 319.

71 Lennox, Lady Algernon Gordon, ed., 337.

72 Neu, 245.

73 Williams, 104.

74 Arthur S. Link, *Wilson, Campaigns for Progressivism and Peace, 1916-1917* (Princeton: Princeton University Press, 1965), 20.

75 PWW, vol. 37, 57-58.

76 Neu, 246.

77 Hansard Parliamentary Debates, 3d series, vol. 82, col. 219, (May 24, 1916).

78 *New York Times,* May 23, 1916, 2.

79 PWW, vol. 37, 104.

80 PWW, vol. 37, 48.

81 *L'Homme Libre,* May 27, 1916, 1.

82 *L'Homme Libre,* May 28, 1916, 1.

83 Link *Campaigns for Progressivism,* 23.

84 PWW, vol. 37, 114-115.

85 PWW, vol. 37, 113.

86 *London Times,* May 29, 1916, 9.

87 PWW, vol. 37, 179.

88 PWW, vol. 37, 412.

89   DLG, *War Memoirs,* vol. 1, 414.

90   *New York Times,* June 16, 1916, 1.

91   Rowland, 346.

92   Stevenson, 114.

93   Gilbert, *Organizer of Victory,* 370.

94   PWW, vol. 38, 497.

95   DLG, *War Memoirs,* vol. 1, 517.

96   Stevenson, 127.

97   Gilbert, *Organizer of Victory,* 390.

98   Hattersley, 409.

99   Hattersley, 418.

100 Stevenson, 133.

CHAPTER SIXTEEN

1   Grigg, *War Leader,* 220-221.

2   George, Lord Riddell, *Lord Riddell's War Diary, 1914-1918* (London: Ivor Nicholson & Watson, 1933), 324.

3   Hattersley, *David Lloyd George,* 439.

4   Owen, *Tempestuous Journey,* 352.

5   PWW, vol. 40, 133.

6   PWW, vol. 40, 189.

7   Sterling Kernek, "The British Government's Reactions to President Wilson's 'Peace' Note of December, 1916," *The Historical Journal* 13, no. 4 (December, 1970), 721.

8   Hansard Parliamentary Debates, 3d. series, vol. 88, cc 1333-94 (December 19, 1916).

9   Hansard Parliamentary Debates, 3d. series, vol. 88, cc 1333-94 (December 19, 1916).

10   *London Times,* Dec 22, 1916, 8.

11   Link, *Campaigns for Progressivism,* 217.

12   FRUS, 1916 Supplement, Dec. 18, 1916, 97-99

13   Seymour, vol. 2, 405.

14   Burton J. Hendrick, ed., *The Life and Letters of Walter H. Page* vol. 2 (New York: Doubelday, Page, 1924), 207.

15   *London Times,* Dec. 22 1916, 9.

16   Link, *Campaigns for Progressivism,* 230.

17   Newhall, *Life at War,* 324.

18   *L'Homme Enchaine,* December 25, 1916, 1.

19   PWW, vol. 40, 356.

20   PWW, vol. 40, 368.

21   Link, *Campaigns for Progressivism,* 248.

22   PWW, vol. 40, 528.

23   PWW, vol. 40, 433-439.

24   *The New York Times,* January 23, 1917, 1.

25   *The New York Times,* February 2, 1917, 2.

26   Link, *Campaigns for Progressivism,* 273.

27   Hendrick, ed., vol. 2, 214.

28 *London Times,* January 24, 1917, 7.

29 DLG, *War Diaries,* vol. 1, 982.

30 *London Times,* Jan 24, 1917, 8.

31 *L'Homme Enchaine,* January 25, 1917, 1.

32 Link, *Campaigns for Progressivism,* 279.

33 Seymour, vol. 2, 436.

34 Link, *Campaigns for Progressivism,* 251.

35 PWW, vol. 41, 100.

36 Houston, *Eight Years,* 229.

37 Link, *Campaigns for Progressivism,* 296.

38 Link, *Campaigns for Progressivism,* 297.

39 PWW, vol. 41, 111.

40 PWW, vol. 41, 111.

41 *London Times,* February 5, 1917, 10.

42 *L'Homme Enchaine,* February 5, 1917, 1.

43 John M. McEwen, ed., *The Riddell Diaries,* (London: Athlone Press, 1986), 184.

44 Link, *Campaigns for Progressivism,* 341.

45 Devlin, *Too Proud to Fight,* 650.

46 *New York Times,* February 4, 1917, 1.

47 *L'Homme Enchaine,* February 6, 1917, 1.

48 Link, *Campaigns for Progressivism,* 316.

49 Link, *Campaigns for Progressivism,* 316.

50 Link, *Campaigns for Progressivism* 318.

51 King, *Generals and Politicians,* 140.

52 Stevenson, *Lloyd George,* 139.

53 Meyer, *A World Undone,* 430.

54 Link, *Campaigns for Progressivism,* 343.

55 Devlin, 651.

56 *New York Times,* February 27, 1917, 1.

57 *L'Homme Enchaine,* March 1, 1917, 1.

58 *New York Times,* February 28, 1917, 1.

59 PWW, vol. 41, 320.

60 PWW, vol. 41, 333.

61 Grigg, *War Leader,* 56.

62 Watson, 258.

63 *New York Times,* March 20, 1917, 2.

64 Link, *Campaigns for Progressivism,* 408.

65 Baker, *Facing War,* 503.

66 *New York Times,* March 22, 1917, 1.

67 *New York Times,* March 22, 1917, 1.

68 Link, *Campaigns for Progressivism,* 414.

69 PWW, vol. 41, 483.

70 *New York Times,* March 30, 1917, 2.

71 Grigg, *War Leader,* 72.

72 PWW, vol. 41, 519-527.

73 *New York Herald,* April 6, 1917, 3.

74 *New York Times,* April 6, 1917, 6.

75 *New York Times,* May 28, 1917, 6.

76 Dallas, *Heart of a Tiger,* 468.

77 King, 145.

78 King, 154.

79 Brogan, *Development of Modern France,* 499.

80 Dallas, 493.

81 Archives of the Senate, Commission de l'Armee, Auditions des Ministres, June 25, 1917, 8991.

82 Dallas, 483.

83 Archives of the Senate, Commission de l'Armee, Auditions des Ministres, June 25, 1917, 8991.

84 Archives of the Senate, Commission de l'Armee, Auditions des Ministres, June 25, 1917, 8993-8994.

85 Dallas, 488.

86 *Journal Officiel du Senat,* July 22, 1917,

87 Holt, *The Tiger,* 181.

88 Holt, 56.

89 *New York Times,* July 24, 1917, 2.

90 DLG, *War Memoirs,* vol. 2, 1283.

91 Meyer, 493.

92 Adam Hochschild, *To End All Wars* (New York: Houghton, Mifflin, 2011), 291.

93 Baker, *War Leader, 1917-1918,* 221.

94 PWW, vol. 44, 57-58.

95 *L'Homme Enchaine,* August 19, 1917, 1.

96 PWW, vol. 44, 125-129.

97 Owen, 432.

98 Rowland, *David Lloyd George,* 422.

99 George, Lord Riddell, *Lord Riddell's War Diary, 1914-1918,* 290.

100 Brogan, 536.

101 Watson, 269

102 Dallas, 496.

103 *L'Homme Enchaine,* November 15, 1917, 1.

CHAPTER SEVENTEEN

1 Grigg, *War Leader,* 533.

2 George, Lord Riddell, *Lord Riddell's War Diary, 1914-1918* (London: Ivor Nicholson & Watson, 1933), 318.

3 George, *War Diary,* 327; 337.

4 Newhall, *Clemenceau,* 381.

5 DLG, *War Diaries,* vol. 2, 1609.

6 Dallas, *Heart of a Tiger,* 502.

7 Dallas, 502-503.

8 Watson, *Georges Clemenceau,* 279.

9 Dallas, 520.

10 Newhall, 365.

11 Newhall, 369.

12 Bruun, *Clemenceau*, 156.

13 PWW, vol. 45, 69.

14 Seymour, vol. 3, 225.

15 *New York Times*, December 9, 1917, 1.

16 Tasker Bliss, "The Evolution of the United Command," *Foreign Affairs,* (December, 1922), 6.

17 PWW, vol. 45, 122.

18 Bruun, 138.

19 Dallas, 516.

20 Seymour, vol. 3, 274.

21 *London Times*, November 30, 1917, 9.

22 Hochschild, *To End all Wars*, 302.

23 George, *War Diary*, 296.

24 *London Times*, December 1, 1917, 9.

25 Seymour, vol. 3, 237.

26 DLG, *War Diaries*, vol. 2, 1618.

27 DLG, *War Diaries*, vol. 2, 1622.

28 King, *Generals and Politicians*, 200.

29 PWW, vol. 45, 166.

30 PWW, vol. 45, 176.

31 *New York Times*, January 6, 1918, 1.

32 Grigg, *War Leader,* 380-382.

33 George, *War Diary*, 304.

34 *London Times*, January 7, 1918, 8.

35 Seymour, vol. 3, 334.

36 *New York Times*, January 9, 1918, 1.

37 PWW, vol. 51, 495.

38 PPW, vol. 51, 476.

39 PWW, vol. 51, 497.

40 PWW, vol. 51, 155-162.

41 PWW, vol. 51, 161.

42 Dallas, 516.

43 Holt, *The Tiger,* 194.

44 Holt, 177-183.

45 King, *Generals and Politicians,* 211.

46 *Archives of the Senate, Commission de l'Armee, Auditions des Ministres,* December 14, 1917, 9420.

47 DLG, *War Memoirs*, vol. 2, 1750.

48 *New York Tribune*, April 7, 1918, 1.

49 Holt, 200.

50 Peter E. Wright, *At the Supreme War Council* (New York: G.P. Putnam's Sons, 1921), 107.

51 Watson, 301.

52 Holt, 203.

53 Watson, 302.

54 George, *War Diary,* 320.

55 King, 216.

56 Holt, 204.

57 Georges Clemenceau, *Grandeur and Misery of Victory* (New York: Harcourt, Brace, 1930), 39.

58 King, *Generals and Politicians*, 216.

59 *Archives of the Senate, Commission de l'Armee, Auditions des Ministres.* April 5, 1918, 10533.

60 DLG, *War Memoirs*, vol. 2, 1743.

61 DLG, *War Memoirs*, vol. 2, 1749.

62 DLG, *War Memoirs*, vol. 2, 1752.

63 Clemenceau, *Grandeur and Misery*, 63; 65.

64 *Archives of the Senate, Commission de l'Armee, Auditions des Ministres.* April 5, 1918, 10555.

65 DLG, *War Memoirs*, vol. 2, 1825.

66 Hattersley, *David Lloyd George*, 469.

67 PPWW-DE, WILS—01-47-02-0361-0001

68 Clemenceau, *Grandeur and Misery*, 53.

69 Grigg, *War Leader*, 523.

70 Dallas, 532.

71 Elizabeth Greenhalgh, "David Lloyd George, Georges Clemenceau and the 1918 Manpower Crisis," *The Historical Journal* 50, no. 2 (June 2007), 406.

72 Greenhalgh, 406.

73 PWW, vol. 48, 226.

74 Baker, *Facing War*, 191.

75 Baker, *Facing War*, 207.

76 Clemenceau, *Grandeur and Misery*, 54.

77 Dallas, 535.

78 Dallas, 535.

79 *Manchester Guardian*, June 5, 1918, 5.

80 Holt, 210.

81 Newhall, 396.

82 Newhall, 399.

83 Dallas, 537.

84 *London Times*, August 2, 1918, 7-8.

85 *New York Times*, August 2, 1918, 1.

86 Seymour, vol. 4, 63.

87 Seth Tillman, *Anglo-American Relations at the Peace Conference of 1919* (Princeton: Princeton University Press, 1961), 8.

88 Tillman, 35.

89 Seymour, vol. 4, 23.

90 Seymour, vol. 4, 49.

91 PPWW-DE, WILS 01-49-02-0300.

92 Holt, 216.

93 Harry R. Rudin, *Armistice 1918* (New Haven CT.: Yale University Press, 1944), 41.

94 Rudin, 41.

95 PWW, vol. 51, 127-130.

96 RUDIN, at 133.

97 DLG, *War Memoirs*, vol. 2, 1953.

98 Rudin, 91.

99 Rudin, 104.

100 Rudin, 104.

101 PWW, vol. 51, 262.

102 Rudin, 107-108.

103 Rudin, 108.

104 Rudin, 126.

105 PWW, vol. 51, 317, n. 6.

106 Seymour, vol. 4, 82.

107 Seymour, vol. 4, 83.

108 *New York Times*, October 15, 1918, 1.

109 Rudin, 133.

110 *New York Times*, October 19, 1918, 3.

111 *London Times*, October 19, 1918, 7.

112 PWW, vol. 51, 411-412.

113 Rudin, 173.

114 PWW, vol. 51, 381-382.

115 Walworth, *Woodrow Wilson*, vol. 2, 202.

116 Walworth, vol. 2, 201.

117 PWW, vol. 51, 463-464.

118 PWW, vol. 51, 473.

119 Seymour, vol. 4, 162-164.

120 Seymour, vol. 4, 166.

121 George, *War Diary*, 380.

122 PWW, vol. 51, 513.

123 DLG, *War Memoirs*, vol. 2, 1978.

124 PWW, vol. 51, 581-582.

125 PWW, vol. 51, 594.

126 George, *War Diary*, 380.

127 Walworth, *Woodrow Wilson*, vol. 2, 204.

128 Walworth, *Woodrow Wilson*, vol. 2, 204.

129 Rudin, 338-340, and Seymour, vol. 4, 137.

130 Rudin, 342.

131 Rudin, 384.

132 Seymour, vol. 4, 143.

133 Holt, 217.

134 Jere Clemens King, *Foch versus Clemenceau* (Cambridge, MA.: Harvard University Press, 1960), 15.

135 Hattersley, 473.

136 Rudin, 387.

137 *London Times*, November 13, 1918, 7.

138 Holt, 219.

CHAPTER EIGHTEEN

1 D. Stevenson, *French War Aims Against Germany, 1914-1919* (Oxford, U.K.: Clarendon Press, 1982), 148.

2 H.W.V. Temperley, ed., *A History of the Peace Conference of Paris* vol. 1 (London: Hodder & Stoughton, 1920), 138.

3 Clemenceau, *France Facing Germany*, 12.

4   Stevenson, *French War Aims*, 118.

5   Inga Floto, *Colonel House in* Paris (Princeton: Princeton University Press, 1973), 82.

6   PWW, vol. 53, 96-97.

7   PWW, vol. 53, 127-128.

8   Winston S. Churchill, *The Aftermath* (London: Macmillan & Co. 1941), 118.

9   Robert A. Burnett, "Georges Clemenceau in the Paris Peace Conference 1919" (Ph.D. diss. University of North Carolina at Chapel Hill, 1967), 82.

10   (Paris) *Temps*, Nov. 3, 1918, 1.

11   Seymour, vol. 4, 218.

12   Seymour, vol. 4, 218.

13   Seymour, vol. 4, 215.

14   PWW, vol. 53, 243.

15   Walworth, *Woodrow Wilson*, vol. 2, 211.

16   Neu, *Colonel House,* 383.

17   Seymour, vol. 4, 206.

18   PWW, vol. 53, 285-286.

19   *New York Tribune*, December 4, 1918, 2.

20   Tumulty, 335.

21   James T. Shotwell, *At the Paris Peace Conference* (New York: Macmillan, 1937), 75-78.

22   *London Times*, November 13, 1918, 9, 12.

23   PWW, vol. 53, 71.

24   George, *War Diary*, vol. 2, 3.

25   Rowland, *David Lloyd George*, 468.

26   Rowland, 469.

27   Rowland, 470.

28   DLG, *The Truth about the Peace Treaties*, vol. 1, (London: Victor Gollancz, 1938), 179.

29   PWW, vol. 53, 293-298; FRUS-PPC, vol. 1, 369.

30   King, *Foch versus Clemenceau,* 16.

31   André Tardieu, *The Truth About the Treaty* (London: Hodder & Stoughton, 1921), 194.

32   Clemenceau, *Grandeur and Misery*, 232-33.

33   DLG, *The Truth,* vol. I, 135.

34   King, *Foch versus Clemenceau*, 24.

35   FRUS-PPC, vol. 1, 343.

36   The *Guardian*, December 10, 1918, 7.

37   Walworth, *Woodrow Wilson*, vol. 2, 222.

38   *New York Tribune*, December 15, 1918, 2.

39   Walworth, *Woodrow Wilson*, vol. 2, 223.

40   Seymour, vol. 4, 252.

41   Seymour, vol. 4, 215.

42   Seymour, vol. 4, 252.

43   Seymour, vol. 4, 253.

44   PWW, vol. 53, 456.

45   Neu, 384.

46   Charles T. Thompson, *The Peace Conference Day by Day* (New York: Brentano's, 1920), 47.

47   *London Times*, December 21, 1918, 9-10.

48   Phyllis Lee Levin, *Edith and Woodrow* (New York: Scribner, 2001), 272.

49   A. Scott Berg, *Wilson* (New York: G.P. Putnam's Sons, 2013), 612.

50   *New York Times*, December 22, 1918, 9.

51   Neu, 384-385.

52   DLG, *Memoirs of the Peace Conference* (New Haven, CT.: Yale University Press, 1960), 144.

53   Thompson, 56.

54   DLG, *The Truth,* vol. 1, 114.

55   DLG, *The Truth,* vol. 1, 119.

56   George Curry, "Woodrow Wilson, Jan Smuts and the Versailles Settlement," *The American Historical Review* 66, no. 4 (July, 1961), 971.

57   Curry, 971.

58   Andrew Tink, *Australia,* 1901-2000 (Sydney, New South Publishing, 2014, unpaginated, chapter 9.)

59   DLG, *The Truth,* vol. 1, 120.

60   DLG, *The Truth,* vol. 1, 121.

61   *New York Times*, December 28, 1918, 1.

62   *London Times*, December 28, 1918, 8.

63   DLG, *Memoirs of the Peace Conference*, 112.

64   *London Times*, December 30, 1918, 3.

65   *New York Times*, December 31, 1918, 1-2.

66   Seymour, vol. 4, 255.

67   Arno Mayer, *Politics and Diplomacy of Peacemaking* (New York: Vintage Books, 1969), 192.

68   Mayer, 192.

69   Thompson, 69.

70   DLG, *Memoirs of the Peace Conference*, 147.

71   Seymour, vol. 4, 270.

72   Stevenson, *French War Aims*, 148.

73   Walworth, *Woodrow Wilson*, vol. 2, 242.

74   Ray Stannard Baker, *Woodrow Wilson and the World Settlement*, vol. 1 (Garden City, NY: Doubleday, Page, 1922) 179-180.

75   DLG, *The Truth,* 9.

CHAPTER NINETEEN

1   Clemenceau, *Grandeur and Misery,* 176-177.

2   DLG, *Memoirs of the Peace Conference*, 149.

3   Harold Nicolson, *Peacemaking 1919* (Gloucester, MA.: Peter Smith, 1984, 72.

4   Tardieu, *Truth About the Treaty*, 91.

5   Seymour, vol. 4, 250.

6   Seymour, vol. 4, 242.

7   FRUS-PPC, vol. 3, 162-163.

8   FRUS-PPC, vol. 3, 164.

9   FRUS-PPC, vol. 3 165.

10   FRUS-PPC, vol. 3, 166.

11   FRUS-PPC, vol. 3, 168.

12   George, Lord Riddell, *Lord Riddell's Intimate Diary of the Peace Conference and After* (London: Victor Gallancz, 1933), 5-6.

13 Lloyd George, *The Truth*, 516.

14 FRUS-PPC, vol. 3, 721.

15 FRUS-PPC, vol. 3, 742.

16 FRUS-PPC, vol. 3, 742.

17 FRUS-PPC, vol. 3, 747.

18 DLG, *Memoirs of the Peace Conference,* 359.

19 DLG, *Memoirs of the Peace Conference,* 752.

20 DLG, *Memoirs of the Peace Conference,* 754.

21 DLG, *Memoirs of the Peace Conference,* 765-766.

22 DLG, *Memoirs of the Peace Conference,* 765-766.

23 Robert Lansing, *The Peace Negotiations, a Personal Narrative* (Boston: Houghton Mifflin, 1931) 253.

24 Riddell, *Intimate Diary,* 17.

25 DLG, *Memoirs of the Peace Conference,* 360.

26 Maurice Hankey, *The Supreme Control at the Paris Peace Conference, 1919.* (London: George Allen and Unwin, 1963), 61.

27 FRUS-PPC, vol. 3, 803-804.

28 FRUS-PPC, vol. 3, 677-678.

29 Stephen Bonsal, *Unfinished Business* (Garden City, NY: Doubleday, Doran, 1944), 17-18.

30 FRUS-PPC, vol. 3, 190.

31 FRUS-PPC, vol. 3, 196-198.

32 FRUS-PPC, vol. 3, 691.

33 FRUS-PPC, vol. 3, 703.

34 FRUS-PPC, vol. 3, 703.

35 FRUS-PPC, vol. 3, 707-708.

36 FRUS-PPC, vol. 3, 712; 901.

37 FRUS-PPC, vol. 3, 931.

38 FRUS-PPC, vol. 3, 931.

39 FRUS-PPC, vol. 3, 903.

40 FRUS-PPC, vol. 3, 975.

41 FRUS-PPC, vol. 3, 975.

42 FRUS-PPC, vol. 3, 976.

43 Henry Wickham Steed, *Through Thirty Years*, vol. 2 (London: William Heinemann, 1924), 275.

44 DLG, *The Truth*, vol. 2, 972.

45 *New York Times*, February 4, 1919, 2.

46 *New York Times*, February 4, 1919, 2.

47 *Le Temps*, February 5, 1919, 1.

48 PWW, vol. 53, 507.

49 Clemenceau, *Grandeur and Misery*, 172.

50 David Hunter Miller, *The Drafting of the Covenant*, vol. 2 (New York: G.P. Putnam's Sons, 1928, 74.

51 Miller, vol. 2, 91.

52 Arthur Walworth, *Wilson and His Peacemakers*, (New York: W.W. Norton, 1986), 54.

53 Miller, vol. 2, 137.

54 Seymour, vol. 4, 304.

55 Walworth, *Wilson and His Peacemakers*, 116.

56 Bonsal, 24.

57 Miller, vol. 1, 133.

58 Miller, vol. 1, 133.

59 Bonsal, at 25.

60 Thompson, *Day by Day,* 176.

61 Bonsal, 29-30.

62 Miller, vol. 2, 329.

63 PWW, vol. 54, 514.

64 James E. Hewes, "Henry Cabot Lodge and the League of Nations" *Proceedings of the American Philosophical Society* 114.4 (1970), 250.

65 Hewes, 294.

66 Paul Birdsall, *Versailles Twenty Years After* (New York: Reynal & Hitchcock, 1941), 132.

67 Bonsal, 30.

68 Bonsal, 44.

69 Bonsal, 44-45.

70 Seymour, vol. 4. 412.

71 Bonsal, 48-49.

72 Hansard Parliamentary Debates, 3d series, vol. 112 cc 51-104, (Feb. 11, 1919.)

73 Hansard Parliamentary Debates, 3d series, vol. 112 cc 51-104, (Feb. 11, 1919.)

74 Miller, vol. 2, 325.

75 Walworth, *Wilson and his Peacemakers,* 145.

76 Miller, vol. 2, 560.

77 Miller, vol. 2, 562-563.

78 Miller, vol. 2, 564.

79 Miller, vol. 2, 572-573.

80 George Bernard Noble, *Policies and Opinions at Paris, 1919* (New York: Macmillan, 1935), 195.

81 Bernard Baruch, *The Making of the Reparation and Economic Sections of the Treaty* (New York: Howard Fertig, 1970), 5.

82 FRUS-PPC, vol. 2, 582.

83 FRUS-PPC, vol. 2, 582.

84 FRUS-PPC, vol. 2, 21.

85 DLG, *Memoirs of the Peace Conference,* 297.

86 Ferdinand Czernin, *Versailles 1919* (New York: G.P. Putnam's Sons, 1964), 269.

87 Czernin, 269.

88 McCormick, 32-33.

89 McCormick, 30.

90 McCormick, 30.

91 Marc Trachtenberg, "Reparations at the Paris Peace Conference," *Journal of Modern History* 51 (March, 1979), 31.

92 FRUS-PPC, vol. 2, 604.

93 Inga Floto, *Colonel House in Paris* (Princeton: Princeton University Press, 1973), 152.

94 FRUS-PPC, vol. 3, 682.

95 DLG, *The Truth,* vol. 2, 461.

96 DLG, *Memoirs* of the Peace Conference, V. 1 at 314.

97 McCormick, at 42.

98 House and Seymour, eds. At 1921.

99 Baruch, at 21-22.

100 Bonsal, at 49.

101 Id.

102 House, V. 4 at 329.

103 Id. at 330.

104 Bonsal, at 58.

CHAPTER TWENTY

. . . .

1   Bonsal, 60.

2   Riddell, *Intimate Diary*, 24.

3   PWW, vol. 55, 224.

4   Allan Nevins, *Henry White: Thirty Years of American Diplomacy* (New York: Harper & Bros., 1930, 390.

5   *The New York Times*, February 25, 1919, 1.

6   Nevins, 391.

7   Walworth, *Woodrow Wilson*, vol. 2, 269.

8   *The New York Times*, February 27, 1919, 1-2.

9   Henry Cabot Lodge, *The Senate and the League of Nations* (New York: Chas. Scribner's Sons, 1925, 100.

10   65th Cong. 3d sess. 4520-28 (February 28, 1919).

11   PWW, vol. 55, 312, n.1.

12   Hewes, "Henry Cabot Lodge and the League of Nations," 248.

13   65th Cong. 3d sess. 4520-28 (February 28, 1919), 4524.

14   65th Cong. 3d sess. 4520-28 (February 28, 1919), 4522.

15   65th Cong. 3d sess. 4520-28 (February 28, 1919), 4525.

16   Hewes, 248.

17   65th Cong. 3d sess. 4520-28 (February 28, 1919), 4527.

18   65th Cong. 3d sess. 4520-28 (February 28, 1919), 4527.

19   PWW, vol. 55, 312.

20   PWW, vol. 55, 310.

21   PWW, vol. 55, 313.

22   PWW, vol. 55, 437.

23   PWW, vol. 55, 492.

24   *The Guardian*, February 22, 1919, 7.

25   *The Guardian*, February 28, 1919, 8.

26   *The Guardian*, March 5, 1919, 4.

27   Stevenson, *Lloyd George,* 169.

28   Seymour, vol. 4, 330.

29   Dallas, *Heart of a Tiger,* 563.

30   Ray Stannard Baker, *Woodrow Wilson and the World Settlement*, vol. 1 (Garden City, NY: Doubleday, Page, 1922), 297.

31   Bonsal, 67.

32   PWW, vol. 55, 212.

33   PWW, vol. 55, 213.

34   Seymour, vol. 4, 335-336.

35   Floto, 123.

36   Bonsal, 65.

37   FRUS-PPC, vol. 4, 85.

38   Walworth, *Peacemakers*, 149.

39   PWW, vol. 55, 233-234.

40   Seymour, vol. 4, 346.

41   Seymour, vol. 4, 346-347.

42   PWW, vol. 55, 245.

43   PWW, vol. 55, 246.

44   Tardieu, *The Truth about the Treaty*, 151.

45   PWW, vol. 55, 210-211.

46   McCormick, 43.

47   PWW, vol. 55, 231.

48   McCormick, 45.

49   McCormick, 45.

50   PWW, vol. 55, 245.

51   Thompson, 236.

52   Seymour, vol. 4, 344.

53   Seymour, vol. 4, 352.

54   Seymour, vol. 4, 352, n.1.

55   Thompson, 239.

56   Stevenson, 170.

57   Bonsal, 68.

58   Bonsal, 71.

59   PWW, vol. 55, 408.

60   *New York Times*, March 4, 1919, 1.

61   *New York Times*, March 5, 1919, 2.

62   *New York Times*, March 5, 1919, 2.

63   *New York Times*, March 5, 1919, 2.

64   PWW, vol. 55, 414-415.

65   PWW, vol. 55, 418.

66   PWW, vol. 55, 420.

67   PWW, vol. 55, 362.

68   PWW, vol. 55, 362

69   Walworth, *Peacemakers*, 175.

70   PWW, vol. 55, 458.

71   PWW, vol. 55, 472.

72   FRUS-PPC, vol. 4, 280-281.

73   FRUS-PPC, vol. 4, 282-283.

74   Lodge, 123.

75   Nevins, 378.

76   Nevins, 383.

CHAPTER TWENTY-ONE

1 PWW, vol. 55, 488, n. 2.
2 PWW, vol. 55, 497.
3 Stevenson, *Lloyd George,* 172.
4 Riddell, 32.
5 PWW, vol. 55, 532.
6 PWW, vol. 55, 538.
7 PWW, vol. 55, 539.
8 Riddell, *Intimate Diary,* 34.
9 Tumulty, 534.
10 Seymour, vol. 4, 390.
11 Riddell, 36.
12 Hankey, 97.
13 Hankey, 101.
14 DLG, *Memoirs of the Peace Conference,* 266-267.
15 DLG, *Memoirs of the Peace Conference,* 267.
16 DLG, *Memoirs of the Peace Conference,* 267.
17 DLG, *Memoirs of the Peace Conference,* 267.
18 DLG, *Memoirs of the Peace Conference,* 268.
19 DLG, *Memoirs of the Peace Conference,* 269.
20 DLG, *Memoirs of the Peace Conference,* 269.
21 DLG, *Memoirs of the Peace Conference,* 270.
22 DLG, *Memoirs of the Peace Conference,* 270.
23 DLG, *Memoirs of the Peace Conference,* 270.
24 DLG, *Memoirs of the Peace Conference,* 269.
25 Stevenson, *Lloyd George,* 175.
26 Stevenson, *Lloyd George,* 276.
27 FRUS-PPC, vol. 4, 417.
28 Seymour, vol. 4, 390.
29 Tumulty, 538.
30 Miller, *The Drafting of the Covenant,* vol. 1, 336.
31 David Hunter Miller, "The Making of the League," in Edward M. House and Charles Seymour, eds., *What Really Happened at Paris,* (London: Hodder & Stoughton, 1921), 403.
32 Miller, *The Drafting of the Covenant,* vol. 1, 421.
33 Miller, *The Drafting of the Covenant,* vol. 1, 420.
34 Miller, *The Drafting of the Covenant,* vol. 1, 443.
35 Miller, *The Drafting of the Covenant,* vol. 1, 444.
36 Miller, *The Drafting of the Covenant,* vol. 1, 444.
37 PWW-DE, vol. 57, 236.
38 PWW-DE, vol. 57, 461.
39 PWW-DE, vol. 57, 462.
40 COF, vol. 1, 4.
41 Seymour, vol. 4, 382.
42 COF, vol. 1, 36, n. 6.
43 COF, vol. 1, 18-19.

44 COF, vol. 1, 20.

45 COF, vol. 1, 19.

46 COF, vol. 1, 31.

47 COF, vol. 1, 32.

48 COF, vol. 1, 32

49 COF, vol. 1, 32-33.

50 COF, vol. 1, 34-35.

51 COF, vol. 1, 29.

52 COF, vol. 1, 52.

53 PWW, vol. 56, 501.

54 PWW, vol. 56, 499.

55 *London Times*, April 3, 1919, 12.

56 Stevenson, *Lloyd George*, 178.

57 McCormick, 65.

58 McCormick, 65.

59 Mayer, *Politics and Diplomacy*, 585-586.

60 PWW-DE, vol. 47, 34.

61 Seymour, vol. 4, 401.

62 COF, vol. 1, 41.

63 Martet, *Georges Clemenceau*, 25.

64 PWW, vol. 56, 349.

65 Isaiah Bowman, "Constantinople and the Balkans" in House & Seymour, eds., *What Really Happened at Paris*, 464-465.

66 Cary Grayson, *Woodrow Wilson, An Intimate Memoir* (Washington, D.C.: Potomac Books, 1960), 77.

67 Grayson, 78.

68 COF, vol. 1, 61.

69 COF, vol. 1, 61

70 COF, vol. 1, 63.

71 COF, vol. 1, 196.

72 COF, vol. 1, 189.

73 COF, vol. 1, 190.

74 COF, vol. 1, 190.

75 COF, vol. 1, 191.

76 COF, vol. 1, 193.

77 COF, vol. 1, 197.

78 COF, vol. 1, 201.

79 COF, vol. 1, 203.

80 Riddell, 51.

81 PWW-DE, vol. 57, 347.

82 DLG, *Memoirs*, 374.

83 Hansard Parliamentary Debates, 3d series, vol. 114, cc 2936 (April 16, 1919).

84 Hansard Parliamentary Debates, 3d series, vol. 114, cc 2953 (April 16, 1919).

85 PWW-DE, vol. 57, 343.

86 PWW-DE, vol. 57, 343-344.

87 PWW-DE, vol. 57, 344.

88 PWW-DE, vol. 57, 345.

89   PWW-DE, vol. 57, 352.

90   COF, vol. 1, 278.

91   COF, vol. 1, 282.

92   COF, vol. 1, 283.

93   COF, vol. 1, 287.

94   COF, vol. 1, 286-287.

95   COF, vol. 1, 289.

96   COF, vol. 1, 291.

97   COF, vol. 1, 291.

98   COF, vol. 1, 292.

99   COF, vol. 1, 293.

100 COF, vol. 1, 294.

101 Stevenson, *Lloyd George*, 182.

102 *New York Times*, April 19, 1919, 1-2.

103 Thompson, 318.

104 Hankey, 131.

105 Hankey, 545.

106 COF, vol. 1, 298.

107 COF, vol. 1, 300.

108 COF, vol. 1, 301.

109 COF, vol. 1, 304.

110 COF, vol. 1, 305.

111 COF, vol. 1, 311.

112 COF, vol. 1, 311-312.

113 PWW-DE, vol. 57, 597.

114 COF, vol. 1, 325.

115 COF, vol. 1, 336.

116 DLG, *The Truth*, vol. 2, 828.

117 COF, vol. 1, 334.

118 COF, vol. 1, 335.

119 COF, vol. 1, 335.

120 COF, vol. 1, 338.

121 COF, vol. 1, 344.

122 Riddell, 56.

123 COF, vol. 1, 350.

124 Thompson, 331.

125 COF, vol. 1, 351.

126 COF, vol. 1, 352.

127 COF, vol. 1, 359.

128 COF, vol. 1, 359.

129 COF, vol. 1, 363.

130 COF, vol. 1, 362.

131 COF, vol. 1, 364.

132 DLG, *The Truth*, vol. 2, 840.

133 Nicolson, 182.

134 PWW-DE, vol. 58, 142.

135 PWW-DE, vol. 58, 70-71.

136 PWW-DE, vol. 58, 175.

137 COF, vol. 1, 399-400.

138 COF, vol. 1, 400.

139 COF, vol. 1, 401.

140 Thompson, 345.

141 Lansing, *Peace Negotiations,* 258.

142 PWW-DE, vol. 58, 327.

143 PWW-DE, vol. 58, 271, n. 1.

144 *New York Times,* April 29, 1919, 1.

145 COF, vol. 1, 421.

146 Temperly, vol. 3, 330.

147 Temperly, vol. 3, 330.

148 FRUS-PPC, vol. 5, 361.

149 *New York Tribune,* May 2, 1919, 1.

150 *New York Times,* May 4, 1919, 1.

151 FRUS-PPC, vol. 5, 425.

152 FRUS-PPC, vol. 5, 434.

153 FRUS-PPC, vol. 5, 435.

154 COF, vol. 1, 469.

155 COF, vol. 1, 469.

156 COF, vol. 1, 470.

157 COF, vol. 1, 477.

158 *The Guardian,* May 6, 1919, 7.

159 FRUS-PPC, vol. 3, 340.

160 FRUS-PPC, vol. 3, 384.

161 Nicolson, 327.

162 Tardieu, 195.

CHAPTER TWENTY-TWO

1   FRUS-PPC, vol. 3, 415-416.

2   FRUS-PPC, vol. 3, 417.

3   Stevenson, *Lloyd George,* 183.

4   FRUS-PPC, vol. 3, 417.

5   Tardieu, *The Truth,* 120.

6   Howard Elcock, *Portrait of a Decision* (London: Eyre Metheun, 1972), 242.

7   Riddell, *Intimate Diary,* 76.

8   Stevenson, 183.

9   COF, vol. 2, 7.

10 COF, vol. 2, 7.

11 COF, vol. 2, 7-8.

12 FRUS-PPC, vol. 5, 563.

13 COF, vol. 2, 19.

14 FRUS-PPC, vol. 5, 564.

15 Riddell, *Intimate Diary,* 78.

16 FRUS-PPC, vol. 5, 564.

17 FRUS-PPC, vol. 5, 740.

18 FRUS-PPC, vol. 5, 818.

19 *New York Times,* May 14, 1919, 1-2.

20 *New York Tribune,* May 14, 1919, 2.

21 COF, vol. 2, 50.

22 COF, vol. 2, 69.

23 COF, vol. 2, 151.

24 COF, vol. 2, 352.

25 COF, vol. 2, 65.

26 COF, vol. 2, 65.

27 COF, vol. 2, 134.

28 FRUS-PPC, vol. 11, 573.

29 Elcock, 247.

30 Elcock, 251.

31 Nicolson, 350.

32 Nicolson, 350.

33 COF, vol. 2, 105.

34 DLG, *The Truth About the Peace Treaties,* vol. 2, 882-883.

35 COF, vol. 2, 259.

36 COF, vol. 2, 259.

37 COF, vol. 2, 260.

38 COF, vol. 2, 263.

39 Elcock, 251.

40 Seymour, vol. 4, 474.

41 DLG, *The Truth about the Peace Treaties,* vol. I, 689.

42 DLG, *The Truth about the Peace Treaties,* vol. 1, 721.

43 DLG, *The Truth about the Peace Treaties,* vol. 1, 720.

44 DLG, *The Truth about the Peace Treaties,* vol. 1, 710.

45 DLG, *The Truth about the Peace Treaties,* vol. 1, 711.

46 DLG, *The Truth about the Peace Treaties,* vol. 1, 700.

47 COF, vol. 2, 268-269.

48 COF, vol. 2, 270-271.

49 COF, vol. 2, 271.

50 COF, vol. 2, 274.

51 COF, vol. 2, 275-276.

52 COF, vol. 2, 276.

53 PWW, vol. 60, 50.

54 McCormick, 95.

55 PWW, vol. 60, 50.

56 PWW, vol. 60, 53.

57 PWW, vol. 60, 69.

58 PWW, vol. 60, 70.

59 PWW, vol. 60, 67.

60   John Maynard Keynes, *The Economic Consequences of the Peace* (New York: The Century Company, 1926), 22.

61   Bert E. Park, "Wilson's Neurologic Illness during the Summer of 1919," in PWW, vol. 62, 628.

62   COF, vol. 2, 281-282.

63   COF, vol. 2, 323, 328.

64   COF, vol. 2, 367.

65   Seymour, vol. 4, 480.

66   Seymour, vol. 4, 481-482.

67   PWW, vol. 60, 398-399.

68   COF, vol. 2, 404.

69   COF, vol. 2, 404.

70   COF, vol. 2, 405.

71   COF, vol. 2, 421.

72   COF, vol. 2, 440.

73   COF, vol. 2, 426.

74   COF, vol. 2, 453-454.

75   COF, vol. 2, 475.

76   FRUS-PPC, vol. 6, 929.

77   FRUS-PPC, vol. 6, 933.

78   FRUS-PPC, vol. 6, 934.

79   FRUS-PPC, vol. 6, 935.

80   Thompson, 397.

81   *New York Times*, June 19, 1919, 2.

82   *New York Times*, June 19, 1919, 2.

83   *New York Times*, June 20, 1919, 1.

84   *New York Times*, June 21, 1919, 1.

85   *New York Times*, June 22, 1919, 3.

86   FRUS-PPC, vol. 6, 610.

87   Watson, 359.

88   PWW, vol. 61, 76-77.

89   *New York Times*, June 24, 1919, 1.

90   COF, vol. 2, 536.

91   COF, vol. 2, 536.

92   COF, vol. 2, 543.

93   FRUS-PPC, vol. 11, 599.

94   Thompson, 419.

95   FRUS-PPC, vol. 11, 601.

96   FRUS-PPC, vol. 11, 603.

97   Seymour, vol. 4, 487.

98   Thompson, 421.

EPILOGUE

1   Watson, 361.

2   *New York Times*, July 11, 1919, 2.

3   Bert E. Park, "Wilson's Neurologic Illness during the Summer of 1919" in PWW, vol. 62, 628-638.

4   *New York Times*, August 20, 1919, 2.

5   PWW, vol. 62, 507, n. 2.

6   DLG, *Memoirs of the Peace Conference*, 154.

7   PWW, vol. 61, 258-259.

8   PWW, vol. 62, 525.

9   PWW, vol. 62, 576.

10   PWW, vol. 62, 574.

11   PWW, vol. 63, 580. The parenthetical is open in the original.

12   PWW, vol. 63, 621.

13   *London Times*, December 12, 1919, 15.

14   Wythe Williams, *The Tiger of France* (New York: Duell, Sloan and Pearce, 1949), 234.

15   DLG, *Memoirs of the Peace Conference*, 154.

INDEX